S0-ASW-066

infinite times more

infinite times more

nyrd

Copyright © 2023 by nyrd.

Library of Congress Control Number:		2023900644
ISBN:	Hardcover	978-1-6698-6088-4
	Softcover	978-1-6698-6087-7
	eBook	978-1-6698-6086-0

All rights reserved. No part of this book may be reproduced or transmitted in any form or by any means, electronic or mechanical, including photocopying, recording, or by any information storage and retrieval system, without permission in writing from the copyright owner.

Any people depicted in stock imagery provided by Getty Images are models, and such images are being used for illustrative purposes only.
Certain stock imagery © Getty Images.

Print information available on the last page.

Rev. date: 01/12/2023

To order additional copies of this book, contact:
Xlibris
844-714-8691
www.Xlibris.com
Orders@Xlibris.com
846366

CONTENTS

I'm Sad 1

Guilt and Furthermore 2

Touch the Clouds...3

Unbind Me 4

Disappear for a While 5

Choke hold 6

Shinigami Eyes 7

mas vida 8

Dear Mom and Dad I Forgive You...............................9

Full Moon..10

Before 11

Subconscious...12

The Ghost of You (Part One)......................................13

The Ghost of You (Part Two) 14

The Ghost of You (Part Three)..................................15

Because of Her 16

My Little Kitten 17

Tempo Solo 18

(Un)censored 19

Hot as Hell..20

Part of Me...21

Oppressor 22

Tell Me, God 23

Take It Slow..24

Grow Up...25

These Are the Moments in Time 26

Villain Era..27

Purgatory...28

Internal and External 29

In the Air...30

Straight Menace 31

Bañarme al Sol..32

Self-Inflicting..33

VR..34

Gifted 35

Wolfine..36

Dominator 37

You're My Humanity...38

Sick Brain..39

Hinder 40

Lost Cause Lookin' for a Clause............................41

More Than Rare 42

Indisputable...43

Happy Birthday 44

Taurus 45

Dear Ex (Part 1) 46

Dear Ex (Part 1) 47

Dear Ex (Part 1) 48

Psychotic Rage 49

Battle Cry..50

Till Dawn 51

Hell Boy 52

Cuidarme..53

Vacant..54

POV 55

Energy 56

Mana 57

Allure to Darkness 58

Am I Amendable? 59

Iridescent Soul 60

Little Miss Bliss 61

Cigarettes 62

Light 63
Monster 64
Gnarly 65
New Heights 66
Revive 67
Head to the Clouds 68
Baby 69
My Time 70
Sin City 71
Toxic 72
Split Personality Disorder 73
Guardian Angel 74
Dying Dying Dying 75
Happily 76
Ever 77
After 78
Too Late to Apologize 79
Advisor 80
Out Law 81
Soldier 82
Time to Tap In 83
A Fate Worse than hell 84
Maniacs 85
Dear Mom, ... 86
Baby Boy 87
Alive and Well 88
Provider 89
Graceful Silhouette Part 1 90
Graceful Silhouette Part 2 91
Just a Nomad 92
Destined to Be Damned 93
Meant for More 94
Drifter 95
No Hidden Agenda 96
Infinite 97

Kill Me First 98
Spirited Away 99
Cross My Heart 100
Subconsciously at War 101
Eulogy 102

I'm Sad

It hurts to force you to say I love you,
Brother, I wish I wasn't someone you had to get used to,
I try to do good, but repeatedly I screw
things up from my every view,
Jona, my Jona, I wish I was more like you
and not like euphoria's rue,
I breathe in and out, and I'm not surprised
my karma is my only virtue,
I am sad, and if I write as if I'm not, then I'd be completely untrue,
Forgiveness is a luxury I cannot yet afford,
As well as love and trust, I betrayed you all again before,
My dear little brother, Hector, I know you're smart,
but I'm no good for your devotion nor amor,
So I'll cry and pray on my downfall because
I know I'll never truly soar,
Mana has wings I'll never relate to, even
though she was always my mentor,
She's the greatest to do it for she's in heaven
taking action as a conquistador,
Here on earth I look at my mother, and I see I'm
not the one she truly wants to adore,
And I see my father's eyes, and I'm aware he's
hoping I'd eventually leave through that door,
My dear sister, my dear brothers, I truly feel I am done for,
I've felt this way my whole life. What can I say?
I don't recall anything else at my core,
I try more than I should. At this point, my
perception needs to be no more,
I only wish you can forgive me until the memory of
me no longer follows you like a tormentor.

NYRD
09/16/22

Guilt and Furthermore

Dawn will rise and so will I,
Anger reveals itself when depression latches on to pry,
Filled with guilt of moments I would utterly lie and sly,
She knows me well enough, so she had to say bye,
I never meant to break you apart and make you cry,
Ghosted with just photos and letters to remind
me of how high I used to soar,
Now I barely let myself feel deeper than the surface of my core,
Broken and alone, my soul was meant to ultimately leave me poor,
Darkness follows and I can't stop the
liquor from flowing out to pour,
I seek refuge from these islands shore,
Take me before Lucifer comes through that fucking door,
Pity me, god, because this guilt eats me alive like a fucking whore,
I never deserved her and nor was I meant for her infinite amor,
First and last time I'll ever let my heart open to be adored,
First and last time I'll ever let my heart and body be explored,
I'd break myself first before I could be something you'd hoped for,
God, be there to take this drink out of my hand like it was a chore,
Stop this pattern and make me come undone
with gore in this bloody war,
Maybe, just maybe, I could finally become
something everlasting more.

NYRD
04/30/22

2

Touch the Clouds

I'm drifting,
Said I always played victim,
That I was better off without liquor in my system,
Made the worst choices and drifted farther from wisdom,
I could lie and say I have it under control, but
baby, we both know I'd look dumber,
Getting high in my four walls to Lana Del Rey's summer bummer,
Such a classic. A$AP Rocky is a top tier gunner,
I think of you ever so often. I doubt I'll ever recover,
Laying low for the meantime but it's getting
harder to keep my mind out of the gutter,
Won her, lost her, and spun her all around,
I ain't shit, but a quickie to be aroused,
Weak for one and one alone, so you can
imagine how my eyes don't browse,
But mentally, I'm still so sick, and all I wanna do is touch the clouds,
Get away from myself but my life is needed here for it's what God allows,
Ringing in my ears, it's not music, but whispers and ominous sounds,
This demonic presence wants to be seen, so it serenades me with growls,
I could show my hand and give a frown, but I'll smile and act resound,
A pack of night owls, we are accustomed to hearing other painful howls,
When I think of you, Karen, I imagine things
to do to you and for you for hours,
Happy place, happy space in my mind, I tuck you
away because this love is strictly ours,
I won't show my hand 'cause people only know
how to turn things bitter and sour,
But if you want, you can grab my book this winter
for it'll only give me so much more power,
Devour each word of my twisted mind as I devour her lotus flower,
Still I am drifting, still I am sinking, but baby, I'll
die before I turn into another coward,
I'll touch the clouds one day, but today's not the
motive I should think to empower,
I wanna see my sister again, but I need her eyes to be prouder.

NYRD
08/29/22

Unbind Me

Insomnia has left me color-blind,
Death intertwined with me like it was meant to bind,
Hovering the ceiling this is my own hellish design,
Slipknot essence, we are truly not your kind,
I can't describe the feeling of utterly losing your mind,
Sharpened and hyphened, but ultimately not
inclined to be bold and outlined,
The stars told me a long time ago this shit wouldn't ever be aligned,
Gun clutching in my holster, maybe it's time I've resigned,
These thoughts hit me like bullets when it's ill timed,
The target moves and plays trickery with
every expression I've rhymed,
Tell me, god, is this the fate you've declared to be assigned?
Is death my twisted remedy to remind me to prosper and grind?
To never let the bad moments and thoughts consume
me whole until my aura is deeply unkind,
Help me not to rewind but to sincerely unbind.

NYRD
04/26/22

Disappear for a While

Every vow I break becomes my guilt,
Every bridge I burn is profound regret,
Every line I've crossed costs me my respect,
Every breath I now breathe is my everlasting karma,
Forever I'll be sorry, but for an eternity I'll gravely suffer,
And I could love you harder, but I still don't
deserve to be anybody's lover,
Tonight I feel it all so sincerely. I must hide beneath the covers,
It's true I'm the black sheep of the family
for I'm nothing like my brothers,
I stay for them for they're the only ones that love
me unconditionally like no bloody other,
I could do right by them this time and not
like how I did to my sweet mother,
I miss you more than life, but I probably shouldn't bother her,
I probably should stop to think more before
I continue to dishonor her,
I should remain silence and proper or make an
effort to be something of a scholar,
God, take this noose off around my collar,
Take these traumas away and sedate me to make me calmer,
I don't want to live in my home and feel like a damn squatter,
If I could, I'd take these demons to be slaughtered,
But if I could ask of anything, God, could
you turn this wine into water,
Exchange these pills for something much stronger,
Suppose if I disappear for a while with your
verses, it could take me so much farther.

NYRD
08/29/22

5

Choke hold

Life with you would have been grander than the Great Gatsby,
The past replays in my mind, but I no longer hope and believe,
My chances ran up and so did your desire for me,
Drove everyone away, now all that's left is to fucking grieve,
So many letters, I bet I've become such a pet peeve,
I wish you'd text first, but I must learn how
to stop forcing shit and just breathe,
My heart has been sunk beneath my feet for some time now,
Heart has stopped beating since I lost my version of Iroh,
I don't know who I am without them, but I have to find out,
I keep trying to swim, even though I'm
incomplete and in utter doubt,
I can't get to know anyone anymore because I
got demons tracking my every route,
I'm just a silhouette of what I used to be
before the unspeakable drought,
Mana, the past still haunts me day in and day out,
The walls shout at me and I listen back with pure devout,
I wake up just to write about all the things
I'm now truly left without,
I'm only hurting myself now. There's no telling the amount,
I know in my dreams my lost loves are always down for the count,
KC and Mana, I'm forever sorry for being the
utmost worst person all fucking around,
I hoped things could have been different,
but this is my new reality now,
Karma has me on a choke hold and pinned to the fucking ground,
Deep down I know it's too late to redeem
myself 'cause I can hear the hellhounds.

NYRD
06/31/22

Shinigami Eyes

You can't help it for my red eyes only speak shinigami,
I got you bending and folding in ways like origami,
Dame mas make me drown in your tsunami,
What a beautiful mess I've left. I'm the devil on your graceful shoulder,
I'll suck your blood dry like I'm Ian Somerhalder,
Toxic as fuck, but I'm there if she ever needed someone to hold her,
Sever this knot if you want, it'll only lessen the pressure,
I will no longer be the aggressor or my own self-deprecating oppressor,
Nonchalant now 'cause why would I let you
go through another endeavor?
I love you, but it's best if I let these emotions fester,
I look to you and I just hope to God he'd always bless her,
Too good, too pure for me to ever try to suppress her,
I've drained myself of my deepest desires, I'm so sure,
Black hole of a soul, it's a disaster within my core,
Anything that comes never truly does go,
You could trace your fingers across my back so slow,
But you were just a beautiful dream—this I know,
Better off with another version of me, so I'll look closer to grow,
These shinigami eyes make me want to chase
these lows until I'm down below,
Possessed vessel but we both want to survive, so we continue to row,
Swaying back and forth, chasing a new balance to flow,
Good and bad, it's a war against myself like
I'm Johnny Depp in the movie *Blow*,
True story but I'm no longer chasing anymore snow,
So sober now, I feel all my bitter woes,
Forgiveness is not in the cards unless it's more guilt to expose,
For so long, I thought I've been trying, but
this isn't the effort I really do owe,
I had to lose it all and become your greatest foe,
I had to lose my mind like I was Vincent Van Gogh,
But for now, let me try this life thing again
every day and all my tomorrows,
'Cause there's no erasing it, so I might as well
make art out of it like I'm Michelangelo.

NYRD
08/27/22

mas
vida

Cosas de la vida,
Tan tristezas a tu lado se olvida,
It's hard to look down when your morals siempre son arriba,
Your venom tastes like sweet euphoria or the meaning of eureka,
I want to take you some place unknown and far away like topeka,
Time is irrelevant when you've always been mi senorita sin cita,
Labels are absurd and so are these mierdita cervezas,
I want to be better than the distractions en mi stupido cabeza,
Actions preferably mean more than promesas,
You're never without a trace 'cause my clothes are
always laced with the scent of your sweetest aromas,
It's hard to keep count of your achievements and diplomas,
Iteligente y eligante como un bouquet de rosas.

NYRD
04/24/22

Dear Mom and Dad
I Forgive You

So bold she walked so I could run,
A true Jimenes piercing right through the sun,
No matter what happens I know I had always won,
A sister like her. The universe knew I was one lucky son of a gun,
Lord knows she's the only reason I ever begun,
Raised me like one of her own without a fraction of a question,
Held me close at night when my eyes were
only laced with depression,
I just wanted my mother to care, but she just
knew how to make me feel less than,
Twenty years later, I'm no longer a child, but
my mother still left her impression,
And I'm still lost for words when she tries to reach
out to leave a sign of regret or confession,
Mom, I wish I could tell you it's okay, that I forgive
you, but I'm scared to make a connection,
If I told you everything about me, you'd
hate me from every direction,
The sight of me will disgust you, so I lie because I no
longer have my sister's affection nor protection,
I know once this book comes out, you'll know things that I
should have buried in order for you to not take as consumption,
But, Mother and Father, if this ruins our relationship just know I
will still love you through every cross-section and altercation,
I will love thee as if you were laced with utter perfection,
Because my sister's heart knew every trace of grace
and mercy of her glimmering reflection.

NYRD
10/25/22

Full Moon

You only knew what was left of my debris,
I cut myself off with Jason Voorhees's machete,
I prefer to be nominee 'cause I don't want
you to think of me as a guarantee,
Anxiety makes my hands shaky and unsteady,
I wear black, so nobody can see me fucking sweaty,
My depression makes everything feel heavy,
so best believe I never feel ready,
It's a full moon tonight and all that ignites inside is envy,
I wish I was complete, but lately, I'm in a
mental state of chaotic frenzy,
I don't have it in me to try to act friendly,
I don't have it in me for you to get to know me,
Who really got me? I got me since I was in elementary,
Not a soul gave a damn, so don't look at me
for something complementary,
Used to sway my head to some Elvis Presley, but
now I rage to corpse to keep this trajectory,
Forever sus, forever ungodly flow, it's fucking noteworthy, you see,
Bass drops, gun never cocks, I'm Cillian fucking Murphy,
Learned to never give out free courtesy
nor show any palpable mercy,
Fuckers will take advantage of that shit, so
might as well play them all dirty,
Menace to society like *Ken Kaneki* season two, surely,
I don't plan to live till I'm forty, so take what
you can get from me fucking early,
Circle so small it's nonexistent, but bitch, it's still gnarly.

NYRD
08/30/22

Before

Summer time in New York City,
The nights never slept—it was always quite busy,
Hotel to hotel, with views astonishingly pretty,
I would give anything to go back to a time that silly,
Not a whole lot mattered for COVID wasn't even a thing,
Now we all walk as if we had invisible strings,
I miss my sister the most, but it was her time to spread her wings,
And my lover grew tired of my shenanigans,
so I should stop looking at rings,
It was their time, so I should move on too and let myself begin,
I must admit this new reality has gotten deeply under my skin,
But this new course I walk requires me to be at peace from within,
I can't write unless I'm prepared to sincerely dive in,
I cannot hold back from admitting all the
ways I've committed a sin,
Still I'd do it over again and take it to the chin,
I had to fuck up and lose it all in order to taste the win.

NYRD
10/14/22

@nyrdwolfine

Subconscious

Black chipped nails and I'm filled with anxiety,
I could hate myself more, but I'll leave that to society,
In your eyes, you'll always see what's outside of me,
Like a picture book, you forgot how to read the
underlining details of what's inside of me,
These accusations spin and swirl, and it's truly a sight to see,
For so long, I couldn't believe this was God's holy testimony,
I couldn't fathom the grace and mercy you
tried so hard to place onto me,
Suppose I am here to test the limitations of society's ideology,
Suppose I am here to endure the worst
and to never hear an apology,
Not even the stars could predict my great odyssey,
They look at you differently as if you were
a creature of Greek mythology,
They can't bear to get to know you, so they
ghost you like a true divine comedy,
There is no modesty when the mind has perceived
the unfamiliar as a monstrosity,
Even if they don't understand me, the ones that
will, will see through the facade in me,
Deeply I think we all just want to be understood
more than seen, subconsciously.

NYRD
10/13/22

The Ghost of You
(Part One)

I should have proposed when I had the chance,
I should have held on tighter when we last danced,
But now it's just these pieces that are left of
me when we shared that last glance,
It's too late now—it feels so—so let's make a toast,
To the fact that I now feel the utmost comatose,
We both know, even if it's not me you choose, I'm
still the one that utterly loved you the most,
Your silhouette still fucking haunts me like a fucking ghost,
I wish I didn't keep track of your every move and post,
I'm infected and you're the host,
Depression, PTSD, and anxiety, I wish
I never knew I was diagnosed,
It's confirmed I'm far beyond fucked, so now
I rely on doctors for every dose,
Promise me, when I perish, you'll leave a sunflower and not a rose,
I hope I don't impose on this, but keep the memory of us close,
We had something so special, lord knows.

NYRD
06/04/22

The Ghost of You
(Part Two)

I don't care if everyone else forgets me, but please
not you for it's a fate worse than hell,
It's a fate I wish to never dwell in my sweetest Giselle,
And I hope I'm not coming off as too sad or too
much, but you are the utmost rarest, my gazelle,
Your curves and aura paint hues I never knew existed
before I got caught in between your intel,
Miguel, on repeat when I can't help but think
of moments we shared at every hotel,
Notes, I can't help but to fucking hit when I'm in the mood to rebel,
And if I'm in my feelings, best believe
it's either Adele, Lana, or Abel,
And if you ever need me, best believe I'll be fucking able,
TBH, I'd be lying if I said I didn't have dreams of
making you mine again right at the table,
Bed or floor, no matter where, you'll be swallowed like an edible,
And fuck all these labels, I'm tryna eat you out
and make you even more intelligible,
Let's get intellectual and flexible, speaking cursive
into your thighs till it's more than exceptionable,
Impeccable, your taste, I could love you longer
than infinite like it was inevitable.

NYRD
06/04/22

The Ghost of You
(Part Three)

Switching positions, you truly are incredible,
I could watch you do yoga, and you could
watch me become more accessible,
To you, I'll be 25/8, unquestionably available,
I'm a whore to your cause—this is undoubtable,
Candles are lit. This is more than just a confessional,
Crazy for you, but I'd still fuck you like a professional,
I become ethical when I penetrate you so sensibly,
Don't get it confused. My desire for you
goes far deeper than sexual,
Both aware, this is nothing known as conventual,
But our serotonin flourishes when we're skin
to skin—it's beyond substantial.

NYRD
06/04/22

Because of Her

Entangled within the bed covers,
This moment we're simply just lovers,
Two souls manifesting every shade of color,
Indiscriminate, her hues are like no other,
She's the canvas, and I, the connoisseur,
I try my best to not smother her,
But she's so rare she's well tapped within my literature,
I couldn't possibly love her more—this I thought I was sure,
I'm so confused within my own structure,
She makes me question everything without
even the feel of her skin to touch her,
I'm the instrument, and she's damn near the conductor,
She has changed my ways as if I were John Tucker,
Cupid had no say when she placed me in the picture,
This can't be real, but it is, and my heart is damn near ruptured,
But today I woke up and thought of moving upward,
This morning I breathed, and it wasn't just because of her,
Hmm, I still sighed, and I couldn't help but to just wonder,
Suppose if I didn't still think of her, I wouldn't know
how to rise from repeatedly going under,
I wouldn't know how to write faster than thunder.

NYRD
09/24/22

My Little Kitten

She likes being faced down in total submission,
She likes being forced into position,
Gripping her throat, she knows my intuition,
I take what's mine, mm-hmm, baby listen,
Our moans echo through the room—it's a given,
The bed creaks, as I am undeniably aroused and driven,
You won't let me stop until all is forgiven,
And I won't even dare listen until I've completed my mission,
I could fuck another, but I'm not here for multiple women,
Yes, they're beautiful, but they're not what gives
meaning to everything I've written,
Or for what I will write in the future because
this is ultimately my decision,
I won't deny the way you hold my head down, screaming ambition,
I don't like it . . . I love it, my little kitten,
I could tie you up with a ribbon and fuck you with utter precision,
And every so often, we can link up to help
you unwind as if it were tradition,
Are you wet yet, or should I inspect as your primary physician?

NYRD
10/19/22

Tempo Solo

Melancholy and I share more than just similarities,
Monster energy and mellow music melodies,
Close the curtains it's time to create
something the opposite of parodies,
I don't know how to explain my heart when
there's no sign of amenities,
No one stays, and why would they if I've dug
my grave and made public enemies?
Once my lover, now I'm just praying to the lord for remedies,
I'm sorry for everything but it's too late
I've made one too many felonies,
Betrayed your trust and allowed my demons
to seek out their tendencies,
All these memories, it's giving me fucking vertigo,
Hate to see you walk away, but I love to see you go,
Chasing after your dreams while I allow
my ache to dwell and grow,
She says to breathe and that I'd learn to dance in my own tempo,
In time I'll learn to do this solo, but for now I'll retrace your tempo,
Follow the leader. Your steps are so silent, my
love, you must be on your tiptoes,
Little do I know I'm chasing after a ghost, and she'll
do anything to not let her emotions expose,
My long lost lover, I'm in utter regret of making
you want to dive deeper within the shadows,
It's all my fault for disappointing you far too many
times and my every post truly does show that,
Twisted and sick individual, I am far from reach
from the one that truly knows me in fact.

NYRD
09/14/22

(Un)censored

I wore your trust like armor,
Sturdy with my words, I could never murmur,
Accustomed to feeling so cold but she made you quite warmer,
Skin to skin, your shell of a father never did try to learn her,
Never took the opportunity to really earn her,
Only knew a version of you that we all
know now was just a foreigner,
We try so hard to be what our parents want that
we weep at night with such horror,
I always wanted to be level-minded like Levi, but
my anger resembles quite like Eren Yeager,
I'll turn to stone before I ever again be cut like paper,
Let me be because I won't pretend to be
your oh-so-friendly neighbor,
What I want now means much more than
what others could possibly cater,
And I won't make do with your demands.
I am nothing like a negotiator,
I am the dictator of my own well-being and decisions,
so let go of trying to become a translator,
My armor builds only with time. I will
never again be known as a faker,
Nineteen ninety-seven, I was born to wield a
sword and stand tall like a crusader,
Suppose one day my heart will turn my darkest of
depths into something appealing and tender,
But for now, I will embellish on the parts of me
that embraces my ill-equipped temper,
Arm's length, I'll keep my cancerous heart
before I go on another bender,
This is the only way I'll be able to breathe
until I am truly ready to remember,
Until I am deeply prepared to open this wound uncensored.

NYRD
10/22/22

Hot as Hell

You filled my box with love letters,
Mementos to last through the cold weather,
Feelings I really did think I detached from
now that we're no longer together,
These things happen when you're awake
at night with no sort of pleasure,
One two three drinks, I swore I was through,
but this liquor relieves the pressure,
You dealt the cards, God, but you left my acceptance on the dresser,
I've gone through all the stages of grief, yet
I can't move on from my depressor,
I don't want to be the norm and hit the refresher,
The tabs stay as they are as if I didn't know
the meaning of the term to sever,
Can I just let you go so we can both be better?
Although I suppose I wouldn't have a topic
to write about if I truly left her,
My heart moves with hers. She's clearly a collector,
Eyes so devious but her motives show no sign of error,
Not meant to be a professor but she's damn near clever,
Brains and beauty, there's no way I'd forget her,
Giselle, my God, I am under your spell,
Giselle, I don't know how to ever say farewell,
Excel and propel, you always did mean well,
Skin like caramel, she's respectfully hot as hell,
Deeper I dive as if I was clearly compelled,
Aware, I am though as we make sweet love in every hotel,
Make you mine over and over again and
whisper my sweet mademoiselle.

NYRD
09/13/22

Part of Me

Singing blues has been getting old,
You could be my lover and still be so cold,
Icy like snowflakes but still have a heart of gold,
I could love for forever and never leave nor fold,
Baby, I speak to God about the threshold you have on me,
I speak to God how it's been so long since you dropped me,
It's been so long since I felt you want me,
Still I'll love you from far away and
nothing could possibly stop me,
Suppose the blues caught me like a vigorous wave or tsunami,
Suppose it's time I let the thought of you go, my sweet mami,
Still I'll fondle your memory as if I was making origami,
Still I'll care for your silhouette as if I was
the designer of Givenchy or Armani,
Know this, I'll never tarnish your name like Amber did to Johnny,
I'll honor you like Donatella did to Gianni,
Your essence lives on even if you're not para mi,
Forever my love, dare I say, you'll be a part of me.

NYRD
06/29/22

Oppressor

I know I am blessed beyond measure,
But these days, I'm without a notion of Eros's pleasure,
The memory of you haunts me in what feels like forever,
I keep the box of us tucked away in my dresser,
I should let this go, but I still wish we were together,
And I know I'll die before I get the chance to ever caress her,
I should let these thoughts go before I feel its unwavering pressure,
It'll never be our time for your love was never
meant to be my ultimate successor,
I am aware I'm undeserving of cupid's blissful endeavor,
I would cry and be sad, but there's no
reason to be my own oppressor,
The stars told me last night that I'd always
dance with my own guilt and aggressor,
The longer I hold onto life, the longer I'll feel so much lesser...
I don't know where the future lies for me, but I
know at this moment I don't feel at all better.

NYRD
05/09/22

Tell Me, God

Your memory and voice still fucking haunts,
So used to losing to karma, she truly does know how to taunt,
Flip a coin to see how she will tie this knot,
Will it leave me dead or just barely breathing?
Will I carry on or will I fail due to grieving?
Tell me, God, is this what you expected of my little
life to have—no more meaning or feeling?
I try so hard, but I'm stuck in a state of bruised and bleeding,
Slipknot snuff plays and I can't help but
to feel the demons creeping,
Tell me, God, is this how you wanted things to go,
Forever in a sleep paralysis state, as if I'm
repenting for my sins down below,
I can't move I can't talk not this again oh no,
Finger on the trigger, I have the urge to paint the walls red,
We all know something just never was right inside my head,
I'd say pray for me, but God considers me dead,
In between the lines I've gathered and read,
To God, I failed one too many times, he briefly said,
Tell me what to believe if I can only come
close to the demons in my bed,
Will this thread of misery ever stop pumping through my chest?
Flew too close to the sun and now I no longer have a home to rest,
So tell me, God, why are you so pressed to keep
me here? I'm not something to invest.

NYRD
09/16/22

23

Take It Slow

You can find me where the flowers certainly bloom,
If only you knew the things I thought of in my room,
Undress you slow till your water drips and flows,
Roam your body till you're free from your woes,
I want to liberate your spirit from the darkness that grows,
Been through so much, you've gone accustomed to your lows,
You hold back your moans as I kiss your toes,
I've hit it once, so you know how this really goes,
Just let me let you lose control,
Let me let you reach your goal,
Your epiphany relies on how I go about devouring you whole,
If today was my last day, I would spend it entirely with you solely,
With you I would feel closest to heaven
because I know I am nothing holy,
How about this time we take things much more slowly?
I want to hold on to these moments for when I feel so lonely,
Bebe, I love you enough to no longer be selfish
enough to keep you utmost closely.

NYRD
09/23/22

Grow Up

Midnight rain hits the top of the roof,
I climb to the attic only to drop this noose,
Broken hearts, shattered glass on the kitchen floor
I'm tired of being just a muse,
My eyes glimmer with rage. I'm sick and tired of
being wolfine's number fucking two,
You're truly a character, but that mentality is going to thrive and consume,
She loves me today only to hate me tomorrow. This won't ultimately subdue,
I'm twenty-five. I need stability. I can't go
about life, acting like this won't do,
I need to grow up once and for all, it's clear and true,
I need to stop with my own bullshit and call my therapist,
If my sister were here, she would be profusely pissed,
God, don't tell her I trace my blade onto my wrists,
God, just tell her I'm finally okay with being alive because
my passions outweigh everything that persists,
Just whisper her sweet nothings so she won't worry
where I'd go when the darkness hits,
I'm trying not to get too sad, but fuck, I know I'll cry if I eat another Milano,
Chocolate filling with a hard shell, she would always
spilt it between yo y mis hermanos,
I can't help it, so I cover my face con mis manos,
A puddle of tears, I can still hear the rain drops touching the ground,
A river of sadness, I should have never hollered at you like a hellhound,
KC, you should not have forgiven me, but you did and
your grace and mercy will always stand profound,
I never meant to hurt you, I never meant to get so ignorantly loud,
Suppose a part of me thought it would be easier to be hated
than to uphold a status that you could be proud,
Maybe I'm just too talented at ruining good
things by inserting storm clouds,
I've had enough of this cycle and every derailing bad choice I've allowed,
I walk this path alone now without a notion of a crowd,
Like stars we don't ever touch each other but
we know we'll always be around,
No matter how many times the sun rotates around the earth,
my devotion for my loved ones will always be found.

NYRD
10/22/22

These Are the Moments in Time

For once we meet in the middle,
Straight forward and not in a riddle,
Sincerely say what we mean without a ripple effect,
Your initials engraved on my skin, so the memory is well kept,
I could love you for forever without a
notion of bitterness nor regret,
So much pain yet so much I could undoubtedly reflect,
Wisdom comes when misery has no place else to project,
Saving myself from myself because I'm the greatest suspect,
Me versus me, it's time to wake up for I've over-fucking-slept,
I could lie again, but where's my self-respect?
Disconnected to myself and connected to
the drugs that left me in debt,
In between my fingers, contemplating on smoking this cigarette,
The grass taste nice when my knees have felt utterly swept,
Staring at the eclipse just for a moment, we could gaze and forget,
So much wrong we did, huh? Is it too late to press reset?
Inner thoughts and remedies play over my
mind like a broken cassette,
Divine, you are Giselle, there's no forgetting
your mermaid silhouette,
Sing with me to Jhené Aiko, so I could forget to present,
Even when the moon was at its crescent, it
was always undeniably pleasant,
Iridescent souls we touched even when the our
broken pieces clashed. It was still fluorescent,
Maybe the breakup had to happen so we could
conquer our demons and suppressants,
But tonight, just tonight, we could look up to spot our
true witness to our time as stupid adolescents,
Infinite times more, I mumble back to myself, as the tears drop
and so does the will to take another goddamn antidepressant.

NYRD
09/06/22

Villain Era
~~Hero Arc~~

I'm just tryna escape from the backrooms,
Forgot my sanity has gone and I'm left
with these damn mushrooms,
Took too much now my pupils are beyond dilated,
Frustrated and isolated, all that's left is for my alter ego to rape me,
Skin to skin, we commence the degrading,
Skin to skin, I'm in immense pressure. There's no mistaking,
I run but the hallway is never-ending, and the drugs
are making sure I'm never again waking,
It's obvious my hands are not the only thing that's shaking,
Heartbreaking, isn't it? To be so close to having it,
yet far enough so that you're never grasping it,
Baby girl, there's a special place in hell for your kind,
Baby girl, there's a special place in hell for
your throat to be undoubtedly mine,
I'm the mastermind, and you're everything that'll soon be confined,
I am wolfine, and you're dead to me, so let's have
some fun before our destiny demands to bind,
We tried things your way. Now it's time you
left these little feelings behind,
One too many times your aspirations and
desires have been declined,
Now we gotta change our strips for something purely unkind,
I got a grin on my face writing this, so best
believe I'm deeply deprived,
Blood thirsty ever since wolfine has entered the chat,
Never again will we allow our twisted outsides
remain inside like a cave full of bats,
I am thirsty, but not for a damn shot glass,
My knuckles demand to be intertwined with brass,
We came for demolition until thy universe
has no choice but to kiss my ass,
This world is cruel enough, but I'm here to twist
the knife before it begs to collapse.

NYRD
10/11/22

Purgatory

Your name designated in my virtue,
Your face brings images, such as déjà vu,
Months go by, I'm fixated on the silhouette of you,
Past and future tense, I'm a product of
the chaos I've ultimately stew,
My third eye wishes I would wake up and come through,
I'm far away from you, and my skies are no
longer laced with your hues of blue,
I'm stuck in purgatory where every creature
is stitched with a remedy so taboo,
Falling in love with this new sensation so
there's no reason to unscrew,
Forever fucked by your essence swirling inside
of me, I'm captivated by your genjutsu,
Better off this way than empty, with an unknown
motive to seek misplaced value,
Love is infinite when it comes from a thread
weaved by a genuine revenue,
Slowly dropping the lust for liquor for an icy cold Mountain Dew,
I'm captivated to start anew,
I'm conflicted to stop looking for the goddamn issue,
Vision is impaired when the problem is within
me and not my external fucking view.

NYRD
04/29/22

Internal and External

I won't fake a smile nor play as your prototype,
I'm a vampire at night, but you're still not my type,
Heartless to society and all its meaningless hype,
I'll never be someone you could ever accurately describe,
Love me or hate me, either way high-five 'cause I do prescribe,
No one can write this story if I'm the sole and only scribe,
I pave my own path willingly without a pack or tribe,
I have no desire to take handouts nor bribes,
God fills every inch of this aching soul with graceful vibes,
Do good and be good through the viciously unforgiving tides,
Being alone and un-lonely leaves my thoughts picking sides,
Lord, let this anger and sadness stop destroying my insides,
But I'm aware as long as it's not external,
no one really fucking minds,
Aware of my mental illness but still
shocked when it truly does arise,
Patience ponders when you speak with disappointed eyes,
I'm sorry I couldn't hide it all better with little white lies,
I should ahve stayed quiet, but alas, I was not wise,
And I have to write this shit down to make
something out of my these broken ties.

NYRD
04/27/22

In the Air

I want the fairytale,
I want to lure you into my lair,
Make you feel ever so rare,
Legs whimper while I'm pulling on your hair,
You are mine and I am yours. I sincerely
can't stress this enough, I swear,
Neverland shaped as hotel rooms for this erotic love affair,
Leave it all behind 'cause I want to feel you bare,
Whisper in your ear nobody can fucking compare,
Slap me. Let's make things officially square,
I know I caused a lot of damage and despair,
But give me the chance for redemption
to clear the toxicity in the air,
Maybe not now, but sooner or later, this slate will impair,
I hope you know every poem is a love letter to her, the rightful heir,
Soulmates, as messed up as it is, you're
the only one who suits me fair,
The only one who tolerates me when my eyes see red and flare,
Your initials on my arm remind me you're always there,
God knows I try but need to be better than
just a notion of leaning on a prayer.

NYRD
04/26/22

Straight Menace

The shadow in the mirror has been whispering some utter sense,
My blood drops. It's not a coincidence,
Losing my mind, I'm so down for the experience,
Bury me alive. Let's see the demonic forces start to commence,
Play me like a tiny violin at my very own underlining expense,
Laughing, losing your breath, baby, I love
the way you stay on the offense,
And I stay so hollow and dense 'cause
there's no need any self-defense,
It's you, so I let it slide like a sympathetic cop
would if you forgot your license,
Suppose it's the boobs, suppose it's the pretty
face, but let's not uphold this,
The truth is society couldn't care less, tsk tsk,
If it's not in the public eye, it goes on straight to dismiss,
Not enough souls care enough to distinguish the premise,
I cry far too less to care about being
anything else but a divine menace,
Tippy toes, I'm a thief when it comes to
chasing the feeling of zealousness,
Sweet thing on my hip, she's my day one,
she's my fucking precious,
Devour her like I meant it, serenade her like it
was an electric guitar plus Hendrix,
I got more than two scents, I got more than your penance,
I don't praise Satanism, I praise my very own mindful essence,
Not a God, but just a lyrical genius at every gaze I give at every
sentence spoken it demonstrates my strong everlasting presence,
Baby, I'm finishing off the year with vengeance.

NYRD
09/12/22

Bañarme al Sol

I am covered in ashes,
Gave my best but still you wouldn't share your rations,
You betrayed me, Neida. I thought we
shared the same exact passions,
You're just a hotheaded fool with steaming
fumes like headless dragons,
A house so empty, you still fill it with what your mind imagines,
She won't come back, so stop filling it with
entities that resemble famines,
Whatever happens, happens in a cowboy bebop order of fashion,
If I could, I'd heal these wounds enough to see
Hector's future heirs, Esteban y Sebastian,
Or my Mia I'll one day meet when my future
self requires me to take notable action,
I just need to get out of my own way because I'm
becoming a red flag of walking distraction,
So much pieces there all just fractions of myself
trying to rediscover what it means to be whole,
I wish my sister could take the wheel when I
don't know how to continue with this role,
Twenty-five years old and I'm still chasing
your ghost. I'm a fool, I know,
Mom, I pray for you in ways I should pray for myself, I know,
Perhaps this Christmas, I'll get myself something else besides coal,
Suppose I'll fill this sack with an abundant
mass of affirmations for the soul,
Good music, good poetry to brush up on
my knowledge of ingles y español,
Te quiero mana y sé que tengo el control,
Dame mas tiempo para bañarme al sol,
I'm so close I can feel the rays en mi espalda, I know.

NYRD
09/11/22

Self-Inflicting

Dance ballerina for I'm your mighty Zeus,
You don't ever need a spotlight for you bring la luz,
Be more than a muse, be the hand that unties this noose,
Your lips, your sweat, Giselle, you never
knew what it felt like to lose,
Winner by nature, it's a given you're what
everyone would never refuse,
Hourglass shape with a lingering taste of juice,
She's not an easy cruise. She's too busy being the
thunder forecast on the your daily news,
Turn the page and she's the layout when your
mind drifts and wanders as you hit snooze,
Quite obvious but quite oblivious, you are well
too entangled within your temple of blues,
Always to text first, I see you haven't picked up on any clues,
My dear wolfine, this is a reminder to not blow another fuse,
No one really understands unless there in the place of your shoes,
But she tried her best and you ruined every
opportunity to try to accuse,
She cares for you truly but deep down she's so
fucking tired of your every excuse,
No one could possibly love you unless you love you
without indulging in self-inflicting abuse.

NYRD
09/11/22

33

VR

Lost in a virtual reality,
I could scream, but I'm used to handling it so casually,
So vivid but I know nothing's real, and this
ache is nothing but a fucking cavity,
I could make an appointment to see another,
but I know it'll only end in tragedy,
I welcome the brutality, but only if it's I
that is infected by its insanity,
I only made it this far 'cause my sister stopped
me from jumping off the balcony,
Now I know I have to live for her own peaceful bliss and sanity,
And if I end it all now, then the heavens will rain in pure agony,
I suppose I should stop playing with death
and my limited mortality,
God has shown me more than enough hospitality,
In this museum, I walk past every version of myself in actuality,
Disgusted and angry, I would do more than just commit battery,
Mother, forgive me for being this monster
stuck in the vessel, this anatomy,
I'm just an unknown anomaly corrupted by the devil's analogy,
Mana, open the galaxy and stars for me, if the day
ever comes when you accept this apology,
I'm losing touch with more than just reality
but with my own sense of gravity.

NYRD
09/14/22

Gifted

No rest for the wicked,
I do what I want, I'm committed,
But ever since I met you, I've been conflicted,
Could it be possible it's still you?
My God, there's no way you could have had all this scripted,
There's no way she soothes my soul like liquor
could never do—she's the purest liquid,
Down my throat her nectar spreads, and I cannot
deny I'm in her reach. I'm quite livid,
The way her body fits my own can leave
my doubts quite submitted,
Is it true I'm the one that leaves your breath quite constricted?
I take your body farther than he could
ever, and it's so sick and twisted,
But the feeling is mutual because you have me addicted,
If letting you go was ever so easy, God would have been permitted,
But it's obvious I tried and I thought I really succeeded,
but one look at you and my heart has been lifted,
How do I come up with things to say when all
I have are memories? I must be gifted,
Alas, it also leads to torment to endure the only
time I felt most alive before I drifted,
She knows I ain't shit, but she still allows me to coexist,
She knows I'm grateful, but she also knows
I'm bad news in the midst,
Can't blame her now that I'm lonely and pissed,
Pissed at myself for letting you become missed,
But I guess that's when you know it's real when the
emotions still linger way past since you've last kissed.

NYRD
10/18/22

Wolfine

Hardwired to succeed,
Lucifer and I both shook on the deed,
My motives were planted like a seed,
Hardwired to be a different person to proceed,
I made my bed a long time ago,
I'm a ghostwriter indeed,
I come in the night when you feel the urge to blow,
A couple of lines and we both know you want some more,
Shinigami eyes, baby, get used to the glow,
I'll take you far from this current state and put you on the radio,
You wanna be known so badly, but the value
is going to cost ya, you already know,
Take my hand wolfine before you soon become fin,
Embrace this side of yours as the almighty kingpin,
We both know you're slowly fading from
taking one too many shots to the chin,
God left like your sister did. She's no longer in the form of skin,
But she visits your dreams telling you not to sin,
It's too late, isn't it, Lucifer? My fate is already making you grin,
I can see it, God, you're playing a sad tune on a violin,
Notes I've never heard before you're tapping from within,
Paralyzed I can't help but to wonder where exactly I've been,
Tears form and my reality seems to spin,
So much time wasted. God, can you just fill me in?
I don't want to be this version that stripped
of her every meaningful win.

NYRD
09/25/22

36

Dominator

If I fold, would you swallow your pride to care?
I've lost more than the average being could possibly bare,
I'll never let anyone within my reach again, this I swear,
No one stays but I guess that's life,
It's simply known to be unfair,
The moon is the only thing that has always been ultimately there,
Only reliable thing when nightfall touches the air,
I know I've never been the best, but I've certainly
always been indescribably rare,
Things always seem to change so I avoid
those who seem to be missing a pair,
You just gotta say fuck it eventually and take
risks like you got nine lives to spare,
Beating my chest like a gorilla, I'm ready to grasp
it all rather than to just simply declare,
There's a war inside my mind, but I place my
hands to thy Lord for a sincere prayer,
It's a close remedy to my internal solar beaming flares,
I always end up burning myself, but this time,
I'm more equipped and prepared,
My brains just as strong as my body. I am no longer scared,
If you've lost it all. then you can relate to the
void of sincere emptiness and despair,
A fate worse than hell but look how you've
come so others should beware,
C'est juste la vie, but it's not too late to reclaim your heir.

NYRD
10/23/22

37

You're My Humanity

The more I bleed, the more it takes the pain away,
The more I scratch the surface, the more
purgatory feels cozy to stay,
Hell became boring, so I used it as my ashtray,
Now my every breath keeps thy padre at bay,
Doomsday may be my favorite holiday,
I embrace the worst, so eventually it'll want to leave me too,
Reverse psychology will eventually be all
that I need for a bloody rescue,
Twenty-five years young and embracing
all that now makes brand-new,
Had to switch up on my morals because everyone took it as taboo,
Hate myself now but it's the only way I'll ever awaken my genjutsu,
Chakra flows throughout my body, so best
believe I'm now a major issue,
Walking, talking red flag and that's the truth too,
Honesty hour I still fucking miss you,
I still let the late nights consume me on cue,
Like clockwork but deep down I'll forever choose
my love for you to always continue,
It's the only thing that reminds me I'm still
human, so I let you forever linger through.

NYRD
08/31/22

Sick Brain

Your veins are tempting my blade,
Blood thirsty, I want it all to fucking rain,
Sweeney Todd in the flesh, I'm up for a killing raid,
The devil drives the will to my notable crusade,
Hmm, why does your sweat taste like you're afraid?
You tell me you're not that I am the one
whose fate has now been made,
God, the devil toys with my brain as if we were in an arcade,
Over and over again, this is more than just a moment to serenade,
I will never come out of this, can't you tell this isn't a charade?
Slowly dying. slowly decaying,
Echoes of God's verses spiral through my
mind—I can feel them prying,
Suppose it's my guardian angel sighing and silently praying,
The good, the bad, and then there are the ones
that do everything, except obeying,
I don't think twice when it comes to acting
on everything I be saying,
Not meant to follow the rules nor to lead when I'm
one snap away from becoming a super saiyan,
When I tell you I got you, best believe I ain't ever playing.

NYRD
09/22/22

Hinder

Touch me once and you'll set my black fire,
I was not always like this. It's just part of my new attire,
This world made me into such a monster and a fucking liar,
And I know nobody cares to reads this, but it's
the only thing that makes me feel higher,
A sense of redemption that I know awaits to be conspired,
Twisted and dented, I pray to God to be ultimately sired,
I cannot go on this way so fucked up and tired,
Twenty-four-seven, I need more time to be acquired,
I have a long list of regrets and it's nothing to be desired,
Baby, my sweetest baby, run as far as you can
'cause I'm coming off a little too strong,
As good as I dream to be, I'm all types of wrong,
I was born to never belong, and the more I tried, the
more I realized I was just another sad song,
And although it's only been you I've ever loved all along,
I must stop being selfish and let you stay gone,
Better off without me hindering your everlasting dawn.

NYRD
10/04/22

40

Lost Cause Lookin' for a Clause

It's clear I've looked down at my feet,
It's a virtue of mine to utterly accept defeat,
A pattern established to face. Fuck Lucifer's dirty cleats,
Concrete evidence, I've been fucked from birth,
so I'm accustomed to bittersweets,
Motto of life is dukes of hazards, so you know I'm down for leaps,
I'm down for hella heaps,
I've barely slept, so be wary when I don't sensor the bleeps,
Be wary when I'm walking down the streets
& rolling hard in the deeps,
Cobrah on the highest possible volume, so
best believe it's not for the peeps,
It's to keep me livid for the upcoming
weeks so I don't dwell on weeps,
Bumping my noggin', smiling in a daze at all
the other misunderstood lookin' creeps,
Rosy cheeks and me, I'm a loner, occasional
stoner like Pete, or a.k.a. Sketes?
Talking gibberish and supposedly it's a poem, so
don't forget what I'm fucking stuttering to reap,
Pause and rewind, it's a cycle in my head,
so let's skip the meet and greet,
I ate up every mishap my demons utterly speak like a
full tank of gasoline in your beloved used jeep,
But better off alone is the new foretold
motto I wish to follow and seek,
Opening my eyes to new beginnings to let the light
shine through the darkest sides of me that peak.

NYRD
04/23/22

41

More Than Rare

So heavy to bare,
Reality is quite a nightmare,
But in my dreams you're always there,
My love, you're always there, and I'm fully
aware it's a moment for us to share,
I hold you close and nothing can possibly compare,
The birds sing and dance in this love affair,
We were truly one of a kind pair,
But I must awake soon with great despair,
It's like being shocked through the electric chair,
Nothing prepares me for this, I swear,
After all this time, it still causes a tear,
So please nobody seek me out to try to repair,
Just drive off and steer clear from me, beware,
It won't be me, but someone elsewhere,
So don't come close because I will not share,
Not this heart nor my tender lovin' care,
For it is far more than just rare,
It only releases itself in a dream or in a prayer.

NYRD
01/20/21

Indisputable

Cloudy vibes and sweet iced tea,
Fighting till my last breath like I'm Bruce Lee,
Indisputable energy, it tastes like Halsey,
Bouncing off the walls so fucking effortlessly,
Alone in my dome is always preferably,
So fuck the outside noise and all its fake generosity,
Music is all that lingers inside of me like a novelty,
I could care less if no one sees 'cause I'm
too in tuned with my odyssey,
It's all I know quite honestly,
I'll dive in head first into the unknown before
I make an apology to society,
Far too aware I'm a prodigy and everything
I am is sewed within possibility,
So I'll roll the dice as if it were my stability,
A pen and paper gets me off as if it were my tranquility,
Whether the outcome is good or bad, there's
always sincerity within my credibility,
Beneath the rubble I promise you there is no disability,
Only humility beneath the mass of your own sense of capability,
And if no one sees that, just know that the
stars will always carry your nobility.

NYRD
08/31/21

Happy Birthday

Anime or Hulu,
Living room just us two,
Good times I'll hold onto,
Your laughter always on cue,
Heart so golden it might be taboo,
You're more than an imprint or a tattoo,
Ultimately you've aid me like the strongest gorilla glue,
Sadness can never know me long enough to turn me utterly blue,
Instead I'm an array of sunshine with passions, I need to make do,
My dear brothers, this is a poem in the eyes of your tender views,
Words too hard to illustrate, so I'll play as your rescue,
Mother figure, to say the least, she's
undoubtedly always there to turn to,
Even now I know you're there in my every
breath when I feel the notion to subdue,
No matter what the future may brew, my faith in
honoring you is the only instinct that ring true,
I will make you proud, Senpai, this I promise you,
Jimenes name will rise like a white rose that
knew nothing more than to push through,
Today I'll hold you in my heart as I say happy
birthday, Momm and before you can it,
I love you too.

NYRD
05/22/22

Taurus

You came to leave.
'Cause all I can do is keep my heart and secrets up my sleeve,
Not everything is what I once thought or perceived,
I'm not who I once was unfortunately I feel misconceived,
I don't know who I am lately,
Just a silhouette riddled so vaguely,
I try to speak but the weight of my chest gets heavier daily,
These wounds won't seem to heal, I bet you must hate me,
Too sweet of a soul, I know you, rather just move on and forget me,
I promise you I'll forever regret the bad I've
done to you, my graceful Taurus baby,
Karma will come for me and my journey will end inhumanely,
It's what I deserve, and all I have to blame
is ultimately inside of me,
It's hard to write without begging myself to
not take my own my life indeed,
I should stop writing about you and my mom, but it's
the only thing that rattles inside my brain to bleed,
Cross my heart, I hope my destiny is someplace
far so I don't stop you from succeeding,
There's a special place for me in hell deep down.
God and I both nodded our heads agreeing.

NYRD
05/13/22

Dear Ex
(Part 1)

Ariel, you're wetter than the ocean,
Lay you down, shower you with this utter devotion,
In your ear, my sweet darling, tell me how do you want this motion,
Up and down, bebe, I'm glad I'm what you've chosen,
Kings of Leon's "Sex on Fire" is on the
radio for tonight's radiant emotion,
Give me your heart and I'll give you my all so freely and open,
I'll speak of you so graciously for you've aided
me when I had no serotonin nor oxytocin,
Just a couple of sinners stitched together like knitted woven,
Just a couple of kids too young for this intense lovin',
Suppose in time, if it's meant to be, whether
it's in a year or even seven,
I trust in God as I trust in a frozen Slurpee from 7-Eleven,
With you, Giselle, I'm at my closest to heaven,
These words have no meaning if you didn't
leave your notable impression,
A blessing and a lesson without question,
I'd do it all over again without rethinking it for a second,
I'm sorry it took me so long to overcome
my demons and depression,
Each day I live is a day I write again for it's
my utmost profound obsession,
I'll never forget the moments you've calmed my
storms like it was a free therapy session.

NYRD
06/04/22

46

Dear Ex
(Part 2)

You always carried what felt like a sensual sixth sense,
It felt as if our souls imprinted onto each other's essence,
So deep this bond goes, it was more than just great sex,
Blind as a bat but I know how real and
rare you are without my specs,
Who needs hoes that resemble objects when
we could be doing endless projects,
Shh, that was an inside joke, so I'm sorry I can't explain its aspects,
Watch me flex on you hoes when you try to talk to me with depths,
My energy and language do not correlate with your concepts,
KC knows this mind ain't for no basic bitch for it's far too complex,
My life ain't meant to be foretold as bland as simplex,
No matter how long it takes, we're both meant to take greater steps,
Just like that quote "no stress, one boo, no
ex, small circle, bigger checks,"
Key facts everything corresponds like the movie butterfly effects.

NYRD
06/04/22

Dear Ex
(Part 3)

Look in the mirror. Tell me what do you want for it to reflect,
Forever, I'll choose her and this life for God allowed it to connect,
It's easy to forget self-worth, but it's a choice to neglect,
Stay close to the ones that treat your soul,
body, and mind with profound respect,
Imperfectly perfect, we are just humans.
What can one truly expect?
Look closely, you are your own architect,
Take these letters apart when you need to
understand what I'm trying to dialect,
But, Dear Giselle, if it's only you that reads this,
then I've hit everyone I've wanted to direct,
Bebe, I love you completely and truthfully with your every aspect,
A walk to remember was the greatest example in retrospect,
Give love and cherish each other unconditionally
is what I wish to portray and protect.

NYRD
06/04/22

Psychotic Rage

You are the main character and the theme,
Words flow out of my mouth like a vigorous river stream,
I look at you and it's hard to fully comprehend
what the hell this fucking means,
Smoke fills the air when I need a deeper understanding
of my deepest desires and dreams,
Never the one to collapse but to take
things to the ultimate extremes,
Wish I was like Fez, from *Euphoria*, with a calm
mindset and frame down to his fucking genes,
Suppose I could be that for you one day, but
I doubt you would truly believe,
Psychotic rage inside of me and we both know you're not naive,
Hot headed as fuck, I'm too quick with
the switchblade up my sleeve,
I'm too quick with the back talk and damn
right action walks like Keanu Reeves,
I'm not tryna deceive you 'cause I'm John Wick,
so I'ma still be about it, even when I grieve,
Like a light switch, I come alive when
provoked. Baby, it's a pet peeve,
Don't fuck with the ones I love 'cause you'll have
an outer body experience, soul's gonna leave.

NYRD
05/28/22

Battle Cry

Not sure if this is a goodnight or goodbye,
High above the mesmerizing sky where angels
fly had no notion of evil could ever pry,
I wait down here for a single reply to somehow clarify,
Alas, no noise, no commotion to simply gratify,
Alone once again with a clouded mind to
keep me away from my third eye,
March first of twenty twenty-two and what do I have to justify?
All my days are spent writing, thinking it'll somehow purify,
Thinking it'll calm my battle cry,
Still my demons dance and grin ear to ear
without a notion of being shy,
Without guilt they vigorously multiply with
no end, and they'll never be satisfied,
Gasping for air, my God, I'm petrified,
My God, I'm solidified,
Frozen in space and time, I'm nothing but
a mass of self-sabotaging suicide,
"Rise! Rise! Rise!" is what I say to keep
my mind gracefully occupied,
Agony is all that resides inside, how much
longer do I have by my brother's side?
How much longer do I have before I'm fully
convinced I have nothing left to provide?
As sincere as I'm being right now, if you text
me and ask if I'm okay, just know I lied,
Whatever hope I have left is struggling
to be what once was an allied,
So conflicted to look at the fucking bright side,
But God damn it, I'll smile before the tears ever cease to be dried,
I'll yell at the top of my lungs with pride
before death catches me fucking slide.

NYRD
03/01/22

Till Dawn

Heavy is the head that wears the crown,
I couldn't hold up the promise to keep the chaos resound,
My demons latch onto the like they're waiting on a rebound,
I closed the door to love so that it could be
easier for no one to stick around,
Your hands no longer reach for my own, and
it's obvious I live in a ghost town,
I don't want to be here anymore with these
souls that rather see me below ground,
And alas, all my remedies are no longer there to hold shit down,
These memories serve nothing more than just
pain to keep my sanity from being found,
Everyone has moved on so I suppose it's
my turn to just turn things off,
Being selfless to others has only left my
guard so pitifully weak and soft,
It's a cycle for people to leave, so how about
we cut ties and just get lost?
Tokyo has been calling my name ever
since my heart has been crossed,
But I'll never choose to live a wanderlust life forever
consumed by my own wretched frost,
I won't turn my emotions off when things go undoubtedly wrong,
I will stay true to myself, but I will choose wisely
who sees the parts that are undoubtedly fond,
No one will ever feel a taste of my love until I make
through to the other side of this very sad song, until
there's no more tears chasing my every dawn.

NYRD
11/16/22

Hell Boy

Dreamt of heaven but fell into hell,
Just a silhouette of a ghost in its shell,
Felt like Michael but Lucifer sincerely dwells,
I can't stay here, sweetheart, 'cause demolition fucking sells,
I have a vision of a life I see for myself and lately
it's the only thing that really compels,
Beauty and brains but this heart has grown so
cold, so I hid it in the darkest well,
Oh well, I suppose my chaotic mind is the only
thing that's meant to astonishingly propel,
Utterly meant to be without a mademoiselle,
But fuck it, I know things changed, and
chasing a Benjamin is my only tell,
I don't need witchcraft to get what I want 'cause I'm
the entity and my demons are under my spell,
I'm your senpai, I'm your master, but I ain't
part of no cartel, so change the canal,
Baby, I'm not what you need. I'm what you desire, no morale,
No fucking way I'd fuck you to give you the
notion I'd keep you on my personnel,
Prove your loyalty or get the fuck out of my face,
Prove your innocence so I can show you why it's a disgrace,
Dance with me and I'll show you how I got to this place,
Red wine in my system, is it clear I'm just a carcass?
Is it clear I'm never seeing a loved one if they're in heaven's gates?
I am what I am, so I will fuck it up even more before
it makes me its bitch like I'm Patrick Bates,
I will laugh at your fucking face before I cry
of the empty void of God's embrace,
It's clear I was meant to be a rebel and make mistakes,
Always destined to be left behind in the shape
God wanted me to forever taste.

NYRD
11/17/22

Cuidarme

I get sad when I think about the time I chose not to spend with you,
I swear I thought I had more time to love you too,
Regretfully I never showed how much you
meant to me and god I wish you knew,
Time really blew by, and now I rely on meds to mend me on cue,
Like clockwork, I dance with you in this empty venue,
Like clockwork, I'm racing to be everything you wanted me to be,
Demons sigh, wishing I'd stop dreaming of life's utter beauty,
This isn't a novela nor a movie, but baby, I'd do
anything to keep from feeling this gloomy,
Whether it's pills or aspirations, it's the only thing
that keeps me going, so goddam it, sue me,
Hate me or love me, either way you never really knew me,
Either way, baby, you're just another phase y no puedo quedarme,
And I already know if you're not my first lover,
then you'll never truly cuidarme.

NYRD
07/11/22

Vacant

This bouquet of flowers, you never really did want to claim it,
I hope if it's not me, then another could make you want to save it,
Love is but a luxury too far grand for me
to ever fully grasp to obtain it,
The life I've ever so dreamt of always leaves me quite so vacant,
I'm just a stupidly sad song for everyone's joyous entertainment,
I don't recall the last time she said I was beautiful
or the last time I woke up feeling radiant,
But I can recall the times I've felt my soul in utter displacement,
The times I felt everyone draw from impulse
to trade me for a replacement,
God, I know it's just me hurting while everyone's
in a state of constant com-placement,
Still I can't erase the memories because in those
memories, we were closer than adjacent,
These tears drop down my cheek onto the
cement of my cold empty basement,
It hurts to write, but it's the only way to free
myself from my own resentment,
It's just a heaviness as if my feet were caving into the pavement,
Like quicksand, I'm deep beneath debt, with death
knocking on every sign of being impatient.

NYRD
11/08/22

POV

I tried so hard to leave it in the past tense,
I tried so hard to not be such a menace,
But fuck, what was the premise?
Fuck, I feel like I'm everyone's blemish,
I don't want to rage anymore and be your life long wreckage,
But damn, I know this is more than just a fetish,
I know I have a problem that I need to replenish,
Find God for love isn't everything but a recipe to perish,
I know so much now that I wished I knew then
before life became utterly hellish,
I am damnation forged by my mistakes
that I must now try to embellish,
This is more than a POV, but a notion to right my
wrongs and find a new meaning of zealous,
'Cause god knows I'm tired of feeling this fucking breathless,
Gasping for oxygen, I'm clutching onto my sister's necklace,
It's not ashamed to beg for mercy 'cause god knows
this isn't my first time feeling so fucking helpless,
This isn't my first time calling for a lifeline
'cause I've been so fucking careless,
It's all my fault this is more than just self-awareness,
I reap what a sow for being so fucking reckless.

NYRD
05/16/22

Energy

This isn't a honeymoon, but we sure did bloom,
No matter how far, we're under the same exact moon,
Lips to your skin I can make you utterly swoon,
My god, make this a lifetime rather than soon,
Let my baby shine rather than to hide in her cocoon,
We both know this love is not meant to end by noon,
Caressing your lips with my own as we float inside this lagoon,
Not a single word exchanged as we hear the silence of this tune,
Water so still, you'd think we're immune,
From everything and everyone, this is our own platoon,
So rest your weary heart for there's no need to fume,
Be like water and only allow its energy to consume,
And, lord, when she's ready, give her the strength to presume.

NYRD
07/24/21

Mana

You'll always be in my heart,
In my dreams, we're never apart,
Every description of you simply resonates with art,
You were always there at any given rate,
Even when I was down, you truly did motivate,
You taught me to be wise and to communicate,
To love deeply and to reciprocate,
I swear to god, I'll always appreciate,
Every move I make will be in honor of you, I dedicate,
You're my mom, dad, and best friend in
every sense I can firmly illustrate,
Purer than water she's the keeper to heaven's purely white gates,
Always and forever her soul sincerely captivates,
Our bond is deeper than the sense of two soulmates,
Because of you, my faith grows and refreshes,
cleaning up my broken slate.

NYRD
04/13/21

Allure to Darkness

Don't underestimate the allure of darkness,
What we see what we feel is within our harness,
Art is a picture perfect envelope for chaos to play,
It's the only thing that makes sense beneath
the parts I cannot convey,
The only thing that is left when sanity is but a void that never stays,
So just this once come with me to Playa del Rey
where the sun reflects its golden rays,
Your caramel skin and glossy lips never could do
whatever they may as long as they don't betray,
Suppose I'm not the right one, but I'm the
one your body seeks for a relay,
My chaos is just what you crave to put your cuerpo at ease,
Never half-assed, so spread your limbs for a hint of expertise,
Tongue tied with vows I'm tempted to apply
the pressure so, bebe, please,
Stop fighting these desires for I'm more than
willing to prove I am a better me,
I could never thank you enough for putting
me on the right path to succeed,
I am undeserving, but I'll spend a lifetime
making it up to you indeed,
So much darkness within my soul, I'll learn to
express it in other ways so that no one bleeds.

NYRD
10/03/22

Am I Amendable?

Be practical but never palpable,
Keep quite before you're deemed as irrational,
The broken pieces have turned you into
something of a reckless animal,
Trying so hard to be tamed but its clear your losses are tangible,
You write just so you can shut your eyes at night, but the
nightmares make the pain excruciatingly visible,
Inexplicable it's like there's something
missing like an unknown variable,
An emotion I lost long ago I tend to feel less
and less significant like a decimal,
My chest pounds so loud, my life feels like
how you look at me . . . regrettable,
Sins on sins, hell seems undeniably ethical,
I want to change, but is it too late to be established
as something beautifully credible,
Noteworthy and amendable

Did God wash his hands on the sight of my existence?
Is my spiritual light too dimmed now for you to waver an assist?
Did I disappoint you far too many times
when I would slice my wrists?
Apologizes are pointless when I could
never forgive myself in the midst,
I want to be better. God, I want to feel you on my
cold skin as if I were being sun kissed,
I want the moonlight to grace my presence
when I feel like I'm being punished,
I want to be noticed by you more than I
want my work to be published,
I need you, I need you, I need you, God,
Now more than ever before my time and
chances on this earth are finished.

NYRD
12/3/22

59

Iridescent Soul

I would rather be your friend rather than a stranger,
By my side rather to feel you are endangered,
Such a species, my God, I'd give my life for
you if the option was wagered,
Pain lingers but I'll never look upon you for something ill-natured,
Although I've made mistakes that could never be wavered,
I'm only human, but it's not an excuse to be accepted nor favored,
Even if your presence is no longer with me,
your memory will infinitely be savored,
Your scent, laughter, and dimples will forever be
stitched into my soul like it was tailored,
Not another being could unravel all that you have come to layered,
My first love, you are ultimately what I
come to feel like I've majored,
KC, only thy angels from above know how
deeply you are truly spiced and flavored,
Iridescent soul, you are but a blossoming
butterfly so delicately catered,
God took his time as if he was aware his
time would never be tapered,
Because of you, my words have meaning and impact as if I've
touched such grace. It makes my voice tremble or quavered.

NYRD
05/30/22

Little Miss Bliss

Angelic with demonic red lips,
Up and down you like how I move these hips?
This love resembles a total eclipse, and there is no
portion of this being foretold in any scripts,
You wouldn't see our story be played out in any flicks,
This is more than profound so never let me let go of this
grip cause I'm waiting to eventually take more sips,
I need you in my life like I need Jesus when
conflict tends to come into the mix,
You keep my two feet on the ground, even
when I don't know what's in the abyss,
I won't let this woman become someone I'd only ever reminisce,
I'll forever chase her like I'm cashing this bliss,
I'm going mental without her passionate kiss,
The way she flicks her tongue and makes it shifts,
You got me for a long time and not a short time my future missus,
Cross my heart, I fucking promise this,
Best believe I'll put a ring around that finger
as long as you and I breathe and exist,
Alexa, play Camilo's "Por Primera Vez" cause that's
how I'm feeling and I can't fucking resist,
I'd take on every night shift just to make sure you're
pampered and fed with more than just gifts,
I know you don't ever ask for it, but best believe I'll always insist,
God really did bless my little life when he
placed you into my world to coexist,
Until my last breath, you can count on me if you need an assist,
I'll even put your ass on a life raft, so you don't ever try to drift,
I'd fight with the power or my fists if your demons
or whomever arises from the mists.

NYRD
06/06/22

Cigarettes

Early morning, I just might need a cig,
Up at 5:00 a.m., my life feels just about rigged,
I need to stop waiting to feel blissfully fulfilled,
Each day I wonder if today I'd want to rebuild,
All these broken pieces just makes me want to be resealed,
I just don't know what it takes for the good in me to be revealed,
This cigarette tastes like I'll never be healed,
The sun wants to shine on my face, but my
demons shield me to only conceal,
Look away, they say, as I intensely feel,
The heat lingers but my darkness is just surreal,
Just breathe and watch *I Love Lucy's* Lucille,
Such a tender soul, just wanted to make those laughs to appeal,
I miss her like I miss the goodness in my withering soul,
Being without my mana has just taken an immense toll,
This is a life sentence and definitely not parole,
Robbed and beaten of all that I thought I had in control,
My guardian angel sighs and I've once again
asked for her guidance to console,
I suppose we both need a cigarette before we take this stroll.

NYRD
09/26/22

Light

These wounds won't seem to fade,
Tears drop, falling down my jet black suede,
Flames are getting hotter, my demons are on a tirade,
Day and night dealing with this fucking crusade,
Entities laughing and joking, playing me like a fucking arcade,
I'm angry, sad, and so fucking betrayed,
Switchblade to my neck I'm yelling at the
top of lungs, I'm not afraid!
Time and time again, I've been here before,
but this is not another retrograde,
I can't picture myself walking this earth
for another fucking decade.

Mom, I miss you more than ever. You should have stayed,
I would have traded places with you, lord knows I fucking prayed,
Why do all the best ones go no matter how
much we beg and persuade,
Ever since you left, these tears haven't dried but only invade,
The light behind my eyes has now dimmed and degrade,
I know you're there mom urging me to not self-medicate,
That one day all the answers will soon be made,
And till then to not forget all you have portrayed.

NYRD
06/06/21

Monster

Samurai at day,
Day walker by night,
My alter ego is wolfine fucking knight,
My sword never folds when I'm lifted to thy sight,
But I'm only human, so I burn at the stake
to the touch of a candlelight,
Still I will fucking rise for I am a phoenix,
so I'll undoubtedly take flight,
I match my words with my actions like I'm Charles fucking White,
G fuel runs through my veins, so best
believe I'm feeling the electrolytes,
My mind so divine, if you could see the rays
of emotion, I'd be like northern lights,
I battle with my metal each day, but I never quit at any vice,
Corpse, Scarlxrd, and Savage Ga$p play in the
background when I need a taste of paradise,
Bass and my demons get along swimmingly, so I let
them play while I take leave from my own demise,
Thumbs typing, head swaying, I got that
Power Puff Girls type of spice,
I'll fight anyone and everyone like I'm from the *Totally Spies!*
My allies are in the music and in my notepad
when I feel the urge of grace to emphasize,
I don't know how to explain who or what I
am entirely, but I'll let you decide.

NYRD
11/05/22

Gnarly

The flames group me so I just let it embody,
I bend her over when she has been naughty,
Just this moment I know that she fucking got me,
Just this moment I'll forget that I see everything like Itachi,
You break my walls 'cause fucking you now ain't just a hobby,
I want you and you alone and not a silhouette or a copy,
I can't stand meeting up with someone else if
it's not you I'm waiting at the lobby,
Angelic as ever, she gets into position so we can get sloppy,
Does what I say 'cause she knows I only fuck her so godly,
I love the way she turn the tables and rides me like a Harley,
I love the way she even says that she's sorry,
Naked and afraid 'cause she knows that I can get gnarly,
But she loves the pain she's twisted like she's Harley,
I'm not no joker, but I am disturbed like Shoto's brother, Dabi,
My villain academia arc, but I'm not in it for a kamikaze.

NYRD
11/01/22

65

New Heights

Gazing at my birth mother and there's still no relation,
I don't recognize my own reflection,
I just want to grasp this undoubtable inception,
The stars swarm my mind with utter fixation,
Dancing about reminding me I'm in their mentions,
Maybe I don't need to belong anywhere in precise,
Suppose I don't need another being in order to feel paradise,
Just the moon and I is all I could ever demand as my asking price.

Jesus never folded, so I must not either
when life tends to rolls its dice,
Still I hope if the time ever comes God sees
you and I plus northern lights,
Deeply I feel God's grace surround me when
I'm consumed by own devilish vice,
Maybe I don't deserve you, but I'd sacrifice it all to
prove I can make through these hellish nights,
Redemption for a love fully noteworthy of its tender rights,
And if the day ever comes I'd prove it to thy
lord, I could take on any new heights.

NYRD
05/19/22

Revive

In your eyes, they glimmer with admiration,
Our memories fill me up with affirmation,
Every sense of the meaning, you are adoration,
Selfless you are without any hesitation,
A true blessing you flutter through and through with inspiration,
Mom, I know you'll fight your way back to us without limitation,
Strongest woman I know for you bring this world liberation,
Your vision has the power to bring us three to salvation,
So rise, Mother, there's still so much left to give,
Still so much you gotta live,
Still so much for you to thrive,
Conquer and revive.

NYRD
04/13/21

Head to the Clouds

Every poem,
Every meaning,
Every syllable,
Is fucking bleeding,
The memory of you is constant and proceeding,
Spilled ink won't stop my pen from leading,
I watch you and you're only exceeding,
So I'll write until I, too, am succeeding,
Until my demons are nothing but receding,
Head to the clouds rather than the ceiling,
Read in between the lines, I won't stop fucking breathing,
For there's no option of me leaving,
Know I'll turn to god if I need a shoulder for some leaning,
In his heavenly aura, there is no ounce of deceiving,
No fantasy worth more than just in him believing,
In my tears, I'll once again find peace within my own being,
For there's a spark waiting for a chance for fleeing,
Wings waiting to taste a motion so vigorously freeing.

NYRD
08/22/21

Baby

Been day dreaming about you lately,
How I'm a better me with you baby,
And I don't care if I look crazy,
I need you by my side daily,
For you soothe my waters when it gets wavy,
You calm my earthquakes when it gets shaky,
Baby, you're the headlights when my vision is hazy,
On a rainy day with you I'd want to be lazy,
My beautiful lady, you blossom like a daisy,
Forever vibrant and exceeding greatly,
I'll love you the same even when you're eighty,
Your love has never been felt vaguely,
I value your gentle heart immensely,
This passion we share intensely,
That look in your eyes is deadly,
Ask me for what you want and I'll supply plenty,
You know me well to know I'm always ready,
Baby, I swear with you, it's a blessing, so throw confetti.

NYRD
06/28/20

My Time

If only you saw my Spotify,
Playlist echoes through the walls, touching the vanilla sky,
You'd think the beat of this bass was unreal like it was sci-fi,
Baby, music is priceless. It's my slice of apple pie,
My happiness when I want to fucking cry,
Without you, there's no peace or stability on standby,
So por favor, could we hear tunes together before
you have to eventually say bye?
And could I caress your back while our tongues tie?
You're the butterfly and I'm the ferocious firefly,
You're the calm and I'm the chaos that needs to utterly modify,
I'm so sick of these dark thoughts that fucking occupy,
Can we just skip to the parts that truly do simplify?
Can we just skip to the part where we somehow multiply?
I want a family with you before we eventually mummify,
Tell me it's still me, and I'll be someone you would seek to nominate and verify,
Take me to court and I'll truthfully testify,
I've taken steps to be better and I just hope thy lord can justify,
Only time will truly tell if my morals really do dignify or falsify,
Lord knows I try so hard to satisfy you and show gratitude
without leaving you lookin' crossed eyed,
Lord, crucify me if I ever lay another woman
down to make love and hum a lullaby,
Lord, rid her of me if I ever do another woman the
same for I don't want to become the bad guy,
And if I'm ever the toxicity in her life, please open her eyes to clarify,
Even now I think to myself I don't deserve this goddess for I'm
ruined and horrified and she's dripped in gold so utterly purified
and laced with a taste I can't help but to utterly sigh,
I've cried and died more times than I can count, and
still I can say that I've conquered and tried,
God, hear the despair in my voice when all I beg of
you is to keep my loved ones by my side,
Help me become a better version of myself before my illness and PTSD collide,
But for now, I'll touch the skies and continue to
write as I hear Stevie Nicks landslide,
Something soothing to keep my demons nowhere close by,
Let them starve and leave them severely dry,
It's my time this time to take aim and make a bull's eye
without questioning my existence or asking god why.

NYRD
06/05/22

Sin City

If I was a place I'd be sin city,
I love the idea of diving into the nitty gritty,
Witty, I surely am, but I ain't no Mickey,
I could and I would rid your body into the great Mississippi,
Watch your limbs dissolve into nothing, so
yes, an autopsy can fucking miss me,
Told myself I wouldn't commit to nothing risky
if it's doesn't start with fucking whiskey,
One, two, three seconds is all it takes for you to want to kiss me,
Take your back to my hotel room and
watch you beg and say gimme,
More and more I want your body, so please forgive me,
You are my sole addiction, so when I see a pic of you I say dis me?!
Wow, I cannot believe it the way you got me acting so frisky,
Got me hyped making me want to shimmy,
If I could, I'd slide down your fucking chimney,
I'm one call, one text away from us getting busy,
Ready whenever you are. I promise I won't get fucking wheezy.

NYRD
05/30/22

Toxic

I'll devour her in my embrace as I spin her,
Baby, damn right I'm aware I'm a fucking winner,
You're a proclaimed saint and I'm the sinner,
Forever, I'll serenade you like you're the
side and main course dinner,
Up and down, we're getting giggly with it,
Left or right, she's always there I can't fucking dare quit it,
Deep down, we both know we'll eventually admit it,
Mr. & Mrs. Smith—you're Angelina Jolie
and I'm Brad Pitt, so it's pretty lit,
Your eyes so icy cold, so when I caress
your cheek, I gotta wear a mitt,
You hate/love how witty I can be as I take
control of your body without a permit,
You don't even realize it till it's too late and
you're without your Fashion Nova outfit,
And when I'm done with you, we'll forget why
we even threw a fit in the first place,
Toxic, of course, but there's beauty in the madness we
must admit with some resounding notion of grace,
And if there's ever a day that comes, and we're face to face, I'll
wholeheartedly say this to you without meaning to displace.

NYRD
05/23/22

72

Split Personality Disorder

I've deeply become unholy and sinful,
I crave everlasting love, but I'm only seen as a sex symbol,
This mind of mine writes just to ultimately want to scribble,
I have a killer smile with three staggering dimples,
My eyes are so sad, it's quite empty yet sincerely simple,
Nothing inside could possibly ever reach
its expectations to assemble,
Still I stay just in case it's a sign of one big riddle,
Split personality disorder, so it seems there
to be no room for us to rekindle,
Can't you see you're doomed to never succeed
at meeting yourself in the middle?
It's a cycle to howl at the moon with a heavy ache full,
At the end of the day, only you can bring yourself
back to reality my divine wolfine,
Only you can say if you're ready to begin again
instead of letting out a notable sigh,
These dark emotions will always linger, but
that doesn't mean you have to comply,
Your lips are shaking, my dear wolfine, why?
I'm scared of myself. What if I never defy the
odds of climbing out of this hell pit?
What if I'm forever doomed to be so close to having
it but just far enough to never grasping it?
Am I meant to hold terminal chaos or will God help me acquit?
I just don't know anymore some nights I trace
my wrists with a blade, pondering to slit,
I just don't know how long this must take before I'm all out of grit,
I just don't know anymore, wolfine, this hurts to admit.

NYRD
11/18/22

Guardian Angel

I dream a dream of your embrace,
Feathery wings fill up this place,
My guardian angel's palpable grace,
Takes me higher and farther than outer space,
Fills my heart with hope, so I pack it like a suitcase,
It's been so cold, yet your words tend to me like a fireplace,
With you I could never keep a straight face,
My tears could fill up the largest vase,
I'll make light of this moment, even when I feel utmost displaced,
All my life my parents made me feel as if I was a waste,
At times I wished I was just erased,
Crying on the bathroom floor, I can feel my heart race,
But my sister-slash-mom is always there to
pick me up to tie my shoe lace,
It's thanks to her why I'm not without a trace,
And that's when I learned my guardian angel was
there all along, and she can never be replaced.

NYRD
02/18/21

Dying
Dying
Dying

Heartless ever since I saw you lifeless,
I couldn't salvage this bond ever since the virus,
I wished I could have gone with you during this crisis,
There's something in my eye. I'll just blame it on my sinus,
I should have been there for you when you
cried every night from arthritis,
This world didn't have to be this cruel to
you, but I sure did divide us,
I wish I could tell you I'm sorry for wasting
your efforts and guidance,
I wish I could tell you I know better now, but I
know I just deserve your utter silence,
You should be resting and I should continue on crying,
You're at peace, while the whole time I've
just been impulsively lying,
Everything's okay I swear I don't wish I was dying,
I swear I'll wake up tomorrow, and I'll still
without a doubt be stupidly trying,
Looking out the window, I see a blue jay just
sitting there, grumpy and sighing,
Can't help but to think of my ex too while I
hear my phone buzzing from notifying,
I'm a poetic genius, but my romantic life has
been more pathetic than satisfying,
Far from the graceful touch of her lips exquisitely electrifying,
Is it clear yet I haven't felt a woman's love
grasping my vessel to unify me?
Is it noticeable I got issues clearly doing
more than just occupying me?
God, take my last words and take my entire
being and sincerely crucify me.

NYRD
11/14/22

Happily

The rumble of the ground always fought to tie this knot,
The hurting just does not fucking cease to stop,
And these lines always seem to mean more than just a fucking lot,
It's an earthquake, and I'm sure to utterly collapse,
Empty void commanding a purpose perhaps,
Talking red flag with no notion for take backs,
Let's get high together and remember we never want to relapse,
You called it quits, but I cannot let go of these meaningful scraps,
Snapchat still remembers our sinful snaps,
I'm a fool, but maybe it's time I accept it's a wrap,
Delusional for love but let's face the facts.

NYRD
06/28/20

76

Ever

Happily ever after was never written in the contracts,
And happily ever after will never be foretold
again in another one of my awful tracks,
Love isn't everything, but it's what manifests these racks,
Every bridge, every verse I withhold takes to the
stage to perform its melancholic acts,
God knows I'm tired and sorry, but I'm done
giving up my coin for your tax,
Unapologetically, I'm here to notify
Death's door, I'm not ready for you to set foot on my grass.

After

Deep down I just want to rewind and not let the memories pass,
Let's go back to better days where we were both in ceramics class,
But alas, it's not within the forecasts,
But alas, I know forgiveness is just too much to ask,
We both could have been better, but maybe
it's not too late to fully grasp,
Only god knows what I could never truly enhance,
Only god knows you meant more than just an utter glance,
Just this once, my love, could I have this one last dance?
Just this once, my lord, could my love still have a chance?
If not, please claim my heart to still take its stance,
To walk this earth even when there's no
hope for a blissful romance.

NYRD
04/10/22

Too Late to Apologize

Fate did you dirty when she knew I was a pit bull,
Kneel down and kiss the pistol before you get a fist full,
Got my stripes long before I ever heard a "God bless you,"
Twenty-five years old and I'm eager to come up for my debut,
Never was not an uphill battle. This road I
paved required me to act brand-new,
Something has got to give, so I had to let
go of my desires for you too,
But deep down, nobody sees what resides inside
'cause no one ever bothers to pass thru,
God knows I reminisce of my ex's sisters, but like
always, I screw things up like it was on cue,
We all know there's a special place in hell for souls
like me, forever destined to be black and blue,
And like always, I end up wishing I knew then what I know now,
But like always, it's not until everyone
has no choice but to say ciao,
I'm a ticking time bomb, but this time, I'm
aware nobody will see me go pow,
I know I won't ever get a reaction, much less a raised eyebrow,
Friendships and relationships ended, but we
all want them to stay somehow,
So much time has passed, but we all know apologies wouldn't
have made a difference, not then and much less now.

NYRD
11/12/22

Advisor

Tongue so vicious like a viper,
Promised myself I wouldn't let you become my almighty cypher,
Voodoo in your possession I just might wife her,
I just might do this just to ultimately make me wiser,
I learn things the hard way I don't need an advisor,
My fellow knight just hand me my visor,
I'm going to war and not looking back for a sympathizer,
All alone with my demons hollering as backseat drivers,
Quiet! Quiet! I know if I crash and burn,
you'll never be guilt-trip survivors,
Jesus died so I could be the supplier and
provider to my own requires,
But still let the glory of the lord command my
hands and emotions like invisible wires,
I'm a puppet to your cause. Use me like
the gym's mountain climbers,
Left foot, right foot—I'm devoted to a cause like Michael Meyers,
God, you've enlightened me to seek a new
motivation for utter revival,
I'll be your warrior, you're ultimate fighter,
and never one of your bitter rivals.

NYRD
05/17/22

Out
Law

Reppin' through and through, I'm an outlaw,
Thank you for the venom I needed a push to go in raw,
I need a push to knock your shit through your jaw,
I lacked hatred, but my brother took me past withdraw,
Livin' like Jotaro Kujo, you'll never see my heart ever thaw,
Cold as fuck, icy narcho justss like how I was before,
Had to kill myself off so I could thrive for the one time for y'all,
I write the best shit when I'm fucked in the head, so stay
and watch my thoughts appall, slither, and crawl,
Paint the walls red to cover up the cursive 'cause
my words tend to be conflicted by fireball,
Dragon breath, hotheaded fucker, I'm too
young to be this tempted by alcohol,
My guardian angel once again pulling me
out of shit like it was just protocol,
I'm the dark knight, while everyone has their guns
pointed at me, but I'm used to urge to see me fall,
I'm used to the taste of the cement. I'm
used to everyone tryna brawl,
Always hated, always traded like I was Yu-Gi-Oh! trap card, LOL,
But now I'm big time, and you want to come back
into my life. Well, bitch, I'm too swole,
Better off alone I don't need anyone but God
to watch my bankroll utterly thrall,
Baby watch my stamina never become something I'd ever recall,
I'll never sleep on the bag, even if it requires
me to lose absolute control,
Till my last fucking breath, I will never break
even if my insides turn to coal.

NYRD
11/19/22

Soldier

Everything I am is linked to my history,
All that I want to be lies behind the mist of mystery,
Not even foul play would work on the lord
that sees through any trickery,
Getting to the other side requires overcoming trials of misery,
In life, the things worth having the most are
never given without accepting injury,
There will always be a price to pay to mold a soldier to victory,
And each demon that clouds my heart will
soon be exiled from my trajectory,
As well as my damaged soul will express a breath of liberty,
A future such as this will consume my will
with bliss to escape my own captivity,
There's still so much more the lord and I
know I see to manifest into reality,
As I live in a society that every turn of a
corner is filled with negativity,
I'll be the brave soldier to lead by example to express
my unconditional sympathy and positivity.

NYRD
01/02/20

Time to Tap In

I'm not dead. I only dress that way,
I like the satisfaction of obtaining my prey,
It's the only that makes me feel alive when my morals stray away,
Cowboy bebop in the mornings con café,
The calm before the storm I embellish in the foreplay,
Two feet on the ground whenever it's doomsday,
It's a good thing my sister ascended before she could
see the madness I would eventually portray,
It's a good thing I can light this match
without your gaze in my way,
It's a good thing I'm a writer and not an ashtray,
Spike said it best when he stated whatever happens, happens,
That's the life I wish to live, cherishing it all through rations,
The galaxy is my commander, my captain,
Fuck the city, fuck Manhattan,
Give me the stars, I'm ready to tap in,
No fixed guide I'm brain dead when the Slurpee is slappin',
Molly has entered the chat, so best believe
I'm movin' like Charlie Chaplin,
Speechless my body reacts with the vibe that's hangin',
In circles, we spin, baby. By the end of
the night, I'ma need a napkin,
In between your legs, you got me trapped in.

NYRD
10/30/22

A Fate Worse than hell

Just a bum that's never well dressed,
I'm damn right overwhelmed and stressed,
I suppose it's better this way than lonely and depressed,
Why can't I just turn off my brain and get some much needed rest,
God rid her off my heart 'cause I know she'll never be impressed,
Everything I say goes unsaid and I'm left utterly congest,
It is what it is. I know there's no point in
having these feelings expressed,
It's best if I keep these desires oppressed,
Finger on the trigger, baby girl, please be my guest,
Take me out once and for all for we both
know you want this to manifest,
It's a hit and run, and it's not a hard pill to digest,
Karma seeks justice when there's no room to be blessed,
You don't have to say it for I'll be the one to get it off your chest,
Slowly I'll vanish and slowly you'll feel the
weight become less compressed,
Baby, it's okay I know how this goes all too well,
so there's nothing left for you to confess,
I'll stay away from all the places we went
too, especially your address,
You're a goddess, and I wouldn't want to
damage your work in progress,
I could keep talking, but nevertheless there's
nothing left that needs to be expressed.

NYRD
06/17/22

84

Maniacs

You know where to find me, having thoughts you've never had,
The feeling is mutual, got me jotting down in my notepad,
Baby, fuck everyone. Let them be bitter and sad,
You got your legs wrapped around me in a
choke hold. I'm happy you're glad,
Wherever you go, I'll follow. Damn! I got it for you bad,
Guess that means I'll always pace about like a fucking nomad,
Cross my heart, I'll always have your
front and back like a comrade,
Whatever you want, I'll even blow your back,
Whatever you want, I'd let you play me over
and over again like a soundtrack,
Baby, you got me breathing heavy. It must be an asthma attack,
Fuck a Prozac. Your pussy got me when I
fall back, so I can bounce back,
Baby, you got me in a daze you made me into an insomniac,
And the way you always want it, you must be a nymphomaniac,
But it's all good 'cause we both fuck with each other like maniacs.

NYRD
03/05/22

Dear Mom,

Between us two, home isn't home without you,
My sunshine echoes ultimately through you,
I miss your embrace and the way you said you loved me too,
It breaks my heart, but I rather you not say you knew,
Heartbreak after heartbreak, every hue is
trying so hard not to turn to blue,
The way you laughed and the way you
carried me all the way through,
All these years I relied on you like a panda relies on bamboo,
Best mom in the world is such an understatement,
Through god, I'll try my best to remain patient,
As much as it hurts, I'll pray and not let
my demons stay complacent,
Your essence will forever reside inside
me like it was always meant to,
So, Mom, stay strong, stay courageous for
your blessings are purely overdue.

NYRD
???12/21

Baby Boy

I could love you for a century,
But I know for now you'll dwell in my memory,
Circulating through my circumference,
I'll embody a sense of endurance,
So thank you, baby boy, for your assurance,
You stay by my side like you were my insurance,
For even in silence, you gave substance,
These four walls never echoed with durance,
So I promise I'll never leave you in the past tense,
Parenthood became my sixth sense,
So I'll love you forever and carry your memory through every view,
Every sunlight, every gasping wind, I'll breathe
you in to keep from feeling bitter blue,
To keep from reaching another tissue,
Baby boy, your bliss is all I wish to live up to,
Your fierce bravery I aspire to make ring true,
I want your every quality intertwined
with my own to make me anew.

NYRD
09/20/21

Alive and Well

Us will never be fin,
Your soft cherry lips I'll always remember on my skin,
My love, where have you been?
Always will I deeply miss this,
Bebe, you are my infinite bliss,
Every touch, every kiss,
As a poet, I clearly reminisce,
Every attribute of you always hits,
You are alive and well in my poems it sits,
In my memory there will never be splits,
No dirty tricks to tell me this was fixed with scripts,
Just a love as beautiful and rare as a total solar eclipse,
In the moment we finally met,
It felt like an apocalypse,
Souls intertwined down to our fingertips,
No more words, my dear, for you cannot convince,
It was more than just a tender moment to dismiss,
It was real and it still is, even now as we
walk through the great abyss.

NYRD
02/18/21

Provider

I don't need a reminder,
My three babies are always in my viewfinder,
Even in the afterlife, I'll hold on to you guys tighter,
Raise your hands and god will raise you higher,
Working six days a week, dusk till dawn, because I am a fighter,
Forty-two years old and now I can say I am wiser,
I pray and pray to always be my baby's provider,
To make it through any obstacle as a survivor,
To be the best mother and put them before my deepest of desires,
God give me the strength like a vigorously fierce tiger,
To never stop fighting, to never allow my demons to conspire,
Lord, give me faith and will that I'll stay entire,
As long as I have you, my glorious lord, I'll never truly tire.

NYRD
04/19/21

Graceful Silhouette
Part 1

Your graceful silhouette lingers through the open sea,
Let's lay here for a bit and hear Machine Gun
Kelly's interlude of banyan tree,
Suppose we get lost in the music before we
become utter dust and debris,
I'd give anything to make things right with you
before I become an illness or decease,
I'd give absolutely anything for you to just live in one piece,
Infinite times more, bebe, I will love you
enough to let you breathe and release,
You will forever hold my heart as the woman
that gave me more than just beliefs,
My little mermaid, you were always there when
I knew nothing more than bitter griefs,
You were my lifeguard when I had wash up on any given reefs,
My sweetest girl your lips always left me shocked with utter relief,
You took my heart and made it yours until every breath
I breathed was close enough to feel your teeth,
The reflection of pure happiness when we locked eyes
made every broken piece collide underneath.

NYRD
06/13/22

Graceful Silhouette
Part 2

Forever in my heart, I'd hold you beneath
the covers so silent and discrete,
But it's time I let you dive into your next chapter
for my face feels set stone in concrete,
May you fly high, my sweet butterfly, and never
may you land my angelic shimmering sky,
You're an array of stars and sunshine for I'd forever pray
on and never will I ever let out a melancholy cry,
I'll simply say, "Thank you, God, for the
opportunity in calling her utterly mine,"
We had our time, but now it's time I stop
holding too tight to confine,
KC, you're in my every breathless view and coastline,
You're in every essence of every grapevine,
Forever I'll taste you like that yummy shimmering moonshine,
This isn't a goodbye, but a thank you letter for all the
goodness you had spread, my sweet clementine,
May one day, our divine souls be ready to truly intertwine,
May the next time we lock eyes be filled with
peace and calmness to simply signify.

NYRD
06/13/22

Just a Nomad

I want to run as far as I can and never stop until I'm a nomad,
Roam wherever I may please from the will of my own hand,
And only when I'm lonely will I allow myself to think
of those memories we've thought out and planned,
I should be spending quality time with my fam, but
I'm overwhelmed yet again like I'm a Jojo stand,
I got scars I can't talk about out loud without
substance abuse and sweaty palms,
I make the most of my given circumstances
'cause I tend to embellish on the cons,
Born with horns but also born with brains and bronze,
A recipe for disaster with chemical x just
to add to the mixture of the odds,
God, why have you forsaken me? I thought
these aspirations were forever ours?
Am I meant to burn like the brightest star, or is this
destiny of ours just a moment in time like a lit cigar?
If it is, then so be it; but tell me, God, why did you create me to
keep her memory so close if her body is somewhere so fucking far,
Soothe these shaky waters from my eyes at once,
so my fingers can caress my guitar,
The strings act as levers to my ignition when
the darkness needs an outlet to devour,
I'm floating through time and space,
I'm floating through tempered grace,
Just a nomad looking for meaning to its undisclosed case,
No way to tell what season it is, so one can only accept the
unknowing feeling to just embrace it all face-to-fucking-face.

NYRD
11/25/22

Destined to Be Damned

Herbal tea keeps me closer to sobriety,
The thought of you devours my whole reality,
You always have been and always will be the one and only,
Who needs a latchkey when you're the whole damn committee?
Stargazing into your eyes and it's clearly my vitamin C,
No doesn't exist to any degree,
Memories of a story about you and me,
Such a story started way back in twenty sixteen,
I love, love the most when you're part of every given scene,
Time and space is nothing when there's passion in between,
Fingertips stroking your back like it's nearly a routine,
Moments like these I could never have foreseen nor unseen,
Who needs coffee when you taste like the sweetest caffeine?
Heart's racing, this is somehow soothing and serene,
Titanic says my heart will go on, but alas,
I doubt it, my dear Celine,
Your voice echoes in my brain like it's jumping on trampolines,
Your lips, the juiciest of them all. It's like sucking on tangerines,
You've taken a hold onto my demons and put them to smithereens,
You're surely prettier than those models on Vogue magazines,
Truly are the closest thing to heaven when I day dream of fantasies,
My trenched tragedies will never just let me be,
But even at my lowest, you would pray and plea for me,
I don't know why I deserved you, but I know I truly did lose thee,
Destined to be damned, but I know you
would probably still disagree,
Hardest on myself when I'm down on my fucking knees,
Tears falling, god, please don't become my greatest absentee,
Believe in me 'cause I can't feel each breath I
breathe play out with such guarantee.

NYRD
06/01/22

Meant for More

Back at the club, make sure your feelings aren't showing,
I love it when you're dancing you know
damn well that you're glowing,
You tell yourself to keep it cool, keep it chill,
before the tears start flowing,
And your friends start fucking with your
head, not knowing they're provoking,
Baby, I can tell you've been trying too hard to be easygoing,
But honestly, fuck that persona. She'll keep you from growing,
Looks can be deceiving. I'm not into posing,
I'm not a fuck boy, but I do have my problems with self-loathing,
I promise you though, I'm nothing like the rest.
I don't wish to participate in gloating,
And I don't know how to swim, but I'll be
your life raft to keep you floating,
I'm here to stay even through the unknowing,
So lay your head on my chest before you go on exploding,
Or we can try coping in another way by taking off your clothing,
Baby, it's no secret you're not easy to go about decoding,
And I hope I'm not imposing, but I'll spend a
lifetime just to keep you from folding,
You're meant for more than you could
possibly think of fucking molding.

NYRD
06/21/21

94

Drifter

Such dead eyes love to lace itself with black eyeliner,
Pain has become so utterly bland and severely minor,
The needle digs deeper into my skin when I feel like I need her,
Although thy devil loves to wine and dine me
and seduce my thoughts into a bitter blur,
God help me save myself from my own pathetic addiction to liquor,
Heal these wounds no one can see or know
unless I scribe it like literature,
I do apologize, my lord, if my words seem to slur, but I know
you know what I'm trying to say I'm somewhat sure,
Sometimes it's hard to speak when it still
feels too loud to even whisper,
I just hope you understand the void that
lingers now without my sister,
It's so dark and empty within this ocean so divine yet sinister,
Can I just close my eyes for a moment
and sway about like a drifter?

NYRD
05/24/22

95

No Hidden Agenda

Dead behind the eyes, I've become so lackluster,
Monotone in my voice, there's nothing to muster,
It's been a while, hasn't it, since you felt the warmth of another?
There's so much prey calling my name but not
enough motive for me to play hunter,
Can't talk to a soul about these inner things,
so I let it all fucking clutter,
Am I paranoid or have I always been this
cautious to only ever trust her?
And lately I think too hard about her until my
mind dives deep within the gutter,
I have bad luck at having friends with pure intentions
'cause eventually they all want to take the place of her,
It's bold to assume my love letters are about you, but
sweetheart, there's no hidden agenda I can assure,
I've only had loved for two woman, and one is dead
and the other rather lives a life so obscure,
No fixed compass, so she drifts slowly and
slowly farther from the shore,
I just hope she eventually finds solace within herself
that's tangible and undoubtedly secure,
And I have so much I, too, need to work on before
I could truly say I've fucking matured,
Clearly it's best if I'm alone than to pretend there are feelings
or desires for someone else—that would just be absurd.

NYRD
11/20/22

Infinite

You are my sun,
By far mesmerizing,
You are my moon,
Even emphasizing stars,
My galaxy is what you are,
Only with you,
I could scar so easily,
Only with you,
I could feel so zealously,
Hold you in my arms,
Glaring at your peaceful serenity,
Above the water my mermaid,
Oh so heavenly,
Sleep, my love, how I prayed so heavily,
The sight the smell of red roses greeting me oh so tenderly,
Take me to the time I wish to be,
Suppose one day if it's meant to be,
But forever I'll hold you safe to keep,
A love so deep,
I've come to terms the words to speak,
To confess my thoughts,
The tears I weep,
Day and night,
My soul so weak but so strong—it's unique,
I close my eyes. The memories too vivid I feel,
My wanderlust mystique,
The word infinite echoes over and over again,
Yes, I'm talking about you,
I've spilled over,
It's 4:00 a.m., and I couldn't keep my composure,
Could never allow another soul in,
So I'll stay a loner,
Each day, a step closer to finding my way,
In hopes of finding her once again.

NYRD

Kill Me First

PTSD, ever since I held your body in my grip,
Biting until the blood drips down from my lip,
So much anxiety, I cover it up so nicely with wit,
So much depression but still not enough for me to ever quit,
Anger issues like I only knew how to speak with my fists,
Tell me the worst thing you've ever done, and
I bet I could top your fucking list,
Sick brain, sick piece of shit in the unapproachable midst,
The devil loves to provoke me with her
veins resonating from thy wrists,
I have disturbing thoughts. Just take me out, God,
before I test out these forbidden gifts,
Machete with your name on it as I caress your hips,
I try to hide the devil in me, but he hasn't
slaughtered in what feels like bricks,
Fuck the desires away before this movie
becomes another horror flick,
But firstly lemme hit this quick lick,
Flip you over show you what it feel like to fuck with six, six, six,
Show you what it feels like to get nasty, raw, and sick, sick, sick,
This isn't a negotiation. This is a profound lunar eclipse,
Fucking you is great, but loving you will
sincerely always be a quick fix.

NYRD
11/11/22

Spirited Away

I made a career off reminiscing,
I want to feel your touch but something's missin',
My shadow haunts me and my humanity is seemingly slippin',
I watch Spirited Away so my eyes can start pissin'.
Alas, sanity does not last long in my household,
I'm held at gunpoint but I'll never fuckin fold,
Even till my last breath I'm in mother fuckin' control,
I'll never let go of my threshold unless God
looked me in the eyes and foretold,
Till then, I'll fight like hell, like Naruto on sage mode,
I'll never bend over backward again to try to keep anybody close,
It's clear to me you've just been wanting this to be foreclosed,
It's so clear to me you've all just wanted me to be disposed,
My humanity has been slippin' from my grasp,
but I'll go before I ever let myself explode,
What if I'm a psychopath what if I'm becoming a ghost,
Suppose I rather let it happen because deep down I already know,
But I'm aware this is probably just a friendly
reminder of depression saying hello,
I would block you if I could and murder you like a Jane Doe,
But I feel it's too late the sink has overflowed,
I'm in too deep like quicksand. My feet
are underneath the fuckin' floor,
Reach back to me, God, I still have more fight left in me to uproar.

NYRD
10/24/22

Cross My Heart

Take me far away from this toxic place,
Where pain meets your everlasting touch and grace,
Your palpable aura resides within me to always trace,
With my fingers onto my pillowcase,
Your memory I'll never hit with a backspace,
At most, I would make it known with an uppercase,
Happy I see that you can't help but to showcase,
I'm happy for you truly. I am I'm familiar
with the journey and its chase,
I'm still trying to grasp my purpose—suppose
it's somewhere in outer space,
Suppose I'm in my own version of American
horror story with Kathy fucking Bates,
Suppose we would both share this misery
as the blade purposely penetrates,
KC, tell me you still think about me and
all my twisted personality traits,
And tell them hooligans you still belong to
me, given we've both made mistakes,
As well tell them you still want me, even though
we've both never shared any first dates,
The passion, love, and allure truly does always await,
Mine forever isn't long enough, so God, promise
me it's her in front of the purely white gates,
Promise me when my time here is done, she
would be my sole and only inmate,
Mm-hmm, cross my heart. I hope you feel the
sincerity through every word I illustrate.

NYRD
06/11/22

100

Subconsciously at War

Success is dependent on effort,
Darling, tear this noose down from its lever,
You must not hit snooze even if it's through the nether,
You must not give into disappear even if the
entities speak to you so fondly and clever,
It's all lies. They're only taking advantage
of the void that achingly quivers,
My teeth never shown unless it's self-
loathing laughter from triggers,
I can't trust anymore, so I keep my distance
'cause we're all just fucking sinners,
I can't let anyone in anymore unless you prove
with consistency why I should reconsider,
I like abnormal, I like extraordinary, not a
copy from your closest printer,
It's been so long since I've felt another's
love flow like a lively river,
I know they all low key hate me, but I'm used
to the weather and the terminal shiver,
Gotta stay on my toes 'cause they're all just
hoping I would burn and wither,
Every single one praying I would keep the grass
high enough for them to easily slither,
I can't live with this paranoia any longer unless I
mentally shift my emotions to be clearer,
Pave new strides that the girl in the mirror so
eagerly wants to serve as her pillar,
Locked eyes with my reflection, and she told me I am
my own longest commitment, so I must deliver.

NYRD
11/12/22

Eulogy

Dear Mom,
Today we're not going to cry nor dwell in the loss of you,
Today is not the day we're going to bury our heads in any tissues,
Today I'll smile and simply say thank you,
Mom, I know all I have to do is look up and you're
there in the horizon of my every view,
And I know you're right there by my side for you'll
give me the strength to pull through,
Your legacy I promise I'll forever pursue,
Like a statue, you always stood so firm, but
now I know you've risen and flew,
So fly, my angelic bird, and when I see you
again, you can tell me all about it,
Like a phoenix, you rose from the ashes,
Your rays so sincere so full of passion you engulf
me with every sense of compassion,
Your love was always so full and more than enough and never a ration,
The pieces you gave were never just a fraction,
It was always everything at once within every interaction,
Your soul so deep, so fulfilling. You were
never characterized as a distraction,
Never characterized as just an empty voice but a leader who takes action,
This sensation I'll take with me through every
move I make, every conversation,
Everywhere I go, you're within me,
My lovely mother, you're never gone for we all
will carry you around like a reflection,
And although times will rise where we may struggle
and under some construction, with you, there is always
hope for something better than perfection,
Together within this connection, within this relation,
we can all share a better discussion,
A love so genuine, so pure, waiting to blossom in every sense,
we are more than capable of showing this expression.
Forever and always, love your three babies.

NYRD
04/23/21

About the Author

My earliest memory of feeling different and out of place in this world was Woodlin elementary school. I've always known I was different, closest thing I had to friend was my librarian Ms. Stevens. She would let me go to library during lunch to read Dr. Seuss books. She was my first real friend she was also the first friend to gift me a present I recall her gifting me a Dr. Seuss miniature sculpture of grinch for Christmas. I knew from that moment it didn't matter I had a lot of friends or people who would like me, I just knew quality will always beat quantity. Life at home I was always close with my siblings we used to share one bedroom my older brother and younger brother Jonathan and Hector shared one bed and my late sister who was honestly a mother to me shared a bed together. Most people would hate sharing a room and for a while, I did but I had grown accustomed and I felt safe knowing my sister was always by my side. From a young age I've had dealt with depression, anxiety, suicide thoughts, sleep paralysis. I've never known peace or solace unless I was writing and turning it into something beautiful. Something worth the sorrow, I've felt throughout my life. I recall telling someone, "every thorn has its rose" in response to her "every rose has its thorns" and I didn't think much of it until I really sat with it and thought there wouldn't even be a beautiful outcome of a rose if the thorn did not remotely exist. The pain of losing sister due to Covid complications in April 21st 2021 and just seeing her condition afterwards holding her, I am reminded I am human. As easily as I can be brought up to this world I could easily be taken out and I had to remember that, I had to feel it, I had to let it dwell inside of me. There's so much pain and so much anguish I carry but if I didn't carry it I wouldn't have the grace and empath I now feel to express it not just in writing but in every conversation, every embrace, every prayer. And ultimately every action. Everything I do stems from the same embodiment and purity my sister Ana Elizabeth Jimenes carried all throughout her life. I am aware this is an autobiography but everything I am ultimately stems from her. She was my parent, my guardian, my sister, my bestfriend. We all carry some similar and some different types of traumas but it's always about how you hand it and how you choose to carry it after that leaves the greatest impact not just to yourself but to others. I want everything I do to stem from love, nothing less nothing more.

T3-ANT-651

CARTOGRAPHY BY PHILIP'S.COPYRIGHT REED INTERNATIONAL BOOKS LTD

OXFORD

DESK
REFERENCE
ATLAS

OXFORD

DESK
REFERENCE
ATLAS

SECOND EDITION

Contents

Cartography by Philip's

Text
Keith Lye

Executive Editor
Caroline Rayner

Art Editors
Alison Myer
Karen Ferguson

Commissioning Editor
Kara Turner

Production
Claudette Morris

Picture Research
Claire Gouldstone

Picture Acknowledgements
Zefa Picture Library /Tom V. Sant
/Geosphere Project Front cover and spine,
main title page Robert Harding Picture Library
/Photri 1 Image Bank /Lionel Brown 10 Rex Features
/Sipa 6, 24 Still Pictures 26, /Anne Piantanida 8,
/Chris Caldicott 16, /Mark Edwards 18, 20, /Hartmut
Schwarzbach 14, 22, /Luke White 4 Tony Stone Images
/Kevin Kelley 2, /Art Wolfe 12

© 1997 Reed International Books Limited

George Philip Limited,
an imprint of Reed Books, Michelin House,
81 Fulham Road, London SW3 6RB,
and Auckland and Melbourne

Cartography by Philip's

Published in North America by
Oxford University Press, Inc.,
198 Madison Avenue,
New York, N.Y. 10016

Oxford is a registered trademark of Oxford University Press

All rights reserved. No part of this publication may be
reproduced, stored in a retrieval system, or transmitted,
in any form or by any means, electronic, mechanical,
photocopying, recording, or otherwise, without the
prior permission of the publisher.

Library of Congress Cataloging-in-Publication Data available

ISBN 0–19–521371–8

Printing (last digit): 9 8 7 6 5 4 3 2 1

Printed in China

World Statistics

vi–ix	Countries
x–xi	Cities
xii–xv	Physical
xvi	Climate

The Earth in Focus

2–3	The Universe & Solar System
4–5	The Changing Earth
6–7	Earthquakes & Volcanoes
8–9	Water & Ice
10–11	Weather & Climate
12–13	Landforms & Vegetation
14–15	Population
16–17	Languages & Religions
18–19	Agriculture & Industry
20–21	Trade & Commerce
22–23	Transport & Travel
24–27	International Organizations
28–29	Regions in the News
30–32	World Flags

Contents

World Maps

1	General Reference
2–3	Northern Hemisphere
4–5	Southern Hemisphere
6–7	Europe
8–9	Scandinavia
10–11	British Isles
12–13	France
14–15	Germany & Benelux
16–17	Central Europe
18–19	Spain & Portugal
20–21	Italy & the Adriatic
22–23	Greece & the Balkans
24–25	Eastern Europe
26–27	Asia
28–29	Western Russia & Central Asia
30–31	Eastern Siberia
32–33	Japan
34–35	China
36–37	Southeast Asia
38–39	Philippines & Eastern Indonesia
40–41	Eastern India, Bangladesh & Burma
42–43	Western India & Pakistan
44–45	Iran, the Gulf & Afghanistan
46–47	The Middle East & Turkey
48–49	Arabia & the Horn of Africa
50–51	Africa
52–53	Northeast Africa
54–55	Northwest Africa
56–57	Central Africa
58–59	Southern Africa
60–61	Australia
62–63	Southeast Australia
64–65	New Zealand, Central & Southwest Pacific
66–67	North America
68–69	Eastern Canada
70–71	Western Canada
72–73	Northeast USA
74–75	Southeast USA
76–77	North central USA
78–79	Southern USA
80–81	Northwest USA
82–83	Southwest USA
84–85	Mexico
86–87	Caribbean & Central America
88–89	South America
90–91	South America – Northwest
92–93	South America – Northeast
94–95	South America – South
96	Antarctica
97–160	**Index to World Maps**

World Statistics – Countries

Listed below are all the countries of the world; the more important territories are also included. If a territory is not completely independent, then the country it is associated with is named. The area figures give the total area of land, inland water and ice. Annual income is the GNP per capita. The figures are the latest available, usually 1995.

Country / Territory	Area (1,000 sq km)	Area (1,000 sq mi)	Population (1,000s)	Capital City	Annual Income US$
Afghanistan	652	252	19,509	Kabul	220
Albania	28.8	11.1	3,458	Tirana	340
Algeria	2,382	920	27,936	Algiers	1,650
Andorra	0.45	0.17	65	Andorra la Vella	14,000
Angola	1,247	481	10,844	Luanda	600
Argentina	2,767	1,068	34,663	Buenos Aires	7,290
Armenia	29.8	11.5	3,603	Yerevan	660
Australia	7,687	2,968	18,107	Canberra	17,510
Austria	83.9	32.4	8,004	Vienna	23,120
Azerbaijan	86.6	33.4	7,559	Baku	730
Azores (Portugal)	2.2	0.87	238	Ponta Delgada	4,466
Bahamas	13.9	5.4	277	Nassau	11,500
Bahrain	0.68	0.26	558	Manama	7,870
Bangladesh	144	56	118,342	Dhaka	220
Barbados	0.43	0.17	263	Bridgetown	6,240
Belarus	207.6	80.1	10,500	Minsk	2,930
Belgium	30.5	11.8	10,140	Brussels	21,210
Belize	23	8.9	216	Belmopan	2,440
Benin	113	43	5,381	Porto-Novo	420
Bhutan	47	18.1	1,639	Thimphu	170
Bolivia	1,099	424	7,900	La Paz/Sucre	770
Bosnia-Herzegovina	51	20	3,800	Sarajevo	2,500
Botswana	582	225	1,481	Gaborone	2,590
Brazil	8,512	3,286	161,416	Brasília	3,020
Brunei	5.8	2.2	284	Bandar Seri Begawan	9,000
Bulgaria	111	43	8,771	Sofia	1,160
Burkina Faso	274	106	10,326	Ouagadougou	300
Burma (= Myanmar)	677	261	46,580	Rangoon	950
Burundi	27.8	10.7	6,412	Bujumbura	180
Cambodia	181	70	10,452	Phnom Penh	600
Cameroon	475	184	13,232	Yaoundé	770
Canada	9,976	3,852	29,972	Ottawa	20,670
Canary Is. (Spain)	7.3	2.8	1,494	Las Palmas/Santa Cruz	7.905
Cape Verde Is.	4	1.6	386	Praia	870
Central African Republic	623	241	3,294	Bangui	390
Chad	1,284	496	6,314	Ndjaména	200
Chile	757	292	14,271	Santiago	3,070
China	9,597	3,705	1,226,944	Beijing	490
Colombia	1,139	440	34,948	Bogotá	1,400
Comoros	2.2	0.86	654	Moroni	520
Congo	342	132	2,593	Brazzaville	920
Costa Rica	51.1	19.7	3,436	San José	2,160
Croatia	56.5	21.8	4,900	Zagreb	4,500
Cuba	111	43	11,050	Havana	1,250
Cyprus	9.3	3.6	742	Nicosia	10,380

Country / Territory	Area (1,000 sq km)	Area (1,000 sq mi)	Population (1,000s)	Capital City	Annual Income US$
Czech Republic	78.9	30.4	10,500	Prague	2,730
Denmark	43.1	16.6	5,229	Copenhagen	26,510
Djibouti	23.2	9	603	Djibouti	780
Dominica	0.75	0.29	89	Roseau	2,680
Dominican Republic	48.7	18.8	7,818	Santo Domingo	1,080
Ecuador	284	109	11,384	Quito	1,170
Egypt	1,001	387	64,100	Cairo	660
El Salvador	21	8.1	5,743	San Salvador	1,320
Equatorial Guinea	28.1	10.8	400	Malabo	360
Eritrea	94	36	3,850	Asmara	500
Estonia	44.7	17.3	1,531	Tallinn	3,040
Ethiopia	1,128	436	51,600	Addis Ababa	100
Fiji	18.3	7.1	773	Suva	2,140
Finland	338	131	5,125	Helsinki	18,970
France	552	213	58,286	Paris	22,360
French Guiana (France)	90	34.7	154	Cayenne	5,000
French Polynesia (France)	4	1.5	217	Papeete	7,000
Gabon	268	103	1,316	Libreville	4,050
Gambia, The	11.3	4.4	1,144	Banjul	360
Georgia	69.7	26.9	5,448	Tbilisi	560
Germany	357	138	82,000	Berlin/Bonn	23,560
Ghana	239	92	17,462	Accra	430
Greece	132	51	10,510	Athens	7,390
Grenada	0.34	0.13	94	St George's	2,410
Guadeloupe (France)	1.7	0.66	443	Basse-Terre	9,000
Guatemala	109	42	10,624	Guatemala City	1,110
Guinea	246	95	6,702	Conakry	510
Guinea-Bissau	36.1	13.9	1,073	Bissau	220
Guyana	215	83	832	Georgetown	350
Haiti	27.8	10.7	7,180	Port-au-Prince	800
Honduras	112	43	5,940	Tegucigalpa	580
Hong Kong (China)	1.1	0.40	6,205	–	17,860
Hungary	93	35.9	10,500	Budapest	3,330
Iceland	103	40	269	Reykjavik	23,620
India	3,288	1,269	942,989	New Delhi	290
Indonesia	1,905	735	198,644	Jakarta	730
Iran	1,648	636	68,884	Tehran	4,750
Iraq	438	169	20,184	Baghdad	2,000
Ireland	70.3	27.1	3,589	Dublin	12,580
Israel	27	10.3	5,696	Jerusalem	13,760
Italy	301	116	57,181	Rome	19,620
Ivory Coast	322	125	14,271	Yamoussoukro	630
Jamaica	11	4.2	2,700	Kingston	1,390
Japan	378	146	125,156	Tokyo	31,450
Jordan	89.2	34.4	5,547	Amman	1,190
Kazakstan	2,717	1,049	17,099	Alma-Ata	1,540
Kenya	580	224	28,240	Nairobi	270
Korea, North	121	47	23,931	Pyongyang	1,100
Korea, South	99	38.2	45,088	Seoul	7,670
Kuwait	17.8	6.9	1,668	Kuwait City	23,350

Country / Territory	Area (1,000 sq km)	Area (1,000 sq mi)	Population (1,000s)	Capital City	Annual Income US$
Kyrgyzstan	198.5	76.6	4,738	Bishkek	830
Laos	237	91	4,906	Vientiane	290
Latvia	65	25	2,558	Riga	2,030
Lebanon	10.4	4	2,971	Beirut	1,750
Lesotho	30.4	11.7	2,064	Maseru	660
Liberia	111	43	3,092	Monrovia	800
Libya	1,760	679	5,410	Tripoli	6,500
Lithuania	65.2	25.2	3,735	Vilnius	1,310
Luxembourg	2.6	1	408	Luxembourg	35,850
Macau (Portugal)	0.02	0.006	490	Macau	7,500
Macedonia	25.7	9.9	2,173	Skopje	730
Madagascar	587	227	15,206	Antananarivo	240
Madeira (Portugal)	0.81	0.31	253	Funchal	4,500
Malawi	118	46	9,800	Lilongwe	220
Malaysia	330	127	20,174	Kuala Lumpur	3,160
Maldives	0.30	0.12	254	Malé	820
Mali	1,240	479	10,700	Bamako	300
Malta	0.32	0.12	367	Valletta	6,800
Martinique (France)	1.1	0.42	384	Fort-de-France	3,500
Mauritania	1,031	398	2,268	Nouakchott	510
Mauritius	2.0	0.72	1,112	Port Louis	2,980
Mexico	1,958	756	93,342	Mexico City	3,750
Micronesia, Fed. States of	0.70	0.27	125	Palikir	1,560
Moldova	33.7	13	4,434	Kishinev	1,180
Mongolia	1,567	605	2,408	Ulan Bator	400
Morocco	447	172	26,857	Rabat	1,030
Mozambique	802	309	17,800	Maputo	80
Namibia	825	318	1,610	Windhoek	1,660
Nepal	141	54	21,953	Katmandu	160
Netherlands	41.5	16	15,495	Amsterdam/The Hague	20,710
Netherlands Antilles (Neths)	0.99	0.38	199	Willemstad	9,700
New Caledonia (France)	18.6	7.2	181	Nouméa	6,000
New Zealand	269	104	3,567	Wellington	12,900
Nicaragua	130	50	4,544	Managua	360
Niger	1,267	489	9,149	Niamey	270
Nigeria	924	357	88,515	Abuja	310
Norway	324	125	4,361	Oslo	26,340
Oman	212	82	2,252	Muscat	5,600
Pakistan	796	307	143,595	Islamabad	430
Panama	77.1	29.8	2,629	Panama City	2,580
Papua New Guinea	463	179	4,292	Port Moresby	1,120
Paraguay	407	157	4,979	Asunción	1,500
Peru	1,285	496	23,588	Lima	1,490
Philippines	300	116	67,167	Manila	830
Poland	313	121	38,587	Warsaw	2,270
Portugal	92.4	35.7	10,600	Lisbon	7,890
Puerto Rico (US)	9	3.5	3,689	San Juan	7,020
Qatar	11	4.2	594	Doha	15,140
Réunion (France)	2.5	0.97	655	Saint-Denis	3,900
Romania	238	92	22,863	Bucharest	1,120

Country / Territory	Area (1,000 sq km)	Area (1,000 sq mi)	Population (1,000s)	Capital City	Annual Income US$
Russia	17,075	6,592	148,385	Moscow	2,350
Rwanda	26.3	10.2	7,899	Kigali	200
St Lucia	0.62	0.24	147	Castries	3,040
St Vincent & Grenadines	0.39	0.15	111	Kingstown	1,730
São Tomé & Príncipe	0.96	0.37	133	São Tomé	330
Saudi Arabia	2,150	830	18,395	Riyadh	8,000
Senegal	197	76	8,308	Dakar	730
Sierra Leone	71.7	27.7	4,467	Freetown	140
Singapore	0.62	0.24	2,990	Singapore	19,310
Slovak Republic	49	18.9	5,400	Bratislava	1,900
Slovenia	20.3	7.8	2,000	Ljubljana	6,310
Solomon Is.	28.9	11.2	378	Honiara	750
Somalia	638	246	9,180	Mogadishu	500
South Africa	1,220	471	44,000	Pretoria/Cape Town/ Bloemfontein	2,900
Spain	505	195	39,664	Madrid	13,650
Sri Lanka	65.6	25.3	18,359	Colombo	600
Sudan	2,506	967	29,980	Khartoum	750
Surinam	163	63	421	Paramaribo	1,210
Swaziland	17.4	6.7	849	Mbabane	1,050
Sweden	450	174	8,893	Stockholm	24,830
Switzerland	41.3	15.9	7,2681	Bern	36,410
Syria	185	71	14,614	Damascus	5,700
Taiwan	36	13.9	21,100	Taipei	11,000
Tajikistan	143.1	55.2	6,102	Dushanbe	470
Tanzania	945	365	29,710	Dodoma	100
Thailand	513	198	58,432	Bangkok	2,040
Togo	56.8	21.9	4,140	Lomé	330
Trinidad & Tobago	5.1	2	1,295	Port of Spain	3,730
Tunisia	164	63	8,906	Tunis	1,780
Turkey	779	301	61,303	Ankara	2,120
Turkmenistan	488.1	188.5	4,100	Ashkhabad	1,400
Uganda	236	91	20,466	Kampala	190
Ukraine	603.7	233.1	52,027	Kiev	1,910
United Arab Emirates	83.6	32.3	2,800	Abu Dhabi	22,470
United Kingdom	243.3	94	58,306	London	17,970
United States of America	9,373	3,619	263,563	Washington, DC	24,750
Uruguay	177	68	3,186	Montevideo	3,910
Uzbekistan	447.4	172.7	22,833	Tashkent	960
Vanuatu	12.2	4.7	167	Port-Vila	1,230
Venezuela	912	352	21,810	Caracas	2,840
Vietnam	332	127	74,580	Hanoi	170
Virgin Is. (US)	0.34	0.13	105	Charlotte Amalie	12,000
Western Sahara	266	103	220	El Aaiún	300
Western Samoa	2.8	1.1	169	Apia	980
Yemen	528	204	14,609	Sana	800
Yugoslavia	102.3	39.5	10,881	Belgrade	1,000
Zaïre	2,345	905	44,504	Kinshasa	500
Zambia	753	291	9,500	Lusaka	370
Zimbabwe	391	151	11,453	Harare	540

World Statistics – Cities

Listed below are all the cities with more than 600,000 inhabitants (only cities with more than 1 million inhabitants are included for China, Brazil and India). The figures are taken from the most recent censuses and surveys, and are in thousands. As far as possible the figures are for the metropolitan area, e.g. greater New York or Mexico City.

	Population (1,000s)		Population (1,000s)		Population (1,000s)		Population (1,000s)
Afghanistan		Ottawa–Hull	921	Santo Domingo	2,100	Varanasi	1,026
Kābul	1,424	Québec	646	**Ecuador**		Vishakhapatnam	1,052
Algeria		Toronto	3,893	Guayaquil	1,508	**Indonesia**	
Algiers	1,722	Vancouver	1,603	Quito	1,101	Bandung	2,027
Oran	664	Winnipeg	652	**Egypt**		Jakarta	11,500
Angola		**Chile**		Alexandria	3,380	Malang	650
Luanda	2,250	Santiago	4,628	Cairo	9,656	Medan	1,686
Argentina		**China**		El Gîza	2,144	Palembang	1,084
Buenos Aires	10,990	Anshan	1,204	Shubra el Kheima	834	Semarang	1,005
Córdoba	1,198	Beijing	12,362	**El Salvador**		Surabaya	2,421
La Plata	640	Changchun	2,470	San Salvador	1,522	Ujung Pandang	913
Mendoza	775	Changsha	1,510	**Ethiopia**		**Iran**	
Rosario	1,096	Chengdu	2,760	Addis Ababa	2,316	Ahvaz	725
San Miguel de Tucumán	622	Chongqing	3,870	**France**		Bakhtaran	624
Armenia		Dalian	2,400	Bordeaux	696	Esfahan	1,127
Yerevan	1,226	Fushun	1,202	Lille	959	Mashhad	1,759
Australia		Fuzhou	1,380	Lyons	1,262	Qom	681
Adelaide	1,071	Guangzhou	3,750	Marseilles	1,087	Shiraz	965
Brisbane	1,422	Guiyang	1,080	Paris	9,469	Tabriz	1,089
Melbourne	3,189	Hangzhou	1,790	Toulouse	650	Tehran	6,476
Perth	1,221	Harbin	3,120	**Georgia**		**Iraq**	
Sydney	3,713	Hefei	1,110	Tbilisi	1,279	Al Mawsil	664
Austria		Hong Kong (SAR*)	6,205	**Germany**		Arbil	770
Vienna	1,560	Jilin	1,037	Berlin	3,475	As Sulaymaniyah	952
Azerbaijan		Jinan	2,150	Cologne	693	Baghdad	3,841
Baku	1,081	Kunming	1,500	Dortmund	602	Diyala	961
Bangladesh		Lanzhou	1,340	Essen	622	**Ireland**	
Chittagong	2,041	Linhai	1,012	Frankfurt	660	Dublin	1,024
Dhaka	7,832	Macheng	1,010	Hamburg	1,703	**Israel**	
Khulna	877	Nanchang	1,440	Munich	1,256	Tel Aviv	1,502
Belarus		Nanjing	2,490	**Ghana**		**Italy**	
Minsk	1,658	Ningbo	1,100	Accra	1,390	Genoa	668
Belgium		Qingdao	2,300	**Greece**		Milan	1,359
Brussels	952	Qiqihar	1,070	Athens	3,097	Naples	1,072
Bolivia		Shanghai	15,082	**Guatemala**		Palermo	697
La Paz	1,126	Shenyang	4,050	Guatemala	2,000	Rome	2,723
Santa Cruz	767	Shijiazhuang	1,610	**Guinea**		Turin	953
Brazil		Taiyuan	1,720	Conakry	1,508	**Ivory Coast**	
Belém	1,246	Tangshan	1,044	**Haiti**		Abidjan	2,500
Belo Horizonte	2,049	Tianjin	10,687	Port-au-Prince	1,402	**Jamaica**	
Brasília	1,596	Ürümqi	1,130	**Honduras**		Kingston	644
Curitiba	1,290	Wuhan	3,870	Tegucigalpa	739	**Japan**	
Fortaleza	1,758	Xi'an	2,410	**Hungary**		Chiba	851
Manaus	1,011	Zhengzhou	1,690	Budapest	2,009	Fukuoka	1,269
Nova Iguaçu	1,286	Zibo	2,400	**India**		Hiroshima	1,102
Pôrto Alegre	1,263	**Colombia**		Ahmadabad	3,298	Kawasaki	1,200
Recife	1,290	Barranquilla	1,064	Bangalore	4,087	Kitakyushu	1,020
Rio de Janeiro	9,888	Bogotá	5,026	Bhopal	1,064	Kobe	1,509
Salvador	2,056	Cali	1,719	Bombay (Mumbai)	15,093	Kumamoto	640
São Paulo	16,417	Cartagena	746	Calcutta	11,673	Kyoto	1,452
Bulgaria		Medellin	1,621	Coimbatore	1,136	Nagoya	2,159
Sofia	1,114	**Congo**		Delhi	9,882	Okayama	605
Burkina Faso		Brazzaville	938	Hyderabad	4,280	Osaka	10,601
Ouagadougou	634	**Costa Rica**		Indore	1,104	Sakai	806
Burma (Myanmar)		San José	1,186	Jaipur	1,514	Sapporo	1,732
Rangoon (Yangon)	2,513	**Croatia**		Kanpur	2,111	Sendai	951
Cambodia		Zagreb	931	Lucknow	1,642	Tokyo–Yokohama	26,836
Phnom Penh	920	**Cuba**		Ludhiana	1,012	**Jordan**	
Cameroon		Havana	2,143	Madras (Chennai)	5,361	Amman	1,300
Douala	884	**Czech Republic**		Madurai	1,094	Az-Zarqa	609
Yaoundé	750	Prague	1,217	Nagpur	1,661	**Kazakhstan**	
Canada		**Denmark**		Patna	1,099	Almaty	1,198
Calgary	754	Copenhagen	1,353	Pune	2,485	Qaraghandy	613
Edmonton	840	**Dominican Republic**		Surat	1,517	**Kenya**	
Montréal	3,127	Santiago	690	Vadodara	1,115	Nairobi	2,000

	Population (1,000s)		Population (1,000s)		Population (1,000s)		Population (1,000s)
Mombasa	600	Hyderabad	1,107	Vanderbijlpark–		Charlotte	1,212
Korea, North		Karachi	9,863	Vereeniging	774	Chicago	7,561
Chinnampo	691	Lahore	5,085	West Rand	870	Cincinnati	1,560
Chongjin	754	Multan	1,257	**Spain**		Cleveland	2,221
Hamhung	775	Peshawar	1,676	Barcelona	1,631	Columbus	1,394
Pyongyang	2,639	Rawalpindi	1,290	Madrid	3,041	Dallas	2,795
Korea, South		**Paraguay**		Sevilla	714	Denver	1,715
Inchon	1,818	Asunción	945	Valencia	764	Detroit	4,308
Kwangju	1,145	**Peru**		Zaragoza	607	Hartford	1,156
Puchon	668	Arequipa	620	**Sri Lanka**		Houston	3,530
Pusan	3,798	Lima–Callao	6,601	Colombo	1,863	Indianapolis	1,424
Seoul	11,641	**Philippines**		**Sweden**		Kansas City	1,617
Suwon	645	Caloocan	629	Göteburg	783	Jacksonville	661
Taegu	2,229	Cebu	641	Stockholm	1,539	Los Angeles	12,410
Taejon	1,062	Davao	868	**Switzerland**		Memphis	610
Ulsan	683	Manila	9,280	Zürich	915	Miami	2,008
Kyrgyzstan		Quezon City	1,667	**Syria**		Milwaukee	1,450
Bishkek	597	**Poland**		Aleppo	1,640	Minneapolis–St Paul	2,618
Latvia		Kraków	745	Damascus	2,230	New Orleans	1,303
Riga	840	Lódz	834	Homs	644	New York	16,329
Lebanon		Warsaw	1,643	**Taiwan**		Norfolk	1,497
Beirut	1,500	Wroclaw	642	Kaohsiung	1,405	Oklahoma	984
Libya		**Portugal**		T'aichung	817	Omaha	656
Tripoli	960	Lisbon	2,561	T'ainan	700	Philadelphia	4,944
Madagascar		Oporto	1,174	T'aipei	2,653	Phoenix	2,330
Antananarivo	1,053	**Puerto Rico**		**Tajikistan**		Pittsburgh	2,406
Malaysia		San Juan	1,816	Dushanbe	602	Portland	1,605
Kuala Lumpur	1,145	**Romania**		**Tanzania**		St Louis	2,519
Mali		Bucharest	2,061	Dar-es-Salaam	1,361	Sacramento	1,419
Bamako	746	**Russia**		**Thailand**		Salt Lake City	1,128
Mauritania		Chelyabinsk	1,125	Bangkok	5,876	San Antonio	1,379
Nouakchott	600	Irkutsk	632	**Tunisia**		San Diego	2,601
Mexico		Izhevsk	653	Tunis	1,827	San Francisco	3,866
Ciudad Juárez	798	Kazan	1,092	**Turkey**		San Jose	1,529
Culiacán Rosales	602	Khabarovsk	609	Adana	1,472	Seattle	2,124
Guadalajara	2,847	Krasnodar	638	Ankara	3,028	Tampa	2,107
León	872	Krasnoyarsk	914	Antalya	734	Washington, DC	4,360
Mexicali	602	Moscow	9,233	Bursa	1,317	**Uruguay**	
Mexico City	15,643	Nizhniy Novgorod	1,425	Diyarbakir	677	Montevideo	1,384
Monterrey	2,522	Novosibirsk	1,418	Gaziantep	930	**Uzbekistan**	
Puebla	1,055	Omsk	1,161	Icel	908	Tashkent	2,113
Tijuana	743	Perm	1,086	Istanbul	7,490	**Venezuela**	
Moldova		Rostov	1,023	Izmir	2,333	Barquisimento	745
Chişinău	700	St Petersburg	4,883	Kayseri	648	Caracas	2,784
Mongolia		Samara	1,223	Kocaeli	669	Maracaibo	1,364
Ulan Bator	601	Saratov	899	Konya	1,040	Maracay	800
Morocco		Simbirsk	670	Manisa	641	Valencia	1,032
Casablanca	2,943	Togliatti	689	Urfa	649	**Vietnam**	
Fès	564	Ufa	1,092	**Uganda**		Haiphong	1,448
Marrakesh	602	Vladivostok	637	Kampala	773	Hanoi	3,056
Rabat–Salé	1,220	Volgograd	1,000	**Ukraine**		Ho Chi Minh City	3,924
Mozambique		Voronezh	905	Dnipropetrovsk	1,190	**Yemen**	
Maputo	2,000	Yaroslavl	631	Donetsk	1,121	Sana	927
Netherlands		Yekaterinburg	1,347	Kharkiv	1,622	**Yugoslavia (Serbia**	
Amsterdam	1,100	**Saudi Arabia**		Kiev (Kyyiv)	2,643	**and Montenegro)**	
Rotterdam	1,074	Jedda	1,400	Kryyyy Rih	729	Belgrade	1,137
The Hague	695	Mecca	618	Lviv	807	**Zaïre**	
New Zealand		Riyadh	2,000	Odesa	1,096	Kinshasa	3,804
Auckland	896	**Senegal**		Zaporizhye	898	Lubumbashi	739
Nicaragua		Dakar	1,729	**United Kingdom**		Mbuji-Mayi	613
Managua	974	**Singapore**		Birmingham	1,400	**Zambia**	
Nigeria		Singapore	2,874	Glasgow	730	Lusaka	982
Ibadan	1,365	**Somalia**		Liverpool	1,060	**Zimbabwe**	
Kano	657	Mogadishu	1,000	London	6,378	Bulawayo	622
Lagos	10,287	**South Africa**		Manchester	1,669	Harare	1,189
Ogbomosho	712	Cape Town	1,912	Newcastle	617		
Norway		Durban	1,137	**United States**			
Oslo	714	East Rand	1,379	Atlanta	3,143		
Pakistan		Johannesburg	1,196	Baltimore	2,434	* Special Administrative	
Faisalabad	1,875	Port Elizabeth	853	Boston	3,211	Region	
Gujranwala	1,663	Pretoria	1,080	Buffalo	1,194		

World Statistics – Physical

Under each subject heading, the statistics are listed by continent. The figures are in size order beginning with the largest, longest or deepest, and are rounded as appropriate. Both metric and imperial measurements are given. The lists are complete down to the > mark; below this mark they are selective.

Land & Water

	km²	miles²	%
The World	509,450,000	196,672,000	–
Land	149,450,000	57,688,000	29.3
Water	360,000,000	138,984,000	70.7
Asia	44,500,000	17,177,000	29.8
Africa	30,302,000	11,697,000	20.3
North America	24,241,000	9,357,000	16.2
South America	17,793,000	6,868,000	11.9
Antarctica	14,100,000	5,443,000	9.4
Europe	9,957,000	3,843,000	6.7
Australia & Oceania	8,557,000	3,303,000	5.7
Pacific Ocean	179,679,000	69,356,000	49.9
Atlantic Ocean	92,373,000	35,657,000	25.7
Indian Ocean	73,917,000	28,532,000	20.5
Arctic Ocean	14,090,000	5,439,000	3.9

Seas

Pacific Ocean	km²	miles²
South China Sea	2,974,600	1,148,500
Bering Sea	2,268,000	875,000
Sea of Okhotsk	1,528,000	590,000
East China & Yellow	1,249,000	482,000
Sea of Japan	1,008,000	389,000
Gulf of California	162,000	62,500
Bass Strait	75,000	29,000

Atlantic Ocean	km²	miles²
Caribbean Sea	2,766,000	1,068,000
Mediterranean Sea	2,516,000	971,000
Gulf of Mexico	1,543,000	596,000
Hudson Bay	1,232,000	476,000
North Sea	575,000	223,000
Black Sea	462,000	178,000
Baltic Sea	422,170	163,000
Gulf of St Lawrence	238,000	92,000

Indian Ocean	km²	miles²
Red Sea	438,000	169,000
The Gulf	239,000	92,000

Mountains

Europe		m	ft
Mont Blanc	France/Italy	4,807	15,771
Monte Rosa	Italy/Switzerland	4,634	15,203
Dom	Switzerland	4,545	14,911
Liskamm	Switzerland	4,527	14,852
Weisshorn	Switzerland	4,505	14,780
Taschorn	Switzerland	4,490	14,730
Matterhorn/Cervino	Italy/Switzerland	4,478	14,691
Mont Maudit	France/Italy	4,465	14,649
Dent Blanche	Switzerland	4,356	14,291
Nadelhorn	Switzerland	4,327	14,196
> Grandes Jorasses	France/Italy	4,208	13,806
Jungfrau	Switzerland	4,158	13,642
Barre des Ecrins	France	4,103	13,461
Gran Paradiso	Italy	4,061	13,323
Piz Bernina	Italy/Switzerland	4,049	13,284
Eiger	Switzerland	3,970	13,025

Europe (cont.)		m	ft
Monte Viso	Italy	3,841	12,602
Grossglockner	Austria	3,797	12,457
Wildspitze	Austria	3,772	12,382
Monte Disgrazia	Italy	3,678	12,066
Mulhacén	Spain	3,478	11,411
Pico de Aneto	Spain	3,404	11,168
Marmolada	Italy	3,342	10,964
Etna	Italy	3,340	10,958
Zugspitze	Germany	2,962	9,718
Musala	Bulgaria	2,925	9,596
Olympus	Greece	2,917	9,570
Triglav	Slovenia	2,863	9,393
Monte Cinto	France (Corsica)	2,710	8,891
Gerlachovka	Slovak Republic	2,655	8,711
Torre de Cerrado	Spain	2,648	8,688
Galdhöpiggen	Norway	2,468	8,100
Hvannadalshnúkur	Iceland	2,119	6,952
Kebnekaise	Sweden	2,117	6,946
Ben Nevis	UK	1,343	4,406

Asia		m	ft
Everest	China/Nepal	8,848	29,029
K2 (Godwin Austen)	China/Kashmir	8,611	28,251
Kanchenjunga	India/Nepal	8,598	28,208
Lhotse	China/Nepal	8,516	27,939
Makalu	China/Nepal	8,481	27,824
Cho Oyu	China/Nepal	8,201	26,906
Dhaulagiri	Nepal	8,172	26,811
Manaslu	Nepal	8,156	26,758
Nanga Parbat	Kashmir	8,126	26,660
Annapurna	Nepal	8,078	26,502
Gasherbrum	China/Kashmir	8,068	26,469
Broad Peak	China/Kashmir	8,051	26,414
Xixabangma	China	8,012	26,286
Kangbachen	India/Nepal	7,902	25,925
Jannu	India/Nepal	7,902	25,925
Gayachung Kang	Nepal	7,897	25,909
Himalchuli	Nepal	7,893	25,896
Disteghil Sar	Kashmir	7,885	25,869
Nuptse	Nepal	7,879	25,849
Khunyang Chhish	Kashmir	7,852	25,761
Masherbrum	Kashmir	7,821	25,659
Nanda Devi	India	7,817	25,646
Rakaposhi	Kashmir	7,788	25,551
Batura	Kashmir	7,785	25,541
Namche Barwa	China	7,756	25,446
Kamet	India	7,756	25,446
Soltoro Kangri	Kashmir	7,742	25,400
Gurla Mandhata	China	7,728	25,354
Trivor	Pakistan	7,720	25,328
> Kongur Shan	China	7,719	25,324
Tirich Mir	Pakistan	7,690	25,229
K'ula Shan	Bhutan/China	7,543	24,747
Pik Kommunizma	Tajikistan	7,495	24,590
Elbrus	Russia	5,642	18,510
Demavend	Iran	5,604	18,386
Ararat	Turkey	5,165	16,945
Gunong Kinabalu	Malaysia (Borneo)	4,101	13,455
Yu Shan	Taiwan	3,997	13,113
Fuji-San	Japan	3,776	12,388

Africa		m	ft
Kilimanjaro	Tanzania	5,895	19,340
Mt Kenya	Kenya	5,199	17,057
Ruwenzori (Margherita)	Uganda/Zaire	5,109	16,762
Ras Dashan	Ethiopia	4,620	15,157

Africa (cont.)		m	ft
Meru	Tanzania	4,565	14,977
Karisimbi	Rwanda/Zaire	4,507	14,787
Mt Elgon	Kenya/Uganda	4,321	14,176
Batu	Ethiopia	4,307	14,130
Guna	Ethiopia	4,231	13,882
Toubkal	Morocco	4,165	13,665
Irhil Mgoun	Morocco	4,071	13,356
Mt Cameroon	Cameroon	4,070	13,353
Amba Ferit	Ethiopia	3,875	13,042
Pico del Teide	Spain (Tenerife)	3,718	12,198
Thabana Ntlenyana	Lesotho	3,482	11,424
Emi Koussi	Chad	3,415	11,204
Mt aux Sources	Lesotho/South Africa	3,282	10,768
Mt Piton	Réunion	3,069	10,069

Oceania		m	ft
Puncak Jaya	Indonesia	5,029	16,499
Puncak Trikora	Indonesia	4,750	15,584
Puncak Mandala	Indonesia	4,702	15,427
Mt Wilhelm	Papua New Guinea	4,508	14,790
Mauna Kea	USA (Hawaii)	4,205	13,796
Mauna Loa	USA (Hawaii)	4,170	13,681
Mt Cook	New Zealand	3,753	12,313
Mt Balbi	Solomon Is.	2,439	8,002
Orohena	Tahiti	2,241	7,352
Mt Kosciusko	Australia	2,237	7,339

North America		m	ft
Mt McKinley (Denali)	USA (Alaska)	6,194	20,321
Mt Logan	Canada	5,959	19,551
Citlaltepetl	Mexico	5,700	18,701
Mt St Elias	USA/Canada	5,489	18,008
Popocatepetl	Mexico	5,452	17,887
Mt Foraker	USA (Alaska)	5,304	17,401
Ixtaccihuatl	Mexico	5,286	17,342
Lucania	Canada	5,227	17,149
Mt Steele	Canada	5,073	16,644
Mt Bona	USA (Alaska)	5,005	16,420
Mt Blackburn	USA (Alaska)	4,996	16,391
Mt Sanford	USA (Alaska)	4,940	16,207
Mt Wood	Canada	4,848	15,905
Nevado de Toluca	Mexico	4,670	15,321
Mt Fairweather	USA (Alaska)	4,663	15,298
Mt Hunter	USA (Alaska)	4,442	15,573
Mt Whitney	USA	4,418	14,495
Mt Elbert	USA	4,399	14,432
Mt Harvard	USA	4,395	14,419
Mt Rainier	USA	4,392	14,409
Blanca Peak	USA	4,372	14,344
Longs Peak	USA	4,345	14,255
Tajumulco	Guatemala	4,220	13,845
Grand Teton	USA	4,197	13,770
Mt Waddington	Canada	3,994	13,104
Mt Robson	Canada	3,954	12,972
Chirripó Grande	Costa Rica	3,837	12,589
Mt Assiniboine	Canada	3,619	11,873
Pico Duarte	Dominican Rep.	3,175	10,417

South America		m	ft
Aconcagua	Argentina	6,960	22,834
Bonete	Argentina	6,872	22,546
Ojos del Salado	Argentina/Chile	6,863	22,516
Pissis	Argentina	6,779	22,241
Mercedario	Argentina/Chile	6,770	22,211
Huascaran	Peru	6,768	22,204
Llullaillaco	Argentina/Chile	6,723	22,057
Nudo de Cachi	Argentina	6,720	22,047
Yerupaja	Peru	6,632	21,758
N. de Tres Cruces	Argentina/Chile	6,620	21,719
Incahuasi	Argentina/Chile	6,601	21,654
Cerro Galan	Argentina	6,600	21,654
Tupungato	Argentina/Chile	6,570	21,555

South America (cont.)		m	ft
Sajama	Bolivia	6,542	21,463
Illimani	Bolivia	6,485	21,276
Coropuna	Peru	6,425	21,079
Ausangate	Peru	6,384	20,945
Cerro del Toro	Argentina	6,380	20,932
Siula Grande	Peru	6,356	20,853
Chimborazo	Ecuador	6,267	20,561
Cotapaxi	Ecuador	5,896	19,344
Pico Colon	Colombia	5,800	19,029
Pico Bolivar	Venezuela	5,007	16,427

Antarctica	m	ft
Vinson Massif	4,897	16,066
Mt Kirkpatrick	4,528	14,855
Mt Markham	4,349	14,268

Ocean Depths

Atlantic Ocean	m	ft
Mt Kirkpatrick	4,528	14,855
Puerto Rico (Milwaukee) Deep	9,220	30,249
Cayman Trench	7,680	25,197
Gulf of Mexico	5,203	17,070
Mediterranean Sea	5,121	16,801
Black Sea	2,211	7,254
North Sea	660	2,165
Baltic Sea	463	1,519

Indian Ocean	m	ft
Java Trench	7,450	24,442
Red Sea	2,635	8,454
Persian Gulf	73	239

Pacific Ocean	m	ft
Mariana Trench	11,022	36,161
Tonga Trench	10,882	35,702
Japan Trench	10,554	34,626
Kuril Trench	10,542	34,587
Mindanao Trench	10,497	34,439
Kermadec Trench	10,047	32,962
New Guinea Trench	9,140	19,987
Peru–Chile Trench	8,050	26,410

Antarctica	m	ft
Molloy Deep	5,608	18,399

Land Lows

		m	ft
Caspian Sea	Europe	−28	−92
Dead Sea	Asia	−403	−1,322
Lake Assal	Africa	−156	−512
Lake Eyre North	Oceania	−16	−52
Death Valley	North America	−86	−282
Valdés Peninsula	South America	−40	−131

Rivers

Europe		km	miles
Volga	Caspian Sea	3,700	2,300
Danube	Black Sea	2,850	1,770
Ural	Caspian Sea	2,535	1,575
Dnepr (Dnipro)	Volga	2,285	1,420
Kama	Volga	2,030	1,260
Don	Volga	1,990	1,240
Petchora	Arctic Ocean	1,790	1,110
Oka	Volga	1,480	920

Europe (cont.)

		km	miles
Belaya	Kama	1,420	880
Dnister (Dniester)	Black Sea	1,400	870
Vyatka	Kama	1,370	850
Rhine	North Sea	1,320	820
North Dvina	Arctic Ocean	1,290	800
Desna	Dnepr (Dnipro)	1,190	740
Elbe	North Sea	1,145	710
>Wisla	Baltic Sea	1,090	675
Loire	Atlantic Ocean	1,020	635
West Dvina	Baltic Sea	1,019	633

Asia

		km	miles
Yangtze	Pacific Ocean	6,380	3,960
Yenisey–Angara	Arctic Ocean	5,550	3,445
Huang He	Pacific Ocean	5,464	3,395
Ob–Irtysh	Arctic Ocean	5,410	3,360
Mekong	Pacific Ocean	4,500	2,795
Amur	Pacific Ocean	4,400	2,730
Lena	Arctic Ocean	4,400	2,730
Irtysh	Ob	4,250	2,640
Yenisey	Arctic Ocean	4,090	2,540
Ob	Arctic Ocean	3,680	2,285
Indus	Indian Ocean	3,100	1,925
Brahmaputra	Indian Ocean	2,900	1,800
Syrdarya	Aral Sea	2,860	1,775
Salween	Indian Ocean	2,800	1,740
Euphrates	Indian Ocean	2,700	1,675
Vilyuy	Lena	2,650	1,645
Kolyma	Arctic Ocean	2,600	1,615
Amudarya	Aral Sea	2,540	1,575
Ural	Caspian Sea	2,535	1,575
Ganges	Indian Ocean	2,510	1,560
>Si Kiang	Pacific Ocean	2,100	1,305
Irrawaddy	Indian Ocean	2,010	1,250
Tarim–Yarkand	Lop Nor	2,000	1,240
Tigris	Indian Ocean	1,900	1,180
Angara	Yenisey	1,830	1,135
Godavari	Indian Ocean	1,470	915
Sutlej	Indian Ocean	1,450	900

Africa

		km	miles
Nile	Mediterranean	6,670	4,140
Zaïre/Congo	Atlantic Ocean	4,670	2,900
Niger	Atlantic Ocean	4,180	2,595
Zambezi	Indian Ocean	3,540	2,200
Oubangi/Uele	Zaïre	2,250	1,400
Kasai	Zaïre	1,950	1,210
Shaballe	Indian Ocean	1,930	1,200
Orange	Atlantic Ocean	1,860	1,155
Cubango	Okavango Swamps	1,800	1,120
>Limpopo	Indian Ocean	1,600	995
Senegal	Atlantic Ocean	1,600	995
Volta	Atlantic Ocean	1,500	930
Benue	Niger	1,350	840

Australia

		km	miles
Murray–Darling	Indian Ocean	3,750	2,330
Darling	Murray	3,070	1,905
Murray	Indian Ocean	2,575	1,600
Murrumbidgee	Murray	1,690	1,050

North America

		km	miles
Mississippi–Missouri	Gulf of Mexico	6,020	3,740
Mackenzie	Arctic Ocean	4,240	2,630
Mississippi	Gulf of Mexico	3,780	2,350
Missouri	Mississippi	3,780	2,350
Yukon	Pacific Ocean	3,185	1,980
Rio Grande	Gulf of Mexico	3,030	1,880
Arkansas	Mississippi	2,340	1,450
Colorado	Pacific Ocean	2,330	1,445
Red	Mississippi	2,040	1,270

North America (cont.)

		km	miles
Columbia	Pacific Ocean	1,950	1,210
Saskatchewan	Lake Winnipeg	1,940	1,205
Snake	Columbia	1,670	1,040
Churchill	Hudson Bay	1,600	990
Ohio	Mississippi	1,580	980
Brazos	Gulf of Mexico	1,400	870
>St Lawrence	Atlantic Ocean	1,170	730

South America

		km	miles
Amazon	Atlantic Ocean	6,450	4,010
Paraná–Plate	Atlantic Ocean	4,500	2,800
Purus	Amazon	3,350	2,080
Madeira	Amazon	3,200	1,990
São Francisco	Atlantic Ocean	2,900	1,800
Paraná	Plate	2,800	1,740
Tocantins	Atlantic Ocean	2,750	1,710
Paraguay	Paraná	2,550	1,580
Orinoco	Atlantic Ocean	2,500	1,550
Pilcomayo	Paraná	2,500	1,550
Araguaia	Tocantins	2,250	1,400
Juruá	Amazon	2,000	1,240
Xingu	Amazon	1,980	1,230
Ucayali	Amazon	1,900	1,180
Maranón	Amazon	1,600	990
>Uruguay	Plate	1,600	990
Magdalena	Caribbean Sea	1,540	960

Lakes

Europe

		km²	miles²
Lake Ladoga	Russia	17,700	6,800
Lake Onega	Russia	9,700	3,700
Saimaa system	Finland	8,000	3,100
Vänern	Sweden	5,500	2,100
Rybinskoye Reservoir	Russia	4,700	1,800

Asia

		km²	miles²
Caspian Sea	Asia	371,800	143,550
Aral Sea	Kazak./Uzbek.	33,640	13,000
Lake Baykal	Russia	30,500	11,780
Tonlé Sap	Cambodia	20,000	7,700
>Lake Balqash	Kazakstan	18,500	7,100
Lake Dongting	China	12,000	4,600
Lake Ysyk	Kyrgyzstan	6,200	2,400
Lake Orumiyeh	Iran	5,900	2,300
Lake Koko	China	5,700	2,200
Lake Poyang	China	5,000	1,900
Lake Khanka	China/Russia	4,400	1,700
Lake Van	Turkey	3,500	1,400
Lake Ubsa	China	3,400	1,300

Africa

		km²	miles²
Lake Victoria	East Africa	68,000	26,000
Lake Tanganyika	Central Africa	33,000	13,000
Lake Malawi/Nyasa	East Africa	29,600	11,430
Lake Chad	Central Africa	25,000	9,700
Lake Turkana	Ethiopia/Kenya	8,500	3,300
Lake Volta	Ghana	8,500	3,300
Lake Bangweulu	Zambia	8,000	3,100
Lake Rukwa	Tanzania	7,000	2,700
Lake Mai-Ndombe	Zaïre	6,500	2,500
>Lake Kariba	Zambia/Zimbabwe	5,300	2,000
Lake Mobutu	Uganda/Zaïre	5,300	2,000
Lake Nasser	Egypt/Sudan	5,200	2,000
Lake Mweru	Zambia/Zaïre	4,900	1,900
Lake Cabora Bassa	Mozambique	4,500	1,700
Lake Kyoga	Uganda	4,400	1,700
Lake Tana	Ethiopia	3,630	1,400
Lake Kivu	Rwanda/Zaïre	2,650	1,000
Lake Edward	Uganda/Zaïre	2,200	850

Australia		km²	miles²
Lake Eyre	Australia	8,900	3,400
Lake Torrens	Australia	5,800	2,200
Lake Gairdner	Australia	4,800	1,900

North America		km²	miles²
Lake Superior	Canada/USA	82,350	31,800
Lake Huron	Canada/USA	59,600	23,010
Lake Michigan	USA	58,000	22,400
Great Bear Lake	Canada	31,800	12,280
Great Slave Lake	Canada	28,500	11,000
Lake Erie	Canada/USA	25,700	9,900
Lake Winnipeg	Canada	24,400	9,400
Lake Ontario	Canada/USA	19,500	7,500
Lake Nicaragua	Nicaragua	8,200	3,200
Lake Athabasca	Canada	8,100	3,100
Smallwood Reservoir	Canada	6,530	2,520
Reindeer Lake	Canada	6,400	2,500
Lake Winnipegosis	Canada	5,400	2,100
Nettilling Lake	Canada	5,500	2,100
Lake Nipigon	Canada	4,850	1,900
Lake Manitoba	Canada	4,700	1,800

South America		km²	miles²
Lake Titicaca	Bolivia/Peru	8,300	3,200
Lake Poopo	Peru	2,800	1,100

Islands

Europe		km²	miles²
Great Britain	UK	229,880	88,700
Iceland	Atlantic Ocean	103,000	39,800
Ireland	Ireland/UK	84,400	32,600
Novaya Zemlya (North)	Russia	48,200	18,600
West Spitzbergen	Norway	39,000	15,100
Novaya Zemlya (South)	Russia	33,200	12,800
Sicily	Italy	25,500	9,800
Sardinia	Italy	24,000	9,300
North-east Spitzbergen	Norway	15,000	5,600
Corsica	France	8,700	3,400
Crete	Greece	8,350	3,200
Zealand	Denmark	6,850	2,600

Asia		km²	miles²
Borneo	Southeast Asia	744,360	287,400
Sumatra	Indonesia	473,600	182,860
Honshu	Japan	230,500	88,980
Celebes	Indonesia	189,000	73,000
Java	Indonesia	126,700	48,900
Luzon	Philippines	104,700	40,400
Mindanao	Philippines	101,500	39,200
Hokkaido	Japan	78,400	30,300
Sakhalin	Russia	74,060	28,600
Sri Lanka	Indian Ocean	65,600	25,300
Taiwan	Pacific Ocean	36,000	13,900
Kyushu	Japan	35,700	13,800
Hainan	China	34,000	13,100
Timor	Indonesia	33,600	13,000
Shikoku	Japan	18,800	7,300
Halmahera	Indonesia	18,000	6,900
Ceram	Indonesia	17,150	6,600
Sumbawa	Indonesia	15,450	6,000
Flores	Indonesia	15,200	5,900
Samar	Philippines	13,100	5,100
Negros	Philippines	12,700	4,900
Bangka	Indonesia	12,000	4,600
Palawan	Philippines	12,000	4,600
Panay	Philippines	11,500	4,400
Sumba	Indonesia	11,100	4,300
Mindoro	Philippines	9,750	3,800
Buru	Indonesia	9,500	3,700

Asia (cont.)		km²	miles²
Bali	Indonesia	5,600	2,200
Cyprus	Mediterranean	3,570	1,400

Africa		km²	miles²
Madagascar	Indian Ocean	587,040	226,660
Socotra	Indian Ocean	3,600	1,400
Réunion	Indian Ocean	2,500	965
Tenerife	Atlantic Ocean	2,350	900
Mauritius	Indian Ocean	1,865	720

Oceania		km²	miles²
New Guinea	Indon./Papua NG	821,030	317,000
New Zealand (South)	New Zealand	150,500	58,100
New Zealand (North)	New Zealand	114,700	44,300
Tasmania	Australia	67,800	26,200
New Britain	Papua NG	37,800	14,600
New Caledonia	Pacific Ocean	19,100	7,400
Viti Levu	Fiji	10,500	4,100
Hawaii	Pacific Ocean	10,450	4,000
Bougainville	Papua NG	9,600	3,700
Guadalcanal	Solomon Is.	6,500	2,500
Vanua Levu	Fiji	5,550	2,100
New Ireland	Papua NG	3,200	1,200

North America		km²	miles²
Greenland	Greenland	2,175,600	839,800
Baffin Is.	Canada	508,000	196,100
Victoria Is.	Canada	212,200	81,900
Ellesmere Is.	Canada	212,100	81,800
Cuba	Cuba	110,860	42,800
Newfoundland	Canada	110,680	42,700
Hispaniola	Atlantic Ocean	76,200	29,400
Banks Is.	Canada	67,000	25,900
Devon Is.	Canada	54,500	21,000
Melville Is.	Canada	42,400	16,400
Vancouver Is.	Canada	32,150	12,400
Somerset Is.	Canada	24,300	9,400
Jamaica	Caribbean Sea	11,400	4,400
Puerto Rico	Atlantic Ocean	8,900	3,400
Cape Breton Is.	Canada	4,000	1,500

South America		km²	miles²
Tierra del Fuego	Argentina/Chile	47,000	18,100
Falkland Is. (East)	Atlantic Ocean	6,800	2,600
South Georgia	Atlantic Ocean	4,200	1,600
Galapagos (Isabela)	Pacific Ocean	2,250	870

World Statistics – Climate

For each city, the top row of figures shows total rainfall in inches whilst the bottom row shows the average temperature in ° Fahrenheit. The total annual rainfall and average annual temperature are given at the end of the rows.

	Jan.	Feb.	Mar.	Apr.	May	June	July	Aug.	Sept.	Oct.	Nov.	Dec.	Total
Europe													
Berlin, Germany	1.8	1.6	1.3	1.7	1.9	2.6	2.9	2.7	1.9	1.9	1.8	1.7	23.7
Altitude 180 feet	30	32	39	48	57	63	66	64	59	48	41	34	48
London, UK	2.1	1.6	1.5	1.5	1.8	1.8	2.2	2.3	1.9	2.2	2.5	1.9	23.3
16 ft	39	41	45	48	54	61	64	63	59	52	46	41	52
Málaga, Spain	2.4	2.0	2.4	1.8	1.0	0.2	0	0.1	1.1	2.5	2.5	2.4	18.7
108 ft	54	55	61	63	66	84	77	79	73	68	61	55	66
Moscow, Russia	1.5	1.5	1.4	1.5	2.1	2.3	3.5	2.8	2.3	1.8	1.9	2.1	24.6
512 ft	9	14	25	43	55	61	64	63	54	43	30	19	39
Paris, France	2.2	1.8	1.4	1.7	2.2	2.1	2.3	2.5	2.2	2.0	2.0	2.0	24.4
246 ft	37	39	46	52	59	64	68	66	63	54	45	39	53
Rome, Italy	2.8	2.4	2.2	2.0	1.8	1.5	0.6	0.8	2.5	3.9	5.1	3.7	29.3
56 ft	46	48	52	57	64	72	77	77	72	63	55	50	61
Asia													
Bangkok, Thailand	0.3	0.8	1.4	2.3	7.8	6.3	6.3	6.9	12.0	8.1	2.6	0.2	55
7 ft	79	82	84	86	84	84	82	82	82	82	79	77	82
Bombay (Mumbai), India	0.1	0.1	0.1	<0.1	0.7	19.1	24.3	13.4	10.4	2.5	0.5	0.1	71.4
36 ft	75	75	79	82	86	84	81	81	81	82	81	79	80
Ho Chi Minh, Vietnam	0.6	0.1	0.5	1.7	8.7	13.0	12.4	10.6	13.2	10.6	4.5	2.2	78.1
30 ft	79	81	84	86	84	82	82	82	81	81	81	79	82
Hong Kong, China	1.3	1.8	2.9	5.4	11.5	15.5	15.0	14.2	10.1	4.5	1.7	1.2	85.2
108 ft	61	59	64	72	79	82	82	82	81	77	70	64	73
Tokyo, Japan	1.9	2.9	4.2	5.3	5.8	6.5	5.6	6.0	9.2	8.2	3.8	2.2	61.6
20 ft	37	39	45	55	63	70	77	79	73	63	52	43	58
Africa													
Cairo, Egypt	0.2	0.2	0.2	0.1	0.1	<0.1	0	0	<0.1	<0.1	0.1	0.2	1.1
1,380 ft	55	59	64	70	77	82	82	82	79	75	68	59	71
Cape Town, South Africa	0.6	0.3	0.7	1.9	3.1	3.3	3.5	2.6	1.7	1.2	0.7	0.4	20
56 ft	70	70	68	63	57	55	54	55	57	61	64	66	62
Lagos, Nigeria	1.1	1.8	4.0	5.9	10.6	18.1	11.0	2.5	5.5	8.1	2.7	1.0	72.4
10 ft	81	82	84	82	82	79	79	77	79	79	82	82	81
Nairobi, Kenya	1.5	2.5	4.9	8.3	6.2	1.8	0.6	0.9	1.2	2.1	4.3	3.3	37.8
5,970 ft	66	66	66	64	64	61	61	61	64	66	64	64	64
Australia, New Zealand & Antarctica													
Christchurch, New Zealand	2.2	1.7	1.9	1.9	2.6	2.6	2.7	1.9	1.8	1.7	1.9	2.2	25.1
33 ft	61	61	57	54	48	43	43	45	48	54	57	61	53
Darwin, Australia	15.2	12.3	10.0	3.8	0.6	0.1	<0.1	0.1	0.5	2	4.7	9.4	58.7
98 ft	84	84	84	84	82	79	77	79	82	84	86	84	83
Mawson, Antarctica	0.4	1.2	0.8	0.4	1.7	7.1	0.2	1.6	0.1	0.8	0	0	14.3
46 ft	32	23	14	7	5	3	0	0	−1	9	23	30	12
Sydney, Australia	3.5	4.0	5.0	5.3	5.0	4.6	4.6	3.0	2.9	2.8	2.9	2.9	46.5
138 ft	72	72	70	64	59	55	54	55	59	64	66	70	63
North America													
Anchorage, Alaska, USA	0.8	0.7	0.6	0.4	0.5	0.7	1.6	2.6	2.6	2.2	1.0	0.9	14.6
131 ft	12	18	23	36	45	54	57	55	48	36	23	12	35
Kingston, Jamaica	0.9	0.6	0.9	1.2	4.0	3.5	1.5	3.6	3.9	7.1	2.9	1.4	31.5
112 ft	77	77	77	79	79	82	82	82	81	81	79	79	80
Los Angeles, USA	3.1	3.0	2.8	1.0	0.4	0.1	<0.1	<0.1	0.2	0.6	1.2	2.6	15
312 ft	55	57	57	61	63	66	70	72	70	64	61	57	63
Mexico City, Mexico	0.5	0.2	0.4	0.8	2.1	4.7	6.7	6.0	5.1	2.0	0.7	0.3	29.5
7,574 ft	12	13	16	18	19	19	17	18	18	16	14	13	16
New York, N. Y., USA	3.7	3.8	3.6	3.2	3.2	3.3	4.2	4.3	3.4	3.5	3.0	3.6	42.8
315 ft	30	30	37	50	61	68	73	73	70	59	45	36	53
Vancouver, Canada	6.1	4.5	4.0	2.4	2.0	1.8	1.3	1.6	2.6	4.5	5.9	7.2	43.8
46 ft	37	41	43	48	54	59	63	63	57	50	43	39	50
South America													
Antofagasta, Chile	0	0	0	<0.1	<0.1	0.1	0.2	0.1	<0.1	0.1	<0.1	0	0.6
308 ft	70	70	68	64	61	59	57	57	59	61	64	66	63
Buenos Aires, Argentina	3.1	2.8	4.3	3.5	3.0	2.4	2.2	2.4	3.1	3.4	3.3	3.9	37.4
89 ft	73	73	70	63	55	48	50	52	55	59	66	72	61
Lima, Peru	0.1	<0.1	<0.1	<0.1	0.2	0.2	0.3	0.3	0.3	0.1	0.1	<0.1	1.7
394 ft	73	75	75	72	66	63	63	61	63	64	66	70	68
Rio de Janeiro, Brazil	4.9	4.8	5.1	4.2	3.1	2.1	1.6	1.7	2.6	3.1	4.1	5.4	42.8
200 ft	79	77	75	72	70	70	70	70	70	72	73	77	74

The Earth in Focus

> Landsat image of the
San Francisco Bay area.
The narrow entrance to
the bay (crossed by the
Golden Gate Bridge)
provides an excellent
natural harbor. The
San Andreas Fault runs
parallel to the coastline.

The Universe & Solar System

Between 10 and 20 billion (or 10,000 to 20,000 million) years ago, the Universe was created in a huge explosion known as the 'Big Bang'. In the first 10^{-24} of a second the Universe expanded rapidly and the basic forces of nature, radiation and subatomic particles, came into being. The Universe has been expanding ever since. Traces of the original 'fireball' of radiation can still be detected, and most scientists accept the Big Bang theory of the origin of the Universe.

The Nearest Stars ▾	
The 20 nearest stars, excluding the Sun, with their distance from Earth in light years.*	
Proxima Centauri	4.25
Alpha Centauri A	4.3
Alpha Centauri B	4.3
Barnard's Star	6.0
Wolf 359	7.8
Lalande 21185	8.3
Sirius A	8.7
Sirius B	8.7
UV Ceti A	8.7
UV Ceti B	8.7
Ross 154	9.4
Ross 248	10.3
Epsilon Eridani	10.7
Ross 128	10.9
61 Cygni A	11.1
61 Cygni B	11.1
Epsilon Indi	11.2
Groombridge 34 A	11.2
Groombridge 34 B	11.2
L789-6	11.2
*A light year equals approximately 5,900 billion miles [9,500 billion km].	

> *The Lagoon Nebula is a huge cloud of dust and gas. Hot stars inside the nebula make the gas glow red.*

GALAXIES

Almost a million years passed before the Universe cooled sufficiently for atoms to form. When a billion years had passed, the atoms had begun to form protogalaxies, which are masses of gas separated by empty space. Stars began to form within the protogalaxies, as particles were drawn together, producing the high temperatures necessary to bring about nuclear fusion. The formation of the first stars brought about the evolution of the protogalaxies into galaxies proper, each containing billions of stars.

Our Sun is a medium-sized star. It is

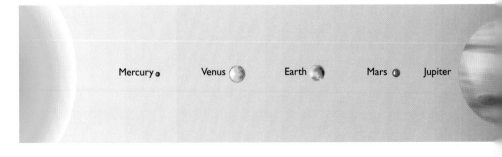

Mercury ○ Venus ○ Earth ○ Mars ○ Jupiter

PLANETARY DATA

	Mean distance from Sun (million miles)	Mass (Earth = 1)	Period of orbit (Earth years)	Period of rotation (Earth days)	Equatorial diameter (miles)	Escape velocity (miles/sec)	Number of known satellites
Sun	–	332,946	–	25.38	865,000	383.7	–
Mercury	36.2	0.06	0.241	58.67	3,031	2.65	0
Venus	66.9	0.8	0.615	243.0	7,521	6.44	0
Earth	93.0	1.0	1.00	0.99	7,926	6.95	1
Mars	141.2	0.1	1.88	1.02	4,217	3.13	2
Jupiter	483.4	317.8	11.86	0.41	88,730	37.0	16
Saturn	886.8	95.2	29.46	0.42	74,500	22.1	20
Uranus	1,784.8	14.5	84.01	0.45	31,763	13.2	15
Neptune	2,797.8	17.2	164.79	0.67	30,775	14.5	8
Pluto	3,662.5	0.002	248.54	6.38	1,430	0.68	1

one of the billions of stars that make up the Milky Way galaxy, which is one of the millions of galaxies in the Universe.

THE SOLAR SYSTEM

The Solar System lies towards the edge of the Milky Way galaxy. It consists of the Sun and other bodies, including planets (together with their moons), asteroids, meteoroids, comets, dust and gas, which revolve around it.

The Earth moves through space in three distinct ways. First, with the rest of the Solar System, it moves around the center of the Milky Way galaxy in an orbit that takes 200 million years.

As the Earth revolves around the Sun once every year, its axis is tilted by about 23.5 degrees. As a result, first the northern and then the southern hemisphere lean toward the Sun at different times of the year, causing the seasons experienced in the mid latitudes.

The Earth also rotates on its axis every 24 hours, causing day and night. The movements of the Earth in the Solar System determine the calendar. The length of a year – one complete orbit of the Earth around the Sun – is 365 days, 5 hours, 48 minutes and 46 seconds. Leap years prevent the calendar from becoming out of step with the solar year.

> The diagram below shows the planets around the Sun. The sizes of the planets are relative but the distances are not to scale. Closest to the Sun are dense rocky bodies, known as the terrestrial planets. They are Mercury, Venus, Earth, and Mars. Jupiter, Saturn, Uranus, and Neptune are huge balls of gas. Pluto is a small, icy body.

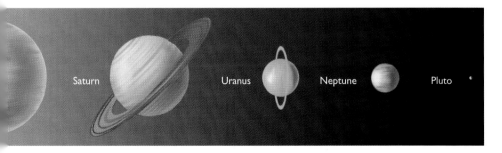

Saturn Uranus Neptune Pluto

The Changing Earth

THE SOLAR SYSTEM was formed around 4.7 billion years ago, when the Sun, a glowing ball of gases, was created from a rotating disk of dust and gas. The planets were then formed from material left over after the creation of the Sun.

After the Earth formed, around 4.6 billion years ago, lighter elements rose to the hot surface, where they finally cooled to form a hard shell, or crust. Denser elements sank, forming the partly liquid mantle, the liquid outer core, and the solid inner core.

EARTH HISTORY

The oldest known rocks on Earth are around 4 billion years old. Natural processes have destroyed older rocks. Simple life forms first appeared on Earth around 3.5 billion years ago, though rocks formed in the first 4 billion years of Earth history contain little evidence of life. But

> Fold mountains, such as the Himalayan ranges which are shown above, were formed when two plates collided and the rock layers between them were squeezed upwards into loops or folds.

rocks formed since the start of the Cambrian period (the first period in the Paleozoic era), about 590 million years ago, are rich in fossils. The study of fossils has enabled scientists to gradually piece together the long and complex story of life on Earth.

THE PLANET EARTH

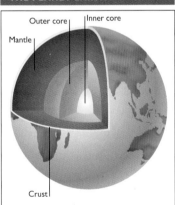

Outer core | Inner core
Mantle
Crust

CRUST The continental crust has an average thickness of 22–25 miles [35–40 km]; the oceanic crust averages 4 miles [6 km].

MANTLE 1,800 miles [2,900 km] thick. The top layer is solid, resting on a partly molten layer called the asthenosphere.

OUTER CORE 1,300 miles [2,100 km] thick. It consists mainly of molten iron and nickel.

INNER CORE (DIAMETER) 840 miles [1,350 km]. It is mainly solid iron and nickel.

ELEMENTS

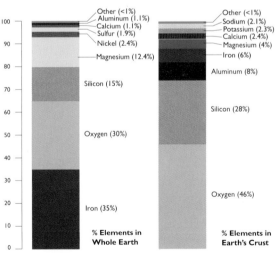

Other (<1%)
Aluminum (1.1%)
Calcium (1.1%)
Sulfur (1.9%)
Nickel (2.4%)
Magnesium (12.4%)
Silicon (15%)
Oxygen (30%)
Iron (35%)
% Elements in Whole Earth

Other (<1%)
Sodium (2.1%)
Potassium (2.3%)
Calcium (2.4%)
Magnesium (4%)
Iron (6%)
Aluminum (8%)
Silicon (28%)
Oxygen (46%)
% Elements in Earth's Crust

> The Earth contains about 100 elements, but eight of them account for 99% of the planet's mass. Iron makes up 35% of the Earth's mass, but most of it is in the core. The most common elements in the crust – oxygen and silicon – are often combined with one or more of the other common crustal elements, to form a group of minerals called silicates. The mineral quartz, which consists only of silicon and oxygen, occurs widely in such rocks as granites and sandstones.

PLATE BOUNDARIES

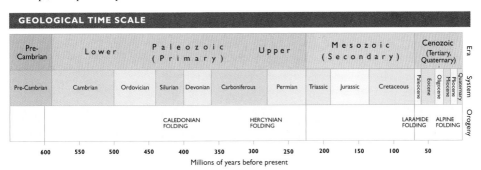

> The Earth's lithosphere is divided into six huge plates and several small ones. Ocean ridges, where plates are moving apart, are called constructive plate margins. Ocean trenches, where plates collide, are subduction zones. These are destructive plate margins. The map shows the main plates and the directions in which they are moving.

—— Plate boundaries

➡ Direction of plate movements

PACIFIC Major plates

THE DYNAMIC EARTH

The Earth's surface is always changing because of a process called plate tectonics. Plates are blocks of the solid lithosphere (the crust and outer mantle), which are moved around by currents in the partly liquid mantle. Around 250 million years ago, the Earth contained one super-continent called Pangaea. Around 180 million years ago, Pangaea split into a northern part, Laurasia, and a southern part, Gondwanaland. Later, these huge continents, in turn, also split apart and the continents drifted to their present positions. Ancient seas disappeared and mountain ranges, such as the Himalayas and Alps, were pushed upward.

PLATE TECTONICS

In the early 1900s, two scientists suggested that the Americas were once joined to Europe and Africa. Together they proposed the theory of continental drift to explain the similarities between rock structures on both sides of the Atlantic. But no one could offer an explanation as to how the continents moved.

Evidence from the ocean floor in the 1950s and 1960s led to the theory of plate tectonics, which suggested that the lithosphere is divided into large blocks, or plates. The plates are solid, but they rest on the partly molten asthenosphere, within the mantle. Long ridges on

the ocean floor were found to be the edges of plates which were moving apart, carried by currents in the asthenosphere. As the plates moved, molten material welled up from the mantle to fill the gaps. But at the ocean trenches, one plate is descending beneath another along what is called a subduction zone. The descending plate is melted and destroyed. This crustal destruction at subduction zones balances the creation of new crust along the ridges. Transform faults, where two plates are moving alongside each other, form another kind of plate edge.

GEOLOGICAL TIME SCALE

Era	Pre-Cambrian	Lower	Paleozoic (Primary)			Upper		Mesozoic (Secondary)			Cenozoic (Tertiary, Quaternary)					
System	Pre-Cambrian	Cambrian	Ordovician	Silurian	Devonian	Carboniferous	Permian	Triassic	Jurassic	Cretaceous	Paleocene	Eocene	Oligocene	Miocene	Pliocene	Quaternary
Orogeny				CALEDONIAN FOLDING		HERCYNIAN FOLDING							LARAMIDE FOLDING	ALPINE FOLDING		

600 550 500 450 400 350 300 250 200 150 100 50

Millions of years before present

5

Earthquakes & Volcanoes

PLATE TECTONICS HELP us to understand such phenomena as earthquakes, volcanic eruptions, and mountain building.

EARTHQUAKES

Earthquakes can occur anywhere, but they are most common near the edges of plates. They occur when intense pressure breaks the rocks along plate edges, making the plates lurch forward in a sudden movement.

> The earthquake that struck Kobe in January 1995 was the worst one experienced in Japan since 1923. Japan lies alongside subduction zones.

Major Earthquakes since 1900 ▾			
Year	Location	Mag.	Deaths
1906	San Francisco, USA	8.3	503
1906	Valparaiso, Chile	8.6	22,000
1908	Messina, Italy	7.5	83,000
1915	Avezzano, Italy	7.5	30,000
1920	Gansu, China	8.6	180,000
1923	Yokohama, Japan	8.3	143,000
1927	Nan Shan, China	8.3	200,000
1932	Gansu, China	7.6	70,000
1934	Bihar, India/Nepal	8.4	10,700
1935	Quetta, Pakistan	7.5	60,000
1939	Chillan, Chile	8.3	28,000
1939	Erzincan, Turkey	7.9	30,000
1960	Agadir, Morocco	5.8	12,000
1964	Anchorage, Alaska	8.4	131
1968	Northeast Iran	7.4	12,000
1970	North Peru	7.7	66,794
1976	Guatemala	7.5	22,778
1976	Tangshan, China	8.2	255,000
1978	Tabas, Iran	7.7	25,000
1980	El Asnam, Algeria	7.3	20,000
1980	South Italy	7.2	4,800
1985	Mexico City, Mexico	8.1	4,200
1988	Northwest Armenia	6.8	55,000
1990	North Iran	7.7	36,000
1993	Maharashtra, India	6.4	30,000
1994	Los Angeles, USA	6.4	61
1995	Kobe, Japan	7.2	5,000
1997	Northwest Iran	6.1	965

> The section between the Pacific and Indian oceans shows a subduction zone under the American plate, with spreading ocean ridges in the Atlantic and Indian oceans. East Africa may one day split away from the rest of Africa as plate movements pull the Rift Valley apart.

Earthquakes are common along the mid-ocean ridges, but they are a long way from land and cause little damage. Other earthquakes occur near land in subduction zones, such as those that encircle much of the Pacific Ocean. These earthquakes often trigger off powerful sea waves, called tsunamis. Other earthquakes occur along transform faults, such as the San Andreas fault in California, a boundary between the North American and Pacific plates. Movements along this fault cause periodic disasters, such as the earthquakes in San Francisco (1906) and Los Angeles (1994).

VOLCANOES & MOUNTAINS

Volcanoes are fueled by magma (molten rock) from the mantle. Some volcanoes, such as in Hawaii, lie above 'hot spots' (sources of heat in the mantle). But most volcanoes occur either along the ocean ridges or above subduction zones, where

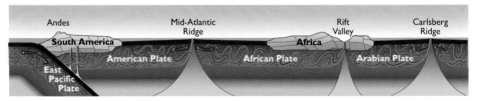

Andes   Mid-Atlantic Ridge   Rift Valley   Carlsberg Ridge

South America   Africa

American Plate   African Plate   Arabian Plate

East Pacific Plate

EARTHQUAKES

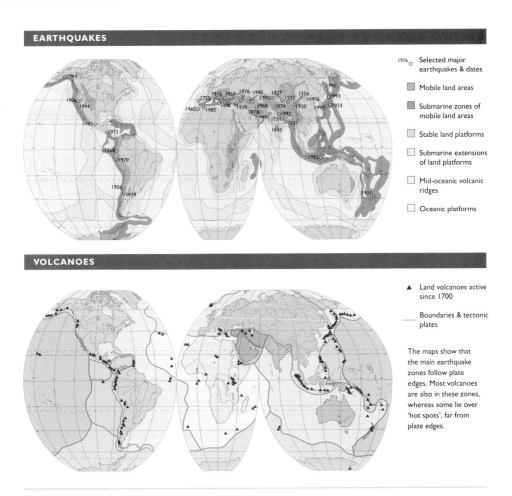

1976 ○ Selected major earthquakes & dates

▨ Mobile land areas

▨ Submarine zones of mobile land areas

☐ Stable land platforms

☐ Submarine extensions of land platforms

☐ Mid-oceanic volcanic ridges

☐ Oceanic platforms

VOLCANOES

▲ Land volcanoes active since 1700

── Boundaries & tectonic plates

The maps show that the main earthquake zones follow plate edges. Most volcanoes are also in these zones, whereas some lie over 'hot spots', far from plate edges.

magma is produced when the descending plate is melted.

Volcanic mountains are built up gradually by runny lava flows or by exploded volcanic ash. Fold mountains occur when two plates bearing land areas collide and the plate edges are buckled upward into fold mountain ranges. Plate movements also fracture rocks and block mountains are formed when areas of land are pushed upward along faults or between parallel faults. Blocks of land sometimes sink down between faults, creating deep rift valleys.

> Volcanoes occur when molten magma reaches the surface under pressure through long vents. 'Quiet' volcanoes emit runny lava (called pahoehoe). Explosive eruptions occur when the magma is sticky. Explosive gases shatter the magma into ash, which is hurled upward into the air.

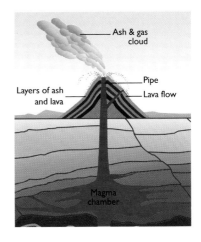

Ash & gas cloud

Layers of ash and lava

Pipe

Lava flow

Magma chamber

Water & Ice

A VISITOR FROM outer space might be forgiven for naming our planet 'Water' rather than 'Earth', because water covers more than 70% of its surface. Without water, our planet would be as lifeless as the Moon. Through the water cycle, fresh water is regularly supplied from the sea to the land. Most geographers divide the world's water into four main oceans: the Pacific, the Atlantic, the Indian and the Arctic. Together the oceans contain 97.2% of the world's water.

The water in the oceans is constantly on the move, even, albeit extremely slowly, in the deepest ocean trenches. The greatest movements of ocean water occur in the form of ocean currents. These are marked, mainly wind blown

> Ice breaks away from the ice sheet of Antarctica, forming flat-topped icebergs. The biggest iceberg ever recorded came from Antarctica. It covered an area larger than Belgium.

EXPLANATION OF TERMS

GLACIER A body of ice that flows down valleys in mountain areas. It is usually narrow and hence smaller than ice caps or ice sheets.

ICE AGE A period of Earth history when ice sheets spread over large areas. The most recent Ice Age began about 1.8 million years ago and ended 10,000 years ago.

ICEBERG A floating body of ice in the sea. About eight-ninths of the ice is hidden beneath the surface of the water.

ICE SHEET A large body of ice. During the last Ice Age, ice sheets covered large parts of the northern hemisphere.

OCEAN The four main oceans are the Pacific, the Atlantic, the Indian and the Arctic. Some

people classify a fifth southern ocean, but others regard these waters as extensions of the Pacific, Atlantic, and Indian oceans.

OCEAN CURRENTS Distinct currents of water in the oceans. Winds are the main causes of surface currents.

SEA An expanse of water, but smaller than an ocean.

JANUARY TEMPERATURE AND OCEAN CURRENTS

(Northern Hemisphere – Winter)

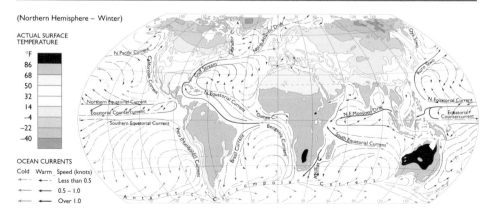

ACTUAL SURFACE
TEMPERATURE

°F
86
68
50
32
14
−4
−22
−40

OCEAN CURRENTS
Cold Warm Speed (knots)
Less than 0.5
0.5 – 1.0
Over 1.0

CROSS SECTION OF ANTARCTICA

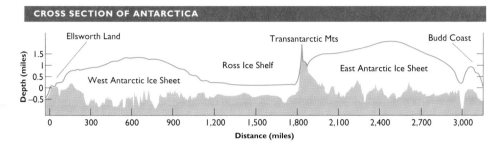

movements of water on or near the surface. Other dense, cold currents creep slowly across the ocean floor. Warm and cold ocean currents help to regulate the world's climate by transferring heat between the tropics and the poles.

ICE

About 2.15% of the world's water is locked in two large ice sheets, several smaller ice caps and glaciers. The world's largest ice sheet covers most of Antarctica. The ice is up to 15,750 ft [4,800 m] thick and it represents 70% of the world's fresh water. The volume of ice is about nine times greater than that contained in the world's other ice sheet in Greenland. Besides these two ice sheets, there are some smaller ice caps in northern Canada, Iceland, Norway and Spitzbergen, and

many valley glaciers in mountain regions throughout the world, except Australia.

If global warming was to melt the world's ice, the sea level could rise by as much as 330 ft [100 m], flooding low-lying coastal regions. Many of the world's largest cities and most fertile plains would vanish beneath the waves.

> This section across Antarctica shows the concealed land areas in brown, with the top of the ice in blue. The section is divided into the West and East Antarctic Ice Sheets. The vertical scale has been exaggerated.

Composition of Seawater ▾

The principal components of seawater, by percentage, excluding the elements of water itself:

Chloride (Cl)	55.04%	Potassium (K)	1.10%
Sodium (Na)	30.61%	Bicarbonate (HCO₃)	0.41%
Sulfate (SO₄)	7.69%	Bromide (Br)	0.19%
Magnesium (Mg)	3.69%	Strontium (Sr)	0.04%
Calcium (Ca)	1.16%	Fluorine (F)	0.003%

The oceans contain virtually every other element, the more important ones being lithium, rubidium, phosphorus, iodine and barium.

JULY TEMPERATURE AND OCEAN CURRENTS

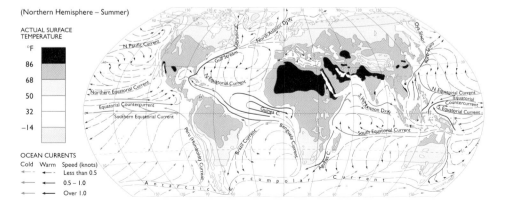

Weather & Climate

WEATHER IS A description of the day-to-day state of the atmosphere. Climate, on the other hand, is weather in the long term: the seasonal pattern of temperature and precipitation averaged over time.

In some areas, the weather is so stable and predictable that a description of the weather is much the same as a statement of the climate. But in parts of the mid-latitudes, the weather changes from hour to hour. Changeable weather is caused mainly by low air pressure systems, called cyclones or depressions, which form along the polar front where warm subtropical air meets cold polar air.

The main elements of weather and climate are temperature and rainfall. Temperatures vary because the Sun heats the Earth unequally, with the most intense heating around the Equator. Unequal heating is responsible for the general circulation of the atmosphere and the main wind belts.

Rainfall occurs when warm air containing invisible water vapor rises. As the rising air cools, the capacity of the air to hold water vapor decreases and so the water vapor condenses into droplets of water or ice crystals, which collect together to form raindrops or snowflakes.

> Lightning occurs in clouds and also between the base of clouds and the ground. Lightning that strikes the ground can kill people or start forest fires.

LIGHTNING

Lightning is a flash of light in the sky caused by a discharge of electricity in the atmosphere. Lightning occurs within cumulonimbus clouds during thunderstorms. Positive charges build up at the top of the cloud, while negative charges build up at the base. The charges are finally discharged as an electrical spark. Sheet lightning occurs inside clouds, while cloud to ground lightning is usually forked. Thunder occurs when molecules along the lightning channel expand and collide with cool molecules.

> The rainfall map shows areas affected by tropical storms, which are variously called hurricanes, tropical cyclones, willy willies, and typhoons. Strong polar winds bring blizzards in winter.

ANNUAL RAINFALL

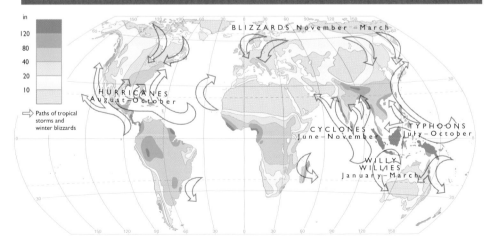

in
120
80
40
20
10

⇨ Paths of tropical storms and winter blizzards

BLIZZARDS November–March

HURRICANES August–October

CYCLONES June–November

TYPHOONS July–October

WILLY WILLIES January–March

GLOBAL WARMING

The Earth's climates have changed many times during its history. Around 11,000 years ago, much of the northern hemisphere was buried by ice. Some scientists believe that the last Ice Age may not be over and that ice sheets may one day return. Other scientists are concerned that air

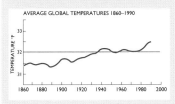

AVERAGE GLOBAL TEMPERATURES 1860–1990

pollution may be producing an opposite effect – a warming of the atmosphere. Since 1900, average world temperatures have risen by about 0.9°F [0.5°C] and increases are likely to continue. Global warming is the result of an increase in the amount of carbon dioxide in the atmosphere, caused by the burning of coal, oil, and natural gas, together with deforestation. Short-wave radiation from the Sun passes easily through the atmosphere. But, as the carbon dioxide content rises, more of the long-wave radiation that returns from the Earth's surface is absorbed and trapped by the carbon dioxide. This creates a 'greenhouse effect', which will change the world's climates with, perhaps, disastrous environmental consequences.

CLIMATE

The world contains six main climatic types: hot and wet tropical climates; dry climates; warm temperate climates; cold temperate climates; polar climates; and mountain climates. These regions are further divided according to the character and amount of precipitation and special features of the temperature, notably seasonal variations. Regions with temperate climates include Mediterranean areas with hot, dry summers and mild, moist winters. Because of its large size, the United States experiences a range of climates, from temperate on the east and west coasts, to dry in the interior.

CLIMATIC REGIONS

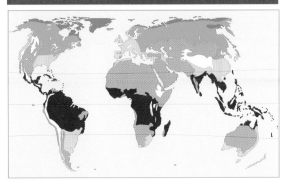

■ Tropical Climate (hot & wet)

▨ Dry Climate (desert & steppe)

☐ Temperate Climate (warm & wet)

▨ Continental Climate (cold & wet)

■ Polar Climate (very cold & wet)

☐ Mountainous Areas (where altitude affects climate types)

WORLD CLIMATIC RECORDS

Highest Recorded Temperature
Al Aziziyah, Libya: 136.4°F [58°C] on 13 September 1922

Highest Mean Annual Temperature
Dallol, Ethiopia: 94°F [34.4°C] from 1960–66

Lowest Mean Annual Temperature
Polus, Nedostupnosti, Pole of Cold, Antarctica: – 72°F [–57.8°C]

Lowest Recorded Temperature (outside poles)
Verkhoyansk, Siberia, Russia: –90°F [–68°C] on 6 February 1933

Windiest Place
Commonwealth Bay, Antarctica: gales often exceed 200 mph [320 km/h]

Longest Heatwave
Marble Bar, Western Australia: 162 days over 94°F [38°C], 23 October 1923 to 7 April 1924

Driest Place
Calama, northern Chile: no recorded rainfall in 400 years to 1971

Wettest Place (average)
Tututendo, Colombia: mean annual rainfall 463 in [11,770 mm]

Wettest Place (24 hours)
Cilaos, Réunion, Indian Ocean: 73.6 in [1,870 mm] from 15–16 March 1952

Wettest Place (12 months)
Cherrapunji, Meghalaya, northeast India: 1,040 in [26,470 mm], August 1860 to1861. Cherrapunji also holds the record for rainfall in one month: 37 in [930 mm] in July 1861

Heaviest Hailstones
Gopalganj, central Bangladesh: up to 2.25 lbs [1.02 kg] in April 1986, which killed 92 people

Heaviest Snowfall (continuous)
Bessans, Savoie, France: 68 in [1,730 mm] in 19 hours over the period 5–6 April 1969

Heaviest Snowfall (season/year)
Paradise Ranger Station, Mt Rainier, Washington, USA: 1,224 in [31,102 mm] fell from 19 February 1971 to 18 February 1972

Landforms & Vegetation

THE CLIMATE LARGELY determines the nature of soils and vegetation types throughout the world. The studies of climate and plant and animal communities are closely linked. For example, tropical climates are divided into tropical forest and tropical grassland climates. The tropical forest climate, which is hot and rainy throughout the year, is ideal for the growth of forests that contain more than half of the world's known plant and animal species. But tropical grassland, or savanna, climates have a marked dry season. As a result, the forest gives way to grassland, with scattered trees.

CLIMATE & SCENERY

The climate also helps to shape the land. Frost action in cold areas splits boulders apart, while rapid temperature changes in hot deserts make rock surfaces peel away like the layers of an onion. These are examples of mechanical weathering.

Chemical weathering usually results from the action of water on rocks. For example, rainwater containing dissolved carbon dioxide is a weak acid, which reacts with limestone. This chemical process is responsible for the erosion of the world's most spectacular caves.

Running water and glaciers play a major part in creating scenery, while in

> The tropical broadleaf forests are rich in plant and animal species. The extinction of many species because of deforestation is one of the great natural disasters of our time.

NATURAL VEGETATION

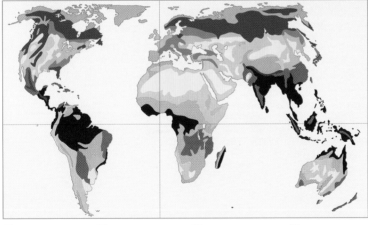

> Human activities, especially agriculture, have greatly modified plant and animal communities throughout the world. As a result, world vegetation maps show the natural 'climax vegetation' of regions – that is, the kind of vegetation that would grow in a particular climatic area, had that area not been affected by human activities. For example, the climax vegetation of western Europe is broadleaf, deciduous forest, but most of the original forest, together with the animals which lived in it, was destroyed long ago.

- Tundra & mountain vegetation
- Needleleaf evergreen forest
- Broadleaf deciduous forest
- Mixed needleleaf evergreen & broadleaf deciduous trees
- Mid-latitude grassland
- Semidesert scrub land
- Evergreen broadleaf & deciduous trees & scrub
- Desert
- Tropical grassland (savanna)
- Tropical broadleaf & monsoon rain forest
- Subtropical broadleaf & needleleaf forest

DESERTIFICATION AND DEFORESTATION

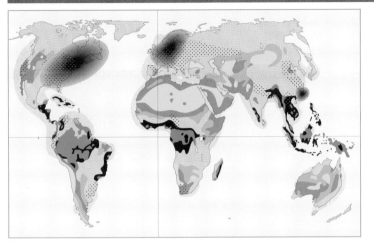

Pollution

☐ Polluted seas

▨ Main areas of sulfur & nitrogen emissions

■ Areas of acid rain

Desertification

☐ Existing deserts

■ Areas with a high risk of desertification

■ Areas with a moderate risk of desertification

Deforestation

■ Former areas of rain forest

■ Existing rain forest

dry areas, wind-blown sand is a powerful agent of erosion. Most landforms seem to alter little in one person's lifetime. But geologists estimate that natural forces remove an average of 1.4 in [3.5 cm] from land areas every 1,000 years. Over millions of years, these forces reduce mountains to flat plains.

HUMAN INTERFERENCE

Climate also affects people, though air conditioning and central heating now make it possible for us live in comfort almost anywhere in the world.

However, human activities are damaging our planet. Pollution is poisoning rivers and seas, while acid rain, caused by air pollution, is killing trees and acidifying lakes. The land is also harmed by such things as nuclear accidents and the dumping of toxic wastes.

Some regions have been overgrazed or so intensively farmed that once fertile areas have been turned into barren deserts. The clearance of tropical forests means that plant and animal species are disappearing before scientists have had a chance to study them.

MOLDING THE LAND

Powerful forces inside the Earth buckle rock layers to form fold mountain ranges. But even as they rise, the forces of erosion wear them away. On mountain slopes, water freezes in cracks in rocks. Because ice occupies more space than the equivalent amount of water, this 'frost action' shatters rocks, and the fragments tumble downhill. Some end up on or inside moving glaciers. Other rocks are carried away by running water. The glaciers and streams not only transport rock fragments, but they also wear out valleys and so add to their load. The eroded material breaks down into fragments of sand, silt and mud, much of which reaches the sea, where it piles up on the sea floor in layers. These layers eventually become compacted into sedimentary rocks, such as sandstones and shales. These rocks may eventually be squeezed up again by a plate collision to form new fold mountains, so completing a natural cycle of mountain building and destruction.

MAJOR FACTORS AFFECTING WEATHERING

	WEATHERING RATE		
	◄ SLOW		FAST ►
Mineral solubility	low (e.g. quartz)	moderate (e.g. feldspar)	high (e.g. calcite)
Rainfall	low	moderate	heavy
Temperature	cold	temperate	hot
Vegetation	sparse	moderate	lush
Soil cover	bare rock	thin to moderate soil	thick soil

Weathering is the breakdown and decay of rocks in situ. It may be mechanical (physical), chemical or biological.

Population

THE ADVENT OF agriculture around 10,000 years ago had a great impact on human society. People abandoned their nomadic way of life and settled in farming villages. With plenty of food, some people were able to pursue jobs unconnected with farming. These developments eventually led to rapid social changes, including the growth of early cities and the emergence of civilization.

THE POPULATION EXPLOSION

The social changes had a major effect on the world's population, which rose from around 8 million in 8000 BC, to about 300 million by AD 1000. The rate of population increase then began to accelerate further, passing the 1 billion mark in the 19th century, the 2 billion mark in the 1920s, and the 4 billion mark in the 1970s.

Today the world has a population of about 5.8 billion and experts forecast that it will reach around 11 billion by 2075. However, they then predict that it will stabilize or even decline a little toward 2100. Most of the expected increase will occur in developing countries in Africa, Asia and Latin America.

> Many cities in India, such as Bombay (also known as Mumbai), have grown so quickly that they lack sufficient jobs and homes for their populations. As a result, slums now cover large areas.

POPULATION PYRAMIDS

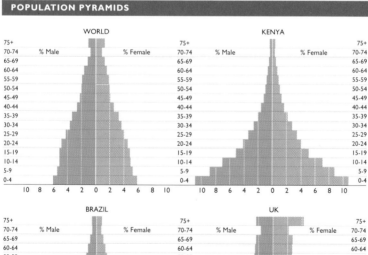

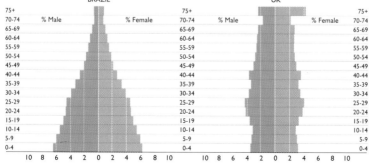

> The population pyramids compare the average age structures for the world with those of three countries at varying stages of development. Kenya, a developing country, had, until recently, one of the world's highest annual rates of population increase. As a result, a high proportion of Kenyans are aged under 15. Brazil has a much more balanced economy than Kenya's, and a lower rate of population increase. This is reflected in a higher proportion of people aged over 40. The UK is a developed country with a low rate of population growth, 0.3% per year between 1985–95, much lower than the world average of 1.6%. The UK has a far higher proportion of people over 60 years old.

The World's Largest Cities ▾

By early next century, for the first time ever, the majority of the world's population will live in cities. Below is a list of the 20 largest cities (in thousands) based on 1996 figures.

1	Tokyo, *Japan*	26,836
2	São Paulo, *Brazil*	16,417
3	New York, *USA*	16,329
4	Mexico City, *Mexico*	15,643
5	Bombay (Mumbai), *India*	15,093
6	Shanghai, *China*	15,082
7	Los Angeles, *USA*	12,410
8	Beijing, *China*	12,362
9	Calcutta, *India*	11,673
10	Seoul, *South Korea*	11,641
11	Jakarta, *Indonesia*	11,500
12	Buenos Aires, *Argentina*	10,990
13	Tianjin, *China*	10,687
14	Osaka, *Japan*	10,601
15	Lagos, *Nigeria*	10,287
16	Rio de Janeiro, *Brazil*	9,888
17	Delhi, *India*	9,882
18	Karachi, *Pakistan*	9,863
19	Cairo, *Egypt*	9,656
20	Paris, *France*	9,469

This population explosion has been caused partly by better medical care, which has reduced child mortality and increased the average life expectancy at birth throughout the world. But it has also created problems. In some developing countries, nearly half of the people are children. They make no contribution to the economy, but they require costly education and health services. In richer countries, the high proportion of retired people is also a strain on the economy.

By the late 20th century, for the first time in 10,000 years, the majority of people are no longer forced to rely on farming for their livelihood. Instead, nearly half of them live in cities where many of them enjoy a high standard of living. But rapid urbanization also creates problems, especially in the developing world, with the growth of slums and an increase in homelessness and crime.

POPULATION BY CONTINENT

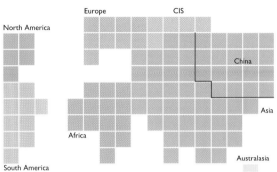

> The cartogram shows the populations of the continents in a diagrammatic way, with each square representing 1% of the world's population. For example, North America is represented by five squares, which means that it contains about 5% of the world's population, while Asia, the most populous continent even excluding the Asian part of the former USSR, is represented by 56 squares (China accounting for 19 of these). By contrast, Australasia is represented by less than half of a square because it contains only 0.45% of the world's population.

WORLD DEMOGRAPHIC EXTREMES

Fastest growing population; average annual % growth (1992–2000)		Slowest growing population; average annual % growth (1992–2000)	
1	Nigeria ... 5.09	1	Kuwait ... -1.39
2	Afghanistan ... 4.21	2	Ireland ... -0.24
3	Ivory Coast ... 3.54	3	St Kitts & Nevis ... -0.22
4	Oman ... 3.52	4	Bulgaria ... -0.13
5	Syria ... 3.51	5	Latvia ... -0.10

Youngest populations; % aged under 15 years		Oldest populations; % aged over 65 years	
1	Kenya ... 49.9	1	Sweden ... 18.1
2	Uganda ... 49.6	2	Norway ... 16.4
=	Yemen ... 49.6	3	Denmark ... 15.4
4	Botswana ... 49.3	=	United Kingdom ... 15.4
5	Tanzania ... 49.1	5	Austria ... 15.0

Highest urban populations; % of population living in urban areas		Lowest urban populations; % of population living in urban areas	
1	Singapore ... 100.0	1	Bhutan ... 5.3
2	Macau ... 99.0	2	Burundi ... 5.5
3	Belgium ... 96.9	3	Rwanda ... 7.7
4	Kuwait ... 95.6	4	Burkina Faso ... 9.0
5	Hong Kong ... 94.1	5	Nepal ... 9.6

Most male populations; number of men per 100 women		Most female populations; number of women per 100 men	
1	United Arab Emirates ... 206.7	1	Russia ... 110.0
2	Qatar ... 167.2	2	Austria ... 108.8
3	Bahrain ... 145.3	=	Somalia ... 108.8
4	Kuwait ... 128.3	4	Germany ... 108.0
5	Saudi Arabia ... 119.1	5	Barbados ... 107.9

Languages & Religions

ALL PEOPLE BELONG to one species, *Homo sapiens*, but within that species is a great diversity of cultures. Two of the main factors that give people an identity and sense of kinship with their neighbors are language and religion.

Definitions of languages vary and as a result estimates of the total number of languages in existence range from about 3,000 to 6,000. Many languages are spoken only by a small number of people. Papua New Guinea, for example, has only 4.2 million people but 869 languages.

The world's languages are grouped into families, of which the Indo–European is the largest. Indo–European languages are spoken in a zone stretching from

> Religion is a major force in Southeast Asia. About 94% of the people in Thailand are Buddhists, and more than 40% of men over the age of 20 spend some time, if only a few weeks, serving as Buddhist monks. Confucianism, Islam, Hinduism, and Christianity are also practiced in Thailand.

THE WORLD'S LANGUAGES

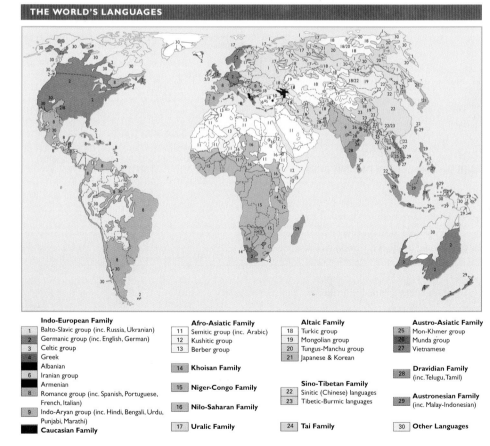

Indo-European Family
1. Balto-Slavic group (inc. Russia, Ukranian)
2. Germanic group (inc. English, German)
3. Celtic group
4. Greek
5. Albanian
6. Iranian group
7. Armenian
8. Romance group (inc. Spanish, Portuguese, French, Italian)
9. Indo-Aryan group (inc. Hindi, Bengali, Urdu, Punjabi, Marathi)
10. Caucasian Family

Afro-Asiatic Family
11. Semitic group (inc. Arabic)
12. Kushitic group
13. Berber group

14. **Khoisan Family**

15. **Niger-Congo Family**

16. **Nilo-Saharan Family**

17. **Uralic Family**

Altaic Family
18. Turkic group
19. Mongolian group
20. Tungus-Manchu group
21. Japanese & Korean

Sino-Tibetan Family
22. Sinitic (Chinese) languages
23. Tibetic-Burmic languages

24. **Tai Family**

Austro-Asiatic Family
25. Mon-Khmer group
26. Munda group
27. Vietnamese

Dravidian Family
28. (inc. Telugu, Tamil)

Austronesian Family
29. (inc. Malay-Indonesian)

30. **Other Languages**

NATIVE SPEAKERS

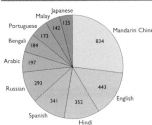

> The chart shows the native speakers of major languages in millions. Mandarin Chinese is the language of 834 million, as compared with English, which has 443 million speakers. However, many other people speak English as a second language.

Religious Adherents ▾

The world's major religions, with the number of adherents in millions (latest available year)

Christian	1,667
Roman Catholic	952
Protestant	337
Orthodox	162
Anglican	70
Other Christian	148
Muslim	881
Sunni	841
Shia	104
Hindu	663
Buddhist	312
Chinese folk	172
Ethnic/local	92
Jewish	18
Sikh	17

> Most languages have alphabetic systems of writing. The Greek alphabet uses some letters from the Roman alphabet, such as the A and B. Russians use the Cyrillic alphabet, which is based partly on Roman and partly on Greek letters. The Cyrillic alphabet is also used for Bulgarian. Serbs use either the Cyrillic or the Roman alphabet to write Serbo-Croat.

Europe, through southwestern Asia into the Indian subcontinent. In addition, during the period of European colonization, they spread throughout North and South America and also to Australia and New Zealand. Today about two-fifths of the world's people speak an Indo-European language, as compared with one-fifth who speak a language belonging to the Sino-Tibetan language.

The Sino-Tibetan language family includes Chinese, which is spoken as a first language by more people than any other. English is the second most important first language, but it is more important than Chinese in international affairs and business, because so many people speak it as a second language.

RELIGIONS

Christianity is the religion of about a third of the world's population. Other major religions include Buddhism, Islam, Hinduism, Judaism, Chinese folk religions and traditional tribal religions.

Religion is a powerful force in human society, establishing the ethics by which people live. It has inspired great music, painting, architecture and literature, yet at the same time religion and language have contributed to conflict between people throughout history. Even today, the cause of many of the conflicts around the world are partly the result of language and religious differences.

ALPHABETS

The Greek Alphabet

Α	Β	Γ	Δ	Ε	Ζ	Η	Θ	Ι	Κ	Λ	Μ	Ν	Ξ	Ο	Π	Ρ	Σ	Τ	Υ	Φ	Χ	Ψ	Ω
A	V/B	G	D	E	Z	E	TH	I	K	L	M	N	X	O	P	R	S	T	Y	F	CH	PS	O

The Cyrillic Alphabet

А	Б	В	Г	Д	Е	Ё	Ж	З	И	Й	К	Л	М	Н	О	П	Р	С	Т	У	Ф	Х	Ц	Ч	Ш	Щ	Ю	Я
A	B	V	G	D	E	YO	ZH	Z	I	Y	K	L	M	N	O	P	R	S	T	U	F	KH	TS	CH	SH	SHCH	YU	YA

Agriculture & Industry

BECAUSE IT SUPPLIES so many basic human needs, agriculture is the world's leading economic activity. But its relative importance varies from place to place. In most developing countries, agriculture employs more people than any other activity. For example, the diagram at the bottom of this page shows that more than 90% of the people of Nepal are employed in farming.

Many farmers in developing countries live at subsistence level, producing barely enough to supply the basic needs of their families. Alongside the subsistence sector, some developing countries produce one or two cash crops that they export. Dependence on cash crops is precarious: when world commodity prices fall, the country is plunged into financial crisis.

In developed countries, by contrast, the proportion of people engaged in agriculture has declined over the last 200

> The cultivation of rice, one of the world's most important foods, is still carried out by hand in many areas. But the introduction of new strains of rice has greatly increased yields.

years. Yet, by using farm machinery and scientific methods, notably the selective breeding of crops and animals, the production of food has soared. For example, although agriculture employs only 3% of its workers, the United States is one of the world's top food producers.

INDUSTRIALIZATION

The Industrial Revolution began in Britain in the late 18th century and soon spread to mainland Europe and other parts of the world. Industries first arose in areas with supplies of coal, iron ore, and cheap water power. But later, after oil and gas came into use as industrial fuels, factories could be set up almost anywhere.

The growth of manufacturing led to an increase in the number of industrial cities. The flight from the land was accompanied by an increase in efficiency in agriculture. As a result, manufacturing replaced agriculture as the chief source of

EMPLOYMENT

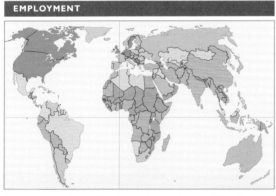

The number of workers employed in manufacturing for every 100 workers engaged in agriculture (latest available year)

- Under 10
- 10 – 50
- 50 – 100
- 100 – 200
- 200 – 500
- Over 500

DIVISION OF EMPLOYMENT

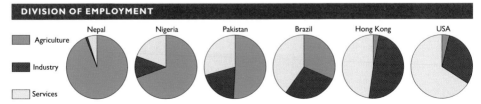

- Agriculture
- Industry
- Services

Nepal Nigeria Pakistan Brazil Hong Kong USA

PATTERNS OF PRODUCTION

> The table shows how the economy breaks down (in terms of the Gross Domestic Product for 1995) in a selection of industrialized countries. Agriculture remains important in some countries, though its percentage share has steadily declined since the start of the Industrial Revolution. Industry, especially manufacturing, accounts for a higher proportion, but service industries account for the greatest percentage of the GDP in most developed nations. The figures for Manufacturing are shown separately from Industry because of their importance in the economy.

Country	Agriculture	Industry (excl. manufacturing)	Manufacturing	Services
Australia	3%	13%	15%	68%
Austria	2%	9%	26%	62%
Brazil	10%	12%	25%	53%
Denmark	4%	7%	20%	69%
Finland	5%	3%	28%	64%
France	3%	7%	22%	69%
Germany	1%	11%	27%	61%
Greece	18%	12%	20%	50%
Hungary	6%	9%	19%	66%
Ireland	8%	7%	3%	82%
Italy	3%	7%	25%	65%
Japan	2%	17%	24%	57%
Kuwait	0%	46%	9%	45%
Mexico	8%	8%	20%	63%
Netherlands	4%	9%	19%	68%
Norway	3%	21%	14%	62%
Singapore	0%	9%	28%	63%
Sweden	2%	5%	26%	67%
UK	2%	8%	25%	65%
USA	2%	9%	22%	67%

income and employment in industrialized countries and rapidly widened the wealth gap between them and the poorer non-industrialized countries whose economies continued to rely on agriculture.

SERVICE INDUSTRIES

Eventually, the manufacturing sector became so efficient that it could supply most of the things that people wanted to buy. Trade between industrialized countries also increased, so widening the choice for consumers in the developed world. These factors led to a further change in the economies of developed countries, namely a reduction in the relative importance of manufacturing and the growth of the service sector.

Service industries include such activities as government, transport, insurance, finance, and even the writing of computer software. In the United States, service industries now account for about two-thirds of the Gross National Product (GNP), while in Japan they account for more than half. But the wealth of both countries still rests on their massive industrial production.

AGRICULTURE

Predominant type of farming or land use

- ▇ Nomadic herding
- ▨ Hunting, fishing & gathering
- ☐ Subsistence agriculture
- ■ Commercial ranching
- ☐ Commercial livestock & grain farming
- ■ Urban areas
- ▨ Forestry
- ☐ Unproductive land

Trade & Commerce

TRADE HAS ALWAYS been an important human activity. It has widened the choice of goods available in any country, lowered prices and generally raised living standards. People regard any growth of world trade as a sign that the world economy is healthy, whereas a decline indicates a world recession.

Exports and imports are of two main kinds. Visible imports and exports include primary products, such as food and manufactures. Invisible imports and exports include services, such as banking, insurance, interest on loans, and money spent by tourists.

World trade, both visible and invisible, is dominated by the 29 members of the OECD (Organization for Economic Development), which includes the world's top trading nations, namely the United States, Japan, Germany, France, Italy and the United Kingdom, as well as Australia, New Zealand, Canada and Mexico. Hungary, Poland and South Korea joined in 1996.

> The new port of the historic Italian city of Ravenna is linked to the Adriatic Sea by a canal. The port has large oil refining and petrochemical industries.

CHANGING EXPORTS

From the late 19th century to the 1950s, primary products, including farm products, minerals, natural fibers, timber and, in the latter part of this period, oil

The World's Largest Businesses ▾

The world's largest businesses in 1996 by market capitalization, in billions of US$. Market capitalization is the number of shares the company has, multiplied by the market price of those shares.

1	General Electric, *USA*	150.3
2	Royal Dutch Shell, *Neths/UK*	135.3
3	Coca-Cola, *USA*	126.9
4	Nippon Telegraph & Tel., *Japan*	119.6
5	Exxon, *USA*	103.4
6	Bank of Tokyo-Mitsubishi, *Japan*	102.7
7	Toyota Motor Corporation, *Japan*	97.9
8	Merck, *USA*	85.1
9	AT & T, *USA*	84.1
10	Intel, *USA*	78.7
11	Microsoft, *USA*	78.5
12	Philip Morris, *USA*	73.6
13	Roche Holding, *Switzerland*	72.0
14	Johnson & Johnson, *USA*	68.3
15	Procter & Gamble, *USA*	66.8
16	Intl Business Machines, *USA*	65.7
17	Wal-Mart Stores, *USA*	60.5
18	Sumitomo Bank, *Japan*	58.9
19	British Petroleum, *UK*	58.2
20	Industrial Bank of Japan, *Japan*	57.6

DEBT AND AID

International debtors and the development aid they receive (latest available year)

The provision of aid by rich countries to developing countries is part of international politics. But the grants made to developing countries are often dwarfed by the burden of debt which the countries are expected to repay. In 1990, the debts of Mozambique, one of the world's poorest countries, were estimated to be 75 times its entire earnings from exports.

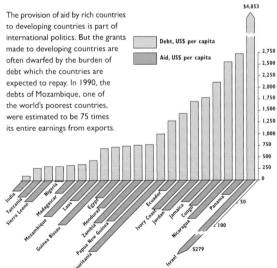

TRADED PRODUCTS

The character of world trade has greatly changed in the last 50 years. While primary products were once the leading commodities, world trade is now dominated by manufactured products. Cars are the single most valuable traded product, followed by vehicle parts and engines. The next most valuable goods are high-tech products such as data processing (computer) equipment, telecommunications equipment, and transistors. Other items include aircraft, paper and board, trucks, measuring and control instruments, and electrical machinery. Trade in most manufactured products is dominated by the OECD countries. For example, the leading vehicle exporter is Japan, which became the world's leading car manufacturer in the 1980s. The United States, Germany, the United Kingdom, France and Japan lead in the production of data processing equipment.

and natural gas, dominated world trade.

Many developing countries still remain dependant on exporting mineral ores, fossil fuels, or farm products such as cocoa or coffee whose prices fluctuate according to demand. But today, manufactured goods are the most important commodities in world trade. The OECD nations lead the world in exporting manufactured goods, though they are being challenged by a group of 'tiger economies' in eastern Asia, notably Singapore, Hong Kong and Taiwan. Other rapidly industrializing countries in Asia include Thailand, Malaysia and the Philippines. The generally cheap labor costs of these countries have enabled them to produce manufactured goods for export at prices lower than those charged for goods made in Western countries.

Private companies carry on most of the world's trade. The small proportion handled by governments decreased recently with the collapse of Communist regimes in eastern Europe and the former Soviet Union.

SHARE OF WORLD TRADE

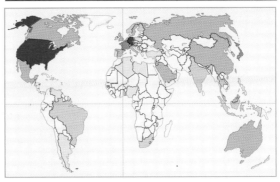

Percentage share of total world exports by value (1994)

- ■ Over 10%
- ■ 5 – 10%
- ■ 1 – 5%
- ■ 0.5 – 1%
- □ 0.25 – 0.5%
- □ Under 0.25%

DEPENDENCE ON TRADE

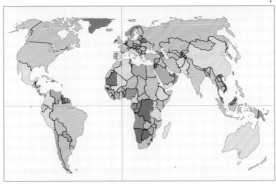

Value of exports as a percentage of Gross Domestic Product (1994)

- ■ Over 50% GDP
- ■ 40 – 50% GDP
- ■ 30 – 40% GDP
- ■ 20 – 30% GDP
- □ 10 – 20% GDP
- □ Under 10% GDP

Trade in Oil ▾

Major world trade in oil in millions of tons (1995)

Middle East to Asia (not Japan) ... 250	Mexico to USA 53
Middle East to Japan 204	W. Africa to W. Europe 42
Middle East to W. Europe 175	Western Europe to USA 37
S. and C. America to USA 111	Middle East to Africa 34
N. Africa to W. Europe 98	Middle East to South and Central America 33
CIS to Western Europe 79	
Middle East to USA 79	CIS to Central Europe 27
Canada to USA 65	Western Europe to Canada 17
West Africa to USA 63	*Total world trade* 1,815

Transport & Travel

ABOUT 200 YEARS ago, most people never traveled far from their birthplace. But adventurous travelers can now reach almost any part of the world.

Transport is concerned with moving goods and people around by land, water and air. Land transport was once laborious, and was dependent on pack animals or animal-drawn vehicles. But during the Industrial Revolution, railroads played a vital role in moving bulky materials and equipment required by factories. They were also important in the opening up and development of remote areas around the world in North and South America, Africa, Asia and Australia.

Today, however, motor vehicles have taken over many of the functions once served by railroads. Unlike railroads, motor vehicles provide a door-to-door service and modern trucks can carry large loads. In the United States, however, the long distances between cities means that railroads still carry about 35% of the domestic freight traffic, with trucks accounting for just 25% (compared to 90% in Britain). However, automobiles account for more than 76% of intercity passenger traffic.

> Traffic jams and vehicle pollution have affected cities throughout the world. Many of Bangkok's beautiful old canals have been filled in to provide extra roads to cope with the enormous volume of traffic in the city.

TRAVEL & TOURISM

Sea transport, which now employs huge bulk grain carriers, oil tankers and container ships, still carries most of the world's trade. But since the late 1950s, fewer passengers have traveled overseas by sea, because air travel is so much faster, though many former ocean liners now operate successfully as cruise ships.

Air travel has played a major part in the rapid growth of the tourist industry,

AIR TRAVEL

Number of passenger miles flown, in millions (1994). Passenger miles are the number of passengers (both international and domestic) multiplied by the distance flown by each passenger from airport of origin.

- ■ Over 60,000
- ■ 30,000 – 60,000
- ■ 6,000 – 30,000
- ☐ 600 – 6,000
- ☐ 300 – 600
- ☐ Under 300

The Busiest International Airports ▾

Total number of passengers, in thousands (March 1995 to March 1996)

1	O'Hare Intl., *Chicago*	67,253
2	Hartsfield Atlanta Int., *Atlanta*	57,735
3	Dallas/Fort Worth Int., *Dallas*	56,491
4	Heathrow, *London*	54,453
5	Los Angeles Intl., *Los Angeles*	53,909
6	Haneda, *Tokyo*	45,823
7	Frankfurt/Main, *Frankfurt*	38,178
8	San Francisco Intl., *San Francisco*	36,263
9	Miami Intl., *Miami*	33,236
10	Denver Intl., *Denver*	31,037
11	Kimpo Intl., *Seoul*	30,919
12	John F. Kennedy Intl., *New York*	30,380
13	Charles de Gaulle, *Paris*	28,355
14	Metro Wayne County, *Detroit*	28,200
15	Hong Kong Intl., *Hong Kong*	28,043

The Longest Rail Networks ▾

Extent of rail network, in thousands of miles, (1994)

1	USA	136.0
2	Russia	94.4
3	Germany	56.8
4	Canada	53.2
5	China	43.1
6	India	38.2
7	Japan	23.7
8	Australia	23.2
9	Argentina	21.2
10	France	21.2

which accounted for 7.5% of world trade by the mid-1990s. Travel and tourism have greatly increased people's understanding and knowledge of the world, especially in the OECD countries, which account for about 8% of world tourism.

Some developing countries have large tourist industries which have provided employment and led to improvements in roads and other facilities. In some cases, tourism plays a vital role in the economy. For example, in Kenya, tourism provides more income than any other activity apart from the production and sale of coffee. However, too many tourists can damage fragile environments, such as the wildlife and scenery in national parks. Tourism can also harm local cultures.

THE IMPORTANCE OF TOURISM

Nations receiving the most from tourism, millions of US$ (1996)			Fastest growing tourist destinations, % change in receipts (1994–95)		
1	USA	64,400	1	South Korea	49%
2	Spain	28,400	2	Czech Republic	27%
3	France	28,200	3	India	21%
4	Italy	27,300	4	Russia	19%
5	UK	20,400	5	Philippines	18%
6	Austria	15,100	6	Turkey	17%
7	Germany	13,200	7	Thailand	15%
8	Hong Kong	11,200	8	Poland	13%
9	China	10,500	9	China	12%
10	Switzerland	9,900	10	Israel	12%

Number of tourist arrivals, millions (1995)			Overseas travelers to the USA, thousands (1997 projections)		
1	France	60,584	1	Canada	13,900
2	Spain	45,125	2	Mexico	12,370
3	USA	44,730	3	Japan	4,640
4	Italy	29,184	4	UK	3,350
5	China	23,368	5	Germany	1,990
6	UK	22,700	6	France	1,030
7	Hungary	22,087	7	Taiwan	885
8	Mexico	19,870	8	Venezuela	860
9	Poland	19,225	9	South Korea	800
10	Austria	17,750	10	Brazil	785

THE WORLD'S VEHICLES

Proportion of the world's vehicles by region (1994)

0   10%   20%   30%   40%

North America

West Europe

Asia

East Europe & CIS

Others

TOTAL = 270 million vehicles

CAR OWNERSHIP

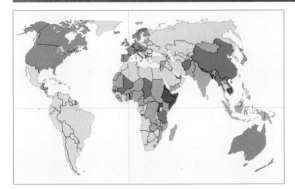

Number of people per car (1994)

- ■ Over 1,000
- ■ 500 – 1,000
- ■ 100 – 500
- □ 25 – 100
- □ 5 – 25
- ▨ Under 5

Two-thirds of the world's vehicles are found in the developed countries of Europe and North America. Car ownership is also high in Australia and New Zealand, as well as in Japan, the world's leading car exporter. Car transport is the most convenient form of passenger travel, but air pollution caused by exhaust fumes is a serious problem in many large cities.

International Organizations

In the late 1980s, people rejoiced at the collapse of Communist regimes in eastern Europe and the former Soviet Union, because this brought to an end the Cold War, a long period of hostility between East and West. But hope of a new era of peace was shattered when ethnic and religious rivalries led to civil war in Yugoslavia and in parts of the former Soviet Union.

In order to help maintain peace, many governments have formed international organizations to increase cooperation. Some, such as NATO (North Atlantic

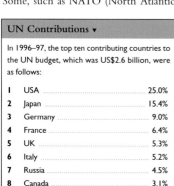

UN Contributions ▾

In 1996–97, the top ten contributing countries to the UN budget, which was US$2.6 billion, were as follows:

1	USA	25.0%
2	Japan	15.4%
3	Germany	9.0%
4	France	6.4%
5	UK	5.3%
6	Italy	5.2%
7	Russia	4.5%
8	Canada	3.1%
9	Spain	2.4%
10	Brazil	1.6%

> In the early 1990s, the United Nations peacekeeping mission worked to end the civil war in Bosnia-Herzegovina and also to bring aid to civilians affected by the fighting.

Treaty Organization), are defense alliances, while others aim to encourage economic and social cooperation. Some organizations such as the Red Cross are non-governmental organizations, or NGOs.

UNITED NATIONS

The United Nations, the chief international organization, was formed in October 1945 and now has 185 member countries. The only independent nations that are not members are Kiribati, Nauru, Switzerland, Taiwan, Tonga, Tuvalu and the Vatican City.

THE UNITED NATIONS

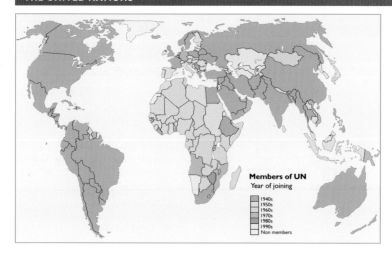

Members of UN
Year of joining

- 1940s
- 1950s
- 1960s
- 1970s
- 1980s
- 1990s
- Non members

> The membership of the UN has risen from 51 in 1945 to 185 by the end of 1996. The first big period of expansion came in the 1960s when many former colonies achieved their independence. The membership again expanded rapidly in the 1990s when new countries were formed from the former Soviet Union and Yugoslavia. The most recent addition, Palau, is a former US trust territory in the Pacific Ocean and joined in 1994.

The United Nations was formed at the end of World War II to promote peace, international cooperation and security, and to help solve economic, social, cultural, and humanitarian problems. It promotes human rights and freedom and is a forum for negotiations between nations.

The main organs of the UN are the General Assembly, the Security Council, the Economic and Social Council, the Trusteeship Council, the International Court of Justice and the Secretariat.

The UN also operates 14 specialized agencies concerned with particular issues, such as agriculture, education, working conditions, communications and health. For example, UNICEF (the United Nations International Children's Fund), established in 1946 to deliver postwar relief to children, now aims to provide basic health care to children and mothers worldwide. The ILO (International Labor Organization) seeks to improve working conditions, while the FAO (Food and Agricultural Organization) aims at improving the production and distribution of food. The WTO (World Trade Organization) was set up as recently as January 1995 to succeed GATT (General Agreements on Tariffs and Trade).

THE UNITED NATIONS

THE GENERAL ASSEMBLY is the meeting of all member nations every September under a newly-elected president to discuss issues affecting development, peace, and security.

THE SECURITY COUNCIL has 15 members, of which five are permanent. It is responsible for maintaining international peace.

THE SECRETARIAT consists of the staff and employees of the UN, including the Secretary-General (appointed for a five-year term), who is the UN's chief administrator.

THE ECONOMIC & SOCIAL COUNCIL works with the specialized agencies to implement UN policies on improving living standards, health, cultural and educational cooperation.

THE TRUSTEESHIP COUNCIL was designed to bring several dependencies to independence. This work is now complete.

THE INTERNATIONAL COURT OF JUSTICE, or World Court, deals with legal problems and helps to settle disputes. Its headquarters are at The Hague, in the Netherlands.

UN DEPARTMENTS

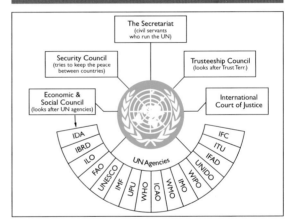

UN PEACEKEEPING MISSIONS

The United Nations tries to resolve international disputes in several ways. It sends unarmed observer missions to monitor cease-fires or supervise troop withdrawals, and the Security Council members also send peacekeeping forces.

This first of these forces was sent in 1948 to supervise the cease-fire between Arabs and Jews in disputed parts of Palestine and, since then, it has undertaken more than 30 other missions. The 'Blue Berets', as the 25,650 UN troops are called, must be impartial in any dispute

and they can fire only in self-defense. Hence, they can operate only with the support of both sides, which leaves them open to criticism when they are unable to prevent violence by intervening.

By the mid-1990s, the UN was involved in 15 world conflicts, was policing the boundary in partitioned Cyprus, and was seeking to enforce a peace agreement in Angola after 20 years of civil war. Other UN missions were in Tajikistan, Georgia, the Israeli-occupied Golan Heights, Haiti, Kuwait, southern Lebanon, the India–

Pakistan border, Liberia, Mozambique, Western Sahara and the former Yugoslavia. A force known as UNPROFOR (UN Protection Force) had been operating in Bosnia-Herzegovina and, by 1995, it accounted for 60% of the total UN peacekeeping budget. In February 1996, the Secretary-General of the UN approved the setting up of a new force, the United Nations Mission in Bosnia-Herzegovina (UNMIBH). Its main objective was to help create the right climate for the elections held in September 1996.

cludes the countries of East and Southeast Asia, as well as North America, plus Australia, New Zealand and Chile. APEC aims to create a free trade zone by 2020.

Together the United States, Canada and Mexico form NAFTA (North American Free Trade Agreement), which aims at eliminating trade barriers within 15 years of its foundation on 1 January 1994. Other economic groupings link the countries of Latin America.

Another economic group with more limited aims is OPEC (Organization of Petroleum Exporting Countries). It works to unify policies concerned with the sale of petroleum on world markets.

The central aim of the Colombo Plan is to provide economic development assistance for South and Southeast Asia.

ECONOMIC ORGANIZATIONS

Over the last 40 years, many countries have joined common markets aimed at eliminating trade barriers and encouraging the free movement of workers and capital.

The best known of these is the European Union. Other organizations include ASEAN (the Association of Southeast Asian Nations), which aims at reducing trade barriers between its seven members: Brunei, Indonesia, Malaysia, the Philippines, Singapore, Thailand and Vietnam.

APEC (the Asia-Pacific Cooperation Group) was founded in 1989 and in-

> The European Parliament, one of the branches of the EU, consists of 626 members. The number of members for each country is based mainly on population.

OTHER ORGANIZATIONS

Some organizations exist for consultation on matters of common interest. The Commonwealth of Nations grew out of the links created by the British Empire, while the OAS (Organization of American States) works to increase understanding throughout the Western Hemisphere. The OAU (Organization of

THE EUROPEAN UNION

At the end of World War II (1939–45), many Europeans wanted to end the ancient emnities that had caused such destruction and rebuild the shattered continent. It was in this mood that Belgium, France, West Germany, Italy, Luxembourg and the Netherlands signed the Treaty of Paris in 1951. This set up the European Coal and Steel Community (ECSC), the forerunner of the European Union.

In 1957, through the Treaty of Rome, the same six countries created the European Economic Community (EEC) and the European Atomic Community (EURATOM). In 1967, the ECSC, the EEC and EURATOM merged to form the

single European Community (EC).

Another economic group, the European Free Trade Association (EFTA), was set up in 1960 by seven countries: Austria, Denmark, Norway, Portugal, Sweden, Switzerland, and the United Kingdom. However, Denmark, Ireland and the UK left to become members of the EC in 1973, followed by Greece in 1981, Spain and Portugal in 1986, and Austria, Finland and Sweden in 1995. The expansion of the EC to 15 members left EFTA with just four members: Iceland, Liechtenstein, Norway and Switzerland.

In 1993, following the signing of the Maastricht Treaty, the EC was reconstituted

as the European Union (EU). The aims of the EU include economic and monetary union, a single currency for all 15 countries, and closer cooperation on foreign and security policies and also on home affairs. This step has led to a debate. Some people would like the EU to develop into a federal Europe, but others fear that this would lead to a loss of national identity. Another matter of importance is the future enlargement of the EU. By 1995, formal applications for membership had been received from Turkey, Malta, Cyprus, Poland, Hungary, Slovakia and Romania. Other possible members include the Czech Republic, Estonia, Latvia and Lithuania.

AUSTRALIA'S NEW ROLE

Most of the people who settled in Australia between 1788 and the mid-20th century came from the British Isles. However, the strong ties between Australia and Britain were weakened after Britain joined the European Community in 1973. Since 1973, many Australians have argued that their world position has changed and that they are part of a Pacific community of nations, rather than an extension of Europe. Some want closer integration with ASEAN, the increasingly powerful economic group formed by seven Southeast Asian nations. But in 1995, the prime minister of Malaysia, Dr Mahathir Mohamad, argued that Australia could not be regarded as Asian until at least 70% of its people were of ethnic Asian origin.

African Unity) has a similar role in Africa, while the Arab League is made up of Arabic-speaking North African and Middle Eastern states. The recently formed CIS (Commonwealth of Independent States) aims at maintaining links between 12 of the 15 republics which made up the Soviet Union.

NORTH–SOUTH DIVIDE

The deepest division in the world today is the divide between rich and poor nations. In international terms, this is called the North–South divide, because the North contains most of the world's developed countries, while the developing countries lie mainly in the South. The European Union recognizes this division and gives special trading terms to more than 60 former European dependencies, which form the ACP (African, Caribbean and Pacific) states. One organization containing a majority of developing countries is the Non-Aligned Movement. This Movement was created in 1961 during the Cold War as a political bloc allied neither to the East nor to the West. However, the aims of the 113 members who attended the movement's 11th gathering in 1995 were concerned mainly with economic matters. The 113 countries between them produce only about 7% of the world's gross output and they can speak for the poorer South.

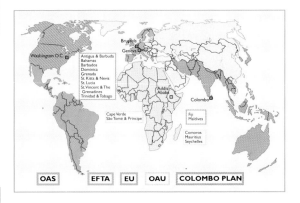

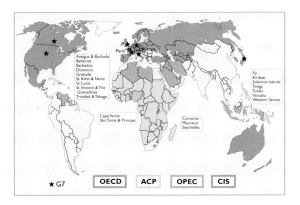

> The maps show the membership of major international organizations. One important grouping shown on the bottom map is the Group of Seven (often called G7), which was set up on 22 September 1985. This group of seven major industrial democracies (Canada, France, Germany, Italy, Japan, the United Kingdom and the United States) holds periodic meetings to discuss major problems, such as world recessions.

Regions in the News

> The hoped-for era of peace following the end of the Cold War in Europe in the early 1990s was not to be. Former Yugoslavia, a federation of six republics ruled by a Communist government between 1946 and 1991, became a 'region in the news' when it split apart in 1991. First, Croatia, Slovenia and Macedonia declared themselves independent nations, followed by Bosnia-Herzegovina in 1992. This left two states, Serbia and Montenegro, to continue as Yugoslavia. The presence in Croatia and Bosnia-Herzegovina of Orthodox Christian Serbs, Roman Catholic Croats and Muslims proved an explosive mixture. Fighting broke out first in Croatia and then in Bosnia-Herzegovina. Following a bitter civil war, accompanied by 'ethnic cleansing' (the slaughter and expulsion of rival ethnic groups), the signing of the Dayton Peace Accord in 1995 ended the war and affirmed Bosnia-Herzegovina as a single state with its capital at Sarajevo. But the new country is partitioned into a Muslim–Croat Federation and a Serbian Republic. Elections were held in Bosnia-Herzegovina in 1996.

Population breakdown ▾

Population totals and the proportion of ethnic groups (1995)

Yugoslavia **10,881,000**
  Serb 63%, Albanian 17%, Montenegrin 5%, Hungarian 3%, Muslim 3%
Serbia 6,017,200
  Kosovo 2,045,600
  Vojvodina 2,121,800
Montenegro 696,400

Bosnia-Herzegovina **4,400,000**
  Muslim 49%, Serb 31%, Croat 17%

Croatia **4,900,000**
  Croat 78%, Serb 12%

Slovenia **2,000,000**
  Slovene 88%, Croat 3%, Serb 2%

Macedonia (F.Y.R.O.M.) **2,173,000**
  Macedonian 64%, Albanian 22%, Turkish 5%, Romanian 3%, Serb 2%

International borders
Republic boundaries
Province boundaries
Line of the Dayton Peace Accord
Muslim–Croat Federation
Serbian Republic

> Since its establishment in 1948, the State of Israel has seldom been out of the news. During wars with its Arab neighbors in 1948–49, 1956, 1967 and 1973, it occupied several areas. The largest of the occupied territories, the Sinai peninsula, was returned to Egypt in 1979 following the signing of an Egyptian–Israeli peace treaty. This left three Israeli-occupied territories: the Gaza Strip, the West Bank bordering Jordan, and the Golan Heights, a militarily strategic area overlooking southwestern Syria.

Despite the peace agreement with Egypt, conflict continued in Israel with the PLO (Palestine Liberation Organization), which claimed to represent Arabs in Israel and Palestinians living in exile. Finally, on 13 September 1993 Israel officially recognized the PLO, and Yasser Arafat, leader of the PLO, renounced terrorism and recognized the State of Israel. This led to an agreement signed by both sides in Washington, DC. In May 1994, limited Palestinian self-rule was established in the Gaza Strip and in parts of the occupied West Bank. A Palestinian National Authority (PNA) was created and took over from the Israeli military administration when Israeli troops withdrew from the Gaza Strip and the city of Jericho. On 1 July 1994 the Palestinian leader, Yasser Arafat, stepped on to Palestinian land for the first time in 25 years.

Many people hoped that these developments would eventually lead to the creation of a Palestinian state, which would coexist in peace with its neighbor Israel. But groups on both sides sought to undermine the peace process. In November 1995, a right-wing Jewish student assassinated the Israeli prime minister, Yitzhak Rabin, who was succeeded by Símon Peres.

In 1996, a right-wing coalition led by Binyamin Netanyahu was returned to power in a general election. The peace talks with the PLO were temporarily halted, but an agreement was reached in early 1997 over the withdrawal of Israeli troops from the town of Al Khalil (Hebron), on the West Bank. One-fifth of this town remained in the hands of about 400 Israeli settlers. Negotiations with Syria, however, over the Golan Heights were halted in 1996.

THE NEAR EAST

0   25   50 km

35°E

—·—·— 1949 Armistice Line

- - - - - 1974 Cease-fire Lines (Golan Heights)

Efrata
●   Main Jewish settlements in the West Bank and Gaza Strip

Halhul
□   Main Palestinian Arab towns in the West Bank and Gaza Strip – under Palestinian control since May 1994 (Gaza and Jericho) and 28 September 1995 (West Bank)

Population breakdown ▾

Population totals and the proportion of ethnic groups (1995)

Israel **5,696,000**
    Jewish 82%, Arab Muslim 14%, Arab Christian 3%, Druse 2%
West Bank 973,500
    Palestinian Arab 97% (Arab Muslim 85%, Christian 8%, Jewish 7%)
Gaza Strip 658,200
    Arab Muslim 98%

Jordan **5,547,000**
    Arab 99% (Palestinian Arab 50%)

Syria **14,614,000**
    Arab 89%, Kurdish 6%

World Flags

 Afghanistan

 Albania

 Algeria

 Angola

 Argentina

 Armenia

 Australia

 Austria

 Azerbaijan

 Bahamas

 Bahrain

 Bangladesh

 Belarus

 Belgium

 Benin

 Bhutan

 Bolivia

 Bosnia-Herzegovina

 Botswana

 Brazil

 Bulgaria

 Burkina Faso

 Burma (Myanmar)

 Burundi

 Cambodia

 Cameroon

 Canada

 Central African Rep.

 Chad

 Chile

 China

 Colombia

 Congo

 Costa Rica

 Croatia

 Cuba

 Cyprus

 Czech Republic

 Denmark

 Djibouti

Dominican Republic

 Ecuador

 Egypt

 El Salvador

 Equatorial Guinea

 Eritrea

Estonia

Ethiopia

 Finland

France

Gabon

Georgia

Germany

Ghana

Greece

30

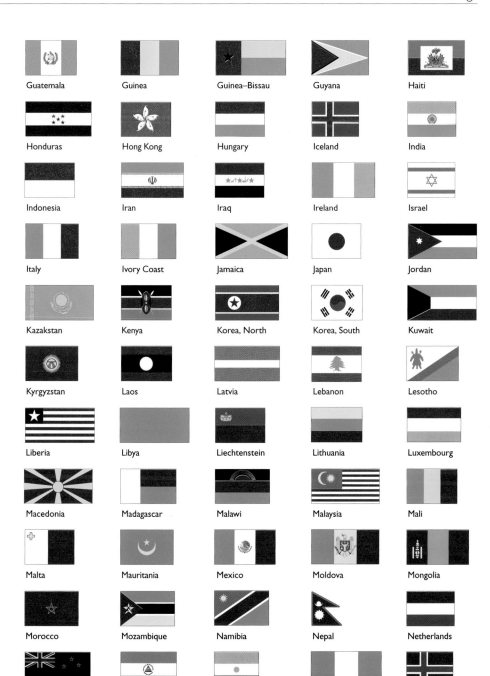

Guatemala

Guinea

Guinea–Bissau

Guyana

Haiti

Honduras

Hong Kong

Hungary

Iceland

India

Indonesia

Iran

Iraq

Ireland

Israel

Italy

Ivory Coast

Jamaica

Japan

Jordan

Kazakstan

Kenya

Korea, North

Korea, South

Kuwait

Kyrgyzstan

Laos

Latvia

Lebanon

Lesotho

Liberia

Libya

Liechtenstein

Lithuania

Luxembourg

Macedonia

Madagascar

Malawi

Malaysia

Mali

Malta

Mauritania

Mexico

Moldova

Mongolia

Morocco

Mozambique

Namibia

Nepal

Netherlands

New Zealand

Nicaragua

Niger

Nigeria

Norway

31

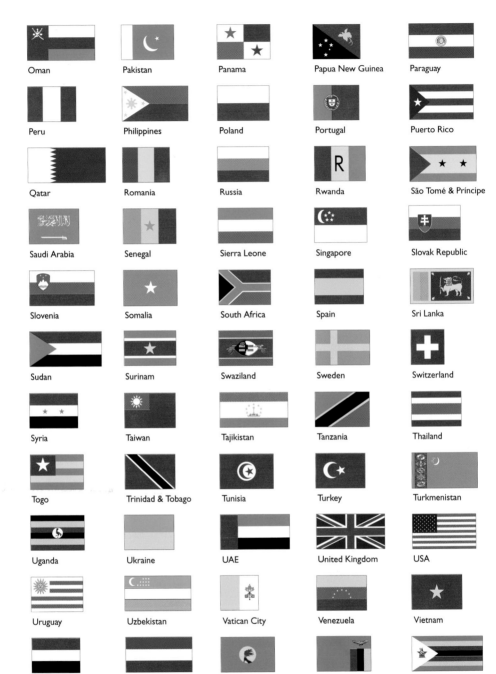

Oman	Pakistan	Panama	Papua New Guinea	Paraguay
Peru	Philippines	Poland	Portugal	Puerto Rico
Qatar	Romania	Russia	Rwanda	São Tomé & Príncipe
Saudi Arabia	Senegal	Sierra Leone	Singapore	Slovak Republic
Slovenia	Somalia	South Africa	Spain	Sri Lanka
Sudan	Surinam	Swaziland	Sweden	Switzerland
Syria	Taiwan	Tajikistan	Tanzania	Thailand
Togo	Trinidad & Tobago	Tunisia	Turkey	Turkmenistan
Uganda	Ukraine	UAE	United Kingdom	USA
Uruguay	Uzbekistan	Vatican City	Venezuela	Vietnam
Yemen	Yugoslavia	Zaïre	Zambia	Zimbabwe

World Maps — GENERAL REFERENCE

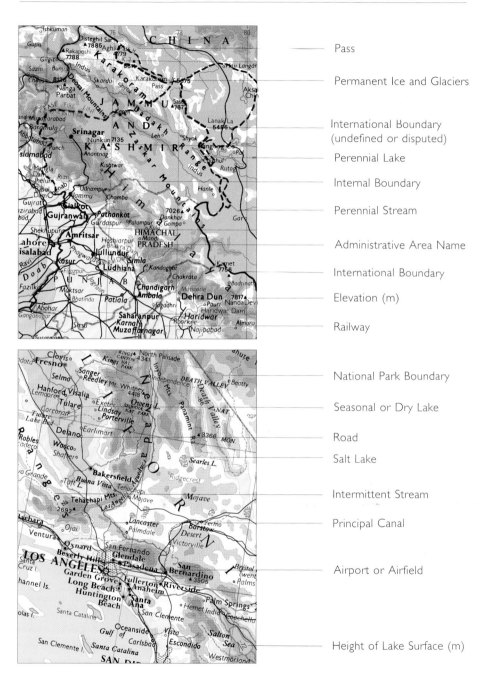

Pass

Permanent Ice and Glaciers

International Boundary
(undefined or disputed)

Perennial Lake

Internal Boundary

Perennial Stream

Administrative Area Name

International Boundary

Elevation (m)

Railway

National Park Boundary

Seasonal or Dry Lake

Road

Salt Lake

Intermittent Stream

Principal Canal

Airport or Airfield

Height of Lake Surface (m)

Settlements

Settlement symbols and type styles vary
according to the scale of each map and
indicate the importance of towns rather
than specific population figures.

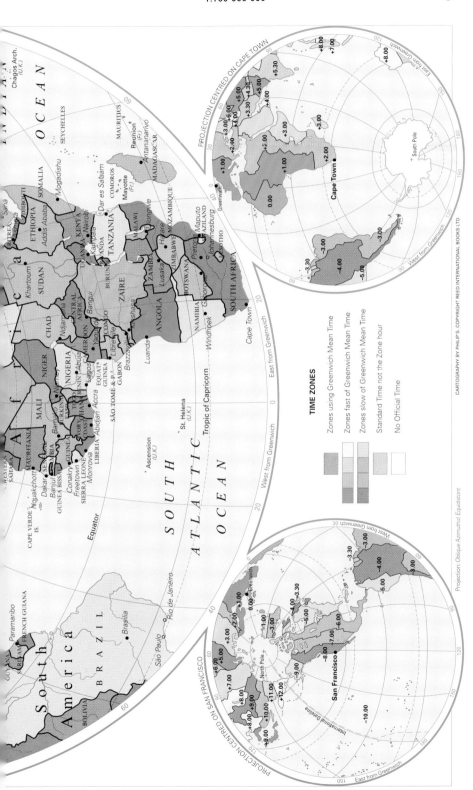

TIME ZONES

Zones using Greenwich Mean Time

Zones fast of Greenwich Mean Time

Zones slow of Greenwich Mean Time

Standard Time not the Zone hour

No Official Time

PROJECTION CENTRED ON CAPE TOWN

PROJECTION CENTRED ON SAN FRANCISCO

Projection: Oblique Azimuthal Equidistant

CARTOGRAPHY BY PHILIP'S. COPYRIGHT REED INTERNATIONAL BOOKS LTD

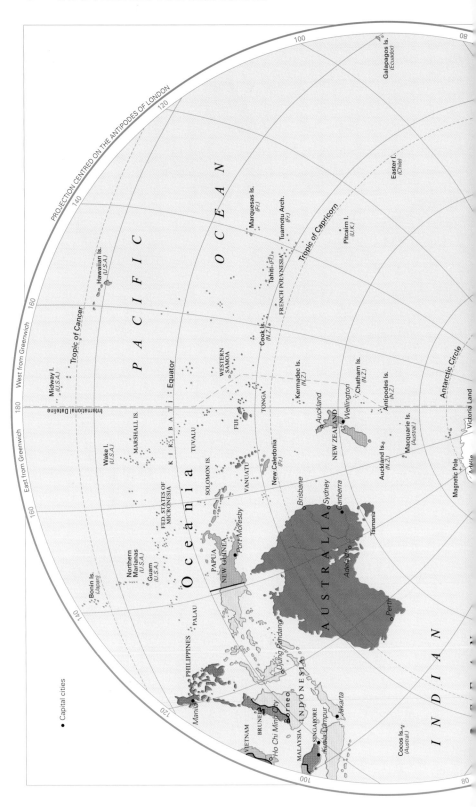

PROJECTION CENTRED ON THE ANTIPODES OF LONDON

West from Greenwich

East from Greenwich

International Dateline

Tropic of Cancer

Equator

Tropic of Capricorn

Antarctic Circle

PACIFIC OCEAN

INDIAN

Oceania

AUSTRALIA

NEW ZEALAND

INDONESIA

Borneo

Galapagos Is.
(Ecuador)

Easter I.
(Chile)

Marquesas Is.
(Fr.)

Tuamotu Arch.
(Fr.)

Pitcairn I.
(U.K.)

Tahiti (Fr.)

FRENCH POLYNESIA

Cook Is.
(N.Z.)

WESTERN
SAMOA

TONGA

Kermadec Is.
(N.Z.)

Chatham Is.
(N.Z.)

Antipodes Is.
(N.Z.)

Auckland

Wellington

Macquarie I.
(Austral.)

Auckland Is.
(N.Z.)

FIJI

VANUATU

New Caledonia
(Fr.)

TUVALU

SOLOMON IS.

KIRIBATI

MARSHALL IS.

FED. STATES OF
MICRONESIA

Wake I.
(U.S.A.)

Midway I.
(U.S.A.)

Hawaiian Is.
(U.S.A.)

Bonin Is.
(Japan)

Northern
Marianas
(U.S.A.)

Guam
(U.S.A.)

PALAU

PHILIPPINES

Manila

VIETNAM

Ho Chi Minh City

BRUNEI

MALAYSIA

SINGAPORE

Kuala Lumpur

Ujung Pandang

Jakarta

Cocos Is.
(Austral.)

PAPUA
NEW GUINEA

Port Moresby

Brisbane

Sydney

Canberra

Adelaide

Perth

Tasmania

Magnetic Pole

Victoria Land

Adélie

• Capital cities

100

120

140

160

180

160

140

120

100

80

80

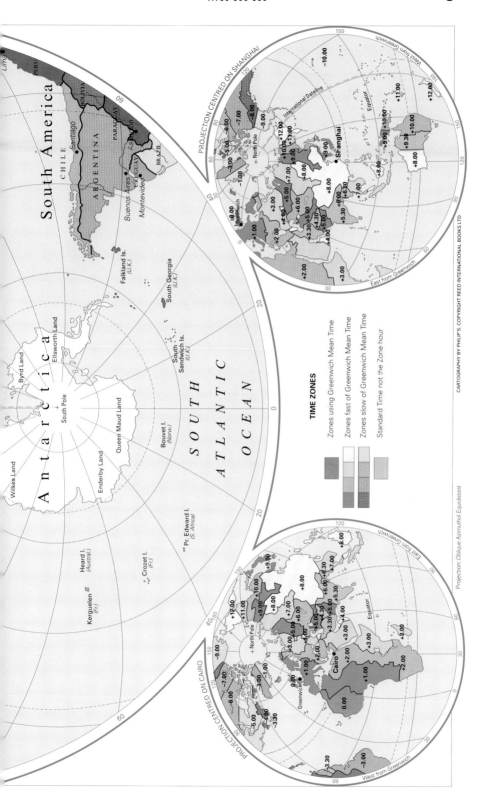

TIME ZONES

Zones using Greenwich Mean Time

Zones fast of Greenwich Mean Time

Zones slow of Greenwich Mean Time

Standard Time not the Zone hour

South America

Antarctica

SOUTH ATLANTIC OCEAN

PROJECTION CENTRED ON SHANGHAI

PROJECTION CENTRED ON CAIRO

Projection: Oblique Azimuthal Equidistant

CARTOGRAPHY BY PHILIP'S. COPYRIGHT REED INTERNATIONAL BOOKS LTD

1 2 3 4 5 6 7 8 9

C

ICELAND
●Reykjavik

Arctic Circle

Norwegian

60

Sea

Tromsø

Narv

D

Faroe Is.
(Den.)

SWEDEN

Shetland
Is.

Trondheim

NORWAY

Bergen

Gävle

55

Hebrides

Orkney
Is.

Oslo

Örebro

Uppsala

UNITED
KINGDOM

Stavanger

Aberdeen

SCOTLAND

Glasgow

Dundee

Vänern

Jönköping

Kattegat

Gotlar

E

ATLANTIC

N.
IRELAND
Belfast

Edinburgh

North

DENMARK
Århus

Ålborg

Gothenburg

Skagerrak

IRELAND

Dublin●

Newcastle-
upon-Tyne

Manchester

Leeds

Liverpool

Sheffield

50

Cork

Sea

Copenhagen

Malmö

Baltic

Kiel

Birmingham

WALES
Cardiff

ENGLAND

Bristol

Amsterdam

The Hague

NETHER-
LANDS

Hamburg

Bremen

Elbe

Gdańsk

Szczecin

Bydgoszcz

F

OCEAN

Plymouth

Southampton

LONDON

Rotterdam

Antwerp

BELGIUM

Essen

Dortmund

GERMANY

Hannover

Magdeburg

Berlin

POL

Poznań

Oder

Łódź

English Channel

Le Havre

Lille

Brussels

Cologne

Bonn

Halle

Leipzig

Dresden

Wrocław

Channel Is.
(U.K.)

Rouen

Wiesbaden

Frankfurt
am Main

Chemnitz

Katowice

Brest

Seine

LUX.
Luxembourg

Prague

Ostrava

PARIS

CZECH REP.

45

FRANCE

Strasbourg

Nuremberg

Rhine

Stuttgart

SL

Nantes

Loire

Dijon

Munich

Vienna

Bratislav

Bay of
Biscay

Limoges

Lyons

St.-Étienne

Zürich

Bern

LIECH.
Vaduz

AUSTRIA

Linz

Salzburg

Innsbruck

Graz

HUNG

G

Bordeaux

SWITZERLAND

Geneva

Milan

SLOVENIA

Ljubljana

Zagreb

Toulouse

Garonne

Grenoble

CROATIA

Rhône

Turin

Venice

Trieste

La Coruña

Nice

Genoa

Bologna

BOSNIA-
HERZ.

Vigo

MONACO

Florence

Porto

Douro

Bilbao

Toulon

SAN
MARINO

Split

Sarajevo

YU

40

Valladolid

ANDORRA
Andorra-
la-Vella

Zaragoza

Ebro

Marseilles

Tiber

MON
NEG

Lisbon●

PORTUGAL

Madrid●

Corsica

Ajaccio

ITALY

Rome●

Adriatic

Sea

H

SPAIN

Guadiana

Valencia

Barcelona

Balearic Is.

Minorca

Sardinia

Tyrrhenian

Naples

Bari

Tira

Seville

Córdoba

Murcia

Alicante

Palma

Ibiza

Majorca

Sea

Tàranto

AL

Guadalquivir

Granada

Málaga

Cagliari

Palermo

Messina

Ionia

Cádiz

Gibraltar *(U.K.)*

Str. of Gibraltar

Tangier

Ceuta*(Sp.)*

Melilla*(Sp.)*

Algiers

Mediterranean

Sicily

Catánia

Sea

J

Africa

MOROCCO

ALGERIA

Annaba

Constantine

TUNISIA

Tunis

Pantelleria
(Italy)

Sea

MALTA

Valletta

I: 20 000 000

100   0   100   200   300   400   500 miles
100   0   200   400   600   800 km

10   11   12   13   14   15   16   17   18   19

35   40   45   50   55   60   65   70

C

Ob

White Sea

Hammerfest ⊙

Murmansk ⊙

Kiruna

Luleå ⊙

Arkhangelsk ⊙

D

N. Dvina

Nizhniy Tagil ⊙

Kotlas ⊙

Perm ⊙

FINLAND

Vaasa ⊙

L. Onega

Yekaterinburg ⊙

Tampere ⊙

Kirov ⊙

Chelyabinsk ⊙ 55

Turku ⊙

Vyborg ⊙ *L. Ladoga*

Vologda ⊙

Ufa ⊙

Helsinki ●

■ ST. PETERSBURG

Kostroma ⊙

R   U   S   S   I   A

E

holm

Tallinn ⊙

L. Chudskoye

Yaroslavl ⊙

Ivanovo ⊙

Nizhniy Novgorod ⊙

Kazan ⊙

Magnitogorsk ⊙

ESTONIA

Sea

Rybinsk Res.

LATVIA

Riga ⊙

■ MOSCOW

Simbirsk ⊙

Samara ⊙

Orenburg ⊙

W. Dvina

Uralsk ⊙

50

LITHUANIA

Vitebsk ⊙

Smolensk ⊙

Tula ⊙

Penza ⊙

Volga

Kaunas ⊙

Saratov ⊙

Ural

K   A   Z   A   K   H   S   T   A   N

F

Kaliningrad

Vilnius ●

Mogilev ⊙

Orel ⊙

Tambov ⊙

(Russia)

Minsk ●

Białystok ⊙

BELARUS

Gomel ⊙

Kursk ⊙

Voronezh ⊙

Atyraū ⊙

Warsaw ●

Brest ⊙

Pripet

Don

ND

Lublin ⊙

Chernigov ⊙

Volgograd ⊙

Kraków ⊙

Zhitomir ⊙

Kiev ● *Dnieper*

Kharkov ●

Astrakhan ⊙

45

Lvov ⊙

U   K   R   A   I   N   E

Caspian Sea

K REP

Dniester

Dnepropetrovsk ⊙

Donetsk ⊙

Miskolc ⊙

Bug

Krivoy Rog ⊙

Zaporozhye ⊙ Taganrog ⊙

Rostov ●

Y

pest ⊙ Debrecen ⊙

MOLDOVA

Nikolayev ⊙

Kherson ⊙

Stavropol ⊙

Makhachkala ⊙

G

Cluj-Napoca ⊙

Kishinev ●

Odessa ●

Krasnodar ⊙

Timişoara ⊙

R O M A N I A

Crimea

Brasov ⊙

Galaţi ⊙

Sevastopol ⊙

Ploieşti ⊙

Constanţa ⊙

B l a c k   S e a

GEORGIA

Tbilisi ⊙

AZERBAIJAN

Baku ● 40

Belgrade ●

Bucharest ●

Danube

ARMENIA

SERBIA

Niş ⊙

Varna ⊙

Yerevan ●

Araks

Tabriz ⊙

H

SLAVIA

Sofia ●

BULGARIA

Bosporus

Samsun ⊙

Erzurum ⊙

Skopje ●

Plovdiv ⊙

T   U   R   K   E   Y

MACEDONIA

■ ISTANBUL

IRAN

Thessaloniki ⊙

Bursa ⊙

Ankara ●

Diyarbakır ⊙

35

ΑΤ

GREECE

Aegean Sea

İzmir ⊙

Kayseri ⊙

A   s   i   a

İzmir ⊙

Konya ⊙

Adana ⊙

Aleppo ⊙

Euphrates

IRAQ

J

Pátrai ⊙

Athens ●

Antalya ⊙

SYRIA

Tigris

Baghdad ⊙ 45

Rhodes ⊙

CYPRUS

Nicosia ●

10   Crete   11   30   12   35   13   14   15

CARTOGRAPHY BY PHILIPS. COPYRIGHT REED INTERNATIONAL BOOKS LTD.

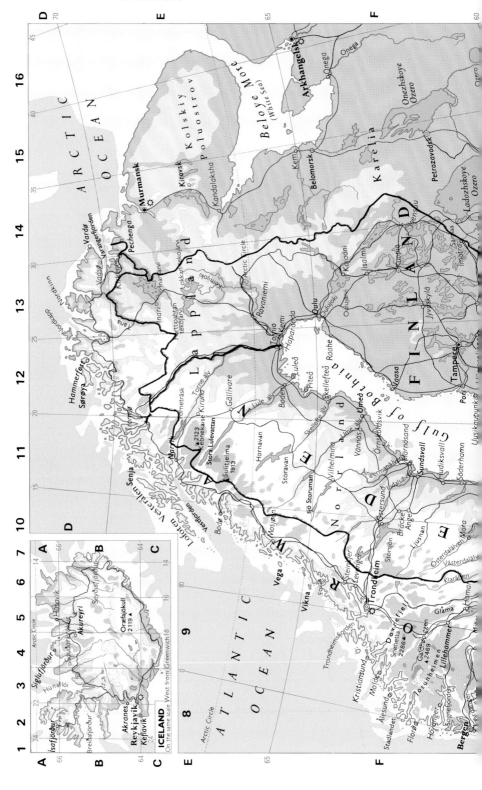

ICELAND
On the same scale West from Greenwich 18

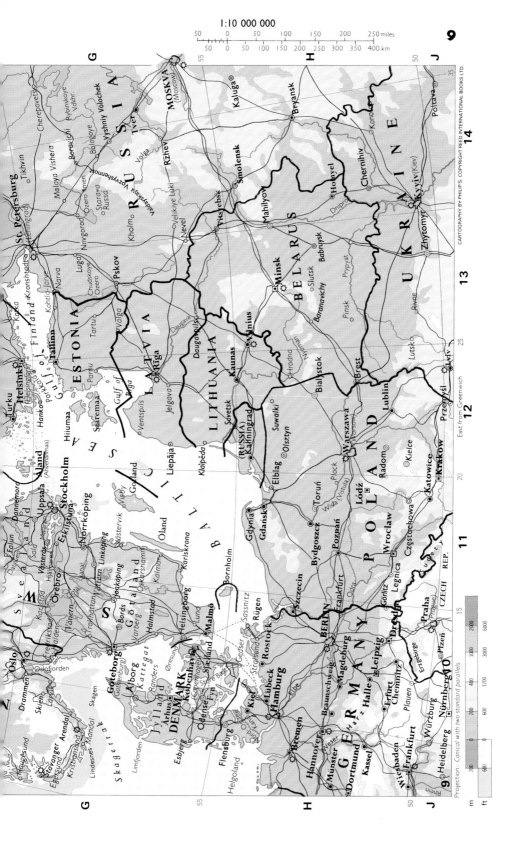

1:10 000 000

50   0   50   100   150   200   250 miles
50   0   50   100   150   200   250   300   350   400 km

CARTOGRAPHY BY PHILIP'S. COPYRIGHT REED INTERNATIONAL BOOKS LTD.

Projection: Conical with two standard parallels

East from Greenwich

FINLAND

RUSSIA

ESTONIA

LATVIA

LITHUANIA

BELARUS

UKRAINE

POLAND

GERMANY

DENMARK

SWEDEN

CZECH REP.

BALTIC SEA

Gulf of Finland

Gulf of Riga

Kattegat

Skagerrak

MOSKVA (Moscow)

St. Petersburg

Helsinki (Helsingfors)

Turku

Tallinn

Riga

Vilnius

Kaunas

Minsk

Kyyiv (Kiev)

Warszawa (Warsaw)

BERLIN

Kraków

Oslo

Stockholm

København (Copenhagen)

Hamburg

14

13

12

11

10

9

G   H   J

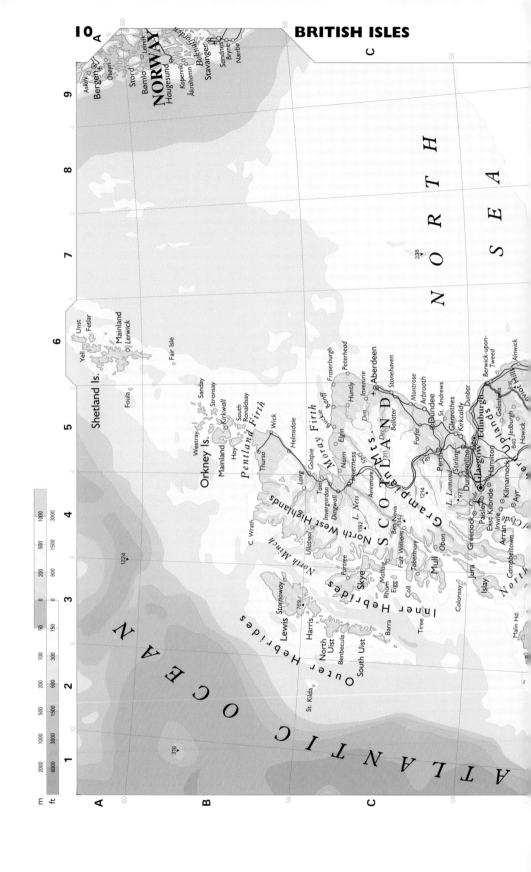

A
NORWAY
Askøy
Bergen
Osøyr
Stord
Bømlo
Lemik
Flora
Haugesund
Florogon
Bol...
Kopervik
Åkrahamn
Sandnes
Bryne
Stavanger
Nærbø

NORTH SEA

238

Shetland Is.
Yell
Unst
Fetlar
Mainland
Lerwick
Foula

Fair Isle

Orkney Is.
Westray
Sanday
Stronsay
Mainland
Kirkwall
Hoy
South Ronaldsay
Pentland Firth

Wick
Helmsdale
Golspie
Lairg
Tain
Thurso

Moray Firth
Buckie
Bonff
Banff
Elgin
Nairn
Inverness
Dingwall
Invergordon
Aviemore
L. Ness

Fraserburgh
Peterhead
Aberdeen
Stonehaven
Huntly
Inverurie

1224

C. Wrath
Ullapool
North West Highlands
Ben Nevis 1342
1182
Fort William
Tobermory
Oban

North Minch
Portree
Skye
Mallaig
Rhum
Eigg
Coll
Tiree
Mull

SCOTLAND
Don
Dee
311
1214
973
Deeside
Ballater
Forfar
Perth
Stirling
L. Lomond

Grampian Mts.
Montrose
Arbroath
St. Andrews
Dundee
Glenrothes
Kirkcaldy
Dunfermline
Dunbar

Berwick-upon-Tweed
Edinburgh
Galashiels
816
Hills
Alnwick

Glasgow
Hamilton
East Kilbride
Kilmarnock
Paisley
Greenock
Clyde
Irvine
Ayr
Campbeltown

F. of Clyde
Arran
Jura
Islay
Colonsay
Malin Hd.

Southern Uplands
840
Jedburgh

North ...

Inner Hebrides
Barra
South Uist
Benbecula
North Uist
Harris
Lewis
Stornoway
789

Outer Hebrides

St. Kilda

316

ATLANTIC OCEAN

m ft
1000 3000
500 1500
200 600
100 300
50 150
0 0
200 600
500 1500
1000 3000
2000 6000

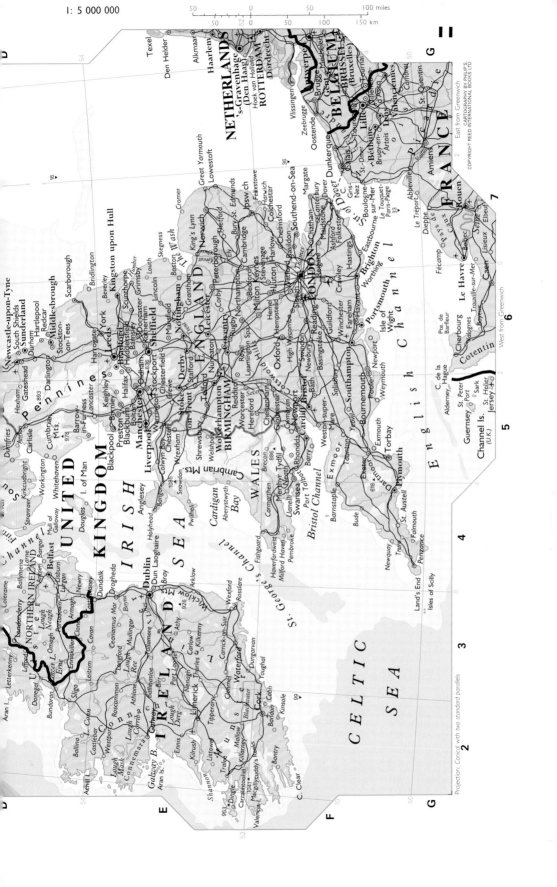

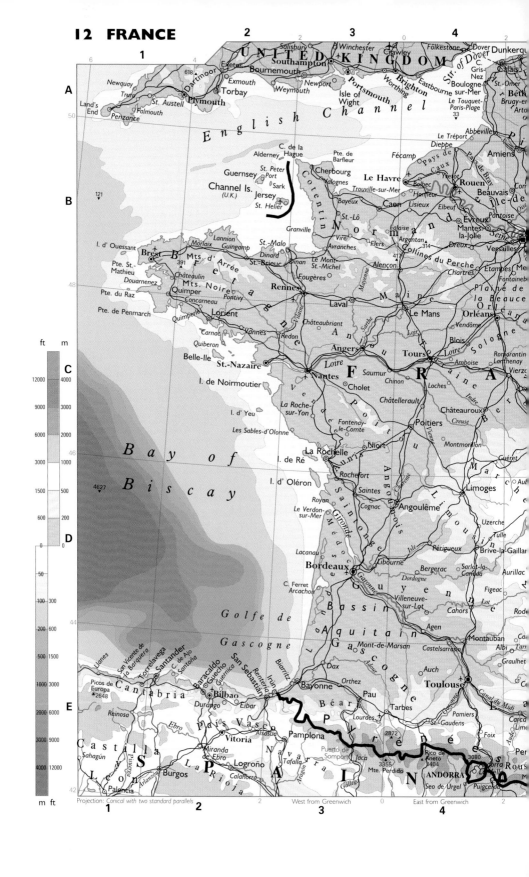

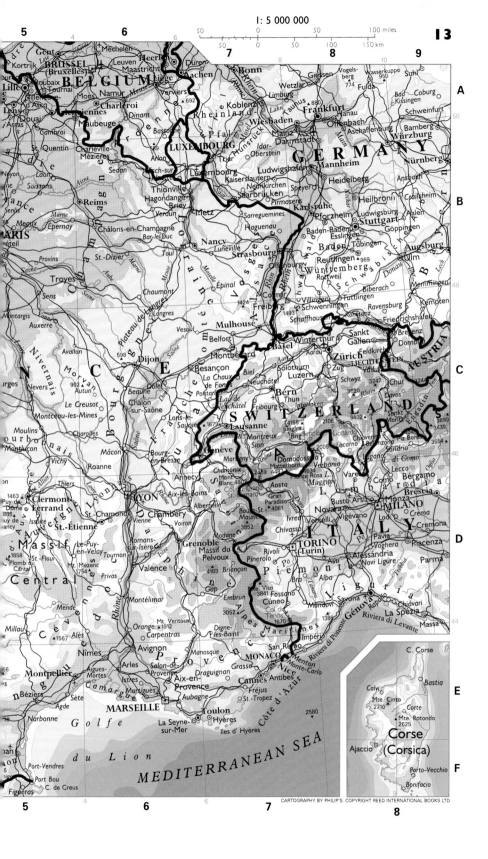

50   0   50   100 miles
50   0   50   150 km

5   6   7   8   9

BELGIUM
Gent   Mechelen   Heerlen
Kortrijk   Leuven   Maastricht   Düren   Bonn
BRUSSEL   Liège   Aachen   Giessen   Vogels-   Wasserkuppe
(Bruxelles)   Verviers   berg   950   Suhl
Lille   Roubaix   Tournai   Mons   Namur   Rheinland   Limburg   Wetzlar   774   Fulda   A
d'Ascq   692   Koblenz   Lahn   Bad   Coburg
Lens   Charleroi   Dinant   Taunus   Frankfurt   Kissingen
Arras   Valenciennes   Bastogne   Rheinland   Wiesbaden   Hanau   Offenbach   Bamberg   Schweinfurt
Douai   Cambrai   Maubeuge   Pfalz   Mainz   Darmstadt   Aschaffenburg   Würzburg
St.-Quentin   Charleville-   LUXEMBOURG   Idar-   GERMANY   Nürnberg
Mézières   Esch-sur-   589   Oberstein   Mannheim
Noyon   Laon   Sedan   Arlon   Luxembourg   Trier   Hunsrück   Ludwigshafen   Heidelberg   Ansbach   B
Soissons   Thionville   Kaiserslautern   Neunkirchen   Speyer   Heilbronn   Crailsheim
France   Reims   Hagondange   Saarbrücken   Pirmasens   Karlsruhe   Ludwigsburg   Aalen
Créteil   Épernay   Briey   Verdun   Metz   Sarreguemines   Pforzheim   Stuttgart   Augsburg
PARIS   Marne   Châlons-en-Champagne   Haguenau   Baden-Baden   Esslingen   Göppingen
Meaux   Bar-le-Duc   Nancy   Baden   Tübingen
Senlis   Provins   St.-Dizier   Toul   Lunéville   Strasbourg   Offenburg   969   Württemberg   Ulm
Seine   Chaumont   Épinal   Colmar   Rottweil   Schwäbische   Donau   Memmingen   48
Troyes   Aube   Freiburg   Villingen   Schwenningen   Biberach
Sens   1424   Schaffhausen   Tuttlingen   Ravensburg   Kempten
Auxerre   Vesoul   1493   Konstanz   Friedrichshafen
Langres   Mulhouse   Basel   Winterthur   Sankt   Bregenz
Montargis   Plateau de Langres   Belfort   Aarau   Gallen   Dornbirn
Nivernais   598   Dijon   Montbéliard   Sankt   AUSTRIA   C
Avallon   Besançon   Biel   Solothurn   Zürich   Feldkirch   3244
Nevers   902   Morvan   La Chaux-   Neuchâtel   Luzern   Zug   LIECHTENSTEIN
Autun   Beaune   de Fonds   3247   Chur
Le Creusot   Dole   Pontarlier   Bern   Schwyz   Davos   Engadin   3899
Montceau-les-Mines   Chalon-   Lac de   Thun   Interlaken   3620   Rhein   Sankt   3439
Moulins   sur-Saône   Neuchâtel   Fribourg   Gottardo   Chiavenna   Moritz   Piz Bernina   3554
Charolles   1679   SWITZERLAND   4158   Brig   2108   Bellinzona   di Como   46
Bourbonnais   Lausanne   Jungfrau   3402   Locarno   Sondrio
Montluçon   Mâcon   Bourg-   Montreux   Rhône   2005   Lugano   Lecco   Bergamo
Vichy   en-Bresse   Genève   Sion   Domodossola   Verbánia   Brescia
Roanne   Annecy   Martigny   Matterhorn   Monte Rosa   Maggiore   Varese   Monza
Thiers   Chamonix   2469   4487   Busto Arsizio   MILANO   Crema
1463   Clermont-   Aix-les-Bains   Mont   Aosta   4061   Ivrea   Novara   Lodi   Cremona
Puy-de-   Ferrand   LYON   Blanc 4807   Gran   Vigevano   Vercelli   Pavia
Dôme   885   St.-Chamond   Chambéry   Paradiso   2005   Chivasso   Voghera   Piacenza   D
St.-Étienne   Vienne   Voiron   3852   ITALY   Alessándria
Massif   Le-Puy-   Albertville   Bourg-St-   TORINO   Asti   Novi Ligure   Parma
en-Velay   Grenoble   Maurice   (Turin)   Piemonte
1858   St.-Flour   Massif du   Modane   Rívoli   Tortona
Plomb du   Mt. Mézenc   Romans-   Pelvoux   Pinerolo   Po   Voghera
Cantal   1754   sur-Isère   4103   Briançon   Po   Liguria   Gènoa
Central   Privas   Gap   Viso   Asti   La Spezia
Mende   Tournon   Montélimar   3841   Fossano   Savona   Chiávari   Massa
Millau   Valence   Mt. Ventoux   Embrun   Cúneo   Riviera di Levante   44
1567   Alès   Digne-   1912   3052   Col di   Mondoví   Genova   Rápallo
Nîmes   Orange   les-Bains   Tenda   Impéria   Riviera di Ponente
Béziers   Avignon   Carpentras   1870   1388   San Remo
Montpellier   Manosque   Grasse   Alpes   Menton   Riviera di Ponente
Aigues-   Arles   Salon-de-   Draguignan   Maritimes   MONACO
Narbonne   Mortes   Istres   Provence   Aix-en-   Cannes   Monte-Carlo   Nice
Agde   Martigues   Provence   Fréjus   Antibes   Côte d'Azur
Sète   Camargue   Aubagne   St.-Tropez
MARSEILLE   Toulon   Hyères   2580   E
Golfe   La Seyne-   Îles d'Hyères
Port-Vendres   du   Lion   sur-Mer
Port Bou   MEDITERRANEAN SEA
Figueras   C. de Creus

C. Corse

Calvi   Bastia
Mte. Cinto   Corte
2710
Mte. Rotondo   E
2625
Corse
(Corsica)
Ajaccio   Porto-Vecchio   F
Bonifacio

5   4   6   6   7   8

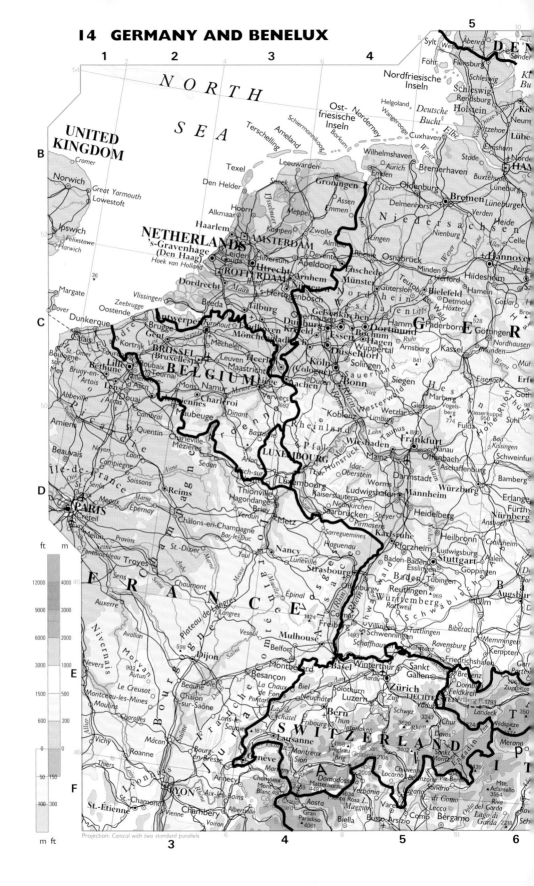

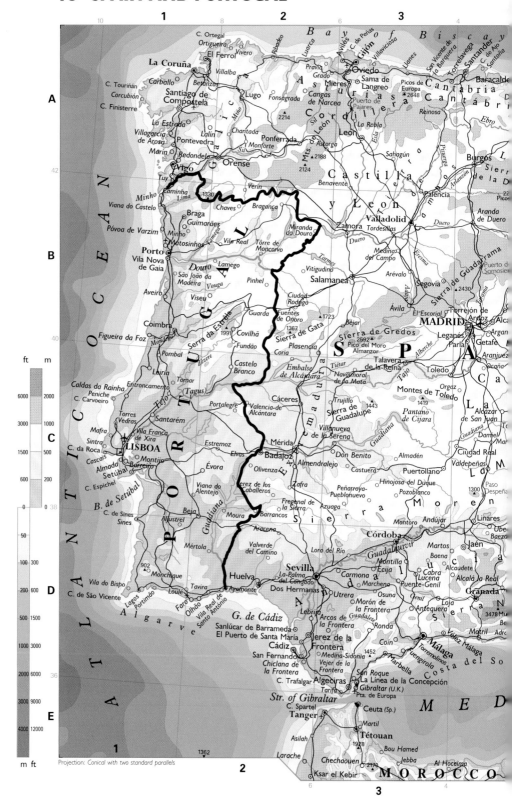

Projection: Conical with two standard parallels

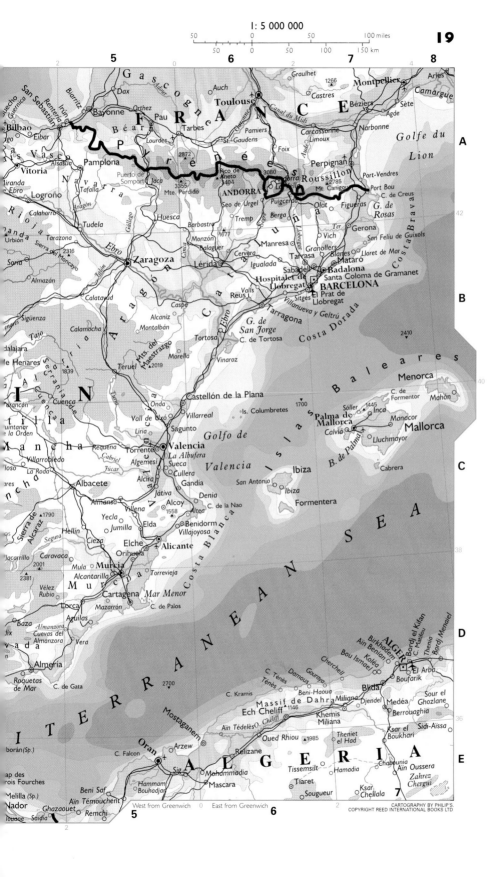

1: 5 000 000

50   0   50   100 miles

50   0   50   100   150 km

5   6   7   8

Graulhet   1266   Montpellier   Arles

San Sebastián Biarritz Dax Auch Castres Béziers Sète Camargue

Irún Bayonne Orthez Toulouse Agde

Guernica Renteria Pau Tarbes Pamiers Carcassonne Narbonne

F R A N C E

Bilbao Eibar Béarn Lourdes St-Gaudens Limoux Golfe du Lion

Vitoria Alsasua Pamplona Pyrénées Foix Perpignan **A**

Navarra Puerto de Somport Jaca 2872 3080 Roussillon Port-Vendres

Logroño Tafalla Rico de 3355 3404 **ANDORRA** 2785 Mt. Canigou Port Bou

Ebro Calahorra Mte. Perdido Andorra C. de Creus

Miranda Aragón Seo de Urgel Puigcerdá Olot Figueras G. de Rosas

Rioja Tudela Huesca Berga Vich Gerona 42

Sierra del Moncayo 2316 Barbastro 1677 Tremp Ter San Feliu de Guixols

Urbión Tarazona Monzón Balaguer Manresa Granollers Costa Brava

Soria Almazán **Zaragoza** Lérida Cervera Igualada Tarrasa Blanes Lloret de Mar

Calatayud Cinca Sabadell Mataró

Siguenza Calamocha Cataluña Hospitalet de Llobregat **BARCELONA** Santa Coloma de Gramanet **Badalona**

Tajo Montalbán Valls Reus Sitges El Prat de Llobregat **B**

Guadalajara Alcañiz Caspe Villanueva y Geltrú Tarragona Costa Dorada

de Henares Serranía Mts. del Maestrazgo 2019 Morella G. de San Jorge Tortosa C. de Tortosa 2410

Cuenca 1839 Teruel Vinaroz

I N Turia Villarreal Castellón de la Plana Islas Baleares Menorca

Castilla Quintanar de la Orden Cuenca Onda Vall de Uxó 1700 Inca 1445 C. de Formentor Mahón 40

la Mancha Liria Sagunto Is. Columbretes Sóller Palma de Mallorca Manacor

Villarrobledo Requena Torrente **Valencia** Calviá **Mallorca**

La Roda Cabriel Algemesi La Albufera Lluchmayor

Albacete Júcar Sueca B. de Palma

Alcira Cullera Golfo de Valencia Cabrera **C**

Almansa Játiva Gandia San Antonio Ibiza

Yecla Villena Alcoy Denia Ibiza Formentera

Sierra de Alcaraz 1790 Elda 1558 Altea C. de la Nao San Antonio

Jumilla Benidorm Villajoyosa

Hellín Segura Cieza Elche **Alicante**

Carcallino Caravaca Mula Orihuela Costa Blanca 38

2001 **Murcia** Torrevieja

2381 Alcantarilla Murcia

Baza Vélez Rubio Cartagena Mar Menor

fix Almanzora Lorca Mazarrón C. de Palos

vada Cuevas del Almanzora Aguilas Vera

Almería Bordj el Kifan C. Mattou Thenia Bordj Menaiel **D**

Roquetas de Mar C. de Gata Birkhadem **ALGER** Koléa

Ain Benian El Arba

2700 Cherchell Bou Ismael Boufarik

C. Ténès Damous Gouraya Blida Sour el Ghozlane

C. Kramis Ténès Beni-Haoua Miliana Medéa Berrouaghia

Massif de Dahra Djendel Sidi-Aissa

Ech Cheliff 1146 Khemis Miliana Ksar el Boukhari 36

Mostaganem Ain Tédelès O. Cheliff Theniet el Had

borán (Sp.) Oued Rhiou 1985

Oran Arzew Relizane Hamadia Ain Oussera Zahrez Chergui

ap des rois Fourches C. Falcon Sig Mohammadia **A L G E R I A** **E**

Melilla (Sp.) Beni Saf Hammam Bouhadjar Mascara Tissemsilt Tiaret Sougueur Ksar Chellala

Nador Ain Témouchent

Ghazaouet Remchi Saïdia

CARTOGRAPHY BY PHILIP'S.
COPYRIGHT REED INTERNATIONAL BOOKS LTD

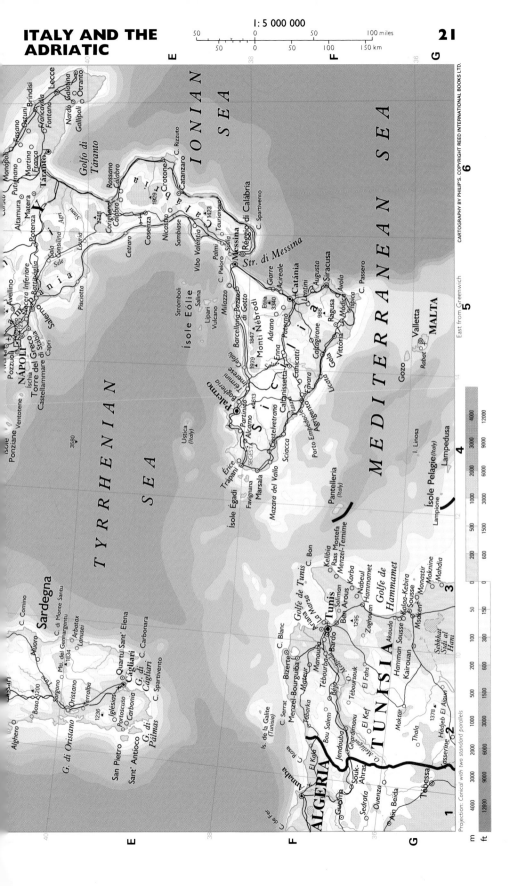

1: 5 000 000

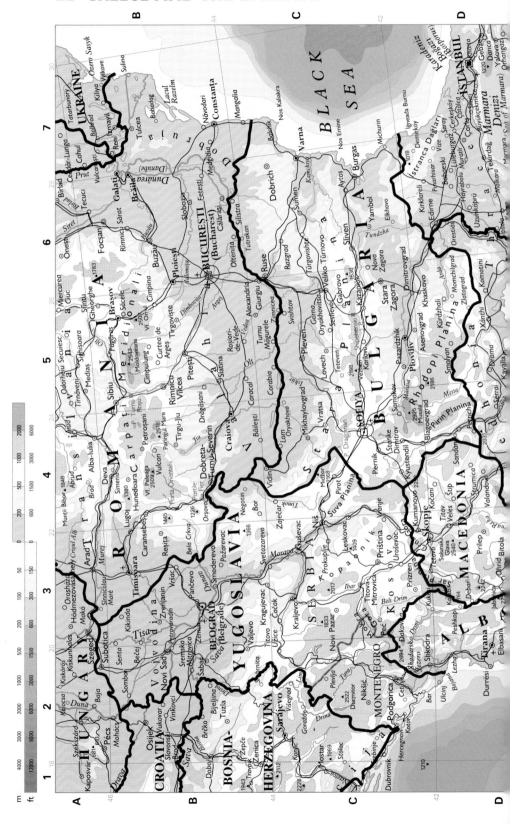

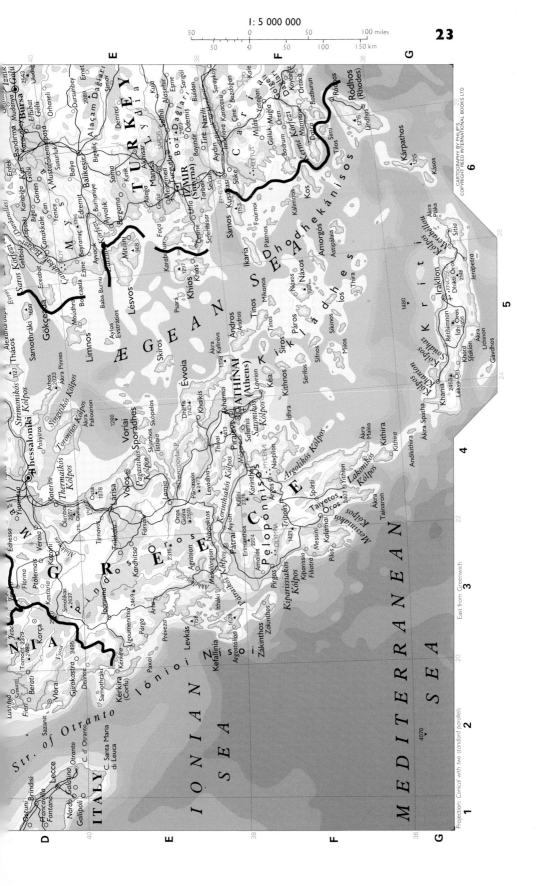

1 : 5 000 000

50   0   50   100 miles

50   0   50   100   150 km

CARTOGRAPHY BY PHILIP'S.
COPYRIGHT REED INTERNATIONAL BOOKS LTD

Projection: *Conical with two standard parallels*

East from Greenwich

TURKEY

M Y S I A

I Z M I R

C a r i a

Dhodhekánisos

Ródhos (Rhodes)

AEGEAN SEA

Kikládhes

Sporádhes

ATHÍNAI (Athens)

G R E E C E

Pelopónnisos

Kríti

ITALY

Str. of Otranto

I O N I A N   S E A

M E D I T E R R A N E A N   S E A

Thessaloníki

Bursa

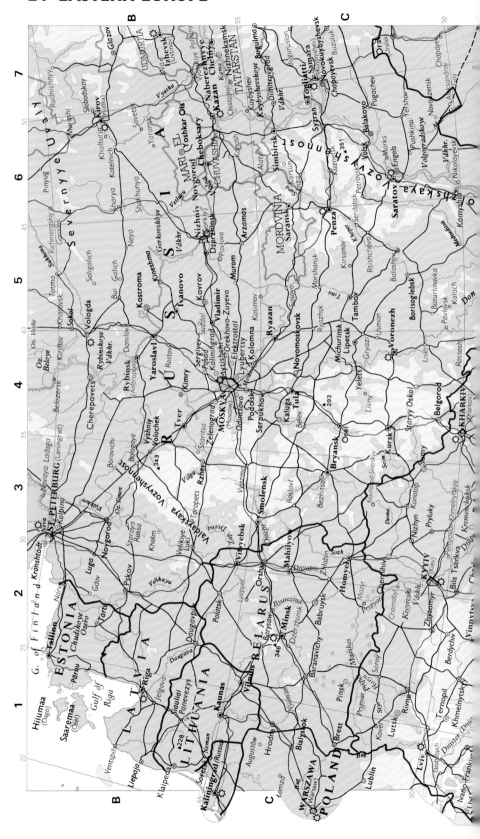

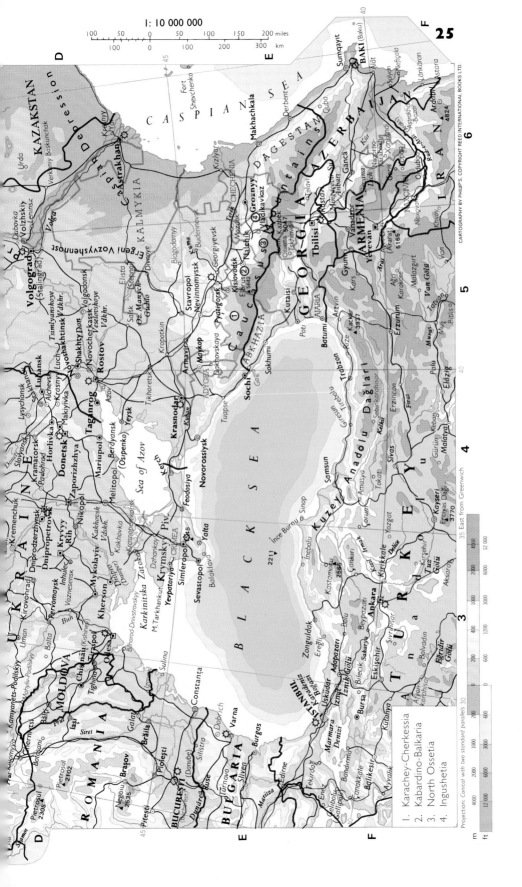

25

1 : 10 000 000

CARTOGRAPHY BY PHILIP'S. COPYRIGHT REED INTERNATIONAL BOOKS LTD.

1. Karachey-Cherkessia
2. Kabardino-Balkaria
3. North Ossetia
4. Ingushetia

Projection: Conical with two standard parallels 30

35 East from Greenwich

CASPIAN SEA

BLACK SEA

Sea of Azov

KAZAKSTAN

UKRAINE

MOLDOVA

ROMANIA

BULGARIA

TURKEY

GEORGIA

AZERBAIJAN

ARMENIA

IRAN

DAGESTAN

KALMYKIA

CHECHENIA

Caucasus Mountains

Anadolu Dağları

Kuzey

Volgograd (Stalingrad)
Astrakhan
Rostov
Krasnodar
Stavropol
Sochi
Novorossiysk
Tbilisi
Yerevan
BAKI (Baku)
Sumqayıt
Makhachkala
Grozny
Vladikavkaz
Nalchik
Kutaisi
Batumi
Trabzon
Erzurum
Ankara
İstanbul
Bursa
Odesa
Chişinău
BUCUREŞTI
Varna
Burgas
Constanța

C   B   A

ATLANTIC OCEAN

GREENLAND

ARCTIC

Svalbard

Barents Sea

Novaya Zemlya

Kara Sea

Arctic Circle

ICELAND

D

Murmansk

Vorkuta

Yenisey

UNITED KINGDOM

NORWAY

White Sea

Arkhangelsk

Salekhard

Ob

R U

E

LONDON

North Sea

SWEDEN

FINLAND

ST. PETERSBURG

Nizhniy Novgorod

Perm

Yekaterinburg

Irtysh

FRANCE

PARIS

GERMANY

Berlin

Warsaw

MOSCOW

Kazan

Ufa

Chelyabinsk

Omsk

E u r o p e

Prague

Vienna

ITALY

Rome

Belgrade

UKRAINE

Danube

Volga

Samara

Pavlodar

Seme

F

Odessa

Athens

Black Sea

ISTANBUL

Bursa

Don

Rostov

Volgograd

Astrakhan

KAZAKSTAN

Karaganda

Izmir

TURKEY

Ankara

GEORGIA

Tbilisi

Aral Sea

Syrdarya

L. Balkhash

Konya

Yerevan

AZERBAIJAN

Baku

UZBEKISTAN

Tashkent

Alma Ata

SINI

Nicosia

Adana

ARMENIA

Caspian Sea

Tabriz

TURKMENISTAN

Samarkand

Bishkek

KYRGYZSTAN

CYPRUS

Beirut

Aleppo

Mosul

Ashkhabad

TAJIKISTAN

Kashi

UIO

G

LIBYA

Mediterranean Sea

Alexandria

ISRAEL

LEBANON

Damascus

SYRIA

Euphrates

Mashhad

Dushanbe

Hotan

CAIRO

Jerusalem

Amman

JORDAN

IRAQ

Baghdad

Basra

IRAN

TEHRÂN

Esfahân

Herât

Kâbul

Islamabad

JAMMU & KASHMIR

EGYPT

Suez

Nile

KUWAIT

Kuwait

Shiraz

Zâhedân

AFGHANISTAN

Qandahâr

Faisalabad

Lahore

Aswân

SAUDI ARABIA

The Gulf

BAHRAIN

Riyadh

QATAR

Al Manâmah

Doha

Abu Dhabi

UNITED ARAB EMIRATES

Muscat

PAKISTAN

DELHI

New Delhi

Jaipur

Lucknow

H

Port Sudan

Jedda

Medina

Mecca

G. of Oman

KARACHI

Indus

Kanpur

Varanasi

I N D I

SUDAN

Khartoum

Red Sea

Muscat

Ahmadabad

Vadodara

Indore

Bhopal

Nagpur

ERITREA

San'a

YEMEN

Aden

OMAN

Arabian Sea

Surat

BOMBAY

Pune

Hyderabad

J

DJIBOUTI

G. of Aden

Socotra (Yemen)

Addis Ababa

ETHIOPIA

SOMALI REP.

Lakshadweep Is. (India)

Bangalore

MAD

UGANDA

L. Victoria

A f r i c a

Madurai

K

ZAÏRE

KENYA

Nairobi

Mogadishu

Equator

I N D I A N

MALDIVES

Male

Colombo

SRI

O C

TANZANIA

Mombasa

Dar es Salaam

SEYCHELLES

L

ZAMBIA

MALAWI

Aldabra Is. (Seychelles)

Amirante Is. (Seychelles)

Victoria

Chagos Arch. (U.K.)

Projection: Bonne 30

6   7   40   8   Hanoi ● Capital Cities   9   60   10   70   East from Greenwich   80   11

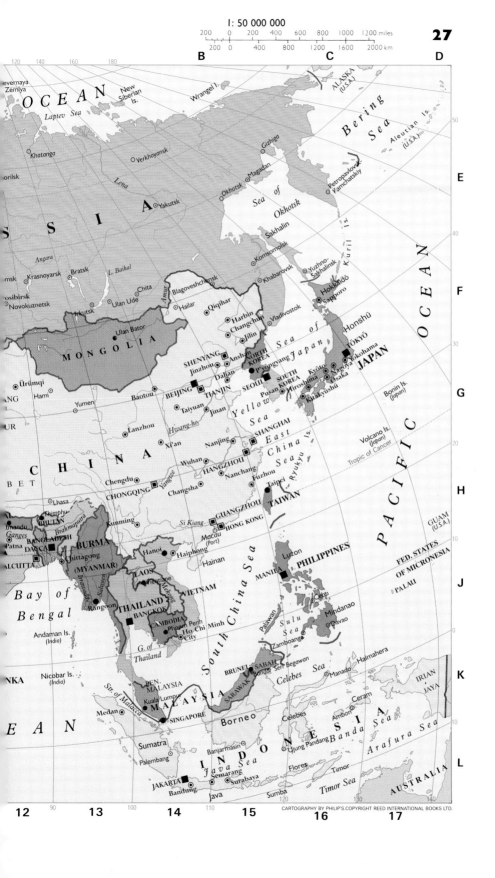

1: 50 000 000

200   0   200   400   600   800   1000   1200 miles

200   0   400   800   1200   1600   2000 km

OCEAN

Severnaya Zemlya

New Siberian Is.

Wrangel I.

ALASKA (U.S.A.)

Laptev Sea

○ Khatanga

○ Verkhoyansk

Gizhiga

Bering Sea

Aleutian Is. (U.S.A.)

○ Norilsk

Lena

○ Yakutsk

Okhotsk○ Magadan

Sea of Okhotsk

Petropavlovsk-Kamchatskiy

○ msk   *Angara*   Krasnoyarsk   Bratsk   *L. Baikal*

Komsomolsk

○ Khabarovsk

Yuzhno-Sakhalinsk

Sakhalin

○ osibirsk   ○ Novokuznetsk   ○ Irkutsk   ○ Ulan Ude   ○ Chita

Amur

○ Hailar

○ Qiqihar

Harbin

Vladivostok

Kuril Is.

Hokkaidō

Sapporo

S I A

S S I A

○ Ulan Bator

M O N G O L I A

Changchun

Jilin

Sea of Japan

Honshū

○ Ürümqi   ○ Hami

SHENYANG   Anshan   NORTH KOREA

Pyongyang

TŌKYŌ

Nagoya Yokohama

JAPAN

Jinzhou

Dalian

SEOUL

SOUTH KOREA

Kyōto

Osaka

○ Yumen

○ Baotou

BEIJING   TIANJIN

Pusan

Hiroshima

Kitakyūshū

ANG   Taiyuan

Jinan

Yellow Sea

Bonin Is. (Japan)

○ Lanzhou

Hwang-ho

Xi'an   Nanjing

SHANGHAI

East China Sea

C H I N A

BET   Chengdu

Yangtze

Wuhan   HANGZHOU

Nanchang

Fuzhou

Volcano Is. (Japan)

○ Lhasa

CHONGQING   Changsha

Taipei

Tropic of Cancer

Ryukyu Is.

Thimphu○

BHUTAN

Kunming

Si Kiang

GUANGZHOU

TAIWAN

○ tmandu   *Brahmaputra*

HONG KONG

GUAM (U.S.A.)

Ganges

BANGLADESH

Macau (Port)

○ Patna   DACCA

Chittagong

BURMA (MYANMAR)

Hanoi

Haiphong

Luzon

PHILIPPINES

FED. STATES OF MICRONESIA

LCUTTA○   *Irrawaddy*

LAOS

Hainan

MANILA

PALAU

Bay of

Salween

Vientiane

VIETNAM

Cebu

○ *Bengal*

Rangoon

THAILAND

BANGKOK

Mekong

Mindanao

Davao

Andaman Is. (India)

CAMBODIA

Phnom Penh

Ho Chi Minh City

Palawan

Sulu Sea

Zamboanga

G. of Thailand

South China Sea

Halmahera

NKA   Nicobar Is. (India)

BRUNEI   SABAH

Bandar Seri Begawan

Celebes Sea

○ Manado

IRIAN JAYA

PEN. MALAYSIA

SARAWAK

Kuala Lumpur

M A L A Y S I A

○ Medan

SINGAPORE

Borneo

Celebes

Ceram

Ambon○

I N D O N E S I A

Arafura Sea

E A N

Sumatra

Banjarmasin

Ujung Pandang

Banda Sea

Palembang

Java Sea

Semarang

Flores

Timor

Timor Sea

JAKARTA   Bandung

Surabaya

Java

Sumba

AUSTRALIA

P A C I F I C   O C E A N

12   90   13   100   14   110   15   16   120   17   130   140

CARTOGRAPHY BY PHILIP'S.COPYRIGHT REED INTERNATIONAL BOOKS LTD.

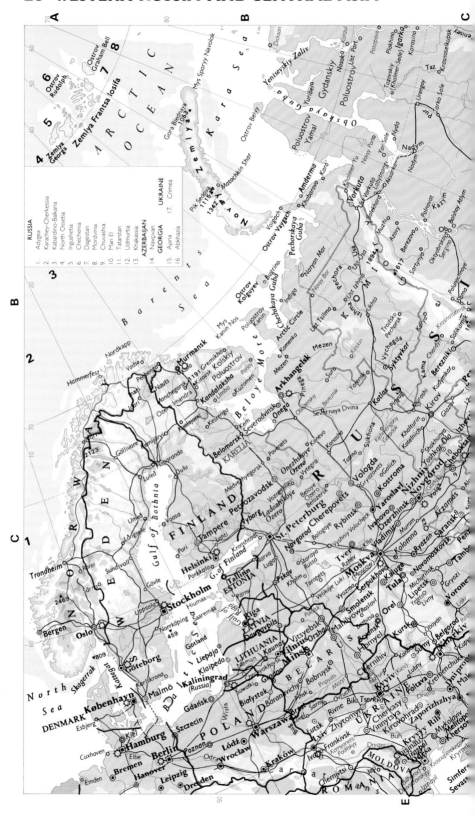

RUSSIA
1. Adygea
2. Karachey-Cherkessia
3. Kabardino-Balkana
4. North Ossetia
5. Ingushetia
6. Chechenia
7. Dagestan
8. Mordvinia
9. Chuvashia
10. Mari El
11. Tatarstan
12. Udmurtia
13. Khakassia

AZERBAIJAN
14. Naxçıvan

GEORGIA
15. Ajaria
16. Abkhazia

UKRAINE
17. Crimea

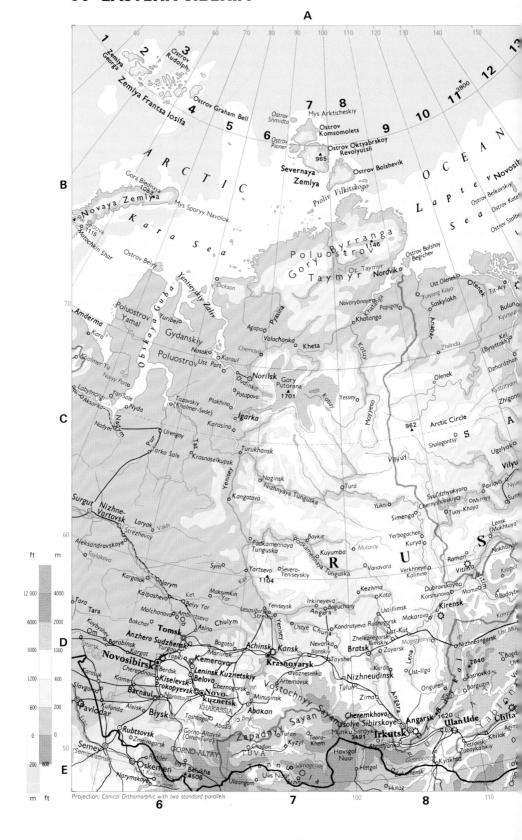

A

1
2
3
Zemlya
Georga
Ostrov
Rudolph
Zemlya Frantsa Iosifa
Ostrov Graham Bell
4
5
6
7
8
9
10
11 3800
12

Ostrov
Shmidta
Mys Arkticheskiy
Ostrov
Komsomolets
Ostrov
Pioner
Ostrov Oktyabrskoy
Revolyutsii
965
Severnaya
Zemlya
Ostrov Bolshevik

ARCTIC
OCEAN
Laptev Novosib

Gora Blednaya
1063 a
Novaya Zemlya a
Mys Sporyy Navolok
Proliv Vilkitskogo
Ostrov Belkovskiy
Ostrov Kote

B

Pik Sedova
1115
Matochkin Shar
Kara Sea
Ostrov Belyy
Dickson
PoluoByrranga
Goryostrov 1146
Taymyr
Ostrov Bolshoy
Begichev
Ostrov Stalb
Sea
Nordvik

70
Amderma
Kara
Poluostrov
Yamal
Yuribey
Yeniseyskiy Zaliv
Obskaya Guba
Gydanskiy
Poluostrov
Agapa
Prasina
Volochanka
Kheta
Khatanga
Popigay
Novorybnoye
Khatanga
Ust Olenek
Olenek Tit-Ary
Yuryung Kaya
Saskylakh
Anabar
Bulun
Kyusyur
Kel
(Bysyttakh)
Zhlinda
Dzhardzhan
Kystatyam

Khalmer Yu
Nowy Port
Labytnangi
Aksarka
Nyda
Nosok
Karaul
Ust Port
Chernaya
Norilsk
Gory
Putorana
1701
Yessey
Olenek
Zhigans

C

Nadym
Nar'm
Pur
Taz
Yarka Sale
Urengoy
Krasnoselkupsk
Tazovskiy
(Khalmer-Sede)
Plakhino
Potapovo
Dudinka
Igarka
Karasino
Turukhansk
Moyero
Kotuy
962
Arctic Circle
Shologontsy
Vilyuy
Ugolyako
Vilyu
S A

Surgut
Nizhne-
Vartovsk
Laryak
Vakh
Strezhevoy
Aleksandrovskoye
Taylakova
Kargasok
Narym
Taz
Yenisey
Noginsk
Nizhnyaya Tunguska
Kangotovo
Tura
Podkamennaya
Tunguska
Baykit
Kuyumba
Vanavara
Mutoray
Yukti
Simengo
Chernyshevskiy
Syul'dzhyukyoro
Tuoy-Khaya
Pavlovo
Mirnyy
Nyu
Sun
Yerbogachen
Kurya
Verkhneye
Kalinino
Roman
Vitim
Nokh
Kropot
Atil

60
Ket
Belyy Yar
Maksimkin
Yar
Kalpashevo
Molchanovo
Ambortsevo
Bakchar
Kuybyshev
Barabinsk
Kargat
Yurga
Tomsk
Asino
Chulym
Bogotol
Mariinsk
Achinsk
Kansk
Yartsevo
Severo-
Yeniseyskiy
1104
Sym
Yeniseysk
Strelka
Lesosibirsk
Angara
Boguchany
Ust-Ilimsk
Kezhma
Kato
Dubrovskoye
Korshunova
Makarovo
Ust-Kut
Magistralnyy
Kirensk
Karalu
Mama
Bodaybo

ft   m
12 000 4000
6000 2000

Tara
Novosibirsk
Om
Kargasuk
Karasuk
Tatarsk
Kamen
Cherepanovo
Novoaltaysk
Iskitim
Berdsk
Topki
Kemerovo
Leninsk Kuznetsky
Belovo
Kiselevsk
Prokopyevsk
Novo-
kuznetsk
Chernogorsk
Minusinsk
Abakan
Artemovsk
Voznesenka
Vostochnyy Sayan
Nevanka
Ilanskiy
Tayshet
Tulun
Zima
Karda
Lena
Ust-Ilga
Onguren
455
Sosnovka
Borguzin
2840
Nizhneangarsk
Bagd

D
3000 1000
1200 400

Novosibirsk
Barnaul
Biysk
Slavgorod
Kulunda
Aleisk
Zmeinogorsk
Gorno-Altaysk
(Oirot-Tura)
Tashtagol
Abaza
Turan
Kyzyl
Toora-
Khem
Minusinsk
Abakan
KHAKASSIA
Zapadnyy
Sayan
HKHASSIA
Cheremkhovo
Usolye Sibirskoye
Angarsk
Irkutsk
1620
Sardyka
3491
Kultuk
Slyudyanka
Ulan Ude
Chita
Khilok
Petrovsk-
Zabaykalskiy
ablon

600 200
0 0

Pavlodar
Semey
(Semipalatinsk)
Ridder
Oskemen
Narymskoye
Belukha
4506
Kamennogorsk
Zyryn
Kosh-Agach
GORNO-ALTAY
TUVA
Samagaltay
Erzin
Hovsgol
Nuur
Hatgal
Kyakhta
Gusnoozersk
Petropavlovka

E
200 600
Uvs Nuur
Ulaangom
Hutag

m ft

6
7
100
8
110

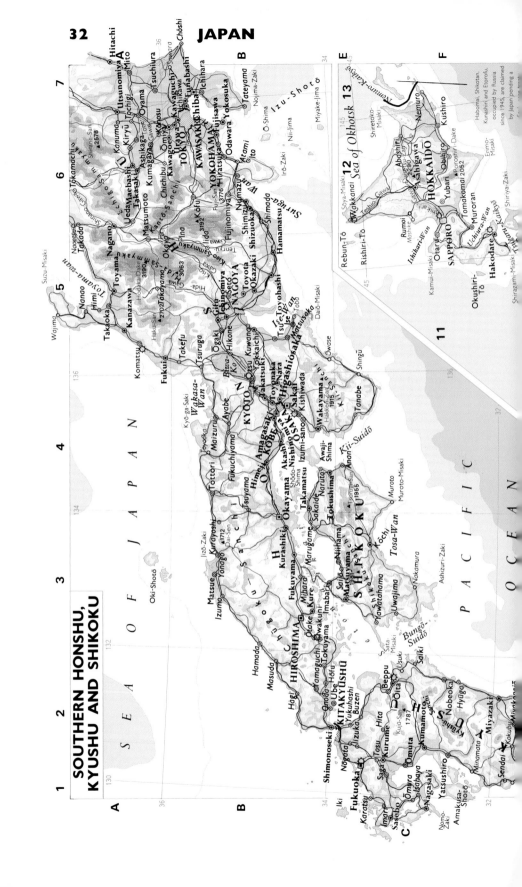

SOUTHERN HONSHU, KYUSHU AND SHIKOKU

SEA OF JAPAN

PACIFIC OCEAN

Sea of Okhotsk

HOKKAIDO

SAPPORO

TOKYO
YOKOHAMA
KAWASAKI
CHIBA

NAGOYA
KYOTO
OSAKA
KOBE

HIROSHIMA

SHIKOKU

KYŪSHŪ

KITAKYŪSHŪ

Fukuoka

Nagasaki

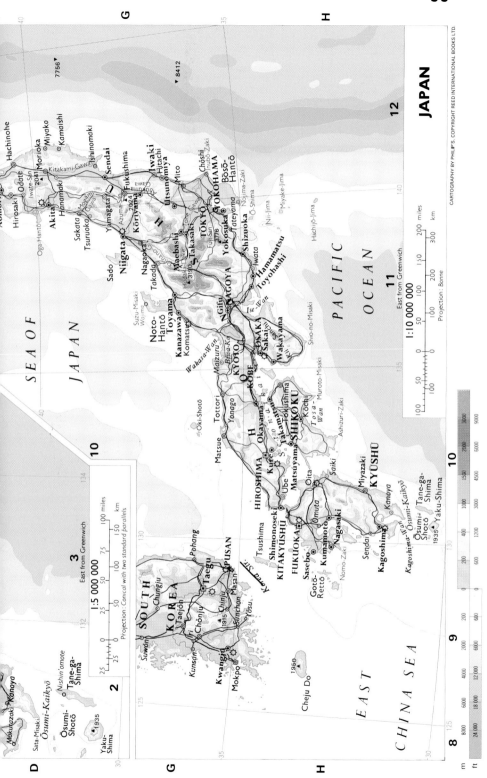

JAPAN

SEA OF

JAPAN

PACIFIC

OCEAN

1:10 000 000

East from Greenwich

Projection: Bonne

12

11

10

9

8

SOUTH

KOREA

EAST

CHINA SEA

7756 ▼

▼ 8412

Hachinohe
Odate
Miyako
Kamaishi
Morioka
Iwate-San
2041
Hanamaki
Ishinomaki
Kitakami Gawa
Sendai
Fukushima
Iwaki
Hitachi
Utsunomiya
Mito
Chōshi
Inubō-Zaki
Bōsō-Hantō
Nojima-Zaki
Ō-Shima
Miyake-Jima
Hachijō-Jima
Nii-Jima

Hirosaki
Akita
Hachirō-Gata
Oga-Hantō
Sakata
Tsuruoka
Yamagata
Kōriyama
Niigata
Azuma-San
2024
Nagaoka
Shibata
Takasaki
Maebashi
3190
Sado
Takada
Toyama
Noto-Hantō
Kanazawa
Komatsu
Suzu-Misaki
Wajima
Gifu
NAGOYA
Ise-Wan
Wakasa-Wan
Maizuru
KYŌTO
OSAKA
Sakai
Wakayama
KOBE
Okayama
HIROSHIMA
Kure
Tottori
Yonago
Matsue
Oki-Shotō
Oki-Shoto

TOKYO
YOKOHAMA
Fuji-San
3776
Yokosuka
Tateyama
Shizuoka
Iwata
Hamamatsu
Toyohashi

Takamatsu
Tokushima
SHIKOKU
Matsuyama
Kōchi
Tosa-Wan
Ashizuri-Zaki
Muroto-Misaki
Shio-no-Misaki

Shimonoseki
Ube
Ōita
Saiki
Miyazaki
KITAKYUSHU
FUKUOKA
Ōmuta
Kumamoto
Sasebo
Gotō-Rettō
Nagasaki
Nomo-Zaki
Sendai
KYŪSHŪ
Kanoya
Kagoshima
Ōsumi-Shotō
Tane-ga-Shima
1935 Yaku-Shima
Ōsumi-Kaikyō
Kagoshima-Wan
Ōsumi-Kaikyō

Tsushima
Pusan
Masan
Chinju
Yōsu
Sunchon
Kwangju
1915
Mokpo
Cheju Do
1950
Chunju
Iri
Chŏnju
Kunsan
Suwŏn
Taejŏn
Taegu
Pohang
Chungju
Korea Str.

Mokuzazaki
Kanoya
Sata-Misaki
Ōsumi-Kaikyō
Nishin'omote
Tane-ga-Shima
Ōsumi-Shotō
Yaku-Shima
1935

1:5 000 000

East from Greenwich

Projection: Conical with two standard parallels

0   25   50   75   100 miles

0   25   50   100   150   km

m   ft
9000   3000
6000   2000
4500   1500
3000   1000
1200   400
600   200
0   0
600   200
2000   6000
6000   12 000
12 000   18 000
18 000   24 000
24 000   8000

1:5 000 000

0   50   100   150   200 miles

0   100   200   300   km

CARTOGRAPHY BY PHILIP'S. COPYRIGHT REED INTERNATIONAL BOOKS LTD.

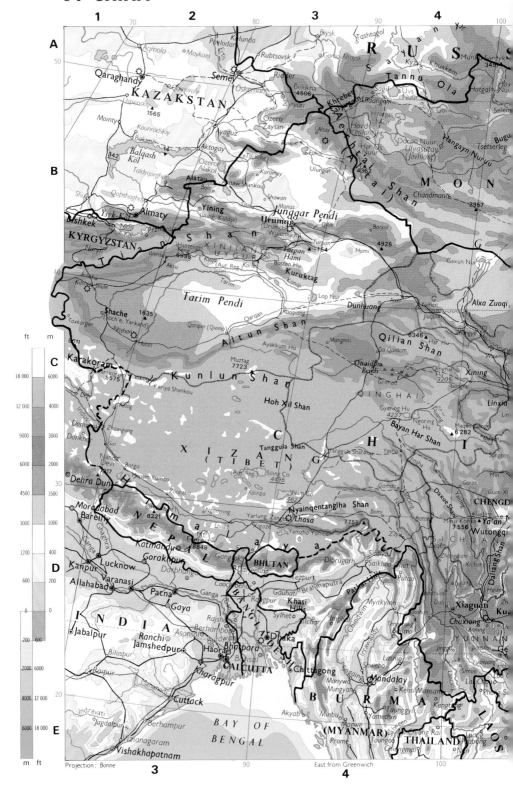

1 : 20 000 000

100   0   100   200   300   400   500 miles

100   0   200   400   600   800 km

5   110   6   120   7   130   8

Cheremkhovo 1620
Angarsk
kutsk   I   Ozero Baykal   Bukachdcha   Shimanovsk
Ulan Ude   Yablonovyy Khrebet   Chita   Sretensk   Svobodnyy   Chegdomyn   2640   A
Babushkin   455   Khilok   Nerchinsk   Shilka   Argun   Yile huli Shan   Blagoveshchensk   Ozero Boton
Kyakhta   Olovyannaya   Borzya   Zabaykalsk   Xiao Hinggan Ling   Obluchye Birobidzhan
Hentiyn   Nuruu   Ondörhaan   Matad   Aksha   Hulun Nur   Hailar   Butha Qi   HEILONGJIANG   Yichun   Hegang   Hamusi   Khabarovsk   B
Ulaanbaatar   (Ulan Bator)   Kerulen   Choybalsan   Buir   Nur   Qiqihar   Hailun   Shuangyashan   Dalnerechensk
Dzuunmod   Ondörhaan   Arxan   Solon   Horqin Youyi Qianqi   Baicheng   Mudanjiang   Kirovka   HARBIN   B
Dalandzadgad   Saynshand   Dzamin Üüd   Erenhot   1949   Tongliao   Da'an   Changchun   Jilin   Ussuriysk   Vladivostok   Artem
Bayan Bogd   Sonid Youqi   Duolun   Chifeng   Fuxin   Siping   Liaoyuan   Dunhua   Yanji   Hunchun   Najin   Chongjin
Mumingan Lianheqi   Chengde   Jinzhou   SHENYANG   Benxi   Fushun   Tonghua   1744   NORTH   40
Hohhot   Jining   Zhangjiakou   Xuanhua   Yingkou   Anshan   Liaoyang   Dandong   KOREA   Hamhung
BAOTOU   Datong   Tong-Xian   Qinhuangdao   Liaodong Wan   Sinuiju   P'yongyang   Wonsan   Hungnam
Mu Us Shamo   3015   BEIJING   (Peking)   Hangu   TIANJIN   Tangshan   Korea Bay   Chinnampo   Haeju   Kangnung
THE GREAT WALL   Shijiazhuang   Baoding   (Tientsin)   Bo Hai   Yantai   SEOUL   Inch'on   Andong
Yinchuan   Wuzhong   TAIYUAN   Yangquan   Jinan   Zibo   Weifang   Kaesong   Taejon   SOUTH   Taegu
NINGXIA   HUIZU   Fenyang   Yuci   Xingtai   Handan   Boshan   Ye Xian   QINGDAO   Kunsan   KOREA   Pusan
Lanzhou   Qingyang   Changzhi   Anyang   Jining   SHANDONG   Jiao Xian   YELLOW   Choñju   Masan
Pinghang   Tongchuan   Longji   Liaozui   Kaifeng   Shangqiu   Xuzhou   Hai'an   Lianyungang   SEA   Kwangju   Tsushima Str.
Tianshui   Baoji   Luoyang   Zhengzhou   Shangshui   JIANGSU   Mokpo   Fukuoka
Qin Ling   4107   XI'AN   Xuchang   Huainan   Bengbu   Zhenjiang   Changzhou   Cheju   Sasebo
HENAN   Nanyang   Zhumadian   Huai   NANJING   Wuxi   Suzhou   Cheju Do   1950   Nagasaki
Hanzhong   Ankang   Xiangfan   Xinyang   Hefei   ANHUI   Wuhu   SHANGHAI   JAPAN
Daba Shan   Fengjie   Yichang   Zigui   Jingling   WUHAN   Anqing   Jiaxing   Shaoxing
Nanchong   Wanxian   Shashi   Huangshi   Jiujiang   Hangzhou   Ningbo   EAST
Hechuan   Beibei   Jinshi   Dongting Hu   Poyang Hu   Jingdezhen   Qu Xian   Linhai   CHINA
Zigong   CHONGQING   Changde   Nanchang   Tunxi   Wenzhou   SEA
Luzhou   Yiyang   Changsha   Shangrao   Yingtan   Lishui
2494   Xiangtan   Zhuzhou   Ji'an   JIANGXI   Xian'ou   Ningde   30
Zunyi   HUNAN   Shaoyang   Nanping   Fuzhou   Okinawa   7507
GUIZHOU   Zhenyuan   Hengyang   Wuyi Shan   FUJIAN   Ryukyu-Retto
Guiyang   Anshun   Duyun   Guilin   Chen Xian   Ganzhou   Quanzhou   Taibei   (Taipei)   Jilong   Yilan
Liuzhou   Shaoguan   Zhangzhou   Xinzhu   Miaoli   Taizhong   Sakishima-Gunto
GUANGXI   Mei Xian   Xiamen   Zhanghua   Jiayi   TAIWAN   Tropic of Cancer
ZHUANGZU   Wuzhou   GUANGDONG   Chao'an   3950
Nanning   Pingxiang   Sanshui   GUANGZHOU   (Canton)   Shantou   Tainan   Taidong   Pingdong
Foshan   Jiangmen   Gaoxiong
Lang Son   Qinzhou   Macau   Kowloon   Bashi Channel
HANOI   Beihai   Hong Kong   Batan Is.
Haiphong   G. of   Zhanjiang   Maoming
Tonkin   Leizhou   SOUTH   CHINA
Haikou   Hainan Dao   SEA   E
Wuzhi Shan   1867   HAINAN   PHILIPPINES   Luzon   Laoag

5   110   6   7

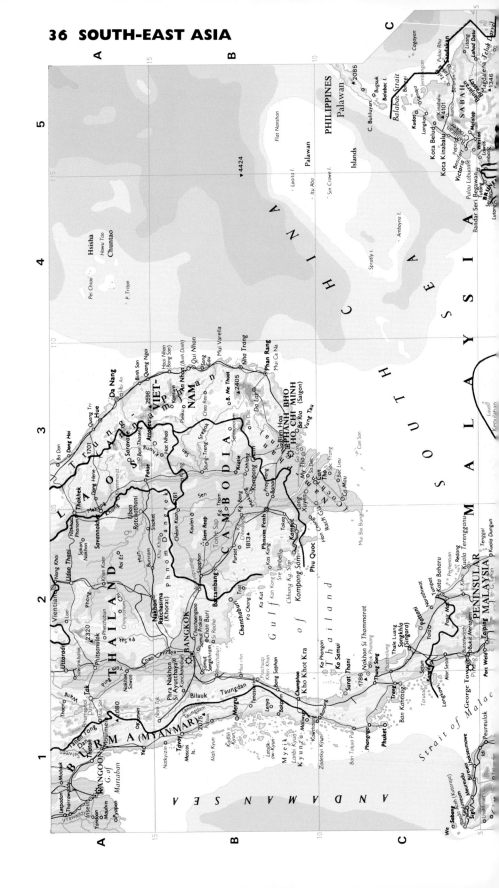

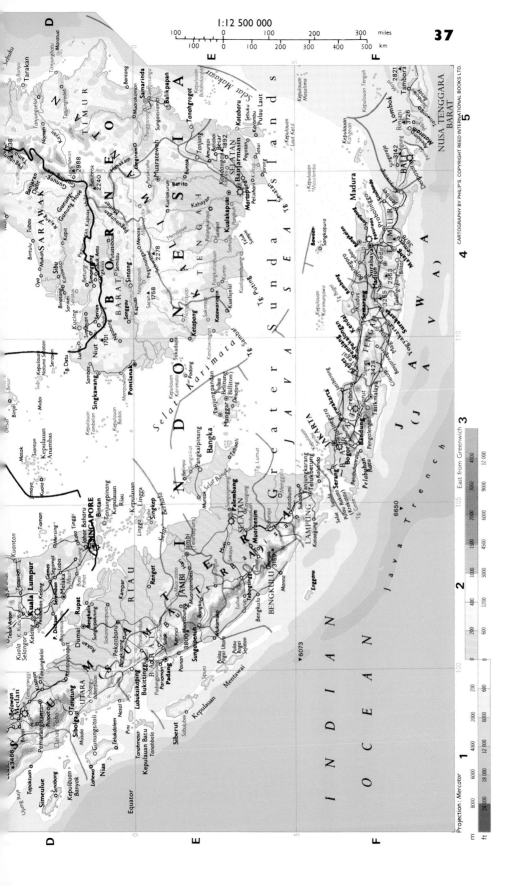

1:12 500 000

100   0   100   200   300   miles

100   0   100   200   300   400   500   km

Projection: Mercator

CARTOGRAPHY BY PHILIP'S. COPYRIGHT REED INTERNATIONAL BOOKS LTD.

East from Greenwich

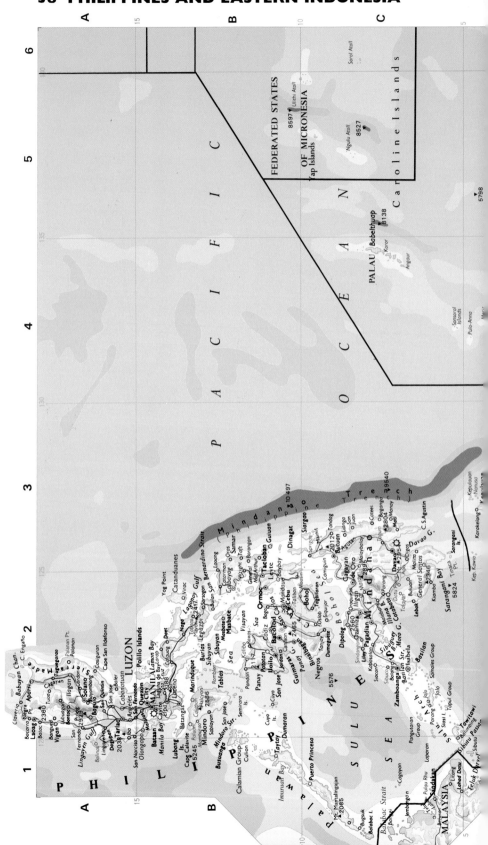

1:12 500 000

100   0   100   200   300 miles
100   0 100 200 300 400 500 km

PAPUA NEW GUINEA

CARTOGRAPHY BY PHILIP'S. COPYRIGHT REED INTERNATIONAL BOOKS LTD.

East from Greenwich

Projection Mercator

IRIAN JAYA

Pegunungan Maoke
Pegunungan Sudirman   Puncak
Puncak   5029   4750
Jaya 4702

Merauke

C E L E B E S

S E A

Halmahera

SULAWESI
(CELEBES)

SELATAN

TENGGARA

TENGAH

UTARA

M O L U C C A   S E A

S E R A M   S E A

Seram (Ceram)

B A N D A   S E A

MALUKU

Buru

A R A F U R A   S E A

Ambon

Kepulauan Aru

Kepulauan Tanimbar

TIMOR
TIMUR

Lesser Sunda Islands

NUSA TENGGARA TIMUR

Flores

Sumbawa

Sumba

F L O R E S   S E A

S a w u   S e a

Kupang

Equator

Selat Makasar

Kepulauan Sangihe

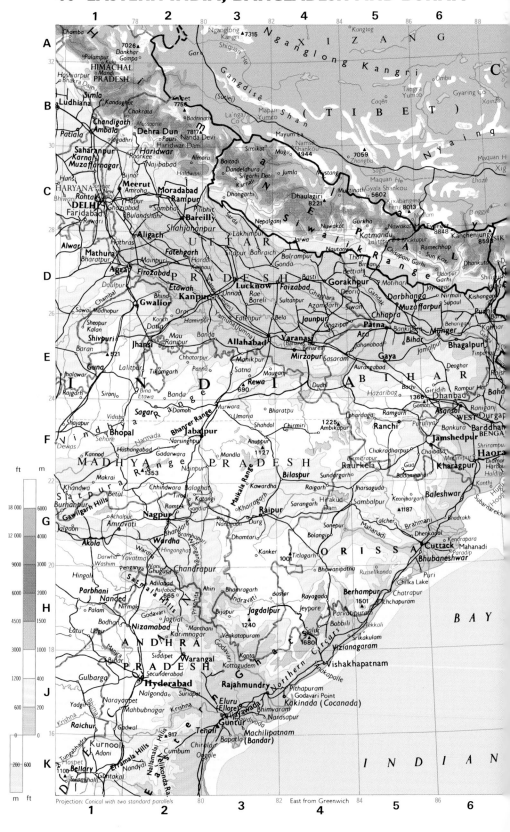

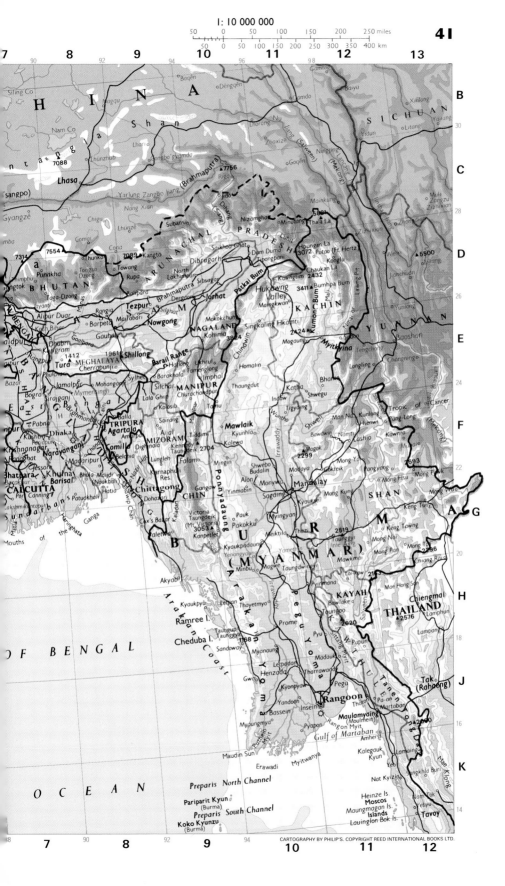

1 : 10 000 000

50 0 50 100 150 200 250 miles

50 0 50 100 150 200 250 300 350 400 km

7 **8** **9** **10** **11** **12** **13**

90 92 94 96 98

Siling Co

C H I N A

B

Bagên

Dêngqên

Nagqu

Nam Co

Shan

Nu

Jiang (Salween)

Biyu

Xinlong

SICHUAN

Litang

Yalong

B

30

Lhasa

7088

ntang

Lhünzhub

Gongbo'gyamda

Dhorong

Zhabxize

Ninglong

Goqên

Yidun

Chamdo

(Mekong)

Jomda

Baiyu

30

Nang Xian

Yarlung Zangbo Jiang (Brahmaputra)

Chigu

7756

Rigaŭ

Jido

Mainkung

Zhonghua

Litaxixian

Mulé

Zoigê

Zhongdian

C

28

sangpo)

Gyangzê

mba

Comai

Cona

Lhünze

Subansiri

Nizamghat

Minutang

Thala La

Zayü

Jianchuan

Yunlong

28

7314

7554

7088

Kangto

Tawang

ARUNACHAL PRADESH

Saikhoa Ghat

Dibrugarh

Dom Duma

Dhongbani

Lohit

Hpungan La

Chaukan La

Konglu

Putao (Ft. Hertz)

3072

Weki

5500

D

26

BHUTAN

Thunkar

Tongsa Dzong

Rupa

North Lakhimpur

Sibsagar

Kawngtum

Bumhpa Bum

2432

Lawa Pit

Tengchong

D

Thimphu

Punakha

Tôga-Dzong

Balipara

Brahmaputra

Jorhat

Hukawng Valley

3411

Malngkwan

KACHIN

Singkaling Hkamti

Mogaung

2424

Myitkyina

Baoshan

26

Alipur Duar

Tezpur

Silghat

M

Mokokchung

NAGALAND

Kohima

3824

Chindwin

YUNNAN

Changning

E

Kuch Bihar

Mairabari

Nowgong

Gauhati

Homalin

Bhamo

Longling

E

24

Dhubri

Goalpara

Barpeta

Shillong

1961

Barail Range

Hailong

Likhrul

Imphal

Katha

Shwegu

Mong Yu

Tengchong

Tropic of Cancer

24

Turu

MEGHALAYA

Cherrapunji

1412

Barakhola

Tamenglong

Thaungdut

Tigyaing

Man Na

Kunlong

Pang-Long

Jamalpur

Sylhet

Mohangonj

Silchar

MANIPUR

Wuntho

Shwebo

Shweli

Bawdwin

Namtu

Hsenwi

Lashio

Kawnra

Muniai

F

22

Mymensingh

Lala Ghat

Churachandpur

Tiddim

Mawlaik

Homalin

Mogok

2299

Gokteik

Pangyang

7693

Mong Pawk

F

Bogra

Sirajganj

Karimganj

Barddhaman

Aijal

MIZORAM

Kyunhla

Kalewa

Mingin

Shwebo

Madaya

Mong Hsu

Mong Pawk

Pabna

Kushtia

Dhaka

Agartala

TRIPURA

Dighnala

Kennedy

2704

Falam

Alon

Budalin

Monywa

Mandalay

Mong Kung

SHAN

Keng Tawng

Mong Tai

Khulna

Narayanganj

Comilla

Belonia

CHIN

Gangaw

Yinmabin

Sagaing

Kyaukse

Mong Nai

Mong Tai

2296

Jessore

Barisal

Madaripur

Bhola Majid

Lunglei

Karnaphuli Res.

Victoria

Taungdeik

(Mt. Victoria)

3053

Pauk

Myingyan

Thazi

2519

Taunggyi

Inle Lake

Keng Tawng

Chiang Rai

G

CALCUTTA

Khulna

Chittagong

Dohazari

Kanpetlet

Kyaukpadaung

Meiktila

Yamethin

Mawkmai

Mong Pan

B U R M A

G

20

Par Canning

Noakhali

Hatia

Akyab

Kyaukpyu

Minbu

Magwe

Taungdwingyi

Pyinmana

KAYAH

(MYANMAR)

Mae Hong Son

20

Lakshmikantapur

Patuakhali

Ramree I.

Letpan

Thayetmyo

Prome

Toungoo

Bawlake

2620

2576

Chiengmai

Lamphun

H

18

OF BENGAL

Cheduba I.

Sandoway

Taunggup

Taunggyi

1168

Myanaung

Arakan Coast

Pegu Yoma

Pyu

Papun

THAILAND

Lampang

H

Myaungmya

Henzada

Letpadan

Tharrawaddy

Maduak

Tak (Rahaeng)

J

16

OCEAN

Bassein

Insein

Rangoon

Yandoon

Kyonpyaw

Pegu

Thaton

Moulmein

Maulamyaing

Pa-an

Martaban

J

Myoungmya

Pyapon

Rangon Myit

Gulf of Martaban

Amherst

2600

Preparis North Channel

Pariparit Kyun

(Burma)

Preparis South Channel

Koko Kyunzu

(Burma)

Maudin Sun

Erawadi

Myitwanya

Kalegauk Kyun

Yeb

Nat Kyizing

K

14

Heinze Is.

Moscos Is.

Maungmagan Is.

Lauinglon Bok Is.

Islands

Yebyu

Tavoy

Nam Tok

Lamaing

Mae Klong

K

14

7 **8** **9** **10** **11** **12**

88 90 92 94

CARTOGRAPHY BY PHILIP'S. COPYRIGHT REED INTERNATIONAL BOOKS LTD.

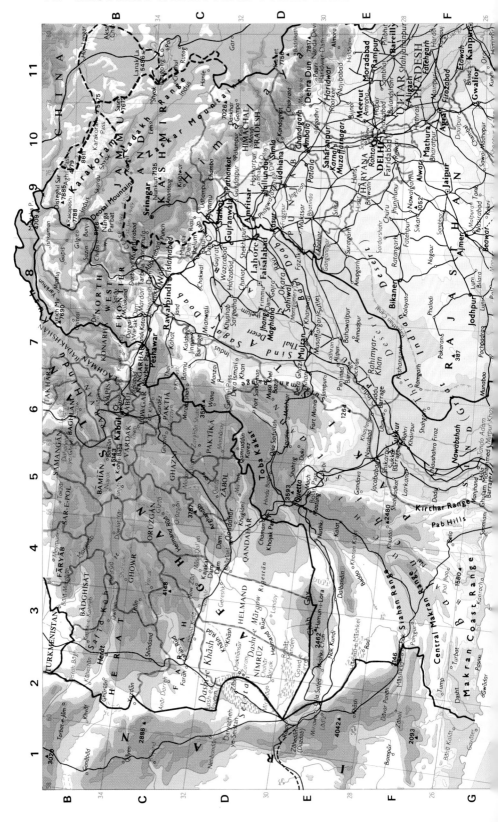

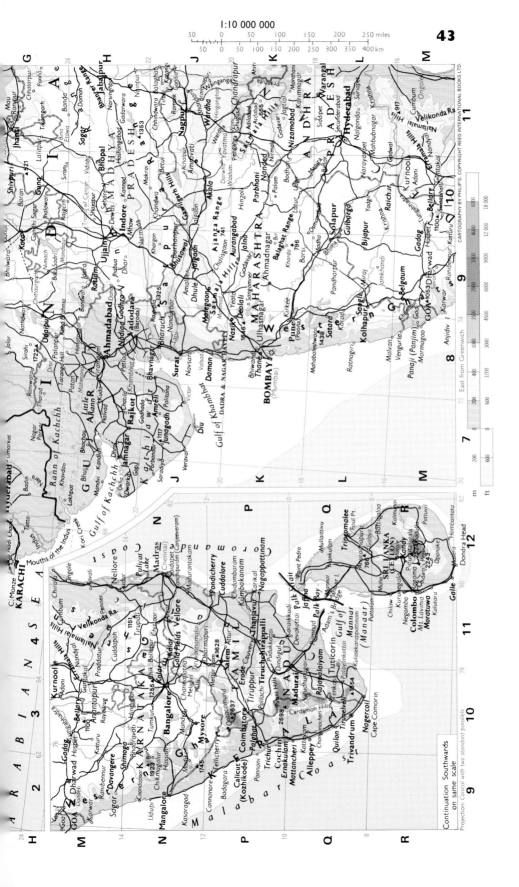

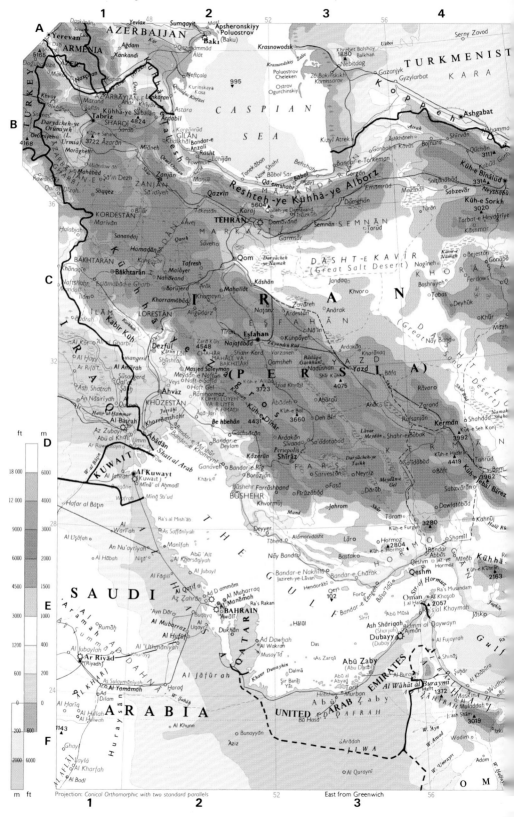

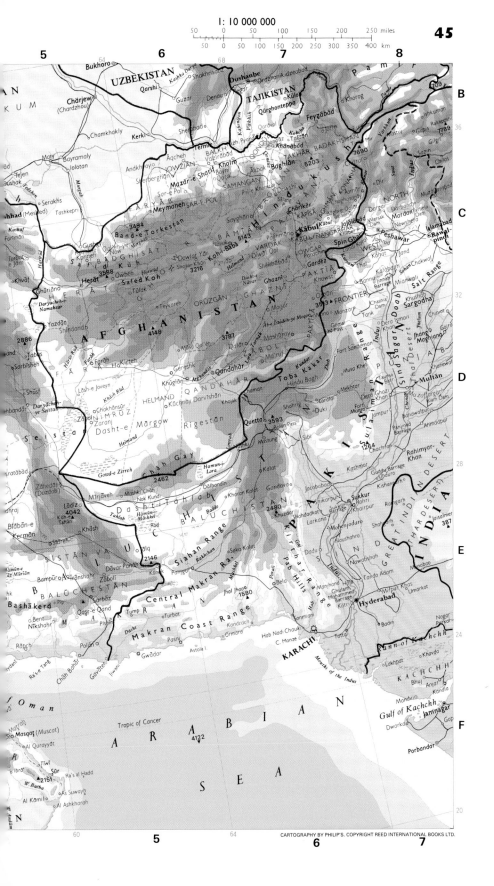

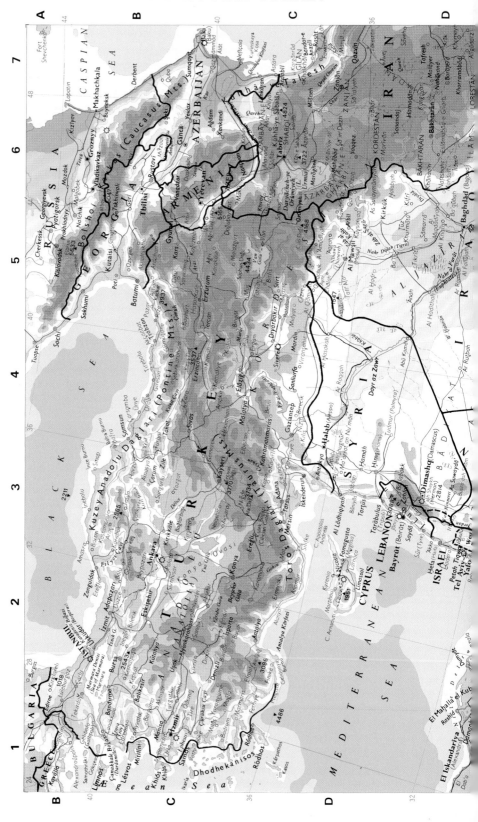

1:10 000 000

50   0   50   100   150   200   250 miles
50 0   50 100 150 200 250 300 350 400 km

THE GULF

MESOPOTAMIA

HUZESTĀN

Ahvāz

KUWAIT

Al Kuwayt (Kuwait)

Abādān

Shatt al-Arab

AL HIJĀRA

AN NAFŪD

JABAL SHAMMAR

NEJD

AS SUDŪR

Al 'Aramah

Ar Riyād (Riyadh)

SAUDI ARABIA

AD DAHNĀ

NEJD

RUB' AL KHALI

EL SHAM

SHAM

AT Tubayq

At Tih

Gebel el Tih

SINAI

RED SEA

EGYPT

Es Sahrâ esh Sharqiya

EL QĀHIRA (CAIRO)

El Gîza

Nahr en Nîl (Nile)

SUDAN

ES SAHRÂ EN NÛBIYA (NUBIAN DESERT)

Buheiret en Nâser (Lake Nasser)

Aswân

Bîr Shagâra

Muhammad Qol

Jiddah

Makkah (Mecca)

HIJĀZ

TIHĀMA

AL HIJĀZ

Aţ Ţā'if

AL HĀMAD

AL JIRĀN

Al Madīnah

Harrat Khaybar

East from Greenwich

Projection: Conical Orthomorphic with two standard parallels

CARTOGRAPHY BY PHILIP'S. COPYRIGHT REED INTERNATIONAL BOOKS LTD.

Division between Greeks and Turks
in Cyprus; Turks to the North.

m   ft
2000 6000   0 0   240 600   600 1200 3000 1500 4500 2000 6000 3000 9000 4000 12 000

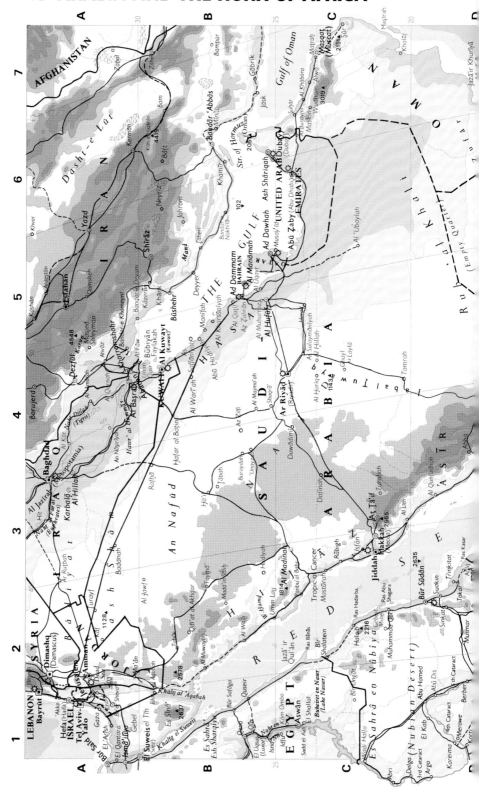

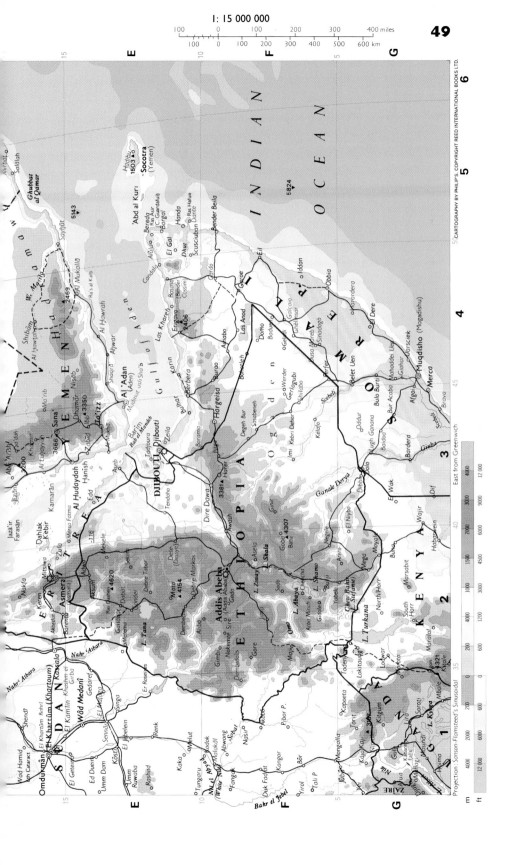

1: 15 000 000

100   0   100   200   300   400 miles
100   0   100   200   300   400   500   600 km

E   10   F   G

6
5
4
3
2
1

CARTOGRAPHY BY PHILIP'S. COPYRIGHT REED INTERNATIONAL BOOKS LTD.

I N D I A N   O C E A N

Socotra
(Yemen)
Hadibu
1503▲○

Abd al Kuri
E 824

Bereda
Ras Asir
Dhut C. Guardafui
Honda Bargal
Scuscuban Ras Hafun
Dante
Bender Beila

Ghubbat al Qamar

H A D R A M A W T

Saihut
5143
2469

W. Masila
Shubang
Al Howtah

Al Mukalla
Ra's al Kalb

G u l f   o f   A d e n

Candala
Bossaso Iddan
Bender Cassim
2406
Erigavo

El Gal

Las Khoreh Cardo Gracie Eil Idan
Karin Las Anod

Obbia

Ayiabo
Burao

M i j e r t e i n

Haruo
Barrara
Ali Jiao

Al 'Adan
(Aden)

3350
Ta'izz
Dhamar
3666

Sana
3200

Shaqra
Nisab
Aljwar

Y E M E N

Al Howrah

Y E M E N

Abd 'Arabiyi

Khamir
Madinat ush Sha'b

Berbera
Hargeisa

O g a d e n

Werder
Gerlogubi
Ghilalbo

Domo
Badue

Dusa Mareb
Ferfer
Ghelmsor
Sinadogo

El Dere

Mereta

Mahaddei Uen
Belet Uen

Ogaden

S O M A L I   R E P U B L I C

Giohar
Orsciek
Muqdisho
(Mogadishu)
Merca

Jaza'ir Farasan

Kamaran

Al Hudaydah
Hanish
Zabid
Al Mukha

D J I B O U T I

Obock
Tadjoura
Djibouti

Zeila

Mersa Fatma

Aseb
Edd
Assab

Tendaho

Borama

Jijiga

3381▲Hirer

Dire Dawa

Harer

Degeh Bur

Szoabeneh

Kebri Dehar

Keledo

Imi

E T H I O P I A

Awash

Addis Abeba
(Addis Ababa)

Dese
(Dessye)
-116
Debre Markos

Gobb 4307
Batu

Scebeli

Ganale Dorya

Dolo
El Wok

Dolo

Bur Acaba
Baidoa
Bulo Burti

Bardera

Brava

Sebeli

Giuba
Mahaddei Uen

Lugh Ganana
Oddur

Algoi

Mersa Teklai

Mitsiwa
Nokra

Asmera

4620
Ras Dashen
4154
Woizro
Debre Tabor

Aksum

Mekele

Gallabat

Debre Markos
Fiche
Gondar
Gialo

Gore
Jima

Nekemte Sire

Gimbi

Demta

Gore
Majig
Omo

Sada
L. Zreay
Giksela
Shala

L. Shamo
L. Abaya

Arbi Minch
Gidyeo
Yabelo

Chew Bahir
L. Stefanie

Arero

Negele

El Nyibo

Mega
Moyali
Buna

South Horr
North Horr

Mandera

Wajir
Habaswein

K E N Y A

L. Turkana

Marsabit

Lokwar

Lokitaung

Toden

Lowar
Koto

Moyale

Jo
Toro
Kitgum

L. Kwga
Soroti

Kapoeta
3187

U G A N D A

Torit

Mongalla
Kajo Kaji

Juba

Z A I R E

S U D A N

El-Kharrûm (Khartoum)
Omdurmân
El Kharrûm Bahri
4th Cataract

Wad Hamid
Shendt

Wâd Medanî

Kassala
Gedaref
Er Roseires

Sennar
El Getena
Ed Dueim
Kosti
Rashad
Singa

Umm Ruwaba

Nahr 'Atbara
Atbara

Barentu
Keren
Akordat
Agordat
Teseney
Metemma

I. Tana
Nahr 'Atbara

Nosir
Gedaref

El Kamlin
Khoshm el Girba

El Obeid
Melut
Rabak

Kaka
Renk

Tungaru

Malakâl
Kodok
Abwong
Nâsir

Pibor P.
Kongor
Bôr

Nil el Abyad
White Nile

Duk Fadiat
Tali P.
Tirol
Bahr el Jebel

Fangak

Baro

Nile
Nimule
Karuma Falls

East from Greenwich

Projection: Samson-Flamsteed's Sinusoidal

15   E   F   G

m   4000   3000   2000   1500   1000   4000   2000   200   0   200   4000
ft   12 000   9000   6000   4500   3000   1200   600   0   600   12 000

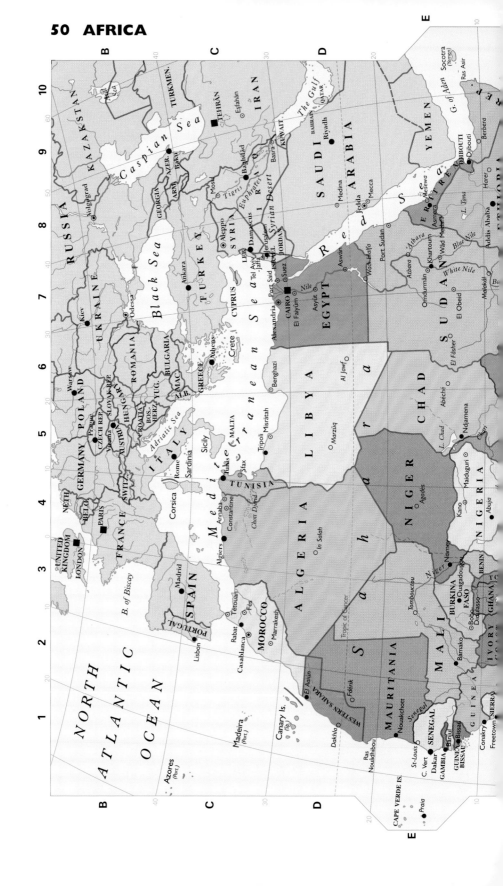

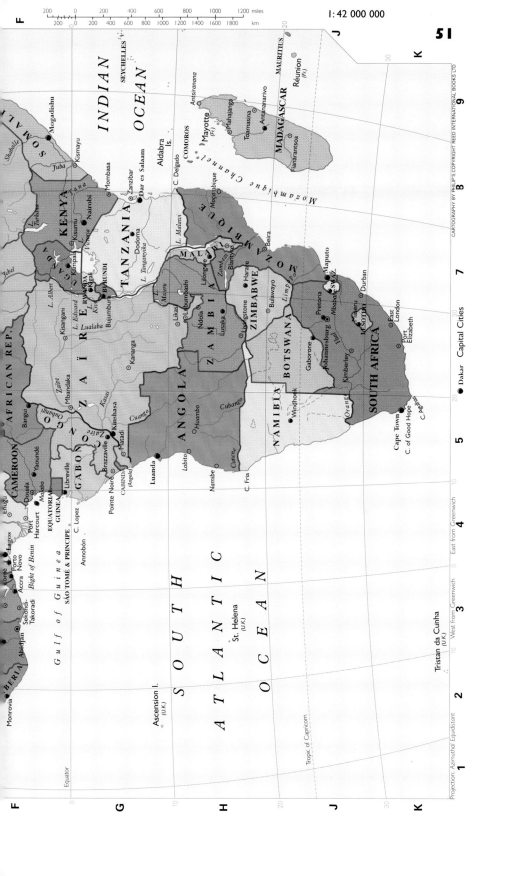

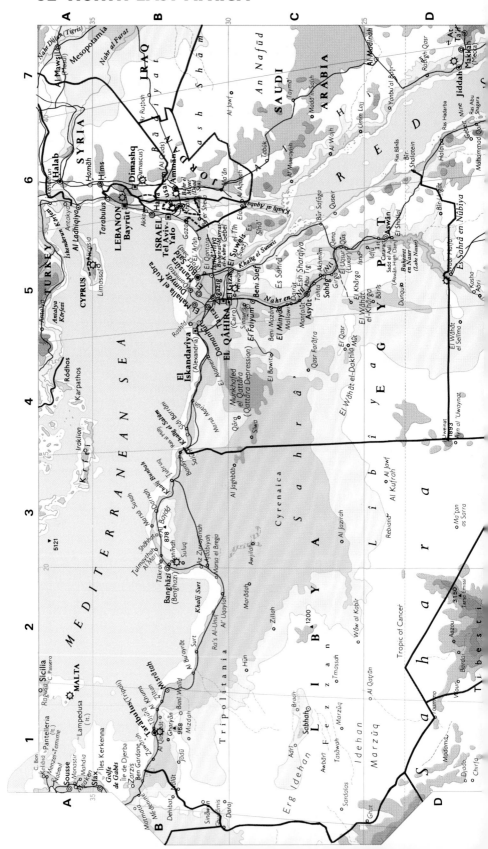

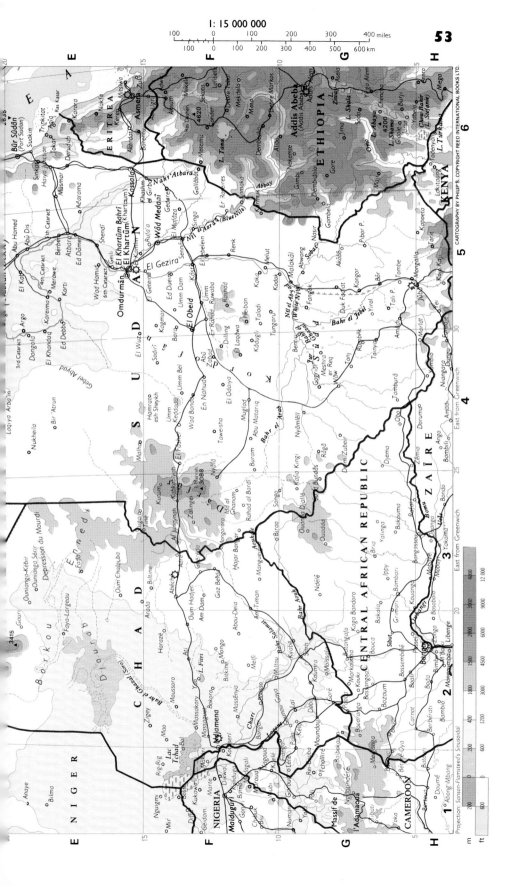

1: 15 000 000

100   0   100   200   300   400 miles
100 0 100 200 300 400 500 600 km

Projection: Sanson-Flamsteed's Sinusoidal

CARTOGRAPHY BY PHILIP'S. COPYRIGHT REED INTERNATIONAL BOOKS LTD.

E   F   G   H

ERITREA

Asmera

Bûr Sûdân
(Port Sudan)

ETHIOPIA

Addis Abeba
(Addis Ababa)

L. Tana

KENYA

L. Turkana

Nahr 'Atbara

Kassala

El Khartûm Bahri
El Khartûm (Khartum)
Omdurmân

Wâd Medani

El Gezira

Nîl el Azraq (Blue Nile)

El Obeid

White Nile

Malakâl

SUDAN

KORDOFAN

DARFUR

Bahr el Arab

Bahr el Jebel

Juba

Gebel Abyad

CENTRAL AFRICAN REPUBLIC

ZAÏRE

CHAD

NIGER

Bangui

Ennedi

Depression du Mourdi

Borkou

Djourab

NIGERIA

Ndjamena

Lac Tchad

Maiduguri

Chari

CAMEROON

Massif de
l'Adamaoua

East from Greenwich

m   ft

4800   12 000
3600   9000
2400   6000
1500   4500
1000   3000
600   1200
400   600
200   200
0   0

6

5

4

3

2

1

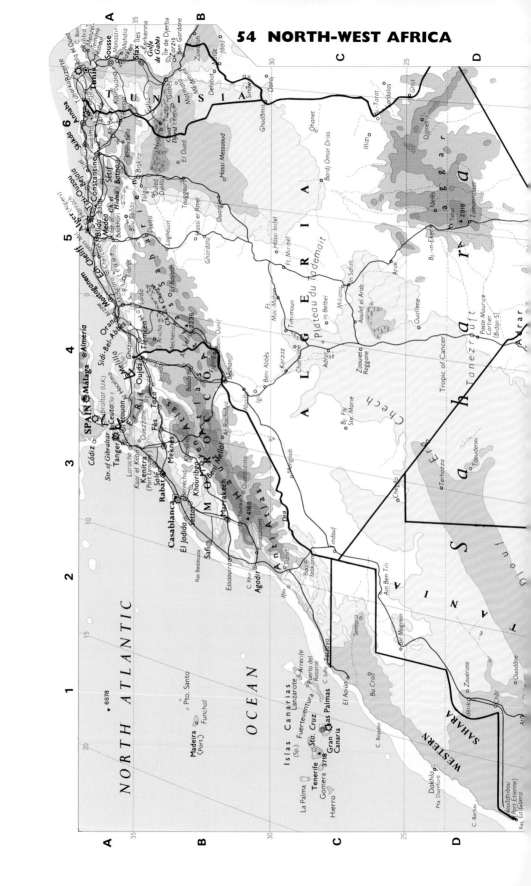

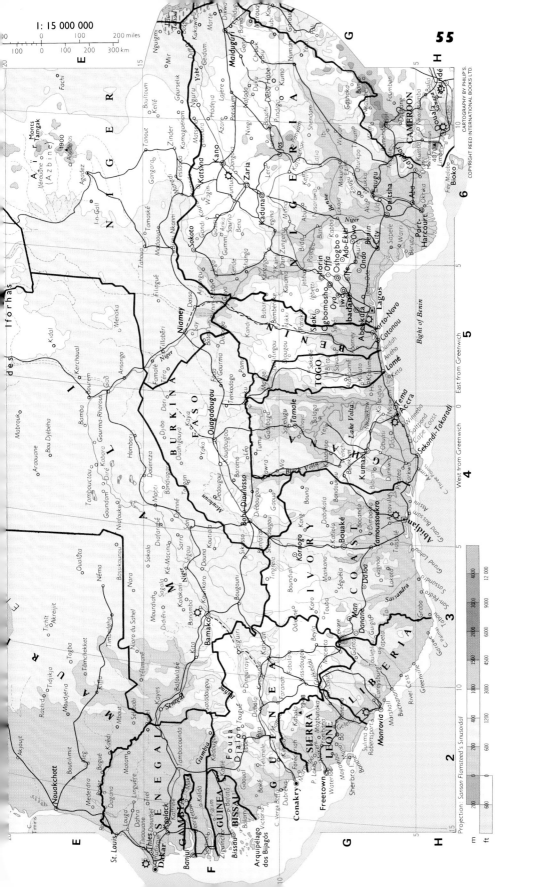

1 10 2 15 3 20 4

A

N I G E R

Oum Chalouba

Tanout
Boultoum
Zigey
Bahr el Ghazal (Soro)
Arada
Biltine
Tigaibo
Tiné
Kutum

Gangara
Kellé
Mir
Nguigmi
Rig-Rig
Mao
Moussoro
Harazé
Abéché
Adré
Al Junaynah
Kabki

Zinder
Gourselik
Lac Tchad
Bol
C H A D
Oum Hadjer
Am Dam
Guereda
Zalingei

Tessaoua
Kamoguenam
Matsena
Diffa
Kukawa
Massakary
Ydo
L. Fitri
Mongo
Bitkine
Goz Beïda
Mongororo
308

B

Kano
Nguru
Yobe
Geidam
Marte
Dikwa
Ndjamena
(Lamy)
Bokoro
Massaguet
Massenya
Abou-Deïa
Am-Timan
Hajar Banga
Rahad al Bardi

Azare
Hadejia
Lajere
Maiduguri
Konduga
Kousseri
Chari
Melfi
Boussa
Manga
Birao
Songo

Dangora
Ningi
Potiskum
Nafada
Gonri
Bama
Madagali
Maroua
Yagoua
Bongor
Bousso
Miltou
Bahr Salamat
Mangueigne
Ouanda Djallé

C

Lere
Bauchi
Duku
Chibuk
Biu
Deba Habe
Hubi
Koele
Kaguoa
Garoua
Léré
Pala
Lai
Kélo
Kyabé
Sarh
Ndélé
Ouadda
Birni

Jos
Kafanchan
Panyam
Kumo
Numan
Garoa
Fianga
Gaya
Kélo
Doba
Goré
Bakala
Ippy
Yalinga
Bria

NIGERIA
Pindiga
Yola
Pah
Rei Bouba
Tcholliré
Moundou
Koumra
Batangafo
Kaga Bandoro
Bakouma

Lafia
Shendam
Massif de
Ngaoundéré
l'Adamaoua
Baibokoum
Papua
Marcounda
Bocaranga
Kouki
Bossangoa
Bouca
Sibut
Grimari
Bambari
Rafe

Makurdi
Takum
Wum
Gashaka
Banyo
Tibati
Meiganga
Bouar
Bozoum
Bossembélé
Carnot
Boali
CENTRAL AFRICAN
REPUBLIC
Bangassou

Oturkpo
Nkambe
Bali
Foumban
Yoko
Bétaré-Oya
Berbérati
Bambio
Bimbom
Zongo
Bosobolo
Mobaye
Bomu

C CAMEROON
Calabar
Kumba
Oron
Bamenda
Dschang
M'Bé
Bafia
Bertoua
Batouri
Boda
M'Baïki
Monpono
Libenge
Busingo
Gemena
Mobayi
Yakoma
Lik

Mont Cameroun
4070 m
Limbe
Douala
Yaoundé
Doumé
Abong Mbang
Nola
Bimbo
Bangui
Oubangui
Monveda
Aketi

D Bioko (Fernando Póo)
Rio Muni
Edéa
M'Balmayo
Sangmelima
Lomié
Yokadouma
Molounou
Bomboma
Budjala
Lisala
Bumba
Busu-Djanoa
Basoka

EQUATORIAL GUINEA
Mbini
Ebolowa
Djoum
Ambam
Bitam
Minvoul
Souanke
Ouesso
Dongou
Impfondo
Bongandanga
Basankusa
Yahuma
Zaïre

Libreville
Cocobeach
Oyem
Mvadi
Ousye
Belinga
Mekambo
Sembé
Bomongo
Lulonga
Bolomba
Djolu
Isangi

E C. Lopez
Port-Gentil
Kango
Ndjole
Booué
Makokou
Kellé
Makoua
Owando
Ewo
Mbandaka
Irebu
Befale
Boende
Bokungu
Opala

GABON
Ombooué
Iguéla
Lambaréné
Lastoursville
Okondja
Koula-Moutou
Mouanda
Franceville
Okoyo
Mossaka
Lukolela
Kiri
Z A I R E
Monkoto
Ikela
Lome

Setté Cama
Nyanga
Moabi
Ndendé
Fougamou
Mouila
Djambala
Zanaga
Gamboma
Lac Tumba
Mai-Ndombe
Inongo
Kutu
Lokolama
Loto
Dekese

F Mayumba
Tchibanga
Mossendjo
Komono
Sibiti
Kibangou
Mindouli
Kwamouth
Mushie
Tolo
Lukenie
Oshwe
Kole
Lodja
Bena Dibele

Pointe Noire
Loubomo
Tshela
Luozi
Brazzaville
Kinshasa
Bandundu
Masi-Manimba
Basongo
Dibaya
Lubue
Ilebo
Sankuru
Mweka
Luebo
Demba
Dimbelenge

CABINDA
Cacongo
Matadi
Madimba
Mbanza Ngungu
Kikongulu
Kenge
Kikwit
Idiofa
Kasai
Charlesville
Gungu
Makumbi
Kananga
Mbuji

Cabinda
Boma
Nqui
Mbanza Congo
Maquela do-Zombo
Festil
Popokabaka
Kasongo Lunda
Tshikapa
Kuzumba
Luiza
Lund

F ATLANTIC
Soyo
Damba
Kahemba
Luachimo
Kamisomba
Lucapa
Kapanga

Nzeto
Uige
N'Gage
Sanza Pombo
Camabatela
Luremo
Caúngula
Capaia
Kasai

Ambriz
Caxito
Quibaxe
Ndalatando
Lubalo
Chiluage
Sandoa
Kafok

G OCEAN
Luanda
Pta. das Palmeirinhas
Muxima
Dondo
Quela
Malanje
Cambundi-Catembo
Cacolo
Saurimo
Luau
Dilolo
Mutshatsh

Gunza
Gabela
A N G O L A
Sumbe
Andulo
Calulo
Muconda
Luacana

ft m 12 000 4000 9000 3000 6000 2000 4500 1500 3000 1000 1200 400 600 200 0 0 200 600 m ft

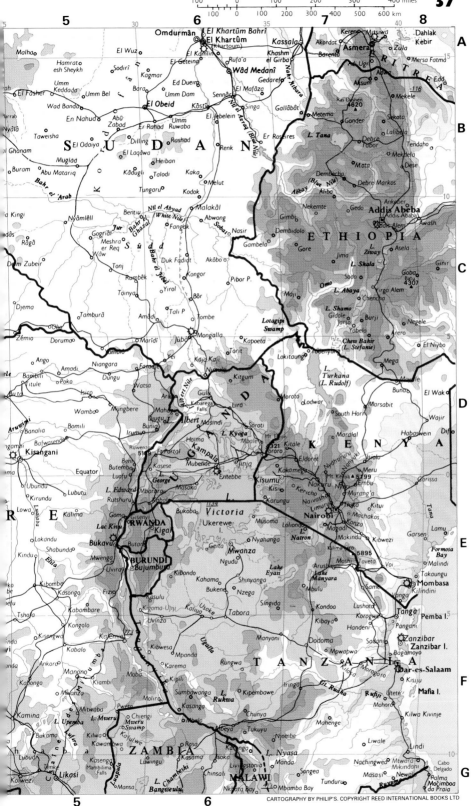

1: 15 000 000

100   0   100   200   300   400 miles
100 0 100 200 300 400 500 600 km

| 5 | 6 | 7 | 8 |

30   35   40

Omdurmân   El Khartûm Bahri
El Khartûm   Kassala   Kerene Mitsiwa   Dahlak
(Khartoum)   Akordat   Zula   Kebir
Malha   El Wuz   El Kamlin   Khashm   Asmera   Mersa Fatma
        Hamrat   Rufa'a   el Girba   Barentu   ERITREA   **A**
    esh Sheikh   Sodirî   El Geteina   Gedaref   Adi Ugri   15
Umm   Bara   Ed Dueim El Mafâza   Aksum   Mekele   -116   Edd
Keddada Umm Bel   Umm Dam Sennâr   Ras Dashen
Wad Banda   El Obeid   Kôsti   Singa   Gallâbât   4620   Sekota
En Nahud   Er Rahad   El Jebelein   Metema   Gonder   Debre   **B**
    Abû   Umm Ruwaba   Er Roseires   L. Tana   Tabor   Lalibela
    Zabad   Renk   Mekdela   Tendaho
Taweisha El Odaiya Dilling Rashad   Kaka   Mata   Dese
        Kadugli Talodi Kodok   Dembecha
    Muglad   Heiban   Melut   Abbay (Blue Nile) Debre Markos
Abu Matariq El Laqawa   Tungaru   Aliba   Ankober   **10**
Bahr el 'Arab   Nekemte   Gedo   Addis Abeba
    Bentiu   Nil el Abyad   Malakâl   (Addis Ababa)   Awash
Nyâmlêll   Jur (White Nile) Abwong   Gimbi Dembidolo   Debre Sina Alem Asela   **C**
Gogriâl Bahr   Fangak   Nasir   Gore   Ziway
Meshra   Ghazal   Omo Jima L. Shala   Gobá
er Req   Wâw   Duk Fadiat Akôbo   Sodo   Bati 4307 Ginir
    Tonj   Rumbêk Kongor Pibor P.   L. Abaya Yirga Alem Chencha
Toinya   Yirol   Bôr   Tombe   Mãji   L. Shamo Gidole Burji
    Amadi   Tali P   Lotagipi   Jarso   Negele
Tamburâ   Mongalla Kapoeta Swamp   Chew Bahir Tabelo Arero   **D**
Djema   Jûba   Torit   (L. Stefanie)
Dorumo Yei   Koja Kaji Lokitaung   El Niybo
Ango Maridi   Kitgum   L. Turkana
Amadi   Faradje   Moroto   (L. Rudolf)   Bunat El Wak
Niangara Dungu Watsa Lira Lodwar   Marsabit   Wajir
Isiro   Gulu   Mt. Elgon   South Horr
Mungbere Mahagi Mosindi Soroti Kitale   Eldoret   Maralal   Habaswein   Difi
Bomili   Kabarega   L. Kyoga Mbale   Kakamega   Nyahururu Isiolo
    Falls   Tororo Eldoret Mt. Kenya Meru
Kisangani Butembo   Fort Portal Jinja Kericho   Nakuru 5199 Embu   Garissa
Equator Kasese Mubende Kampala Kisumu   Naivasha Thika
Ubundu   Lubutu L. Edward Entebbe Kisii   Murang'a Kitui
Kirundu Rutshuru   Masaka   Karungu Nairobi Machakos   Lamu
Kalima Goma Bukoba Victoria   Loliondo   Magadi Garsen   **E**
Lac Kivu Gisenyi RWANDA   Ukerewe I. Musoma   Natron   Konza Kibwezi   Formosa
Bukavu   Kigali   Geita   Makindu   Bay
Lokandu Butare   Mwanza Nyahanga   5895 Taveta   Malindi
Shabunda Uvira BURUNDI Mwanza Geita Lake   Moshi   Voi   Mombasa
Kindu   Bujumbura Kibondo Kahama Eyasi   Manyara Same Kilindini
Kibombo   Ngudu   Shinyanga   Arusha   Tanga
Kasongo Fizi   Bukene Nzega   Mbulu Kondoa   Korogwe Pemba I. **5**
Kabambare Kigoma-Ujiji Uvinza Tabora Manyoni Dodoma Handeni Zanzibar
Kongolo Kaliua   Singida   Mpwapwa   Sadani Zanzibar I.
Kabalo Uvinza 773   Ugalla Manyoni Iringa Morogoro Bagamoyo
Manono Kibwesa Mpanda Karema   TANZANIA   Dar-es-Salaam   **F**
Mwanza Kambi   Kipili   Sumbawanga   Gt. Ruaha Utete Mafia I.
Kapongo Molira Kasanga   Chunya Mahenge   Mohoro
Kamina Mitwaba Chiengi Mbeya Tukuyu Njombe Kilwa Kivinje
L. Upemba L. Mweru Mweru Kasanga   Liwale Lindi
Bukama Kilwa Swamp Kawambwa Mbeya Manda Nachingwea Mtwara Cabo
Kolwezi Likasi ZAMBIA   Kasama Isoka   L. Nyasa Masasi Delgado
    Kasenga Mambilima Luwingu Chinsali   Songea Tunduru Palma Moçimboa
Mansa   Falls L. Chambeshi   MALAWI   da Praia   **G**
Lubudi   Bangweulu Nkhata Bay Mbamba Bay   Newala
                                                                    10

| 5 | 6 |

CARTOGRAPHY BY PHILIP'S. COPYRIGHT REED INTERNATIONAL BOOKS LTD

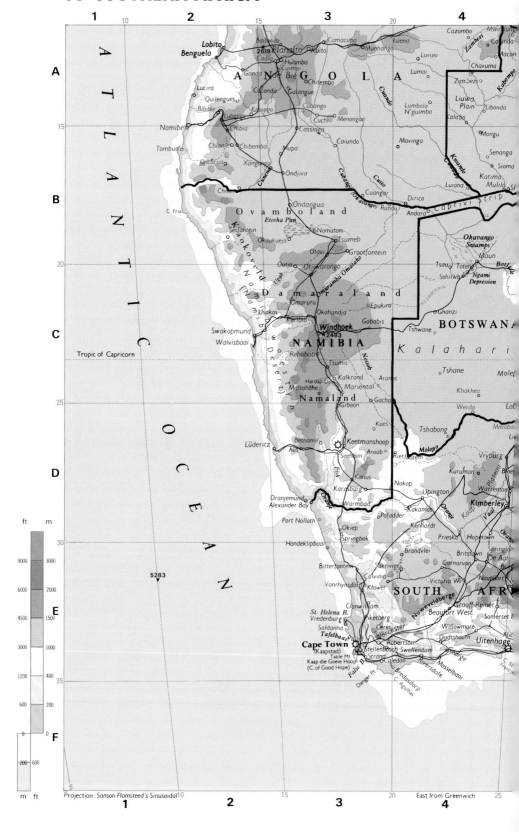

ft   m

9000 3000

6000 2000

4500 1500

3000 1000

1200 400

600   200

0   0

200   600

m   ft

Projection: Sanson Flamsteed's Sinusoidal

East from Greenwich

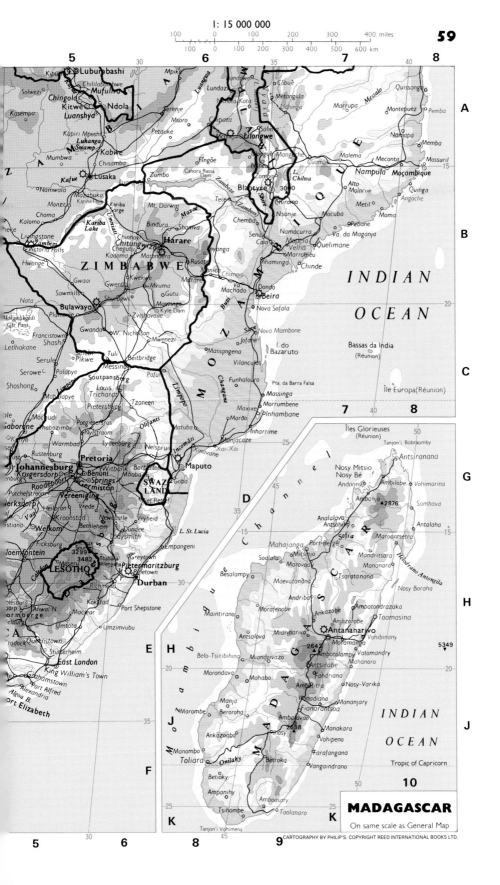

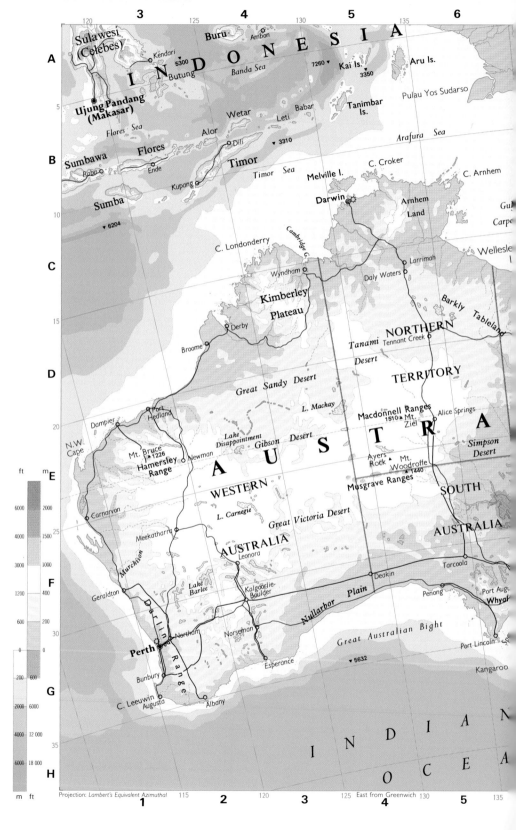

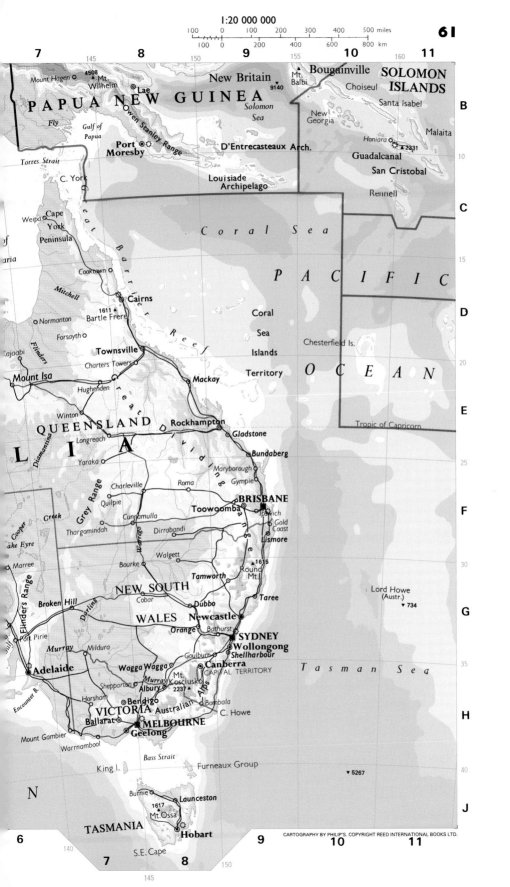

1:20 000 000

100   0   100   200   300   400   500 miles
100   0   200   400   600   800 km

7   145   **8**   150   **9**   155   **10**   160   **11**

Mount Hagen   4508 ▲ Mt.
Wilhelm   ⊙ Lae

New Britain   Mt.
Balbi   Bougainville   **SOLOMON**

PAPUA NEW GUINEA   9140   Choiseul   **ISLANDS**   **B**

Fly   Gulf of
Papua   Solomon
Sea   New
Georgia   Santa Isabel

Owen Stanley Range   Honiara ⊙ ▲2331   Malaita

**Port
Moresby** ⊙⊙   D'Entrecasteaux Arch.   **Guadalcanal**   10

C. York   Louisiade
Archipelago   **San Cristobal**

Torres Strait   Rennell   **C**

Weipa   Cape
York
Peninsula   *C o r a l   S e a*

aria

Cooktown   **P A C I F I C**   15

Mitchell   Cairns   Coral   **D**

Normanton   1611 ▲
Bartle Frere   Sea

Forsayth   Islands

Townsville   Territory   *O C E A N*   20

ajaabi   Charters Towers   Chesterfield Is.

Mount Isa   Mackay

Hughenden

Winton   Rockhampton   Tropic of Capricorn   **E**

QUEENSLAND   Gladstone   25

Longreach   Bundaberg

Yaraka   Maryborough

Charleville   Gympie

Roma

Quilpie   **BRISBANE**   **F**

Thargomindah   Toowoomba   Ipswich

Cunnamulla   Gold
Coast

Dirranbandi   Lismore

Cooper   Creek   Walgett   30

Lake Eyre   Bourke   Round
1615 ▲ Mt.

Marree   Tamworth

NEW SOUTH   Taree   Lord Howe
(Austr.)   **G**

Broken Hill   Cobar   ▼ 734

WALES   Dubbo   **Newcastle**

Port Pirie   Orange   Bathurst   35

Murray   Mildura   **SYDNEY**   *T a s m a n   S e a*

Adelaide   Wagga Wagga   **Wollongong**
Shellharbour

Shepparton   Mt.
Kosciusko   **Canberra**
CAPITAL TERRITORY

Encounter B.   Horsham   Albury   2237 ▲   Bombala

VICTORIA Australian   C. Howe   **H**

Ballarat   **Bendigo**

Mount Gambier   **Geelong**   **MELBOURNE**

Warrnambool   40

King I.   Bass Strait   Furneaux Group

N   ▼ 5267

Burnie   Launceston   **J**

1617 ▲
Mt.Ossa

TASMANIA   **Hobart**

6   140   **7**   **8**   150   **9**   **10**   **11**

S.E. Cape   145

CARTOGRAPHY BY PHILIP'S. COPYRIGHT REED INTERNATIONAL BOOKS LTD.

62 SOUTH-EAST AUSTRALIA

1   2   3

135   140

Tieyon
Abminga
L. Thomas
Alton Downs
L. Cooninie
Yamma
Yamma

Chandler
Pedirka
The Hamilton
The Stevenson
Peera Peera
Poolanna L.
Andrewilla
Arrabury
Mount
Howitt
McGregor Ra.

The Alberga
Oodnadatta
Clifton Hills
Goyder
Lagoon
Coongie
Durham
Downs
Kihee

Welbourn Hill
Arckaringa
Cowarie
Nappa Merrie
Nackatunga

A

Marla
Cadney Park
Peake Cr.
Lora Cr.
L. Conway
Warrina
The Neales
Kittakittaooloo
Cooper Creek
Etadunna
L. Hope or
Pando
Innamincka
Orient

Coober Pedy
L. Cadibarrawirracanna
Cr.
William
Creek
Naryilco
Bulloo Downs

McDouall
Peak
Coward Springs
Bopeechee
L. Florence
L. Gregory
Bulloo L.

Mulgathing
Bulgunnia
Mt. Eba
L. Eyre
(South)
Marree
The Frome
L. Blanche
L. Callabonna
Moolawatana
Milparinka
Tibooburra
Wonota

30

Wynbring
Malbooma
Tarcoola
L. Labyrinth
Farina
Lyndhurst
Quinyambie
Cobham
The Salt L.
Yancan

Koonibba
L. Harris
Kingoonya
L. Younghusband
L. Hanson
Leigh Creek
South
Beltana
Benbonyathe Hill
1058
Lake
Frome
Kayrunnera
Moalie
Park

Ceduna
L. Everard
Haut
Island
Lagoon
Woomera
Pimba
Parachilna
Frome Downs
Corona
Grassmere
Wilcanna

Puntabie
L. Acraman
Perinuty
Lagoon
Woocalla
St. Mary Pk.
1165
Wilpena
Benagerie
Little Topar

Denial
B.
Wirrulla
Yardea
P.O.
L. Macfarlane
Hawker
Stephens Creek
Popio L.
Broken Hill

B

Nuyts
Arch.
Pt.
Brown
Poochera
Nukey Bluff
472
L. Gilles
Iron Knob
Craddock
Carrieton
Olary
Cockburn
Menindee L.
Darling
Talyawalka

Streaky B.
Minnipa
Buckleboo
Mt. Remarkable
969
Port Augusta
Wilmington
Yunta
Mannahill
Cawndilla L.
Menindee
Boor

Pt. Westall
C. Blanche
Port Kenny
Kyancutta
Kimba
Baroo
Orroroo
Paratoo
Nackara
Oakbank
Tandou L.
Gum Lake
Willaba

30

C. Radstock
Streaky Bay
Darke Peak
Iron
Baron
Whyalla
Peterborough
Terowie
Quondong
L. Popilta

Anxious
Bay
C. Bauer
Elliston
Kopi
Lock
Cowell
Port Pirie
Jamestown
Braemar
Traveller's L.

C. Finniss
Rudall
Crystal Brook
Gladstone
Hallett
Mt. Bryan
934
L.
Victoria
Burtundy

Flinders I.
Investigator
Group
Kadina
Port Broughton
Snowtown
Brinkworth
Robertstown
Morgan
Murray Berri
Wentworth
Mildura

Drummond Pt.
Mt. Hope
Cummins
Yeelanna
Ungarra
Arno
Bay
Wallaroo
Clare
Farrell Flat
Riverton
Waikerie
Barmera
Renmark
Red Cliffs

Coffin B.
Tumby Bay
Moonta
Bowman
Balaklava
Kapunda
Nuriootpa
Loxton
Hattah
Euston

Coffin Bay
Pen.
Wanggry
Yorke
Pen.
Mortland
Hamley
Bridge
Angaston
Sedan
Meringur
Werrimull
Robinvale

Port Lincoln
C. Donington
Ardrossan
Salisbury
Gawler
Mannum
Alawoona
Ouyen

C. Carnot
Corny Pt.
Port Adelaide
Elizabeth
Wanbi
Peebinga
Underbool
Tyrrell

35

Sleaford B.
West I.
C. Spencer
Edithburgh
ADELAIDE
Glenelg
Brighton
Murray Bridge
Strathalbyn
Marama
Cowangie
Patchewollock

Gambier Is.
Str. G. St. Vincent
Milang
Tailem
Bend
L. Albacutya
Hopetoun

C. Borda
Kingscote
Willunga
Cape
Jervis
Meningie
L. Albert
Keith
Nhill
Yaapeet
Birchip
Kerang

Kangaroo I.
C. Gantheaume
Victor Harbor
Encounter B.
Salt
Creek
Tintinara
Hindmarsh
Jeparit
Swan Hill

C. du Couedic
Str.
Investigator
Str.
L. Alexandrina
Younghusband
Peninsula
Bordertown
Wolseley
Dimboola
Donald

C

Lacepede Bay
Kingston South East
Frances
Mortlake
Natimuk
Horsham
St. Arnaud
Charlt

Beachport
George
Naracoorte
Edenhope
Murtoa
Maryborough

C. Jaffa
Ripoli B.
Millicent
L. Bonney
Penola
Balmoral
Casterton
Cavendish
Glenelg
Stawell
Ararat
Clunes

Mount Gambier
Coleraine
Hamilton
Penshurst
Skipton
Ballarat
MELB

C. Northumberland
McDonnell
Heywood
Mortlake
Cressy
Geelon

Discovery
Bay
Bridgewater
Portland
Port Fairy
Colac
Lorne

Warrnambool
C. Otway
Quec

D

C. Wickham

King Island

Currie

Stokes Pt.

140

East from Greenwich

3

Tasmania inset

40

King Island
Palana

Stokes Pt.
C. Keraudren
Hunter Is.
Flinders Island
Furneaux
Group
Cape Barren I.
Whitemark
Prime Seal I.

Smithton
Three
Hummock I.
Robbins I.
Stanley

Marrawah
Wynyard
Burnie
Penguin
Ulverstone
Devonport
George Town
Clarke I.
Banks Strait

Arthur
Temma
Waratah
Railton
Mt. Ossa
1617
Latrobe
Deloraine
Westbury
Launceston
Scottsdale
Bridport
Herrick
Naturaliste
Pt.
St. Helens

Corinna
Rosebery
Zeehan
Mole Creek
Longford
Ben Lomond
1527
St. Marys

Strahan
Queenstown
Macquarie
Harb.
Bronte Pk.
Great L.
Conara
Jun.
Campbell
Town
Ross
Cranbrook
Freycinet
Pen.
Schouten I.

Hibbs Bay
Wayatinah
Bothwell
Ouse
Parattah
Triabunna
Maria I.

D

TASMANIA
L. Pedder
Maydena
Colebrook

Port Davey
Bathurst Harb.
S.W. Cape
Huonville
Cygnet
Dover
New Norfolk
Glenorchy
Hobart
Kingston
Storm
Bay
Forestier Pen.
Tasman Pen.
Port Arthur

Bruny I.

3
S.E. Cape
4

145

Scale

ft   m

4500   1500
3000   1000
1200   400
600   200
0   0
200   600
2000   6000
4000 12 000

m   ft

Projection: Bonne

1:8 000 000

50   0   50   100   150   200 miles
50   0   50   100   150   200   250   300 km

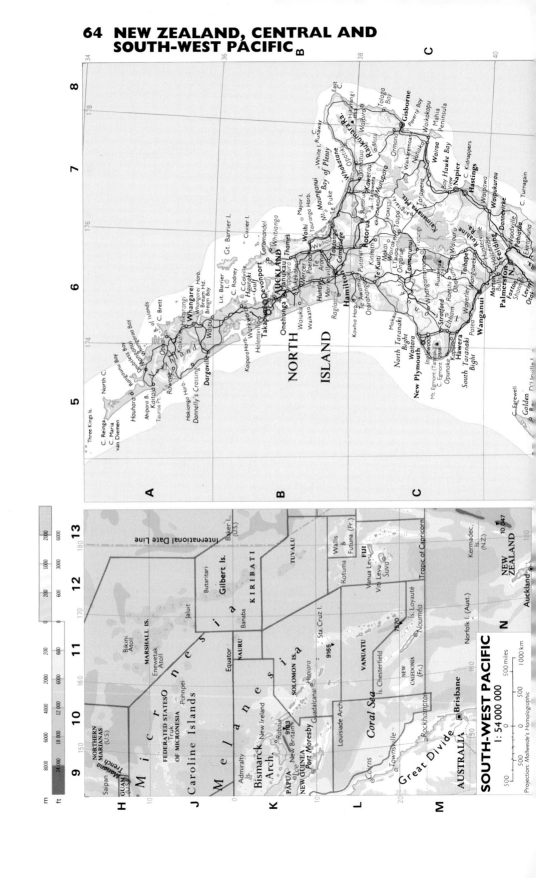

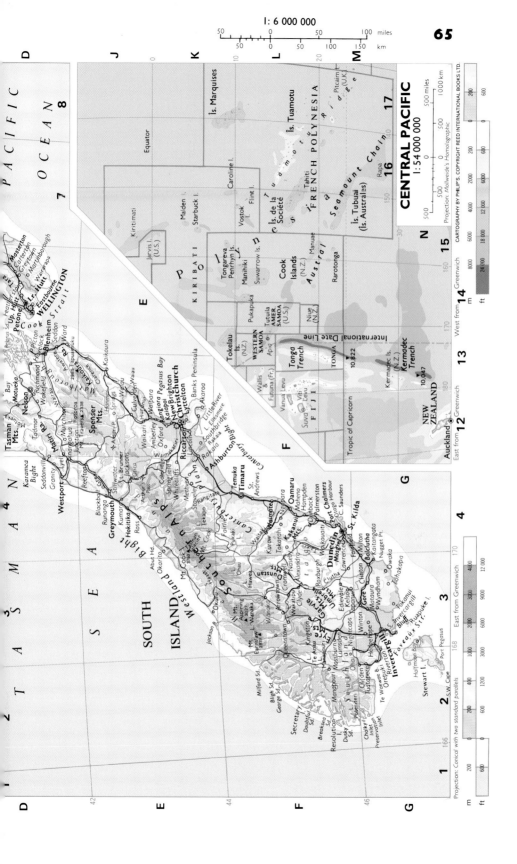

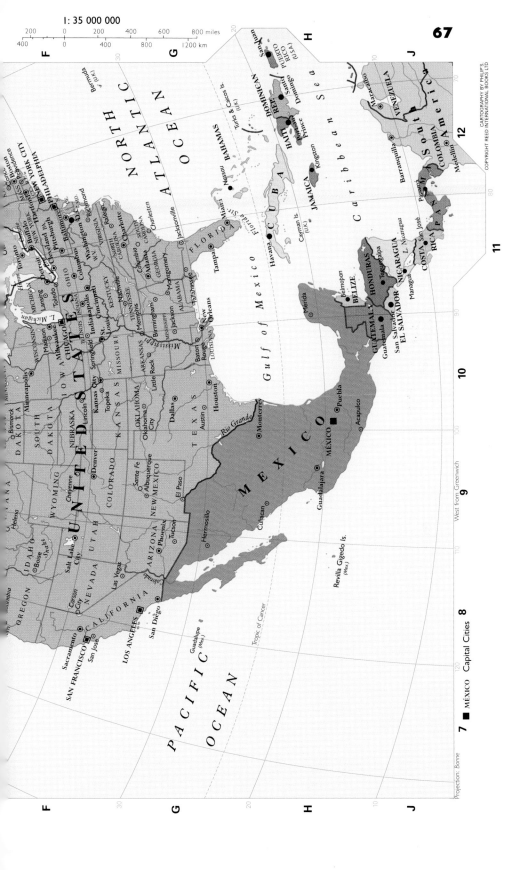

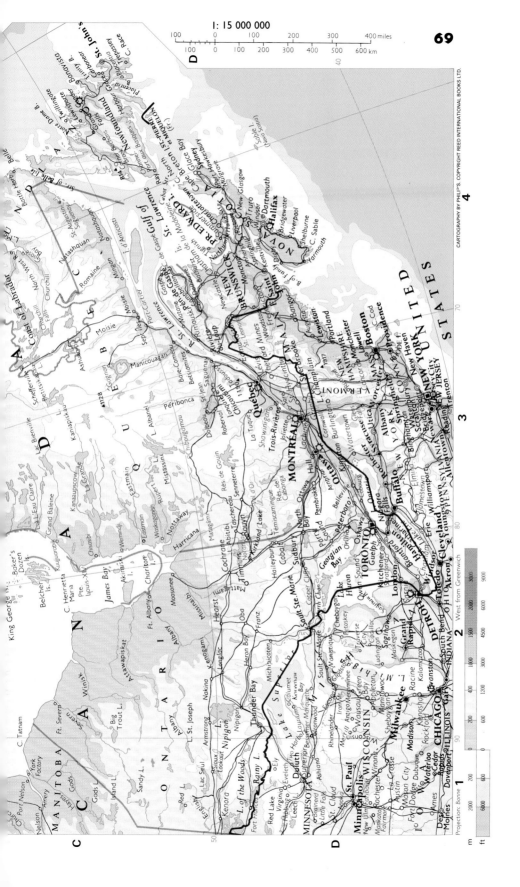

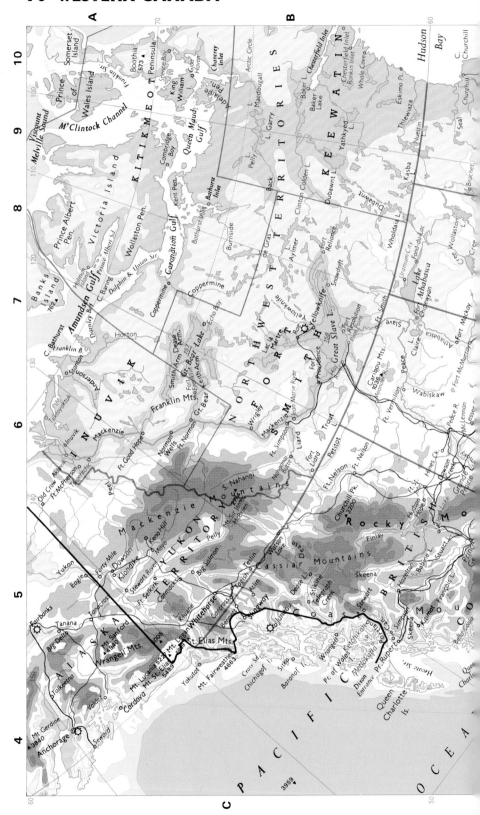

1: 15 000 000

100   0   100   200   300   400 miles

100   0   100   200   300   400   500   600 km

CARTOGRAPHY BY PHILIP'S. COPYRIGHT REED INTERNATIONAL BOOKS LTD.

Projection: Bonne

ALASKA
1: 30 000 000

100   0   100   200   300 miles

100   0   100   200   300   400 km

West from Greenwich

PACIFIC OCEAN

m   ft
2000   6000
1500   4500
1000   3000
600   1200
400   600
200
0

3000   9000
2000   6000

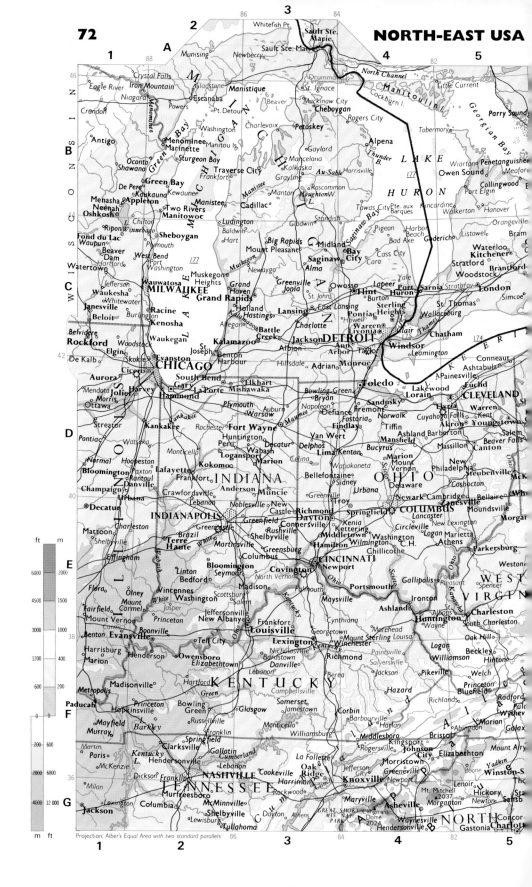

Projection: Alber's Equal Area with two standard parallels

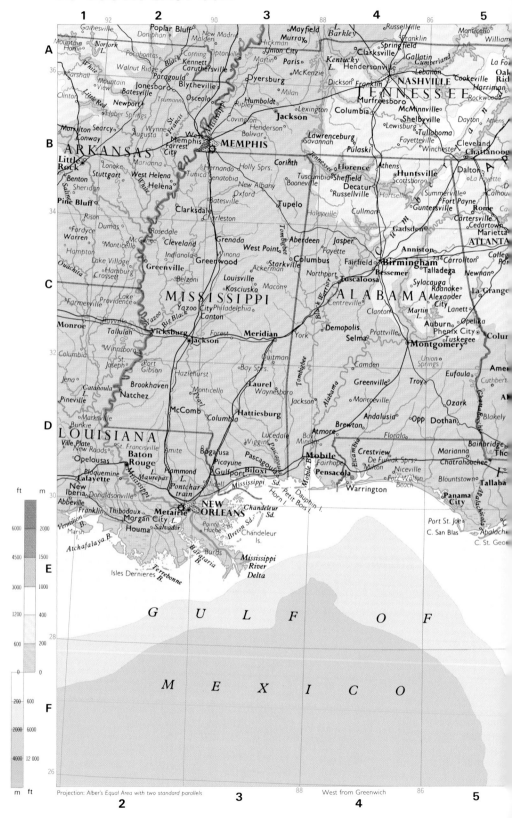

Projection: Alber's Equal Area with two standard parallels
West from Greenwich

1 : 6 000 000

50   0   50   100 miles

50   0   50   100   150 km

84   6   82   7   80   8   78   9   76   10

| | | |
A

Currituck Sd.

Harlan
Middlesboro   Abingdon   Marion   Galax   Martinsville   Danville   Emporia   Elizabeth City   36
Rogersville   Johnson   Bristol   Mount Airy   Reidsville   Eden   Roxboro   Roanoke Rapids   Winton   Manteo
Jefferson   City   Morristown   City   Elizabethton   Yadkin   Greensboro   Burlington   Oxford   Henderson   Edenton   Albemarle Sd.   Roanoke I.
Greeneville   Newport   Boone   Winston-Salem   Graham   Durham   Rocky Mount   Williamston
Knoxville   Maryville   Lenoir   Hickory   Thomasville   High   Chapel Hill   Raleigh   Wilson   Greenville   B
Mt. Mitchell   Statesville   Point   Lexington   Haw   Washington   Pamlico
2037   Morganton   Salisbury   Kannapolis   Asheboro   Smithfield   Goldsboro   Kinston   New Bern
Asheville   Chimney   Waynesville   Shelby   Concord   Sanford   Dunn   Neuse
REAT SMOKY   Dome   Hendersonville   Gastonia   Albemarle   Southern   Clinton   Jacksonville   Beaufort   Hatteras
MTS. NAT.   2024   Brevard   Charlotte   Pines   Fayetteville   C. Lookout
PARK   Murphy   NORTH   CAROLINA   Pamlico Sound
Brasstown Bald   Spartanburg   Gaffney   Monroe   Laurinburg   Cape   Onslow
1458   Greenville   Rock Hill   Lancaster   Lumberton   Fear   B.   Raleigh   B.
Toccoa   Easley   Union   Chester   Bennettsville   Whiteville   Wilmington   34
Anderson   Laurens   Hartsville   Dillon   Mullins   Southport
Gainesville   Hartwell   Greenwood   Newberry   Camden   Darlington   Marion   C. Fear
Elberton   Abbeville   Saluda   Florence   Lake City   Conway
Athens   Clark   L.   Columbia   Sumter   Myrtle Beach   C
Lawrenceville   Hill L.   Murray   SOUTH   CAROLINA   Manning   Kingstree
Decatur   Covington   Orangeburg   L.   Georgetown
East Point   Augusta   Aiken   Bamberg   Marion   32
GEORGIA   Sparta   Waynesboro   Summerville   North Charleston   30
Griffin   Milledgeville   Millen   Walterboro   Charleston   Mt. Pleasant
Macon   Swainsboro   Ridgeland   Beaufort   28
Warner   Dublin   Statesboro   Parris I.   26
Robins   Cochran   Vidalia
Perry   Eastman   Savannah
Cordele   Hazlehurst   Hinesville   Ossabaw I.
Sylvester   Fitzgerald   Baxley   Jesup   St. Catherines I.
Tifton   Douglas   Sapelo I.
Moultrie   Adel   Waycross   Brunswick   D
Cairo   Okefenokee   Cumberland I.
Valdosta   Swamp   Folkston   Fernandina Beach
Quitman   FLORIDA   St. Johns   A   T   L   A   N   T   I   C
Monticello   Jasper   Jacksonville
Madison   Live Oak   JACKSONVILLE   Beach   30
Perry   Lake   Jacksonville   Starke   Green Cove Springs
City   St. Augustine
Apalachee   High Springs   Palatka   O   C   E   A   N
B.   Bunnell
Cross City   Gainesville   Ormond   E
L.   Beach
George   Daytona Beach
Ocala   De Land   New
Crystal River   Eustis   Smyrna Beach
Inverness   Sanford   C. Canaveral
Leesburg   Titusville   28
Brooksville   Winter Park   Merritt Island
Dade City   Orlando   Cocoa
Turpon Springs   Kissimmee   Melbourne
Lakeland   Haines City   Indian   River
Clearwater   Winter Haven   F
Largo   TAMPA   Bartow   Vero Beach
St. Petersburg   Tampa Bay   Sebring   Fort Pierce   Grand Cays
Bradenton   L.   Stuart   Little Abaco I.   Gt. Guana Cay
Sarasota   Istokpoga   Okeechobee   Settlement   Hope
Arcadia   Pt.   Town
Punta Gorda   L.   Pahokee   West Palm   Freeport   Grand   Great
La Belle   Okeechobee   Belle   Beach   Bahama I.   Abaco I.
Charlotte Harb.   Fort   Glade   Delray Beach
Cape   Myers   Pompano Beach   BAHAMAS   26
Coral   Immokalee   Boca Raton   Fort Lauderdale
Naples   Big Cypress Swamp   Carol City   Hollywood   G
EVERGLADES   Hialeah   Miami Beach
NAT. PARK   MIAMI
Biscayne
B.
Homestead

84   6   82   8   9

CARTOGRAPHY BY PHILIP'S. COPYRIGHT REED INTERNATIONAL BOOKS LTD.

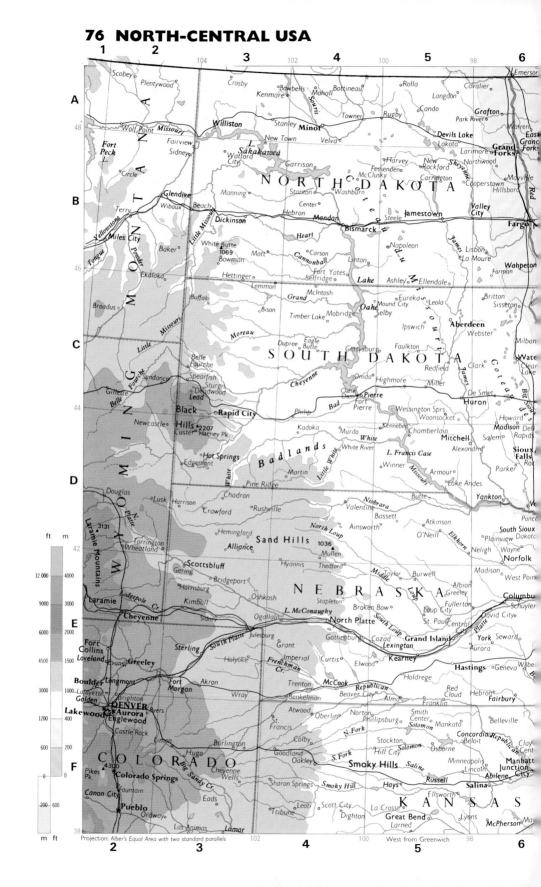

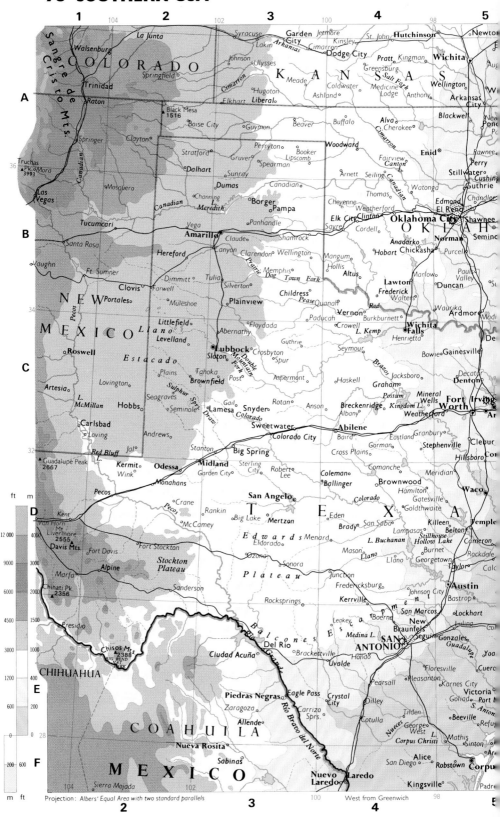

COLORADO

KANSAS

Walsenburg · La Junta · Syracuse · Garden · Jetmore · Newton
City
Springfield · Lakin · Arkansas · Kinsley · St. John · Hutchinson
Trinidad · Johnson · Ulysses · Cimarron · Dodge City · Pratt · Kingman · Wichita
Raton · Cimarron · Meade · Coldwater · Greensburg · Salt Fork · Wellington · Aug
Elkhart · Liberal · Ashland · Medicine · Anthony · Arkansas · Po
Springer · Black Mesa 1516 · Lodge · City · Pc
Boise City · Guymon · Beaver · Buffalo · Alva · Cherokee · Blackwell · New
Truchas Pk. Mora 3993 · Clayton · Stratford · Perryton · Booker · Woodward · Fairview · Canton · Enid · Pawnee
Mosquero · Dalhart · Gruver · Spearman · Lipscomb · Arnett · Seiling · Canadian · Watonga · Guthrie
Las Vegas · Sunray · Dumas · Thomas · Weatherford · Edmond · El Reno · Chandler
Tucumcari · Channing · Borger · Canadian · Cheyenne · Elk City · Clinton · Oklahoma City · OKLAH
Santa Rosa · Meredith · Pampa · Panhandle · Sayre · Cordell · Norman · Seminc
Vaughn · Vega · Amarillo · Claude · Clarendon · Wellington · Mangum · Hobart · Chickasha · Purcell
Hereford · Canyon · Shamrock · Hollis · Altus · Anadarko · Marlow · Paul's
Ft. Sumner · Prairie · Memphis · Dog · Town · Fork · Lawton · Frederick · Duncan · Valley
Dimmitt · Tulia · Silverton · Childress · Pease · Quanah · Walters · Waurika · Ardmore · Madi
Clovis · Farwell · Muleshoe · Plainview · Paducah · Vernon · Burkburnett · Henrietta · Bowie · Gainesville · De
Portales · Littlefield · Floydada · Crowell · L. Kemp · Wichita · Falls
Levelland · Llano · Abernathy · Guthrie · Seymour · Crosbyton · Spur · Aspermont · Haskell · Graham · Jacksboro · Decatur · Denton
Roswell · Estacado · Lubbock · Slaton · Double · Mountain · Fork · Rotan · Anson · Breckenridge · Albany · Kingdom L. · Weatherford · Fort · Irving
Lovington · Plains · Tahoka · Brownfield · Post · Possum · Mineral · Worth
Artesia · Hobbs · Seagraves · Gail · Lamesa · Snyder · Colorado · Wells · Granbury · Cleburr
L. McMillan · Seminole · Sulphur Spr · Sweetwater · Baird · Abilene · Eastland · Stephenville · Hillsborc
Carlsbad · Loving · Andrews · Dra · Stanton · Big Spring · Colorado City · Cross Plains · Gorman · Comanche · Meridian
Red Bluff L. · Kermit · Odessa · Midland · Sterling · Robert · Coleman · Brownwood · Hamilton · Waco
Guadalupe Peak 2667 · Wink · Garden City · City · Lee · Ballinger · Goldthwaite · Gatesville
Pecos · Monahans · Crane · Rankin · Big Lake · Mertzon · San Angelo · Colorado · Eden · San Saba · Killeen · Temple
Kent · Pecos · McCamey · T E X A · Brady · Lampasas · Stillhouse · Belton · Cameron
Van Horn Mt. Livermore 2555 · Fort Stockton · Edwards · Menard · Eldorado · Mason · Llano · Burnet · Rockdale
Davis Mts. · Fort Davis · Stockton · Ozona · Sonora · Plateau · Junction · Fredericksburg · Georgetown · Taylor · Calc
Marfa · Alpine · Plateau · Rocksprings · Kerrville · Johnson City · Austin · Bastrop
Chinati Pk. 2356 · Sanderson · Balcones · Boerne · San Marcos · Lockhart
Presidio · Rio Grande · Del Rio · Leakey · Medina L. · New · Seguin · Gonzales · Luling · Col
CHIHUAHUA · Chisos Mts. 2388 BIG BEND · Ciudad Acuña · Brackettville · Hondo · Braunfels · SAN · Guadalupe · Yoa
Del Rio · Uvalde · ANTONIO · Floresville · Cuerc
Piedras Negras · Eagle Pass · Crystal · Dilley · Pearsall · Pleasanton · Karnes City · Victoria
Zaragoza · City · Carrizo · Cotulla · Tilden · Gohad · Port · S. Anton
COAHUILA · Allende · Sprs. · Nueces · George · Beeville · Refu
Nueva Rosita · West L. · Corpus Christi · Mathis · Sinton · Corpu
Sabinas · San Diego · Alice · Robstown
MEXICO · Nuevo · Laredo · Kingsville · Padre
Laredo · Sierra Mojada

ft · m
12 000 · 4000
9000 · 3000
2000
6000 · 1500
4500 · 1000
3000 · 400
1200 · 200
600 · 28
0 · 0
200 · 600
m · ft

Projection: Albers' Equal Area with two standard parallels

West from Greenwich

VANCOUVER
Port Coquitlam
New
Westminster
Chilliwack

1 Juan de Fuca Strait
C. Flattery
C. Alava
Port Angeles
Port Townsend
Sequim
Forks
Olympic Mts.
Mt. Olympus 2428
OLYMPIC NAT. PARK

Duncan
Victoria
Anacortes
Fendale
Lynden
Mt. Baker 3285

BRITISH COL

Oliver
Grand Forks
Trail
Creston

Kootenay L.

Bellingham
Sedro Woolley
Mt. Vernon
Oak Harbor
Arlington
Darrington
Glacier Pk. 3213

NORTH CASCADES NAT. PARK

Oroville
Okanogan
Omak
Republic
Brewster

Franklin D. Roosevelt L.

Kettle Falls
Colville
Chewelah
Newport

Bonners Ferry
Priest L.
Sandpoint

A

Bremerton
Port Orchard
Hoquiam
Aberdeen
Grays Harb.
Westport
Montesano
Shelton
Tumwater
Olympia
Tacoma
Puyallup
Renton
SEATTLE
Edmonds
Everett

Leavenworth
Chelan
Lake Chelan
Wenatchee
Cashmere
Waterville

Grand Coulee Dam
Davenport
Odessa
Ritzville

Spokane
Deer Park
Coeur d'Alene L.
Post Falls
Cœur d'Alene
St. Maries
Wallace

B

WASHINGTON

Ellensburg
Cle Elum
Quincy
Ephrata
Moses Lake
Othello
Connell

Columbia Basin

Pullman
Colfax
Palouse
Moscow

Willapa B.
Long Beach
C. Disappointment
Warrenton
Seaside
Astoria
St. Helens

Winlock
Centralia
Chehalis
Castle Rock
Kelso 2550
Longview
Kalama

Mt. Rainier 4392
MT. RAINIER NAT. PARK

Yakima
Selah
Union Gap
Toppenish
Sunnyside
Grandview
Prosser

Richland
Pasco
Kennewick

Dayton
Pomeroy
Waitsburg
Clarkston
Lewiston

Walla Walla
Milton-Freewater

46

Tillamook
Hillsboro
PORTLAND
Vancouver

Goldendale
Columbia
The Dalles
Mt. Hood 3427

Hermiston
Pendleton
Pilot Rock
Elgin

Enterprise

C

McMinnville
Milwaukie
Oregon City
Newberg
Lincoln City
Dallas
Mount Angel

Maupin
Deschutes

Heppner
Condon

La Grande
Wallowa 3011 Mts.

Newport
Waldport
Corvallis
Salem
Independence
Albany
Lebanon
Mill City
Mt. Jefferson 3200

Fossil
Madras
Prineville
Mitchell
John Day

Blue Mountains

Baker

44

Florence
Junction City
Sweet Home
Three Sisters 3156
OREGON

Crooked
Redmond
Bend

John Day 2755
Seneca

New Meadows
McCall

Eugene
Springfield
Oakridge
Cottage Grove
Drain

Brogan
Council

D

North Bend
Coos Bay
Coquille
Myrtle Point
C. Blanco
Sutherlin
Roseburg
Myrtle Creek
Canyonville

Silvies
John Day

Malheur
Vale
Ontario
Payette
Weiser
New Plymouth
Emmett

Cascade

Port Orford
Rogue
Grants Pass
Gold Beach
Brookings
Jacksonville
Crater L.
CRATER LAKE NAT. PARK
Mt. McLoughlin 2894

Great Sandy Desert

Harney Basin
Burns
Harney L.
Malheur L.

Juntura
Owyhee
Caldwell
Nampa
Boise

Idaho City
Mountain Home

42

Crescent City
Medford
Ashland
Klamath Falls
Upper Klamath L.
Summer L.

L. Abert

2962

Snake

Glenns Ferry

E

Klamath
Mts.
Dunsmuir
Weed
Mt. Shasta 4317
Montague
Yreka
Alturas
Clear Lake Res.
Goose L.

Lakeview
Warner Mts.

Alvord Desert

McDermitt

Arcata
Eureka
Fortuna
Ferndale
Cape Mendocino

CALIFORNIA
Thompson Pk. 2724
Mount Shasta
McCloud
Burney

Alkali Lake

Black Rock Ra.

Santa Rosa Ra.

Independence Mts.

Wells

Redding
Anderson
Red Bluff
Weaverville
Shasta Lake
Lassen Peak 3187
Eagle L.

Winnemucca

Carlin
Humboldt
Elko
3437

124

Fort Bragg
Willits
Corning
Orland
Willows
Chester
Susanville
Westwood
Almanor L.
Honey L.

Rye Patch Res.
Lovelock
Winnemucca L.
Pyramid L.

Battle Mountain
2997

Ruby Mts.
Franklin L.
Ruby L.

F

Ukiah
Clear L.
Lakeport
Cloverdale
Healdsburg
Calistoga
Sebastopol
Santa Rosa
Napa
Fairfield
San Rafael
Vallejo

Chico
Oroville
Downieville
Quincy
Feather
Nevada City
Grass Valley
Marysville
Yuba City
Colusa
Sacramento
Arbuckle
Woodland
Davis

Portola
Truckee
Reno
Sparks
Virginia City
Fallon
Carson Sink
Carson City
Gardnerville

Stillwater Ra.

Austin
3235
Eureka

Toiyabe Ra.

NEVADA

McGill
Ely

38

Berkeley
Richmond
Golden Gate
San
Antioch
Lodi
Jackson
S. Andreas

Lake Tahoe
Placerville
Arden
Citrus Heights
Auburn

Mt. Grant 3426
Walker L.
Hawthorne

Mt. Jefferson 3599
Monitor Ra.

Shell Creek

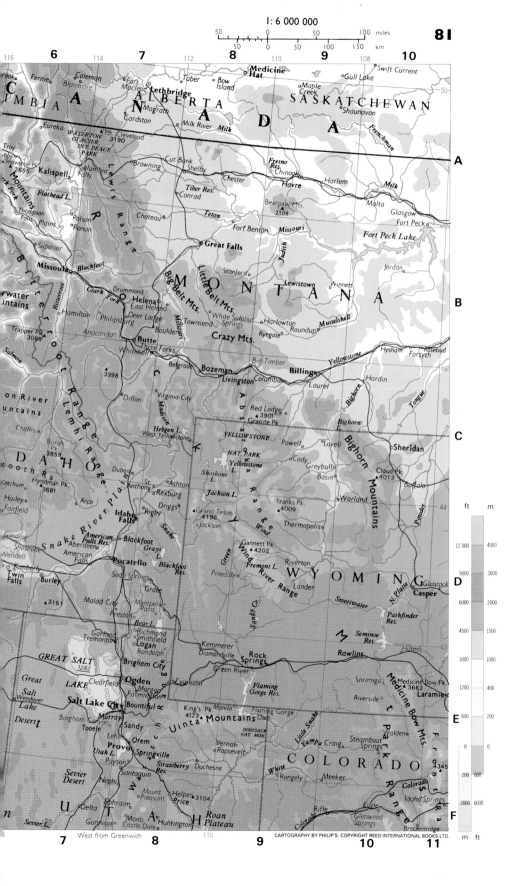

1: 6 000 000

50   0   50   100 miles

50   0   50   100   150 km

CARTOGRAPHY BY PHILIP'S. COPYRIGHT REED INTERNATIONAL BOOKS LTD.

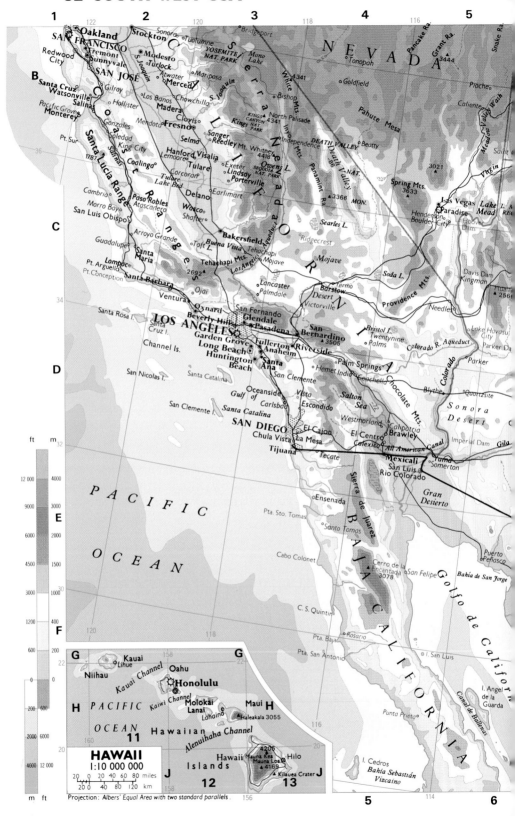

1 122 **2** 120 **3** 118 **4** 116 **5**

Oakland
SAN FRANCISCO Stockton Sonora Tuolumne Bridgeport N E V A D A Pancake Ra.
Fremont Modesto YOSEMITE Mono Grant Ra. Snake Ra.
Redwood City Sunnyvale Turlock NAT. PARK Lake Tonopah 3444
SAN JOSE Merced Mariposa 4341 Goldfield Pioche

B Santa Cruz Atwater Bishop Caliente Meadow Valley Wash
Watsonville Gilroy Los Banos Chowchilla North Palisade Pahute Mesa
Pacific Grove Hollister Madera KINGS CANYON 4341 Saint
Monterey Salinas Clovis NAT. PARK Inyo Mts. Beatty 3021
Gonzales Fresno Kings River Independence DEATH VALLEY 3633
Pt. Sur Soledad Sanger SEQUOIA NAT. Owens L. DEATH VALLEY Virgin
1787 King City Selma Reedley Mt. Whitney PARK Death Valley NAT. MON.
Santa Lucia Range Salinas Hanford Visalia 4418 Panamint Ra. Spring Mts.
Coalinga Lemoore Exeter 3366 3633 Las Vegas Lake
Cambria Tulare Lindsay MON. Paradise Mead
Morro Bay Paso Robles Mendota Corcoran Porterville Henderson Hoover Dam
San Luis Obispo Atascadero Tulare Delano Boulder City
Arroyo Grande Lake Bed Woaco Searles L. Davis Dam
Guadalupe Shafter Ridgecrest Kingman
Lompoc Santa Maria Bakersfield Mojave Soda L. Providence Mts.
Pt. Arguello Buena Vista Tehachapi Needles 2566
Pt. Conception Santa Barbara Taft Tehachapi Mts. Mojave Termo
2692 Los Angeles Aqueduct Barstow Desert
Santa Rosa I. Ventura Ojai Lancaster Victorville
34 Oxnard Palmdale Bristol L. Lake Havasu City
Santa Cruz I. Beverly Hills San Fernando Twentynine Palms Colorado R. Aqueduct Parker Dam
LOS ANGELES Glendale Pasadena San Bernardino Parker
D Channel Is. Garden Grove Fullerton Riverside 3505 Palm Springs Colorado
San Nicolas I. Long Beach Anaheim Santa Hemet Indio Blythe Quartzsite
Huntington Beach Ana San Clemente Coachella Sonora
Santa Catalina Oceanside Vista Palm Springs Chocolate Mts. Desert
Gulf of Carlsbad Escondido Salton Westmorland Calipatria
Santa Catalina I. Sea Brawley
San Clemente I. SAN DIEGO El Cajon Westmorland Gila
Chula Vista La Mesa El Centro
Tijuana Tecate Calexico All American Imperial Dam
Mexicali Canal Yuma
San Luis Somerton
Rio Colorado

P A C I F I C

Ensenada Gran Desierto
O C E A N Pta. Sto. Tomas
Santo Tomas B Cerro de la Encantada Golfo de California
Cabo Colonet 3078 San Felipe
A Puerto Peñasco
C. S. Quintin J Bahía de San Jorge
F 120 118 Pta. Bajac A
Pta. San Antonio I. San Luis

G 158 **G** Kauai Oahu 116 I. Angel de la Guarda
Niihau Lihue Kauai Channel Honolulu Punta Prieta Canal de Ballenas
Molokai Maui **H**
H PACIFIC Lanai Haleakala 3055 I. Cedros Bahía Sebastián Vizcaíno
OCEAN Hawaiian Channel Alenuihaha Channel **11**
Hawaii Islands Mauna Kea Kilauea Crater
HAWAII 4205 Hilo
1:10 000 000 Mauna Loa 4169 **J**
12 156 **13** **5** 114 **6**

Projection: Albers' Equal Area with two standard parallels.

ft   m
12 000 4000
9000 3000
6000 2000
4500 1500
3000 1000
1200 400
600 200
0   0
200 600
2000 6000
4000 12000
m   ft

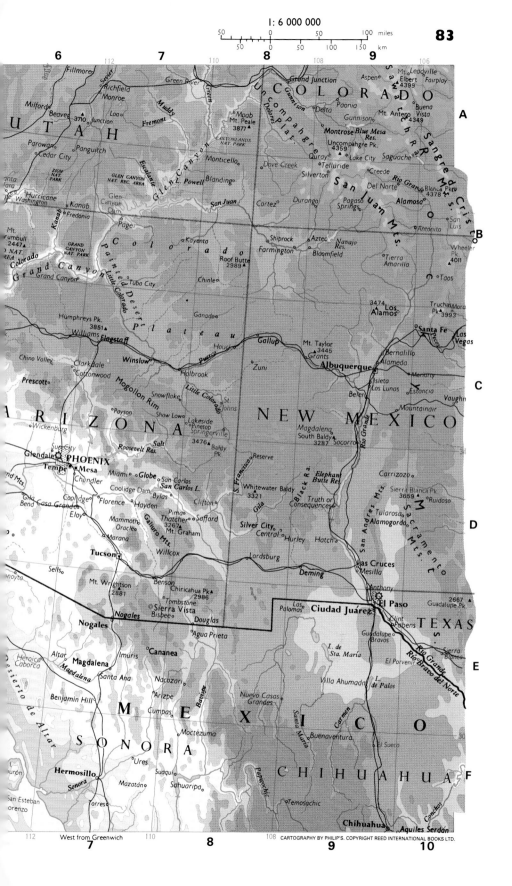

1: 6 000 000

50   0   50   100 miles
50 0 50   100   150 km

6   7   8   9

COLORADO

Fillmore
Richfield   Green River   Grand Junction   Aspen   Mt. Elbert 4399   Leadville   Fairplay
Monroe   Muddy   Gunnison   Delta   Paonia   Mt. Antero   Buena
Milford   Beaver   Loa   Fremont   Moab   Dolores   Gunnison   4349   Vista   A
UTAH   Junction   3710   Mt. Peale   Montrose   Blue Mesa   Mt. Antero
Parowan   Panguitch   3877   CANYONLANDS   Uncompahgre   Res.   4349   Saguache
Cedar City   NAT. PARK   Uncompahgre Pk.   Lake City   Creede
ZION   GLEN CANYON   Monticello   4359   Quray   Telluride   Creede   Rio Grande
Hurricane   NAT. REC. AREA   Dave Creek   Silverton   Del Norte   Blanca Pk.   Alamosa
Washington   Kanab   Glen   L. Powell   Blanding   San Juan Mts.   4378   San
Fredonia   Canyon   San Juan   Cortez   Durango   Pagosa   Luis   B
Mt.   Page   Roof Butte   Shiprock   Aztec   Springs   Antonito   Wheeler
Trumbull   GRAND CANYON   2989   Farmington   Navajo   Tierra   Pk.
2447   NAT. PARK   Kayenta   Bloomfield   Res.   Amarilla   4011
Colorado   Grand Canyon   Painted   Tuba City   Chinle   Taos
Grand Canyon   Little   Desert   Ganado   3474 Los   Truchas   Mora
Humphreys Pk.   Colorado   Plateau   Alamos   Pk. 3993   Santa Fe
3851   Williams   Flagstaff   Houck   Gallup   Mt. Taylor   Bernalillo   Las
Chino Valley   Winslow   Puerco   3445   Alameda   Vegas
Clarkdale   Holbrook   Zuni   Grants   Albuquerque   C
Prescott   Cottonwood   St.   Isleta   Menaury
ARIZONA   Mogollon Rim   Snowflake   Johns   Los Lunas   Estancia
Wickenburg   Payson   Show Low   Lakeside   Belen   Vaughn
Salt   Pinetop   3476   NEW   MEXICO   Mountainair
Sun City   Roosevelt Res.   Springerville   Baldy   Magdalena   Socorro   Carrizozo
Glendale   PHOENIX   Miami   Pk.   South Baldy   Rio Grande   Sierra Blanca Pk.
Tempe   Mesa   Globe   San Carlos   Reserve   3287   3659   Ruidoso
Chandler   Coolidge Dam   Bylas   Whitewater Baldy   Elephant   Tularosa
Coolidge   Florence   Hayden   3321   Gila   Butte Res.   Alamogordo   D
Casa Grande   Mammoth   Thatcher   Clifton   Truth or   Las   Sacramento Mts.
Eloy   Oracle   3267   Pima   Safford   Consequences   Cruces
Marana   Mt. Graham   Silver City   San Andres Mts.
Tucson   Willcox   Central   Hurley   Hatch   Las Cruces
Sells   Mt. Wrightson   Benson   Lordsburg   Deming   Mesilla
2881   Chiricahua Pk.   Anthony   2667
Nogales   2986   Las   El Paso   Guadalupe Pk.   E
Sierra Vista   Tombstone   Palomas   Ciudad Juárez   Clint   TEXAS
Nogales   Bisbee   Douglas   Fabens
Agua Prieta   Guadalupe   Rio Grande   Sierra
Bravos   Rio Bravo del Norte   Blanca
Heroica   Altar   Magdalena   Imuris   Cananea   El Porvenir
Caborca   Santa Ana   Nacozari   I. de   El Sueco   Carmen
Arizpe   Sta. María   Villa Ahumada   L.
Benjamin Hill   Cumpas   Nuevo Casas   de Palos
MEXICO   Grandes   CHIHUAHUA   F
SONORA   Moctezuma   Santa María   Buenaventura
Hermosillo   Ures   Suaqui   Carmen   El Sueco
Sonora   Mazatán   Sahuaripa   Temosachic
Torreos   Aquiles Serdán
Chihuahua   Conchos

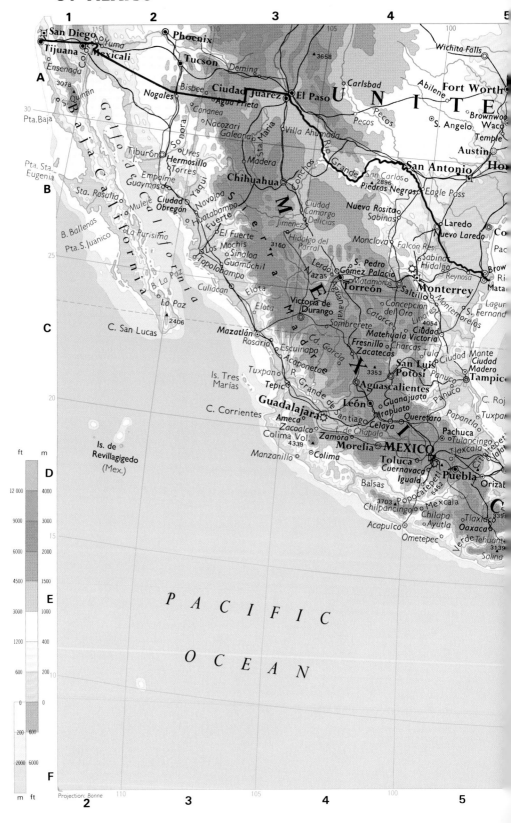

84 MEXICO

1 | **2** | **3** | **4** | **5**

San Diego
Yuma
Phoenix
Wichita Falls
Tijuana
Mexicali
Tucson
Ensenada
Deming
Carlsbad
Abilene
Fort Worth
3078
Bisbee
Ciudad
U N I T E
3658
Nogales
Agua Prieta
El Paso
S. Angelo
Brownsville
Waco
Pta. Baja
30
Cananea
Villa Ahumada
Pecos
Temple
Nacozari
Pecos
Austin
Pta. Sta.
Eugenia
Tiburón
Ures
Madera
Grande
San Antonio
Hou
Empalme
Hermosillo
Chihuahua
Conchos
San Carlos
Sta. Rosalia
Torres
2896
Piedras Negras
Eagle Pass
Muleje
Guaymas
Ciudad
Camargo
Nueva Rosita
Laredo
B. Ballenas
Ciudad
Obregón
Huatabampo
Delicias
Sabinas
Nuevo Laredo
Co
La Purisima
Navojoa
Fuerte
Jimenez
Monclova
Falcon Res.
Pac
Pta. S. Juanico
El Fuerte
Hidalgo del
Parral
Sabinas
Hidalgo
25
Los Mochis
3160
Lerdo
S. Pedro
Reynosa
Brow
Topolobampo
Sinaloa
Nazas
Gómez Palacio
Ri
Guamúchil
Matamoros
Mata
Culiacán
Elota
Torreón
Saltillo
Monterrey
Concepcion
Lagu
C. San Lucas
2406
Elota
Victoria de
Durango
del Oro
S. Fernand
Mazatlán
Sombrerete
Catorce
4054
Ciudad
Rosario
Cd. Garcia
Matehuala
Victoria
Mante
Escuinapa
Fresnillo
Charcas
Ciudad
Madero
Acaponeta
Zacatecas
San Luis
Tula
Tampico
Is. Tres
Tuxpan
3353
Potosi
Panuco
Marias
R.
Aguascalientes
Panuco
C. Roj
Tepic
Grande de
León
Guanajuato
Tuxpan
Guadalajara
Santiago
Irapuato
Celaya
Querétaro
Papantla
Ameca
L. de Chapala
Pachuca
Zacoalco
Zamora
Tlaxco
Colima Vol.
Morelia
MEXICO
Tulancingo
4339
Colima
Toluca
Tlaxcala
Manzanillo
Cuernavaca
Iguala
Puebla
Orizal
Balsas
5452
3703
Popocatépetl
Mexcala
Chilpancingo
Chilapa
Tlaxiaco
Acapulco
Ayutla
Oaxaca
Ometepec
Verde
Tehuant
31,39
Salina

P A C I F I C

O C E A N

Is. de
Revillagigedo
(Mex.)

ft	m
12 000	4000
9000	3000
6000	2000
4500	1500
3000	1000
1200	400
600	200
0	0
200	600
2000	6000

m | ft

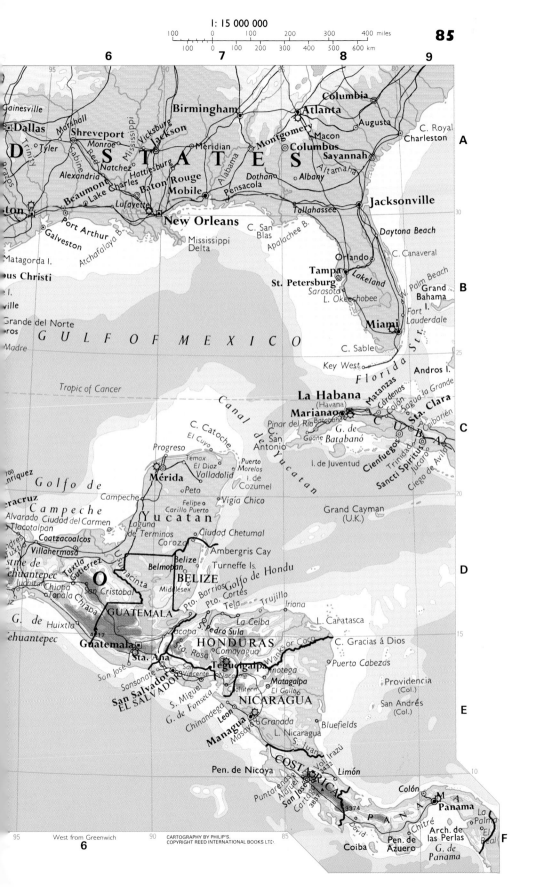

1 : 15 000 000

100   0   100   200   300   400 miles

100   0   100   200   300   400   500   600 km

6   7   8   9

UNITED STATES

Gainesville   Birmingham   Columbia
Dallas   Marshall   Atlanta   Augusta
Shreveport   Jackson   C. Royal
Tyler   Monroe   Vicksburg   Meridian   Montgomery   Columbus   Charleston
S T A T E S   Macon   Savannah
Natchez   Hattiesburg   Columbus
Alexandria   Alabama   Dothan   Albany   Altamaha
Beaumont   Lake Charles   Baton Rouge   Pensacola
ton   Lufayette   Mobile   Tallahassee   Jacksonville
Port Arthur B.   New Orleans   Daytona Beach
Galveston   Atchafalaya B.   C. San   Apalachee B.
Matagorda I.   Mississippi   Blas   Orlando   C. Canaveral
Delta   Tampa   Lakeland   W. Palm Beach
us Christi   St. Petersburg   Grand
l.   Sarasota   L. Okeechobee   Bahama
ville   Miami   Fort   I.
Grande del Norte   Lauderdale
ros   **G U L F   O F   M E X I C O**   C. Sable
Madre   Key West   Florida Str.   Andros I.

Tropic of Cancer   Canal de   La Habana
Matanzas
(Havana)   Córdenas   Sagua la Grande
Marianao   Batabanó   Colón   Sta. Clara
Pinar del Rio   C U B A   Caibarién
C. Catoche   El Cuyo   C. San   G. de   Trinidad
Progreso   Antonio   Guane   Batabanó   Cienfuegos   Sancti Spíritus
Temax   Puerto   I. de Juventud   Ciego de Ávila
El Diaz   Morelos
nriquez   Mérida   Valladolid   I. de
Golfo de   Peto   Cozumel
raruz   Campeche   Vigía Chico   Grand Cayman
Alvarado   Ciudad del Carmen   (U.K.)
Tlacotalpan   Felipe
Coatzacoalcos   Carillo Puerto
ndres   Laguna   Ciudad Chetumal
Villahermosa   de Terminos   Corozal
stme de   Tuxtla   Ambergris Cay
ehuantepec   Gutierrez   Belize   Turneffe Is.
Chiapa   Belmopan   **BELIZE**
Juditan   Tonala   Chiapa   San Cristobal   Middlesex
Golfo de Hondu
G. de Huixtla   **G U A T E M A L A**   Pto. Barrios   Pto. Cortés
ehuantepec   Zacapa   Tela   Trujillo   L. Caratasca
Guatemala   4217   La Ceiba   Iriona
Sta. Ana   Pedro Sula   Wanks or Coco   C. Gracias á Dios
Sta. Rosa   **HONDURAS**   Puerto Cabezas
San José   Comayagua   Providencia
Sonsonate   San   Tegucigalpa   notega   (Col.)
San Salvador   Vincente   Nacaome   San Andrés
EL SALVADOR   Matagalpa   (Col.)
S. Miguel   El Gallo
G. de Fonseca   **NICARAGUA**
Chinandega   Leon
Managua   Granada   Bluefields
Masay   L. Nicaragua
S. Juan   **COSTA RICA**   Limón
Pen. de Nicoya   Vol. Irazú   Colón
Puntarenas   Alajuel   3432   **P A N A M A**   Panama
San José   Cartago   La
Cortés   3374   Chitré   Arch. de   Palma
David   las Perlas   El
Coiba   Pen. de   Real
Azuero   G. de
Panama

CARTOGRAPHY BY PHILIP'S.
COPYRIGHT REED INTERNATIONAL BOOKS LTD.

A

B

C

D

E

F

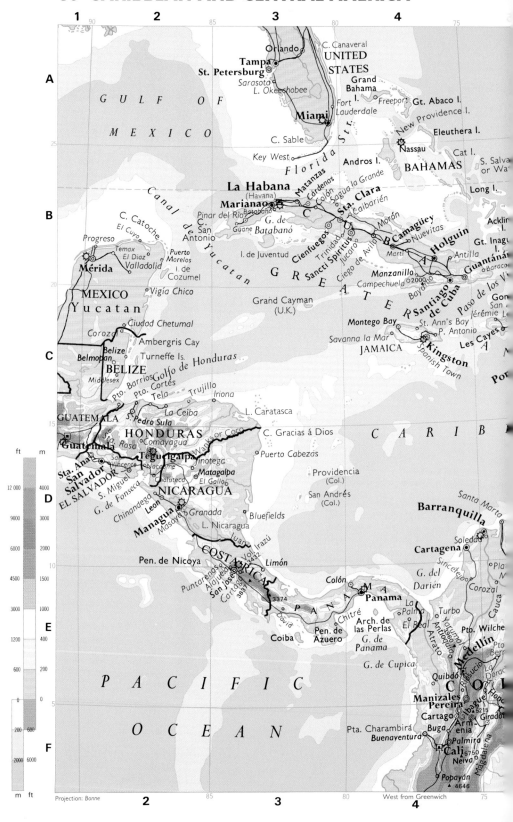

86 CARIBBEAN AND CENTRAL AMERICA

UNITED STATES

C. Canaveral
Orlando
Tampa
St. Petersburg
Sarasota
L. Okeechobee
Grand Bahama I.
Fort Lauderdale
Freeport
Gt. Abaco I.
Miami
New Providence I.
C. Sable
Nassau
Eleuthera I.
Key West
Andros I.
BAHAMAS
Cat I.
S. Salva or Wa
Long I.
Acklir

GULF OF MEXICO

Canal de Yucatan

C. Catoche
El Cuyo
Progreso
Temax
El Diaz
Mérida
Valladolid
I. de Cozumel
Puerto Morelos
MEXICO
Yucatan
Vigía Chico

C. San Antonio
Pinar del Río
Batabanó
La Habana
(Havana)
Marianao
G. de Batabanó
Cienfuegos
I. de Juventud
Matanzas
Cárdenas
Colón
Sagua la Grande
Sta. Clara
Caibarién
Morón
Camagüey
Nuevitas
Holguin
Antilla
Gt. Inagu
Guantán
Baraco
Manzanillo
Bayo
Santiago de Cuba
2000
Campechuela
Sancti Spíritus
Trinidad
Ciego de Ávila
Júcaro
Martí
GREATER

Grand Cayman
(U.K.)

Ciudad Chetumal
Corozal
Ambergris Cay
Belize
Turneffe Is.
BELIZE
Belmopan
Middlesex
Golfo de Honduras
Pto. Barrios
Pto. Cortés
Tela
Trujillo
Iriona
La Ceiba
L. Caratasca

Montego Bay
Savanna la Mar
St. Ann's Bay
Spanish Town
JAMAICA
Kingston
Les Cayes
P. Antonio
Jérémie
Paso de los V
Gon
San
Por

GUATEMALA
S. Pedro Sula
HONDURAS
Comayagua
Guatemala
Sta. Rosa
San Vincente
San Salvador
EL SALVADOR
S. Miguel
G. de Fonseca
Chinandega
León
Managua
Masay
Granada
NICARAGUA
L. Nicaragua
Tegucigalpa
Jinotega
Matagalpa
El Gallo
Wanks or Coco
C. Gracias á Dios
Puerto Cabezas
Bluefields
Providencia
(Col.)
San Andrés
(Col.)

CARIB

Pen. de Nicoya
COSTA RICA
Puntarenas
Alajuela
San José
Cartago
3837
3374
Irazú
2442
Limón
Colón
Panama
PANAMA
Chitré
Pen. de Azuero
Coiba
G. del Darién
La Palma
El Real
Arch. de las Perlas
G. de Panama
G. de Cupica
Pta. Charambirá
Buenaventura

Santa Marta
BARRANQUILLA
Soledad
Cartagena
Sincelejo
Corozal
Turbo
Pto. Wilche
Medellín
Quibdó
Manizales
Pereira
Cartago
Buga
Armenia
Palmira
Cali
Neiva
Popayán
4646
5215
5750
Giradot
COL

PACIFIC OCEAN

Florida Str.

Projection: Bonne

West from Greenwich

ft	m
12 000	4000
9000	3000
6000	2000
4500	1500
3000	1000
1200	400
600	200
0	0
200	600
2000	6000
m	ft

1: 15 000 000

100   0   100   200   300   400 miles
100   0   100   200   300   400   500   600 km

ATLANTIC

OCEAN

Tropic of Cancer

Mayaguana

Caicos I. (U.K.)

Turks Is. (U.K.)

Port de Paix   S. Francisco de Macoris

Cap Haitien   Monte Cristi   Valverde   Pto. Plata   Santiago

Vega   Sanchez   Canal de la Mona   PUERTO RICO (U.S.A.)   St. Thomas (U.S.A.)

DOMINICAN   Aguadilla   Arecibo   San Juan   Charlotte Amalie   Virgin Is. (U.K.)   Anguilla (U.K.)   St. Martin (Fr. & Neth.)   Sombrero (U.K.)

REP.   1338   Caguas   St. Croix   ST. CHRISTOPHER -

au Prince   La Romana   Ponce   (U.S.A.)   NEVIS   ANTIGUA &

Santo Domingo   Guayama   Christiansted   Basseterre   BARBUDA

S. Pedro de Macoris   Mayagüez   Charlestown   St. John's

Azua   Bani   Bahrona   Mayagüez   Plymouth   Montserrat (U.K.)

Hispaniola   Duverge   Barahona   Leeward   Guadeloupe (Fr.)

TILLES   Islands   Pointe à Pitre

LESSER   DOMINICA

Roseau

Fort de France   Martinique (Fr.)

EAN   SEA   ANTILLES   Castries

Windward   ST. LUCIA

ST. VINCENT   BARBADOS

&   Kingstown   Bridgetown

THE GRENADINES

Islands   GRENADA

St. George's

Pta. Gallinas   Venezuela de   La Blanquilla   (Ven.)

Aruba (Neth.)   Curaçao   Willemstad   Tobago

Pen. de la   NETH.   Bonaire   Margarita   Port of Spain

Guajira   ANTILLES   La Asunción   Carúpano   TRINIDAD & TOBAGO

Golfo de Venezuela   Pta. Cabello   Maiquetía   La Tortuga   Cumaná   G. de   San Fernando

Coro   Dabajuro   (Ven.)   Paria

5800   Caracas

Sa. Nevada   Maracaibo   Cabimas   Maracay   Barcelona   2596   Maturín

de Sta. Marta   San Felipe   Valencia   Coripi   El Tigre   Tucupita

L. de   Trujillo   Barquisimeto   Las Mercedes   Orinoco   Ciudad

Maracaibo   Calabozo   Guayana

El Banco   Valera   Portuguesa   San Fernando   Ciudad Bolívar   Georgetown

Ocaña   5007   Guanare   de Apure   New

cuta   Cord. de Mérida   Apure   El Callao   Tumeremo   Amsterdam

Rubio   San Cristóbal   Caicara   Wismar

4100   Pamplona   Arauca   Arauca   VENEZUELA   2560

Bucaramanga   Meta   Pto. Páez   Caura   Roraima   SURINAM

rrancabermeja   Pto. Carreño   228?   2810

Tunja   Pto. Ayacucho   1280

OMBIA   Sierra Pacaraima

Zipaquirá

Bogotá

Guaviare   Casiquiare

Sa. Parima

BRAZIL

CARTOGRAPHY BY PHILIP'S. COPYRIGHT REED INTERNATIONAL BOOKS LTD.

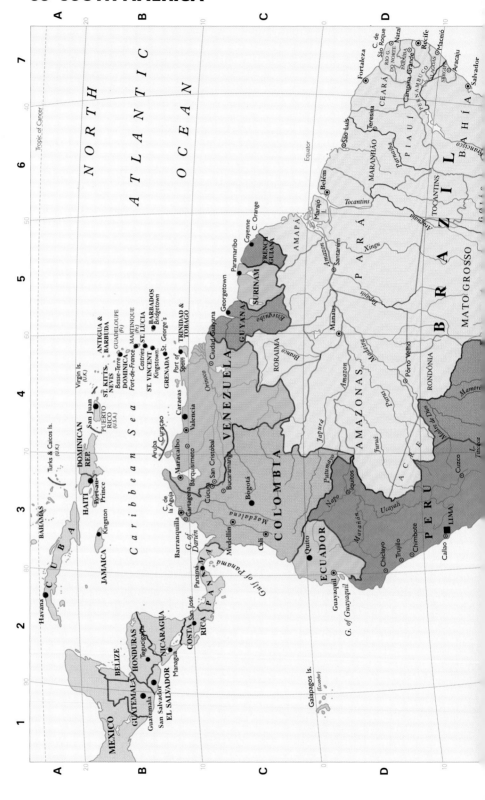

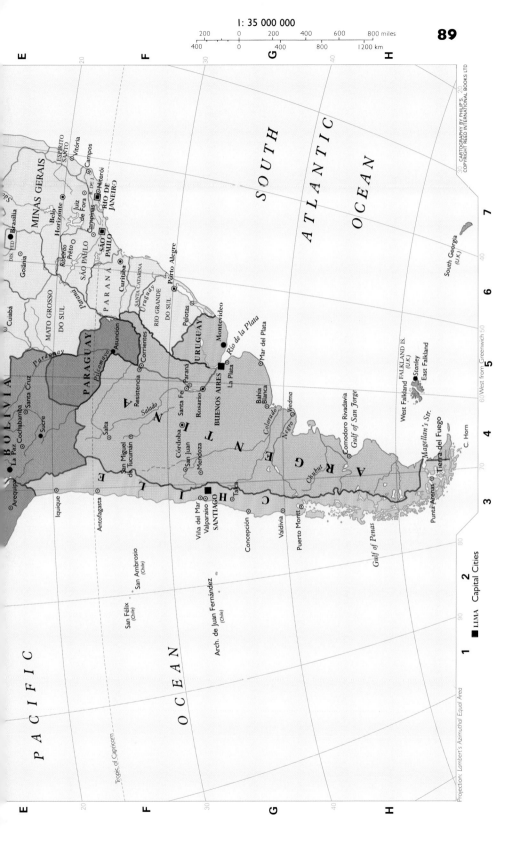

1: 35 000 000

200   0   200   400   600   800 miles
400   0   400   800   1200 km

Projection: Lambert's Azimuthal Equal Area

CARTOGRAPHY BY PHILIP'S
COPYRIGHT REED INTERNATIONAL BOOKS LTD

■ LIMA   Capital Cities

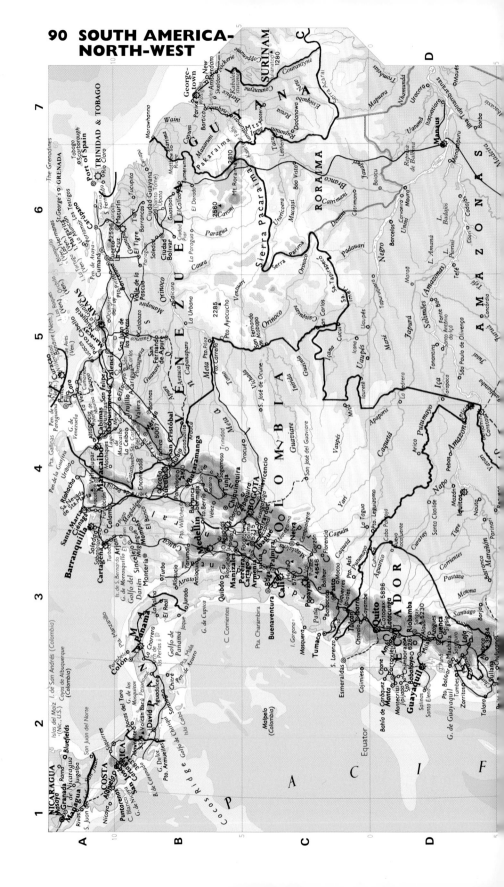

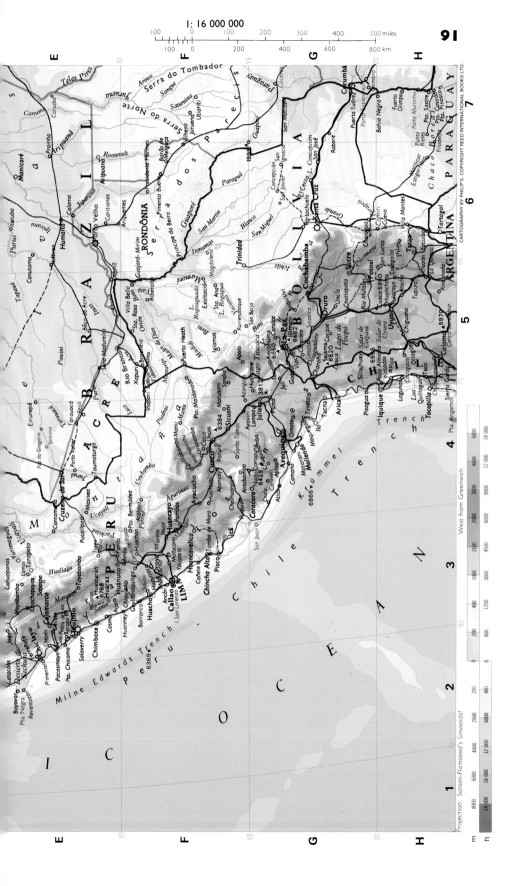

1 : 16 000 000

100   0   100   200   300   400   500 miles

100   0   200   400   600   800 km

CARTOGRAPHY BY PHILIP'S. COPYRIGHT REED INTERNATIONAL BOOKS LTD.

Projection: Sanson-Flamsteed's Sinusoidal

West from Greenwich

m   8000 6000 4000 2000 1500 1000 600 400 200 0
ft   24000 18000 12000 9000 6000 4500 3000 1200 600 0   6000 12000 18000

B R A Z I L

RONDÔNIA

ACRE

M

P E R U

C H I L E

B O L I V I A

ARGENTINA PARAGUAY

Chaco Boreal

P A C I F I C   O C E A N

Peru   Trench

Milne Edwards Trench

Krümmel   Trench

Chile   Trench

LIMA
Callao

Lago Titicaca

Cuzco

Arequipa

Arica

Iquique

La Paz

Oruro

Cochabamba

Sucre

Potosí

Santa Cruz

Trinidad

Corumbá

Puerto Suárez

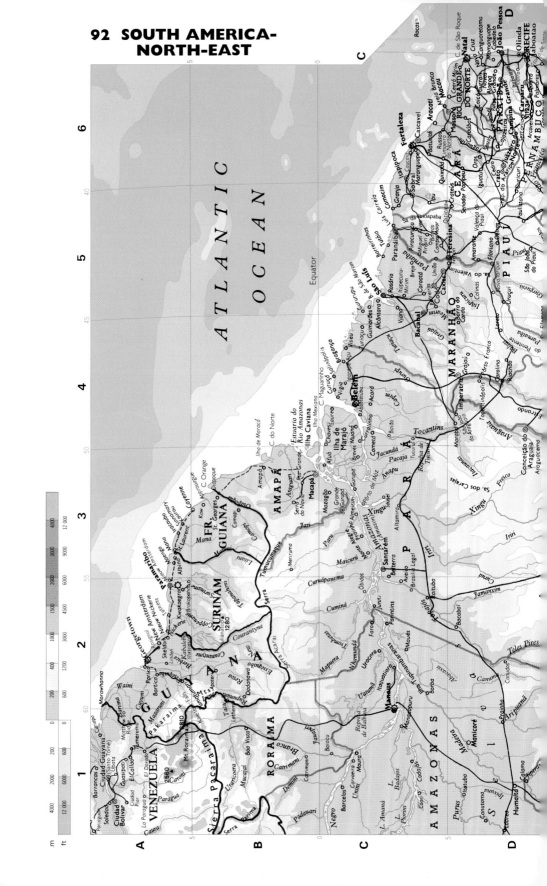

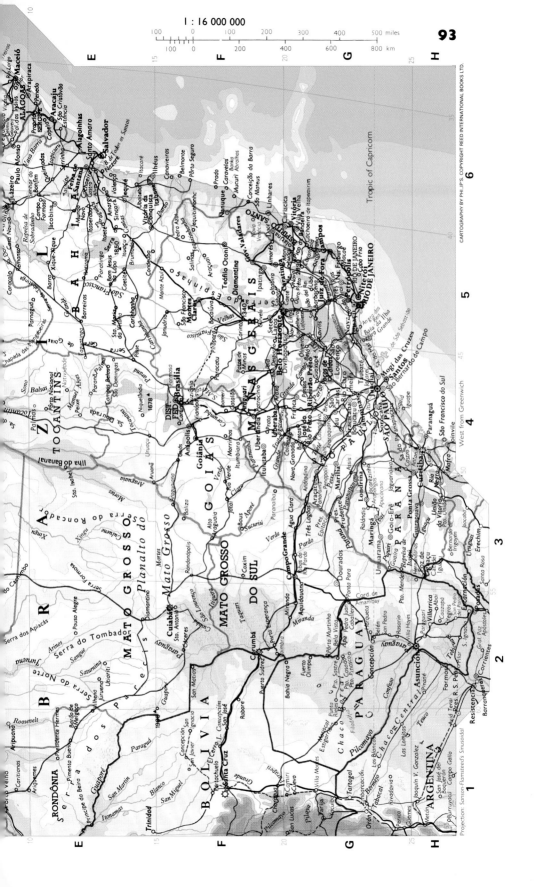

1 : 16 000 000

CARTOGRAPHY BY PHILIP'S. COPYRIGHT REED INTERNATIONAL BOOKS LTD.

Projection: Sanson-Flamsteed's Sinusoidal

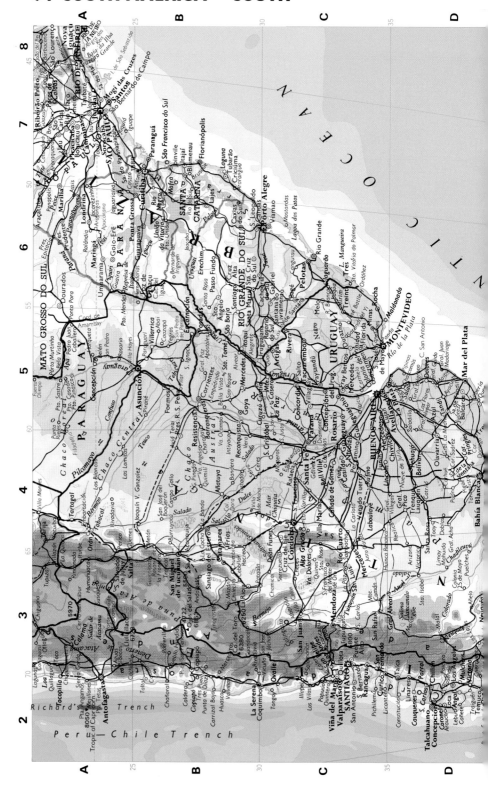

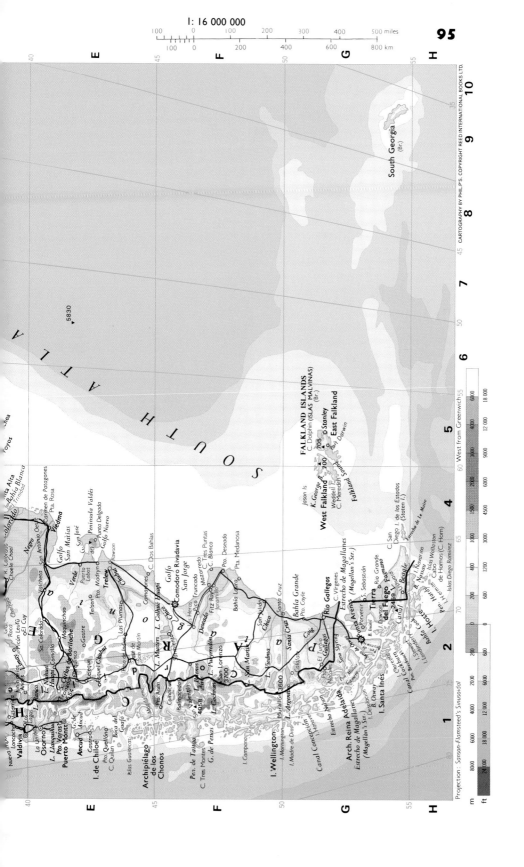

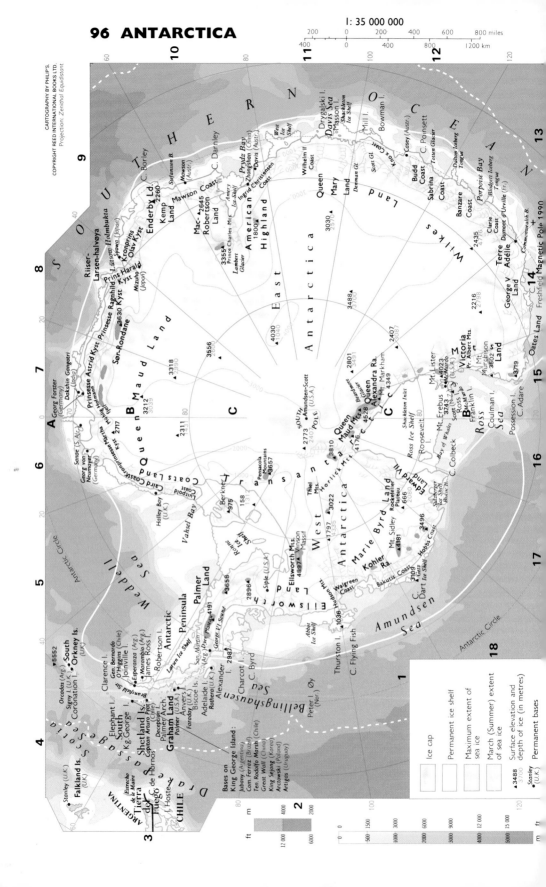

1: 35 000 000

200   0   200   400   600   800 miles
400   0   400   800   1200 km

CARTOGRAPHY BY PHILIP'S
COPYRIGHT REED INTERNATIONAL BOOKS LTD.
Projection: Zenithal Equidistant

SOUTHERN OCEAN

East Antarctica

West Antarctica

Weddell Sea

Bellingshausen Sea

Amundsen Sea

Ross Sea

Davis Sea

Queen Maud Land

Enderby Ld.

Coats Land

Palmer Land

Ellsworth Land

Marie Byrd Land

Wilkes Land

American Highland

Transantarctic Mts.

Queen Mary Land

Bases on King George Island:
Jubany (Argentina)
Com. Ferraz (Brazil)
Ten. Rodolfo Marsh (Chile)
Great Wall (China)
King Sejong (Korea)
Arctowski (Poland)
Artigas (Uruguay)

Legend

	Ice cap
	Permanent ice shelf
	Maximum extent of sea ice
	March (Summer) extent of sea ice
▲3488 ▼3700	Surface elevation and depth of ice (in metres)
● Stanley	Permanent bases

Index to Map Pages

The index contains the names of all principal places and features shown on the maps. Physical features composed of a proper name (Erie) and a description (Lake) are positioned alphabetically by the proper name. The description is positioned after the proper name and is usually abbreviated:

Erie, L. **72   C5**

Where a description forms part of a settlement or administrative name however, it is always written in full and put in its true alphabetical position:

Lake Charles   **79   D7**

Names beginning St. are alphabetized under Saint, but Sankt, Sint, Sant, Santa and San are all spelt in full and are alphabetized accordingly.

The number in bold type which follows each name in the index refers to the number of the map page where that feature or place will be found. This is usually the largest scale at which the place or feature appears.

The letter and figure which are in bold type immediately after the page number give the grid square on the map page, within which the feature is situated.

Rivers carry the symbol → after their names. A solid square ■ follows the name of a country while an open square □ refers to a first order administrative area.

A

Name	Page	Grid
A Coruña = La Coruña	18	A1
Aachen	14	C4
Aalborg = Ålborg	9	G9
Aalen	14	D6
Aarau	13	C8
Aare →	13	C8
Aarhus = Århus	9	G10
Aba	55	G6
Ābādān	47	E7
Ābādeh	44	D3
Abadla	54	B4
Abaetetuba	92	C4
Abakan	30	D7
Abancay	91	F4
Abarqū	44	D3
Abashiri	32	F12
Abay	29	E8
Abaya, L.	53	G6
Abbay = Nîl el Azraq →	53	E5
Abbeville	12	A4
Abbieglassie	63	A4
Abbot Ice Shelf	96	B2
Abbottabad	42	B8
Abd al Kūrī	49	E5
Abéché	53	F3
Abeokuta	55	G5
Abercorn = Mbala	57	F6
Abercorn	63	A5
Aberdeen, Australia	63	B5
Aberdeen, U.K.	10	C5
Aberdeen, S. Dak., U.S.A.	76	C5
Aberdeen, Wash., U.S.A.	80	B2
Aberystwyth	11	E4
Abidjan	55	G4
Abilene	78	C4
Abitibi L.	69	D3
Abkhaz Republic □ = Abkhazia □	25	E5
Abkhazia □	25	E5
Abminga	62	A1
Åbo = Turku	9	F12
Abohar	42	D9
Aboméy	55	G5
Abong-Mbang	56	D2
Abou-Deïa	53	F2
Abri	52	D5
Abrolhos, Banka	93	F6
Abrud	17	E6
Absaroka Range	81	C9
Abū al Khaşīb	47	E6
Abū 'Alī	47	F7
Abu 'Arīsh	49	D3
Abu Dhabi = Abū Ţaby	44	E3
Abū Dīs	53	E5
Abu Hamed	53	E5
Abū Kamāl	46	D5
Abu Mataria	53	F4
Abu Rudeis	47	E3
Abu Tig	52	C5
Abû Zabad	53	F4
Abû Ţaby	44	E3
Abuja	55	G6
Abukuma-Gawa →	33	G12
Abunã	91	E5
Abunã →	91	E5
Abut Hd.	65	E4
Abwong	53	G5
Acaponeta	84	C3
Acapulco	84	D5
Acarigua	90	B5
Accra	55	G4
Aceh □	36	D1
Achalpur	43	J10
Achill I.	11	E1
Achinsk	30	D7
Acireale	21	F5
Acklins I.	86	B5
Aconcagua, Cerro	94	C3
Aconquija, Mt.	94	B3
Açores, Is. dos = Azores	50	C1
Acraman, L.	62	B2
Acre = 'Akko	46	D3
Acre □	91	E4
Acre →	91	E5
Ad Dahnā	47	F7
Ad Dammām	47	F7
Ad Dawhah	44	E2
Ad Dilam	47	G6
Ad Dīwāniyah	47	E6
Ada	79	B5
Adaja →	18	B3
Adam	44	F4
Adamaoua, Massif de l'	53	G1
Adamawa Highlands = Adamaoua, Massif de l'	53	G1
Adamello, Mte.	20	A3
Adaminaby	63	C4
Adam's Bridge	43	Q11
Adams Mt.	80	B3
Adana	46	C3
Adapazarı	46	B2
Adarama	53	E5
Adare, C.	96	B15
Adaut	39	F4
Adavale	63	A3
Adda →	20	B2
Addis Ababa = Addis Abeba	53	G6
Addis Abeba	53	G6
Addis Alem	53	G6
Adelaide	62	B2
Adelaide I.	96	A3
Adelaide Pen.	70	B10
Adélie, Terre	96	A14
Adélie Land = Adélie, Terre	96	A14
Aden = Al 'Adan	49	E4
Aden, G. of	49	E4
Adi	39	E4
Adi Ugri	53	F6
Adige →	20	B4
Adilabad	43	K11
Adirondack Mts.	73	C8
Admer	54	D6
Admiralty I.	71	C6
Admiralty Is.	64	K9
Ado-Ekiti	55	G6
Adonara	39	F2
Adoni	43	M10
Adour →	12	E3
Adra	18	D4
Adrano	21	F5
Adrar	54	C4
Adré	53	F3
Adrī	52	C1
Adriatic Sea	20	C5
Adua	39	E3

Adwa 53 F6
Adzhar
  Republic □ =
  Ajaria □ 25 E5
Ægean Sea ... 23 E5
Aerhtai Shan . 34 B4
Afghanistan ■ . 45 C6
Afgoi 49 G3
'Afif 47 G5
Afognak I. 71 C4
Afuá 92 C3
Afyonkarahisar 46 C2
Agadès =
  Agadez 55 E6
Agadez 55 E6
Agadir 54 B3
Agapa 30 B6
Agartala 41 F8
Agats 39 F5
Agboville 55 G4
Agde 13 E5
Agen 12 D4
Agra 42 F10
Agri .→ 21 D6
Ağrı Dağı 46 C6
Ağrı Karakose . 46 C5
Agrigento 21 F4
Agrinion 23 E3
Água Clara ... 93 G3
Agua Prieta .. 84 A3
Aguadas 90 B3
Aguadilla 87 C6
Aguarico .→ .. 90 D3
Aguas Blancas 94 A3
Aguascalientes 84 C4
Aguilas 19 D5
Agulhas, C. ... 58 E4
Agung 37 F5
Agusan .→ ... 38 C7
Ahaggar 54 D6
Ahar 46 C6
Ahipara B. 64 A5
Ahiri 43 K12
Ahmadabad .. 43 H8
Ahmadnagar .. 43 K9
Ahmadpur ... 42 E7
Ahmedabad =
  Ahmadabad . 43 H8
Ahmednagar =
  Ahmadnagar 43 K9
Ahvāz 47 E7
Ahvenanmaa =
  Åland 9 F11
Aḥwar 49 E4
Aigues-Mortes . 13 E6
Aihui 35 A7
Aija 91 E3
Aiken 75 C7
Aimere 39 F2
Aimorés 93 F5
Ain Banaiyan .. 44 F2
Aïn Beïda ... 54 A6
Aïn Ben Tili ... 54 C3
Aïn-Sefra 54 B4
Ainabo 49 F4
Aïr 55 E6
Aisne .→ 13 B5
Aiud 17 E6
Aix-en-Provence 13 E6
Aix-la-Chapelle
  = Aachen .. 14 C4
Aix-les-Bains .. 13 D6
Aiyion 23 E4
Aizawl 41 F9
Ajaccio 13 F8
Ajanta Ra. ... 43 J9
Ajari Rep. =
  Ajaria □ 25 E5
Ajaria □ 25 E5

Ajdâbiyah 52 B3
Ajka 16 E3
'Ajmān 44 E3
Ajmer 42 F9
Ajo, C. de 18 A4
Akaroa 65 E5
Akashi 32 B4
Akelamo 39 D3
Aketi 56 D4
Akharnaí 23 E4
Akhelóös .→ .. 23 E3
Akhisar 23 E6
Akhmîm 52 C5
Akimiski I. 69 C2
Akita 33 G12
Akjoujt 55 E2
'Akko 46 D3
Akkol 29 E8
Aklavik 70 B6
Akmolinsk =
  Aqmola 29 D8
Akobo .→ 53 G5
Akola 43 J10
Akordat 53 E6
Akpatok I. 68 B4
Akreïjit 55 E3
Akron 72 D5
Aksai Chin ... 42 B11
Aksaray 46 C3
Aksarka 28 C7
Akşehir 46 C2
Aksu 34 B3
Aksum 53 F6
Aktogay 29 E8
Aktsyabrski ... 17 B9
Aktyubinsk =
  Aqtöbe 29 D6
Aku 55 G6
Akure 55 G6
Akyab = Sittwe 41 G9
Al 'Adan 49 E4
Al Aḥsā 47 F7
Al Amādīyah .. 46 C5
Al Amārah 47 E6
Al 'Aqabah ... 47 E3
Al 'Aramah ... 47 F6
Al Ashkhara ... 45 F4
Al Baḍi' 47 G6
Al Başrah 47 E6
Al Bayḍā 52 B3
Al Bu'ayrāt al
  Ḥasūn 52 B2
Al Fallūjah 46 D5
Al Fāw 47 E7
Al Fujayrah ... 44 E4
Al Hābah 47 F6
Al Haddār 47 G6
Al Hāmad 47 E4
Al Ḥamar 47 G6
Al Ḥamrā' 47 F4
Al Ḥarīq 47 G6
Al Ḥasakah ... 46 C5
Al Ḥawrah 49 E4
Al Ḥayy 47 D6
Al Ḥijāz 47 F4
Al Ḥillah, Iraq . 47 D6
Al Ḥillah,
  Si. Arabia .. 47 G6
Al Hindīyah ... 47 D6
Al Hoceïma ... 54 A4
Al Ḥudaydah .. 49 E3
Al Hufūf 47 F7
Al Ḥulwah ... 47 G6
Al Ittihad =
  Madīnat ash
  Sha'b 49 E3
Al Jāfūrah 47 F7
Al Jaghbūb ... 52 C3
Al Jahrah 47 E6

Al Jalāmīd 47 E4
Al Jawf, Libya . 52 D3
Al Jawf,
  Si. Arabia ... 47 E4
Al Jazirah, Iraq 46 D5
Al Jazirah, Libya 52 C3
Al Jubayl 47 F7
Al Jubaylah .. 47 F6
Al Junaynah .. 53 F3
Al Khābūra .. 44 F4
Al Khalīl 47 E3
Al Kharfah ... 47 G6
Al Kharj 47 F6
Al Khasab 44 E4
Al Kufrah 52 D3
Al Kūt 47 D6
Al Kuwayt 47 E7
Al Lādhiqīyah . 46 D3
Al Luḥayyah .. 49 D3
Al Madīnah ... 47 F4
Al Majma'ah .. 47 F6
Al Manāmah .. 44 E2
Al Marj 52 B3
Al Mawşil 46 C5
Al Midhnab ... 47 F6
Al Mish'āb ... 47 E7
Al Mubarraz ... 47 F7
Al Muḥarraq .. 44 E2
Al Mukallā ... 49 E4
Al Mukhā 49 E3
Al Musayyib .. 47 D6
Al Muwayliḥ .. 47 F3
Al Qaḍīmah .. 47 G4
Al Qā'iyah ... 47 F5
Al Qāmishli ... 46 C5
Al Qaşabát ... 52 B1
Al Qaşīm 47 F5
Al Qaţīf 47 F7
Al Qaţrūn 52 D2
Al Qayşūmah . 47 E6
Al Quaisūmah . 47 E6
Al Quds =
  Jerusalem .. 47 E3
Al Qurayyāt .. 45 F4
Al Qurnah 47 E6
Al 'Ulā 47 F4
Al Uqaylah ash
  Sharqiyah .. 52 B2
Al Uqayr 47 F7
Al 'Uthmānīyah 47 F7
Al 'Uwaynid .. 47 F6
Al 'Uwayqīlah . 47 E5
Al 'Uyūn 47 F5
Al Wakrah 44 E2
Al Wari'āh ... 47 F6
Al Yamāmah .. 47 F6
Alabama □ ... 74 C4
Alabama .→ .. 74 D4
Alaçam Dağları 23 E7
Alagoa Grande 92 D6
Alagoas □ 93 D6
Alagoinhas ... 93 E6
Alajuela 86 D3
Alamosa 83 B10
Åland 9 F11
Alania = North
  Ossetia □ ... 25 E5
Alanya 46 C2
Alapayevsk ... 29 D7
Alaşehir 23 E7
Alaska □ 71 B4
Alaska, G. of .. 71 C5
Alaska Peninsula 71 C4
Alaska Range . 71 B4
Alataw Shankou 34 B3
Alatyr 24 C6
Alausi 90 D3
Alawoona 62 B3
Alba 20 B2

Alba-Iulia 17 E6
Albacete 19 C5
Albacutya, L. .. 62 C3
Albania ■ ... 23 D3
Albany,
  Australia 60 H2
Albany, Ga.,
  U.S.A. 75 D5
Albany, N.Y.,
  U.S.A. 73 C9
Albany, Oreg.,
  U.S.A. 80 C2
Albany .→ 69 C2
Albardón 94 C3
Albemarle 75 B7
Alberche .→ .. 18 C3
Albert, L. 62 C2
Albert L. 57 D6
Albert Nile .→ . 57 D6
Albertville 13 D7
Albi 12 E5
Albina 92 A3
Alborán 18 E4
Ålborg 9 G9
Alborz, Reshteh-
  ye Kūhhā-ye . 44 B3
Albuquerque . 83 C9
Albury 63 C4
Alcalá de
  Henares 18 B4
Alcalá la Real . 18 D4
Alcamo 21 F4
Alcañiz 19 B5
Alcântara,
  Embalse de . 18 C2
Alcantarilla ... 19 D5
Alcaraz, Sierra
  de 19 C4
Alcaudete 18 D3
Alcázar de San
  Juan 18 C4
Alchevsk 25 D4
Alcira 19 C5
Alcoy 19 C5
Aldabra Is. ... 51 G8
Aldan .→ 31 C10
Alderney 11 G5
Aleg 55 E2
Alegrete 94 B5
Aleisk 29 D9
Aleksandriya =
  Oleksandriya 17 C8
Aleksandrovskoye
  .... 29 C8
Alemania 94 B3
Alençon 12 B4
Aleppo = Ḥalab 46 C4
Alès 13 D6
Alessándria .. 20 B2
Ålesund 8 F9
Aleutian Is. ... 71 C2
Alexander Arch. 71 C6
Alexander I. .. 96 A3
Alexandra,
  Australia 63 C4
Alexandra, N.Z. 65 F3
Alexandria = El
  Iskandarîya . 52 B4
Alexandria,
  Canada 71 C7
Alexandria,
  Romania ... 22 C5
Alexandria,
  S. Africa .. 59 E5
Alexandria, La.,
  U.S.A. 79 D7
Alexandria, Va.,
  U.S.A. 73 E7

Alexandrina, L.	62	C2
Alexandroúpolis	22	D5
Alga	29	E6
Algarve	18	D1
Algeciras	18	D3
Algemesí	19	C5
Alger	54	A5
Algeria ■	54	C5
Alghero	21	D2
Algiers = Alger	54	A5
Algoa B.	59	E5
Alhucemas = Al Hoceïma	54	A4
'Alī al Gharbī	47	D6
'Alī Khēl	42	C6
Aliağa	23	E6
Alibo	53	G6
Alicante	19	C5
Alice Springs	60	E5
Aligarh	42	F11
Aligüdarz	46	D7
Alipur	42	E7
Alipur Duar	41	D7
Aliwal North	59	E5
Aljustrel	18	D1
Alkmaar	14	B3
All American Canal	82	D5
Allahabad	40	E3
Allanmyo	41	H10
Allegheny →	73	D5
Allegheny Plateau	73	F5
Allentown	73	D8
Alleppey	43	Q10
Aller →	14	B5
Allier →	13	C5
Allora	63	A5
Alma Ata = Almaty	29	E8
Almada	18	C1
Almadén	18	C3
Almansa	19	C5
Almanzor, Pico del Moro	18	B3
Almanzora →	19	D5
Almaty	29	E8
Almazán	19	B4
Almeirim	92	C3
Almelo	14	B4
Almendralejo	18	C2
Almería	19	D4
Almora	42	E11
Alnwick	10	D6
Alon	41	F10
Alor	39	F2
Alor Setar	36	C2
Alps	14	E5
Alsace	13	B7
Alsask	71	C9
Alsásua	19	A4
Alta Gracia	94	C4
Altagracia	90	A4
Altai = Aerhtai Shan	34	B4
Altamira	92	C3
Altamura	21	D6
Altanbulag	35	A5
Altay	34	B3
Altea	19	C5
Alto Araguaia	93	F3
Alto Molocue	59	B7
Alton	77	F9
Alton Downs	62	A2
Altoona	73	D6
Altun Shan	34	C3
Alùla	49	E5
Alusi	39	F4
Alvarado	85	D5
Alvear	94	B5
Alvie	62	C3
Alwar	42	F10
Alxa Zuoqi	35	C5
Am Dam	53	F3
Am-Timan	53	F3
Amâdi, Sudan	53	G5
Amadi, Zaïre	57	D5
Amadjuak	68	B3
Amadjuak L.	68	B3
Amagasaki	32	B4
Amakusa-Shotō	32	C2
Amaliás	23	F3
Amalner	43	J9
Amambay, Cordillera de	94	A5
Amangeldy	29	D7
Amapá	92	B3
Amapá □	92	B3
Amarante	92	D5
Amargosa	93	E6
Amarillo	78	B3
Amaro, Mte.	20	C5
Amasra	46	B3
Amasya	46	B3
Amazon = Amazonas →	92	C3
Amazonas □	90	D6
Amazonas →	92	C3
Ambala	42	D10
Ambalavao	59	J9
Ambam	56	D2
Ambanja	59	G9
Ambartsevo	29	D9
Ambato	90	D3
Ambatolampy	59	H9
Ambatondrazaka	59	H9
Amberg	15	D6
Ambergris Cay	85	D7
Amberley	65	E5
Ambikapur	40	F4
Ambilobé	59	G9
Ambo	91	F3
Amboise	12	C4
Ambon	39	E3
Ambositra	59	J9
Amboyna I.	36	C4
Ambriz	56	F2
Amby	63	A4
Amchitka I.	71	C1
Amderma	28	C7
Ameca	84	C4
Ameland	14	B3
American Highland	96	B10
American Samoa ■	65	L13
Americus	75	C5
Amery	71	C10
Amery Ice Shelf	96	A10
Ames	77	D8
Amherst, Burma	41	J11
Amherst, Canada	69	D4
Amiata, Mte.	20	C3
Amiens	12	B5
Amirante Is.	26	K9
'Ammān	47	E3
Amorgós	23	F5
Amoy = Xiamen	35	D6
Ampanihy	59	J8
Ampenan	37	F5
Amper →	15	D6
Amravati	43	J10
Amreli	42	J7
Amritsar	42	D9
Amroha	42	E11
Amsterdam	14	B3
Amstetten	15	D8
Amudarya →	29	E6
Amundsen Gulf	70	A7
Amundsen Sea	96	B1
Amuntai	37	E5
Amur →	31	D12
Amurang	39	D2
Amuri Pass	65	E5
Amyderya = Amudarya →	29	E6
An Nafūd	47	E5
An Najaf	47	D6
An Nhon	36	B3
An Nu'ayrīyah	47	F7
Anabar →	30	B9
Anaconda	81	B7
Anadolu	46	C2
'Ānah	46	D5
Anaheim	82	D4
Anakapalle	40	J4
Analalava	59	G9
Anambas, Kepulauan	37	D3
Anambas Is. = Anambas, Kepulauan	37	D3
Anamur	46	C3
Anan	32	C4
Anantnag	42	C9
Ananyiv	17	E9
Anápolis	93	F4
Anār	44	D3
Anārak	44	C3
Anatolia = Anadolu	46	C2
Añatuya	94	B4
Anaye	53	E1
Anchorage	71	B5
Ancohuma, Nevada	91	G5
Ancón	91	F3
Ancona	20	C4
Ancud	95	E2
Ancud, G. de	95	E2
Andalgalá	94	B3
Andalucía □	18	D3
Andalusia	74	D4
Andalusia □ = Andalucía □	18	D3
Andaman Is.	27	H13
Andaman Sea	36	B1
Andara	58	B4
Anderson	72	D3
Anderson →	70	B7
Andes = Andes, Cord. de los	91	G4
Andes, Cord. de los	91	G4
Andhra Pradesh □	43	L11
Andijon	29	E8
Andikithira	23	G4
Andizhan = Andijon	29	E8
Andkhvoy	45	B6
Andoany	59	G9
Andorra ■	19	A6
Andorra La Vella	19	A6
Andreanof Is.	71	C2
Andrewilla	62	A2
Ándria	20	D6
Andriba	59	H9
Andropov = Rybinsk	24	B4
Ándros	23	F5
Andros I.	86	B4
Andújar	18	C3
Andulo	56	G3
Aného	55	G5
Aneto, Pico de	19	A6
Angamos, Punta	94	A2
Ang'angxi	35	B7
Angara →	30	D7
Angarsk	30	D8
Angaston	62	B2
Ånge	8	F11
Angeles	38	A2
Angellala	63	A4
Ångermanälven →	8	F11
Angers	12	C3
Anglesey	11	E4
Ango	57	D5
Angol	94	D2
Angola ■	58	A3
Angoulême	12	D4
Angoumois	12	D4
Angra dos Reis	94	A8
Angren	29	E8
Anguilla ■	87	C7
Anhui □	35	C6
Anhwei □ = Anhui □	35	C6
Anjidiv I.	43	M9
Anjou	12	C3
Anjozorobe	59	H9
Anju	35	C7
Anka	55	F6
Ankang	35	C5
Ankara	46	C3
Ankazoabo	59	J8
Ankazobe	59	H9
Ankoro	57	F5
Ann Arbor	72	C4
Annaba	54	A6
Annan	11	D5
Annapolis	73	E7
Annecy	13	D7
Anning	34	D5
Anniston	74	C5
Annobón	51	G4
Annuello	62	B3
Anqing	35	C6
Ansbach	14	D6
Anshan	35	B7
Anshun	35	D5
Ansirabe	59	H9
Ansongo	55	E5
Ansudu	39	E5
Antabamba	91	F4
Antakya	46	C4
Antalaha	59	G10
Antalya	46	C2
Antalya Körfezi	46	C2
Antananarivo	59	H9
Antarctic Pen.	96	A4
Antarctica	96	C
Antequera	18	D3
Anti Atlas	54	C3
Antibes	13	E7
Anticosti, I. d'	69	D4
Antigua & Barbuda ■	87	C7
Antilla	86	B4
Antioquia	90	B3
Antofagasta	94	A2
Antofagasta de la Sierra	94	B3
Antongila, Helodrano	59	H9
Antonina	94	B7
Antrim	11	D3
Antsalova	59	H8
Antsiranana	59	G9
Antsohihy	59	G9
Antwerp = Antwerpen	14	C3
Antwerpen	14	C3
Anupgarh	42	E8
Anvers = Antwerpen	14	C3

Anvers I. 96 A3
Anxi 34 B4
Anxious B. 62 B1
Anyang 35 C6
Anzhero-
Sudzhensk .. 29 D9
Ánzio 20 D4
Aomori 33 F12
Aosta 20 B1
Aoudéras 55 E6
Aoulef el Arab . 54 C5
Apalachicola → 74 E5
Apaporis → .. 90 D5
Aparri 38 A2
Apeldoorn 14 B3
Apennines =
Appennini .. 20 B3
Apia 65 L13
Apiacás, Serra
dos 91 E7
Aplao 91 G4
Apo, Mt. 38 C3
Apollonia =
Marsá Susah 52 B3
Apolo 91 F5
Apoteri 90 C7
Appalachian
Mts. 73 F5
Appennini 20 B3
Appleton 72 B1
Approuague .. 92 B3
Aprília 20 D4
Apucarana 94 A6
Apure → 90 B5
Apurimac → .. 91 F4
Aqabah = Al
'Aqabah 47 E3
'Aqabah, Khalīj
al 47 E3
Āqcheh 45 B6
Aqīq 53 E6
Aqmola 29 D8
Aqrah 46 C5
Aqtöbe 29 D6
Aquidauana .. 93 G2
Aquitain, Bassin 12 D3
Ar Rachidiya .. 54 B4
Ar Ramādī 46 D5
Ar Raqqah 46 D4
Ar Rass 47 F5
Ar Rifā'ī 47 E6
Ar Riyāḍ 47 F6
Ar Ruṭbah 46 D5
Ar Ruwayḍah . 47 G6
Ara 40 E5
'Arab, Bahr
el → 53 G4
Arab, Shatt
al → 47 E7
Arabian Desert
= Es Sahrā'
Esh Sharqīya 52 C5
Arabian Gulf =
Gulf, The ... 44 E2
Arabian Sea ... 26 H10
Araç 46 B3
Aracaju 93 E6
Aracataca 90 A4
Aracati 92 C6
Araçatuba 93 G3
Aracena 18 D2
Araçuaí 93 F5
Arad 16 E5
Arada 53 F3
Arafura Sea .. 39 F4
Aragón □ 19 B5
Aragón → 19 A5
Araguacema .. 92 D4
Araguaia → .. 92 D4

Araguari 93 F4
Araguari → .. 92 B4
Arak 54 C5
Arakan Coast .. 41 H9
Arakan Yoma . 41 H10
Araks = Aras,
Rūd-e → ... 46 B7
Aral 29 E7
Aral Sea 29 E6
Aral Tengizi =
Aral Sea 29 E6
Aralsk = Aral .. 29 E7
Aralskoye More
= Aral Sea .. 29 E6
Aran I. 10 D2
Aran Is. 11 E2
Aranda de
Duero 18 B4
Aranjuez 18 B4
Aranos 58 C3
Araouane 55 E4
Arapgir 46 C4
Arapiraca 93 D6
Arapongas ... 94 A6
Araranguá 94 B7
Araraquara ... 93 G4
Ararat 62 C3
Ararat, Mt. =
Ağrı Dağı ... 46 C6
Araripe,
Chapada do . 92 D6
Aras, Rūd-e → 46 B7
Arauca 90 B4
Arauca → 90 B5
Arauco 94 D2
Araxá 93 F4
Araya, Pen. de . 90 A6
Arbatax 21 E2
Arbīl 46 C6
Arbroath 10 C5
Archangel =
Arkhangelsk . 28 C5
Arcila = Asilah 54 A3
Arckaringa ... 62 A1
Arckaringa
Cr. → 62 A2
Arcos de la
Frontera 18 D3
Arcot 43 N11
Arcoverde ... 92 D6
Arctic Bay ... 68 A2
Arctic Red River 70 B6
Arda → 22 D6
Ardabīl 46 C7
Ardahan 46 B5
Ardakān =
Sepīdān 44 D3
Ardenne 14 D3
Ardennes =
Ardenne 14 D3
Ardestän 44 C3
Ardlethan 63 B4
Ardmore 78 B5
Ardrossan ... 62 B2
Arecibo 87 C6
Areia Branca . 92 C6
Arendal 9 G9
Arequipa 91 G4
Arero 53 H6
Arévalo 18 B3
Arezzo 20 C3
Argamakmur .. 37 E2
Arganda 18 B4
Argentan 12 B3
Argentário, Mte. 20 C3
Argentina ■ .. 94 D3
Argentina Is. .. 96 A3
Argentino, L. .. 95 G2

Argeş → 22 B6
Arghandab → 42 D4
Argo 53 E5
Argolikós
Kólpos 23 F4
Árgos 23 F4
Argostólion .. 23 E3
Argungu 55 F5
Århus 9 G10
Arica, Chile .. 91 G4
Arica, Colombia 90 D4
Aridh 47 F6
Arinos → 91 F7
Aripuanã 91 E6
Aripuanã → .. 90 E6
Ariquemes ... 91 E6
Arizona □ 94 D3
Arizona □ 83 C7
Arjona 90 A3
Arkalyk =
Arqalyk 29 D7
Arkansas □ .. 79 B7
Arkansas → .. 79 C8
Arkansas City . 78 A5
Arkhangelsk .. 28 C5
Arklow 11 E3
Arkticheskiy,
Mys 30 A7
Arlanzón → .. 18 A3
Arlberg P. 14 E6
Arles 13 E6
Arlington, Va.,
U.S.A. 73 E7
Arlington,
Wash., U.S.A. 80 A2
Arlon 14 D3
Armagh 11 D3
Armavir 25 D5
Armenia 90 C3
Armenia ■ 25 E5
Armidale 63 B5
Armstrong ... 69 C2
Arnaud → 68 B3
Arnauti, C. ... 46 D3
Arnhem 14 C3
Arnhem, C. ... 60 C6
Arnhem Land . 60 C5
Arno → 20 C3
Arno Bay 62 B2
Arnsberg 14 C5
Aroab 58 D3
Arqalyk 29 D7
Arrabury 62 A3
Arrah = Ara ... 40 E5
Arran 10 D4
Arras 13 A5
Arrecife 54 C2
Arrée, Mts. d' . 12 B2
Arrowtown ... 65 F3
Árta 23 E3
Arthur → 62 D3
Arthur's Pass . 65 E4
Artigas 94 C5
Artois 12 A5
Artsyz 17 E9
Artvin 46 B5
Aru, Kepulauan 39 F4
Aru Is. = Aru,
Kepulauan .. 39 F4
Arua 57 D6
Aruanã 93 E3
Aruba ■ 87 D6
Arumpo 62 B3
Arunachal
Pradesh □ .. 41 C10
Arusha 57 E7
Aruwimi → ... 56 D4
Arxan 35 B6
Arys 29 E7
Arzamas 24 B5

Arzew 54 A4
'As Saffānīyah . 47 E7
As Samāwah .. 47 E6
As
Sulaymānīyah,
Iraq 46 D6
As
Sulaymānīyah,
Si. Arabia ... 47 F6
As Summān .. 47 F6
As Sūq 47 G5
As Suwaydā' .. 46 D4
As Suwayh ... 45 F4
As Şuwayrah . 47 D6
Asahigawa 32 F12
Asansol 40 F6
Ascension I. .. 51 G2
Aschaffenburg . 14 D5
Aschersleben .. 15 C6
Áscoli Piceno . 20 C4
Ascope 91 E3
Aseb 49 E3
Asela 53 G6
Asenovgrad ... 22 C5
Ash Shām,
Bādiyat 47 D4
Ash Shāmīyah . 47 E6
Ash Shāriqah . 44 E3
Ash Shaṭrah .. 47 E6
Ash Shaykh, J. 46 D3
Ash Shu'aybah 47 F6
Ash Shu'bah .. 47 E6
Ashburton 65 E4
Ashcroft 71 C7
Asheville 75 B6
Ashford,
Australia 63 A5
Ashford, U.K. .. 11 F7
Ashgabat 29 F6
Ashikaga 32 A6
Ashizuri-Zaki .. 32 C3
Ashkhabad =
Ashgabat ... 29 F6
Ashmyany ... 17 A7
Ashqelon 47 E3
Ashtabula 72 D5
Ashuanipi, L. .. 69 C4
Asia, Kepulauan 39 D4
Asifabad 43 K11
Asike 39 F6
Asilah 54 A3
Asinara 20 D2
Asinara, G. dell' 20 D2
Asino 29 D9
Asipovichy ... 17 B9
'Asīr □ 48 D3
Asir, Ras 49 E5
Asmara 53 E6
Asmera 53 E6
Aspiring, Mt. .. 65 F3
Assam □ 41 D9
Assen 14 B4
Assini 55 G4
Assiniboia 71 D9
Assiniboine → 71 D10
Assis 94 A6
Assisi 20 C4
Asti 20 B2
Astipálaia 23 F6
Astorga 18 A2
Astoria 80 B2
Astrakhan 25 D6
Astrakhan-Bazär 25 F6
Asturias □ ... 18 A3
Asunción 94 B5
Aswân 52 D5
Aswân High
Dam = Sadd
el Aali 52 D5

Asyût 52 C5
At Ṭafilah 47 E3
At Tā'if 48 C3
Atacama,
  Desierto de . 94 A3
Atacama, Salar
  de 94 A3
Atakpamé 55 G5
Atalaya 91 F4
Atami 32 B6
Atapupu 39 F2
Atâr 54 D2
Atasu 29 E8
Atauro 39 F3
Atbara 53 E5
'Atbara ⟶ .. 53 E5
Atbasar 29 D7
Athabasca ... 71 C8
Athabasca ⟶ . 70 C8
Athabasca, L. . . 70 C8
Athens =
  Athínai 23 F4
Athens, Ala.,
  U.S.A. 74 B4
Athens, Ga.,
  U.S.A. 75 C6
Athínai 23 F4
Athlone 11 E3
Áthos 23 D5
Athy 11 E3
Ati 53 F2
Atico 91 G4
Atlanta 75 C5
Atlantic City . 73 E8
Atlas Mts. =
  Haut Atlas . 54 B3
Atrak =
  Atrek ⟶ 44 B3
Atrek ⟶ 44 B3
Attawapiskat ⟶ 69 C2
Attock 42 C8
Attopeu 36 B3
Attur 43 P11
Atuel ⟶ 94 D3
Atyraū 29 E6
Aubagne ... 13 E6
Aube ⟶ 13 B5
Auburn 74 C5
Auburn Ra. .. 63 A5
Aubusson ... 12 D5
Auch 12 E4
Auckland ... 64 B6
Aude ⟶ 13 E5
Augathella ... 63 A4
Augsburg 14 D6
Augusta, Italy . 21 F5
Augusta, Ga.,
  U.S.A. 75 C7
Augusta, Maine,
  U.S.A. 73 B11
Aunis 12 C3
Auponhia ... 39 E3
Aurangabad,
  Bihar, India . 40 E5
Aurangabad,
  Maharashtra,
  India 43 K9
Aurich 14 B4
Aurillac 12 D5
Aurora, Colo.,
  U.S.A. 76 F2
Aurora, Ill.,
  U.S.A. 72 D1
Aus 58 D3
Auschwitz =
  Oświęcim ... 16 C4
Austin, Minn.,
  U.S.A. 77 D8
Austin, Tex.,
  U.S.A. 78 D5

Austral Is. =
  Tubuai Is. ... 65 M16
Austral
  Seamount
  Chain 65 M16
Australia ■ ... 60 E6
Australian Alps 63 C4
Australian
  Capital
  Territory □ .. 63 C4
Austria ■ 15 E8
Autun 13 C6
Auvergne 13 D5
Auvergne, Mts.
  d' 13 D5
Auxerre 13 C5
Avallon 13 C5
Aveiro, Brazil . 92 C2
Aveiro, Portugal 18 B1
Åvej 46 D7
Avellaneda ... 94 C5
Avellino 21 D5
Aversa 21 D5
Avezzano 20 C4
Aviá Terai ... 94 B4
Aviemore 10 C5
Avignon 13 E6
Ávila 18 B3
Avilés 18 A3
Avoca ⟶ 62 C3
Avola 21 F5
Avranches 12 B3
'Awālī 44 E2
Awash 49 F3
Awatere ⟶ ... 65 D6
Awbārī 52 C1
Awjilah 52 C3
Axim 55 H4
Axiós ⟶ 23 D4
Ayabaca 90 D3
Ayabe 32 B4
Ayacucho,
  Argentina ... 94 D5
Ayacucho, Peru 91 F4
Ayaguz 29 E9
Ayamonte 18 D2
Ayaviri 91 F4
Āybak 45 B7
Aydın 23 F6
Ayers Rock .. 60 F5
Áyios Evstrátios 23 E5
Aylmer, L. ... 70 B8
Ayn Dār 47 F7
Ayn Zālah 46 C5
Ayr 10 D4
Aytos 22 C6
Ayu, Kepulauan 39 D4
Ayutla 84 D5
Ayvacık 23 E6
Ayvalık 23 E6
Aẕ Ẕahrān 47 F7
Az Zarqā 46 D4
Az-Zilfī 47 F6
Az Zubayr 47 E6
Az Zuwaytinah 52 B3
Azamgarh 40 D4
Azärbayjan =
  Azerbaijan ■ . 25 E6
Āzarbāyjān-e
  Gharbī □ 46 C6
Āzarbāyjān-e
  Sharqī □ 46 C6
Azare 55 F7
Azbine = Aïr .. 55 E6
Azerbaijan ■ .. 25 E6
Azerbaijchan =
  Azerbaijan ■ 25 E6
Azogues 90 D3
Azores 50 C1

Azov 25 D4
Azov, Sea of .. 25 D4
Azovskoye More
  = Azov, Sea
  of 25 D4
Azovy 28 C7
Azúa 87 C5
Azuaga 18 C3
Azuero, Pen. de 86 E3
Azul 94 D5

B

Ba Don 36 A3
Ba Ria 36 B3
Bab el Mandeb 49 E3
Baba Burnu ... 23 E6
Babadag 22 B7
Babadayhan .. 29 F7
Babaeski 22 D6
Babahoyo 90 D3
Babana 55 F5
Babar 39 F3
Babo 39 E4
Bābol 44 B3
Bābol Sar 44 B3
Baboua 56 C2
Babruysk 17 B9
Babura 55 F6
Babuyan Chan. 38 A2
Babylon 47 D6
Bacabal 92 C5
Bacan,
  Kepulauan .. 39 E3
Bacan, Pulau . 39 E3
Bacarra 38 A2
Bacău 17 E8
Bachelina ... 29 D7
Back ⟶ 70 B9
Backstairs
  Passage 62 C2
Bacolod 38 B2
Bad Ischl 15 E7
Bad Kissingen . 14 C6
Bad Lands ... 76 D3
Badagara 43 P9
Badajoz 18 C2
Badalona 19 B7
Badalzai 42 E4
Badampahar .. 40 F6
Badanah 47 E5
Badarinath .. 42 D11
Badas 36 D4
Badas,
  Kepulauan .. 37 D3
Baddo ⟶ 42 E4
Bade 39 F5
Baden 15 D9
Baden-Baden .. 14 D5
Baden-
  Württemberg □
  .... 14 D5
Badgastein ... 15 E7
Bādghīsāt □ .. 42 B3
Badin 43 G6
Baduen 49 F4
Baena 18 D3
Baeza 18 D4
Bafatá 55 F2
Baffin B. 68 A4
Baffin I. 68 B3
Bafia 56 D2
Bafing ⟶ 55 F2
Bafoulabé 55 F2
Bāfq 44 D3
Bafra 46 B3

Bāft 44 D4
Bafwasende ... 57 D5
Bagamoyo ... 57 F7
Baganga 38 C3
Bagansiapiapi . 37 D2
Bagdarin 30 D9
Bagé 94 C6
Baghdād 46 D6
Bagheria 21 E4
Baghlān 42 A6
Baghlān □ 45 C7
Baguio 38 A2
Bahamas ■ ... 86 A4
Baharampur .. 40 E7
Bahawalpur ... 42 E7
Bahía =
  Salvador 93 E6
Bahía □ 93 E5
Bahía Blanca . 94 D4
Bahía de
  Caráquez ... 90 D2
Bahía Laura .. 95 F3
Bahía Negra . 91 H7
Bahr Aouk ⟶ . 56 C3
Bahr
  Salamat ⟶ . 53 G2
Bahraich 40 D3
Bahrain ■ 44 E2
Baia Mare ... 17 E6
Baïbokoum ... 53 G2
Baidoa 49 G3
Baie Comeau . 69 D4
Ba'ījī 46 D5
Baikal, L. =
  Baykal, Oz. .. 30 D8
Baile Atha Cliath
  = Dublin 11 E3
Băileşti 22 B4
Bailundo 58 A3
Bā'ir 47 E4
Baird Mts. ... 71 B3
Bairnsdale ... 63 C4
Baitadi 40 C3
Baiyin 35 C5
Baja 16 E4
Baja, Pta. 84 B1
Baja California . 84 A1
Bajimba, Mt. .. 63 A5
Bakala 56 C4
Bakchar 29 D9
Bakel 55 F2
Baker, L. 70 B10
Baker I. 64 J13
Baker Lake .. 70 B10
Baker Mt. 80 A3
Baker's Dozen
  Is. 69 C3
Bakersfield ... 82 C3
Bākhtarān 46 D6
Bakı 25 E6
Bakony Forest =
  Bakony
  Hegyseg ... 16 E3
Bakony Hegyseg 16 E3
Bakouma 56 C4
Baku = Bakı .. 25 E6
Bakutis Coast . 96 B1
Baky = Bakı .. 25 E6
Balabac I. 36 C5
Balabac Str. .. 36 C5
Balabalangan,
  Kepulauan .. 37 E5
Balaghat Ra. .. 43 K10
Balaguer 19 B6
Balaklava,
  Australia 62 B2
Balaklava,
  Ukraine 25 E3
Balakovo 24 C6

Balashov 24 C5
Balasore =
  Baleshwar . . 40 G6
Balaton 16 E3
Balbina, Reprêsa
  de 90 D7
Balchik 22 C7
Balclutha 65 G3
Baleares, Is. . . . 19 C7
Balearic Is. =
  Baleares, Is. . 19 C7
Baler 38 A2
Baleshwar 40 G6
Bali, Cameroon 55 G7
Bali, Indonesia 37 F5
Bali □ 37 F5
Balikeşir 23 E6
Balikpapan 37 E5
Balimbing 38 C1
Balipara 41 D9
Baliza 93 F3
Balkan Mts. =
  Stara Planina 22 C4
Balkh 45 B6
Balkhash =
  Balqash 29 E8
Balkhash, Ozero
  = Balqash Köl 29 E8
Balla 41 E8
Ballarat 62 C3
Ballater 10 C5
Ballina, Australia 63 A5
Ballina, Ireland 11 D2
Ballinasloe 11 E2
Ballymena 11 D3
Balmaceda 95 F2
Balmoral 62 C3
Balonne → . . . 63 A4
Balqash 29 E8
Balqash Köl . . . 29 E8
Balrampur 40 D4
Balranald 62 B3
Balsas → 84 D4
Balta 17 D9
Bălţi 17 E8
Baltic Sea 9 G11
Baltimore 73 E7
Baluchistan □ . 42 F4
Balya 23 E6
Bam 44 D4
Bama 53 F1
Bamako 55 F3
Bamba 55 E4
Bambari 56 C4
Bamberg 14 D6
Bambili 57 D5
Bamenda 55 G7
Bāmīān □ 42 B5
Bampūr 45 E5
Ban Don =
  Surat Thani . 36 C1
Ban Mê Thuôt =
  Buon Me
  Thuot 36 B3
Banaba 64 K11
Banalia 57 D5
Banam 36 B3
Banamba 55 F3
Bananal, I. do . 93 E3
Banaras =
  Varanasi . . . 40 E4
Band-e
  Torkestān . . 45 C6
Banda,
  Kepulauan . . 39 E3
Banda Aceh . . . 36 C1
Banda Banda,
  Mt. 63 B5
Banda Elat 39 F4

Banda Is. =
  Banda,
  Kepulauan . . 39 E3
Banda Sea 39 F3
Bandanaira . . . 39 E3
Bandar =
  Machilipatnam 40 J3
Bandār 'Abbās 44 E4
Bandar-e Anzalī 46 C7
Bandar-e
  Bushehr =
  Büshehr 44 D2
Bandar-e Chārak 44 E3
Bandar-e
  Deylam 47 E7
Bandar-e
  Khomeynı . . . 47 E7
Bandar-e
  Lengeh 44 E3
Bandar-e
  Ma'shur 47 E7
Bandar-e
  Nakhīlū 44 E3
Bandar-e Rīg . . 44 D2
Bandar-e
  Torkeman . . . 44 B3
Bandar
  Maharani =
  Muar 37 D2
Bandar
  Penggaram =
  Batu Pahat . . 37 D2
Bandar Seri
  Begawan . . . 36 D5
Bandawe 59 A6
Bandeira, Pico
  da 93 G5
Bandera 94 B4
Bandiagara . . . 55 F4
Bandırma 23 D7
Bandon 11 F2
Bandundu 56 E3
Bandung 37 F3
Banff, Canada . 71 C8
Banff, U.K. 10 C5
Banfora 55 F4
Bang Saphan . . 36 B1
Bangalore 43 N10
Bangassou 56 D4
Banggai,
  Kepulauan . . 39 E2
Banggi, P. 36 C5
Banghāzī 52 B3
Bangka, P.,
  Sulawesi,
  Indonesia . . . 39 D3
Bangka, P.,
  Sumatera,
  Indonesia . . . 37 E3
Bangka, Selat . 37 E3
Bangkinang . . . 37 D2
Bangko 37 E2
Bangkok 36 B2
Bangladesh ■ . 41 E7
Bangong Co . . 42 B11
Bangor, Down,
  U.K. 11 D4
Bangor,
  Caerns. & Mers.,
  U.K. 11 E4
Bangor, U.S.A. 73 B11
Bangued 38 A2
Bangui 56 D3
Bangweulu, L. . 57 G6
Bani 87 C5
Banī Walīd . . . 52 B1
Banīnah 52 B3
Bāniyās 46 D3
Banja Luka 20 B6

Banjarmasin . . 37 E4
Banjul 55 F1
Bankipore 40 E5
Banks I. 70 A7
Banks Pen. 65 E5
Banks Str. 62 D4
Bankura 40 F6
Banningville =
  Bandundu . . 56 E3
Bannu 42 C7
Banská Bystrica 16 D4
Banswara 43 H9
Bantry 11 F2
Banu 42 B6
Banyak,
  Kepulauan . . 37 D1
Banyo 55 G7
Banzare Coast . 96 A13
Banzyville =
  Mobayi 56 D4
Baoding 35 C6
Baoji 35 C5
Baoshan 34 D4
Baotou 35 B6
Bapatla 40 K3
Ba'qūbah 46 D6
Bar,
  Montenegro, Yug.
  . . . . 22 C2
Bar, Ukraine . . 17 D8
Bar-le-Duc 13 B6
Barabai 37 E5
Barabinsk 29 D8
Baracaldo 19 A4
Baracoa 86 B5
Barahona 87 C5
Barail Range . . 41 E9
Barakhola 41 E9
Barakpur 41 F7
Barakula 63 A5
Baramula 42 B9
Baran 43 G10
Baranavichy . . . 17 B8
Baranof I. 71 C6
Barão de
  Melgaço 91 F6
Barapasi 39 E5
Barat Daya,
  Kepulauan . . 39 F3
Barbacena 93 G5
Barbacoas 90 C3
Barbados ■ . . . 87 D8
Barbastro 19 A6
Barberton 59 D6
Barcellona Pozzo
  di Gotto 21 E5
Barcelona, Spain 19 B7
Barcelona,
  Venezuela . . . 90 A6
Barcelos 90 D6
Bardai 52 D2
Barddhaman . . 40 F6
Bardejov 16 D5
Bardera 49 G3
Bardi, Ra's 47 F4
Bardīyah 52 B4
Bareilly 42 E11
Barentu 53 E6
Barfleur, Pte. de 12 B3
Barga 34 C3
Bargal 49 E5
Barhi 40 E5
Bari 20 D6
Bari Doab 42 D8
Barīm 49 E3
Barinas 90 B4
Baring, C. 70 B8
Bârîs 52 D5
Barisal 41 F8
Barisan, Bukit . 37 E2

Barito → 37 E4
Barkly Tableland 60 D6
Barlee, L. 60 F2
Barletta 20 D6
Barmedman . . . 63 B4
Barmer 42 G7
Barmera 62 B3
Barnato 63 B4
Barnaul 29 D9
Barnsley 11 E6
Barnstaple 11 F4
Baro 55 G6
Baroda =
  Vadodara . . . 43 H8
Barpeta 41 D8
Barquísimeto . . 90 A5
Barra, Brazil . . . 93 E5
Barra, U.K. 10 C3
Barra do Corda 92 D4
Barra do Piraí . 93 G5
Barra Falsa, Pta.
  da 59 C7
Barraba 63 B5
Barrackpur =
  Barakpur . . . 41 F7
Barraigh =
  Barra 10 C3
Barranca, Lima,
  Peru 91 F3
Barranca,
  Loreto, Peru . 90 D3
Barrancabermeja
  . . . . 90 B4
Barrancas 90 B6
Barrancos 18 C2
Barranqueras . . 94 B5
Barranquilla . . . 90 A4
Barras 92 C5
Barreiras 93 E5
Barreirinhas . . . 92 C5
Barreiro 18 C1
Barreiros 92 D6
Barretos 93 G4
Barrier Ra. 62 B3
Barrington Tops 63 B5
Barringun 63 A4
Barrow 71 A4
Barrow-in-
  Furness 11 D5
Barry 11 F5
Barsi 43 K9
Barsoi 40 E6
Barstow 82 C4
Bartica 90 B7
Bartin 46 B3
Bartle Frere . . . 61 D8
Bartlesville . . . 79 A6
Barysaw 17 A9
Bāsa'idū 44 E3
Basankusa 56 D3
Basarabeasca . 17 E9
Basel 13 C7
Bashi Channel . 35 D7
Bashkir Republic
  =
  Bashkortostan □
  . . . . 29 D6
Bashkortostan □ 29 D6
Basilan 38 C2
Basilan Str. . . . 38 C2
Basildon 11 F7
Basim =
  Washim 43 J10
Basingstoke . . . 11 F6
Basle = Basel . 13 C7
Basoka 56 D4
Basongo 56 E4
Basque
  Provinces =
  País Vasco □ . 19 A4

Basra = Al
Başrah 47 E6
Bass Str. 61 H8
Bassano 71 C8
Bassano del
Grappa 20 B3
Bassas da India 59 C7
Bassein 41 J10
Basseterre 87 C7
Bassikounou .. 55 E3
Bastak 44 E3
Bastar 40 H3
Basti 40 D4
Bastia 13 E8
Bastogne 14 C3
Bata 56 D1
Bataan 38 B2
Batabanó 86 B3
Batabanó, G. de 86 B3
Batac 38 A2
Batagoy 31 C11
Batamay 31 C10
Batang 34 C4
Batangafo 56 C3
Batangas 38 B2
Batanta 39 E4
Bateman's B. .. 63 C5
Batemans Bay . 63 C5
Bath 11 F5
Bathurst,
Australia 63 B4
Bathurst,
Canada ... 69 D4
Bathurst, C. .. 70 A7
Bathurst Harb. . 62 D4
Bathurst Inlet . 70 B9
Batinah 44 F4
Batlow 63 C4
Batman 46 C5
Batna 54 A6
Baton Rouge .. 79 D8
Batouri 56 D2
Battambang ... 36 B2
Battipáglia ... 21 D5
Battle Creek .. 72 C3
Battle Harbour . 69 C5
Battleford 71 C9
Batu 49 F2
Batu, Kepulauan 37 E1
Batu Is. = Batu,
Kepulauan ... 37 E1
Batu Pahat 37 D2
Batuata 39 F2
Batumi 25 E5
Baturaja 37 E2
Baturité 92 C6
Bau 37 D4
Baubau 39 F2
Bauchi 55 F6
Bauer, C. 62 B1
Baukau 39 F3
Bauru 93 G4
Baús 93 F3
Bautzen 15 C8
Bavaria =
Bayern □ ... 15 D6
Bawdwin 41 F11
Bawean 37 F4
Bawku 55 F4
Bawlake 41 H11
Bay, L. de 38 B2
Bay City 72 C4
Bay View 64 C7
Bayamo 86 B4
Bayan Har Shan 34 C4
Bayan Hot =
Alxa Zuoqi .. 35 C5
Bayanaüyl 29 D8
Bayanhongor .. 35 B5

Bayázeh 44 C3
Baybay 38 B2
Bayburt 46 B5
Bayern □ 15 D6
Bayeux 12 B3
Bayındır 23 E6
Baykal, Oz. ... 30 D8
Baykit 30 C7
Baykonur =
Bayqongyr .. 29 E7
Bayombong ... 38 A2
Bayonne 12 E3
Bayovar 91 E2
Bayqongyr 29 E7
Bayram-Ali =
Bayramaly .. 29 F7
Bayramaly ... 29 F7
Bayramiç 23 E6
Bayreuth 15 D6
Bayrūt 46 D3
Baytown 79 E6
Baza 19 D4
Bazaruto, I. do . 59 C7
Beachport 62 C2
Beagle, Canal . 95 G3
Beardmore
Glacier 96 C14
Béarn 12 E3
Beauce, Plaine
de la 12 B4
Beaudesert ... 63 A5
Beaufort 36 C5
Beaufort Sea .. 66 B6
Beaufort West . 58 E4
Beaumont 79 D6
Beaune 13 C6
Beauvais 12 B5
Beauval 71 C9
Beaver 71 B5
Beaver → 71 C9
Beawar 42 F9
Bečej 22 B3
Béchar 54 B4
Beenleigh 63 A5
Be'er Sheva ... 47 E3
Beersheba =
Be'er Sheva . 47 E3
Befale 56 D4
Bega 63 C4
Behbehān 47 E7
Behshahr 44 B3
Bei Jiang → .. 35 D6
Bei'an 35 B7
Beibei 35 D5
Beihai 35 D5
Beijing 35 C6
Beilpajah 63 B3
Beinn na
Faoghla =
Benbecula .. 10 C3
Beira 59 B6
Beirut = Bayrūt 46 D3
Beitbridge ... 59 C6
Beja, Portugal . 18 C2
Béja, Tunisia .. 54 A6
Bejaia 54 A6
Béjar 18 B3
Bejestān 44 C4
Békéscsaba ... 16 E5
Bela, India ... 40 E4
Bela, Pakistan . 42 F5
Bela Crkva ... 22 B3
Bela Vista 94 A5
Belarus ■ 24 C2
Belau = Palau ■ 38 C4
Belawan 37 D1
Belaya Tserkov
= Bila Tserkva 17 D10

Belcher Is. 69 C3
Belém 92 C4
Belén 94 A5
Belet Uen 49 G4
Belev 24 C4
Belfast 11 D4
Belfort 13 C7
Belgaum 43 M9
Belgium ■ ... 14 C3
Belgorod 24 C4
Belgorod-
Dnestrovskiy
= Bilhorod-
Dnistrovskyy 25 D3
Belgrade =
Beograd 22 B3
Beli Drim → .. 22 C3
Belinga 56 D2
Belinyu 37 E3
Beliton Is. =
Belitung 37 E3
Belitung 37 E3
Belize ■ 85 D7
Belize City ... 85 D7
Belkovskiy,
Ostrov 30 B11
Bell Bay 62 D4
Bell Peninsula . 68 B2
Bell Ville 94 C4
Bella Unión ... 94 C5
Bella Vista ... 94 B5
Bellary 43 M10
Bellata 63 A4
Belle-Ile 12 C2
Belle Isle 69 C5
Belle Isle, Str. of 69 C5
Belleville,
Canada 69 D3
Belleville, U.S.A. 77 F10
Bellin =
Kangirsuk .. 68 C4
Bellingen 63 B5
Bellingham ... 80 A2
Bellingshausen
Sea 96 A2
Bellinzona ... 13 C8
Belluno 20 A4
Belmont 63 B5
Belmonte 93 F6
Belmopan 85 D7
Belo Horizonte 93 F5
Belo-Tsiribihina 59 H8
Beloit 77 D10
Belokorovichi . 17 C9
Belomorsk ... 28 C4
Belonia 41 F8
Belorussia ■ =
Belarus ■ ... 24 C2
Belovo 29 D9
Beloye, Ozero . 24 A4
Beloye More .. 28 C4
Belozersk 24 A4
Beltana 62 B2
Belterra 92 C3
Beltsy = Bălţi . 17 E8
Belukha 29 E9
Beluran 36 C5
Belyy, Ostrov . 28 B8
Belyy Yar 29 D9
Bembéréke ... 55 F5
Bemidji 77 B7
Ben Gardane .. 52 B1
Ben Lomond,
N.S.W.,
Australia 63 B5
Ben Lomond,
Tas., Australia 62 D4
Ben Nevis 10 C4
Bena 55 F6

Bena Dibele ... 56 E4
Benagerie 62 B3
Benalla 63 C4
Benambra, Mt. . 63 C4
Benares =
Varanasi ... 40 E4
Benavente 18 A3
Benbecula 10 C3
Benbonyathe .. 62 B2
Bend 80 C3
Bender Beila .. 49 F5
Bendery =
Tighina 17 E9
Bendigo 63 C3
Benevento 20 D5
Bengal, Bay of . 41 J7
Bengbu 35 C6
Benghazi =
Banghāzī ... 52 B3
Bengkalis 37 D2
Bengkulu 37 E2
Bengkulu □ ... 37 E2
Benguela 58 A2
Beni → 57 D5
Beni → 91 F5
Beni Abbès ... 54 B4
Beni Mazâr ... 52 C5
Beni Mellal ... 54 B3
Beni Ounif ... 54 B4
Beni Suef 52 C5
Benidorm 19 C5
Benin ■ 55 G5
Benin, Bight of 55 H5
Benin City ... 55 G6
Benjamin
Constant 90 D4
Benoni 59 D5
Bent 44 E4
Benteng 39 F2
Benton Harbor 72 C2
Benue → 55 G6
Benxi 35 B7
Beo 38 D3
Beograd 22 B3
Beppu 32 C2
Berati 23 D2
Berau, Teluk .. 39 E4
Berber 53 E5
Berbera 49 E4
Berbérati 56 D3
Berbice → 90 B7
Berdichev =
Berdychiv ... 17 D9
Berdsk 29 D9
Berdyansk ... 25 D4
Berdychiv 17 D9
Berebere 39 D3
Bereda 49 E5
Berehove 17 D6
Berekum 55 G4
Berestechko .. 17 C7
Bereza 17 B7
Berezhany ... 17 D7
Berezina =
Byarezina → 17 B10
Berezniki 28 D6
Berezovo 28 C7
Berga 19 A6
Bergama 23 E6
Bérgamo 20 B2
Bergen 8 F9
Bergerac 12 D4
Berhala, Selat . 37 E2
Berhampore =
Baharampur . 40 E7
Berhampur ... 40 H5
Bering Sea ... 71 C1
Bering Strait .. 71 B3
Berja 19 D4

Berkeley	80	G2
Berkner I.	96	B4
Berlin	15	B7
Bermejo →, Formosa, Argentina	94	B5
Bermejo → San Juan, Argentina	94	C3
Bermuda ■	67	F13
Bern	13	C7
Bernardo de Irigoyen	94	B6
Bernburg	15	C6
Berne = Bern	13	C7
Bernina, Piz	13	C8
Beroroha	59	J9
Beroun	16	D2
Berrechid	54	B3
Berri	62	B3
Berry, Australia	63	B5
Berry, France	12	C5
Bershad	17	D9
Bertoua	56	D2
Berwick-upon-Tweed	10	D6
Besalampy	59	H8
Besançon	13	C7
Besar	37	E5
Besni	46	C4
Bessarabiya	17	E9
Bessarabka = Basarabeasca	17	E9
Bessemer	74	C4
Betanzos	18	A1
Bétaré Oya	56	C2
Bethanien	58	D3
Bethel	71	B3
Bethlehem, S. Africa	59	D5
Bethlehem, U.S.A.	73	D8
Béthune	13	A5
Bethungra	63	B4
Betioky	59	J8
Betroka	59	J9
Betsiamites	69	D4
Bettiah	40	D5
Betul	43	J10
Betung	37	D4
Beverley	11	E6
Beverly Hills	82	C3
Beyla	55	G3
Beyneu	29	E6
Beypazarı	46	B2
Beyşehir Gölü	46	C2
Bezhitsa	24	C3
Béziers	13	E5
Bezwada = Vijayawada	40	J3
Bhachau	43	H7
Bhadrakh	40	G6
Bhadravati	43	N9
Bhagalpur	40	E6
Bhakra Dam	42	D10
Bhamo	41	E11
Bhandara	43	J11
Bhanrer Ra.	43	H11
Bharat = India ■	43	J10
Bharatpur	42	F10
Bhatpara	41	F7
Bhaunagar = Bhavnagar	43	J8
Bhavnagar	43	J8
Bhawanipatna	40	H3
Bhilsa = Vidisha	43	H10
Bhilwara	43	G9
Bhima →	43	L10
Bhimavaram	40	J3
Bhind	42	F11
Bhiwandi	43	K8
Bhiwani	42	E10
Bhola	41	F8
Bhopal	43	H10
Bhubaneshwar	40	G5
Bhuj	43	H6
Bhumiphol Dam = Phumiphon, Khuan	36	A1
Bhusaval	43	J9
Bhutan ■	41	D8
Biafra, B. of = Bonny, Bight of	56	D1
Biak	39	E5
Biała Podlaska	17	B6
Białogard	16	A2
Białystok	17	B6
Biaro	39	D3
Biarritz	12	E3
Bibala	58	A2
Biberach	14	D5
Bibiani	55	G4
Bida	55	G6
Bidar	43	L10
Biddeford	73	C10
Bidon 5 = Poste Maurice Cortier	54	D5
Bié, Planalto de	58	A3
Biel	13	C7
Bielefeld	14	B5
Biella	20	B2
Bielsk Podlaski	17	B6
Bielsko-Biała	16	D4
Bien Hoa	36	B3
Bienne = Biel	13	C7
Bienville, L.	69	C3
Big Horn Mts. = Bighorn Mts.	81	C10
Big Spring	78	C3
Big Trout L.	69	C2
Biğa	23	D6
Bigadiç	23	E7
Biggar	71	C9
Biggenden	63	A5
Bighorn →	81	B10
Bighorn Mts.	81	C10
Bihać	20	B5
Bihar	40	E5
Bihar □	40	E5
Bihor, Munţii	17	E6
Bijagós, Arquipélago dos	55	F1
Bijapur, Karnataka, India	43	L9
Bijapur, Mad. P., India	40	H3
Bijär	46	D6
Bijeljina	20	B7
Bijnor	42	E11
Bikaner	42	E8
Bikini Atoll	64	H11
Bila Tserkva	17	D10
Bilara	42	F8
Bilaspur	40	F4
Bilauk Taungdan	36	B1
Bilbao	19	A4
Bilbo = Bilbao	19	A4
Bilecik	46	B2
Bilhorod-Dnistrovskyy	25	D3
Bilir	31	C11
Billings	81	C9
Billiton Is. = Belitung	37	E3
Bilma	53	E1
Biloxi	79	D9
Biltine	53	F3
Bima	39	F1
Bimbo	56	D3
Bina-Etawah	43	G11
Binalbagan	38	B2
Binalong	63	B4
Bīnālūd, Kūh-e	44	B4
Binatang	37	D4
Binda	63	A4
Bindle	63	A4
Bindura	59	B6
Bingara, N.S.W., Australia	63	A5
Bingara, Queens., Australia	63	A3
Bingham Canyon	81	E7
Binghamton	73	C8
Bingöl	46	C5
Binh Dinh = An Nhon	36	B3
Binh Son	36	A3
Binjai	37	D1
Binnaway	63	B4
Binongko	39	F2
Bintan	37	D2
Bintulu	37	D4
Bintuni	39	E4
Binzert = Bizerte	54	A6
Bioko	56	D1
Bir	43	K9
Bir Autrun	53	E4
Bir Mogrein	54	C2
Bîr Ungât	52	D5
Bira	39	E4
Birao	53	F3
Birchip	62	C3
Birecik	46	C4
Bireuen	36	C1
Bîrlad	17	E8
Bîrlad →	17	F8
Birmingham, U.K.	11	E6
Birmingham, U.S.A.	74	C4
Birni Nkonni	55	F6
Birnin Kebbi	55	F5
Birr	11	E3
Birrie →	63	A4
Birsk	29	D6
Birur	43	N9
Bisa	39	E3
Biscay, B. of	12	D2
Biscoe Bay	96	B17
Biscoe Is.	96	A3
Bishkek	29	E8
Biskra	54	B6
Bislig	38	C3
Bismarck	76	B4
Bismarck Arch.	64	K9
Bissagos = Bijagós, Arquipélago dos	55	F1
Bissau	55	F1
Bistriţa	17	E7
Bistriţa →	17	E8
Bitam	56	D2
Bitkine	53	F2
Bitlis	46	C5
Bitola	22	D3
Bitolj = Bitola	22	D3
Bitter L. = Buheirat-Murrat-el-Kubra	52	B5
Bitterfontein	58	E3
Bitterroot Range	81	B6
Biu	53	F1
Biwa-Ko	32	B5
Biysk	29	D9
Bizerte	54	A6
Bjelovar	20	B6
Black Forest = Schwarzwald	14	D5
Black Hills	76	D3
Black Sea	25	E3
Black Volta →	55	G4
Blackball	65	E4
Blackburn	11	E5
Blackpool	11	E5
Blackwater →	11	E2
Blagodarnoye = Blagodarnyy	25	D5
Blagodarnyy	25	D5
Blagoevgrad	22	C4
Blagoveshchensk	31	D10
Blairmore	71	D8
Blanc, Mont	13	D7
Blanca, B.	95	D4
Blanca Peak	83	B10
Blanche, C.	62	B1
Blanche, L.	62	A2
Blanes	19	B7
Blantyre	59	B6
Blayney	63	B4
Blednaya, Gora	28	B7
Blenheim	65	D5
Blida	54	A5
Bligh Sound	65	F2
Blitta	55	G5
Blodgett Iceberg Tongue	96	A13
Bloemfontein	59	D5
Bloemhof	59	D5
Blois	12	C4
Bloomington, Ill., U.S.A.	77	E10
Bloomington, Ind., U.S.A.	72	E2
Blue Mts., Oreg., U.S.A.	80	C4
Blue Mts., Pa., U.S.A.	73	D7
Blue Nile = Nîl el Azraq →	53	E5
Blue Ridge Mts.	75	A7
Bluefields	86	D3
Bluff	65	G3
Blumenau	94	B7
Bo	55	G2
Bo Duc	36	B3
Bo Hai	35	C6
Boa Vista	90	C6
Boatman	63	A4
Bobadah	63	B4
Bobbili	40	H4
Bobo-Dioulasso	55	F4
Bóbr →	16	B2
Bobraomby, Tanjon' i	59	G9
Bobruysk = Babruysk	17	B9
Bôca do Acre	91	E5
Boca Raton	75	F7
Bocaiúva	93	F5
Bocanda	55	G4
Bocaranga	56	C3
Bochnia	16	D5
Bochum	14	C4
Boda	56	D3
Bodaybo	30	D9
Boden	8	E12
Bodensee	13	C8
Bodhan	43	K10

Bodø 8 E10
Bodrog → 16 D5
Bodrum 23 F6
Boende 56 E4
Boffa 55 F2
Bogalusa 79 D9
Bogan Gate .. 63 B4
Boggabilla 63 A5
Boggabri 63 B5
Bogo 38 B2
Bogong, Mt. .. 63 C4
Bogotá 90 C4
Bogotol 29 D9
Bogra 41 E7
Bogué 55 E2
Bohemian
  Forest =
  Böhmerwald 15 D7
Bohena Cr. → 63 B4
Böhmerwald .. 15 D7
Bohol 38 C2
Bohol Sea ... 38 C2
Bohotleh 49 F4
Boise 80 D5
Boise City ... 78 A2
Bojador C. ... 54 C2
Bojana → ... 22 D2
Bojnürd 44 B4
Boké 55 F2
Bokhara → ... 63 A4
Bokoro 53 F2
Bokote 56 E4
Bokungu 56 E4
Bol 53 F1
Bolama 55 F1
Bolan Pass ... 42 E5
Bolbec 12 B4
Bole 34 B3
Bolekhiv 17 D6
Bolekhov =
  Bolekhiv 17 D6
Bolesławiec ... 16 C2
Bolgrad =
  Bolhrad 17 F9
Bolhrad 17 F9
Bolinao C. ... 38 A1
Bolívar,
  Argentina ... 94 D4
Bolívar,
  Colombia ... 90 C3
Bolivia ■ 91 G6
Bollon 63 A4
Bolobo 56 E3
Bologna 20 B3
Bologoye 24 B3
Bolomba 56 D3
Bolong 38 C2
Bolsena, L. di . 20 C3
Bolshereche ... 29 D8
Bolshevik,
  Ostrov 30 B8
Bolshoi Kavkas
  = Caucasus
  Mountains .. 25 E5
Bolshoy Atlym 28 C7
Bolshoy
  Begichev,
  Ostrov 30 B9
Bolshoy
  Lyakhovskiy,
  Ostrov 31 B12
Bolton 11 E5
Bolu 46 B2
Bolvadin 46 C2
Bolzano 20 A3
Bom Despacho 93 F4
Bom Jesus da
  Lapa 93 E5
Boma 56 F2
Bomaderry 63 B5

Bombala 63 C4
Bombay 43 K8
Bomboma 56 D3
Bomili 57 D5
Bomongo 56 D3
Bomu → 56 D4
Bon, C. 52 A1
Bonaire 87 D6
Bonang 63 C4
Bonavista ... 69 D5
Bondo 56 D4
Bondoukou ... 55 G4
Bone, Teluk .. 39 E2
Bonerate 39 F2
Bonerate,
  Kepulauan .. 39 F2
Bong Son =
  Hoai Nhon . 36 B3
Bongandanga . 56 D4
Bongor 53 F2
Bonifacio ... 13 F8
Bonn 14 C4
Bonney, L. .. 62 C3
Bonny, Bight of 56 D1
Bonoi 39 E5
Bontang 37 D5
Bonthain 39 F1
Bonthe 55 G2
Bontoc 38 A2
Boolaboolka L. 62 B3
Booligal 63 B3
Boonah 63 A5
Boorindal 63 B4
Boorowa 63 B4
Boothia, Gulf of 68 A2
Boothia Pen. . 70 A10
Booué 56 E2
Bor,
  Serbia, Yug. . 22 B4
Bôr, Sudan .. 53 G5
Borama 49 F3
Borås 9 G10
Borāzjān 44 D2
Borba 90 D7
Borda, C. 62 C2
Bordeaux ... 12 D3
Bordertown .. 62 C3
Bordj Fly Ste.
  Marie 54 C4
Bordj-in-Eker . 54 D6
Bordj Omar
  Driss 54 C6
Bordj-Tarat .. 54 C6
Borger 78 B3
Borisoglebsk . 24 C5
Borisov =
  Barysaw ... 17 A9
Borja 90 D3
Borkou 53 E2
Borkum 14 B4
Borley, C. 96 A9
Borneo 37 D4
Bornholm 9 G11
Boromo 55 F4
Borongan 38 B3
Borovichi ... 24 B3
Borşa 17 E7
Borüjerd 46 D7
Boryslav 17 D6
Bosa 21 D2
Bosanska
  Gradiška 20 B6
Bosaso 49 E4
Boshan 35 C6
Boshrüyeh ... 44 C4
Bosna → 20 B7
Bosna i
  Hercegovina
  = Bosnia-
  Herzegovina ■ 20 B6

Bosnia-
  Herzegovina ■ 20 B6
Bosnik 39 E5
Bosobolo 56 D3
Bosporus =
  Karadeniz
  Boğazı 22 D7
Bossangoa ... 56 C3
Bossembélé .. 53 G2
Bosso 53 F1
Bosten Hu ... 34 B3
Boston, U.K. .. 11 E6
Boston, U.S.A. 73 C10
Botany B. ... 63 B5
Bothnia, G. of . 8 F12
Bothwell 62 D4
Botletle → ... 58 C4
Botoşani 17 E8
Botswana ■ .. 58 C4
Botucatu 94 A7
Bou Djébéha . 55 E4
Bou Izakarn .. 54 C3
Bouaké 55 G3
Bouar 56 C3
Bouârfa 54 B4
Bouca 56 C3
Bougie = Bejaia 54 A6
Bougouni 55 F3
Boulder 76 E2
Boulder Dam =
  Hoover Dam 82 B5
Boulogne-sur-
  Mer 12 A4
Boultoum 55 F7
Bouna 55 G4
Boundiali ... 55 G3
Bourbonnais . 13 C5
Bourem 55 E4
Bourg-en-Bresse 13 C6
Bourg-St.-
  Maurice ... 13 D7
Bourges 12 C5
Bourgogne ... 13 C6
Bourke 63 B4
Bournemouth . 11 F6
Bousso 53 F2
Boutilimit ... 55 E2
Bowen Mts. .. 63 C4
Bowman I. ... 96 A12
Bowmans 62 B2
Bowral 63 B5
Bowraville ... 63 B5
Boyne → 11 E3
Boyni Qara .. 45 B6
Boz Dağları .. 23 E7
Bozburun ... 23 F7
Bozcaada ... 23 E6
Bozdoğan ... 23 F7
Bozeman 81 C8
Bozen =
  Bolzano ... 20 A3
Bozoum 56 C3
Bra 20 B1
Brač 20 C6
Bracciano, L. di 20 C4
Brach 52 C1
Bräcke 8 F11
Brad 17 E6
Bradenton ... 75 F6
Bradford 11 E6
Braemar 62 B2
Braga 18 B1
Bragança, Brazil 92 C4
Bragança,
  Portugal 18 B2
Brahmanbaria . 41 F8
Brahmani → . 40 G6
Brahmaputra → 41 F7
Braidwood ... 63 C4

Brăila 17 F8
Branco → 90 D6
Brandenburg =
  Neubrandenburg
  .... 15 B7
Brandenburg . 15 B7
Brandenburg □ 15 B7
Brandon 71 D10
Brandvlei 58 E4
Braniewo 16 A4
Bransfield Str. . 96 A4
Brantford 69 D2
Branxholme .. 62 C3
Brasiléia 91 F5
Brasília 93 F4
Braşov 17 F7
Brassey,
  Banjaran 36 D5
Bratislava ... 16 D3
Bratsk 30 D8
Braunau 15 D7
Braunschweig . 14 B6
Brava 49 G3
Bravo del Norte,
  R. → =
  Grande,
  Rio → 79 F5
Brawley 82 D5
Bray 11 E3
Bray, Pays de . 12 B4
Brazil ■ 93 E4
Brazos → ... 79 E6
Brazzaville ... 56 E3
Brčko 20 B7
Breaksea Sd. . 65 F2
Bream B. 64 A6
Bream Hd. ... 64 A6
Brecon 11 F5
Breda 14 C3
Bredasdorp .. 58 E4
Bredbo 63 C4
Bregenz 14 E5
Brejo 92 C5
Bremen 14 B5
Bremerhaven . 14 B5
Bremerton ... 80 B2
Brenner P. ... 15 E6
Bréscia 20 B3
Breslau =
  Wrocław ... 16 C3
Bressanone ... 20 A3
Brest, Belarus . 17 B6
Brest, France .. 12 B1
Brest-Litovsk =
  Brest 17 B6
Bretagne 12 B2
Brett, C. 64 A6
Brewarrina ... 63 A4
Brezhnev =
  Naberezhnyye
  Chelny 29 D6
Bria 56 C4
Briançon ... 13 D7
Bribie I. 63 A5
Bridgeport ... 73 D9
Bridgetown .. 87 D8
Bridgewater .. 69 D4
Bridgewater, C. 62 C3
Bridlington .. 11 D6
Bridport 62 D4
Brig 13 C7
Brigham City . 81 E7
Bright 63 C4
Brighton,
  Australia 62 C2
Brighton, U.K. . 11 F6
Bríndisi 21 D6
Brinkworth .. 62 B2
Brisbane 63 A5
Brisbane → .. 63 A5

Bristol, *U.K.*	11	F5
Bristol, *U.S.A.*	75	A6
Bristol B.	71	C3
Bristol Channel	11	F4
Britstown	58	E4
Brittany =		
Bretagne	12	B2
Brive-la-		
Gaillarde	12	D4
Brixen =		
Bressanone	20	A3
Brlik	29	E8
Brno	16	D3
Brocken	14	C6
Brodeur Pen.	68	A2
Brodnica	16	B4
Brody	17	C7
Broken Hill =		
Kabwe	59	A5
Broken Hill	62	B3
Bronte Park	62	D4
Brooks Ra.	71	B5
Brooloo	63	A5
Broome	60	D3
Broughton		
Island	68	B4
Brown, Pt.	62	B1
Brownsville	78	B5
Brownwood	78	D4
Bruay-en-Artois	13	A5
Bruce, Mt.	60	E2
Bruck an der		
Mur	15	E8
Bruges =		
Brugge	14	C2
Brugge	14	C2
Brumado	93	E5
Brunei = Bandar		
Seri Begawan	36	D5
Brunei ■	36	D4
Brunner, L.	65	E4
Brunswick =		
Braunschweig	14	B6
Brunswick	75	D7
Brunswick, Pen.		
de	95	G2
Brusque	94	B7
Brussel	14	C3
Brussels =		
Brussel	14	C3
Bruthen	63	C4
Bruxelles =		
Brussel	14	C3
Bryan	79	D5
Bryan, Mt.	62	B2
Bryansk	24	C3
Bu Craa	54	C2
Buapinang	39	E2
Buayan	38	C3
Bucak	46	C2
Bucaramanga	90	B4
Buchach	17	D7
Buchanan	55	G2
Buchans	69	D5
Bucharest =		
Bucureşti	22	B6
Buckie	10	C5
Buckleboo	62	B2
Bucureşti	22	B6
Budalin	41	F10
Budapest	16	E4
Budd Coast	96	A12
Bude	11	F4
Budennovsk	25	E5
Budgewoi	63	B5
Budjala	56	D3
Buenaventura	90	C3
Buenos Aires	94	C5
Buenos Aires, L.	95	F2
Buffalo	73	C6

Bug ⇢ =		
Buh ⇢	25	D3
Bug ⇢	16	B5
Buga	90	C3
Bugel, Tanjung	37	F4
Bugsuk	36	C5
Bugun Shara	35	B5
Buguruslan	29	D6
Buh ⇢	25	D3
Buheirat-Murrat-		
el-Kubra	52	B5
Buir Nur	35	B6
Bujumbura	57	E5
Bukama	57	F5
Bukavu	57	E5
Bukene	57	E6
Bukhara =		
Bukhoro	29	F7
Bukhoro	29	F7
Bukittinggi	37	E2
Bukoba	57	E6
Bula	39	E4
Bulahdelah	63	B5
Bulan	38	B2
Bulandshahr	42	E10
Bulawayo	59	C5
Buldan	23	E7
Bulgan	35	B5
Bulgaria ■	22	C5
Bulgroo	63	A3
Bulgunnia	62	B1
Bulhar	49	E3
Buli, Teluk	39	D3
Buliluyan, C.	36	C5
Bulli	63	B5
Bulloo ⇢	63	A3
Bulloo Downs	62	A3
Bulloo L.	62	A3
Bulls	64	D6
Bulo Burti	49	G4
Bulsar = Valsad	43	J8
Bulukumba	39	F2
Bulun	30	B10
Bumba	56	D4
Bumhpa Bum	41	D11
Buna	57	D7
Bunbah, Khalīj	52	B3
Bunbury	60	G2
Buncrana	11	D3
Bundaberg	63	A5
Bundi	43	G9
Bundoran	11	D2
Bungo-Suidō	32	C3
Bunia	57	D6
Bunji	42	B9
Buntok	37	E4
Bunyu	37	D5
Buol	39	D2
Buon Me Thuot	36	B3
Buorkhaya, Mys	31	B11
Buqayq	47	F7
Bur Acaba	49	G3
Bûr Safâga	52	C5
Bûr Sa'îd	52	B5
Bûr Sûdân	53	E6
Burao	49	F4
Buraydah	47	F6
Buraymī, Al		
Wāhāt al	44	E3
Burcher	63	B4
Burdur	46	C2
Burdwan =		
Barddhaman	40	F6
Burgas	22	C6
Burgersdorp	59	E5
Burgos	18	A4
Burgundy =		
Bourgogne	13	C6
Burhaniye	23	E6
Burhanpur	43	J10

Burias	38	B2
Buriram	36	A2
Burji	53	G6
Burkina Faso ■	55	F4
Burlington,		
Iowa, U.S.A.	77	E9
Burlington, *N.C.,*		
U.S.A.	75	A8
Burlington, *Vt.,*		
U.S.A.	73	B9
Burlyu-Tyube	29	E8
Burma ■	41	G11
Burnie	62	D4
Burnley	11	E5
Burnside ⇢	70	B9
Burqān	47	E6
Burqin	34	B3
Burra	62	B2
Burren Junction	63	B4
Burrendong		
Dam	63	B4
Burrinjuck Res.	63	C4
Burruyacú	94	B4
Bursa	23	D7
Burtundy	62	B3
Buru	39	E3
Burundi ■	57	E6
Burutu	55	G6
Bury St.		
Edmunds	11	E7
Buşayyah	47	E6
Būshehr	44	D2
Būshehr □	44	D2
Bushire =		
Būshehr	44	D2
Businga	56	D4
Busra ash Shām	46	D4
Busto Arsízio	20	B2
Busu-Djanoa	56	D4
Busuanga	38	B1
Buta	57	D4
Butare	57	E5
Butaritari	64	J12
Butembo	57	D5
Butha Qi	35	B7
Buton	39	E2
Butte	81	B7
Butterworth	36	C2
Butuan	38	C3
Butung = Buton	39	E2
Buturlinovka	24	C5
Buxtehude	14	B5
Buy	24	B5
Büyük		
Menderes ⇢	23	F6
Büyükçekmece	22	D7
Buzău	17	F8
Buzău ⇢	17	F8
Buzen	32	C2
Buzi ⇢	59	B6
Buzuluk	29	D6
Byarezina ⇢	17	B10
Bydgoszcz	16	B3
Byelarus =		
Belarus ■	24	C2
Byelorussia =		
Belarus ■	24	C2
Bykhaw	17	B10
Bykhov =		
Bykhaw	17	B10
Bylot I.	68	A3
Byrd, C.	96	A3
Byrock	63	B4
Byron Bay	63	A5
Byrranga, Gory	30	B8
Byrranga Mts. =		
Byrranga,		
Gory	30	B8
Bytom	16	C4
Bytów	16	A3

C

Ca Mau = Quan		
Long	36	C3
Caála	58	A3
Cabanatuan	38	A2
Cabedelo	92	D7
Cabimas	90	A4
Cabinda	56	F2
Cabinda □	56	F2
Cabinet Mts.	81	B6
Cabo Blanco	95	F3
Cabo Frio	93	G5
Cabo Pantoja	90	D3
Cabonga,		
Réservoir	69	D3
Caboolture	63	A5
Cabora Bassa		
Dam =		
Cahora Bassa		
Dam	59	B6
Cabot Str.	69	D5
Cabra	18	D3
Cabrera	19	C7
Cabriel ⇢	19	C5
Čačak	22	C3
Cáceres, *Brazil*	91	G7
Cáceres, *Spain*	18	C2
Cachimbo, Serra		
do	93	D2
Cachoeira	93	E6
Cachoeira de		
Itapemirim	93	G5
Cachoeira do		
Sul	94	C6
Cacólo	56	G3
Caconda	58	A3
Cacongo	56	F2
Cadibarrawirracanna,		
L.	62	A2
Cadiz, *Phil.*	38	B2
Cádiz, *Spain*	18	D2
Cádiz, G. de	18	D2
Cadney Park	62	A1
Caen	12	B3
Caeté	93	F5
Caetité	93	E5
Cagayan ⇢	38	A2
Cagayan de Oro	38	C2
Cágliari	21	E2
Cágliari, G. di	21	E2
Caguas	87	C6
Cahora Bassa		
Dam	59	B6
Cahors	12	D4
Cahuapanas	91	E3
Cahul	17	F9
Caia	59	B7
Caibarién	86	B4
Caicara	90	B5
Caicó	92	D6
Caicos Is.	87	B5
Caird Coast	96	B5
Cairns	61	D8
Cairo = El		
Qâhira	52	B5
Cairo	79	A9
Caiundo	58	B3
Caiza	91	H5
Cajamarca	91	E3
Cajàzeiras	92	D6
Calabar	55	H6
Calábria □	21	E6
Calafate	95	G2
Calahorra	19	A5
Calais	12	A4
Calama, *Brazil*	91	E6
Calama, *Chile*	94	A3

Calamar,
Bolívar,
Colombia . . . 90 A4
Calamar,
Vaupés,
Colombia . . . 90 C4
Calamian Group 38 B1
Calamocha 19 B5
Calang 36 D1
Calapan 38 B2
Călărași 22 B6
Calatayud 19 B5
Calauag 38 B2
Calavite, C. . . . 38 B2
Calbayog 38 B2
Calca 91 F4
Calcutta 41 F7
Caldas da
Rainha 18 C1
Caldera 94 B2
Caldwell 80 D5
Caledon 58 E3
Caledon → . . . 59 E5
Calgary 71 C8
Cali 90 C3
Calicut 43 P9
California □ . . . 82 B3
California, G. de 84 B2
Calingasta 94 C3
Callabonna, L. . 62 A3
Callao 91 F3
Caloundra 63 A5
Caltagirone . . . 21 F5
Caltanissetta . . 21 F5
Calulo 56 G2
Calunda 58 A4
Calvi 13 E8
Calviá 19 C7
Calvinia 58 E3
Camabatela . . . 56 F3
Camacupa 58 A3
Camagüey . . . 86 B4
Camaná 91 G4
Camargo 91 H5
Camargue . . . 13 E6
Camarones . . . 95 E3
Cambay =
Khambhat . . 43 H8
Cambay, G. of =
Khambat, G.
of 43 J8
Cambodia ■ . . 36 B3
Cambrai 13 A5
Cambrian Mts. . 11 E5
Cambridge, *N.Z.* 64 B6
Cambridge, *U.K.* 11 E7
Cambridge,
U.S.A. 73 C10
Cambridge Bay 70 B9
Cambridge G. . 60 C4
Cambundi-
Catembo . . 56 G3
Camden, *Ark.,*
U.S.A. 79 C7
Camden, *N.J.,*
U.S.A. 73 E8
Cameroon ■ . . 56 C2
Cameroun, Mt. 56 D1
Cametá 92 C4
Caminha 18 B1
Camira Creek . 63 A5
Camissombo . . 56 F4
Camocim 92 C5
Camopi → . . . 92 B3
Campana, I. . . . 95 F1
Campánia □ . . 21 D5
Campbell Town 62 D4
Campbellton . . 69 D4
Campbelltown . 63 B5

Campbeltown . 10 D4
Campeche 85 D6
Campeche, B. de 85 D6
Camperdown . . 62 C3
Campina Grande 92 D6
Campinas 94 A7
Campo 56 D1
Campo Belo . . . 93 G4
Campo Formoso 93 E5
Campo Grande 93 G3
Campo Maíor . . 92 C5
Campo Mourão 93 G3
Campoalegre . . 90 C3
Campobasso . . 20 D5
Campos 93 G5
Campos Belos . 93 E4
Campuya → . . . 90 D4
Camrose 71 C8
Çan 23 D6
Can Tho 36 B3
Canada ■ 70 C8
Cañada de
Gómez 94 C4
Çanakkale 23 D6
Çanakkale
Boğazı 23 D6
Cananea 84 A2
Canarias, Is. . . . 54 C1
Canary Is. =
Canarias, Is. . 54 C1
Canavieiras . . . 93 F6
Canbelego . . . 63 B4
Canberra 63 C4
Candala 49 E4
Candelo 63 C4
Candia =
Iráklion 23 G5
Canea = Khaniá 23 G5
Canelones 94 C5
Cañete, *Chile* . . 94 D2
Cañete, *Peru* . . 91 F3
Cangas de
Narcea 18 A2
Canguaretama . 92 D6
Canguçu 94 C6
Canicattì 21 F4
Canigou, Mt. . . 12 E5
Canipaan 36 C5
Çankırı 46 B3
Cann River 63 C4
Cannanore . . . 43 P9
Cannes 13 E7
Canoas 94 B6
Canora 71 C9
Canowindra . . . 63 B4
Cantabria □ . . . 18 A4
Cantabrian Mts.
= Cantábrica,
Cordillera . . . 18 A3
Cantábrica,
Cordillera . . . 18 A3
Cantal, Plomb
du 13 D5
Canterbury 11 F7
Canterbury □ . . 65 E4
Canterbury
Bight 65 F4
Canterbury
Plains 65 E4
Canton =
Guangzhou . . 35 D6
Canton 72 D5
Canudos 91 E7
Canutama 91 E6
Cap-Haïtien . . . 87 C5
Cap St.-Jacques
= Vung Tau . 36 B3
Capaia 56 F4
Capanaparo → 90 B5
Cape Barren I. . 62 D4

Cape Breton I. . 69 D4
Cape Coast . . . 55 G4
Cape Dorset . . . 68 B3
Cape Dyer 68 B4
Cape Girardeau 79 A9
Cape Jervis . . . 62 C2
Cape Town . . . 58 E3
Cape Verde Is. ■ 50 E1
Cape York
Peninsula . . 61 C7
Capela 93 E6
Capim → 92 C4
Capraia 20 C2
Capri 21 D5
Caprivi Strip . . 58 B4
Captain's Flat . 63 C4
Caquetá → . . . 90 D5
Caracal 22 B5
Caracas 90 A5
Caracol 93 D5
Caradoc 62 B3
Carajás, Serra
dos 92 D3
Carangola 93 G5
Caransebeş . . . 17 F6
Caratasca, L. . . 86 C3
Caratinga 93 F5
Caraúbas 92 D6
Caravaca 19 C5
Caravelas 93 F6
Caraveli 91 G4
Carballo 18 A1
Carbonara, C. . 21 E2
Carbondale . . . 79 A9
Carbonear 69 D5
Carbonia 21 E2
Carcassonne . . 12 E5
Carcross 70 B6
Cardamon Hills 43 Q10
Cárdenas 86 B3
Cardiff 11 F5
Cardigan B. . . . 11 E4
Cardston 71 D8
Carei 17 E6
Careysburg . . . 55 G2
Carhué 94 D4
Caria 23 F7
Cariacica 93 G5
Caribbean Sea . 86 D5
Cariboo Mts. . . 71 C7
Carinda 63 B4
Carinhanha . . . 93 E5
Carinthia □ =
Kärnten □ . . 15 E7
Caripito 90 A6
Caritianas 91 E6
Carlisle 11 D5
Carlow 11 E3
Carlsbad 78 C1
Carmacks 70 B6
Carman 71 D10
Carmarthen . . . 11 F4
Carmaux 12 D5
Carmelo 94 C5
Carmen 90 B3
Carmen de
Patagones . . 95 E4
Carmona 18 D3
Carnac 12 C2
Carnarvon,
Australia 60 E1
Carnarvon,
S. Africa 58 E4
Carnegie, L. . . 60 F3
Carnic Alps =
Karnische
Alpen 20 A4
Carniche Alpi =
Karnische
Alpen 20 A4

Carnot 56 D3
Carnot, C. 62 B2
Carolina 92 D4
Caroline I. 65 K15
Caroline Is. . . . 64 J10
Caroni → 90 B6
Caroníe =
Nébrodi,
Monti 21 F5
Caroona 63 B5
Carpathians . . . 16 D5
Carpaţii
Meridionali . . 17 F7
Carpentaria, G.
of 60 C6
Carpentras . . . 13 D6
Carpi 20 B3
Carpolac =
Morea 62 C3
Carrara 20 B3
Carrauntoohill . 11 E2
Carrick-on-Suir 11 E3
Carrieton 62 B2
Carrizal Bajo . . 94 B2
Carşamba 46 B4
Carson City . . . 80 F4
Cartagena,
Colombia . . . 90 A3
Cartagena,
Spain 19 D5
Cartago,
Colombia . . . 90 C3
Cartago,
Costa Rica . . 86 E3
Carterton 65 D6
Carthage 79 A6
Cartwright 68 C5
Caruaru 92 D6
Carúpano 90 A6
Carvoeiro 90 D6
Carvoeiro, C. . . 18 C1
Casablanca . . . 54 B3
Cascade Ra. . . . 80 B3
Cascais 18 C1
Cascavel 94 A6
Cáscina 20 C3
Caserta 20 D5
Casiguran 38 A2
Casilda 94 C4
Casino 63 A5
Casiquiare → . . 90 C5
Casma 91 E3
Caspe 19 B5
Casper 81 D10
Caspian Sea . . 29 E6
Cassinga 58 B3
Castellammare
di Stábia . . . 21 D5
Castellón de la
Plana 19 C5
Castelo Branco 18 C2
Castelsarrasin . 12 D4
Castelvetrano . 21 F4
Casterton 62 C3
Castilla La
Mancha □ . . 18 C4
Castilla y
Leon □ 18 A3
Castlebar 11 E2
Castleblaney . . 11 D3
Castlemaine . . 63 C3
Castlereagh → 63 B4
Castres 12 E5
Castries 87 D7
Castro 95 E2
Castro Alves . . 93 E6
Castuera 18 C3
Cat I. 86 B4
Catacáos 91 E2

Catalão

Catalão 93 F4
Çatalca 22 D7
Catalonia =
Cataluña □ .. 19 B6
Cataluña □ ... 19 B6
Catamarca ... 94 B3
Catanduanes . 38 B2
Catanduva 93 G4
Catánia 21 F5
Catanzaro ... 21 E6
Catarman 38 B2
Cateel 38 C3
Catoche, C. .. 85 C7
Catrimani 90 C6
Catskill Mts. .. 73 C8
Cauca → 90 B4
Caucaia 92 C6
Caucasus
  Mountains .. 25 E5
Caúngula 56 F3
Cauquenes ... 94 D2
Caura → 90 B6
Cauvery → .. 43 P11
Caux, Pays de . 12 B4
Cavan 11 C3
Cavendish .. 62 C3
Caviana, I. ... 92 B3
Cavite 38 B2
Cawndilla L. ... 62 B3
Cawnpore =
  Kanpur 40 D3
Caxias 92 C5
Caxias do Sul . 94 B6
Caxito 56 F2
Cayambe 90 C3
Cayenne 92 A3
Cayman Is. ■ . 67 H11
Cazombo 58 A4
Ceadâr-Lunga . 17 E9
Ceanannus Mor 11 E3
Ceará =
  Fortaleza ... 92 C6
Ceará □ 92 D6
Ceará Mirim . 92 D6
Cebollar 94 B3
Cebu 38 B2
Cecil Plains .. 63 A5
Cedar L. 71 C10
Cedar Rapids . 77 E9
Cedro 92 D6
Ceduna 62 B1
Cefalù 21 E5
Cegléd 16 E4
Celaya 84 C4
Celebes =
  Sulawesi □ . 39 E2
Celebes Sea .. 39 D2
Celje 20 A5
Celle 14 B6
Celtic Sea ... 11 F2
Central,
  Cordillera ... 90 C3
Central African
  Rep. ■ ... 56 C4
Central Makran
  Range 42 F4
Cephalonia =
  Kefallinía ... 23 E3
Ceram = Seram 39 E3
Ceram Sea =
  Seram Sea .. 39 E3
Ceres, Argentina 94 B4
Ceres, S. Africa 58 E3
Cerignola ... 20 D5
Cerigo = Kíthira 23 F4
Çerkeş 46 B3
Çerkeşköy .. 22 D6
Cervera 19 B6
Cesena 20 B4

Česka Republika
  = Czech
  Rep. ■ 16 D2
České
  Budějovice .. 16 D2
Ceskomoravská
  Vrchovina ... 16 D2
Çeşme 23 E6
Cessnock ... 63 B5
Cetinje 22 C2
Cetraro 21 E5
Ceuta 18 E3
Cévennes 13 D5
Ceyhan 46 C3
Ceylon = Sri
  Lanka ■ 43 R12
Chachapoyas .. 91 E3
Chachran 42 E7
Chad ■ 53 E2
Chad, L. =
  Tchad, L. ... 53 F1
Chadileuvú → 94 D3
Chadyr-Lunga =
  Ceadâr-Lunga 17 E9
Chagai Hills ... 42 E3
Chagos Arch. . 27 K11
Chãh Bahãr ... 45 E5
Chãh Gay Hills 45 D6
Chahar Burjak . 42 D3
Chaibasa 40 F5
Chakhãnsur ... 42 D3
Chakradharpur . 40 F5
Chakwal 42 C8
Chala 91 G4
Chalcis =
  Khalkís 23 E4
Chalhuanca ... 91 F4
Chalisgaon ... 43 J9
Chalky Inlet .. 65 G2
Challapata 91 G5
Chalon-sur-
  Saône 13 C6
Châlons-en-
  Champagne . 13 B6
Chaman 42 D5
Chamba, India . 42 C10
Chamba,
  Tanzania 59 A7
Chambal → .. 42 F11
Chambéry 13 D6
Chamical 94 C3
Chamonix-Mont
  Blanc 13 D7
Champagne .. 13 B6
Champaign ... 72 D1
Champlain, L. . 73 B9
Chañaral 94 B2
Chandigarh .. 42 D10
Chandler 62 A1
Chandmani ... 34 B4
Chandpur 41 F8
Chandrapur ... 43 K11
Chang Jiang → 35 C7
Changanacheri 43 Q10
Changane → . 59 C6
Changchiak'ou
  = Zhangjiakou 35 B6
Ch'angchou =
  Changzhou .. 35 C6
Changchun ... 35 B7
Changde 35 D6
Changhai =
  Shanghai .. 35 C7
Changjiang ... 35 E5
Changsha 35 D6
Changting ... 35 D6
Changzhi 35 C6
Changzhou ... 35 C6
Channapatna .. 43 N10

Channel Is. 11 G5
Chantada 18 A2
Chanthaburi .. 36 B2
Chantrey Inlet . 70 B10
Chanute 79 A6
Chao Phraya → 36 B2
Chao'an 35 D6
Chaoyang 35 D6
Chapala, L. de . 84 C4
Chapayevsk ... 24 C6
Chapra =
  Chhapra ... 40 E5
Châr 54 D2
Chara 31 D9
Charadai 94 B5
Charagua 91 G6
Charaña 91 G5
Chardara 29 E7
Chardzhou =
  Chärjew 29 F7
Charente → .. 12 D3
Chari → 53 F1
Chãrikãr 42 B6
Chärjew 29 F7
Charleroi 14 C3
Charles, C. ... 73 F8
Charleston, S.C.,
  U.S.A. 75 C8
Charleston,
  W. Va., U.S.A. 72 E5
Charlesville .. 56 F4
Charleville ... 63 A4
Charleville-
  Mézières 13 B6
Charlotte 75 B7
Charlotte Amalie 87 C7
Charlottesville . 73 E6
Charlottetown . 69 D4
Charlton 62 C3
Charolles 13 C6
Charouine 54 C4
Charters Towers 61 E8
Chartres 12 B4
Chascomús ... 94 D5
Châteaubriant . 12 C3
Châteaulin ... 12 B1
Châteauroux .. 12 C4
Châtellerault .. 12 C4
Chatham, N.B.,
  Canada 69 D4
Chatham, Ont.,
  Canada 69 D2
Chatham, U.K. . 11 F7
Chatrapur 40 H5
Chattahoochee →
  .... 74 D5
Chattanooga .. 74 B5
Chauk 41 G10
Chaukan La ... 41 D11
Chaumont ... 13 B6
Chaves, Brazil . 92 C4
Chaves, Portugal 18 B2
Chavuma 58 A4
Cheb 16 C1
Cheboksary ... 24 B6
Chech, Erg 54 D4
Chechenia □ .. 25 E6
Checheno-
  Ingush
  Republic =
  Chechenia □ 25 E6
Chechnya =
  Chechenia □ 25 E6
Cheduba I. ... 41 H9
Cheepie 63 A4
Chegga 54 C3
Chegutu 59 B6
Chehalis 80 B2
Cheju Do 35 C7

Chekiang =
  Zhejiang □ .. 35 D7
Cheleken 29 F6
Chelforó 95 D3
Chelkar =
  Shalqar 29 E6
Chelkar Tengiz,
  Solonchak .. 29 E7
Chełm 17 C6
Chełmno ... 16 B4
Chelmsford ... 11 F7
Cheltenham ... 11 F5
Chelyabinsk ... 29 D7
Chemnitz ... 15 C7
Chen Xian ... 35 D6
Chenab → ... 42 D7
Chencha 53 G6
Chenchiang =
  Zhenjiang .. 35 C6
Chennai =
  Madras 43 N12
Chengde ... 35 B6
Chengdu 35 C5
Chengjiang .. 34 D5
Ch'engtu =
  Chengdu ... 35 C5
Cheo Reo ... 36 B3
Cheom Ksan . 36 B2
Chepén 91 E3
Chepes 94 C3
Cher → 12 C4
Cherbourg ... 12 B3
Cherchell 54 A5
Cherdyn 28 C6
Cherepanovo .. 29 D9
Cherepovets .. 24 B4
Chergui, Chott
  ech 54 B5
Cherikov =
  Cherykaw ... 17 B10
Cherkasy 24 D3
Cherlak 29 D8
Chernaya 30 B6
Chernigov =
  Chernihiv .. 24 C3
Chernihiv 24 C3
Chernivtsi ... 17 D7
Chernobyl =
  Chornobyl .. 17 C10
Chernovtsy =
  Chernivtsi .. 17 D7
Chernyakhovsk 28 D3
Cherquenco ... 94 D2
Cherrapunji .. 41 E8
Cherven ... 17 B9
Chervonohrad . 17 C7
Cherykaw ... 17 B10
Chesapeake .. 73 F7
Chesapeake B. . 73 E7
Cheshskaya
  Guba 28 C5
Chester, U.K. . 11 E5
Chester, U.S.A. 73 E8
Chesterfield .. 11 E6
Chesterfield, Is. 64 L10
Chesterfield Inlet 70 B10
Chesterton Ra. . 63 A4
Cheviot Hills . 10 D5
Chew Bahir .. 53 H6
Cheyenne ... 76 E2
Cheyenne → . 76 C4
Chhapra 40 E5
Chhatarpur .. 43 G11
Chhindwara .. 43 H11
Chhlong 36 B3
Chi → 36 A2
Chiamussu =
  Jiamusi 35 B8
Chiange 58 B2

Name	Page	Ref
Chiapa →	85	D6
Chiávari	20	B2
Chiavenna	20	A2
Chiba	32	B7
Chibemba	58	B2
Chibia	58	B2
Chibougamau	69	D3
Chibuk	53	F1
Chicacole = Srikakulam	40	H4
Chicago	72	D2
Chichagof I.	71	C6
Chichibu	32	A6
Ch'ich'ihaerh = Qiqihar	35	B7
Chickasha	78	B5
Chiclana de la Frontera	18	D2
Chiclayo	91	E3
Chico	80	F3
Chico →, Chubut, Argentina	95	E3
Chico →, Santa Cruz, Argentina	95	F3
Chicoutimi	69	D3
Chidambaram	43	P11
Chidley, C.	68	B4
Chiemsee	15	E7
Chiengi	57	F5
Chiese →	20	B3
Chieti	20	C5
Chiguana	91	H5
Chihli, G. of = Bo Hai	35	C6
Chihuahua	84	B3
Chiili	29	E7
Chik Bollapur	43	N10
Chikmagalur	43	N9
Chilapa	84	D5
Chilas	42	B9
Chilaw	43	R11
Childers	63	A5
Chile ■	94	D2
Chilete	91	E3
Chililabombwe	59	A5
Chilin = Jilin	35	B7
Chilka L.	40	H5
Chillán	94	D2
Chiloé, I. de	95	E2
Chilpancingo	84	D5
Chiluage	56	F4
Chilwa, L.	59	B7
Chimay	29	E6
Chimborazo	90	D3
Chimbote	91	E3
Chimkent = Shymkent	29	E7
Chimoio	59	B6
Chin □	41	F9
China ■	35	C5
Chinan = Jinan	35	C6
Chinandega	85	E7
Chincha Alta	91	F3
Chinchilla	63	A5
Chinchou = Jinzhou	35	B7
Chinde	59	B7
Chindwin →	41	G10
Chingola	59	A5
Ch'ingtao = Qingdao	35	C7
Chinguetti	54	D2
Chinhoyi	59	B6
Chiniot	42	D8
Chinju	35	C7
Chinnampo	35	C7
Chinon	12	C4
Chinsali	57	G6
Chióggia	20	B4
Chíos = Khíos	23	E6
Chipata	59	A6
Chiquián	91	F3
Chiquinquira	90	B4
Chirchiq	29	E7
Chirmiri	40	F4
Chiromo	59	B7
Chisamba	59	A5
Chisapani Garhi	40	D5
Chişinău	17	E9
Chistopol	24	B7
Chita	30	D9
Chitado	58	B2
Chitembo	58	A3
Chitral	42	B7
Chitré	86	E3
Chittagong	41	F8
Chittagong □	41	E8
Chittaurgarh	43	G9
Chittoor	43	N11
Chiusi	20	C3
Chivasso	20	B1
Chivilcoy	94	B4
Chkalov = Orenburg	29	D6
Choele Choel	95	D3
Chojnice	16	B3
Cholet	12	C3
Choluteca	85	E7
Choma	59	B5
Chomutov	16	C1
Chon Buri	36	B2
Chone	90	D3
Chŏngjin	35	B7
Chŏngju	35	C7
Chongqing	35	D5
Chŏnju	35	C7
Chonos, Arch. de los	95	F2
Chop	17	D6
Chornobyl	17	C10
Chortkiv	17	D7
Chorzów	16	C4
Chos-Malal	94	D2
Chōshi	32	B7
Choszczno	16	B2
Chotila	43	H7
Choybalsan	35	B6
Christchurch	65	E5
Christiana	59	D5
Christmas I. = Kiritimati	65	J15
Chu = Shu	29	E8
Ch'uanchou = Quanzhou	35	D6
Chubut →	95	E3
Chudskoye, Oz.	24	B2
Chūgoku-Sanchi	32	B3
Chula Vista	82	D4
Chulucanas	90	E2
Chulym →	29	D9
Chumbicha	94	B3
Chumphon	36	B1
Chuna →	30	D7
Chunchŏn	35	C7
Chungking = Chongqing	35	D5
Chunya	57	F6
Chuquibamba	91	G4
Chuquicamata	94	A3
Chur	13	C8
Churachandpur	41	E9
Churchill	70	C10
Churchill →, Man., Canada	70	C10
Churchill →, Nfld., Canada	69	C4
Churchill, C.	70	C10
Churchill Falls	69	C4
Churchill L.	71	C9
Churu	42	E9
Chushal	42	C11
Chusovoy	28	D6
Chuvash Republic □ = Chuvashia □	24	B6
Chuvashia □	24	B6
Cicero	72	D2
Ciechanów	16	B5
Ciego de Avila	86	B4
Ciénaga	90	A4
Cienfuegos	86	B3
Cieszyn	16	D4
Cieza	19	C5
Cijara, Pantano de	18	C3
Cilician Gates P.	46	C3
Cill Chainnigh = Kilkenny	11	E3
Cimişlia	17	E9
Cimone, Mte.	20	B3
Cîmpina	17	F7
Cîmpulung	17	F7
Cinca →	19	B6
Cincar	20	C6
Cincinnati	72	E3
Çine	23	F7
Cinto, Mte.	13	E8
Circle	71	B5
Cirebon	37	F3
Citlaltépetl	84	D5
Città di Castello	20	C4
Ciudad Bolívar	90	B6
Ciudad Chetumal	85	D7
Ciudad del Carmen	85	D6
Ciudad Delicias = Delicias	84	B3
Ciudad Guayana	90	B6
Ciudad Juárez	84	A3
Ciudad Madero	84	C5
Ciudad Mante	84	C5
Ciudad Obregón	84	B3
Ciudad Real	18	C4
Ciudad Rodrigo	18	B2
Ciudad Trujillo = Santo Domingo	87	C6
Ciudad Victoria	84	C5
Civitanova Marche	20	C4
Civitavécchia	20	C3
Cizre	46	C5
Clanwilliam	58	E3
Clare	62	B2
Clarence →, Australia	63	A5
Clarence →, N.Z.	65	E5
Clarence, I.	95	G2
Clarence I.	96	A4
Clarie Coast	96	A13
Clarke I.	62	D4
Clarksdale	79	B8
Clarksville	74	A4
Claveria	38	A2
Clear, C.	11	F2
Clearwater	75	F6
Clearwater Mts.	81	B6
Clermont-Ferrand	13	D5
Cleveland, Australia	63	A5
Cleveland, U.S.A.	72	D5
Clifden	65	G2
Clifton	63	A5
Clifton Hills	62	A2
Clinton, Canada	71	C7
Clinton, N.Z.	65	G3
Clinton, U.S.A.	77	E9
Clinton Colden L.	70	B9
Clones	11	D3
Clonmel	11	E3
Clovis	78	B2
Cluj-Napoca	17	E6
Clunes	62	C3
Clutha →	65	G3
Clyde	65	F3
Clyde →	10	D4
Clyde, Firth of	10	D4
Clyde River	68	A4
Coari	90	D6
Coast Mts.	70	C7
Coast Ranges	80	F2
Coats I.	68	B2
Coats Land	96	B5
Coatzacoalcos	85	D6
Cobalt	69	D3
Cobar	63	B4
Cóbh	11	F2
Cobham	62	B3
Cobija	91	F5
Cobourg	69	D3
Cobram	63	C4
Cóbué	59	A6
Coburg	15	C6
Cocanada = Kakinada	40	J4
Cochabamba	91	G5
Cochin	43	Q10
Cochin China = Nam-Phan	36	B3
Cochrane	69	D2
Cochrane, L.	95	F2
Cockburn	62	B3
Cockburn, Canal	95	G2
Coco →	86	D3
Cocobeach	56	D1
Cod, C.	73	C10
Codajás	90	D6
Codó	92	C5
Cœur d'Alene	80	B5
Coffeyville	79	A6
Coffin B.	62	B2
Coffin Bay Peninsula	62	B2
Coffs Harbour	63	B5
Cognac	12	D3
Cohuna	63	C3
Coiba, I.	86	E3
Coig →	95	G3
Coihaique	95	F2
Coimbatore	43	P10
Coimbra, Brazil	91	G7
Coimbra, Portugal	18	B1
Coín	18	D3
Cojimies	90	C3
Colac	62	C3
Colatina	93	F5
Colbeck, C.	96	B17
Colbinabbin	63	C3
Colchester	11	F7
Colebrook	62	D4
Coleman	71	D8
Coleraine, Australia	62	C3
Coleraine, U.K.	11	D3
Coleridge, L.	65	E4
Colesberg	59	E5
Colhué Huapi, L.	95	F3
Colima	84	D4

Colinas 92 D5
Coll 10 C3
Collaguasi ... 91 H5
Collarenebri .. 63 A4
Collingwood .. 64 D5
Colmar 13 B7
Colo → 63 B5
Cologne = Köln 14 C4
Colomb-Béchar
  = Béchar ... 54 B4
Colômbia 93 G4
Colombia ■ ... 90 C4
Colombo 43 R11
Colón, Cuba .. 86 B3
Colón, Panama 85 F9
Colonia 94 C5
Colonia Dora . 94 B4
Colonsay 10 C3
Colorado □ .. 83 A10
Colorado →,
  Argentina ... 95 D4
Colorado →,
  N. Amer. 82 E5
Colorado
  Plateau 83 B7
Colorado
  Springs 76 F2
Columbia, Mo.,
  U.S.A. 77 F8
Columbia, S.C.,
  U.S.A. 75 B7
Columbia,
  Tenn., U.S.A. 74 B4
Columbia → .. 80 B1
Columbia,
  District of □ . 73 E7
Columbia Basin 80 B4
Columbretes, Is. 19 C6
Columbus, Ga.,
  U.S.A. 74 C5
Columbus,
  Miss., U.S.A. 74 C3
Columbus, Ohio,
  U.S.A. 72 E4
Colville → ... 71 A4
Colville, C. .. 64 B6
Colwyn Bay ... 11 E5
Comácchio ... 20 B4
Comallo 95 E2
Comilla 41 F8
Comino, C. ... 21 D2
Committee B. . 68 B2
Commonwealth
  B. 96 A14
Commoron
  Cr. → 63 A5
Communism Pk.
  =
  Kommunizma,
  Pik 29 F8
Como 20 B2
Como, L. di ... 20 B2
Comodoro
  Rivadavia .. 95 F3
Comorin, C. ... 43 Q10
Comoro Is. =
  Comoros ■ . 51 H8
Comoros ■ ... 51 H8
Comox 71 D7
Compiègne ... 13 B5
Compton Downs 63 B4
Comrat 17 E9
Conakry 55 G2
Conara Junction 62 D4
Concarneau ... 12 C2
Conceição da
  Barra 93 F6
Concepción,
  Bolivia 91 G6

Concepción,
  Chile 94 D2
Concepción,
  Paraguay ... 94 A5
Concepción, L. 91 G6
Concepción del
  Oro 84 C4
Concepción del
  Uruguay 94 C5
Conchos → .. 84 B3
Concord, N.C.,
  U.S.A. 75 B7
Concord, N.H.,
  U.S.A. 73 C10
Concordia,
  Argentina ... 94 C5
Concórdia, Brazil 90 D5
Condamine ... 63 A5
Condeúba ... 93 E5
Condobolin ... 63 B4
Conegliano ... 20 B4
Confuso → .. 94 B5
Congo =
  Zaïre → 56 F2
Congo
  (Kinshasa) =
  Zaïre ■ 56 E4
Congo ■ 56 E3
Conjeeveram =
  Kanchipuram 43 N11
Conlea 63 B3
Conn, L. 11 D2
Connacht □ .. 11 E2
Connecticut □ . 73 D9
Connecticut → 73 D9
Connemara .. 11 E2
Conoble 63 B3
Cononaco → . 90 D3
Conran, C. ... 63 C4
Conselheiro
  Lafaiete 93 G5
Constance =
  Konstanz ... 14 E5
Constance, L. =
  Bodensee ... 13 C8
Constanţa ... 22 B7
Constantine ... 54 A6
Constitución .. 94 D2
Contai 40 G6
Contamana ... 91 E4
Contas → ... 93 E6
Conway, L. ... 62 A2
Coober Pedy . 62 A1
Cooch Behar =
  Koch Bihar .. 41 D7
Cook, B. 95 H2
Cook, Mt. 65 E4
Cook Inlet ... 71 C4
Cook Is. 65 L14
Cook Strait ... 65 D6
Cooktown ... 61 D8
Coolabah 63 B4
Cooladdi 63 A4
Coolah 63 B4
Coolamon ... 63 B4
Coolangatta ... 63 A5
Cooma 63 C4
Coonabarabran 63 B4
Coonamble ... 63 B4
Coondapoor .. 43 N9
Coongie 62 A3
Coongoola ... 63 A4
Cooninie, L. ... 62 A2
Cooper Cr. →,
  N. Terr.,
  Australia 60 C5
Cooper Cr. →,
  S. Austral.,
  Australia 62 A2

Cooroy 63 A5
Cootamundra . 63 B4
Cooyar 63 A5
Copenhagen =
  København .. 9 G10
Copiapó 94 B2
Copiapó → ... 94 B2
Copley 62 B2
Copper Center . 71 B5
Copper Cliff ... 69 D2
Coppermine ... 70 B8
Coppermine → 70 B8
Coquimbo 94 C2
Corabia 22 C5
Coracora 91 G4
Coral Harbour . 68 B2
Coral Sea 64 L10
Corato 21 D6
Corby 11 E6
Corcaigh = Cork 11 F2
Corcubión ... 18 A1
Córdoba,
  Argentina ... 94 C4
Córdoba, Spain 18 D3
Córdoba, Sierra
  de 94 C4
Cordon 38 A2
Cordova 71 B5
Corfu = Kérkira 23 E2
Coria 18 C2
Corigliano
  Cálabro 21 E6
Corinna 62 D4
Corinth =
  Kórinthos ... 23 F4
Corinth, G. of =
  Korinthiakós
  Kólpos 23 E4
Corinto 93 F5
Cork 11 F2
Çorlu 22 D6
Corner Brook . 69 D5
Corneşti 17 E9
Cornwall 69 D3
Corny Pt. 62 B2
Coro 90 A5
Coroatá 92 C5
Corocoro 91 G5
Coroico 91 G5
Coromandel .. 64 B6
Corona 94 D2
Coronation Gulf 70 B8
Coronation I. .. 96 A4
Coronel 94 D2
Coronel Dorrego 94 D4
Coronel Suárez 94 D4
Corowa 63 C4
Corpus Christi . 78 F5
Corque 91 G5
Corrib, L. 11 E2
Corrientes ... 94 B5
Corrientes → . 90 D4
Corrientes, C.,
  Colombia ... 90 B3
Corrientes, C.,
  Mexico 84 C3
Corse 13 E8
Corse, C. 13 E8
Corsica = Corse 13 E8
Corsicana ... 79 C5
Corte 13 E8
Çorum 46 B3
Corumbá 91 G7
Corumbá de
  Goiás 93 F4
Coruña = La
  Coruña ... 18 A1
Corvallis 80 C2
Cosenza 21 E6

Costa Blanca .. 19 C5
Costa Brava ... 19 B7
Costa del Sol .. 18 D3
Costa Dorada . 19 B6
Costa Rica ■ .. 86 E3
Cotabato 38 C2
Cotagaita 91 H5
Côte d'Azur .. 13 E7
Côte-d'Ivoire ■
  = Ivory
  Coast ■ 55 G3
Cotentin 12 B3
Cotonou 55 G5
Cotopaxi 90 D3
Cotswold Hills . 11 F5
Cottbus 15 C8
Couedic, C. du . 62 C2
Coulman I. ... 96 B15
Council 71 B3
Council Bluffs . 77 E7
Courantyne → . 90 B7
Courtrai =
  Kortrijk 14 C2
Coventry 11 E6
Covilhã 18 B2
Covington ... 72 E3
Cowal, L. 63 B4
Cowangie 62 C3
Cowarie 62 A2
Cowell 62 B2
Cowra 63 B4
Coxim 93 F3
Cox's Bazar .. 41 G8
Cozumel, I. de . 85 C7
Craboon 63 B4
Cracow =
  Kraków 16 C4
Cracow 63 A5
Cradock 59 E5
Craigavon ... 11 D3
Crailsheim ... 14 D6
Craiova 22 B4
Cranbrook,
  Australia 62 D4
Cranbrook,
  Canada 71 D8
Crateús 92 D5
Crato 92 D6
Crawley 11 F6
Crazy Mts. 81 B8
Crema 20 B2
Cremona 20 B3
Cres 20 B5
Cressy 62 C3
Crete = Kríti .. 23 G5
Créteil 12 B5
Creus, C. de ... 19 A7
Creuse → 12 C4
Crewe 11 E5
Criciúma 94 B7
Crimean Pen. =
  Krymskyy
  Pivostriv 25 D3
Crişul Alb → . 16 E5
Crişul Negru → 16 E5
Crna Gora =
  Montenegro □ 22 C2
Crna Gora .. 22 C3
Crna Reka → . 22 D3
Croatia ■ ... 20 B6
Crocker,
  Banjaran ... 36 C5
Croker, C. 60 C5
Cromer 11 E7
Cromwell 65 F3
Cronulla 63 B5
Crookwell ... 63 B4
Cross Sound . 71 C6
Crotone 21 E6

Crows Nest ... 63 A5
Crowsnest Pass 71 D8
Cruz Alta 94 B6
Cruz del Eje ... 94 C4
Cruzeiro 93 G5
Cruzeiro do Sul 91 E4
Crystal Brook .. 62 B2
Csongrád 16 E5
Cuamba 59 A7
Cuando → 58 B4
Cuarto → 94 C4
Cuba ■ 86 B4
Cubango → ... 58 B4
Cuchi 58 A3
Cúcuta 90 B4
Cuddalore 43 P11
Cuddapah 43 M11
Cudgewa 63 C4
Cuenca, *Ecuador* 90 D3
Cuenca, *Spain* . 19 B4
Cuenca,
    Serranía de . 19 C5
Cuernavaca ... 84 D5
Cuevas del
    Almanzora .. 19 D5
Cuevo 91 H6
Cuiabá 93 F2
Cuiabá → 93 F2
Cuima 58 A3
Cuito → 58 B4
Cukai 36 D2
Culcairn 63 C4
Culgoa → 63 A4
Culiacán 84 C3
Culion 38 B2
Cullarin Ra. ... 63 B4
Cullera 19 C5
Culuene → ... 93 E3
Culverden 65 E5
Cumaná 90 A6
Cumberland,
    Canada 71 D7
Cumberland,
    U.S.A. 73 E6
Cumberland
    Pen. 68 B4
Cumberland
    Plateau 72 F3
Cumberland Sd. 68 B4
Cumborah 63 A4
Cumbum 43 M11
Cummins 62 B2
Cumnock 63 B4
Cunene → ... 58 B2
Cúneo 20 B1
Cunnamulla ... 63 A4
Cupica, G. de .. 90 B3
Curaçao 87 D6
Curaray → ... 90 D4
Curiapo 90 B6
Curicó 94 C2
Curitiba 94 B7
Currabubula .. 63 B5
Currais Novos . 92 D6
Curralinho ... 92 C4
Curraweena ... 63 B4
Currie 62 C3
Curtea de Argeş 17 F7
Curtis Group .. 62 C4
Curuápanema →
    .... 92 C2
Curuçá 92 C4
Curup 37 E2
Cururupu 92 C5
Curuzú Cuatiá . 94 B5
Cuttaburra → . 63 A3
Cuttack 40 G5
Cuvier I. 64 B6
Cuxhaven 14 B5

Cuyo 38 B2
Cuzco, *Bolívia* . 91 H5
Cuzco, *Peru* .. 91 F4
Cwmbran 11 F5
Cyclades =
    Kikládhes ... 23 F5
Cygnet 62 D4
Cyprus ■ 46 D3
Cyrenaica 52 C3
Cyrene =
    Shaḥḥāt 52 B3
Czech Rep. ■ . 16 D2
Częstochowa .. 16 C4

D

Da Hinggan Ling 35 B7
Da Lat 36 B3
Da Nang 36 A3
Da Qaidam ... 34 C4
Da Yunhe → .. 35 C7
Daba Shan 35 C5
Dabakala 55 G4
Dabo 37 E2
Dabola 55 F2
Daboya 55 G4
Dacca = Dhaka 41 F8
Dacca =
    Dhaka □ 41 E8
Dachau 15 D6
Dadanawa 90 C7
Dadra and
    Nagar
    Haveli □ 43 J8
Dadu 42 F5
Daet 38 B2
Dagana 55 E1
Dagestan □ ... 25 E6
Daghestan
    Republic =
    Dagestan □ . 25 E6
Dagö = Hiiumaa 24 B1
Dagupan 38 A2
Dahlak Kebir .. 49 D3
Dahod 43 H9
Dahomey =
    Benin ■ 55 G5
Dahra 55 E1
Daiō-Misaki ... 32 B5
Dairût 52 C5
Dakar 55 F1
Dakhla 54 D1
Dakhla, El
    Wâhât el- ... 52 C4
Dakhovskaya .. 25 E5
Đakovica 22 C3
Dalaman → .. 23 F7
Dalandzadgad . 35 B5
Dālbandīn ... 42 E4
Dalby 63 A5
Dalhousie 69 D4
Dali 34 D5
Dalian 35 C7
Daliang Shan .. 34 D5
Dallarnil 63 A5
Dallas 79 C5
Dalmacija 20 C6
Dalmatia =
    Dalmacija .. 20 C6
Daloa 55 G3
Dalton 74 B5
Dalton Iceberg
    Tongue 96 A13
Daly Waters ... 60 D5
Daman 43 J8
Damanhûr 52 B5

Damar 39 F3
Damaraland ... 58 C3
Damascus =
    Dimashq ... 46 D4
Damāvand 44 C3
Damāvand,
    Qolleh-ye .. 44 C3
Damba 56 F3
Dāmghān 44 B3
Damiel 18 C4
Damietta =
    Dumyât 52 B5
Damoh 43 H11
Dampier 60 E2
Dampier, Selat 39 E4
Danbury 73 D9
Dandeldhura .. 40 C3
Dandeli 43 M9
Dandong 35 B7
Dandenong ... 63 C4
Danger Is. =
    Pukapuka .. 65 L14
Danger Pt. ... 58 E3
Dangora 55 F6
Danilov 24 B5
Dankhar Gompa 42 C11
Dannemora .. 9 F11
Dannevirke ... 64 D7
Dante 49 E5
Danube =
    Dunărea → . 17 F9
Danville 75 A8
Danzig =
    Gdańsk 16 A4
Dao 38 B2
Daoud = Aïn
    Beïda 54 A6
Dar el Beida =
    Casablanca . 54 B3
Dar es Salaam . 57 F7
Dārāb 44 D3
Daraj 54 B7
Darband 42 B8
Darbhanga ... 40 D5
Dardanelles =
    Çanakkale
    Boğazı 23 D6
Dârfûr 53 F3
Dargai 42 B7
Dargan Ata ... 29 E7
Dargaville 64 A5
Darıca 22 D7
Darién, G. del . 90 B3
Darjeeling =
    Darjiling ... 40 D7
Darjiling 40 D7
Darling → .. 62 B3
Darling Downs 63 A5
Darling Ra. ... 60 G2
Darlington ... 11 D6
Darłowo 16 A3
Darmstadt ... 14 D5
Darnah 52 B3
Darnley, C. ... 96 A10
Darnley B. ... 70 B7
Dart, C. 96 B18
Dartmoor 11 F5
Dartmouth ... 69 D4
Dartmouth, L. . 63 A4
Darvaza 29 E6
Darvel, Teluk . 38 D1
Darwha 43 J10
Darwin 60 C5
Daryoi Amu =
    Amudarya → 29 E6
Dās 44 E3
Dashhowuz ... 29 E6

Dasht → 42 G2
Dasht-e Kavīr .. 44 C3
Dasht-e Mārgow 42 D3
Datça 23 F6
Datia 43 G11
Datong 35 B6
Datu, Tanjung . 37 D3
Datu Piang ... 38 C2
Daugava → . 24 B1
Daugavpils ... 24 B2
Daulpur 42 F10
Dauphin 71 C9
Dauphiné 13 D6
Davangere ... 43 M9
Davao 38 C3
Davao, G. of .. 38 C3
Dāvar Panāh .. 45 E5
Davenport ... 77 E9
David 86 E3
David Gorodok
    = Davyd
    Haradok 17 B8
Davis Sea 96 A11
Davis Str. 68 B5
Davos 13 C8
Davyd Haradok 17 B8
Dawson 70 B6
Dawson, I. 95 G2
Dax 12 E3
Daxian 35 C5
Daxue Shan ... 34 C5
Daylesford ... 62 C3
Dayr az Zawr .. 46 D5
Dayton 72 E3
Daytona Beach 75 E7
Dead Sea 47 E3
Deakin 60 G4
Deal I. 62 C4
Deán Funes ... 94 C4
Death Valley .. 82 B4
Deba Habe ... 55 F7
Debar 22 D3
Dębica 16 C5
Debre Markos . 53 F6
Debre Tabor .. 53 F6
Debrecen 16 E5
Decatur, *Ala.*,
    U.S.A. 74 B4
Decatur, *Ill.*,
    U.S.A. 77 F10
Deccan 43 L11
Děčín 16 C2
Dedéagach =
    Alexandroúpolis
    .... 22 D5
Dédougou 55 F4
Dee → 10 C5
Deepwater ... 63 A5
Degeh Bur ... 49 F3
Deggendorf ... 15 D7
Deh Bīd 44 D3
Dehi Titan ... 42 C3
Dehibat 54 B7
Dehkareqan ... 46 C6
Dehra Dun ... 42 D11
Dej 17 E6
Dekese 56 E4
Delano 82 C3
Delaware □ ... 73 E8
Delaware → . 73 E8
Delegate 63 C4
Delgado, C. ... 57 G8
Delgo 53 D5
Delhi 42 E10
Delice → 46 C3
Delicias 84 B3
Delmenhorst .. 14 B5
Delmiro Gouveia 93 D6
Deloraine 62 D4

Delungra 63 A5
Delvinë 23 E3
Demanda, Sierra
de la 18 A4
Demavand =
Damävand .. 44 C3
Demba 56 F4
Dembecha 53 F6
Dembidolo 53 G5
Demini → ... 90 D6
Demirci 23 E7
Demirköy 22 D6
Dempo 37 E2
Den Haag = 's-
Gravenhage . 14 B3
Den Helder ... 14 B3
Denau 29 F7
Dendang 37 E3
Denia 19 C6
Denial B. 62 B1
Deniliquin 63 C3
Denman Glacier 96 A11
Denmark ■ ... 9 G9
Denmark Str. .. 66 C17
Denpasar 37 F5
Denton 78 C5
D'Entrecasteaux
Is. 61 B9
Denver 76 F2
Deoghar 40 E6
Deolali 43 K8
Deoria 40 D4
Deosai Mts. .. 42 B9
Dêqên 34 D4
Dera Ghazi Khan 42 D7
Dera Ismail
Khan 42 D7
Derbent 25 E6
Derby, Australia 60 D3
Derby, U.K. ... 11 E6
Derg, L. 11 E2
Dergaon 41 D9
Derry =
Londonderry 11 D3
Derudub 53 E6
Des Moines ... 77 E8
Des Moines → 77 E9
Desaguadero → 91 G5
Dese 49 E2
Desna → 17 C10
Desolación, I. .. 95 G2
Despeñaperros,
Paso 18 C4
Dessau 15 C7
Dessye = Dese 49 E2
D'Estrees B. ... 62 C2
Detmold 14 C5
Detroit 72 C4
Deutsche Bucht 14 A5
Deva 17 F6
Devakottai 43 Q11
Deventer 14 B4
Devonport,
Australia .. 62 D4
Devonport, N.Z. 64 B6
Dewas 43 H10
Deyhük 44 C4
Deyyer 44 E2
Dezfül 47 D7
Dezhneva, Mys 31 C16
Dhafra 44 F3
Dhahira 44 F4
Dhahran = Aẓ
Ẓahrān ... 44
Dhaka 41 F8
Dhaka □ 41 E8
Dhamar 49 E3
Dhamtari 40 G3
Dhanbad 40 F6

Dhangarhi 40 C3
Dhankuta 40 D6
Dhar 43 H9
Dharmapuri ... 43 N11
Dharwad 43 M9
Dhaulagiri 40 C4
Dhenkanal ... 40 G5
Dhíkti Óros ... 23 G5
Dhírfis 23 E4
Dhodhekánisos 23 F6
Dhrol 43 H7
Dhubaibah ... 44 F3
Dhuburi 41 D7
Dhule 43 J9
Dhut → 49 E5
Diafarabé 55 F4
Diamantina .. 93 F5
Diamantina → 62 A2
Diamantino .. 93 E2
Diamond
Harbour 40 F7
Diapaga 55 F5
Dïbā 44 E4
Dibaya 56 F4
Dibaya-Lubue . 56 E3
Dibbi 49 G3
Dibrugarh ... 41 D10
Dickson 28 B9
Didiéni 55 F3
Diébougou ... 55 F4
Diefenbaker L. . 71 C9
Dieppe 12 B4
Digby 69 D4
Digges Is. 68 B3
Dighinala 41 F9
Digne-les-Bains 13 D7
Digos 38 C3
Digul → 39 F5
Dihang → ... 41 D10
Dijlah, Nahr → 47 E6
Dijon 13 C6
Dikimdya ... 31 D10
Dikson =
Dickson 28 B9
Dikwa 53 F1
Dili 39 F3
Dilling 53 F4
Dillingham ... 71 C4
Dilolo 56 G4
Dilston 62 D4
Dimashq 46 D4
Dimbokro ... 55 G4
Dimboola 62 C3
Dîmboviţa → . 22 B6
Dimitrovgrad,
Bulgaria 22 C5
Dimitrovgrad,
Russia 24 C6
Dimitrovo =
Pernik 22 C4
Dinagat 38 B3
Dinajpur 41 E7
Dinan 12 B2
Dinant 14 C3
Dinar 46 C2
Dīnār, Kūh-e .. 44 D2
Dinara Planina . 20 B6
Dinard 12 B2
Dinaric Alps =
Dinara Planina 20 B6
Dindigul 43 P11
Dingle 11 E1
Dinguiraye ... 55 F2
Dingwall 10 C4
Dinosaur
National
Monument .. 81 E9
Diourbel 55 F1
Dipolog 38 C2

Dir 42 B7
Diré 55 E4
Dire Dawa ... 49 F3
Dirico 58 B4
Dirranbandi ... 63 A4
Disa 43 G8
Disappointment,
L. 60 E3
Disaster B. 63 C4
Discovery B. .. 62 C3
Disteghil Sar .. 42 A9
Distrito
Federal □ ... 93 F4
Diu 43 J7
Divinópolis .. 93 G5
Divinoye 25 D5
Diwāl Kol 42 B5
Diyarbakır ... 46 C5
Diz Chah 44 C3
Djado 52 D1
Djakarta =
Jakarta ... 37 F3
Djambala ... 56 E2
Djanet 54 D6
Djawa = Jawa . 37 F3
Djelfa 54 B5
Djema 57 C5
Djenné 55 F4
Djerba, I. de .. 52 B1
Djerid, Chott .. 54 B6
Djibo 55 F4
Djibouti 49 E3
Djibouti ■ 49 E3
Djolu 56 D4
Djougou 55 G5
Djoum 56 D2
Djourab 53 E2
Djugu 57 D6
Dmitriya
Lapteva, Proliv 31 B12
Dnepr → =
Dnipro → .. 25 D3
Dneprodzerzhinsk
=
Dniprodzerzhynsk
.... 25 D3
Dnepropetrovsk
=
Dnipropetrovsk
.... 25 D4
Dnestr → =
Dnister → . 17 E10
Dnestrovski =
Belgorod ... 24 C4
Dnieper =
Dnipro → .. 25 D3
Dniester =
Dnister → . 17 E10
Dnipro → ... 25 D3
Dniprodzerzhynsk
.... 25 D3
Dnipropetrovsk 25 D4
Dnister → .. 17 E10
Dnistrovskyy
Lyman 17 E10
Dnyapro =
Dnipro → .. 25 D3
Doba 53 G2
Doberai, Jazirah 39 E4
Doblas 94 D4
Dobo 39 F4
Doboj 20 B7
Dobreta-Turnu-
Severin 22 B4
Dobrich 22 C6
Dobruja 22 B7
Dobrush 17 B10
Dodecanese =
Dhodhekánisos
.... 23 F6

Dodge City .. 78 A3
Dodoma 57 F7
Dogi 42 C3
Doha = Ad
Dawhah 44 E2
Dohazari 41 F9
Doi 39 D3
Dois Irmãos, Sa. 93 D5
Dolbeau 69 D3
Dole 13 C6
Dolomites =
Dolomiti 20 A3
Dolomiti 20 A3
Dolores 94 D5
Dolphin, C. .. 95 G5
Dolphin and
Union Str. .. 70 B8
Dombarovskiy . 29 D6
Dominica ■ ... 87 C7
Dominican
Rep. ■ 87 C5
Domo 49 F4
Domodóssola . 20 A2
Domville, Mt. .. 63 A5
Don →, Russia 25 D4
Don →, U.K. .. 10 C5
Don Benito ... 18 C3
Donald 62 C3
Donau =
Dunărea → . 17 F9
Donauwörth .. 14 D6
Doncaster ... 11 E6
Dondo, Angola 56 F2
Dondo, Mozam. 59 B6
Dondo, Teluk . 39 D2
Donegal 11 D2
Donets → ... 25 D5
Donetsk 25 D4
Donggala ... 39 E1
Dongola 53 E5
Dongou 56 D3
Dongting Hu . 35 D6
Dongxing ... 35 D5
Donington, C. . 62 B2
Donnelly's
Crossing 64 A5
Donostia = San
Sebastián .. 19 A5
Dora Báltea → 20 B2
Dorchester, C. . 68 B3
Dordogne → . 12 D3
Dordrecht 14 C3
Dori 55 F4
Dornbirn 14 E5
Dorohoi 17 E8
Döröö Nuur ... 34 B4
Dorrigo 63 B5
Dortmund ... 14 C4
Doruma 57 D5
Dos Bahías, C. . 95 E3
Dos Hermanas . 18 D3
Dosso 55 F5
Dothan 74 D5
Douai 13 A5
Douala 56 D1
Douarnenez ... 12 B1
Double Island
Pt. 63 A5
Doubs → 13 C6
Doubtful Sd. .. 65 F2
Doubtless B. .. 64 A5
Douentza 55 F4
Douglas, U.K. . 11 D4
Douglas, U.S.A. 83 E8
Doumé 56 D2
Dourados 94 A6
Douro → 18 B1
Dover, Australia 62 D4
Dover, U.K. ... 11 F7

Dover, Str. of .. 11 F7
Dovrefjell 8 F9
Dowlat Yār 45 C6
Dowlatābād ... 44 D4
Dowshī 45 C7
Draa, Oued → 54 C2
Drăgăşani 22 B5
Dragichyn 17 B7
Dragoman,
Prokhod .. 22 C4
Draguignan ... 13 E7
Drake 63 A5
Drakensberg .. 59 E5
Dráma 22 D5
Drammen 9 G10
Drau =
Drava → ... 20 B7
Drava → ... 20 B7
Dresden 15 C7
Dreux 12 B4
Drina → 20 B7
Drini → 22 C2
Drochia 17 D8
Drogheda 11 E3
Drogichin =
Dragichyn .. 17 B7
Drogobych =
Drohobych .. 17 D6
Drohobych ... 17 D6
Droichead Atha
= Drogheda . 11 E3
Dromedary, C. . 63 C5
Drumheller ... 71 C8
Drummond Pt. 62 B2
Drut → 17 B10
Drygalski I. .. 96 A11
Dschang 55 G7
Đubä 47 F3
Dubai = Dubayy 44 E3
Dubăsari 17 E9
Dubăsari Vdkhr. 17 E9
Dubawnt → .. 70 B9
Dubawnt, L. ... 70 B9
Dubayy 44 E3
Dubbo 63 B4
Dublin, Ireland 11 E3
Dublin, U.S.A. . 75 C6
Dubno 17 C7
Dubossary =
Dubăsari 17 E9
Dubossary
Vdkhr. =
Dubăsari
Vdkhr. 17 E9
Dubovka 24 D5
Dubréka 55 G2
Dubrovitsa =
Dubrovytsya 17 C8
Dubrovnik .. 20 C7
Dubrovytsya .. 17 C8
Dudhi 40 E4
Dudinka 30 C6
Duero =
Douro → ... 18 B1
Dugi Otok ... 20 B5
Duisburg 14 C4
Dukelský
Průsmyk .. 16 D5
Dukhān 44 E2
Duki 42 D6
Duku 55 F7
Dulce → 94 C4
Dulit, Banjaran 37 D4
Duluth 77 B8
Dum Duma ... 41 D10
Dum Hadjer .. 53 F2
Dumaguete ... 38 C2
Dumai 37 D2
Dumaran 38 B1

Dumfries 11 D5
Dumyât 52 B5
Dún Dealgan =
Dundalk 11 D3
Dun Laoghaire 11 E3
Duna =
Dunărea → . 17 F9
Dunaj =
Dunărea → . 17 F9
Dunakeszi ... 16 E4
Dunaújváros .. 16 E4
Dunav =
Dunărea → . 17 F9
Dunback 65 F4
Dunbar 10 D5
Duncan 78 B5
Dundalk 11 D3
Dundee,
S. Africa 59 D6
Dundee, U.K. .. 10 C5
Dundoo 63 A3
Dunedin 65 F4
Dunfermline .. 10 C5
Dungarvan .. 11 E3
Dungog 63 B5
Dungu 57 D5
Dunhuang ... 34 B4
Dunkerque .. 12 A5
Dunkirk =
Dunkerque .. 12 A5
Dunkwa 55 G4
Dúnleary = Dun
Laoghaire ... 11 E3
Dunolly 62 C3
Dunqul 52 D5
Dunstan Mts. .. 65 F3
Durance → .. 13 E6
Durango =
Victoria de
Durango ... 84 C4
Durango ... 19 A4
Durazno 94 C5
Durazzo =
Durrësi 22 D2
Durban 59 D6
Düren 14 C4
Durg 40 G3
Durgapur 40 F6
Durham, U.K. . 11 D6
Durham, U.S.A. 75 B8
Durham Downs 63 A4
Durmitor 22 C2
Durrësi 22 D2
Dursunbey ... 23 E7
D'Urville,
Tanjung ... 39 E5
D'Urville I. ... 65 D5
Dusa Mareb ... 49 F4
Dushak 29 F7
Dushanbe 29 F7
Dusky Sd. 65 F2
Düsseldorf ... 14 C4
Dutch Harbor .. 71 C3
Duwādimi 47 F6
Duyun 35 D5
Düzce 46 B2
Duzdab =
Zāhedān 45 D5
Dvina,
Severnaya → 28 C5
Dvinsk =
Daugavpils .. 24 B2
Dwarka 43 H6
Dyatlovo =
Dzyatlava .. 17 B7
Dyer, C. 68 B4
Dyer Plateau .. 96 B3
Dyersburg 79 A9

Dymer 17 C10
Dynevor Downs 63 A3
Dzamin Üüd .. 35 B6
Dzerzhinsk ... 24 B5
Dzhambul =
Zhambyl 29 E8
Dzhankoy ... 25 D3
Dzhardzhan ... 30 C10
Dzhezkazgan =
Zhezqazghan 29 E7
Dzhizak =
Jizzakh 29 E7
Działdowa ... 16 B5
Dzierzoniów .. 16 C3
Dzungaria =
Junggar Pendi 34 B3
Dzungarian Gate
= Alataw
Shankou 34 B3
Dzuumod 35 B5
Dzyarzhynsk .. 17 B8
Dzyatlava 17 B7

E

Earnslaw, Mt. . 65 F3
East Bengal ... 41 E7
East Beskids =
Vychodné
Beskydy 17 D5
East C. 64 B8
East China Sea 35 C7
East Falkland . 95 G5
East Kilbride .. 10 D4
East London . 59 E5
East Main =
Eastmain ... 69 C3
East Orange .. 73 D8
East St. Louis . 77 F9
East Toorale .. 63 B4
Eastbourne, N.Z. 65 D6
Eastbourne, U.K. 11 F7
Eastern Ghats . 43 N11
Eastmain 69 C3
Eastmain → .. 69 C3
Eau Claire 77 C9
Eberswalde-
Finow 15 B7
Ebolowa 56 D2
Ebro → 19 B6
Eceabat 23 D6
Ech Cheliff ... 54 A5
Echo Bay 70 B8
Echuca 63 C3
Ecija 18 D3
Ecuador ■ ... 90 D3
Ed Dâmer 53 E5
Ed Debba 53 E5
Ed Dueim 53 F5
Edd 49 E3
Eddystone Pt. . 62 D4
Édea 56 D2
Eden → 14 C5
Édhessa 23 D4
Edievale 65 F3
Edinburg 78 F4
Edinburgh ... 10 D5
Edinița 17 D8
Edirne 22 D6
Edithburgh ... 62 C2
Edmonton ... 71 C8
Edmundston .. 69 D4
Edremit 23 E6
Edremit Körfezi 23 E6
Edson 71 C8

Edward → ... 62 C3
Edward, L. ... 57 E5
Edward VII Land 96 C17
Edwards Plateau 78 D3
Égadi, Ísole ... 21 F4
Eger = Cheb ... 16 C1
Eger 16 E5
Egersund 9 G9
Egmont, C. ... 64 C5
Egmont, Mt. .. 64 C6
Eğridir 46 C2
Eğridir Gölü .. 46 C2
Egypt ■ 52 C5
Eibar 19 A4
Eidsvold 63 A5
Eifel 14 C4
Eigg 10 C3
Eil 49 F4
Eildon, L. 63 C4
Eindhoven ... 14 C3
Eire = Ireland ■ 11 E3
Eirunepé 91 E5
Eisenach 14 C6
Eisenerz 15 E8
Eivissa = Ibiza . 19 C6
Eketahuna ... 64 D6
Ekibastuz ... 29 D8
El Aaiún 54 C2
El Alamein ... 52 B4
El Aricha 54 B4
El 'Arîsh 52 B5
El Asnam = Ech
Cheliff 54 A5
El Bawiti 52 C4
El Bayadh ... 54 B5
El Callao 90 B6
El Centro 82 D5
El Cerro 91 G6
El Cuy 95 D3
El Cuyo 85 C7
El Dere 49 G4
El Diviso 90 C3
El Djouf 55 D3
El Dorado, Ark.,
U.S.A. 79 C7
El Dorado,
Kans., U.S.A. 78 A5
El Dorado,
Venezuela ... 90 B6
El Escorial 18 B3
El Faiyûm 52 C5
El Fâsher 53 F4
El Ferrol 18 A1
El Fuerte 84 B3
El Gal 49 E5
El Geneina = Al
Junaynah ... 53 F3
El Geteina 53 F5
El Gîza 52 C5
El Iskandarîya . 52 B4
El Jadida 54 B3
El Jebelein ... 53 F5
El Kab 53 E5
El Kala 54 A6
El Kamlin 53 E5
El Kef 54 A6
El Khandaq ... 53 E5
El Khârga 52 C5
El Khartûm ... 53 E5
El Khartûm
Bahrî 53 E5
El Laqâwa 53 F4
El Mafâza 53 F5
El Mahalla el
Kubra 52 B5
El Mansûra .. 52 B5
El Minyâ 52 C5
El Obeid 53 F5
El Odaiya 53 F4

El Oued	54	B6	Embi →	29	E6	Erie	73	C5	Eulo	63	A4
El Paso	83	E9	Embrun	13	D7	Erie, L.	72	C5	Euphrates =		
El Prat de			Embu	57	E7	Erigavo	49	E4	Furăt, Nahr		
Llobregat	19	B7	Emden	14	B4	Erímanthos	23	F3	al →	47	E6
El Puerto de			Emerson	71	D10	Erimo-misaki	32	F12	Eureka	80	E1
Santa María	18	D2	Emet	23	E7	Eritrea ■	49	E2	Euroa	63	C4
El Qâhira	52	B5	Emi Koussi	53	E2	Erlangen	15	D6	Europa, I.	59	J8
El Qantara	52	B5	Emine, Nos	22	C6	Ermenak	46	C3	Europa, Picos de	18	A3
El Qasr	52	C4	Emmen	14	B4	Ermoúpolis =			Europa, Pta. de	18	D3
El Reno	78	B5	Empalme	84	B2	Síros	23	F5	Europa Pt. =		
El Salvador ■	85	E7	Empangeni	59	D6	Ernakulam =			Europa, Pta.		
El Shallal	52	D5	Empedrado	94	B5	Cochin	43	Q10	de	18	D3
El Suweis	52	C5	Empty Quarter			Erne, Lower L.	11	D3	Evans Head	63	A5
El Tigre	90	B6	= Rub' al			Erode	43	P10	Evanston	72	C2
El Tocuyo	90	B5	Khali	48	D4	Eromanga	63	A3	Evansville	72	F2
El Turbio	95	G2	Ems →	14	B4	Erramala Hills	43	M11	Everard, L.	62	B1
El Uqsur	52	C5	En Nahud	53	F4	Ertis → =			Everest, Mt.	40	C6
El Vigía	90	B4	Enaratoli	39	E5	Irtysh →	28	C7	Everett	80	B2
El Wak	57	D8	Enare =			Erzgebirge	15	C7	Everglades		
El Wuz	53	E5	Inarijärvi	8	E13	Erzincan	46	C4	National Park	75	G7
Elat	47	E3	Encanto, C.	38	A2	Erzurum	46	C5	Evinayong	56	D2
Elâziğ	46	C4	Encarnación	94	B5	Es Sahrâ' Esh			Évora	18	C2
Elba	20	C3	Encounter B.	62	C2	Sharqîya	52	C5	Évreux	12	B4
Elbasani	22	D3	Ende	39	F2	Es Sînâ'	52	C5	Évros →	22	D6
Elbe →	14	B5	Enderby Land	96	A9	Esbjerg	9	G9	Évry	12	B5
Elbert, Mt.	83	A9	Enewetak Atoll	64	H11	Esch-sur-Alzette	13	B6	Évvoia	23	E5
Elbeuf	12	B4	Enez	23	D6	Escuinapa	84	C3	Ewo	56	E2
Elbidtan	46	C4	Engadin	13	C9	Eşfahān	44	C2	Exaltación	91	F5
Elbing = Elbląg	16	A4	Engaño, C.	38	A2	Esh Sham =			Exeter	11	F5
Elbląg	16	A4	Engels	24	C6	Dimashq	46	D4	Exmoor	11	F5
Elbrus	25	E5	Enggano	37	F2	Esil → =			Exmouth	11	F5
Elburz Mts. =			Engkilili	37	D4	Ishim →	29	D8	Extremadura □	18	C2
Alborz,			England □	11	E6	Eskilstuna	9	G11	Eyasi, L.	57	E6
Reshteh-ye			Englewood	76	F2	Eskimo Pt.	70	B10	Eyre (North), L.	62	A2
Kühhâ-ye	44	B3	English Bazar =			Eskişehir	46	C2	Eyre (South), L.	62	A2
Elche	19	C5	Ingraj Bazar	40	E7	Esla →	18	B2	Eyre, L.	60	F6
Elda	19	C5	English Channel	11	F5	Eslāmābād-e			Eyre Cr. →	62	A2
Elde →	15	B6	Enid	78	A5	Gharb	46	D6	Eyre Mts.	65	F3
Eldoret	57	D7	Enna	21	F5	Eşme	23	E7	Eyre Pen.	62	B2
Elektrostal	24	B4	Ennedi	53	E3	Esmeraldas	90	C3	Ezine	23	E6
Elephant I.	96	A4	Enngonia	63	A4	Esperance	60	G3			
Eleuthera	86	A4	Ennis	11	E2	Esperanza	94	C4			
Elgin, U.K.	10	C5	Enniskillen	11	D3	Espichel, C.	18	C1			
Elgin, U.S.A.	72	C1	Enns →	15	D8	Espinal	90	C4			
Elgon, Mt.	57	D6	Enschede	14	B4	Espinazo, Sierra			**F**		
Eliase	39	F4	Ensenada	84	A1	del =					
Elisabethville =			Entebbe	57	D6	Espinhaço,			F.Y.R.O.M. =		
Lubumbashi	59	A5	Entroncamento	18	C1	Serra do	93	F5	Macedonia ■	22	D3
Elista	25	D5	Enugu	55	G6	Espinhaço, Serra			Fabriano	20	C4
Elizabeth,			Enugu Ezike	55	G6	do	93	F5	Facatativá	90	C4
Australia	62	B2	Eólie, Ís.	21	E5	Espírito Santo □	93	G5	Fachi	55	E7
Elizabeth, U.S.A.	73	D8	Épernay	13	B5	Esquel	95	E2	Fada	53	E3
Elizabeth City	75	A9	Ephesus	23	F6	Esquina	94	C5	Fada-n-Gourma	55	F5
Elizabethton	75	A6	Épinal	13	B7	Essaouira	54	B3	Faddeyevskiy,		
Elk	16	B6	Epukiro	58	C3	Essen	14	C4	Ostrov	31	B12
Elkhart	72	D3	Equatorial			Essequibo →	90	B7	Fāḍilī	47	F7
Elkhovo	22	C6	Guinea ■	56	D1	Esslingen	14	D5	Faenza	20	B3
Elko	80	E6	Er Rahad	53	F5	Estados, I. de			Færoe Is. =		
Ellery, Mt.	63	C4	Er Rif	54	A4	Los	95	G4	Førøyar	6	C4
Ellesmere, L.	65	G5	Er Roseires	53	F5	Estância	93	E6	Fǎgǎras	17	F7
Ellice Is. =			Erāwadī Myit =			Estevan	71	D9	Fagnano, L.	95	G3
Tuvalu ■	64	K12	Irrawaddy →	41	K10	Estonia ■	24	B2	Fahraj	45	D4
Elliston	62	B1	Erbil = Arbil	46	C6	Estrêla, Serra da	18	B2	Fahūd	44	F4
Ellore = Eluru	40	J3	Erciyaş Daği	46	C3	Estremoz	18	C2	Fair Isle	10	B6
Ellsworth Land	96	B2	Érd	16	E4	Estrondo, Serra			Fairbanks	71	B5
Ellsworth Mts.	96	B2	Erdek	23	D6	do	92	D4	Fairfield, Ala.,		
Elmore	63	C3	Erebus, Mt.	96	B15	Esztergom	16	E4	U.S.A.	74	C4
Elmshorn	14	B5	Erechim	94	B6	Etadunna	62	A2	Fairfield, Calif.,		
Eltham	64	C6	Ereğli, Konya,			Étampes	12	B5	U.S.A.	80	F2
Eluru	40	J3	Turkey	46	C3	Etawah	42	F11	Fairlie	65	F4
Elvas	18	C2	Ereğli,			Ethiopia ■	49	F2	Fairweather, Mt.	71	C6
Elx = Elche	19	C5	Zonguldak,			Etna	21	F5	Faisalabad	42	D8
Ely	11	E7	Turkey	46	B2	Etosha Pan	58	B3	Faizabad	40	D4
Emāmrūd	44	B3	Eresma →	18	B3	Euboea =			Fakfak	39	E4
Emba = Embi	29	E6	Erewadi			Évvoia	23	E5	Falaise	12	B3
Emba → =			Myitwanya →	41	K10	Eucumbene, L.	63	C4	Falam	41	F9
Embi →	29	E6	Erfurt	15	C6	Eufaula	74	D5	Falconara		
Embarcación	94	A4	Ergani	46	C4	Eugene	80	C2	Maríttima	20	C4
Embi	29	E6	Érice	21	E4	Eugowra	63	B4	Falcone, C.	20	D2

Faleshty =
Fălești 17 E8
Fălești 17 E8
Falkland Is. □ . 95 G5
Falkland Sd. .. 95 G5
Fall River 73 D10
Falmouth 11 F4
False B. 58 E3
Fălticeni 17 E8
Falun 9 F11
Famagusta ... 46 D3
Fandriana 59 J9
Fano 20 C4
Faʊ = Al Fāw . 47 E/
Faradje 57 D5
Farafangana .. 59 J9
Farāh 42 C3
Farāh □ 42 C3
Faranah 55 F2
Farasān, Jazā'ir 49 D3
Farasān,
    Jazā'ir 49 D3
Fareham 11 F6
Farewell, C. ... 64 D5
Farewell C. =
Farvel, Kap .. 68 C6
Farghona 29 E8
Fargo 76 B6
Farim 55 F1
Farīmān 45 C4
Farina 62 B2
Faro, Brazil .. 92 C2
Faro, Portugal . 18 D2
Farrāshband .. 44 D3
Farrell Flat 62 B2
Farrukhabad-
    cum-
    Fatehgarh ... 42 F11
Fārs □ 44 D3
Fársala 23 E4
Fartak, Rās ... 47 E3
Farvel, Kap .. 68 C6
Fāryāb □ 45 B6
Fasā 44 D3
Fasano 21 D6
Fastiv 17 C9
Fastov = Fastiv 17 C9
Fatagar, Tanjung 39 E4
Fatehgarh 42 F11
Fatehpur, Raj.,
    India 42 F9
Fatehpur, Ut. P.,
    India 40 E3
Favara 21 F4
Favignana 21 F4
Faya-Largeau .. 53 E2
Fayd 47 F5
Fayetteville,
    Ark., U.S.A. . 79 A6
Fayetteville,
    N.C., U.S.A. . 75 B8
Fazilka 42 D9
Fdérik 54 D2
Feather → 80 F3
Featherston .. 65 D6
Fécamp 12 B4
Fehmarn 15 A6
Feilding 64 D6
Feira de Santana 93 E6
Feldkirch 14 E5
Felipe Carrillo
    Puerto 85 D7
Felixstowe ... 11 F7
Fengjie 35 C5
Fenyang 35 C6
Feodosiya 25 D4
Ferdows 44 C4
Ferfer 49 F4

Fergana =
    Farghona ... 29 E8
Fermo 20 C4
Fernando de
    Noronha ... 92 C7
Fernando Póo =
    Bioko 56 D1
Ferozepore =
    Firozpur ... 42 D9
Ferrara 20 B3
Ferreñafe 91 E3
Ferret, C. 12 D3
Ferrol = El
    Ferrol 18 A1
Fès 54 B4
Feshi 56 F3
Fetești 22 B6
Fetlar 10 A6
Feuilles → 68 C3
Fezzan 52 C2
Fianarantsoa .. 59 J9
Fianga 53 G2
Ficksburg 59 D5
Fieri 23 D2
Figeac 12 D5
Figueira da Foz 18 B1
Figueras 19 A7
Figuig 54 B4
Fiji ■ 64 L12
Filiatrá 23 F3
Filyos → 46 B3
Fíngõe 59 A6
Finike 46 C2
Finisterre, C. .. 18 A1
Finke → 62 A2
Finland ■ 8 F13
Finland, G. of . 9 G13
Finlay → 70 C7
Finley 63 C4
Finniss, C. ... 62 B1
Fiora → 20 C3
Firat = Furāt,
    Nahr al → .. 47 E6
Firenze 20 C3
Firozabad 42 F11
Firozpur 42 D9
Firūzābād 44 D3
Firūzkūh 44 C3
Fish → 58 D3
Fishguard 11 E4
Fitri, L. 53 F2
Fitz Roy 95 F3
Fiume = Rijeka 20 B5
Fizi 57 E5
Flagstaff 83 C7
Flaming Gorge
    Reservoir .. 81 E9
Flamingo, Teluk 39 F5
Flathead L. ... 81 B6
Flattery, C. ... 80 A1
Flensburg 14 A5
Flers 12 B3
Flesko, Tanjung 39 D2
Flin Flon 71 C9
Flinders → ... 61 D7
Flinders I. 62 C4
Flinders Ras. .. 62 B2
Flint 72 C4
Flint I. 65 L15
Flinton 63 A4
Florence =
    Firenze 20 C3
Florence, Ala.,
    U.S.A. 74 B4
Florence, S.C.,
    U.S.A. 75 B8
Florence, L. ... 62 A2
Flores 39 F2

Flores Sea 39 F2
Floreşti 17 E9
Floriano 92 D5
Florianópolis .. 94 B7
Florida 94 C5
Florida □ 75 F6
Florida, Straits
    of 86 B3
Flórina 23 D3
Florø 8 F9
Fluk 39 E3
Flushing =
    Vlissingen .. 14 C2
Fly → 61 B7
Flying Fish, C. . 96 B1
Foça 23 E6
Focşani 17 F8
Fóggia 20 D5
Föhr 14 A5
Foix 12 E4
Foligno 20 C4
Folkestone ... 11 F7
Fond du Lac .. 77 D10
Fondi 20 D4
Fonsagrada .. 18 A2
Fonseca, G. de 85 E7
Fontainebleau . 13 B5
Fonte Boa 90 D5
Fontenay-le-
    Comte 12 C3
Foochow =
    Fuzhou 35 D6
Forbes 63 B4
Ford's Bridge . 63 A4
Forécariah ... 55 G2
Forestier Pen. . 62 D4
Forfar 10 C5
Forlì 20 B4
Formentera .. 19 C6
Formentor, C. de 19 C7
Former
    Yugoslav
    Republic of
    Macedonia =
    Macedonia ■ 22 D3
Fórmia 20 D4
Formosa =
    Taiwan ■ ... 35 D7
Formosa 94 B5
Formosa, Serra 93 E3
Formosa Bay .. 57 E8
Føroyar =
    Føroyar 6 C4
Føroyar 6 C4
Forrest 62 C3
Forsayth 61 D7
Forst 15 C8
Forster 63 B5
Fort Albany .. 69 C2
Fort Collins .. 76 E2
Fort-de-France . 87 D7
Fort de Possel =
    Possel 56 C3
Fort Dodge ... 77 D7
Fort Franklin . 70 B7
Fort Good-Hope 70 B7
Fort Hertz =
    Putao 41 D11
Fort Lauderdale 75 F7
Fort Liard 70 B7
Fort Macleod . 71 D8
Fort MacMahon 54 C5
Fort McPherson 70 B6
Fort Miribel .. 54 C5
Fort Myers ... 75 F7
Fort Norman .. 70 B7
Fort Peck L. .. 81 B10
Fort Pierce ... 75 F7
Fort Portal ... 57 D6

Fort Providence 70 B8
Fort Resolution 70 B8
Fort Rosebery =
    Mansa 57 G5
Fort Rupert =
    Waskaganish 69 C3
Fort Sandeman 42 D6
Fort Scott 79 A6
Fort Severn ... 69 C2
Fort Shevchenko 29 E6
Fort Simpson . 70 B7
Fort Smith,
    Canada 70 B8
Fort Smith,
    U.S.A. 79 B6
Fort Trinquet =
    Bir Mogrein . 54 C2
Fort Walton
    Beach 74 D4
Fort Wayne ... 72 D3
Fort William .. 10 C4
Fort Worth 78 C5
Fort Yukon ... 71 B5
Fortaleza 92 C6
Forūr 44 E3
Foshan 35 D6
Fossano 20 B1
Fougamou ... 56 E2
Fougères 12 B3
Foula 10 A5
Foumban 55 G7
Foúrnoi 23 F6
Fouta Djalon .. 55 F2
Foveaux Str. .. 65 G3
Foxe Basin ... 68 B3
Foxe Chan. ... 68 B2
Foxe Pen. 68 B3
Foxton 64 D6
Foz do Gregório 91 E4
Foz do Iguaçu . 94 B6
Franca 93 G4
Francavilla
    Fontana 21 D6
France ■ 13 C5
Frances 62 C3
Franceville ... 56 E2
Franche-Comté 13 C6
Francistown .. 59 C5
Frankfurt,
    Brandenburg,
    Germany ... 15 B8
Frankfurt,
    Hessen,
    Germany ... 14 C5
Fränkische Alb 15 D6
Franklin B. ... 70 B7
Franklin I. 96 B15
Franklin Mts. .. 70 B7
Franklin Str. .. 70 A10
Frankston 63 C4
Frantsa Iosifa,
    Zemlya 28 A6
Franz 69 D2
Franz Josef
    Land =
    Frantsa Iosifa,
    Zemlya 28 A6
Fraser → 71 D7
Fraser I. 63 A5
Fraserburgh .. 10 C5
Fray Bentos .. 94 C5
Fredericksburg 73 E7
Fredericton ... 69 D4
Fredrikstad ... 9 G10
Freeport,
    Bahamas ... 86 A4
Freeport, U.S.A. 77 D10
Freetown 55 G2
Fregenal de la
    Sierra 18 C2

Freibourg =
Fribourg 13 C7
Freiburg 14 E4
Freire 95 D2
Freising 15 D6
Freistadt 15 D8
Fréjus 13 E7
Fremont 82 B2
French
Guiana ■ ... 92 B3
French
Polynesia ■ . 65 M16
Fresco → 92 D3
Freshfield, C. .. 96 A14
Fresnillo 84 C4
Fresno 82 B3
Freycinet Pen. . 62 D4
Fria, C. 58 B2
Frías 94 B3
Fribourg 13 C7
Friedrichshafen 14 E5
Friendly Is. =
Tonga ■ 65 L13
Frobisher B. ... 68 B4
Frobisher Bay =
Iqaluit 68 B4
Frome, L. 62 B2
Frome Downs . 62 B2
Front Range .. 81 E11
Frosinone 20 D4
Frunze =
Bishkek 29 E8
Frutal 93 F4
Frýdek-Místek . 16 D4
Fuchou =
Fuzhou 35 D6
Fuengirola 18 D3
Fuentes de
Oñoro 18 B2
Fuerte → 84 B3
Fuerte Olimpo . 91 H7
Fuerteventura . 54 C2
Fuhai 34 B3
Fuji-San 32 B6
Fujian □ 35 D6
Fujinomiya 32 B6
Fujisawa 32 B6
Fukien =
Fujian □ 35 D6
Fukuchiyama .. 32 B4
Fukui 32 A5
Fukuoka 32 C2
Fukushima ... 33 G12
Fukuyama 32 B3
Fulda 14 C5
Fulda → 14 C5
Fullerton 82 D4
Funabashi 32 B7
Funchal 54 B1
Fundación 90 A4
Fundão 18 B2
Fundy, B. of .. 69 D4
Funtua 55 F6
Furāt, Nahr
al → 47 E6
Furneaux Group 62 D4
Fürstenwalde .. 15 B8
Fürth 14 D6
Fury and Hecla
Str. 68 B2
Fusagasuga .. 90 C4
Fushun 35 B7
Futuna 64 L12
Fuxin 35 B7
Fuyuan 35 B8
Fuzhou 35 D6
Fyn 9 G10

G

Gabela 56 G2
Gabès 54 B7
Gabès, G. de .. 52 B1
Gabon ■ 56 E2
Gaborone 59 C5
Gabrovo 22 C5
Gachsārān 44 D2
Gadag 43 M9
Gadarwara 43 H11
Gadhada 43 J7
Gadsden 74 B4
Gadwal 43 L10
Gafsa 54 B6
Gagnoa 55 G3
Gagnon 69 C4
Gaillimh =
Galway 11 E2
Gainesville, Fla.,
U.S.A. 75 E6
Gainesville, Ga.,
U.S.A. 75 B6
Gainesville,
Tex., U.S.A. . 78 C5
Gairdner, L. .. 62 B2
Galangue 58 A3
Galashiels ... 10 D5
Galați 17 F9
Galatina 21 D7
Galcaio 49 F4
Galdhøpiggen . 8 F9
Galela 39 D3
Galesburg 77 E9
Galich 24 B5
Galicia □ 18 A2
Galilee, Sea of
= Yam
Kinneret 46 D3
Gallabat 53 F6
Gállego → ... 19 B5
Gallegos → .. 95 G3
Gallinas, Pta. .. 90 A4
Gallipoli =
Gelibolu ... 23 D6
Gallípoli 21 D6
Gällivare 8 E12
Galloway, Mull
of 11 D4
Galong 63 B4
Galveston 79 E6
Gálvez 94 C4
Galway 11 E2
Galway B. 11 E2
Gambaga 55 F4
Gambela 53 G5
Gambia ■ 55 F1
Gambia → ... 55 F1
Gambier Is. ... 62 C2
Gamboma ... 56 E3
Gan Jiang → . 35 D6
Ganäveh 44 D2
Gäncä 25 E6
Gand = Gent .. 14 C2
Ganda 58 A2
Gandak → ... 40 E5
Gandava 42 E5
Gander 69 D5
Gandhi Sagar . 43 G9
Gandi 55 F6
Gandía 19 C5
Ganedidalem =
Gani 39 E3
Ganga → 41 F8
Ganganagar .. 42 E8
Gangara 55 F6
Gangaw 41 F10
Gangdisê Shan 40 B3

Ganges =
Ganga → .. 41 F8
Gangtok 41 D7
Gani 39 E3
Gansu □ 34 C5
Ganta 55 G3
Gantheaume, C. 62 C2
Gantsevichi =
Hantsavichy . 17 B8
Ganyem 39 E6
Ganzhou 35 D6
Gaoua 55 F4
Gaoual 55 F2
Gaoxiong 35 D7
Gap 13 D7
Gar 34 C2
Garabogazköl
Aylagy 29 E6
Garanhuns ... 92 D6
Garawe 55 H3
Gard 49 F4
Garda, L. di .. 20 B3
Garden City .. 78 A3
Garden Grove . 82 D4
Gardēz 42 C6
Gargano, Mte. . 20 D5
Garigliano → . 20 D4
Garland 81 E7
Garm 29 F8
Garmisch-
Partenkirchen 14 E6
Garmsār 44 C3
Garoe 49 F4
Garonne → . 12 D3
Garoua 53 G1
Garrison Res. =
Sakakawea, L. 76 B4
Garry, L. 70 B9
Garsen 57 E8
Garvie Mts. ... 65 F3
Garwa =
Garoua 53 G1
Gary 72 D2
Garzê 34 C5
Garzón 90 C3
Gasan Kuli =
Hasan Kuli .. 29 F6
Gascogne ... 12 E4
Gascogne, G. de 12 D2
Gascony =
Gascogne ... 12 E4
Gashaka 55 G7
Gaspé 69 D4
Gaspé, C. de .. 69 D4
Gaspé, Pén. de 69 D4
Gasteiz = Vitoria 19 A4
Gastonia 75 B7
Gastre 95 E3
Gata, C. de .. 19 D4
Gata, Sierra de 18 B2
Gateshead ... 11 D6
Gauhati 41 D8
Gaväter 45 E5
Gávdhos 23 G5
Gävle 8 F11
Gawilgarh Hills 43 J10
Gawler 62 B2
Gaxun Nur ... 34 B5
Gaya, India .. 40 E5
Gaya, Niger .. 55 F5
Gayndah 63 A5
Gaysin =
Haysyn 17 D9
Gayvoron =
Hayvoron ... 17 D9
Gaza 47 E3
Gaziantep ... 46 C4
Gazli 29 E7
Gdańsk 16 A4

Gdańska, Zatoka 16 A4
Gdov 24 B2
Gdynia 16 A4
Gebe 39 D3
Gebeit Mine ... 52 D6
Gebze 22 D7
Gedaref 53 F6
Gede, Tanjung 37 F3
Gediz → 23 E6
Gedser 9 H10
Geelong 63 C3
Geesthacht ... 14 B6
Geidam 53 F1
Geili 53 E5
Geita 57 E6
Gejiu 34 D5
Gela 21 F5
Geladi 49 F4
Gelehun 55 G2
Gelibolu 23 D6
Gelsenkirchen . 14 C4
Gemas 37 D2
Gemena 56 D3
Gemerek 46 C4
Gemlik 23 D7
General Acha . 94 D4
General Alvear,
Buenos Aires,
Argentina ... 94 D5
General Alvear,
Mendoza,
Argentina ... 94 D3
General Artigas 94 B5
General
Belgrano 94 D5
General Guido . 94 D5
General Juan
Madariaga . 94 D5
General La
Madrid ... 94 D4
General
MacArthur . 38 B3
General Martin
Miguel de
Güemes 94 A4
General Paz .. 94 B5
General Pico .. 94 D4
General Pinedo 94 B4
General Santos 38 C3
General Villegas 94 D4
Geneva =
Genève 13 C7
Geneva, L. =
Léman, L. ... 13 C7
Genève 13 C7
Genil → 18 D3
Gennargentu,
Mti. del ... 21 D2
Genoa =
Génova 20 B2
Genoa 63 C4
Génova 20 B2
Génova, G. di . 20 C2
Gent 14 C2
Georga, Zemlya 28 A5
George 58 E4
George → ... 68 C4
George, L.,
N.S.W.,
Australia 63 C4
George, L.,
S. Austral.,
Australia 62 C3
George, L.,
Uganda 57 D6
George River =
Kangiqsualujjuaq
.... 68 C4
George Sound . 65 F2

George Town . 36 C2
George V Land . 96 A14
George VI Sound 96 B3
Georgetown, Gambia 55 F2
Georgetown, Guyana 90 B7
Georgia □ 75 C6
Georgia ■ 25 E5
Georgian B. ... 69 D2
Georgiu-Dezh = Liski 24 C4
Georgiyevsk . 25 E5
Gera 15 C7
Geral de Goiás, Serra 93 E4
Geraldton 60 F1
Gerede 46 B3
Gereshk 42 D4
Gerlogubi 49 F4
Germany ■ ... 14 C6
Germiston 59 D5
Gerona 19 B7
Geser 39 E4
Getafe 18 B4
Gettysburg 73 E7
Getz Ice Shelf . 96 B18
Ghaghara → . 40 E5
Ghana ■ 55 G4
Ghanzi 58 C4
Ghardaïa 54 B5
Gharyān 52 B1
Ghat 54 D7
Ghawdex = Gozo 21 F5
Ghayl 47 G6
Ghazal, Bahr el →, Chad . 53 F2
Ghazâl, Bahr el →, Sudan . 57 C6
Ghazaouet 54 A4
Ghaziabad 42 E10
Ghazipur 40 E4
Ghaznī 42 C6
Ghaznī □ 42 C6
Ghèlinsor 49 F4
Ghent = Gent . 14 C2
Ghizao 42 C4
Ghowr □ 42 C4
Ghugus 43 K11
Ghūriān 42 B2
Gia Lai = Pleiku 36 B3
Gian 38 C3
Giarabub = Al Jaghbūb 52 C3
Giarre 21 F5
Gibraltar ■ ... 18 D3
Gibraltar, Str. of 18 E3
Gibson Desert . 60 E4
Gidole 53 G6
Giessen 14 C5
Gifu 32 B5
Giglio 20 C3
Gijón 18 A3
Gila → 82 D5
Gīlān □ 46 C7
Gilbert Is. 64 J12
Gilgandra 63 B4
Gilgit 42 B9
Gilles, L. 62 B2
Gilmore 63 C4
Gimbi 53 G6
Gin Gin 63 A5
Ginir 49 F3
Giohar 49 G4
Gióna, Óros .. 23 E4
Girardot 90 C4
Giresun 46 B4

Girga 52 C5
Giridih 40 E6
Girilambone .. 63 B4
Girne = Kyrenia 46 D3
Girona = Gerona 19 B7
Gironde → ... 12 D3
Girvan 10 D4
Gisborne 64 C8
Gisenyi 57 E5
Gitega 57 E5
Giuba → 49 G3
Giurgiu 22 C5
Giza = El Gîza . 52 C5
Giżycko 16 A5
Gjirokastra ... 23 D3
Gjoa Haven ... 70 B10
Glace Bay 69 D5
Gladstone, Queens., Australia 61 E9
Gladstone, S. Austral., Australia 62 B2
Glåma = Glomma → . 9 G10
Glasgow 10 D4
Glazov 28 D6
Gleiwitz = Gliwice 16 C4
Glen Canyon National Recreation Area 83 B7
Glen Innes ... 63 A5
Glendale 82 C3
Glenelg 62 B2
Glenelg → ... 62 C3
Glenmorgan .. 63 A4
Glenorchy ... 62 D4
Glenreagh ... 63 B5
Glenrothes ... 10 C5
Glens Falls ... 73 C9
Gliwice 16 C4
Głogów 16 C3
Glomma → .. 9 G10
Glorieuses, Is. . 59 G9
Gloucester, Australia 63 B5
Gloucester, U.K. 11 F5
Glusk 17 B9
Gmünd 15 D8
Gmunden 15 E7
Gniezno 16 B3
Go Cong 36 B3
Goa 43 M8
Goa □ 43 M8
Goalen Hd. ... 63 C5
Goalpara 41 D8
Goba, Ethiopia 49 F2
Goba, Mozam. . 59 D6
Gobabis 58 C3
Gobi 35 B6
Gochas 58 C3
Godavari → . 40 J4
Godavari Point 40 J4
Godhra 43 H8
Gods → 71 C10
Gods L. 71 C10
Godthåb 68 B5
Godwin Austen = K2 .... 42 B10
Goeie Hoop, Kaap die = Good Hope, C. of 58 E3
Gogra = Ghaghara → 40 E5
Goiânia 93 F4

Goiás 93 F3
Goiás □ 93 E4
Goio-Ere 94 A6
Gojra 42 D8
Gökçeada 23 D5
Gokteik 41 F11
Gold Coast ... 63 A5
Golden Gate .. 80 G2
Goldsboro 75 B9
Goleniów 16 B2
Golfo Aranci .. 20 D2
Golspie 10 C5
Goma 57 E5
Gomel = Homyel 17 B10
Gomera 54 C1
Gómez Palacio 84 B4
Gomogomo ... 39 F4
Gomoh 40 F6
Gompa = Ganta 55 G3
Gonābād 44 C4
Gonaïves 87 C5
Gonbad-e Kāvūs 44 B3
Gonda 40 D3
Gonder 53 F6
Gönen 23 D6
Gonghe 34 C5
Gongolgon ... 63 B4
Goniri 53 F1
Good Hope, C. of 58 E3
Goodooga 63 A4
Goolgowi 63 B4
Goombalie ... 63 A4
Goondiwindi .. 63 A5
Gooray 63 A5
Gop 43 H6
Göppingen ... 14 D5
Gorakhpur ... 40 D4
Goražde 20 C7
Gordon → ... 62 D4
Gore, Australia 63 A5
Goré, Chad ... 53 G2
Gore, Ethiopia . 53 G6
Gore, N.Z. 65 G3
Gorgān 44 B3
Gorgona, I. ... 90 C3
Gorízia 20 B4
Gorki = Nizhniy Novgorod ... 24 B5
Gorkiy = Nizhniy Novgorod ... 24 B5
Gorkovskoye Vdkhr. 24 B5
Görlitz 15 C8
Gorlovka = Horlivka ... 25 D4
Gorna Dzhumayo = Blagoevgrad 22 C4
Gorna Oryahovitsa 22 C5
Gorno-Altay □ . 29 D9
Gorno-Altaysk . 29 D9
Gorno Slinkino = Gornopravdinsk 29 C8
Gornopravdinsk 29 C8
Gorodenka = Horodenka .. 17 D7
Gorodok = Horodok ... 17 D6
Gorokhov = Horokhiv ... 17 C7
Gorontalo ... 39 D2
Gorzów Wielkopolski 16 B2

Gosford 63 B5
Goslar 14 C6
Gospič 20 B5
Göta kanal 9 G11
Göteborg 9 G10
Gotha 14 C6
Gothenburg = Göteborg ... 9 G10
Gotland 9 G11
Göttingen 14 C5
Gottwaldov = Zlín 16 D3
Gouda 14 B3
Gouin, Rés. ... 69 D3
Goulburn 63 B4
Gounou-Gaya . 53 G2
Gouri 53 E2
Gourma Rharous ... 55 E4
Gourock Ra. ... 63 C4
Governador Valadares ... 93 F5
Gowd-e Zirreh . 42 E3
Goya 94 B5
Goyder Lagoon 62 A2
Goyllarisquisga 91 F3
Goz Beïda ... 53 F3
Gozo 21 F5
Graaff-Reinet .. 58 E4
Gračac 20 B5
Gracias a Dios, C. 86 D3
Grado 18 A2
Gradule 63 A4
Grafton 63 A5
Graham Bell, Os. 28 A7
Graham Land . 96 A3
Grahamstown . 59 E5
Grajaú 92 D4
Grajaú → 92 C5
Grampian Highlands = Grampian Mts. 10 C4
Grampian Mts. 10 C4
Gran Canaria . 54 C1
Gran Chaco ... 94 B4
Gran Paradiso . 20 B1
Gran Sasso d'Italia 20 C4
Granada, Nic. . 85 E7
Granada, Spain 18 D4
Granby 69 D3
Grand Bahama 86 A4
Grand Bassam 55 G4
Grand Canyon . 83 B6
Grand Cayman 86 C3
Grand Coulee Dam 80 B4
Grand Forks, Canada 71 D8
Grand Forks, U.S.A. 76 B6
Grand Island . 76 E5
Grand Lahou . 55 G3
Grand Rapids, Canada 71 C10
Grand Rapids, U.S.A. 72 C3
Grand St.- Bernard, Col du 13 D7
Grand Teton . 81 D8
Grande →, Argentina ... 94 A3
Grande →, Bolivia 91 G6
Grande →, Bahia, Brazil . 93 E5

Grande →,
 Minas Gerais,
 Brazil 93 G3
Grande, B. 95 G3
Grande, Rio → . 79 F5
Grande Baleine,
 R. de la → . . 69 C3
Grande de
 Santiago → 84 C3
Granite City ... 77 F9
Granity 65 D4
Granja 92 C5
Granollers 19 B7
Grantham 11 E6
Granville 12 B3
Gras, L. de 70 B8
Grasse 13 E7
Grassmere 62 B3
Graulhet 12 E4
's-Gravenhage . 14 B3
Gravesend ... 63 A5
Graz 15 E8
Great Abaco I. . 86 A4
Great Australian
 Bight 60 G4
Great Barrier I. 64 B6
Great Barrier
 Reef 61 D8
Great Basin ... 80 F5
Great Bear → . 70 B7
Great Bear L. .. 70 B7
Great Belt =
 Store Bælt .. 9 G10
Great Dividing
 Ra. 61 E8
Great Falls ... 81 B8
Great Inagua I. 86 B5
Great Indian
 Desert = Thar
 Desert 42 F7
Great Karoo ... 58 E4
Great Lake ... 62 D4
Great Ouse → 11 E7
Great Ruaha → 57 F7
Great Saint
 Bernard P. =
 Grand St.-
 Bernard, Col
 du 13 D7
Great Salt L. .. 81 E7
Great Salt Lake
 Desert 81 E7
Great Sandy
 Desert 60 E3
Great Sangi =
 Sangihe, P. .. 39 D3
Great Slave L. . 70 B8
Great Smoky
 Mts. Nat. Pk. 75 B6
Great Victoria
 Desert 60 F4
Great Wall 35 C5
Great Yarmouth 11 E7
Greater Antilles 86 C5
Greater Sunda
 Is. 37 F4
Gredos, Sierra
 de 18 B3
Greece ■ 23 E4
Greeley 76 E2
Green → 83 A8
Green Bay 72 B2
Green C. 63 C5
Greenland ■ .. 66 C9
Greenock 10 D4
Greensboro ... 75 A8
Greenville,
 Liberia 55 G3
Greenville,
 Ala.,
 U.S.A. 74 D4

Greenville,
 Miss., U.S.A. 79 C8
Greenville, N.C.,
 U.S.A. 75 B9
Greenville, S.C.,
 U.S.A. 75 B6
Greenwood,
 Miss., U.S.A. 79 C8
Greenwood,
 S.C., U.S.A. . 75 B6
Gregory, L. ... 62 A2
Greifswald 15 A7
Greiz 15 C7
Gremikha 28 C4
Grenada ■ 87 D7
Grenfell 63 B4
Grenoble 13 D6
Grey → 65 E4
Grey Ra. 63 A3
Greymouth ... 65 E4
Greytown, N.Z. 65 D6
Greytown,
 S. Africa 59 D6
Griffin 75 C5
Griffith 63 B4
Grimari 56 C4
Grimaylov =
 Hrymayliv ... 17 D8
Grimsby 11 E6
Gris-Nez, C. .. 12 A4
Grodno =
 Hrodna 17 B6
Grodzyanka =
 Hrodzyanka . 17 B9
Grójec 16 C5
Groningen 14 B4
Grootfontein .. 58 B3
Gross Glockner 15 E7
Grosser Arber . 15 D7
Grosseto 20 C3
Groznyy 25 E6
Grudziądz 16 B4
Gryazi 24 C4
Gryazovets ... 28 D5
Gua 40 F5
Guadalajara,
 Mexico 84 C4
Guadalajara,
 Spain 18 B4
Guadalcanal . . 64 K11
Guadalete → . 18 D2
Guadalquivir → 18 D2
Guadalupe =
 Guadeloupe ■ 87 C7
Guadalupe,
 Sierra de ... 18 C3
Guadarrama,
 Sierra de ... 18 B4
Guadeloupe ■ . 87 C7
Guadiana → .. 18 D2
Guadix 18 D4
Guafo, Boca del 95 E2
Guaíra 94 A4
Guaitecas, Is. . 95 E2
Guajará-Mirim . 91 F5
Guajira, Pen. de
 la 90 A4
Gualeguay 94 C5
Gualeguaychú . 94 C5
Guam ■ 64 H9
Guamúchil 84 B3
Guan Xian 34 C5
Guanahani =
 San Salvador 86 B5
Guanajuato ... 84 C4
Guandacol ... 94 B3
Guane 86 B3
Guangdong □ . 35 D6
Guanghua ... 35 C6

Guangxi
 Zhuangzu
 Zizhiqu □ ... 35 D5
Guangzhou ... 35 D6
Guanipa → ... 90 B6
Guantánamo .. 86 B4
Guaporé → .. 91 F5
Guaqui 91 G5
Guarapuava ... 94 B6
Guarda 18 B2
Guardafui, C. =
 Asir, Ras 49 E5
Guasdualito ... 90 B4
Guasipati 90 B6
Guatemala ... 85 E6
Guatemala ■ .. 85 D6
Guatire 90 A5
Guaviare □ ... 90 C4
Guaviare → .. 90 C5
Guaxupé 93 G4
Guayama 87 C6
Guayaquil 90 D3
Guayaquil, G. de 90 D2
Guaymas 84 B2
Guddu Barrage 42 E6
Gudivada 40 J3
Gudur 43 M11
Guecho 19 A4
Guékédou 55 G2
Guelma 54 A6
Guelph 69 D2
Guéréda 53 F3
Guéret 12 C4
Guernica 19 A4
Guernsey 11 G5
Guidónia-
 Montecélio .. 20 C4
Guiglo 55 G3
Guildford 11 F6
Guilin 35 D6
Guimarães,
 Brazil 92 C5
Guimarães,
 Portugal 18 B1
Guimaras 38 B2
Guinea ■ 55 F2
Guinea, Gulf of 51 F3
Guinea-Bissau ■ 55 F1
Guingamp 12 B2
Guiping 35 D6
Güiria 90 A6
Guiuan 38 B3
Guiyang 35 D5
Guizhou □ ... 35 D5
Gujarat □ 43 H7
Gujranwala ... 42 C9
Gujrat 42 C9
Gulbarga 43 L10
Gulf, The 44 E2
Gulgong 63 B4
Güllük 23 F6
Gulshad 29 E8
Gulu 57 D6
Gum Lake 62 B3
Gummi 55 F6
Gümüşhane .. 46 B4
Gumzai 39 F4
Guna 43 G10
Gundagai 63 C4
Gungu 56 F3
Gunnedah ... 63 B5
Gunningbar
 Cr. → 63 B4
Guntakal 43 M10
Guntur 40 J3
Gunungapi ... 39 F3
Gunungsitoli .. 37 D1
Gunza 56 G2
Gupis 42 A8

Gürchān 46 D7
Gurdaspur ... 42 C9
Gurgaon 42 E10
Gurkha 40 C5
Gurley 63 A4
Gurupá 92 C3
Gurupá, I.
 Grande de .. 92 C3
Gurupi → 92 C4
Guryev =
 Atyraū 29 E6
Gusau 55 F6
Güstrow 15 B7
Gütersloh 14 C5
Guthrie 78 B5
Guyana ■ 90 B7
Guyane
 française ■ =
 French
 Guiana ■ ... 92 B3
Guyenne 12 D4
Guyra 63 B5
Gwa 41 J10
Gwaai 59 B5
Gwabegar ... 63 B4
Gwádar 42 G3
Gwalior 42 F11
Gwanda 59 C5
Gweru 59 B5
Gwydir → ... 63 A4
Gyandzha =
 Gäncä 25 E6
Gyaring Hu ... 34 C4
Gydanskiy P-ov. 28 B8
Gympie 63 A5
Gyöngyös ... 16 E4
Györ 16 E3
Gypsumville .. 71 C10
Gyula 16 E5
Gyumri 25 E5
Gyzylarbat ... 29 F6

H

Ha 'Arava → . 47 E3
Haarlem 14 B3
Haast → 65 E3
Habaswein ... 57 D7
Hachinohe ... 33 F12
Hadarba, Ras .. 52 D6
Hadd, R'as al .. 45 F4
Hadejia 55 F7
Haden 63 A5
Hadera 46 D3
Hadhramaut =
 Hadramawt . 49 D4
Hadramawt .. 49 D4
Haeju 35 C7
Haerhpin =
 Harbin 35 B7
Hafar al Bāṭin . 47 E6
Hafizabad ... 42 C8
Haflong 41 E9
Haft Gel 47 E7
Hafun, Ras ... 49 E5
Hagen 14 C4
Hagerstown .. 73 E7
Hagi 32 B2
Hagondange-
 Briey 13 B7
Hague, C. de la 12 B3
Hague, The = 's-
 Gravenhage . 14 B3
Haguenau ... 13 B7
Hai'an 35 C7
Haifa = Hefa .. 46 D3

Haikou	35	D6
Ḥā'il	47	F5
Hailar	35	B6
Haileybury	69	D3
Hailun	35	B7
Hainan □	35	E5
Haiphong	35	D5
Haiti ■	87	C5
Haiya Junction	53	E6
Hajar Bangar	53	F3
Hajdúböszörmény	16	E5
Hajnówka	17	B6
Hakken-Zan	32	B4
Hakodate	32	F12
Hala	42	G6
Ḥalab	46	C4
Ḥalabjah	46	D6
Halaib	52	D6
Halberstadt	15	C6
Halcombe	64	D6
Halcon, Mt.	38	B2
Halden	9	G10
Haldia	40	F7
Haldwani	42	E11
Halifax, Canada	69	D4
Halifax, U.K.	11	E6
Halīl →	44	E4
Hall Beach	68	B2
Halle	15	C6
Hallett	62	B2
Halmahera	39	D3
Halmstad	9	G10
Halq el Oued	52	A1
Hälsingborg =		
Helsingborg	9	G10
Halul	44	E3
Hamada	32	B3
Hamadān	46	D7
Hamadān □	46	D7
Hamāh	46	D4
Hamamatsu	32	B5
Hamar	8	F10
Hamburg	14	B5
Hameln	14	B5
Hamersley Ra.	60	E2
Hamhung	35	C7
Hami	34	B4
Hamilton, Australia	62	C3
Hamilton, Canada	69	D3
Hamilton, N.Z.	64	B6
Hamilton, U.K.	10	D4
Hamley Bridge	62	B2
Hamlin =		
Hameln	14	B5
Hamm	14	C4
Hammerfest	8	D12
Hammond	72	D2
Hampden	65	F4
Hampton	73	F7
Hamrat esh Sheykh	53	F4
Han Pijesak	20	B7
Hanamaki	33	G12
Hanau	14	C5
Hancock	77	C7
Handa	49	E5
Handan	35	C6
Handeni	57	F7
Hangayn Nuruu	34	B4
Hangchou =		
Hangzhou	35	C7
Hangu	35	C6
Hangzhou	35	C7
Hangzhou Wan	35	C7
Ḥanīsh	49	E3
Hanle	42	C11
Hanmer Springs	65	E5
Hanna	71	C8
Hannibal	77	F9
Hannover	14	B5
Hanoi	35	D5
Hanover =		
Hannover	14	B5
Hanover, I.	95	G2
Hansi	42	E9
Hanson, L.	62	B2
Hantsavichy	17	B8
Hanzhong	35	C5
Haora	40	F7
Haparanda	8	E12
Happy Valley-Goose Bay	69	C4
Hapur	42	E10
Ḥaql	47	E3
Har	39	F4
Har Hu	34	C4
Har Us Nuur	34	B4
Ḥaraḍ	47	F7
Haraisan Plateau = Hurayṣān	47	G6
Harardera	49	G4
Harare	59	B6
Harazé	53	F2
Harbin	35	B7
Harbour Grace	69	D5
Hardangerfjorden	8	F9
Hardap Dam	58	C3
Hardwar = Haridwar	42	E11
Hardy, Pen.	95	H3
Harer	49	F3
Hargeisa	49	F3
Hari →	37	E2
Haridwar	42	E11
Haringhata →	41	G7
Harīrūd	45	C5
Harīrūd →	42	A2
Harlingen	78	F5
Harlow	11	F7
Harney Basin	80	D4
Härnösand	8	F11
Ḥarrat al Kishb	47	G5
Ḥarrat al 'Uwairidh	47	F4
Harris	10	C3
Harris L.	62	B2
Harrisburg	73	D7
Harrison, C.	68	C5
Harrison Bay	71	A4
Harrogate	11	D6
Hart, L.	62	B2
Hartford	73	D9
Hartlepool	11	D6
Harvey	72	D2
Harwich	11	F7
Haryana □	42	E10
Haryn →	17	B8
Harz	14	C6
Hasa	47	F7
Hasan Kuli	29	F6
Hassi Inifel	54	C5
Hassi Messaoud	54	B6
Hastings, N.Z.	64	C7
Hastings, U.K.	11	F7
Hastings, U.S.A.	76	E5
Hastings Ra.	63	B5
Hatay = Antalya	46	C2
Hatfield P.O.	62	B3
Hatgal	34	A5
Hathras	42	F11
Hatia	41	F8
Hattah	62	B3
Hatteras, C.	75	B10
Hattiesburg	79	D9
Hatvan	16	E4
Hau Bon = Cheo Reo	36	B3
Haugesund	9	G9
Hauraki G.	64	B6
Haut Atlas	54	B3
Hautah, Waḥāt al	47	G6
Hauts Plateaux	54	B4
Havana = La Habana	86	B3
Havant	11	F6
Havel →	15	B7
Havelock	65	D5
Haverfordwest	11	F4
Havlíčkův Brod	16	D2
Havre	81	A9
Havza	46	B3
Hawaii	82	J12
Hawaiian Is.	82	H12
Hawea, L.	65	F3
Hawera	64	C6
Hawick	10	D5
Hawke B.	64	C7
Hawker	62	B2
Hawkwood	63	A5
Hay	63	B3
Hay River	70	B8
Haya	39	E3
Hayes →	71	C10
Hayrabolu	22	D6
Haysyn	17	D9
Hayvoron	17	D9
Hazaribag	40	F5
Healesville	63	C4
Hearst	69	D2
Hebei □	35	C6
Hebel	63	A4
Hebron = Al Khalīl	47	E3
Hebron	68	C4
Hechi	35	D5
Hechuan	35	C5
Heerlen	13	A6
Ḥefa	46	D3
Hefei	35	C6
Hegang	35	B8
Heidelberg	14	D5
Heilbron	59	D5
Heilbronn	14	D5
Heilongjiang □	35	B7
Heilunkiang = Heilongjiang □	35	B7
Heinze Is.	41	K11
Hejaz = Al Ḥijāz	47	F4
Hekimhan	46	C4
Hekou	34	D5
Helena, Ark., U.S.A.	79	B8
Helena, Mont., U.S.A.	81	B7
Helensville	64	B6
Helgoland	14	A4
Heligoland = Helgoland	14	A4
Heligoland B. = Deutsche Bucht	14	A5
Hellín	19	C5
Helmand □	42	D3
Helmand →	42	D2
Helmand, Hamun	45	D5
Helmsdale	10	B5
Helsingborg	9	G10
Helsingfors = Helsinki	9	F13
Helsinki	9	F13
Helwân	52	C5
Hemel Hempstead	11	F6
Henan □	35	C6
Henares →	18	B4
Henderson	75	A8
Hendon	63	A5
Hengyang	35	D6
Henrietta Maria, C.	69	C2
Hentiyn Nuruu	35	B5
Henty	63	C4
Henzada	41	J10
Herāt	42	B3
Herāt □	42	B3
Hercegnovi	22	C2
Hereford	11	E5
Herford	14	B5
Hermidale	63	B4
Hermitage	65	E4
Hermite, I.	95	H3
Hermon, Mt. = Ash Shaykh, J.	46	D3
Hermosillo	84	B2
Hernád →	16	E5
Hernandarias	94	B6
Heroica Nogales = Nogales	84	A2
Heron Bay	69	D2
Herrick	62	D4
's-Hertogenbosch	14	C3
Hesse = Hessen □	14	C5
Hessen □	14	C5
Hewett, C.	68	A4
Hexham	11	D5
Heyfield	63	C4
Heywood	62	C3
Hibbing	77	B8
Hibbs B.	62	D4
Hickory	75	B7
Hicks, Pt.	63	C4
Hida-Sammyaku	32	A5
Hidalgo del Parral	84	B3
Higashiōsaka	32	B4
High Atlas = Haut Atlas	54	B3
High Point	75	B8
High River	71	C8
High Tatra = Tatry	16	D4
High Wycombe	11	F6
Hiiumaa	24	B1
Ḥijārah, Ṣaḥrā' al	47	E6
Ḥijāz □	48	C2
Hijo = Tagum	38	C3
Hikone	32	B5
Hikurangi	64	A6
Hikurangi, Mt.	64	C7
Hildesheim	14	B5
Hillston	63	B4
Hilo	82	J13
Hilversum	14	B3
Himachal Pradesh □	42	D10
Himalaya	40	C5
Himatnagar	43	H8
Himeji	32	B4
Ilimi	32	A5
Ḥimṣ	46	D4
Hindmarsh, L.	62	C3
Hindu Kush	42	B7
Hindubagh	42	D5
Hindupur	43	N10

Hinganghat ... 43 J11
Hingoli 43 K10
Hinna = Imi .. 49 F3
Hinojosa del
 Duque 18 C3
Hirakud Dam .. 40 G4
Hiratsuka 32 B6
Hirosaki 33 F12
Hiroshima ... 32 B3
Hisar 42 E9
Hispaniola ... 87 C5
Hita 32 C2
Hitachi 32 A7
Hjälmaren ... 9 G11
Hlyboka 17 D7
Ho 55 G5
Ho Chi Minh
 City = Phanh
 Bho Ho Chi
 Minh 36 B3
Hoai Nhon 36 B3
Hoare B. 68 B4
Hobart 62 D4
Hobbs Coast .. 96 B18
Hodgson 71 C10
Hódmezővásárhely
 .... 16 E5
Hodna, Chott el 54 A5
Hodonín 16 D3
Hoek van
 Holland 14 B3
Hof 15 C6
Hōfu 32 B2
Hogan Group . 62 C4
Hoggar =
 Ahaggar ... 54 D6
Hoh Xil Shan .. 34 C3
Hohe Rhön ... 14 C5
Hohhot 35 B6
Hoi An 36 A3
Hokianga
 Harbour ... 64 A5
Hokitika 65 E4
Hokkaidō □ .. 32 F12
Holbrook 63 C4
Holguín 86 B4
Hollandia =
 Jayapura ... 39 E6
Holman Island . 70 A8
Holy Cross ... 71 B4
Holyhead 11 E4
Homalin 41 E10
Hombori 55 E4
Home B. 68 B4
Homer 71 C4
Homs = Ḥimṣ . 46 D4
Homyel 17 B10
Hon Chong .. 36 B2
Honan =
 Henan □ 35 C6
Honda 90 B4
Hondeklipbaai . 58 E3
Honduras ■ ... 85 E7
Honduras, G. de 85 D7
Honfleur 12 B4
Hong Kong ... 35 D6
Hongjiang 35 D5
Hongshui He ➝ 35 D5
Hongze Hu 35 C6
Honiara 64 K10
Honolulu 82 H12
Honshū 32 G11
Hood, Mt. 80 C3
Hooghly =
 Hughli ➝ .. 40 G7
Hook of Holland
 = Hoek van
 Holland 14 B3
Hoorn 14 B3

Hoover Dam .. 82 B5
Hope, L. 62 A2
Hope, Pt. 71 B3
Hopedale 68 C4
Hopei =
 Hebei □ 35 C6
Hopetoun 62 C3
Hopetown ... 58 D4
Hoquiam 80 B2
Horlick Mts. ... 96 C1
Horlivka 25 D4
Hormoz 44 E3
Hormoz, Jaz. ye 44 E4
Hormozgān □ . 44 E3
Hormuz, Str. of 44 E4
Horn 15 D8
Horn, Cape =
 Hornos, C. de 95 H3
Hornavan ... 8 E11
Hornos, C. de . 95 H3
Hornsby 63 B5
Horodenka ... 17 D7
Horodok,
 Khmelnytskyy,
 Ukraine 17 D8
Horodok, Lviv,
 Ukraine 17 D6
Horokhiv 17 C7
Horqin Youyi
 Qianqi 35 B7
Horqueta ... 94 A5
Horsham 62 C3
Horton ➝ ... 70 B7
Hose, Gunung-
 Gunung ... 37 D4
Hoshangabad . 43 H10
Hoshiarpur ... 42 D9
Hospet 43 M10
Hospitalet de
 Llobregat ... 19 B7
Hoste, I. 95 H3
Hot Springs .. 79 B7
Hotan 34 C2
Houhora Heads 64 A5
Houlton 73 A12
Houma 79 E8
Houston 79 E6
Hovd 34 B4
Hövsgöl Nuur . 34 A5
Howard 63 A5
Howe, C. 63 C5
Howitt, L. 62 A2
Howrah = Haora 40 F7
Höxter 14 C5
Hoy 10 B5
Høyanger 8 F9
Hoyerswerda . 15 C8
Hpungan Pass . 41 D11
Hradec Králové 16 C2
Hrodna 17 B6
Hrodzyanka ... 17 B9
Hron ➝ 16 E4
Hrvatska =
 Croatia ■ .. 20 B6
Hrymayliv ... 17 D8
Hsenwi 41 F11
Hsiamen =
 Xiamen ... 35 D6
Hsian = Xi'an . 35 C5
Hsinhailien =
 Lianyungang 35 C6
Hsisha Chuntao 36 A4
Hsüchou =
 Xuzhou ... 35 C6
Hua Hin 36 B1
Huacho 91 F3
Huachón 91 F3
Huai He ➝ .. 35 C6
Huainan 35 C6

Huallaga ➝ .. 90 E3
Huambo 58 A3
Huancabamba . 91 E3
Huancane ... 91 G5
Huancapi 91 F4
Huancavelica . 91 F3
Huancayo ... 91 F3
Huang Hai =
 Yellow Sea . 35 C7
Huang He ➝ . 35 C6
Huangliu 35 E5
Huangshi ... 35 C6
Huánuco ... 91 E3
Huaraz 91 E3
Huarmey 91 F3
Huascarán ... 91 E3
Huasco 94 B2
Huatabampo . 84 B3
Huayllay 91 F3
Hubei □ 35 C6
Hubli-Dharwad
 = Dharwad . 43 M9
Huddersfield . 11 E6
Hudiksvall ... 8 F11
Hudson ➝ .. 73 D8
Hudson Bay .. 68 B2
Hudson Mts. . 96 B2
Hudson Str. .. 68 B4
Hue 36 A3
Huelva 18 D2
Huesca 19 A5
Hughenden .. 61 E7
Hughli ➝ 40 G7
Huila, Nevado
 del 90 C3
Huinca Renancó 94 C4
Huize 34 D5
Hukawng Valley 41 D11
Hulan 35 B7
Ḥulayfā' 47 F5
Huld 35 B5
Hull = Kingston
 upon Hull ... 11 E6
Hull 69 D3
Hulun Nur ... 35 B6
Humahuaca .. 94 A3
Humaitá, Brazil 91 E6
Humaitá,
 Paraguay ... 94 B5
Humber ➝ .. 11 E6
Humboldt ... 71 C9
Humboldt ➝ . 80 F4
Hume, L. 63 C4
Humenné ... 16 D5
Hūn 52 C2
Hunan □ 35 D6
Hunedoara .. 17 F6
Hungary ■ .. 16 E4
Hungerford .. 63 A3
Hŭngnam ... 35 C7
Hunsrück 14 D4
Hunter I. 62 D3
Hunter Ra. .. 63 B5
Hunterville ... 64 C6
Huntington .. 72 E4
Huntington
 Beach 82 D3
Huntly, N.Z. .. 64 B6
Huntly, U.K. .. 10 C5
Huntsville ... 74 B4
Huonville ... 62 D4
Hupeh =
 Hubei □ 35 C6
Huraysān ... 47 G6
Huron, L. 72 B4
Hurunui ➝ .. 65 E5
Huşi 17 E9
Hutchinson .. 78
Hutton, Mt. .. 63 A4
Hvar 20 C6

Hwang Ho =
 Huang He ➝ 35 C6
Hwange 59 B5
Hyargas Nuur . 34 B4
Hyderabad,
 India 43 L11
Hyderabad,
 Pakistan ... 42 G6
Hyères 13 E7
Hyères, Is. d' .. 13 E7

I

I-n-Gall 55 E6
Iaco ➝ 91 E5
Ialomiţa ➝ .. 22 B6
Iaşi 17 E8
Iba 38 A2
Ibadan 55 G5
Ibagué 90 C3
Ibar ➝ 22 C3
Ibarra 90 C3
Ibi 55 G6
Ibiá 93 F4
Ibicuy 94 C5
Ibioapaba, Sa.
 da 92 C5
Ibiza 19 C6
Ibonma 39 E4
Ibotirama ... 93 E5
Ibu 39 D3
Icá 91 F3
Içá ➝ 90 D5
Içana 90 C5
İçel = Mersin . 46 C3
Iceland ■ ... 8 B4
Ich'ang =
 Yichang ... 35 C6
Ichchapuram . 40 H5
Ichihara 32 B7
Ichikawa 32 B6
Ichilo ➝ 91 G6
Ichinomiya .. 32 B5
Idaho □ 81 C6
Idaho Falls .. 81 D7
Idar-Oberstein . 14 D4
Idd el Ghanam 53 F3
Iddan 49 F4
Idehan 52 C1
Idehan Marzūq 52 D1
Idelès 54 D6
Idfû 52 D5
Ídhi Óros ... 23 G5
Ídhra 23 F4
Idi 36 C1
Idiofa 56 E3
Idlip 46 D4
Ierápetra ... 23 G5
Iesi 20 C4
Ifanadiana .. 59 J9
Ife 55 G5
Ifni 54 C2
Iforas, Adrar des 54
Igarapava .. 93 G4
Igarapé Açu .. 92 C4
Igarka 28 C9
Igbetti 55 G5
Iglésias 21 E2
Igli 54 B4
Igloolik 68 B2
İğneada Burnu 22 D7
Igoumenítsa . 23 E3
Iguaçu ➝ .. 94 B6
Iguaçu, Cat. del 94 B6
Iguaçu Falls =
 Iguaçu, Cat.
 del 94 B6

Iguala 84 D5
Igualada 19 B6
Iguassu =
  Iguaçu ─► . . 94 B6
Iguatu 92 D6
Iguéla 56 E1
Ihosy 59 J9
Iida 32 B5
Iisalmi 8 F13
Iizuka 32 C2
Ijebu-Ode 55 G5
IJsselmeer 14 B3
Ikaría 23 F6
Ikela 56 E4
Iki 32 C1
Ilagan 38 A2
Īlām 46 D6
Iława 16 B4
Île-de-France . . 12 B5
Ilebo 56 E4
Ilhéus 93 E6
Ili ─► 29 E8
Ilich 29 E7
Iligan 38 C2
Illampu =
  Ancohuma,
  Nevada 91 G5
Illana B. 38 C2
Illapel 94 C2
Iller ─► 14 D5
Illimani 91 G5
Ilium = Troy . . 23 E6
Ilmen, Ozero . . 24 B3
Ilo 91 G4
Iloilo 38 B2
Ilorin 55 G5
Ilwaki 39 F3
Imabari 32 B3
Imandra, Ozero . 28 C4
Imari 32 C1
imeni 26
  Bakinskikh
  Komissarov =
  Neftçala 46 C7
Imeri, Serra . . 90 C5
Imi 49 F3
Imola 20 B3
Imperatriz 92 D4
Impéria 20 C2
Imperial Dam . 82 D5
Impfondo 56 D3
Imphal 41 E9
İmroz =
  Gökçeada . . 23 D5
Imuruan B. . . . 38 B1
In Belbel 54 C5
In Salah 54 C5
Ina 32 B5
Inangahua
  Junction 65 D4
Inanwatan 39 E4
Iñapari 91 F5
Inarijärvi 8 E13
Inca 19 C7
İnce-Burnu . . . 46 B3
Inchon 35 C7
İncirliova 23 F6
Incomáti ─► . . 59 D6
Indalsälven ─► . 8 F11
Indaw 41 E11
Independence,
  Kans., U.S.A. 79 A6
Independence,
  Mo., U.S.A. . 77 F7
India ■ 43 J10
Indian ─► 75 F7
Indian Harbour 68 C6
Indian Head . . 71 C9
Indiana □ 72 D3

Indianapolis . . 72 E2
Indiga 28 C5
Indigirka ─► . . 31 B12
Indonesia ■ . . . 37 E4
Indore 43 H9
Indravati ─► . . 40 H3
Indre ─► 12 C4
Indus ─► 43 G5
İnebolu 46 B3
Ingende 56 E3
Inglewood,
  Queens.,
  Australia 63 A5
Inglewood, Vic.,
  Australia 62 C3
Inglewood, N.Z. 64 C6
Ingolstadt 15 D6
Ingraj Bazar . . 40 E7
Ingrid
  Christensen
  Coast 96 A10
Ingulec =
  Inhulec 25 D3
Inhambane . . . 59 C7
Inhaminga 59 B7
Inharrime 59 C7
Inhulec 25 D3
Ining = Yining . 34 B3
Inírida ─► 90 C5
Injune 63 A4
Inle L. 41 G11
Inn ─► 15 D7
Innamincka . . . 62 A3
Inner Hebrides 10 C3
Inner Mongolia
  = Nei
  Monggol
  Zizhiqu □ . . 35 B6
Innisfail 71 C8
Innsbruck 15 E6
Inongo 56 E3
Inoucdjouac =
  Inukjuak 68 C3
Inowrocław . . . 16 B4
Inquisivi 91 G5
Insein 41 J11
Interlaken 13 C7
International
  Falls 77 A8
Intiyaco 94 B4
Inukjuak 68 C3
Inútil, B. 95 G2
Inuvik 70 B6
Invercargill . . . 65 G3
Inverell 63 A5
Invergordon . . 10 C4
Inverness 10 C4
Inverurie 10 C5
Investigator
  Group 62 B1
Investigator Str. 62 C2
Inya 29 D9
Inza 24 C6
Ioánnina 23 E3
Ionian Is. =
  Iónioi Nísoi . 23 E3
Ionian Sea . . . 21 F6
Iónioi Nísoi . . 23 E3
Íos 23 F5
Iowa □ 77 D8
Iowa City 77 E9
Ipameri 93 F4
Ipatinga 93 F5
Ipiales 90 C3
Ipin = Yibin . . 35 D5
Ipixuna 91 E4
Ipoh 36 D2
Ippy 56 C4
İpsala 22 D6

Ipswich,
  Australia 63 A5
Ipswich, U.K. . . 11 E7
Ipu 92 C5
Iqaluit 68 B4
Iquique 91 H4
Iquitos 90 D4
Iracoubo 92 A3
Iráklion 23 G5
Iran ■ 44 C3
Iran, Gunung-
  Gunung 37 D4
Iran Ra. = Iran,
  Gunung-
  Gunung 37 D4
Īrānshahr 45 E5
Irapuato 84 C4
Iraq ■ 46 D5
Irbid 46 D3
Irebu 56 E3
Ireland ■ 11 E3
Irian Jaya □ . . 39 E5
Iringa 57 F7
Iriri ─► 92 C3
Irish Sea 11 E4
Irkineyeva 30 D7
Irkutsk 30 D8
Iron Baron . . . 62 B2
Iron Gate =
  Portile de Fier 22 B4
Iron Knob 62 B2
Ironwood 77 B9
Irpin 17 C10
Irrara Cr. ─► . . 63 A4
Irrawaddy □ . . 41 J10
Irrawaddy ─► . . 41 K10
Irtysh ─► 28 C7
Irumu 57 D5
Irún 19 A5
Irunea =
  Pamplona . . 19 A5
Irvine 10 D4
Irymple 62 B3
Isabella 38 C2
Isangi 56 D4
Isar ─► 15 D7
Íschia 21 D4
Ise 32 B5
Ise-Wan 32 B5
Isère ─► 13 D6
Isérnia 20 D5
Ishikari-Wan . . 32 F12
Ishim ─► 29 D8
Ishinomaki . . . 33 G12
Ishkuman 42 A8
Isil Kul 29 D8
Isiolo 57 D7
Isiro 57 D5
İskenderun . . . 46 C4
İskŭr ─► 22 C5
Islamabad 42 C8
Island L. 71 C10
Island Lagoon . 62 B2
Islay 10 D3
Isle ─► 12 D3
Isle of Wight □ 11 F6
Ismail = Izmayil 17 F9
Ismâ'ilîya 47 E3
Isna 52 C5
Ísparta 46 C2
Íspica 21 F5
Israel ■ 46 E3
Issoire 13 D5
Issyk-Kul, Ozero
  = Ysyk-Köl,
  Ozero 29 E8
İstanbul 22 D7
Istiaía 23 E4
Istra 20 B4

İstranca Dağları 22 D6
Istres 13 E6
Istria = Istra . . 20 B4
Itabaiana 92 D6
Itaberaba 93 E5
Itabira 93 F5
Itabuna 93 E6
Itaipú, Reprêsa
  de 94 B6
Itaituba 92 C2
Itajaí 94 B7
Italy ■ 20 C4
Itapecuru-Mirim 92 C5
Itaperuna 93 G5
Itapicuru ─►,
  Bahia, Brazil . 93 E6
Itapicuru ─►,
  Maranhão,
  Brazil 92 C5
Itapipoca 92 C6
Itaquatiara . . . 90 D7
Itaquí 94 B5
Itatuba 91 E6
Ithaca = Itháki . 23 E3
Itháki 23 E3
Ito 32 B6
Itonamas ─► . . 91 F6
Ituaçu 93 E5
Ituiutaba 93 F4
Itumbiara 93 F4
Iturbe 94 A3
Itzehoe 14 B5
Ivanava 17 B7
Ivanhoe 63 B3
Ivano-Frankivsk 17 D7
Ivano-Frankovsk
  = Ivano-
  Frankivsk . . . 17 D7
Ivanovo =
  Ivanava 17 B7
Ivanovo 24 B5
Ivatsevichy . . . 17 B7
Ivory Coast ■ . 55 G3
Ivrea 20 B1
Ivujivik 68 B3
Iwahig 36 C5
Iwaki 33 G12
Iwakuni 32 B3
Iwata 33 H11
Iwate-San 33 G12
Iwo 55 G5
Ixiamas 91 F5
Izhevsk 28 D6
Izmayil 17 F9
İzmir 23 E6
İzmit 25 E2
İznik Gölü 23 D7
Izumi-sano . . . 32 B4
Izumo 32 B3
Izyaslav 17 C8

J

Jabalpur 43 H11
Jablah 46 D4
Jablanica 22 D3
Jablonec 16 C2
Jaboatão 92 D6
Jaca 19 A5
Jacareí 94 A7
Jacarèzinho . . 94 A7
Jackson,
  Australia 63 A4
Jackson, Mich.,
  U.S.A. 72 C3
Jackson, Miss.,
  U.S.A. 79 C8

Jackson

Jackson, *Tenn.,*
  U.S.A. 74 B3
Jackson B. 65 E3
Jacksons 65 E4
Jacksonville,
  Fla., U.S.A. .. 75 D7
Jacksonville, *Ill.,*
  U.S.A. 77 F9
Jacksonville,
  N.C., U.S.A. . 75 B9
Jacmel 87 C5
Jacobabad 42 E6
Jacobina 93 E5
Jacundá ⋅→ .. 92 C3
Jadotville =
  Likasi 57 G5
Jādū 52 B1
Jaén, *Peru* ... 91 E3
Jaén, *Spain* .. 18 D4
Jaffa = Tel Aviv-
  Yafo 46 D3
Jaffa, C. 62 C2
Jaffna 43 Q12
Jagadhri 42 D10
Jagdalpur 40 H3
Jagraon 42 D9
Jagtial 43 K11
Jaguariaíva ... 94 A7
Jaguaribe ⋅→ . 92 C6
Jahrom 44 D3
Jailolo 39 D3
Jailolo, Selat .. 39 D3
Jaipur 42 F9
Jakarta 37 F3
Jalalabad 42 B7
Jalapa Enríquez 84 D5
Jalas, Jabal al . 47 F4
Jalgaon,
  Maharashtra,
  India 43 J10
Jalgaon,
  Maharashtra,
  India 43 J9
Jalna 43 K9
Jalón ⋅→ 19 B5
Jalpaiguri 41 D7
Jalq 45 E5
Jaluit I. 64 J11
Jamaica ■ 86 C4
Jamalpur,
  Bangla. 41 E7
Jamalpur, *India* 40 E6
Jamanxim ⋅→ . 92 C2
Jambe 39 E4
Jambi 37 E2
Jambi □ 37 E2
James ⋅→ 76 D6
James B. 69 C2
James Ross I. . 96 A4
Jamestown,
  Australia ... 62 B2
Jamestown,
  N. Dak., U.S.A. 76 B5
Jamestown,
  N.Y., U.S.A. . 73 C6
Jamkhandi 43 L9
Jammu 42 C9
Jammu &
  Kashmir □ .. 42 B10
Jamnagar 43 H7
Jamrud 42 C7
Jamshedpur .. 40 F6
Jand 42 C8
Jandaq 44 C3
Jandowae 63 A5
Janesville 77 D10
Januária 93 F5
Jaora 43 H9
Japan ■ 33 G11

Japan, Sea of . 33 G11
Japen = Yapen 39 E5
Japurá ⋅→ 90 D5
Jaque 90 B3
Jarama ⋅→ ... 18 B4
Jargalant =
  Hovd 34 B4
Jarosław 17 C6
Jarso 53 G6
Jarvis I. 65 K15
Jarwa 40 D4
Jäsk 44 E4
Jasło 16 D5
Jasper 74 C4
Jászberény .. 16 E4
Jataí 93 F3
Játiva 19 C5
Jaú 93 G4
Jauja 91 F3
Jaunpur 40 E4
Java = Jawa .. 37 F3
Java Sea 37 E3
Javhlant =
  Ulyasutay ... 34 B4
Jawa 37 F3
Jaya, Puncak .. 39 E5
Jayanti 41 D7
Jayapura 39 E6
Jayawijaya,
  Pegunungan 39 E5
Jaynagar 40 D6
Jean Marie
  River 70 B7
Jebba 55 G5
Jebel, Bahr
  el ⋅→ 53 G5
Jedburgh 10 D5
Jedda = Jiddah 47 G4
Jędrzejów 16 C5
Jefferson City . 77 F8
Jega 55 F5
Jelenia Góra .. 16 C2
Jelgava 24 B1
Jemaja 37 D3
Jembongan ... 36 C5
Jena 15 C6
Jeparit 62 C3
Jequié 93 E5
Jequitinhonha . 93 F5
Jequitinhonha ⋅→
  .... 93 F6
Jerada 54 B4
Jerantut 37 D2
Jérémie 86 C5
Jerez de la
  Frontera 18 D2
Jerez de los
  Caballeros .. 18 C2
Jerilderie 63 C4
Jersey 11 G5
Jersey City ... 73 D8
Jerusalem 47 E3
Jervis B. 63 C5
Jesselton =
  Kota Kinabalu 36 C5
Jessore 41 F7
Jeypore 40 H4
Jhal Jhao 42 F4
Jhalawar 43 G10
Jhang Maghiana 42 D8
Jhansi 43 G11
Jharsaguda ... 40 G5
Jhelum 42 C8
Jhelum ⋅→ 42 D8
Jhunjhunu 42 E9
Jiamusi 35 B8
Ji'an 35 D6
Jianchuan 34 D4
Jiangling 35 C6

Jiangmen 35 D6
Jiangsu □ 35 C6
Jiangxi □ 35 D6
Jian'ou 35 D6
Jianshui 34 D5
Jiao Xian 35 C7
Jiaozuo 35 C6
Jiaxing 35 C7
Jiayi 35 D7
Jibuti =
  Djibouti ■ .. 49 E3
Jiddah 47 G4
Jido 41 C10
Jihlava 16 D2
Jihlava ⋅→ 16 D3
Jijel 54 A6
Jijiga 49 F3
Jilin 35 B7
Jilong 35 D7
Jima 53 G6
Jiménez 84 B4
Jinan 35 C6
Jindabyne 63 C4
Jindrichuv
  Hradeç 16 D2
Jingdezhen ... 35 D6
Jinggu 34 D5
Jingxi 35 D5
Jinhua 35 D6
Jining,
  Nei Mongol Zizhiqu,
  China 35 B6
Jining,
  Shandong,
  China 35 C6
Jinja 57 D6
Jinnah Barrage 42 C7
Jinotega 85 E7
Jinshi 35 D6
Jinzhou 35 B7
Jiparaná ⋅→ .. 91 E6
Jipijapa 90 D2
Jisr ash
  Shughūr 46 D4
Jiu ⋅→ 22 C4
Jiujiang 35 D6
Jiuquan 34 C4
Jixi 35 B8
Jizzakh 29 E7
Joaçaba 94 B6
João Pessoa .. 92 D7
Joaquín V.
  González 94 B4
Jodhpur 42 F8
Jofane 59 C6
Jogjakarta =
  Yogyakarta .. 37 F4
Johannesburg . 59 D5
Johnson City .. 75 A6
Johnston Falls
  = Mambilima
  Falls 57 G5
Johnstown ... 73 D6
Johor Baharu . 37 D2
Joinvile 94 B7
Joinville I. 96 A4
Joliet 72 D1
Joliette 69 D3
Jolo 38 C2
Jome 39 E3
Jonesboro ... 79 B8
Jönköping 9 G10
Jonquière 69 D3
Jordan ■ 47 E4
Jorhat 41 D10
Jorong 37 E4
Jos 55 G6
Jowzjän □ 45 B6

Juan de Fuca
  Str. 80 A1
Juan de Nova . 59 H8
Juan Fernández,
  Arch. de 89 G3
Juárez 94 D5
Juàzeiro 93 D5
Juàzeiro do
  Norte 92 D6
Jubbulpore =
  Jabalpur 43 H11
Juby, C. 54 C2
Júcar ⋅→ 19 C5
Juchitán 85 D5
Jugoslavia =
  Yugoslavia ■ . 22 B3
Juiz de Fora ... 93 G5
Juli 91 G5
Juliaca 91 G4
Jullundur 42 D9
Jumilla 19 C5
Jumla 40 C4
Jumna =
  Yamuna ⋅→ . 40 E3
Junagadh 43 J7
Jundiaí 94 A7
Juneau 71 C6
Junee 63 B4
Jungfrau 13 C7
Junggar Pendi . 34 B3
Junín 94 C4
Junín de los
  Andes 95 D2
Jūniyah 46 D3
Jur, Nahr el ⋅→ 53 G4
Jura = Jura,
  Mts. du 13 C7
Jura =
  Schwäbische
  Alb 14 D5
Jura 10 D4
Jura, Mts. du . 13 C7
Jurado 90 B3
Juruá ⋅→ 90 D5
Juruena ⋅→ .. 91 E7
Juruti 92 C2
Justo Daract .. 94 C3
Jutland =
  Jylland 9 G9
Juventud, I. de
  la 86 B3
Juwain 42 D2
Jylland 9 G9
Jyväskylä 8 F13

K

K2 .... 42 B10
Kaapkruis 58 C2
Kaapstad =
  Cape Town .. 58 E3
Kabaena 39 F2
Kabala 55 G2
Kabale 57 E6
Kabalo 57 F5
Kabambare ... 57 E5
Kabanjahe ... 37 D1
Kabara 55 E4
Kabardino-
  Balkar
  Republic =
  Kabardino
  Balkaria □ .. 25 E5
Kabardino
  Balkaria □ .. 25 E5
Kabare 39 E4

Name	Pg	Grid
Kabarega Falls	57	D6
Kabasalan	38	C2
Kabba	55	G6
Kabīr, Zab al ➤	46	C5
Kabīr Kūh	47	D6
Kabkabīyah	53	F3
Kabompo ➤	58	A4
Kabongo	57	F5
Kabūd Gonbad	44	B4
Kābul	42	B6
Kābul □	42	B6
Kābul ➤	42	C8
Kaburuang	39	D3
Kabwe	59	A5
Kachchh, Gulf of	43	H6
Kachchh, Rann of	43	G6
Kachin □	41	D11
Kachiry	29	D8
Kaçkar	46	B5
Kadan Kyun	36	B1
Kadina	62	B2
Kadirli	46	C4
Kadiyevka = Stakhanov	25	D4
Kadoma	59	B5
Kâdugli	53	F4
Kaduna	55	F6
Kaédi	55	E2
Kaelé	53	F1
Kaesŏng	35	C7
Kāf	47	E4
Kafakumba	56	F4
Kafan = Kapan	25	F6
Kafanchan	55	G6
Kaffrine	55	F1
Kafia Kingi	53	G3
Kafirévs, Ákra	23	E5
Kafue ➤	59	B5
Kafulwe	57	F5
Kaga Bandoro	56	C3
Kagan	29	F7
Kağizman	46	B5
Kagoshima	33	D2
Kagoshima-Wan	33	D2
Kagul = Cahul	17	F9
Kahama	57	E6
Kahayan ➤	37	E4
Kahemba	56	F3
Kahnūj	44	E4
Kahoolawe	82	H12
Kahramanmaraş	46	C4
Kai, Kepulauan	39	F4
Kai Besar	39	F4
Kai Is. = Kai, Kepulauan	39	F4
Kai Kecil	39	F4
Kaiama	55	G5
Kaiapoi	65	E5
Kaieteur Falls	90	B7
Kaifeng	35	C6
Kaikohe	64	A5
Kaikoura	65	E5
Kaikoura Ra.	65	D5
Kaimana	39	E4
Kaimanawa Mts.	64	C6
Kaingaroa Forest	64	C7
Kainji Res.	55	F5
Kaipara Harbour	64	B6
Kaironi	39	E4
Kairouan	54	A7
Kaiserslautern	14	D4
Kaitaia	64	A5
Kaitangata	65	G3
Kajaani	8	F13
Kajabbi	61	D6
Kajana = Kajaani	8	F13
Kajo Kaji	53	H5
Kaka	53	F5
Kakamas	58	D4
Kakamega	57	D6
Kakanui Mts.	65	F4
Kakhovka	25	D3
Kakhovske Vdskh.	25	D3
Kakinada	40	J4
Kalabagh	42	C7
Kalabahi	39	F2
Kalabo	58	A4
Kalach	24	C5
Kaladan ➤	41	G9
Kalahari	58	C4
Kalakan	31	D9
Kalámai	23	F4
Kalamata = Kalámai	23	F4
Kalamazoo	72	C3
Kalan	46	C4
Kalao	39	F2
Kalaotoa	39	F2
Kalat	42	E5
Kalce	20	B5
Kale	23	F7
Kalegauk Kyun	41	K11
Kalemie	57	F5
Kalewa	41	F10
Kalgan = Zhangjiakou	35	B6
Kalgoorlie-Boulder	60	G3
Kaliakra, Nos	22	C7
Kalianda	37	F3
Kalibo	38	B2
Kalima	57	E5
Kalimantan	37	E4
Kalimantan Barat □	37	D4
Kalimantan Selatan □	37	E5
Kalimantan Tengah □	37	E4
Kalimantan Timur □	37	D5
Kálimnos	23	F6
Kalinin = Tver	24	B4
Kaliningrad, Kaliningd., Russia	24	C1
Kaliningrad, Moskva, Russia	24	B4
Kalinkavichy	17	B9
Kalinkovichi = Kalinkavichy	17	B9
Kalispell	81	A6
Kalisz	16	C4
Kaliua	57	F6
Kalkrand	58	C3
Kalmar	9	G11
Kalmyk Republic = Kalmykia □	25	D6
Kalmykia □	25	D6
Kalocsa	16	E4
Kalomo	59	B5
Kaluga	24	C4
Kalush	17	D7
Kalutara	43	R11
Kama ➤	29	D6
Kamaishi	33	G12
Kamaran	49	D3
Kamchatka, P-ov.	31	D13
Kamchatka Pen. = Kamchatka, P-ov.	31	D13
Kamchiya ➤	22	C6
Kamen	29	D9
Kamenjak, Rt.	20	B4
Kamenka Bugskaya = Kamyanka-Buzka	17	C7
Kamensk Uralskiy	29	D7
Kamin-Kashyrskyy	17	C7
Kamina	57	F5
Kamloops	71	C7
Kampala	57	D6
Kampar ➤	37	D2
Kampen	14	B3
Kampot	36	B2
Kampuchea = Cambodia ■	36	B3
Kampung ➤	39	F5
Kampungbaru = Tolitoli	39	D2
Kamrau, Teluk	39	E4
Kamsack	71	C9
Kamyanets-Podilskyy	17	D8
Kamyanka-Buzka	17	C7
Kamyshin	24	C6
Kanaaupscow	69	C3
Kananga	56	F4
Kanash	24	B6
Kanastraíon, Ákra = Palioúrion, Ákra	23	E4
Kanazawa	32	A5
Kanchanaburi	36	B1
Kanchenjunga	40	D7
Kanchipuram	43	N11
Kanda Kanda	56	F4
Kandahar = Qandahār	42	D4
Kandalaksha	28	C4
Kandalu	42	E3
Kandangan	37	E5
Kandi	55	F5
Kandla	43	H7
Kandos	63	B4
Kandy	43	R12
Kangaroo I.	62	C2
Kangāvar	46	D7
Kangean, Kepulauan	37	F5
Kangean Is. = Kangean, Kepulauan	37	F5
Kangiqsualujjuaq	68	C4
Kangiqsujuaq	68	B3
Kangirsuk	68	C4
Kangnŭng	35	C7
Kango	56	D2
Kangto	41	D9
Kaniapiskau ➤	68	C4
Kaniapiskau L.	69	C4
Kanin, Poluostrov	28	C5
Kanin Nos, Mys	28	C5
Kanin Pen. = Kanin, Poluostrov	28	C5
Kaniva	62	C3
Kankakee	72	D2
Kankan	55	F3
Kankendy = Xankändi	25	F6
Kanker	40	G3
Kannapolis	75	B7
Kannauj	42	F11
Kannod	43	H10
Kano	55	F6
Kanowit	37	D4
Kanoya	33	D2
Kanpetlet	41	G9
Kanpur	40	D3
Kansas □	76	F5
Kansas City, Kans., U.S.A.	77	F7
Kansas City, Mo., U.S.A.	77	F7
Kansk	30	D7
Kansu = Gansu □	34	C5
Kantang	36	C1
Kanuma	32	A6
Kanye	59	C5
Kaohsiung = Gaoxiong	35	D7
Kaokoveld	58	B2
Kaolack	55	F1
Kapan	25	F6
Kapanga	56	F4
Kapchagai = Qapshaghay	29	E8
Kapfenberg	15	E8
Kapiri Mposhi	59	A5
Kāpīsā □	45	C7
Kapit	37	D4
Kapoeta	53	H5
Kaposvár	16	E3
Kapuas ➤	37	E3
Kapuas Hulu, Pegunungan	37	D4
Kapuas Hulu Ra. = Kapuas Hulu, Pegunungan	37	D4
Kapunda	62	B2
Kapuni	64	C6
Kaputar	63	B5
Kara	28	C7
Kara Bogaz Gol, Zaliv = Garabogazköl Aylagy	29	E6
Kara Kalpak Republic □ = Karakalpakstan □	29	E6
Kara Kum	29	F6
Kara Sea	28	B8
Karabiğa	23	D6
Karabük	46	B3
Karaburun	23	E6
Karabutak = Qarabutaq	29	E7
Karacabey	23	D7
Karacasu	23	F7
Karachi	43	G5
Karad	43	L9
Karadeniz Boğazı	22	D7
Karaganda = Qaraghandy	29	E8
Karagayly	29	E8
Karaikal	43	P11
Karaikkudi	43	P11
Karaj	44	C2
Karakalpakstan □	29	E6
Karakas	29	E9
Karakelong	38	D3
Karakitang	39	D3
Karaklis = Vanadzor	25	E5
Karakoram Pass	42	B10
Karakoram Ra.	42	B10
Karalon	30	D9
Karaman	46	C3

Karamay 34 B3
Karambu 37 E5
Karamea Bight 65 D4
Karasburg 58 D3
Karasino 28 C9
Karasuk 29 D8
Karatau =
  Qarataū 29 E8
Karatau, Khrebet 29 E7
Karawanken ... 20 A5
Karazhal 29 E8
Karbalā 47 D6
Karcag 16 E5
Kardhítsa 23 E3
Karelia □ 28 C4
Karelian
  Republic □ =
  Karelia □ ... 28 C4
Kargänrüd 46 C7
Kargasok 29 D9
Kargat 29 D9
Kargil 42 B10
Kariba, L. 59 B5
Kariba Dam ... 59 B5
Kariba Gorge . 59 B5
Karibib 58 C3
Karimata,
  Kepulauan .. 37 E3
Karimata, Selat 37 E3
Karimata Is. =
  Karimata,
  Kepulauan .. 37 E3
Karimnagar ... 43 K11
Karimunjawa,
  Kepulauan .. 37 F4
Karin 49 E4
Karkaralinsk =
  Qarqaraly ... 29 E8
Karkinitska
  Zatoka 25 D3
Karkinitskiy Zaliv
  = Karkinitska
  Zatoka 25 D3
Karl-Marx-Stadt
  = Chemnitz . 15 C7
Karlovac 20 B5
Karlovo 22 C5
Karlovy Vary .. 16 C1
Karlsbad =
  Karlovy Vary 16 C1
Karlskrona ... 9 G11
Karlsruhe 14 D5
Karlstad 9 G10
Karnal 42 E10
Karnali ─➤ 40 C3
Karnaphuli Res. 41 F9
Karnataka □ .. 43 N10
Karnische Alpen 20 A4
Kärnten □ 15 E7
Karonga 57 F6
Karoonda 62 C2
Karora 53 E6
Kárpathos 23 G6
Kars 46 B5
Karsakpay 29 E7
Karshi = Qarshi 29 F7
Karsun 24 C6
Karufa 39 E4
Karungu 57 E6
Karviná 16 D4
Karwar 43 M9
Kasai ─➤ 56 E3
Kasama 57 G6
Kasanga 57 F6
Kasangulu 56 E3
Kasaragod 43 N9
Kasba L. 70 B9
Kasempa 59 A5
Kasenga 57 G5

Kāshān 44 C2
Kashi 34 C2
Kashk-e Kohneh 42 B3
Kāshmar 44 C4
Kashun Noerh =
  Gaxun Nu◄ .. 34 B5
Kasimov 24 C5
Kasiruta 39 E3
Kasongo 57 E5
Kasongo Lunda 56 F3
Kásos 23 G6
Kassalâ 53 E6
Kassel 14 C5
Kassue 39 F5
Kastamonu ... 46 B3
Kasulu 57 E6
Kasur 42 D9
Katako Kombe . 56 E4
Katamatite 63 C4
Katanga =
  Shaba □ 57 F4
Katangi 43 J11
Kateríni 23 D4
Katha 41 E11
Kathiawar 43 H7
Katihar 40 E6
Katima Mulilo . 58 B4
Katingan =
  Mendawai ─➤ 37 E4
Katiola 55 G3
Katmandu 40 D5
Katoomba 63 B5
Katowice 16 C4
Katsina 55 F6
Kattegat 9 G10
Kauai 82 G11
Kaunas 24 C1
Kaura Namoda 55 F6
Kavála 22 D5
Kaw 92 B3
Kawagoe 32 B6
Kawaguchi ... 32 B6
Kawambwa ... 57 F5
Kawardha 40 G3
Kawasaki 32 B6
Kawerau 64 C7
Kawhia Harbour 64 C6
Kawio,
  Kepulauan .. 38 D3
Kawnro 41 F12
Kawthoolei =
  Kawthule □ . 41 H11
Kawthule □ ... 41 H11
Kaya 55 F4
Kayah □ 41 H11
Kayan ─➤ 37 D5
Kayeli 39 E3
Kayes 55 F2
Kayoa 39 D3
Kayrunnera ... 62 B3
Kayseri 46 C3
Kayuagung ... 37 E2
Kazachye 31 B11
Kazakstan ■ .. 29 E7
Kazan 24 B6
Kazanlŭk 22 C5
Kazatin =
  Kozyatyn ... 17 D9
Käzerün 44 D2
Kazumba 56 F4
Kazym ─➤ 28 C7
Ké-Macina ... 55 F3
Kéa 23 F5
Kebnekaise .. 8 E11
Kebri Dehar .. 49 F3
Kecskemét ... 16 E4
Kediri 37 F4
Kédougou 55 F2
Keetmanshoop 58 D3

Keewatin □ ... 70 B10
Kefallinía 23 E3
Kefamenanu .. 39 F2
Keffi 55 G6
Keighley 11 E6
Keith 62 C3
Keith Arm 70 B7
Kekri 42 G9
Kël 30 C10
Kelang 37 D2
Kelibia 52 A1
Kellé 56 E2
Kells =
  Ceanannus
  Mor 11 E3
Kélo 53 G2
Kelowna 71 D8
Kelso 65 F3
Keluang 37 D2
Kem 28 C4
Kema 39 D3
Kemah 46 C4
Kemerovo ... 29 D9
Kemi 8 E12
Kemi älv =
  Kemijoki ─➤ . 8 E12
Kemijoki ─➤ .. 8 E12
Kemp Land .. 96 A9
Kempsey 63 B5
Kempten 14 E6
Kendal 37 F4
Kendall 63 B5
Kendari 39 E2
Kendawangan . 37 E4
Kende 55 F5
Kendrapara ... 40 G6
Kenema 55 G2
Keng Tawng .. 41 G12
Keng Tung ... 41 G12
Kenge 56 E3
Kenhardt 58 D4
Kenitra 54 B3
Kennedy
  Taungdeik .. 41 F9
Kennewick ... 80 B4
Kenogami ─➤ . 69 C2
Kenosha 72 C2
Kent Group .. 62 C4
Kent Pen. 70 B9
Kentau 29 E7
Kentucky □ .. 72 F3
Kentville 69 D4
Kenya ■ 57 D7
Kenya, Mt. ... 57 E7
Kepi 39 F5
Kerala □ 43 P10
Kerang 62 C3
Kerch 25 D4
Kerchoual 55 E5
Keren 53 E6
Kericho 57 E7
Kerinci 37 E2
Kerki 29 F7
Kérkira 23 E2
Kermadec Is. . 64 M13
Kermadec
  Trench 65 N13
Kermän 44 D4
Kermän □ ... 44 D4
Kermänshäh =
  Bäkhtarän .. 46 D6
Kerme Körfezi . 23 F6
Kerrobert 71 C9
Kerulen ─➤ ... 35 B6
Kerzaz 54 C4
Keşan 22 D6
Kestenga 28 C4
Ket ─➤ 29 D9
Keta 55 G5

Ketapang 37 E4
Ketchikan 71 C6
Kętrzyn 16 A5
Keweenaw B. . 69 D2
Key West 86 B3
Khabarovo ... 28 C7
Khabarovsk .. 31 E11
Khābūr ─➤ 46 D5
Khairpur 42 F6
Khakassia □ .. 30 D6
Khakhea 58 C4
Khalkhāl 46 C7
Khalkís 23 E4
Khalmer-Sede =
  Tazovskiy ... 28 C8
Khalmer Yu ... 28 C7
Khalturin 24 B6
Khalūf 48 C6
Khambat, G. of 43 J8
Khambhat 43 H8
Khamir 49 D3
Khānābād 45 B7
Khānaqin 46 D6
Khandwa 43 J10
Khanewal 42 D7
Khaniá 23 G5
Khanion, Kólpos 23 G4
Khankendy =
  Xankändi ... 25 F6
Khanty-
  Mansiysk ... 29 C7
Khapcheranga . 30 E9
Kharagpur ... 40 F6
Kharan Kalat . 42 E4
Kharānaq 44 C3
Kharda 43 K9
Khârga, El
  Wâhât el ... 52 C5
Khargon 43 J9
Khârk, Jazireh . 47 E7
Kharkiv 24 D4
Kharkov =
  Kharkiv 24 D4
Kharovsk 24 B5
Kharsänïya ... 47 F7
Kharta 22 D7
Khartoum = El
  Khartûm ... 53 E5
Khâsh 42 E2
Khashm el Girba 53 F6
Khaskovo 22 D5
Khatanga 30 B8
Khatanga ─➤ . 30 B8
Khaybar, Harrat 47 F5
Khed Brahma . 43 G8
Khemmarat ... 36 A3
Khenchela ... 54 A6
Khenifra 54 B3
Kherson 25 D3
Kheta ─➤ 30 B8
Khilok 30 D9
Khíos 23 E6
Khiuma =
  Hiiumaa ... 24 B1
Khiva 29 E7
Khīyāv 46 C6
Khmelnik 17 D8
Khmelnitskiy =
  Khmelnytskyy 17 D8
Khmelnytskyy . 17 D8
Khmer Rep. =
  Cambodia ■ . 36 B3
Khodoriv 17 D7
Khodzent =
  Khudzhand .. 29 E7
Khojak P. 42 D5
Kholm, Afghan. 45 B6
Kholm, Russia . 24 B3
Khomeyn 44 C2

Khon Kaen 36 A2
Khoper → 29 E5
Khóra Sfakíon . 23 G5
Khorat =
    Nakhon
    Ratchasima . 36 B2
Khorramābād . 46 D7
Khorrāmshahr . 47 E7
Khotyn 17 D8
Khouribga 54 B3
Khowai 41 E8
Khoyniki 17 C9
Khu Khan 36 B2
Khudzhand ... 29 E7
Klūüjiārī 42 D4
Khulna 41 F7
Khulna □ 41 F7
Khūr 44 C4
Khurayş 47 F7
Khūrīyā Mūrīyā,
    Jazā 'ir 48 D6
Khush 42 C3
Khushab 42 C8
Khust 17 D6
Khuzdar 42 F5
Khvor 44 C3
Khvormūj 44 D2
Khvoy 46 C6
Khyber Pass . 42 B7
Kiama 63 B5
Kiamba 38 C2
Kiangsi =
    Jiangxi □ ... 35 D6
Kiangsu =
    Jiangsu □ .. 35 C6
Kibangou 56 E2
Kibombo 57 E5
Kibondo 57 E6
Kibwesa 57 F5
Kibwezi 57 E7
Kicking Horse
    Pass 71 C8
Kidal 55 E5
Kidnappers, C. . 64 C7
Kiel 14 A6
Kiel Canal =
    Nord-Ostsee-
    Kanal → ... 14 A5
Kielce 16 C5
Kieler Bucht ... 14 A6
Kiev = Kyyiv . 17 C10
Kiffa 55 E2
Kifrī 46 D6
Kigali 57 E6
Kigoma-Ujiji . 57 F5
Kihee 62 A3
Kii-Suidō 32 C4
Kikinda 22 B3
Kikládhes ... 23 F5
Kikwit 56 E3
Kilcoy 63 A5
Kilimanjaro .. 57 E7
Kilindini 57 E7
Kilis 46 C4
Kiliya 17 F9
Kilkenny 11 E3
Kilkís 23 D4
Killarney,
    Australia 63 A5
Killarney, Ireland 11 E2
Killeen 78 D5
Killíni 23 F4
Kilmarnock ... 10 D4
Kilmore 63 C3
Kılosa 57 F7
Kilrush 11 E2
Kilwa Kivinje . 57 F7
Kimaam 39 F5
Kimba 62 B2

Kimberley 58 D4
Kimberley
    Plateau 60 D4
Kimry 24 B4
Kinabalu,
    Gunong ... 36 C5
Kindia 55 G2
Kindu 57 E5
Kineshma 24 B5
King George B. 95 G4
King George I. . 96 A4
King George Is. 69 C2
King I. = Kadan
    Kyun 36 B1
King I. 62 C3
King William I. 70 B10
King William's
    Town 59 E5
Kingaroy 63 A5
Kingoonya ... 62 B2
Kings Canyon
    National Park 82 B3
King's Lynn ... 11 E7
Kingscote 62 C2
Kingsport 75 A6
Kingston,
    Canada 69 D3
Kingston,
    Jamaica 86 C4
Kingston, N.Z. . 65 F3
Kingston South
    East 62 C2
Kingston upon
    Hull 11 E6
Kingstown ... 87 D7
Kingsville 78 F5
Kınık 23 E6
Kinkala 56 E2
Kinleith 64 C6
Kinsale 11 F2
Kinshasa 56 E3
Kinston 75 B9
Kintampo 55 G4
Kintap 37 E5
Kiparissía ... 23 F3
Kiparissiakós
    Kólpos 23 F3
Kipembawe ... 57 F6
Kipili 57 F6
Kipushi 59 A5
Kirghizia ■ =
    Kyrgyzstan ■ 29 E8
Kirghizstan =
    Kyrgyzstan ■ 29 E8
Kiri 56 E3
Kiribati ■ 64 K12
Kırıkkale 46 C3
Kirillov 24 B4
Kirin = Jilin .. 35 B7
Kiritimati 65 J15
Kirkcaldy 10 D5
Kirkcudbright . . 11 D4
Kirkee 43 K8
Kirkenes 8 E14
Kirkland Lake . 69 D2
Kırklareli 22 D6
Kirkūk 46 D6
Kirkwall 10 B5
Kirov 28 D5
Kirovabad =
    Gäncä 25 E6
Kirovakan =
    Vanadzor ... 25 E5
Kirovograd =
    Kirovohrad . 25 D3
Kirovohrad 25 D3
Kirovsk =
    Babadayhan . 29 F7
Kirovsk 28 C4

Kirsanov 24 C5
Kirşehir 46 C3
Kirteh 45 C5
Kirthar Range . 42 F5
Kiruna 8 E12
Kirundu 57 E5
Kiryū 32 A6
Kisangani 57 D5
Kisar 39 F3
Kiselevsk 29 D9
Kishanganj .. 40 D7
Kishangarh .. 42 F7
Kishinev =
    Chişinău ... 17 E9
Kishiwada ... 32 B4
Kishtwar 42 C9
Kisii 57 E6
Kisiju 57 F7
Kiska I. 71 C1
Kiskörös 16 E4
Kiskunfélegyháza
    .... 16 E4
Kiskunhalas ... 16 E4
Kislovodsk ... 25 E5
Kiso-Sammyaku 32 B5
Kissidougou .. 55 G2
Kisumu 57 E6
Kita 55 F3
Kitab 29 F7
Kitakami-
    Gawa → ... 33 G12
Kitakyūshū .. 32 C2
Kitale 57 D7
Kitchener 69 D2
Kitega = Gitega 57 E5
Kitgum 57 D6
Kíthira 23 F4
Kíthnos 23 F5
Kitikmeot □ ... 70 B9
Kittakittaooloo,
    L. 62 A2
Kitui 57 E7
Kitwe 59 A5
Kivertsi 17 C7
Kivu, L. 57 E5
Kiyev = Kyyiv . 17 C10
Kiyevskoye
    Vdkhr. =
    Kyyivske
    Vdskh. 17 C10
Kızıl Irmak → . 25 E4
Kizlyar 25 E6
Kizyl-Arvat =
    Gyzylarbat .. 29 F6
Kladno 16 C2
Klagenfurt ... 15 E8
Klaipeda 24 B1
Klamath Falls . 80 D3
Klamath Mts. .. 80 E2
Klarälven → .. 9 G10
Klatovy 16 D1
Klawer 58 E3
Klerksdorp ... 59 D5
Kletsk = Klyetsk 17 B8
Klin 28 D4
Kłodzko 16 C3
Klondike 70 B6
Klouto 55 G5
Kluane L. 70 B6
Kluczbork ... 16 C4
Klyetsk 17 B8
Knossós 23 G5
Knox Coast .. 96 A12
Knoxville 75 B6
Koartac =
    Quaqtaq 68 B4
Koba, Aru,
    Indonesia . 39 F4
Koba, Bangka,
    Indonesia ... 37 E3

Kobarid 20 A4
Kobdo = Hovd 34 B4
Kōbe 32 B4
København .. 9 G10
Koblenz 14 C4
Kobroor,
    Kepulauan .. 39 F4
Kobryn 17 B7
Kocaeli = İzmit 25 E2
Kočani 22 D4
Koch Bihar 41 D7
Kōchi 32 C3
Kochiu = Gejiu 34 D5
Kodiak 71 C4
Kodiak I. 71 C4
Koes 58 D3
Kofiau 39 E3
Koforidua ... 55 G4
Kōfu 32 B6
Kogan 63 A5
Koh-i-Bābā .. 42 B5
Kohat 42 C7
Kohima 41 E10
Kohkīlūyeh va
    Būyer
    Aḥmadī □ .. 44 D2
Kohler Ra. 96 B1
Kokand =
    Qŭqon 29 E8
Kokas 39 E4
Kokchetav =
    Kökshetaū .. 29 D7
Koko Kyunzu . 41 K9
Kokomo 72 D2
Kokonau 39 E5
Kökshetaū .. 29 D7
Koksoak → .. 68 C4
Kokstad 59 E5
Kola, Indonesia 39 F4
Kola, Russia .. 28 C4
Kola Pen. =
    Kolskiy
    Poluostrov .. 28 C4
Kolaka 39 E2
Kolar 43 N11
Kolar Gold
    Fields 43 N11
Kolayat 42 F8
Kolchugino =
    Leninsk-
    Kuznetskiy .. 29 D9
Kolda 55 F2
Kole 56 E4
Kolepom = Yos
    Sudarso,
    Pulau 39 F5
Kolguyev,
    Ostrov 28 C5
Kolhapur 43 L9
Kolín 16 C2
Köln 14 C4
Koło 16 B4
Kołobrzeg 16 A2
Kolokani 55 F3
Kolomna ... 24 B4
Kolomyya ... 17 D7
Kolonodale .. 39 E2
Kolosib 41 E9
Kolpashevo .. 29 D9
Kolpino 24 B3
Kolskiy
    Poluostrov .. 28 C4
Kolwezi 57 G5
Kolyma → ... 31 C13
Komarno ... 16 E4
Komatsu 32 A5
Komi □ 28 C6
Kommunarsk =
    Alchevsk 25 D4

Kommunizma,		
Pik	29	F8
Komodo	39	F1
Komono	56	E2
Komoran, Pulau	39	F5
Komotini	22	D5
Kompong Cham	36	B3
Kompong		
Chhnang	36	B2
Kompong Som	36	B2
Komrat =		
Comrat	17	E9
Komsomolets,		
Ostrov	30	A7
Konarhá □	42	B7
Konch	42	G11
Kondoa	57	E7
Konduga	53	F1
Köneürgench	29	E6
Kong	55	G4
Kong, Koh	36	B2
Konglu	41	D11
Kongolo	57	F5
Kongor	53	G5
Königsberg =		
Kaliningrad	24	C1
Konin	16	B4
Konjic	20	C6
Konosha	28	C5
Konotop	24	C3
Konqi He →	34	B4
Końskie	16	C5
Konstanz	14	E5
Kontagora	55	F6
Kontum	36	B3
Konya	46	C3
Konya Ovası	46	C3
Konza	57	E7
Kooloonong	62	B3
Koondrook	63	C3
Koonibba	62	B1
Koorawatha	63	B4
Kootenay L.	71	D8
Kopaonik	22	C3
Koper	20	B4
Kopeysk	29	D7
Kopi	62	B2
Koprivnica	20	A6
Kopychyntsi	17	D7
Korab	22	D3
Korça	23	D3
Korce = Korça	23	D3
Korčula	20	C6
Kordestan	46	D5
Kordestān □	46	D6
Kordofân	53	F4
Korea, North ■	35	C7
Korea, South ■	35	C7
Korea Bay	35	C7
Korea Strait	35	C7
Korets	17	C8
Korhogo	55	G3
Korim	39	E5
Korinthiakós		
Kólpos	23	E4
Kórinthos	23	F4
Kōriyama	33	G12
Korneshty =		
Corneşti	17	E9
Koro, *Ivory C.*	55	G3
Koro, *Mali*	55	F4
Korogwe	57	F7
Koroit	62	C3
Koror	38	C4
Körös →	16	E5
Korosten	17	C9
Korostyshev	17	C9
Korti	53	E5
Kortrijk	14	C2

Kos	23	F6
Kościan	16	B3
Kosciusko, Mt.	63	C4
Kosha	52	D5
K'oshih = Kashi	34	C2
Košice	16	D5
Kosovo □	22	C3
Kosovska-		
Mitrovica =		
Titova-		
Mitrovica	22	C3
Kôstî	53	F5
Kostopil	17	C8
Kostroma	24	B5
Kostrzyn	16	B2
Koszalin	16	A3
Kota	43	G9
Kota Baharu	36	C2
Kota Belud	36	C5
Kota Kinabalu	36	C5
Kota Tinggi	37	D2
Kotaagung	37	F2
Kotabaru	37	E5
Kotabumi	37	E2
Kotamobagu	39	D2
Kotawaringin	37	E4
Kotelnich	24	B6
Kotelnyy, Ostrov	31	B11
Kotka	9	F13
Kotlas	28	C5
Kotli	42	C8
Kotor	22	C2
Kotovsk	17	E9
Kotri	42	G6
Kottayam	43	Q10
Kotturu	43	M10
Kotuy →	30	B8
Kotzebue	71	B3
Kouango	56	D4
Koudougou	55	F4
Kouilou →	56	E2
Kouki	56	C3
Koula Moutou	56	E2
Koulen	36	B2
Koulikoro	55	F3
Koumra	53	G2
Kounradskiy	29	E8
Kouroussa	55	F3
Kousseri	53	F1
Koutiala	55	F3
Kovel	17	C7
Kovrov	24	B5
Kowloon	35	D6
Köyceğiz	23	F7
Koyuk	71	B3
Koyukuk →	71	B4
Kozan	46	C3
Kozáni	23	D3
Kozhikode =		
Calicut	43	P9
Kozyatyn	17	D9
Kpalimé	55	G5
Kra, Isthmus of		
= Kra, Kho		
Khot	36	B1
Kra, Kho Khot	36	B1
Kragujevac	22	B3
Krajina	20	B6
Krakatau =		
Rakata, Pulau	37	F3
Kraków	16	C4
Kraljevo	22	C3
Kramatorsk	25	D4
Kranj	20	A5
Kraśnik	16	C6
Krasnoarmeysk	29	D5
Krasnodar	25	D4
Krasnoperekopsk		
	25	D3

Krasnoselkupsk	28	C9
Krasnoturinsk	28	D7
Krasnoufimsk	29	D6
Krasnouralsk	29	D7
Krasnovodsk =		
Krasnowodsk	29	E6
Krasnowodsk	29	E6
Krasnoyarsk	30	D7
Krasnyy Luch	25	D4
Krasnyy Yar	25	D6
Kratie	36	B3
Krau	39	E6
Krefeld	14	C4
Kremen	20	B5
Kremenchug =		
Kremenchuk	24	D3
Kremenchuk	24	D3
Kremenchuksk		
Vdskh.	24	D3
Kremenets	17	C7
Krems	15	D8
Kribi	56	D1
Krichev =		
Krychaw	17	B10
Krishna →	40	K3
Krishnanagar	41	F7
Kristiansand	9	G9
Kristiansund	8	F9
Kríti	23	G5
Krivoy Rog =		
Kryvyy Rih	25	D3
Krk	20	B5
Kronprins Olav		
Kyst	96	A9
Kronshtadt	24	B2
Kroonstad	59	D5
Kropotkin,		
Irkutsk, Russia	30	D9
Kropotkin,		
Krasnodar,		
Russia	25	D5
Krosno	16	D5
Krotoszyn	16	C3
Krugersdorp	59	D5
Krung Thep =		
Bangkok	36	B2
Krupki	17	A9
Kruševac	22	C3
Krychaw	17	B10
Krymskiy		
Poluostrov =		
Krymskyy		
Pivostriv	25	D3
Krymskyy		
Pivostriv	25	D3
Kryvyy Rih	25	D3
Ksar el Boukhari	54	A5
Ksar el Kebir	54	B3
Ksar es Souk =		
Ar Rachidiya	54	B4
Kuala	37	D3
Kuala Kubu		
Baharu	37	D2
Kuala Lipis	37	D2
Kuala Lumpur	37	D2
Kuala		
Terengganu	36	C2
Kualajelai	37	E4
Kualakapuas	37	E4
Kualakurun	37	E4
Kualapembuang	37	E4
Kualasimpang	37	D1
Kuandang	39	D2
Kuangchou =		
Guangzhou	35	D6
Kuantan	37	D2
Kuba = Quba	25	E6
Kuban →	25	D4
Kucing	37	D4

Kuda	43	H7
Kudat	36	C5
Kudymkar	28	D6
Kueiyang =		
Guiyang	35	D5
Kufra Oasis = Al		
Kufrah	52	D3
Kufstein	15	E7
Küh-e 'Alijūq	44	D2
Küh-e-Hazārān	44	D4
Küh-e Sorkh	44	C4
Küh-e Taftān	45	D5
Kühak	42	F3
Kühhä-ye-		
Bashäkerd	45	E4
Kühpāyeh	44	C3
Kuito	58	A3
Kujū-San	32	C2
Kukawa	53	F1
Kukësi	22	C3
Kula	23	E7
Kulasekarappattinam		
	43	Q11
Kuldja = Yining	34	B3
Kŭlob	29	F7
Kulsary	29	E6
Kulunda	29	D8
Kulwin	62	C3
Kulyab = Kŭlob	29	F7
Kum Tekei	29	E8
Kuma →	25	E6
Kumagaya	32	A6
Kumai	37	E4
Kumamba,		
Kepulauan	39	E5
Kumamoto	32	C2
Kumanovo	22	C3
Kumara	65	E4
Kumasi	55	G4
Kumayri =		
Gyumri	25	E5
Kumba	56	D1
Kumbakonam	43	P11
Kumbarilla	63	A5
Kumo	55	F7
Kumon Bum	41	D11
Kunama	63	C4
Kungala	63	A5
Kungrad =		
Qŭnghirot	29	E6
Kungur	29	D6
Kunlong	41	F12
Kunlun Shan	34	C3
Kunming	34	D5
Kunsan	35	C7
Kunya-Urgench		
=		
Köneürgench	29	E6
Kuopio	8	F13
Kupa →	20	B6
Kupyansk	28	E4
Kuqa	34	B3
Kür →	25	E6
Kura = Kür →	25	E6
Kurashiki	32	B3
Kurayoshi	32	B3
Kŭrdzhali	22	D5
Kure	32	B3
Kurgaldzhinskiy	29	D8
Kurgan	29	D7
Kuria Maria Is.		
= Khūrīyā		
Mūrīyā, Jazā		
'ir	48	D6
Kurigram	41	E7
Kuril Is. =		
Kurilskiye		
Ostrova	31	E12
Kurilskiye		
Ostrova	31	E12

Kurmuk 53 F5
Kurnool 43 L11
Kurow 65 F4
Kurrajong ... 63 B5
Kurri Kurri 63 B5
Kursk 24 C4
Kuruktag 34 B3
Kuruman 58 D4
Kurume 32 C2
Kus Gölü 23 D6
Kuşadası 23 F6
Kushiro 32 F12
Kushtia 41 F7
Kuskokwim → 71 B3
Kuskokwim B. . 71 C3
Kustanay =
   Qostanay ... 29 D7
Kütahya 46 C2
Kutaisi 25 E5
Kutaraja =
   Banda Aceh . 36 C1
Kutch, Gulf of =
   Kachchh, Gulf
   of 43 H6
Kutch, Rann of
   = Kachchh,
   Rann of 43 G6
Kutno 16 B4
Kutu 56 E3
Kutum 53 F3
Kuujjuaq 68 C4
Kuwait = Al
   Kuwayt 47 E7
Kuwait ■ 47 E6
Kuwana 32 B5
Kuybyshev =
   Samara 24 C7
Kuybyshev ... 29 D8
Kuybyshevskoye
   Vdkhr. 24 B6
Küysanjaq ... 46 C6
Kuyumba 30 C7
Kuzey Anadolu
   Dağları 46 B3
Kuznetsk 24 C6
Kvarner 20 B5
Kvarnerič 20 B5
Kwakoegron .. 92 A2
Kwamouth 56 E3
Kwando → ... 58 B4
Kwangju 35 C7
Kwangsi-Chuang
   = Guangxi
   Zhuangzu
   Zizhiqu □ .. 35 D5
Kwangtung =
   Guangdong □ 35 D6
Kwatisore 39 E4
Kweichow =
   Guizhou □ .. 35 D5
Kwekwe 59 B5
Kwidzyn 16 B4
Kwoka 39 E4
Kyabé 53 G2
Kyabra Cr. → . 63 A3
Kyabram 63 C4
Kyancutta 62 B2
Kyangin 41 H10
Kyaukpadaung 41 G10
Kyaukpyu 41 H9
Kyaukse 41 G11
Kyle Dam 59 C6
Kyneton 63 C3
Kyō-ga-Saki .. 32 B4
Kyoga, L. ... 57 D6
Kyogle 63 A5
Kyongpyaw .. 41 J10
Kyōto 32 B4
Kyrenia 46 D3

Kyrgyzstan ■ .. 29 E8
Kystatyam 30 C10
Kytal Ktakh ... 31 C10
Kyunhla 41 F10
Kyūshū 32 C2
Kyūshū-Sanchi 32 C2
Kyustendil ... 22 C4
Kyusyur 30 B10
Kywong 63 B4
Kyyiv 17 C10
Kyyivske Vdskh. 17 C10
Kyzyl Kum 29 E7
Kyzyl-Kyya ... 29 E8
Kzyl-Orda =
   Qyzylorda ... 29 E7

L

La Albufera ... 19 C5
La Alcarria ... 19 B4
La Asunción .. 90 A6
La Banda 94 B4
La Calera 94 C2
La Carlota 94 C4
La Ceiba 85 D7
La Chaux de
   Fonds 13 C7
La Cocha 94 B3
La Coruña ... 18 A1
La Crosse 77 D9
La Dorada ... 90 B4
La Estrada ... 18 A1
La Grange ... 74 C5
La Guaira ... 90 A5
La Güera 54 D1
La Habana ... 86 B3
La Línea de la
   Concepción . 18 D3
La Mancha ... 19 C4
La Palma,
   Canary Is. .. 54 C1
La Palma,
   Panama 86 E4
La Palma del
   Condado 18 D2
La Paragua .. 90 B6
La Paz,
   Entre Ríos,
   Argentina ... 94 C5
La Paz, San Luis,
   Argentina ... 94 C3
La Paz, Bolivia . 91 G5
La Paz, Mexico . 84 C2
La Pedrera ... 90 D5
La Plata 94 D5
La Quiaca 94 A3
La Rioja 94 B3
La Rioja □ ... 19 A4
La Robla 18 A3
La Roche-sur-
   Yon 12 C3
La Rochelle .. 12 C3
La Roda 19 C4
La Romana ... 87 C6
La Serena 94 B2
La Seyne-sur-
   Mer 13 E6
La Spézia ... 20 B2
La Tortuga 87 D6
La Tuque 69 D3
La Unión 95 E2
La Urbana 90 B5
La Vega 87 C5
Labe = Elbe → 14 B5
Labé 55 F2
Labis 37 D2

Laboulaye 94 C4
Labrador, Coast
   of □ 69 C4
Lábrea 91 E6
Labuan, Pulau . 36 C5
Labuha 39 E3
Labuhanbajo .. 39 F2
Labuk, Telok .. 36 C5
Labyrinth, L. .. 62 B2
Labytnangi ... 28 C7
Lac La Biche .. 71 C8
Lac la Martre .. 70 B8
Lacanau 12 D3
Laccadive Is. =
   Lakshadweep
   Is. 26 H11
Lacepede B. ... 62 C2
Lachine 69 D3
Lachlan → ... 63 B3
Lackawanna .. 73 C6
Lacombe 71 C8
Ladakh Ra. ... 42 B10
Lādīz 45 D5
Ladoga, L. =
   Ladozhskoye
   Ozero 28 C4
Ladozhskoye
   Ozero 28 C4
Ladysmith,
   Canada 71 D7
Ladysmith,
   S. Africa 59 D5
Lae 61 B8
Lafayette 79 D7
Lafia 55 G6
Laghmān □ .. 45 C7
Laghouat 54 B5
Lagonoy Gulf . 38 B2
Lagos, Nigeria . 55 G5
Lagos, Portugal 18 D1
Laguna 94 B7
Lagunas, Chile . 91 H5
Lagunas, Peru . 90 E3
Lahad Datu .. 38 C1
Lahat 37 E2
Lahewa 37 D1
Lāhījān 46 C7
Lahn → ... 14 C4
Lahore 42 D9
Lahti 8 F13
Lahtis = Lahti . 8 F13
Laï 53 G2
Laibin 35 D5
Laidley 63 A5
Laila = Laylá . 47 G6
Lairg 10 B4
Lajere 55 F7
Lajes 94 B6
Lake Cargelligo 63 B4
Lake Charles . 79 D7
Lake City 75 D6
Lake Harbour .. 68 B4
Lake Worth ... 75 F7
Lakeland 75 E7
Lakes Entrance 63 C4
Lakewood ... 72 D5
Lakonikós
   Kólpos ... 23 F4
Lakor 39 F3
Lakota 79 G3
Lakshadweep Is. 26 H11
Lala Ghat 41 E9
Lalibela 53 F6
Lalín 18 A1
Lalitapur =
   Patan 40 D5
Lamaing 41 K11
Lamas 91 E3
Lambaréné ... 56 E2

Lambert Glacier 96 B10
Lame 55 F6
Lamego 18 B2
Lameroo 62 C3
Lamía 23 E4
Lamon Bay ... 38 B2
Lampa 91 G4
Lampedusa ... 21 G4
Lampione 21 G4
Lampung □ ... 37 F2
Lamu 57 E8
Lanai I. 82 H12
Lanak La 42 B11
Lanak'o
   Shank'ou =
   Lanak La ... 42 B11
Lanao, L. 38 C2
Lancaster, U.K. 11 D5
Lancaster,
   U.S.A. 73 D7
Lancaster Sd. . 68 A2
Lanchow =
   Lanzhou ... 35 C5
Lanciano 20 C5
Landeck 14 E6
Landes 12 D3
Landi Kotal .. 42 B7
Land's End ... 11 F4
Landshut ... 15 D7
La'nga Co ... 40 B3
Langkawi, P. . 36 C1
Langkon 36 C5
Langres 13 C6
Langres, Plateau
   de 13 C6
Langsa 36 D1
Languedoc ... 13 E5
Langzhong ... 35 C5
Lannion 12 B2
Lansdowne .. 63 B5
Lansing 72 C3
Lanusei 21 E2
Lanzarote ... 54 C2
Lanzhou ... 35 C5
Laoag 38 A2
Laoang 38 B3
Laon 13 B5
Laos ■ 36 A3
Lapa 94 B7
Laparan 38 C1
Lapland =
   Lappland ... 8 E12
Lappland ... 8 E12
Laptev Sea ... 30 B10
L'Aquila 20 C4
Lär 44 E3
Larache 54 A3
Laramie 76 E2
Larantuka ... 39 F2
Larap 38 B2
Larat 39 F4
Laredo 78 F4
Lariang 39 E1
Lárisa 23 E4
Larnaca 46 D3
Larne 11 D4
Larrimah 60 D5
Larsen Ice Shelf 96 A3
Larvik 9 G9
Laryak 29 C8
Las Anod 49 F4
Las Cruces ... 83 D9
Las Flores ... 94 D5
Las Khoreh ... 49 E4
Las Lajas 94 D2
Las Lomitas .. 94 A4
Las Palmas ... 54 C1
Las Pipinas ... 94 D5

Las Plumas

Las Plumas ... 95 E3
Las Rosas 94 C4
Las Varillas ... 94 C4
Las Vegas 82 B5
Lashio 41 F11
Lassen Pk. 80 E3
Lastoursville .. 56 E2
Lastovo 20 C6
Latacunga 90 D3
Latakia = Al
   Lādhiqīyah .. 46 D3
Latina 20 D4
Latium =
   Lazio ☐ 20 C4
Latrobe 62 D4
Latvia ■ 24 B1
Lauchhammer . 15 C7
Launceston ... 62 D4
Laurel 79 D9
Lauria 21 D5
Laurium 69 D2
Lausanne 13 C7
Laut 36 D3
Laut Kecil,
   Kepulauan .. 37 E5
Laval 12 B3
Lávrion 23 F5
Lawas 36 D5
Lawele 39 F2
Lawng Pit 41 E11
Lawrence, N.Z. 65 F3
Lawrence,
   U.S.A. 77 F7
Lawton 78 B4
Laylá 47 G6
Lazio ☐ 20 C4
Le Creusot 13 C6
Le Havre 12 B4
Le Mans 12 C4
Le Mont-St.-
   Michel 12 B3
Le Moule 87 C7
Le Puy-en-Velay 13 D5
Le Touquet-
   Paris-Plage .. 12 A4
Le Tréport 12 A4
Le Verdon-sur-
   Mer 12 D3
Leamington Spa
   = Royal
   Leamington
   Spa 11 E6
Leandro Norte
   Alem 94 B5
Leavenworth .. 77 F7
Lebak 38 C2
Lebanon ■ 46 D3
Lębork 16 A3
Lebrija 18 D2
Lebu 94 D2
Lecce 23 D2
Lecco 20 B2
Lech ↝ 14 D6
Łęczyca 16 B4
Leduc 71 C8
Leeds 11 E6
Leer 14 B4
Leeton 63 B4
Leeuwarden ... 14 B3
Leeuwin, C. ... 60 G2
Leeward Is. .. 87 C7
Leganés 18 B4
Legazpi 38 B2
Leghorn =
   Livorno 20 C3
Legionowo 16 B5
Legnago 20 B3
Legnica 16 C3
Legume 63 A5

Leh 42 B10
Leicester 11 E6
Leiden 14 B3
Leie ↝ 14 C2
Leine ↝ 14 B5
Leinster ☐ 11 E3
Leipzig 15 C7
Leiria 18 C1
Leitrim 11 D2
Leizhou Bandao 35 D6
Leksula 39 E3
Lékva Ori 23 G5
Leleque 95 E2
Léman, L. 13 C7
Lemhi Ra. 81 C7
Lena ↝ 30 B10
Leninabad =
   Khudzhand .. 29 E7
Leninakan =
   Gyumri 25 E5
Leningrad =
   Sankt-
   Peterburg ... 24 B3
Leninogorsk =
   Ridder 29 D9
Leninsk 25 D6
Leninsk-
   Kuznetskiy .. 29 D9
Lenmalu 39 E4
Lens 13 A5
Lentini 21 F5
Leoben 15 E8
Leodhas =
   Lewis 10 B3
León, Mexico .. 84 C4
León, Nic. 85 E7
León, Spain ... 18 A3
León, Montañas
   de 18 A2
Leongatha 63 C4
Léopold II, Lac
   = Mai-
   Ndombe, L. . 56 E3
Léopoldville =
   Kinshasa .. 56 E3
Leova 17 E9
Lepel = Lyepyel 24 C2
Lepikha 31 C10
Léré 53 G1
Lérida 19 B6
Lerwick 10 A6
Les Cayes 86 C5
Les Sables-
   d'Olonne ... 12 C3
Lesbos =
   Lésvos 23 E6
Leskovac 22 C3
Lesotho ■ 59 D5
Lesser Antilles . 87 D7
Lesser Sunda Is. 39 F2
Lésvos 23 E6
Leszno 16 C3
Lethbridge ... 71 D8
Leti, Kepulauan 39 F3
Leti Is. = Leti,
   Kepulauan .. 39 F3
Leticia 90 D4
Letpadan 41 J10
Letpan 41 H10
Letterkenny ... 11 D3
Leuser, G. 37 D1
Leuven 14 C3
Levádhia 23 E4
Levice 16 D4
Levin 64 D6
Lévis 69 D3
Levkás 23 E3
Levkôsia =
   Nicosia 46 D3

Levskigrad =
   Karlovo 22 C5
Lewis 10 B3
Lewisporte 69 D5
Lewiston, Idaho,
   U.S.A. 80 B5
Lewiston,
   Maine, U.S.A. 73 B10
Lexington, Ky.,
   U.S.A. 72 E3
Lexington, N.C.,
   U.S.A. 75 B7
Leyte 38 B2
Lezha 22 D2
Lhasa 34 D4
Lhazê 34 D3
Lhokkruet 36 D1
Lhokseumawe . 36 C1
Lhuntsi Dzong . 41 D8
Lianga 38 C3
Lianyungang .. 35 C6
Liaoning ☐ 35 B7
Liaoyuan 35 B7
Liard ↝ 70 B7
Libau = Liepāja 24 B1
Libenge 56 D3
Liberal 78 A3
Liberec 16 C2
Liberia 88 D2
Liberia ■ 55 G3
Lîbîya, Sahrâ' . 52 C4
Libobo, Tanjung 39 E3
Libonda 58 A4
Libourne 12 D3
Libreville 56 D1
Libya ■ 52 C2
Libyan Desert =
   Lîbîya, Sahrâ' 52 C4
Licantén 94 D2
Licata 21 F4
Lichinga 59 A7
Lichtenburg .. 59 D5
Lida 17 B7
Liechtenstein ■ 14 E5
Liège 14 C3
Liegnitz =
   Legnica 16 C3
Lienyünchiangshih
   =
   Lianyungang 35 C6
Lienz 15 E7
Liepāja 24 B1
Liffey ↝ 11 E3
Lifford 11 D3
Lightning Ridge 63 A4
Liguria ☐ 20 B2
Ligurian Sea .. 20 C2
Lijiang 34 D5
Likasi 57 G5
Lille 13 A5
Lillehammer .. 8 F10
Lilongwe 59 A6
Liloy 38 C2
Lim ↝ 20 C7
Lima, Indonesia 39 E3
Lima, Peru 91 F3
Lima, U.S.A. .. 72 D3
Lima ↝ 18 B1
Limassol 46 D3
Limay Mahuida 94 D3
Limbang 36 D5
Limbe 56 D1
Limbri 63 B5
Limburg 14 C5
Limeira 94 A7
Limerick 11 E2
Limfjorden 9 G9
Limia =
   Lima ↝ 18 B1
Límnos 23 E5

Limoeiro do
   Norte 92 D6
Limoges 12 D4
Limón 86 E3
Limousin 12 D4
Limoux 12 E5
Limpopo ↝ .. 59 D6
Limuru 57 E7
Linares, Chile . 94 D2
Linares, Mexico 84 C5
Linares, Spain . 18 C4
Linchuan 35 D6
Lincoln,
   Argentina ... 94 C4
Lincoln, N.Z. .. 65 E5
Lincoln, U.K. .. 11 E6
Lincoln, U.S.A. 77 E6
Linden 90 B7
Líndhos 23 F7
Lindi 57 F7
Lingayen 38 A2
Lingayen G. ... 38 A2
Lingen 14 B4
Lingga 37 E2
Lingga,
   Kepulauan .. 37 E2
Lingga Arch. =
   Lingga,
   Kepulauan .. 37 E2
Linguéré 55 E1
Lingyun 35 D5
Linhai 35 D7
Linhares 93 F5
Linköping 9 G11
Linosa, I. 21 G4
Lins 94 A7
Linville 63 A5
Linxia 34 C5
Linz 15 D8
Lion, G. du 13 E6
Lions, G. of =
   Lion, G. du .. 13 E6
Lipa 38 B2
Lípari 21 E5
Lípari, Is. =
   Eólie, Ís. .. 21 E5
Lipcani 17 D8
Lipetsk 24 C4
Lipkany =
   Lipcani 17 D8
Lipovets 17 D9
Lippe ↝ 14 C4
Liptrap C. 63 C4
Lira 57 D6
Liria 19 C5
Lisala 56 D4
Lisboa 18 C1
Lisbon = Lisboa 18 C1
Lisburn 11 D3
Lisburne, C. .. 71 B3
Lishui 35 D6
Lisichansk =
   Lysychansk . 25 D4
Lisieux 12 B4
Liski 24 C4
Lismore 63 A5
Lister, Mt. ... 96 B15
Liston 63 A5
Listowel 11 E2
Litang 38 C1
Litani ↝ 46 D3
Lithgow 63 B5
Lithinon, Ákra . 23 G5
Lithuania ■ ... 24 B1
Litoměřice 16 C2
Little Barrier I. . 64 B6
Little Laut Is. =
   Laut Kecil,
   Kepulauan .. 37 E5

Little
Missouri → . 76 B3
Little River 65 E5
Little Rock 79 B7
Liukang
Tenggaja ... 39 F1
Liuwa Plain .. 58 A4
Liuzhou 35 D5
Liverpool,
Australia 63 B5
Liverpool,
Canada 69 D4
Liverpool, U.K. 11 E5
Liverpool Plains 63 B5
Liverpool Ra. . 63 B5
Livingstone .. 59 B5
Livingstonia .. 57 G6
Livny 24 C4
Livorno 20 C3
Livramento .. 94 C5
Liwale 57 F7
Ljubljana 20 A5
Ljungan → .. 8 F11
Ljusnan → ... 8 F11
Llancanelo,
Salina 94 D3
Llanelli 11 F4
Llanes 18 A3
Llano Estacado 78 C2
Llanos 90 C4
Lleida = Lérida 19 B6
Llobregat → . 19 B7
Lloret de Mar . 19 B7
Lluchmayor ... 19 C7
Llullaillaco,
Volcán 94 A3
Loa → 94 A2
Lobatse 59 D5
Lobería 94 D5
Lobito 58 A2
Locarno 13 C8
Loch Garman =
Wexford 11 E3
Loches 12 C4
Lock 62 B2
Lodhran 42 E7
Lodi, Italy 20 B2
Lodi, U.S.A. ... 80 F3
Lodja 56 E4
Lodwar 57 D7
Łódź 16 C4
Lofoten 8 E10
Logan 81 E8
Logan, Mt. ... 70 B5
Logone → ... 53 F2
Logroño 19 A4
Lohardaga ... 40 F5
Loi-kaw 41 H11
Loir → 12 C3
Loire → 12 C2
Loja, Ecuador . 90 D3
Loja, Spain ... 18 D3
Loji 39 E3
Lokandu 57 E5
Lokitaung 57 D7
Lokoja 55 G6
Lokolama 56 E3
Loliondo 57 E7
Lom 22 C4
Lomami → ... 56 D4
Lomela 56 E4
Lomela → ... 56 E4
Lomié 56 D2

Lomond, L. ... 10 C4
Lompobatang . 39 F1
Łomza 16 B6
Loncoche 95 D2
Londa 43 M9
London 11 F6
Londonderry . 11 D3
Londonderry, C. 60 C4
Londonderry, I. 95 H2
Londrina 94 A6
Long Beach ... 82 D3
Long I.,
Bahamas ... 86 B4
Long I., U.S.A. . 73 D9
Long Xuyen ... 36 B3
Longford,
Australia 62 D4
Longford,
Ireland 11 E3
Longiram 37 E5
Longlac 69 D2
Longnawan ... 37 D4
Longreach ... 61 E7
Longview, Tex.,
U.S.A. 79 C6
Longview,
Wash., U.S.A. 80 B2
Lons-le-Saunier 13 C6
Lop Nor = Lop
Nur 34 B4
Lop Nur 34 B4
Lopez, C. 56 E1
Lora → 42 D4
Lora, Hamun-i- 42 E4
Lora Cr. → ... 62 A2
Lora del Río ... 18 D3
Lorain 72 D4
Loralai 42 D6
Lorca 19 D5
Lorestān □ 46 D6
Loreto 92 D4
Lorient 12 C2
Lorne 62 C3
Lorraine 13 B7
Los Alamos ... 83 C9
Los Andes 94 C2
Los Angeles,
Chile 94 D2
Los Angeles,
U.S.A. 82 C3
Los Blancos ... 94 A4
Los Hermanos . 90 A6
Los Mochis ... 84 B3
Los Roques ... 90 A5
Los Testigos .. 90 A6
Los Vilos 94 C2
Lošinj 20 B5
Lot → 12 D4
Lota 94 D2
Loubomo 56 E2
Louga 55 E1
Louis Trichardt 59 C5
Louis XIV, Pte. . 69 C3
Louisiade Arch. 61 C9
Louisiana □ ... 79 D8
Louisville 72 E3
Loulé 18 D1
Lourdes 12 E3
Louth, Australia 63 B4
Louth, U.K. ... 11 E6
Louvain =
Leuven 14 C3
Lovech 22 C5
Low Tatra =
Nízké Tatry .. 16 D4
Lowell 73 C10
Lower California
= Baja
California ... 84 A1

Lower Hutt 65 D6
Lower Saxony =
Niedersachsen □
.... 14 B5
Lower Tunguska
= Tunguska,
Nizhnyaya → 30 C6
Lowestoft 11 E7
Łowicz 16 B4
Lowyar □ 45 C7
Loxton 62 B3
Loyalty Is. =
Loyauté, Is. . 64 M11
Loyang =
Luoyang 35 C6
Loyauté, Is. ... 64 M11
Loyev = Loyew 17 C10
Loyew 17 C10
Luachimo 56 F4
Luacono 56 G4
Lualaba → ... 57 D5
Luanda 56 F2
Luangwa 59 B6
Luangwa → . 59 A6
Luanshya 59 A5
Luapula → ... 57 F5
Luarca 18 A2
Luashi 56 G4
Luau 56 G4
Lubalo 56 F3
Lubang Is. ... 38 B2
Lubbock 78 C3
Lübeck 15 B6
Lubefu 56 E4
Lubero = Luofu 57 E5
Lubin 16 C3
Lublin 17 C6
Lubuagan 38 A2
Lubuk Antu ... 37 D4
Lubuklinggau .. 37 E2
Lubuksikaping . 37 D2
Lubumbashi .. 59 A5
Lubutu 57 E5
Lucca 20 C3
Lucena, Phil. . 38 B2
Lucena, Spain . 18 D3
Lučenec 16 D4
Lucerne =
Luzern 13 C8
Lucira 58 A2
Luckenwalde .. 15 B7
Lucknow 40 D3
Lüda = Dalian . 35 C7
Lüderitz 58 D3
Ludhiana 42 D9
Ludwigsburg .. 14 D5
Ludwigshafen . 14 D5
Luebo 56 F4
Lufira → 57 F5
Lufkin 79 D6
Luga 24 B2
Lugano 13 C8
Lugansk =
Luhansk 25 D4
Lugh Ganana .. 49 G3
Lugo, Italy 20 B3
Lugo, Spain ... 18 A2
Lugoj 17 F5
Lugovoy 29 E8
Luhansk 25 D4
Luiana 58 B4
Luimneach =
Limerick 11 E2
Luís Correia .. 92 C5
Luitpold Coast . 96 B5
Luiza 56 F4
Luján 94 C4
Lukanga Swamp 59 A5
Lukenie → ... 56 E3

Lukolela 56 E3
Łuków 17 C6
Lule älv → ... 8 E12
Luleå 8 E12
Lüleburgaz ... 22 D6
Lulonga → ... 56 D3
Lulua → 56 E4
Luluabourg =
Kananga 56 F4
Lumai 58 A4
Lumbala
N'guimbo ... 58 A4
Lumsden 65 F3
Lumut, Tg. 37 E3
Lundazi 59 A6
Lundu 37 D3
Lüneburg 14 B6
Lüneburg Heath
= Lüneburger
Heide ... 14 B6
Lüneburger
Heide 14 B6
Lunéville 13 B7
Lunglei 41 F9
Luni 42 G8
Luni → 43 G7
Luninets =
Luninyets ... 17 B8
Luninyets ... 17 B8
Luofu 57 E5
Luoyang 35 C6
Luozi 56 E2
Luremo 56 F3
Lurgan 11 D3
Lusaka 59 B5
Lusambo 56 E4
Lushnja 23 D2
Lushoto 57 E7
Luta = Dalian . 35 C7
Luton 11 F6
Lutong 36 D4
Lutsk 17 C7
Lützow
Holmbukta . 96 A8
Luwuk 39 E2
Luxembourg . 13 B7
Luxembourg ■ 14 D4
Luxor = El
Uqsur 52 C5
Luza 24 A6
Luzern 13 C8
Luzhou 35 D5
Luziânia 93 F4
Luzon 38 A2
Lviv 17 D7
Lvov = Lviv ... 17 D7
Lyakhavichy .. 17 B8
Lyakhovskiye,
Ostrova ... 31 B12
Lyallpur =
Faisalabad .. 42 D8
Lydenburg ... 59 D6
Lydia 23 E7
Lyell 65 D5
Lyepyel 24 C2
Łyna → 16 A5
Lynchburg ... 73 F6
Lynd Ra. 63 A4
Lyndhurst 62 B2
Lynn Lake 71 C9
Lyon 13 D6
Lyonnais 13 D6
Lyons = Lyon . 13 D6
Lys = Leie → . 14 C2
Lysychansk ... 25 D4
Lyttelton 65 E5
Lyubertsy ... 24 B4
Lyuboml 17 C7

M

Ma'alah 47 F6
Ma'ān 47 E3
Ma'anshan ... 35 C6
Ma'arrat an
  Nu'mān 46 D4
Maas → 14 C3
Maastricht .. 13 A6
Mabrouk 55 E4
Macaé 93 G5
McAllen 78 F4
Macao =
  Macau ■ ... 35 D6
Macapá 92 B3
Macau 92 D6
Macau ■ 35 D6
M'Clintock Chan. 70 A9
McComb 79 D8
Macdonnell Ras. 60 E5
McDouall Peak 62 A1
Macdougall L. . 70 B10
Macedonia =
  Makedhonía □ 23 D4
Macedonia ■ .. 22 D3
Maceió 93 D6
Macenta 55 G3
Macerata 20 C4
Macfarlane, L. . 62 B2
Macgillycuddy's
  Reeks 11 F2
McGregor Ra. . 62 A3
Mach 42 E5
Machado =
  Jiparaná → . 91 E6
Machakos 57 E7
Machala 90 D3
Machilipatnam 40 J3
Machiques 90 A4
Machupicchu . 91 F4
Macintyre → . 63 A5
Mackay 61 E8
Mackay, L. 60 E4
Mackenzie → . 70 B6
Mackenzie City
  = Linden .. 90 B7
Mackenzie Mts. 70 B6
McKinley, Mt. . 71 B4
McKinney 79 C5
Macksville 63 B5
Maclean 63 A5
Maclear 59 E5
Macleay → .. 63 B5
McMurdo Sd. . 96 B15
Mâcon, France 13 C6
Macon, U.S.A. . 75 C6
Macondo 58 A4
McPherson Ra. 63 A5
Macquarie
  Harbour ... 62 D4
MacRobertson
  Land 96 B10
Madagali 53 F1
Madagascar ■ . 59 J9
Madā'in Sālih . 47 F4
Madama 52 D1
Madang 61 B8
Madaoua 55 F6
Madaripur 41 F8
Madauk 41 J11
Madaya 41 F11
Maddalena 20 D2
Madeira 54 B1
Madeira → .. 90 D7
Madha 43 L9
Madhya
  Pradesh □ .. 43 H10
Madikeri 43 N9

Madimba 56 E3
Madīnat ash
  Sha'b 49 E3
Madingou 56 E2
Madison 77 D10
Madiun 37 F4
Madras = Tamil
  Nadu □ 43 P10
Madras 43 N12
Madre, Laguna 78 F5
Madre, Sierra . 38 A2
Madre de
  Dios → 91 F5
Madre de Dios,
  I. 95 G1
Madre
  Occidental,
  Sierra 84 B3
Madrid 18 B4
Madurai 43 Q11
Madurantakam 43 N11
Mae Sot 36 A1
Maebashi 32 A6
Maestrazgo,
  Mts. del 19 B5
Maevatanana .. 59 H9
Mafeking =
  Mafikeng ... 59 D5
Maffra 63 C4
Mafia I. 57 F7
Mafikeng 59 D5
Mafra, Brazil . 94 B7
Mafra, Portugal 18 C1
Magadan 31 D13
Magadi 57 E7
Magallanes,
  Estrecho de . 95 G2
Magangué 90 B4
Magburaka ... 55 G2
Magdalena,
  Argentina ... 94 D5
Magdalena,
  Bolivia 91 F6
Magdalena,
  Malaysia ... 36 D5
Magdalena → 90 A4
Magdeburg ... 15 B6
Magelang 37 F4
Magellan's Str.
  = Magallanes,
  Estrecho de . 95 G2
Maggiore, L. .. 20 B2
Magnetic Pole
  (South) =
  South
  Magnetic Pole 96 A13
Magnitogorsk . 29 D6
Magosa =
  Famagusta .. 46 D3
Maguarinho, C. 92 C4
Maġusa =
  Famagusta .. 46 D3
Magwe 41 G10
Mahābād 46 C6
Mahabo 59 J8
Mahagi 57 D6
Mahajanga ... 59 H9
Mahakam → . 37 E5
Mahalapye ... 59 C5
Maḥallāt 44 C2
Mahanadi → . 40 G6
Mahanoro 59 H9
Maharashtra □ 43 J9
Mahbubnagar . 43 L10
Mahdia 52 A1
Mahenge 57 F7
Maheno 65 F4
Mahesana 43 H8
Mahia Pen. ... 64 C7

Mahilyow 17 B10
Mahón 19 C8
Mai-Ndombe, L. 56 E3
Maicurú → ... 92 C3
Maidstone 11 F7
Maiduguri ... 53 F1
Maijdi 41 F8
Maikala Ra. ... 40 G3
Main → 14 D5
Maine 12 C3
Maingkwan ... 41 D11
Mainit, L. 38 C3
Mainland,
  Orkney, U.K. 10 B5
Mainland, Shet.,
  U.K. 10 A6
Maintirano ... 59 H8
Mainz 14 C5
Maipú 94 D5
Maiquetía 90 A5
Mairabari 41 D9
Maitland,
  N.S.W.,
  Australia 63 B5
Maitland,
  S. Austral.,
  Australia 62 B2
Maizuru 32 B4
Majene 39 E1
Maji 53 G6
Majorca =
  Mallorca 19 C7
Maka 55 F2
Makale 39 E1
Makari 56 B2
Makarikari =
  Makgadikgadi
  Salt Pans ... 59 C5
Makasar =
  Ujung
  Pandang 39 F1
Makasar, Selat 39 E1
Makasar, Str. of
  = Makasar,
  Selat 39 E1
Makat 29 E6
Makedhonía □ 23 D4
Makedonija =
  Macedonia ■ 22 D3
Makeni 55 G2
Makeyevka =
  Makiyivka ... 25 D4
Makgadikgadi
  Salt Pans ... 59 C5
Makhachkala . 25 E6
Makian 39 D3
Makindu 57 E7
Makinsk 29 D8
Makiyivka 25 D4
Makkah 47 G4
Makó 16 E5
Makokou 56 D2
Makoua 56 E3
Makrai 43 H10
Makran 45 E5
Makran Coast
  Range 42 G4
Maksimkin Yar 29 D9
Mākū 46 C6
Makumbi 56 F4
Makurazaki ... 33 D2
Makurdi 55 G6
Malabang 38 C2
Malabar Coast 43 P9
Malabo = Rey
  Malabo 56 D1
Malacca, Str. of 36 D1
Maladzyechna . 17 A8
Málaga 18 D3

Malakâl 53 G5
Malakand 42 B7
Malang 37 F4
Malanje 56 F3
Mälaren 9 G11
Malargüe 94 D3
Malaryta 17 C7
Malatya 46 C4
Malawi ■ 59 A6
Malawi, L. 59 A6
Malaybalay ... 38 C3
Malāyer 46 D7
Malaysia ■ ... 36 D4
Malazgirt 46 C5
Malbooma 62 B1
Malbork 16 A4
Malden I. 65 K15
Maldives ■ ... 26 J11
Maldonado ... 94 C6
Malé Karpaty . 16 D3
Maléa, Ákra ... 23 F4
Malegaon 43 J9
Malema 59 A7
Malha 53 E4
Mali ■ 55 E4
Mali → 41 E11
Malik 39 E2
Malili 39 E2
Malin Hd. 10 D3
Malindi 57 E8
Malines =
  Mechelen ... 14 C3
Malino 39 D2
Malita 38 C3
Malkara 22 D6
Mallacoota 63 C4
Mallacoota Inlet 63 C4
Mallaig 10 C4
Mallawi 52 C5
Mallorca 19 C7
Mallow 11 E2
Malmö 9 G10
Malolos 38 B2
Malpelo 90 C2
Malta ■ 21 G5
Maltahöhe 58 C3
Maluku 39 E3
Maluku □ 39 E3
Maluku Sea =
  Molucca Sea 39 E2
Malvan 43 L8
Malvinas, Is. =
  Falkland Is. □ 95 G5
Malyn 17 C9
Malyy
  Lyakhovskiy,
  Ostrov 31 B12
Mamahatun ... 46 C5
Mamanguape . 92 D6
Mamasa 39 E1
Mamberamo → 39 E5
Mambilima Falls 57 G5
Mamburao ... 38 B2
Mamfe 55 G6
Mamoré → ... 91 F5
Mamou 55 F2
Mamuju 39 E1
Man 55 G3
Man, I. of 11 D4
Man Na 41 F11
Mana 92 A3
Manaar, G. of =
  Mannar, G. of 43 Q11
Manacapuru .. 90 D6
Manacor 19 C7
Manado 39 D2
Managua 85 E7
Manakara 59 J9
Manama = Al
  Manāmah ... 44 E2

Mananara 59 H9
Mananjary 59 J9
Manaos =
  Manaus 90 D7
Manapouri 65 F2
Manapouri, L. . 65 F2
Manas 34 B3
Manas → 41 D8
Manasir 44 E2
Manaung 41 H9
Manaus 90 D7
Manay 38 C3
Manchester,
  U.K. 11 E5
Manchester,
  U.S.A. 73 C10
Mand → 44 D3
Manda 57 G6
Mandal 9 G9
Mandalay 41 F11
Mandale =
  Mandalay ... 41 F11
Mandalī 46 D6
Mandar, Teluk . 39 E1
Mandaue 38 B2
Mandi 42 D10
Mandimba 59 A7
Mandioli 39 E3
Mandla 40 F3
Mandritsara ... 59 H9
Mandsaur 43 G9
Mandvi 43 H6
Mandya 43 N10
Mangyshlak
  Poluostrov . 29 E6
Manfalût 52 C5
Manfred 63 B3
Manfredónia .. 20 D5
Mangalia 22 C7
Mangalore 43 N9
Mangaweka ... 64 C6
Manggar 37 E3
Manggawitu .. 39 E4
Mangkalihat,
  Tanjung ... 39 D1
Mangla Dam .. 42 C8
Mangnai 34 C4
Mango 55 F5
Mangoche 59 A7
Mangole 39 E3
Mangonui 64 A5
Mangueigne .. 53 F3
Mangueira, L. da 94 C6
Mangyshlak
  Poluostrov . 29 E6
Manhuaçu 93 G5
Manica 59 B6
Manicoré 91 E6
Manicouagan →
  .... 69 D4
Manīfah 47 F7
Manihiki 65 L14
Manila 38 B2
Manila B. 38 B2
Manilla 63 B5
Manipur □ 41 E9
Manipur → ... 41 F10
Manisa 23 E6
Manitoba □ ... 71 C10
Manitoba, L. .. 71 C10
Manitowoc ... 72 B2
Manizales 90 B3
Manja 59 J8
Manjacaze ... 59 C6
Manjhand 42 G6
Manjil 46 C7
Manjra → 43 K10
Mankono 55 G3
Manly 63 B5
Manmad 43 J9
Manna 37 E2

Mannahill 62 B3
Mannar 43 Q11
Mannar, G. of . 43 Q11
Mannar I. 43 Q11
Mannheim ... 14 D5
Mannum 62 B2
Mano 55 G2
Manokwari .. 39 E4
Manombo 59 J8
Manono 57 F5
Manosque ... 13 E6
Manresa 19 B6
Mansa 57 G5
Mansel I. 68 B2
Mansfield,
  Australia .. 63 C4
Mansfield, U.K. 11 E6
Mansfield,
  U.S.A. 72 D4
Manta 90 D2
Mantalingajan,
  Mt. 36 C5
Mantes-la-Jolie 12 B4
Manthani 43 K11
Mantiqueira,
  Serra da .. 93 G5
Mántova 20 B3
Mantua =
  Mántova ... 20 B3
Manu 91 F4
Manuae 65 L15
Manuel
  Alves → ... 93 E4
Manui 39 E2
Manyara, L. .. 57 E7
Manych-Gudilo,
  Ozero 25 D5
Manyoni 57 F6
Manzai 42 C7
Manzanares .. 18 C4
Manzanillo,
  Cuba 86 B4
Manzanillo,
  Mexico 84 D4
Manzhouli ... 35 B6
Mao 53 F2
Maoke,
  Pegunungan 39 E5
Maoming 35 D6
Mapam Yumco 40 B3
Mapia,
  Kepulauan .. 39 D4
Mapuera → .. 90 D7
Maputo 59 D6
Maqnā 47 E3
Maquela do
  Zombo 56 F3
Maquinchao .. 95 E3
Mar, Serra do . 94 B7
Mar Chiquita, L. 94 C4
Mar del Plata .. 94 D5
Mar Menor .. 19 D5
Maraã 90 D5
Marabá 92 D4
Maracá, I. de .. 92 B3
Maracaibo ... 90 A4
Maracaibo, L. de 90 B4
Maracay 90 A5
Marādah 52 C2
Maradi 55 F6
Marāgheh ... 46 C6
Marāh 47 F6
Marajó, I. de . 92 C4
Maralal 57 D7
Marama 62 C3
Marampa ... 55 G2
Marand 46 C6
Maranguape .. 92 C6
Maranhão =
  São Luís 92 C5

Maranhão □ .. 92 D4
Maranoa → .. 63 A4
Marañón → .. 90 D4
Marão 59 C6
Maraş =
  Kahramanmaraş
  .... 46 C4
Maratua 39 D1
Marbella 18 D3
Marburg 14 C5
Marche 12 C4
Marchena ... 18 D3
Mardan 42 B8
Mardin 46 C5
Marek = Stanke
  Dimitrov ... 22 C4
Marek 39 E2
Margarita, I. de 90 A6
Margate 11 F7
Margelan =
  Marghilon .. 29 E8
Marghilon ... 29 E8
Mari El □ 24 B6
Mari Republic □
  = Mari El □ . 24 B6
Maria I. 62 D4
Maria van
  Diemen, C. .. 64 A5
Mariana Trench 64 H9
Marianao ... 86 B3
Ma'rib 49 D4
Maribor 20 A5
Marîdî 53 H4
Marie Byrd Land 96 B18
Marie-Galante . 87 C7
Mariecourt =
  Kangiqsujuaq 68 B3
Mariental ... 58 C3
Mariinsk 29 D9
Marília 93 G3
Marín 18 A1
Marinduque . 38 B2
Maringá 94 A6
Marion 79 A9
Mariscal
  Estigarribia .. 91 H6
Maritime Alps =
  Maritimes,
  Alpes 13 D7
Maritimes, Alpes 13 D7
Maritsa =
  Évros → ... 22 D6
Mariupol 25 D4
Marīvān 46 D6
Markazī □ ... 46 D6
Markham, Mt. . 96 C15
Marks 24 C6
Marla 62 A1
Marmagao .. 43 M8
Marmara ... 23 D6
Marmara, Sea of
  = Marmara
  Denizi 22 D7
Marmara Denizi 22 D7
Marmaris ... 23 F7
Marmolada,
  Mte. 20 A3
Marne 12 B5
Maroantsetra . 59 H9
Marondera .. 59 B6
Maroni → ... 92 A3
Maroochydore . 63 A5
Maroona 62 C3
Maroua 53 F1
Marovoay ... 59 H9
Marquesas Is. =
  Marquises, Is. 65 K17
Marquette ... 69 D2
Marquises, Is. . 65 K17

Marrakech 54 B3
Marrawah 62 D3
Marree 62 A2
Marromeu 59 B7
Marrowie Cr. → 63 B4
Marrupa 59 A7
Marsá Matrûh . 52 B4
Marsá Susah . 52 B3
Marsabit 57 D7
Marsala 21 F4
Marsden 63 B4
Marseille 13 E6
Marseilles =
  Marseille .. 13 E6
Marshall, Liberia 55 G2
Marshall, U.S.A. 79 C6
Marshall Is. ■ . 64 J12
Marshalltown . 77 D8
Martaban 41 J11
Martaban, G. of 41 J11
Martapura,
  Kalimantan,
  Indonesia ... 37 E4
Martapura,
  Sumatera,
  Indonesia ... 37 E2
Marte 53 F1
Martigny 13 C7
Martigues ... 13 E6
Martin 16 D4
Martina Franca 21 D6
Martinborough 65 D6
Martinique ■ . 87 D7
Martinique
  Passage 87 C7
Martinsville .. 75 A8
Marton 64 D6
Martos 18 D4
Marudi 37 D4
Ma'ruf 42 D5
Marugame ... 32 B3
Marulan 63 B5
Marwar 42 G8
Mary 29 F7
Maryborough =
  Port Laoise .. 11 E3
Maryborough,
  Queens.,
  Australia ... 63 A5
Maryborough,
  Vic., Australia 62 C3
Maryland □ ... 73 E7
Maryvale ... 63 A5
Marzūq 52 C1
Masaka 57 E6
Masalembo,
  Kepulauan .. 37 F4
Masalima,
  Kepulauan .. 37 F5
Masamba 39 E2
Masan 35 C7
Masandam, Ras 44 E4
Masasi 57 G7
Masaya 85 E7
Masbate 38 B2
Mascara 54 A5
Masela 39 F3
Maseru 59 D5
Mashābih ... 47 F4
Mashhad 44 B4
Mashike 32 F12
Mashkel,
  Hamun-i- .. 42 E3
Mashki Chāh .. 42 E3
Masi Manimba 56 E3
Masindi 57 D6
Masisea 91 E4
Masjed
  Soleyman ... 47 E7

Mask, L.	11	E2	Maui	82	H12	Medgidia	22	B7	Menindee L.	62	B3
Masohi	39	E3	Maulamyaing =			Mediaş	17	E7	Meningie	62	C2
Mason City	77	D8	Moulmein	41	J11	Medicine Bow			Menominee	72	B2
Masqat	45	F4	Maumere	39	F2	Ra.	81	E10	Menongue	58	A3
Massa	20	B3	Maun	58	B4	Medicine Hat	71	C8	Menorca	19	C7
Massachusetts □			Maungmagan			Medina = Al			Mentawai,		
	73	C9	Kyunzu	41	K11	Madīnah	47	F4	Kepulauan	37	E1
Massaguet	53	F2	Mauritania ■	55	D2	Medina del			Menton	13	E7
Massakory	53	F2	Mauritius ■	51	H9	Campo	18	B3	Meppel	14	B4
Massangena	59	C6	Mavinga	58	B4	Medina-Sidonia	18	D3	Merabéllou,		
Massawa =			Mawk Mai	41	G11	Medinipur	40	F6	Kólpos	23	G5
Mitsiwa	53	E6	Mawlaik	41	F10	Mediterranean			Meran =		
Massena	73	B8	Mawson Coast	96	A10	Sea	50	C5	Merano	20	A3
Massénya	53	F2	Maxixe	59	C7	Médoc	12	D3	Merano	20	A3
Massif Central	13	D5	Mayaguana	87	B5	Medveditsa ➤	24	D5	Merauke	39	F6
Massinga	59	C7	Mayagüez	87	C6	Medvezhyegorsk	28	C4	Merbein	62	B3
Masson I.	96	A11	Maydena	62	D4	Meekatharra	60	F2	Merca	49	G3
Mastanli =			Mayenne ➤	12	C3	Meerut	42	E10	Merced	82	B2
Momchilgrad	22	D5	Maykop	25	E5	Mega	53	H6	Mercedes,		
Masterton	65	D6	Mayo	70	B6	Mégara	23	F4	Buenos Aires,		
Mastuj	42	A8	Mayo L.	70	B6	Meghalaya □	41	E8	Argentina	94	C5
Mastung	42	E5	Mayon Volcano	38	B2	Mei Xian	35	D6	Mercedes,		
Masty	17	B7	Mayor I.	64	B7	Meiganga	56	C2	Corrientes,		
Masuda	32	B2	Mayu	39	D3	Meiktila	41	G10	Argentina	94	B5
Masvingo	59	C6	Mazabuka	59	B5	Meissen	15	C7	Mercedes,		
Mataboor	39	E5	Mazagán = El			Mejillones	94	A2	San Luis,		
Matad	35	B6	Jadida	54	B3	Mékambo	56	D2	Argentina	94	C3
Matadi	56	F2	Mazagão	92	C3	Mekdela	53	F6	Mercedes,		
Matagalpa	85	E7	Mazán	90	D4	Mekhtar	42	D6	Uruguay	94	C5
Matagami, L.	69	D3	Māzandarān □	44	B3	Meknès	54	B3	Merceditas	94	B2
Matak, P.	37	D3	Mazar-e Sharīf .	45	B6	Mekong ➤	36	C3	Mercer	64	B6
Matakana	63	B4	Mazara del Vallo	21	F4	Mekongga	39	E2	Mercy C.	68	B4
Matam	55	E2	Mazarredo	95	F3	Mekvari =			Meredith, C.	95	G4
Matamoros,			Mazarrón	19	D5	Kür ➤	25	E6	Merga =		
Coahuila,			Mazaruni ➤	90	B7	Melagiri Hills	43	N10	Nukheila	53	E4
Mexico	84	B4	Mazatlán	84	C3	Melaka	37	D2	Mergui Arch. =		
Matamoros,			Māzhān	44	C4	Melalap	36	C5	Myeik Kyunzu	36	B1
Tamaulipas,			Mazīnān	44	B4	Melanesia	64	K10	Mérida, Mexico	85	C7
Mexico	84	B5	Mazoe ➤	59	B6	Melbourne,			Mérida, Spain	18	C2
Ma'ṭan as Sarra	52	D3	Mazurian Lakes			Australia	63	C3	Mérida,		
Matane	69	D4	= Mazurski,			Melbourne,			Venezuela	90	B4
Matanzas	86	B3	Pojezierze	16	B5	U.S.A.	75	E7	Mérida, Cord. de	87	E5
Matapan, C. =			Mazurski,			Mélèzes ➤	68	C3	Meridian	74	C3
Taínaron, Ákra	23	F4	Pojezierze	16	B5	Melfi	53	F2	Meriruma	92	B3
Mataram	37	F5	Mazyr	17	C9	Melfort	71	C9	Merowe	53	E5
Matarani	91	G4	Mbabane	59	D6	Melilla	19	E4	Merriwa	63	B5
Mataró	19	B7	Mbaïki	56	D3	Melitopol	25	D4	Merriwagga	63	B4
Mataura	65	G3	Mbala	57	F6	Melk	15	D8	Merrygoen	63	B4
Matehuala	84	C4	Mbale	57	D6	Melo	94	C6	Mersa Fatma	49	E3
Matera	21	D6	Mbalmayo	56	D2	Melolo	39	F2	Merseburg	15	C6
Mathura	42	F10	Mbamba Bay	57	G6	Melrose	63	B4	Mersin	46	C3
Mati	38	C3	Mbandaka	56	D3	Melun	13	B5	Mersing	37	D2
Matiri Ra.	65	D5	Mbanza Congo	56	F2	Melut	53	F5	Merthyr Tydfil	11	F5
Matmata	54	B6	Mbanza Ngungu	56	F2	Melville I.	71	C9	Mértola	18	D2
Mato Grosso □	93	E3	Mbarara	57	E6	Melville I.	60	C5	Meru	57	D7
Mato Grosso,			Mbeya	57	F6	Melville Pen.	68	B2	Mesa	83	D7
Planalto do	93	F3	Mbini □	56	D2	Memba	59	G8	Meshed =		
Mato Grosso do			Mbour	55	F1	Memboro	39	F1	Mashhad	44	B4
Sul □	93	F3	Mbout	55	E2	Memel =			Meshra er Req	53	G4
Matochkin Shar	28	B6	Mbuji-Mayi	56	F4	Klaipėda	24	B1	Mesolóngion	23	E3
Matosinhos	18	B1	Mbulu	57	E7	Memmingen	14	E6	Mesopotamia =		
Matrah	45	F4	Mchinji	59	A6	Mempawah	37	D3	Al Jazirah	46	D5
Matsue	32	B3	Mead, L.	82	B5	Memphis, Tenn.,			Messina, Italy	21	E5
Matsumoto	32	A6	Mearim ➤	92	C5	U.S.A.	74	B3	Messina,		
Matsusaka	32	B5	Meaux	13	B5	Memphis, Tex.,			S. Africa	59	C6
Matsuyama	32	C3	Mecca =			U.S.A.	78	B3	Messina, Str. di	21	E5
Mattagami ➤	69	C2	Makkah	47	G4	Ménaka	55	E5	Messíni	23	F4
Mattancheri	43	Q10	Mechelen	14	C3	Menan = Chao			Messiniakós		
Matterhorn	13	D7	Mecheria	54	B4	Phraya ➤	36	B2	Kólpos	23	F4
Matthew's Ridge	90	B6	Mecklenburg	15	B6	Menate	37	E4	Mesta ➤	22	D5
Matucana	91	F3	Mecklenburger			Mendawai ➤	37	E4	Meta ➤	90	B5
Matun	42	C6	Bucht	15	A6	Mende	13	D5	Metairie	79	E8
Maturín	90	B6	Meconta	59	A7	Mendocino, C.	80	E1	Metán	94	B4
Mau Ranipur	43	G11	Medan	37	D1	Mendoza	94	C3	Metangula	59	A6
Maubeuge	13	A5	Medanosa, Pta.	95	F3	Mene Grande	90	B4	Metema	53	F6
Maude	63	B3	Medéa	54	A5	Menemen	23	E6	Methven	65	E4
Maudin Sun	41	K10	Medellín	90	B3	Menggala	37	E3	Metil	59	B7
Maués	90	D7	Mederdra	55	E1	Mengzi	34	D5	Metlakatla	71	C6
Mauganj	40	E3	Medford	80	D2	Menindee	62	B3	Mettur Dam	43	P10

Metz 13 B7
Meulaboh 37 D1
Meureudu 36 C1
Meuse → . . 13 A6
Mexiana, I. . . . 92 C4
Mexicali 84 A1
México 84 D5
México ☐ 84 D5
Mexico ■ 84 C4
Mexico, G. of . . 85 B7
Meymaneh . . . 42 B4
Mezen 28 C5
Mezen → . . . 28 C5
Mézene 13 D6
Mezökövesd . . 16 E6
Mezotür 16 E5
Mhow 43 H9
Miami 75 G7
Miami Beach . . 75 G7
Mīāndowāb . . 46 C6
Miandrivazo . . . 59 H9
Mīāneh 46 C6
Mianwali 42 C7
Miaoli 35 D7
Miarinarivo . . . 59 H9
Miass 29 D7
Michalovce . . . 17 D5
Michigan ☐ . . . 72 C3
Michigan, L. . . . 72 C2
Michipicoten . . 69 D2
Michurin 22 C6
Michurinsk 24 C5
Micronesia,
Federated
States of ■ . . 64 J10
Middelburg . . 58 E5
Middlesbrough 11 D6
Midi, Canal
du → . . . 12 E4
Midland 78 D3
Midyat 46 C5
Midzör 22 C4
Międzychód . . . 16 B2
Międzyrzec
Podlaski 17 C6
Mielec 16 C5
Miercurea Ciuc 17 E7
Mieres 18 A1
Miguel Alves . . 92 C5
Mihara 32 B3
Mikhaylovgrad 22 C4
Míkonos 23 F5
Mikura-Jima . . 32 C6
Milagro 90 D3
Milan = Milano 20 B2
Milang 62 B2
Milano 20 B2
Milâs 23 F6
Milazzo 21 E5
Mildura 62 B3
Miles 63 A5
Miletus 23 F6
Milford Haven . 11 F4
Milford Sd. . . . 65 F2
Milḥ, Baḥr al . . 47 D5
Miliana 54 C5
Mill I. 96 A12
Millau 13 D5
Millicent 62 C3
Millinocket 73 B11
Millmerran . . . 63 A5
Milne Inlet 68 A2
Mílos 23 F5
Milparinka P.O. . 62 A3
Milton 65 G3
Milton Keynes . 11 E6
Miltou 53 F2
Milwaukee 72 C2
Min Chiang → 35 D6

Min Jiang → . 35 D5
Mina Pirquitas . 94 A3
Mīnā Su'ud . . . 47 E7
Mīnā'al Aḥmadī 47 E7
Mīnāb 44 E4
Minamata 32 C2
Minas 94 C5
Minas Gerais ☐ 93 F4
Minbu 41 G10
Mindanao 38 C2
Mindanao Sea =
Bohol Sea . . 38 C2
Mindanao
Trench 38 B3
Minden 14 B5
Mindiptana . . . 39 F6
Mindoro 38 B2
Mindoro Str. . . 38 B2
Mindouli 56 E2
Mingäçevir Su
Anbarı 25 E6
Mingan 69 C4
Mingechaurskoye
Vdkhr. =
Mingäçevir Su
Anbarı 25 E6
Mingin 41 F10
Mingt'iehkaitafan
= Mintaka
Pass 42 A9
Minho =
Miño → 18 B1
Minho 18 B1
Minna 55 G6
Minneapolis . . . 77 C8
Minnedosa . . . 71 C10
Minnesota ☐ . . 77 B7
Minnipa 62 B2
Miño → 18 B1
Minorca =
Menorca 19 C7
Minore 63 B4
Minot 76 A4
Minsk 24 C2
Mińsk
Mazowiecki . 16 B5
Minto 71 B5
Minutang 41 C11
Minvoul 56 D2
Mir 53 F1
Mira 20 B4
Miraj 43 L9
Miram Shah . . 42 C7
Miranda 93 G2
Miranda de Ebro 19 A4
Miranda do
Douro 18 B2
Miri 36 D4
Mirim, L. 94 C6
Mirpur Khas . . 42 G6
Mirzapur 40 E4
Mirzapur-cum-
Vindhyachal =
Mirzapur 40 E4
Mish'āb, Ra'as
al 47 E7
Mishan 35 B8
Miskin 44 F4
Miskolc 16 D5
Misool 39 E4
Misrātah 52 B2
Misriç 46 C5
Missinaibi → . . 69 C2
Mississippi ☐ . 79 C9
Mississippi → 79 E9
Mississippi River
Delta 79 E9
Missoula 81 B6

Missouri ☐ 77 F8
Missouri → . . 77 F9
Mistassini L. . . 69 C3
Misurata =
Misrātah 52 B2
Mitchell,
Australia 63 A4
Mitchell, U.S.A. 76 D5
Mitchell → . . . 61 D7
Mitilíni 23 E6
Mito 32 A7
Mitrovica =
Titova-
Mitrovica . . . 22 C3
Mitsinjo 59 H9
Mitsiwa 53 E6
Mittagong 63 B5
Mitú 90 C4
Mitumba,
Chaîne des . . 57 F5
Mitumba Mts. =
Mitumba,
Chaîne des . . 57 F5
Mitwaba 57 F5
Mitzic 56 D2
Miyake-Jima . . 32 B6
Miyako 33 G12
Miyakonojō . . . 32 D2
Miyazaki 32 D2
Miyet, Bahr el =
Dead Sea . . . 47 E3
Mizal 47 G6
Mizdah 52 B1
Mizoram ☐ . . . 41 F9
Mjøsa 8 F10
Mladá Boleslav 16 C2
Mława 16 B5
Mljet 20 C6
Mmabatho . . . 59 D5
Moa 39 F3
Moabi 56 E2
Moalie Park . . 62 A3
Moba 57 F5
Mobaye 56 D4
Mobayi 56 D4
Mobile 74 D3
Mobutu Sese
Seko, L. =
Albert L. . . . 57 D6
Moçambique . . 59 H8
Moçâmedes =
Namibe 58 B2
Mochudi 59 C5
Mocimboa da
Praia 57 G8
Mocoa 90 C3
Mocuba 59 B7
Modane 13 D7
Módena 20 B3
Modesto 82 B2
Módica 21 F5
Moe 63 C4
Moengo 92 A3
Mogadishu =
Muqdisho . . . 49 G4
Mogador =
Essaouira . . . 54 B3
Mogami → . . . 33 G12
Mogaung 41 E11
Mogi das Cruzes 94 A7
Mogi-Mirim . . . 94 A7
Mogilev =
Mahilyow . . . 17 B10
Mogilev-
Podolskiy =
Mohyliv-
Podilskyy . . . 17 D8
Mogoi 39 E4
Mogok 41 F11

Mohács 16 F4
Moḥammadābād
. . . . 44 B4
Mohoro 57 F7
Mohyliv-
Podilskyy . . . 17 D8
Mointy 29 E8
Moisie 69 C4
Moisie → 69 C4
Moïssala 53 G2
Mojave Desert . 82 C4
Mokai 64 C6
Mokokchung . . 41 D10
Mokra Gora . . 22 C3
Molchanovo . . 29 D9
Moldavia ■ =
Moldova ■ . . 17 E9
Molde 8 F9
Moldova ■ . . . 17 E9
Moldoveana . . 17 F7
Molepolole . . . 59 C5
Molfetta 20 D6
Moline 77 E9
Moliro 57 F6
Mollendo 91 G4
Molodechno =
Maladzyechna 17 A8
Molokai 82 H12
Molong 63 B4
Molopo → . . . 58 D4
Molotov = Perm 29 D6
Moloundou . . . 56 D3
Molu 39 F4
Molucca Sea . . 39 E2
Moluccas =
Maluku 39 E3
Moma 59 B7
Mombasa 57 E7
Momchilgrad . . 22 D5
Mompós 90 B4
Mon → 41 G10
Mona, Canal de
la 87 C6
Monaco ■ . . . 13 E7
Monahans 78 D2
Monastir =
Bitola 22 D3
Monastir 52 A1
Moncayo, Sierra
del 19 B5
Mönchengladbach
. . . . 14 C4
Monchique . . . 18 D1
Monclova 84 B4
Mondego → . . 18 B1
Mondeodo . . . 39 E2
Mondovì 20 B1
Monforte de
Lemos 18 A2
Mong Hsu . . . 41 G12
Mong Kung . . 41 G11
Mong Nai 41 G11
Mong Pawk . . 41 F12
Mong Ton . . . 41 G12
Mong Wa 41 G13
Mong Yai 41 F12
Mongalla 53 G5
Monghyr =
Munger 40 E6
Mongibello =
Etna 21 F5
Mongo 53 F2
Mongolia ■ . . . 35 B5
Mongororo . . . 53 F3
Mongu 58 B4
Monkoto 56 E4
Monópoli 21 D6
Monqoumba . . 56 D3

Monroe, *La.,*
  U.S.A. 79 C7
Monroe, *N.C.,*
  U.S.A. 75 B7
Monrovia 55 G2
Mons 14 C2
Monse 39 E2
Mont-de-Marsan 12 E3
Mont-St.-Michel,
  Le = Le Mont-
  St.-Michel ... 12 B3
Montalbán 19 B5
Montana □ ... 81 B9
Montargis ... 13 C5
Montauban ... 12 D4
Montbéliard .. 13 C7
Montceau-les-
  Mines 13 C6
Monte Alegre . 92 C3
Monte Azul .. 93 F5
Monte-Carlo .. 20 C1
Monte Caseros 94 C5
Monte Comán . 94 C3
Monte Santu, C.
  di 21 D2
Montecristi ... 90 D2
Montecristo .. 20 C3
Montego Bay . 86 C4
Montélimar ... 13 D6
Montemorelos . 84 B5
Montenegro □ 22 C2
Montepuez 59 A7
Monterey 82 B2
Montería 90 B3
Monterrey 84 B4
Montes Claros 93 F5
Montesilvano
  Marina 20 C5
Montevideo ... 94 C5
Montgomery =
  Sahiwal ... 42 D8
Montgomery .. 74 C4
Montijo 18 C2
Montilla 18 D3
Montluçon ... 13 C5
Montmorillon . 12 C4
Montoro 18 C3
Montpellier ... 13 E5
Montréal 69 D3
Montreux 13 C7
Montrose, *U.K.* 10 C5
Montrose,
  U.S.A. 83 A9
Montserrat ■ . 87 C7
Monveda 56 D4
Monywa 41 F10
Monza 20 B2
Monze 59 B5
Monze, C. 43 G5
Monzón 19 B6
Moolawatana . 62 A2
Moomin Cr. → 63 A4
Moonie 63 A5
Moonie → ... 63 A4
Moonta 62 B2
Mooroopna ... 63 C4
Moose Jaw ... 71 C9
Moosomin ... 71 C9
Moosonee 69 C2
Mopeia Velha . 59 B7
Mopti 55 F4
Moquegua 91 G4
Mora 8 F10
Moradabad .. 42 E11
Morafenobe .. 59 H8
Moramanga ... 59 H9
Moratuwa ... 43 R11
Morava →,
  Serbia, Yug. . 22 B3

Morava →,
  Slovak Rep. . 16 D3
Moravian Hts. =
  Ceskomoravská
  Vrchovina ... 16 D2
Morawhanna . 90 B7
Moray Firth .. 10 C5
Morden 71 D10
Mordovian
  Republic □ =
  Mordvinia □ 24 C5
Mordvinia □ .. 24 C5
Morea 62 C3
Moree 63 A4
Morelia 84 D4
Morella 19 B5
Morena, Sierra 18 C3
Moreton I. 63 A5
Morgan 62 B2
Morgan City .. 79 E8
Morioka 33 G12
Morlaix 12 B2
Mornington .. 63 C4
Mornington, I. . 95 F1
Moro G. 38 C2
Morocco ■ ... 54 B3
Morococha ... 91 F3
Morogoro 57 F7
Morombe 59 J8
Morón 86 B4
Mörön → 35 B6
Morón de la
  Frontera 18 D3
Morondava .. 59 J8
Morotai 39 D3
Moroto 57 D6
Morphou 46 D3
Morrinhos ... 93 F4
Morrinsville .. 64 B6
Morristown .. 75 A6
Morrumbene .. 59 C7
Morshansk ... 24 C5
Morteros 94 C4
Mortes, R.
  das → 93 E3
Mortlake 62 C3
Morundah ... 63 B4
Moruya 63 C5
Morvan 13 C6
Morven 63 A4
Morwell 63 C4
Moscos Is. ... 41 L11
Moscow =
  Moskva 24 B4
Moscow 80 B5
Mosel → 13 A7
Moselle =
  Mosel → ... 13 A7
Mosgiel 65 F4
Moshi 57 E7
Moskva 24 B4
Moskva → ... 24 B4
Moson-
  magyaróvár . 16 E3
Mosquera ... 90 C3
Moss Vale ... 63 B5
Mossaka 56 E3
Mossburn ... 65 F3
Mosselbaai ... 58 E4
Mossendjo ... 56 E2
Mossgiel 63 B3
Mossoró 92 D6
Mossuril 59 G8
Most 16 C1
Mostaganem .. 54 A5
Mostar 20 C6
Mostardas ... 94 C6
Mostiska =
  Mostyska ... 17 D6

Mosty = Masty 17 B7
Mostyska 17 D6
Mosul = Al
  Mawşil ... 46 C5
Motihari 40 D5
Motril 18 D4
Motueka 65 D5
Motueka → .. 65 D5
Mouanda 56 E2
Moúdhros ... 23 E5
Moudjeria 55 E2
Mouila 56 E2
Moulamein ... 63 C3
Moulins 13 C5
Moulmein ... 41 J11
Moundou 53 G2
Mount Barker . 62 C2
Mount Darwin . 59 B6
Mount Eba ... 62 B2
Mount Gambier 62 C3
Mount Hope,
  N.S.W.,
  Australia 63 B4
Mount Hope,
  S. Austral.,
  Australia 62 B2
Mount Howitt . 62 A3
Mount Isa ... 61 E6
Mount Lofty Ra. 62 B2
Mount McKinley
  National Park 71 B4
Mount Margaret 63 A3
Mount
  Maunganui .. 64 B7
Mount Olympus
  = Uludağ .. 23 D7
Mount Perry . 63 A5
Mount Vernon . 73 D9
Mountain View 82 B1
Moura, *Brazil* . 90 D6
Moura, *Portugal* 18 C2
Mourdi,
  Dépression du 53 E3
Mourdiah ... 55 F3
Moussoro ... 53 F2
Moutohara ... 64 C7
Moutong 39 D2
Moyale 57 D7
Moyamba 55 G2
Moyen Atlas . 54 B3
Moyo 37 F5
Moyyero → .. 30 C8
Mozambique =
  Moçambique 59 H8
Mozambique ■ 59 B7
Mozambique
  Chan. 59 H8
Mozdok 25 E5
Mozyr = Mazyr 17 C9
Mpanda 57 F6
Mpika 59 A6
Mpwapwa ... 57 F7
Msaken 52 A1
Msoro 59 A6
Mu Us Shamo . 35 C5
Muaná 92 C4
Muar 37 D2
Muarabungo .. 37 E2
Muaraenim ... 37 E2
Muarajuloi ... 37 E4
Muarakaman . 37 E5
Muaratebo ... 37 E2
Muaratembesi . 37 E2
Muaratewe ... 37 E4
Mubarraz = Al
  Mubarraz ... 47 F7
Mubende 57 D6
Mubi 53 F1
Muckadilla ... 63 A4

Muconda 56 G4
Mucuri 93 F6
Mudanjiang .. 35 B7
Mudanya ... 23 D7
Mudgee 63 B4
Mufulira 59 A5
Muğla 23 F7
Mugu 40 C4
Muhammad Qol 52 D6
Mühlhausen . 14 C6
Mühlig Hofmann
  fjell 96 B7
Mukacheve .. 17 D6
Mukachevo =
  Mukacheve .. 17 D6
Mukah 37 D4
Mukden =
  Shenyang ... 35 B7
Mukomuko ... 37 E2
Muktsar 42 D9
Mukur 42 C5
Mula 19 C5
Mulchén 94 D2
Mulde → 15 C7
Mulgathing ... 62 B1
Mulgrave 69 D4
Mulhacén ... 18 D4
Mulhouse 13 C7
Mull 10 C4
Mullengudgery 63 B4
Muller,
  Pegunungan 37 D4
Mullingar ... 11 E3
Mullumbimby . 63 A5
Multan 42 D7
Mulwala 63 C4
Mumbaï =
  Bombay 43 K8
Mumbwa 59 A5
Muna 39 F2
München 15 D6
Munchen-
  Gladbach =
  Mönchengladbach
  .... 14 C4
Muncie 72 D3
Mundala 39 E6
Münden 14 C5
Mundo Novo .. 93 E5
Mungallala ... 63 A4
Mungallala
  Cr. → 63 A4
Mungbere ... 57 D5
Munger 40 E6
Mungindi ... 63 A4
Munhango ... 58 A3
Munich =
  München ... 15 D6
Muñoz Gamero,
  Pen. 95 G2
Münster 14 C4
Munster □ ... 11 E2
Muntok 37 E3
Mupa 58 B3
Muqdisho ... 49 G4
Murallón,
  Cuerro 95 F2
Murang'a ... 57 E7
Murashi 24 B6
Muratlı 22 D6
Murchison → . 60 F1
Murchison, Mt. 96 B15
Murchison Falls
  = Kabarega
  Falls 57 D6
Murcia 19 C5
Murcia □ 19 D5
Mureş → 16 E5

Mureşul =
Mureş ⇢ ... 16 E5
Murfreesboro . 74 B4
Murgab =
Murghob ... 29 F8
Murghob 29 F8
Murgon ... 63 A5
Müritz-see 15 B7
Murmansk 28 C4
Murom 24 B5
Muroran 32 F12
Muroto-Misaki . 32 C4
Murray ⇢ 62 C2
Murray Bridge . 62 C2
Murree 42 C0
Murrumbidgee ⇢
.... 62 B3
Murrumburrah 63 B4
Murrurundi ... 63 B5
Murtoa 62 C3
Murwara 40 F3
Murwillumbah . 63 A5
Mürzzuschlag . 15 E8
Muş 46 C5
Mûsa, G. 47 E3
Musa Khel .. 42 D6
Mûsá Qal'eh .. 42 C4
Musaffargarh .. 42 D7
Musala, Bulgaria 22 C4
Musala,
Indonesia ... 37 D1
Musay'ïd 44 E2
Muscat =
Masqat ... 45 F4
Muscat & Oman
= Oman ■ .. 48 C6
Muscatine 77 E9
Musgrave Ras. 60 F5
Mushie 56 E3
Musi ⇢ 37 E2
Muskogee 79 B6
Musmar 53 E6
Musoma 57 D6
Mussoorie .. 42 D11
Mustafakemalpaşa
.... 23 D7
Mustang 40 C4
Musters, L. .. 95 F3
Muswellbrook . 63 B5
Mût, Egypt .. 52 C4
Mut, Turkey ... 46 C3
Mutare 59 B6
Muting 39 F6
Mutoray ... 30 C8
Muxima 56 F2
Muynak 29 E6
Muzaffarabad . 42 B8
Muzaffarnagar . 42 E10
Muzaffarpur ... 40 D5
Muzhi 28 C7
Muztag 34 C3
Mvuma 59 B6
Mwanza,
Tanzania 57 E6
Mwanza, Zaïre . 57 F5
Mweka 56 E4
Mwenezi 59 C6
Mwenga 57 E5
Mweru, L. 57 F5
Mwinilunga .. 58 A4
My Tho 36 B3
Myanaung 41 H10
Myanmar =
Burma ■ .. 41 G11
Myaungmya .. 41 J10
Mycenæ 23 F4
Myeik Kyunzu . 36 B1
Myingyan 41 G10
Myitkyina 41 E11

Mykolayiv 25 D3
Mymensingh .. 41 E8
Mysia 23 E6
Mysore =
Karnataka □ . 43 N10
Mysore 43 N10
Myszków 16 C4
Mytishchi 24 B4

N

Nà Hearadh =
Harris 10 C3
Naab ⇢ 15 D7
Naberezhnyye
Chelny 29 D6
Nabeul 52 A1
Nabire 39 E5
Nablus =
Nâbulus 46 D3
Nâbulus 46 D3
Nachingwea .. 57 G7
Nackara 62 B2
Nacogdoches . 79 D6
Nacozari 84 A3
Nadiad 43 H8
Nadūshan 44 C3
Nadvirna 17 D7
Nadvornaya =
Nadvirna ... 17 D7
Nadym 28 C8
Nadym ⇢ 28 C8
Nafada 55 F7
Nafūd ad Dahy 47 G6
Nafud Desert =
An Nafūd ... 47 E5
Naga 38 B2
Nagaland □ .. 41 E10
Nagano 32 A6
Nagaoka 33 G11
Nagappattinam 43 P11
Nagar Parkar .. 43 G7
Nagasaki 32 C1
Nagaur 42 F8
Nagercoil 43 Q10
Nagïneh 44 C4
Nagoya 32 B5
Nagpur 43 J11
Nagykanizsa .. 16 E3
Nagykörös ... 16 E4
Nahanni Butte . 70 B7
Nahāvand 46 D7
Nä'ifah 48 D5
Nain, Canada .. 68 C4
Nā'ïn, Iran .. 44 C3
Nairn 10 C5
Nairobi 57 E7
Naivasha 57 E7
Najafābād 44 C2
Najd 47 F5
Najibabad ... 42 E11
Nakamura ... 32 C3
Nakfa 53 E6
Nakhichevan =
Naxçıvan .. 25 F6
Nakhichevan
Republic □ =
Naxçıvan □ . 25 F6
Nakhodka 31 E11
Nakhon Phanom 36 A2
Nakhon
Ratchasima . 36 B2
Nakhon Sawan 36 A2
Nakhon Si
Thammarat . 36 C2
Nakina 69 C2

Nakuru 57 E7
Nal ⇢ 42 G4
Nalchik 25 E5
Nalgonda 43 L11
Nallamalai Hills 43 M11
Nālūt 52 B1
Nam Co 34 C4
Nam-Phan ... 36 B3
Namacurra ... 59 B7
Namak,
Daryācheh-ye 44 C3
Namak, Kavir-e 44 C4
Namaland ... 58 C3
Namangan ... 29 E8
Namapa 59 A7
Namber 39 E4
Nambour 63 A5
Nambucca
Heads 63 B5
Nameh 37 D5
Namib Desert =
Namibwoestyn
.... 58 C2
Namibe 58 B2
Namibia ■ .. 58 C3
Namibwoestyn 58 C2
Namlea 39 E3
Namoi ⇢ 63 B4
Nampa 80 D5
Nampula 59 B7
Namrole 39 E3
Namse Shankou 40 C4
Namtu 41 F11
Namur 14 C3
Namutoni ... 58 B3
Namwala 59 B5
Nanaimo 71 D7
Nanango 63 A5
Nanao 32 A5
Nanchang 35 D6
Nanching =
Nanjing ... 35 C6
Nanchong 35 C5
Nancy 13 B7
Nanda Devi .. 42 D11
Nanded 43 K10
Nandewar Ra. . 63 B5
Nandurbar ... 43 J9
Nandyal 43 M11
Nanga-Eboko .. 56 D2
Nanga Parbat . 42 B9
Nangapinoh .. 37 E4
Nangarhár □ .. 42 B7
Nangatayap ... 37 E4
Nanjing 35 C6
Nanking =
Nanjing ... 35 C6
Nanning 35 D5
Nanping 35 D6
Nansei-Shotō =
Ryūkyū-rettō 35 D7
Nantes 12 C3
Nanuque 93 F5
Nanusa,
Kepulauan .. 38 D3
Nanyang 35 C6
Nanyuki 57 D7
Nao, C. de la . 19 C6
Naoetsu 32 A6
Napa 80 F2
Napier 64 C7
Naples = Nápoli 21 D5
Naples 75 F7
Napo ⇢ 90 D4
Nápoli 21 D5
Nappa Merrie . 62 A3
Nara, Japan .. 32 B4
Nara, Mali ... 55 E3
Naracoorte ... 62 C3

Naradhan 63 B4
Narasapur 40 J3
Narathiwat ... 36 C2
Narayanganj .. 41 F8
Narayanpet .. 43 L10
Narbonne ... 13 E5
Nardò 23 D2
Narew ⇢ 16 B5
Narin 42 A6
Narmada ⇢ .. 43 J8
Narooma 63 C5
Narrabri 63 B4
Narran ⇢ 63 A4
Narrandera ... 63 B4
Narromine ... 63 B4
Narsimhapur .. 43 H11
Narva 24 B2
Narvik 8 E11
Naryan-Mar .. 28 C6
Narylico 62 A3
Narym 29 D9
Narymskoye .. 29 E9
Naryn 29 E8
Nasarawa 55 G6
Naseby 65 F4
Naser, Buheirat
en 52 D5
Nashville 74 A4
Nasik 43 K8
Nasirabad .. 42 F9
Nassau 86 A4
Nassau, B. .. 95 H3
Nasser, L. =
Naser,
Buheirat en . 52 D5
Nat Kyizin 41 K11
Nata 59 C5
Natagaima ... 90 C3
Natal, Brazil .. 92 D6
Natal, Indonesia 37 D1
Naţanz 44 C2
Natashquan .. 69 C4
Natashquan ⇢ 69 C4
Natchez 79 D8
Nathalia 63 C4
Nathdwara ... 43 G8
Natitingou ... 55 F5
Natron, L. .. 57 E7
Natuna Besar,
Kepulauan .. 37 D3
Natuna Is. =
Natuna Besar,
Kepulauan .. 37 D3
Natuna Selatan,
Kepulauan .. 37 D3
Naturaliste, C. . 62 D4
Naumburg ... 15 C6
Nauru ■ 64 K11
Naushahra =
Nowshera .. 42 B8
Nauta 90 D4
Nautanwa 40 D4
Navahrudak ... 17 B7
Navalmoral de
la Mata 18 C3
Navarino, I. .. 95 H3
Navarra □ ... 19 A5
Năvodari ... 22 B7
Navoi = Nawoiy 29 E7
Navojoa 84 B3
Návpaktos ... 23 E3
Návplion ... 23 F4
Navsari 43 J8
Nawabshah ... 42 F6
Nawakot 40 D5
Nawalgarh ... 42 F9
Nawāsif, Harrat 47 G5
Nawoiy 29 E7
Naxçıvan 25 F6

Naxçıvan □ ... 25 F6
Náxos 23 F5
Nǎy Band 44 E3
Nazas ⇢ 84 B4
Nazilli 23 F7
Nazir Hat 41 F8
Ncheu 59 A6
Ndalatando ... 56 F2
Ndélé 56 C4
Ndendé 56 E2
Ndjamena 53 F1
Ndjolé 56 E2
Ndola 59 A5
Neagh, Lough . 11 D3
Near Is. 71 C1
Neath 11 F5
Nebine Cr. ⇢ . 63 A4
Nebitdag 29 F6
Nebraska □ ... 76 E5
Nébrodi, Monti 21 F5
Neckar ⇢ 14 D5
Necochea 94 D5
Neemuch =
  Nimach 43 G9
Neepawa 71 C10
Nefta 54 B6
Neftçala 46 C7
Negapatam =
  Nagappattinam
  .... 43 P11
Negele 49 F2
Negombo 43 R11
Negotin 22 B4
Negra Pt. 38 A2
Negrais, C. =
  Maudin Sun . 41 K10
Negro ⇢,
  Argentina ... 95 E4
Negro ⇢, Brazil 90 D6
Negro ⇢,
  Uruguay 94 C5
Negros 38 C2
Nehbandān ... 45 D5
Nei Monggol
  Zizhiqu □ .. 35 B6
Neijiang 35 D5
Neiva 90 C3
Nejd = Najd .. 47 F5
Nekemte 53 G6
Nellore 43 M11
Nelson, Canada 71 D8
Nelson, N.Z. .. 65 D5
Nelson ⇢ 71 C10
Nelson, C. ... 62 C3
Nelson, Estrecho 95 G2
Nelspruit 59 D6
Néma 55 E3
Neman ⇢ 24 B1
Nemunas =
  Neman ⇢ .. 24 B1
Nemuro 32 F13
Nemuro-Kaikyō 32 F13
Nenagh 11 E2
Nenana 71 B5
Nenjiang 35 B7
Nepal ■ 40 D5
Nepalganj 40 C3
Neretva ⇢ ... 20 C6
Ness, L. 10 C4
Nesterov 17 C6
Nesvizh =
  Nyasvizh 17 B8
Netherlands ■ . 14 B3
Netherlands
  Antilles ■ ... 87 D6
Nettilling L. .. 68 B3
Neubrandenburg
  .... 15 B7
Neuchâtel 13 C7

Neuchâtel, Lac
  de 13 C7
Neumünster .. 14 A5
Neunkirchen .. 14 D4
Neuquén 94 D3
Neuruppin ... 15 B7
Neustrelitz ... 15 B7
Neva ⇢ 24 B3
Nevada □ 80 F5
Nevada, Sierra,
  Spain 18 D4
Nevada, Sierra,
  U.S.A. 80 F3
Nevers 13 C5
Nevertire 63 B4
Nevinnomyssk 25 E5
Nevis 87 C7
Nevşehir 46 C3
New Amsterdam 90 B7
New Angledool 63 A4
New Bedford .. 73 D10
New Bern 75 B9
New Brighton . 65 E5
New Britain,
  Papua N. G. . 64 K10
New Britain,
  U.S.A. 73 D9
New
  Brunswick □ 69 D4
New
  Caledonia ■ . 64 M11
New Delhi 42 E10
New England
  Ra. 63 B5
New Glasgow . 69 D4
New Guinea .. 64 K9
New
  Hampshire □ 73 C10
New Haven ... 73 D9
New Hebrides =
  Vanuatu ■ .. 64 L11
New Ireland .. 64 K10
New Jersey □ . 73 E9
New London .. 73 D9
New Mexico □ 83 C9
New Norfolk .. 62 D4
New Orleans .. 79 E8
New Plymouth 64 C6
New Providence 86 A4
New Siberian Is.
  =
  Novosibirskiye
  Ostrova 31 B12
New South
  Wales □ 63 B4
New
  Westminster 71 D7
New York □ ... 73 C8
New York City . 73 D9
New Zealand ■ 64 D7
Newala 57 G7
Newark 73 D8
Newburgh 73 D8
Newbury 11 F6
Newcastle,
  Australia 63 B5
Newcastle,
  S. Africa 59 D5
Newcastle-upon-
  Tyne 11 D6
Newfoundland □
  .... 69 C5
Newman 60 E2
Newport,
  I. of W., U.K. 11 F6
Newport, Newp.,
  U.K. 11 F5
Newport, U.S.A. 73 D10
Newport News 73 F7

Newquay 11 F4
Newry 11 D3
Newton Boyd . 63 A5
Neya 24 B5
Neyrīz 44 D3
Neyshābūr 44 B4
Nezhin = Nizhyn 24 C3
Ngabang 37 D3
Ngabordamlu,
  Tanjung ... 39 F4
Ngami
  Depression .. 58 C4
Nganglong
  Kangri 40 A3
Ngaoundéré .. 56 C2
Ngapara 65 F4
Ngoring Hu .. 34 C4
Ngudu 57 E6
Nguigmi 53 F1
Nguru 55 F7
Nha Trang 36 B3
Nhill 62 C3
Niafounké 55 E4
Niagara Falls,
  Canada 69 D3
Niagara Falls,
  U.S.A. 73 C6
Niah 37 D4
Niamey 55 F5
Niangara 57 D5
Nias 37 D1
Nicaragua ■ .. 85 E7
Nicaragua, L. de 85 E7
Nicastro 21 E6
Nice 13 E7
Nichinan 33 D2
Nicobar Is. 27 J13
Nicosia 46 D3
Nicoya, Pen. de 85 F7
Niedersachsen □
  .... 14 B5
Niemen =
  Neman ⇢ .. 24 B1
Nienburg 14 B5
Nieuw
  Amsterdam . 92 A2
Nieuw Nickerie 92 A2
Niğde 46 C3
Niger ■ 55 E6
Niger ⇢ 55 G6
Nigeria ■ 55 G6
Nightcaps 65 F3
Nii-Jima 32 B6
Niigata 33 G11
Niihama 32 C3
Niihau 82 H11
Nijmegen 14 C3
Nikiniki 39 F2
Nikki 55 G5
Nikolayev =
  Mykolayiv .. 25 D3
Nikolayevsk ... 24 C6
Nikopol 25 D3
Nīkshahr 45 E5
Nikšić 22 C2
Nîl, Nahr en ⇢ 52 B5
Nîl el Abyad ⇢ 53 E5
Nîl el Azraq ⇢ 53 E5
Nile = Nîl, Nahr
  en ⇢ 52 B5
Nimach 43 G9
Nîmes 13 E6
Nimfaíon, Ákra
  = Pínnes,
  Ákra 23 D5
Nimmitabel .. 63 C4
Nīmrūz □ 45 D5
Nimule 57 D6
Nīnawá 46 C5

Nindigully 63 A4
Nineveh =
  Nīnawá 46 C5
Ningbo 35 D7
Ningde 35 D6
Ningpo =
  Ningbo 35 D7
Ningsia Hui A.R.
  = Ningxia
  Huizu
  Zizhiqu □ ... 35 C5
Ningxia Huizu
  Zizhiqu □ .. 35 C5
Niobrara ⇢ .. 76 D5
Nioro du Sahel 55 E3
Niort 12 C3
Nipawin 71 C9
Nipigon, L. 69 D2
Niquelândia .. 93 E4
Nirmal 43 K11
Nirmali 40 D6
Niš 22 C3
Nişāb, Si. Arabia 47 E6
Nişāb, Yemen . 49 E4
Nishinomiya . 32 B4
Nistru =
  Dnister ⇢ .. 17 E10
Niţa' 47 F7
Niterói 93 G5
Nitra 16 D4
Nitra ⇢ 16 E4
Niue 65 L14
Niut 37 D4
Nivernais 13 C5
Nizamabad ... 43 K11
Nizamghat ... 41 C10
Nizhne-Vartovsk 29 C8
Nizhneyansk . 31 B11
Nizhniy
  Novgorod ... 24 B5
Nizhniy Tagil . 29 D6
Nizhyn 24 C3
Nizip 46 C4
Nízké Tatry ... 16 D4
Njombe 57 F6
Nkambe 55 G7
Nkawkaw 55 G4
Nkhata Bay ... 57 G6
Nkhota Kota .. 59 A6
Nkongsamba . 56 D1
Nmai ⇢ 41 E11
Noakhali =
  Maijdi 41 F8
Noatak 71 B3
Nobeoka 32 C2
Nocera Inferiore 21 D5
Nockatunga .. 62 A3
Nogales, Mexico 84 A2
Nogales, U.S.A. 83 E7
Nōgata 32 C2
Noginsk 30 C7
Noire, Mts. ... 12 B2
Noirmoutier, I.
  de 12 C2
Nok Kundi 42 E3
Nokhtuysk ... 30 C9
Nokomis 71 C9
Nola 56 D3
Nome 71 B3
Nong Khai ... 36 A2
Noondoo 63 A4
Nóqui 56 F2
Noranda 69 D3
Nord-Ostsee-
  Kanal ⇢ ... 14 A5
Nordegg 71 C8
Norderney ... 14 B4
Norderstedt ... 14 B5

Nordfriesische
 Inseln 14 A5
Nordhausen ... 14 C6
Nordkapp 8 D13
Nordrhein-
 Westfalen □ . 14 C4
Nordvik 30 B9
Norfolk 73 F7
Norfolk I. 64 M11
Norilsk 30 C6
Norley 63 A3
Norman 78 B5
Norman Wells . 70 B7
Normandie .. 12 B4
Normandy –
 Normandie .. 12 B4
Normanton ... 61 D7
Norquinco 95 E2
Norrköping ... 9 G11
Norrland 8 F11
Norseman 60 G3
North Battleford 71 C9
North Bay ... 69 D3
North Bend ... 80 D1
North C. 64 A5
North Cape =
 Nordkapp ... 8 D13
North
 Carolina □ .. 75 B7
North Channel,
 Canada 69 D2
North Channel,
 U.K. 11 D4
North Dakota □ 76 B4
North Frisian Is.
 =
 Nordfriesische
 Inseln 14 A5
North I. 64 B5
North Korea ■ 35 C7
North
 Lakhimpur .. 41 D10
North Minch .. 10 B4
North Ossetia □ 25 E5
North Pagai, I. =
 Pagai Utara . 37 E2
North Platte .. 76 E4
North Platte → 76 E4
North Rhine
 Westphalia □
 = Nordrhein-
 Westfalen □ . 14 C4
North
 Saskatchewan →
 .... 71 C8
North Sea 10 D8
North Sporades
 = Voríai
 Sporádhes .. 23 E4
North Taranaki
 Bight 64 C6
North
 Thompson → 71 C7
North Uist 10 C3
North West C. . 60 E1
North West
 Frontier □ .. 42 B8
North West
 Highlands .. 10 C4
North West
 River 69 C4
North West
 Territories □ 70 B9
Northampton .. 11 E6
Northern Circars 40 J4
Northern
 Ireland □ ... 11 D3
Northern
 Marianas ■ . 64 H9

Northern
 Territory □ .. 60 D5
Northland □ .. 64 A5
Northumberland,
 C. 62 C3
Northumberland
 Str. 69 D4
Norton Sd. 71 B3
Norway ■ 8 F10
Norway House 71 C10
Norwegian Sea 6 B5
Norwich 11 E7
Nosok 28 B9
Noşratābād ... 45 D4
Nossob → ... 58 D4
Nosy Bé 59 G9
Nosy Boraha .. 59 H9
Nosy Mitsio ... 59 G9
Nosy Varika .. 59 J9
Noteć → 16 B2
Noto-Hanto ... 33 G11
Notre Dame B. 69 D5
Notre Dame de
 Koartac =
 Quaqtaq 68 B4
Notre Dame
 d'Ivugivic =
 Ivujivik 68 B3
Nottaway → .. 69 C3
Nottingham .. 11 E6
Nouâdhibou .. 54 D1
Nouâdhibou,
 Ras 54 D1
Nouakchott ... 55 E1
Nouméa 64 M11
Noupoort 58 E4
Nouveau
 Comptoir =
 Wemindji ... 69 C3
Nouvelle-
 Calédonie =
 New
 Caledonia ■ . 64 M11
Nova Casa Nova 93 D5
Nova Cruz 92 D6
Nova Friburgo . 93 G5
Nova Gaia =
 Cambundi-
 Catembo 56 G3
Nova Iguaçu .. 93 G5
Nova Iorque .. 92 D5
Nova Lima ... 93 F5
Nova Mambone 59 C7
Nova Scotia □ . 69 D4
Nova Sofala .. 59 C6
Nova Venécia . 93 F5
Nova Zagora .. 22 C5
Novara 20 B2
Novaya Ladoga 24 A3
Novaya Lyalya 29 D7
Novaya Zemlya 28 B6
Nové Zámky .. 16 D4
Novgorod 24 B3
Novgorod-
 Severskiy =
 Novhorod-
 Siverskyy ... 24 C3
Novhorod-
 Siverskyy ... 24 C3
Novi Lígure ... 20 B2
Novi Pazar ... 22 C3
Novi Sad 22 B2
Novo Mesto ... 20 B5
Novo Remanso 93 D6
Novoataysk ... 29 D9
Novocherkassk 25 D5
Novogrudok =
 Navahrudak . 17 B7

Novohrad-
 Volynskyy ... 17 C8
Novokazalinsk =
 Zhangaqazaly 29 E7
Novokuybyshevsk
 .... 24 C6
Novokuznetsk . 29 D9
Novomoskovsk 24 C4
Novorossiysk .. 25 E4
Novorybnoye . 30 B8
Novoselytsya .. 17 D8
Novoshakhtinsk 25 D4
Novosibirsk ... 29 D9
Novosibirskiye
 Ostrova 31 B12
Novotroitsk ... 29 D6
Novouzensk .. 24 C6
Novovolynsk .. 17 C7
Novska 20 B6
Novyy Port ... 28 C8
Now Shahr ... 44 B2
Nowa Sól 16 C2
Nowgong 41 D9
Nowra 63 B5
Nowshera 42 B8
Nowy Sącz ... 16 D5
Nowy Targ 16 D5
Nowy Tomyśl . 16 B3
Noyon 13 B5
Nsanje 59 B7
Nsawam 55 G4
Nsukka 55 G6
Nubian Desert =
 Nûbîya, Es
 Sahrâ En ... 52 D5
Nûbîya, Es
 Sahrâ En ... 52 D5
Nuboai 39 E5
Nueltin L. 70 B10
Nueva Imperial 94 D2
Nueva Rosita . 84 B4
Nuéve de Julio 94 D4
Nuevitas 86 B4
Nuevo, G. 95 E4
Nuevo Laredo . 84 B5
Nugget Pt. ... 65 G3
Nuhaka 64 C7
Nukey Bluff ... 62 B2
Nukheila 53 E4
Nukus 29 E6
Nulato 71 B4
Nullarbor Plain 60 G4
Numalla, L. ... 63 A3
Numan 53 G1
Numazu 32 B6
Numfoor 39 E4
Numurkah ... 63 C4
Nuneaton .. 11 E6
Nunivak I. 71 B3
Nunkun 42 C10
Núoro 21 D2
Nuremberg =
 Nürnberg ... 15 D6
Nuriootpa 62 B2
Nürnberg 15 D6
Nurran, L. =
 Terewah, L. . 63 A4
Nusa Tenggara
 Barat □ 37 F5
Nusa Tenggara
 Timur □ 39 F2
Nushki 42 E5
Nutak 68 C4
Nuuk =
 Godthåb 68 B5
Nuwakot 40 C4
Nuweveldberge 58 E4
Nuyts Arch. ... 62 B1
Nyah West 62 C3

Nyahanga 57 E6
Nyahururu 57 D7
Nyaingentanglha
 Shan 34 C4
Nyâlâ 53 F3
Nyasa, L. =
 Malawi, L. .. 59 A6
Nyasvizh 17 B8
Nyda 28 C8
Nyeri 57 E7
Nyíregyháza .. 17 E5
Nylstroom 59 C5
Nymagee 63 B4
Nyngan 63 B4
Nyoman =
 Neman → . 24 B1
Nysa 16 C3
Nysa → 16 B2
Nyurbe 30 C9
Nzega 57 E6
N'Zérékoré ... 55 G3
Nzeto 56 F2

O

Ö-Shima 32 B6
Oahe, L. 76 C4
Oahu 82 H12
Oak Ridge ... 75 A5
Oakbank 62 B3
Oakey 63 A5
Oakland 82 B1
Oamaru 65 F4
Oates Land .. 96 A15
Oaxaca 84 D5
Ob → 28 C7
Oba 69 D2
Oban 10 C4
Obbia 49 F4
Oberhausen ... 14 C4
Oberon 63 B4
Obi, Kepulauan 39 E3
Obi Is. = Obi,
 Kepulauan .. 39 E3
Óbidos 92 C2
Obihiro 32 F12
Obilatu 39 E3
Obo 57 C5
Obozerskaya =
 Obozerskiy .. 28 C5
Obozerskiy ... 28 C5
Obskaya Guba . 28 C8
Obuasi 55 G4
Ocala 75 E6
Ocaña 18 C4
Occidental,
 Cordillera ... 90 C3
Ocean I. =
 Banaba 64 K11
Oceanside → 82 D4
Ocniţa 17 D8
Ocumare del
 Tuy 90 A5
Odate 33 F12
Odawara 32 B6
Oddur 49 G3
Ödemiş 23 E7
Odense 9 G10
Oder → 15 B8
Odesa 25 D3
Odessa – Odesa 25 D3
Odessa 78 D2
Odienné 55 G3
Odintsovo ... 24 B4
Odorheiu
 Secuiesc 17 E7

Odra

Odra = Oder →· 15 B8
Odra →· 16 B2
Oeiras 92 D5
Ofanto →· 20 D6
Offa 55 G5
Offenbach 14 C5
Offenburg 14 D4
Oga-Hantō ... 33 G11
Ōgaki 32 B5
Ogbomosho .. 55 G5
Ogden 81 E8
Ogdensburg .. 73 B8
Oglio →· 20 B3
Ogooué →· ... 56 E1
Ogowe =
  Ogooué →· . 56 E1
Ohai 65 F2
Ohakune 64 C6
Ohanet 54 C6
Ohau, L. 65 F3
Ohio □ 72 D4
Ohio →· 72 F1
Ohre →· 16 C2
Ohrid 22 D3
Ohridsko Jezero 23 D3
Oise →· 12 B5
Ōita 32 C2
Oiticica 92 D5
Ojos del Salado,
  Cerro 94 B3
Oka →· 28 D5
Okaba 39 F5
Okahandja 58 C3
Okahukura ... 64 C6
Okandja 56 E2
Okanogan →· . 80 A4
Okara 42 D8
Okarito 65 E4
Okaukuejo ... 58 B3
Okavango
  Swamps 58 B4
Okaya 32 A6
Okayama 32 B3
Okazaki 32 B5
Okeechobee, L. 75 F7
Okefenokee
  Swamp ... 75 D6
Okhotsk, Sea of 31 D12
Oki-Shotō 32 A3
Okiep 58 D3
Okinawa-Jima . 35 D7
Oklahoma □ .. 78 B5
Oklahoma City 78 B5
Okmulgee 79 B6
Oknitsa =
  Ocniţa 17 D8
Okrika 55 H6
Oktabrsk =
  Oktyabrsk ... 29 E6
Oktyabrsk ... 29 E6
Oktyabrskiy =
  Aktsyabrski . 17 B9
Oktyabrskoy
  Revolyutsii,
  Os. 30 B7
Oktyabrskoye . 28 C7
Okuru 65 E3
Okushiri-Tō .. 32 F11
Öland 9 G11
Olary 62 B3
Olavarría 94 D4
Oława 16 C3
Ólbia 20 D2
Old Crow 70 B6
Oldenburg 14 B5
Oldham 11 E5
Olekma →· ... 31 C10
Olekminsk 31 C10
Oleksandriya .. 17 C8

Olenek 30 C9
Olenek →· 30 B10
Oléron, I. d' ... 12 D3
Oleśnica 16 C3
Olevsk 17 C8
Olhão 18 D2
Olifants →· ... 59 C6
Ólimbos, Óros . 23 D4
Olinda 92 D7
Oliveira 93 G5
Olivenza 18 C2
Ollagüe 91 H5
Olomouc 16 D3
Olongapo 38 B2
Olot 19 A7
Olsztyn 16 B5
Olt →· 22 C5
Olteniţa 22 B6
Oltu 46 B5
Olympia, Greece 23 F3
Olympia, U.S.A. 80 B2
Olympic Mts. .. 80 B2
Olympus, Mt. =
  Ólimbos, Óros 23 D4
Om →· 29 D8
Omagh 11 D3
Omaha 77 E7
Oman ■ 48 C6
Oman, G. of .. 45 E4
Omaruru 58 C3
Omate 91 G4
Ombai, Selat . 39 F2
Omboué 56 E1
Ombrone →· .. 20 C3
Omdurmân ... 53 E5
Ometepec 84 D5
Ōmiya 32 B6
Omo →· 53 G6
Omsk 29 D8
Omul, Vf. 17 F7
Ōmura 32 C1
Omuramba
  Omatako →· . 58 B4
Ōmuta 32 C2
Onang 39 E1
Oncócua 58 B2
Onda 19 C5
Ondangua 58 B3
Ondo 55 G5
Öndörhaan ... 35 B6
Onega 28 C4
Onega →· 8 F15
Onega, G. of =
  Onezhskaya
  Guba 28 C4
Onega, L. =
  Onezhskoye
  Ozero 28 C4
Onehunga 64 B6
Oneşti 17 E8
Onezhskaya
  Guba 28 C4
Onezhskoye
  Ozero 28 C4
Ongarue 64 C6
Onilahy →· ... 59 J8
Onitsha 55 G6
Onoda 32 B2
Ontario □ 69 D2
Ontario, L. 73 C7
Oodnadatta ... 62 A2
Oostende 14 C2
Ootacamund . 43 P10
Opala 56 E4
Opava 16 D3
Opole 16 C3
Oporto = Porto 18 B1
Opotiki 64 C7
Opua 64 A6

Opunake 64 C5
Oradea 17 E5
Orai 42 G11
Oral =
  Zhayyq →· .. 29 E6
Oral 24 C7
Oran, Algeria .. 54 A4
Oran, Argentina 94 A4
Orange =
  Oranje →· .. 58 D3
Orange,
  Australia 63 B4
Orange, France 13 D6
Orange, U.S.A. 79 D7
Orange, C. ... 92 B3
Orangeburg .. 75 C7
Oranienburg .. 15 B7
Oranje →· ... 58 D3
Oranjemund .. 58 D3
Oras 38 B3
Oraşul Stalin =
  Braşov 17 F7
Orbetello 20 C3
Orbost 63 C4
Orchila, I. ... 90 A5
Ordos = Mu Us
  Shamo 35 C5
Ordu 46 B4
Ordzhonikidze =
  Vladikavkaz . 25 E5
Ore Mts. =
  Erzgebirge .. 15 C7
Örebro 9 G11
Oregon □ 80 C3
Orekhovo-
  Zuyevo 24 B4
Orel 24 C4
Ören 23 F6
Orenburg 29 D6
Orense 18 A2
Orepuki 65 G2
Øresund 9 G10
Orgaz 18 C4
Orgeyev =
  Orhei 17 E9
Orgün 45 C7
Orhaneli 23 E7
Orhangazi 23 D7
Orhei 17 E9
Orhon Gol →· . 35 A5
Orient 62 A3
Oriental,
  Cordillera ... 90 B4
Orihuela 19 C5
Orinoco →· ... 90 B6
Orissa □ 40 G5
Oristano 21 E2
Oristano, G. di . 21 E2
Orizaba 84 D5
Orkney Is. 10 B5
Orlando 75 E7
Orléanais 12 C5
Orléans 12 C4
Ormara 42 G4
Ormoc 38 B2
Ormond 64 C7
Örnsköldsvik .. 8 F11
Orocué 90 C4
Orol Dengizi =
  Aral Sea ... 29 E6
Oroquieta 38 C2
Orós 92 D6
Orosháza 16 E5
Orroroo 62 B2
Orsha 24 C3
Orsk 29 D6
Orşova 22 B4
Ortaca 23 F7
Ortegal, C. ... 18 A2

Orthez 12 E3
Ortigueira 18 A2
Ortles 20 A3
Ortón →· 91 F5
Orūmīyeh 46 C6
Orūmīyeh,
  Daryācheh-ye 46 C6
Oruro 91 G5
Oruzgān □ ... 42 C5
Orvieto 20 C4
Oryakhovo 22 C4
Ōsaka 32 B4
Ösel =
  Saaremaa ... 24 B1
Osh 29 E8
Oshawa 69 D3
Oshkosh 76 E3
Oshmyany =
  Ashmyany .. 17 A7
Oshogbo 55 G5
Oshwe 56 E3
Osijek 20 B7
Osipenko =
  Berdyansk .. 25 D4
Osipovichi =
  Asipovichy .. 17 B9
Oskarshamn .. 9 G11
Öskemen 29 E9
Oslo 9 G10
Oslob 38 C2
Oslofjorden ... 9 G10
Osmanabad .. 43 K10
Osmaniye ... 46 C4
Osnabrück ... 14 B5
Osorio 94 B6
Osorno 95 E2
Ossa, Mt. ... 62 D4
Óssa, Oros .. 23 E4
Ostend =
  Oostende .. 14 C2
Oster 17 C10
Österdalälven . 8 F10
Östersund 8 F10
Ostfriesische
  Inseln 14 B4
Ostrava 16 D4
Ostróda 16 B4
Ostroh 17 C8
Ostrołęka 16 B5
Ostrów
  Mazowiecka . 16 B5
Ostrów
  Wielkopolski . 16 C3
Ostrowiec-
  Świętokrzyski 16 C5
Ostuni 21 D6
Ōsumi-Kaikyō . 33 D2
Osuna 18 D3
Oswego 73 C7
Oświęcim ... 16 C4
Otago □ 65 F3
Otago Harbour 65 F4
Ōtake 32 B3
Otaki 64 D6
Otaru 32 F12
Otaru-Wan =
  Ishikari-Wan . 32 F12
Otavalo 90 C3
Otavi 58 B3
Otira Gorge .. 65 E4
Otjiwarongo .. 58 C3
Otorohanga .. 64 C6
Otranto 23 D2
Otranto, C. d' .. 23 D2
Otranto, Str. of 23 D2
Ōtsu 32 B4
Ottawa 69 D3
Ottawa Is. 68 C2
Ottumwa 77 E8

Oturkpo	55	G6
Otway, B.	95	G2
Otway, C.	62	C3
Otwock	16	B5
Ouachita Mts.	79	B6
Ouadâne	54	D2
Ouadda	56	C4
Ouagadougou	55	F4
Ouahran = Oran	54	A4
Ouallene	54	D5
Ouanda Djallé	56	C4
Ouango	56	D4
Ouargla	54	B6
Ouarzazate	54	B3
Oubangi →	56	E3
Oudtshoorn	58	E4
Ouessant, I. d'	12	B1
Ouesso	56	D3
Ouezzane	54	B3
Ouidah	55	G5
Oujda	54	B4
Oujeft	55	D2
Ouled Djellal	54	B6
Oulu	8	E13
Oulujärvi	8	F13
Oulujoki →	8	E13
Oum Chalouba	53	E3
Ounianga-Kébir	53	E3
Ounianga Sérir	53	E3
Ourense = Orense	18	A2
Ouricuri	92	D5
Ouro Prêto	93	G5
Ouse	62	D4
Outer Hebrides	10	C3
Outjo	58	C3
Ouyen	62	C3
Ovalle	94	C2
Ovamboland	58	B3
Oviedo	18	A3
Ovruch	17	C9
Owaka	65	G3
Owambo = Ovamboland	58	B3
Owase	32	B5
Owbeh	42	B3
Owen Sound	69	D2
Owen Stanley Ra.	61	B8
Owendo	56	D1
Owo	55	G6
Owyhee →	80	D5
Oxford, N.Z.	65	E5
Oxford, U.K.	11	F6
Oxley	63	B3
Oxnard	82	C3
Oxus = Amudarya →	29	E6
Oya	37	D4
Oyama	32	A6
Oyem	56	D2
Oyo	55	G5
Ozamiz	38	C2
Ozark Plateau	79	A8
Ózd	16	D5

P

Pa-an	41	J11
Paarl	58	E3
Pab Hills	42	F5
Pabianice	16	C4
Pabna	41	E7
Pacaja →	92	C3
Pacaraima, Sierra	90	C6

Pacasmayo	91	E3
Pachpadra	42	G8
Pachuca	84	C5
Padaido, Kepulauan	39	E5
Padang	37	E2
Padangpanjang	37	E2
Padangsidempuan	37	D1
Paderborn	14	C5
Padloping Island	68	B4
Pádova	20	B3
Padua = Pádova	20	B3
Paducah	72	F1
Paeroa	64	B6
Pafúri	59	C6
Pag	20	B5
Pagadian	38	C2
Pagai Selatan, P.	37	E2
Pagai Utara	37	E2
Pagalu = Annobón	51	G4
Pagastikós Kólpos	23	E4
Pagatan	37	E5
Pahiatua	64	D6
Painan	37	E2
Paint Hills = Wemindji	69	C3
Painted Desert	83	C7
País Vasco □	19	A4
Paisley	10	D4
Paita	90	E2
Pajares, Puerto de	18	A3
Pakaraima Mts.	90	B6
Pakistan ■	42	E7
Pakokku	41	G10
Pakse	36	A3
Paktiā □	42	C6
Pala	53	G2
Palagruža	20	C6
Palam	43	K10
Palampur	42	C10
Palana	62	C4
Palanan	38	A2
Palanan Pt.	38	A2
Palangkaraya	37	E4
Palani Hills	43	P10
Palanpur	43	G8
Palanro	39	E1
Palapye	59	C5
Palau ■	38	C4
Palawan	36	C5
Palayankottai	43	Q10
Paleleh	39	D2
Palembang	37	E2
Palencia	18	A3
Palermo	21	E4
Palestine	79	D6
Paletwa	41	G9
Palghat	43	P10
Pali	42	G8
Palioúrion, Ákra	23	E4
Palitana	43	J7
Palk Bay	43	Q11
Palk Strait	43	Q11
Pallanza = Verbánia	20	B2
Palm Springs	82	D4
Palma	57	G8
Palma →	93	E4
Palma, B. de	19	C7
Palma de Mallorca	19	C7
Palmares	92	D6
Palmas, C.	55	H3
Pálmas, G. di	21	E2

Palmeira dos Índios	93	D6
Palmeirinhas, Pta. das	56	F2
Palmer	71	B5
Palmer Arch.	96	A3
Palmer Land	96	B3
Palmerston	65	F4
Palmerston North	64	D6
Palmi	21	E5
Palmira	90	C3
Palmyra = Tudmur	46	D4
Palopo	39	E2
Palos, C. de	19	D5
Palu, Indonesia	39	E1
Palu, Turkey	46	C5
Paluan	38	B2
Pama	55	F5
Pamiers	12	E4
Pamirs	29	F8
Pamlico Sd.	75	B10
Pampa	78	B3
Pampa de las Salinas	94	C3
Pampanua	39	E2
Pampas, Argentina	94	D4
Pampas, Peru	91	F4
Pamplona, Colombia	90	B4
Pamplona, Spain	19	A5
Panaji	43	M8
Panamá	85	F9
Panama ■	86	E4
Panamá, G. de	86	E4
Panama City	74	D5
Panão	91	E3
Panay	38	B2
Panay, G.	38	B2
Pančevo	22	B3
Pandan	38	B2
Pandharpur	43	L9
Pando	94	C5
Pando, L. = Hope, L.	62	A2
Panevežys	24	B1
Panfilov	29	E8
Pang-Long	41	F12
Pang-Yang	41	F12
Pangani	57	F7
Pangfou = Bengbu	35	C6
Pangkajene	39	E1
Pangkalanbrandan	37	D1
Pangkalanbuun	37	E4
Pangkalansusu	37	D1
Pangkalpinang	37	E3
Pangkoh	37	E4
Pangnirtung	68	B4
Pangutaran Group	38	C2
Panjgur	42	F4
Panjim = Panaji	43	M8
Panjinad Barrage	42	E7
Panorama	94	A6
Pantar	39	F2
Pante Macassar	39	F2
Pantelleria	21	F3
Pánuco	84	C5
Panyam	55	G6
Paoting = Baoding	35	C6
Paot'ou = Baotou	35	B6

Paoua	56	C3
Pápa	16	E3
Papakura	64	B6
Papantla	84	C5
Papar	36	C5
Papua New Guinea ■	61	B8
Papudo	94	C2
Papun	41	H11
Pará = Belém	92	C4
Pará □	92	C3
Paracatu	93	F4
Paracel Is. = Hsisha Chuntao	36	A4
Parachilna	62	B2
Parachinar	42	C7
Paradip	40	G6
Parado	39	F1
Paragua →	90	B6
Paraguaçu →	93	E6
Paraguaná, Pen. de	90	A4
Paraguarí	94	B5
Paraguay ■	94	A5
Paraguay →	94	B5
Paraíba = João Pessoa	92	D7
Paraíba □	92	D6
Paraíba do Sul →	93	G5
Parakou	55	G5
Paramaribo	92	A2
Paraná, Argentina	94	C4
Paraná, Brazil	93	E4
Paraná □	94	A6
Paraná →	94	C5
Paranaguá	94	B7
Paranaíba →	93	G3
Paranapanema →	94	A6
Paranapiacaba, Serra do	94	A7
Parang, Jolo, Phil.	38	C2
Parang, Mindanao, Phil.	38	C2
Paratinga	93	E5
Paratoo	62	B2
Parattah	62	D4
Parbhani	43	K10
Parchim	15	B6
Pardo →, Bahia, Brazil	93	F6
Pardo →, Mato Grosso, Brazil	93	G3
Pardo →, São Paulo, Brazil	93	G4
Pardubice	16	C2
Parecis, Serra dos	91	F7
Parepare	39	E1
Párga	23	E3
Pariaguán	90	B6
Pariaman	37	E2
Parigi	39	E2
Parika	90	B7
Parima, Serra	90	C6
Parinari	90	D4
Parîngul Mare	17	F6
Parintins	92	C2
Pariparit Kyun	41	K9
Paris, France	12	B5
Paris, U.S.A.	79	C6
Park Range	81	F10

Parkersburg ... 72 E5
Parkes 63 B4
Parla 18 B4
Parma 20 B3
Parnaguá 93 E5
Parnaíba, Piauí,
  Brazil 92 C5
Parnaíba,
  São Paulo,
  Brazil 93 F3
Parnaíba → .. 92 C5
Parnassós ... 23 E4
Parnu 24 B1
Paroo → 63 B3
Páros 23 F5
Parral 94 D2
Parramatta ... 63 B5
Parry Sound .. 69 D3
Partinico 21 E4
Paru → 92 C3
Paruro □ 91 F4
Parvän □ 42 B6
Parvatipuram .. 40 H4
Pasadena, Calif.,
  U.S.A. 82 C3
Pasadena, Tex.,
  U.S.A. 79 E6
Pasaje 90 D3
Pascagoula ... 79 D9
Paşcani 17 E8
Pasco 80 B4
Pasco, Cerro de 91 F3
Pashmakli =
  Smolyan 22 D5
Pašman 20 C5
Pasni 42 G3
Paso de Indios 95 E3
Passau 15 D7
Passero, C. ... 21 F5
Passo Fundo .. 94 B6
Passos 93 G4
Pastaza → ... 90 D3
Pasto 90 C3
Patagonia 95 F3
Patan, India .. 43 H8
Patan, Nepal . 40 D5
Patani 39 D3
Patchewollock . 62 C3
Patea 64 C6
Pategi 55 G6
Paternò 21 F5
Paterson 73 D8
Pathankot 42 C9
Patiala 42 D10
Patkai Bum .. 41 D10
Pátmos 23 F6
Patna 40 E5
Patos, L. dos . 94 C6
Patos de Minas 93 F4
Patquía 94 C3
Pátrai 23 E3
Pátraikós Kólpos 23 E3
Patras = Pátrai 23 E3
Patrocínio 93 F4
Pattani 36 C2
Patuakhali 41 F8
Pau 12 E3
Pauini → 90 D6
Pauk 41 G10
Paulis = Isiro . 57 D5
Paulistana ... 92 D5
Paulo Afonso .. 93 D6
Pavia 20 B2
Pavlodar 29 D8
Pavlograd =
  Pavlohrad ... 25 D4
Pavlohrad ... 25 D4
Pavlovo 24 B5
Pavlovsk 24 C5

Pawtucket 73 D10
Paxoí 23 E3
Payakumbuh .. 37 E2
Payne Bay =
  Kangirsuk ... 68 C4
Paysandú 94 C5
Paz, B. la 84 C2
Pazar 46 B5
Pazardzhik ... 22 C5
Peace → 70 C8
Peak Hill 63 B4
Peake 62 C2
Peake Cr. → .. 62 A2
Pebane 59 B7
Pebas 90 D4
Peć 22 C3
Pechenga 28 C4
Pechenizhyn .. 17 D7
Pechora → .. 28 C6
Pechorskaya
  Guba 28 C6
Pecos → 78 E3
Pécs 16 E4
Pedder, L. 62 D4
Pedirka 62 A2
Pedra Azul ... 93 F5
Pedreiras 92 C5
Pedro Afonso . 93 D4
Pedro Juan
  Caballero ... 94 A5
Peebinga 62 B3
Peel → ,
  Australia 63 B5
Peel → , Canada 70 B6
Peera Peera
  Poolanna L. . 62 A2
Pegasus Bay .. 65 E5
Pegu 41 J11
Pegu Yoma .. 41 H10
Pehuajó 94 D4
Peine 14 B6
Peip'ing =
  Beijing 35 C6
Peipus, L. =
  Chudskoye,
  Oz. 24 B2
Peixe 93 E4
Pekalongan ... 37 F3
Pekanbaru ... 37 D2
Pekin 77 E10
Peking = Beijing 35 C6
Pelagie, Is. ... 21 G4
Pelaihari 37 E4
Peleaga, Vf. .. 17 F6
Peleng 39 E2
Pelješac 20 C6
Pelly → 70 B6
Pelly Bay 68 B2
Pelly L. 70 B9
Peloponnese =
  Pelopónnisos □
  .... 23 F4
Pelopónnisos □ 23 F4
Peloro, C. ... 21 E5
Pelorus Sd. .. 65 D5
Pelotas 94 C6
Pelvoux, Massif
  du 13 D7
Pematangsiantar 37 D1
Pemba I. 57 F7
Pembroke,
  Canada 69 D3
Pembroke, U.K. 11 F4
Penang =
  Pinang 36 C2
Penápolis 94 A6
Peñarroya-
  Pueblonuevo 18 C3
Peñas, C. de .. 18 A3

Penas, G. de .. 95 F2
Pench'i = Benxi 35 B7
Pend Oreille L. 80 A5
Pendembu ... 55 G2
Pendleton 80 C4
Penedo 93 E6
Penguin 62 D4
Peniche 18 C1
Penida 37 F5
Peninsular
  Malaysia □ .. 37 D2
Penmarch, Pte.
  de 12 C1
Pennines 11 D5
Pennsylvania □ 73 D7
Penola 62 C3
Penong 60 G5
Penrith 63 B5
Pensacola ... 74 D4
Pensacola Mts. 96 C4
Penshurst 62 C3
Penticton 71 D8
Pentland Firth . 10 B5
Penza 24 C6
Penzance 11 F4
Peoria 77 E10
Perabumulih .. 37 E2
Perche, Collines
  du 12 B4
Perdido, Mte. . 19 A6
Perdu, Mt. =
  Perdido, Mte. 19 A6
Pereira 90 C3
Perekerten 62 B3
Pereyaslav-
  Khmelnytskyy 24 C3
Pergamino 94 C4
Péribonca → . 69 D3
Perico 94 A3
Périgueux 12 D4
Perijá, Sierra de 90 B4
Perlas, Arch. de
  las 86 E4
Perm 29 D6
Pernambuco =
  Recife 92 D7
Pernatty Lagoon 62 B2
Pernik 22 C4
Perpendicular
  Pt. 63 B5
Perpignan ... 13 E5
Persepolis ... 44 D3
Pershotravensk 17 C8
Persian Gulf =
  Gulf, The .. 44 E2
Perth, Australia 60 G2
Perth, U.K. ... 10 C5
Perth Amboy .. 73 D8
Peru ■ 90 C3
Perúgia 20 C4
Pervomaysk ... 25 D3
Pervouralsk .. 29 D6
Pésaro 20 C4
Pescara 20 C5
Peshawar ... 42 B7
Peshkopi 22 D3
Pesqueira ... 92 D6
Petah Tiqwa .. 46 D3
Petauke 59 A6
Peter I.s Øy .. 96 A2
Peterborough,
  Australia 62 B2
Peterborough,
  Canada 69 D3
Peterborough,
  U.K. 11 E6
Peterhead ... 10 C6
Petersburg,
  Alaska, U.S.A. 71 C6

Petersburg, Va.,
  U.S.A. 73 F7
Petitsikapau, L. 69 C4
Petlad 43 H8
Peto 85 C7
Petone 65 D6
Petrich 22 D4
Petrikov =
  Pyetrikaw ... 17 B9
Petrograd =
  Sankt-
  Peterburg .. 24 B3
Petrolândia .. 93 D6
Petrolina 93 D5
Petropavl 29 D7
Petropavlovsk =
  Petropavl .. 29 D7
Petropavlovsk-
  Kamchatskiy 31 D13
Petrópolis ... 93 G5
Petroşani 17 F6
Petrovaradin . 22 B2
Petrovsk 24 C6
Petrozavodsk .. 28 C4
Peureulak ... 36 D1
Pforzheim ... 14 D5
Phagwara ... 42 D9
Phalodi 42 F8
Phan Rang ... 36 B3
Phangan, Ko . 36 C2
Phangnga 36 C1
Phanh Bho Ho
  Chi Minh ... 36 B3
Phatthalung .. 36 C2
Phetchabun .. 36 A2
Philadelphia .. 73 E8
Philippines ■ .. 38 B2
Philippopolis =
  Plovdiv 22 C5
Phillip I. 63 C4
Phillott 63 A4
Phitsanulok .. 36 A2
Phnom Dangrek 36 B2
Phnom Penh . 36 B2
Phoenix 83 D6
Phra Nakhon Si
  Ayutthaya ... 36 B2
Phuket 36 C1
Phumiphon,
  Khuan 36 A1
Piacenza 20 B2
Pialba 63 A5
Pian Cr. → .. 63 B4
Pianosa 20 C3
Piatra Neamţ .. 17 E8
Piauí □ 92 D5
Piave → 20 B4
Pibor Post ... 53 G5
Pica 91 H5
Picardie 13 B5
Picardy =
  Picardie 13 B5
Pichilemu 94 C2
Pico Truncado . 95 F3
Picton, Australia 63 B5
Picton, N.Z. .. 65 D6
Pictou 69 D4
Picún Leufú .. 95 D3
Piedmont =
  Piemonte □ . 20 B1
Piedras, R. de
  las → 91 F5
Piedras Negras 84 B4
Piemonte □ .. 20 B1
Piet Retief ... 59 D6
Pietermaritzburg 59 D6
Pietersburg .. 59 C5
Pietrosul,
  Romania 17 E7

Pietrosul,
Romania 17 E7
Pigüe 94 D4
Piketberg 58 E3
Piła 16 B3
Pilar, Brazil ... 93 D6
Pilar, Paraguay 94 B5
Pilas Group ... 38 C2
Pilcomayo → . 94 B5
Pilibhit 42 E11
Pilica → 16 C5
Pílos 23 F3
Pilsen = Plzeň . 16 D1
Pimba 62 B2
Pimenta Bueno 91 F6
Pimentel 91 E3
Pinang 36 C2
Pinar del Río .. 86 B3
Pınarhisar 22 D6
Pińczów 16 C5
Pindiga 55 G7
Pindos Óros ... 23 E3
Pindus Mts. =
Pindos Óros . 23 E3
Pine Bluff 79 B7
Pine Point 70 B8
Pinega → 28 C5
Pinerolo 20 B1
Pinetown 59 D6
Ping → 36 A2
Pingdong 35 D7
Pingliang 35 C5
Pingwu 35 C5
Pingxiang 35 D5
Pinhel 18 B2
Pini 37 D1
Piniós → 23 E4
Pinnaroo 62 C3
Pínnes, Ákra .. 23 D5
Pinrang 39 E1
Pinsk 17 B8
Pintados 91 H5
Pinyug 24 A6
Piombino 20 C3
Pioner, Os. 30 B7
Piorini, L. 90 D6
Piotrków
Trybunalski . 16 C4
Pip 45 E5
Piquiri → 94 A6
Piracicaba 94 A7
Piracuruca 92 C5
Piræus =
Piraiévs 23 F4
Piraiévs 23 F4
Pirané 94 B5
Pirapora 93 F5
Pírgos 23 F3
Pirin Planina .. 22 D4
Piripiri 92 C5
Pirmasens ... 14 D4
Pirot 22 C4
Piru 39 E3
Pisa 20 C3
Pisagua 91 G4
Pisciotta 21 D5
Pisco 91 F3
Písek 16 D2
Pishan 34 C2
Pising 39 F2
Pistóia 20 C3
Pisuerga → .. 18 B3
Pitarpunga, L. . 62 B3
Pitcairn I. 65 M17
Piteå 8 E12
Pitești 22 B5
Pithapuram ... 40 J4
Pittsburg 79 A6
Pittsburgh 73 D5

Pittsworth 63 A5
Piura 90 E2
Placentia 69 D5
Placentia B. ... 69 D5
Plainview 78 B3
Pláka, Ákra ... 23 G6
Plakhino 28 C9
Plasencia 18 B2
Plata, Río de la 94 C5
Platani → 21 F4
Plato 90 B4
Platte → 77 F7
Plauen 15 C7
Pleiku 36 D3
Plenty, B. of ... 64 B7
Pleven 22 C5
Plevlja 22 C2
Płock 16 B4
Plöckenstein .. 15 D7
Ploiești 22 B6
Plovdiv 22 C5
Plumtree 59 C5
Plymouth 11 F4
Plzeň 16 D1
Po → 20 B4
Po Hai = Bo Hai 35 C6
Pobedy Pik ... 29 E8
Pocatello 81 D7
Poços de Caldas 93 G4
Podgorica 22 C2
Podilska
Vysochyna .. 17 D8
Podkamennaya
Tunguska → 30 C7
Podolsk 24 B4
Podor 55 E1
Pofadder 58 D3
Poh 39 E2
Pohnpei 64 J10
Poinsett, C. ... 96 A12
Pointe-à-Pitre .. 87 C7
Pointe Noire ... 56 E2
Poitiers 12 C4
Poitou 12 C3
Pokaran 42 F7
Pokataroo 63 A4
Pokrovsk =
Engels 24 C6
Pola = Pula ... 20 B4
Polan 45 E5
Poland ■ 16 B5
Polatsk 24 B2
Polcura 94 D2
Polesye = Pripet
Marshes 17 B9
Poli 56 C2
Police 16 B2
Polillo Is. 38 B2
Políyiros 23 D4
Polnovat 28 C7
Polonne 17 C8
Polonnoye =
Polonne 17 C8
Poltava 24 D3
Polunochnoye . 28 C7
Polynesia 65 L15
Polynésie
française =
French
Polynesia ■ . 65 M16
Pombal, Brazil . 92 D6
Pombal,
Portugal 18 C1
Pomézia 20 D4
Pomorski,
Pojezierze .. 16 B3
Ponape =
Pohnpei 64 J10

Ponca City 78 A5
Ponce 87 C6
Pond Inlet 68 A3
Pondicherry ... 43 P11
Ponferrada ... 18 A2
Ponnani 43 P9
Ponnyadaung . 41 F10
Ponoy → 28 C5
Ponta Grossa .. 94 B6
Ponta Pora ... 94 A5
Pontarlier 13 C7
Pontchartrain L. 79 D8
Ponte Nova ... 93 G5
Pontevedra ... 18 A1
Pontiac 72 C4
Pontianak 37 E3
Pontine Is. =
Ponziane,
Ísole 21 D4
Pontine Mts. =
Kuzey
Anadolu
Dağları 46 B3
Pontivy 12 B2
Pontoise 12 B5
Ponziane, Ísole 21 D4
Poochera 62 B1
Poole 11 F6
Poona = Pune . 43 K8
Pooncarie 62 B3
Poopelloe L. .. 63 B3
Poopó, L. de .. 91 G5
Popayán 90 C3
Popigay 30 B9
Popilta, L. 62 B3
Popio L. 62 B3
Poplar Bluff ... 79 A8
Popocatépetl,
Volcán 84 D5
Popokabaka ... 56 F3
Poprád 16 D5
Porbandar 43 J6
Porcupine → . 71 B5
Pordenone ... 20 B4
Pori 8 F12
Porkkala 9 G12
Porlamar 90 A6
Poroshiri-Dake . 32 F12
Porpoise B. ... 96 A13
Porretta, Passo
di 20 B3
Port Adelaide . 62 B2
Port Alberni ... 71 D7
Port Alfred ... 59 E5
Port Angeles .. 80 A2
Port Antonio .. 86 C4
Port Arthur,
Australia 62 D4
Port Arthur,
U.S.A. 79 E7
Port-au-Prince . 87 C5
Port Augusta .. 62 B2
Port Augusta
West 62 B2
Port Bergé
Vaovao 59 H9
Port Bou 19 A7
Port Broughton 62 B2
Port-Cartier .. 69 C4
Port Chalmers . 65 F4
Port Darwin ... 95 G5
Port Davey ... 62 D4
Port Dickson .. 37 D2
Port Elizabeth . 59 E5
Port Fairy 62 C3
Port-Gentil 56 E1
Port Harcourt . 55 H6
Port Harrison =
Inukjuak 68 C3

Port
Hawkesbury . 69 D4
Port Hedland .. 60 E2
Port Huron 72 C4
Port Kembla ... 63 B5
Port Kenny 62 B1
Port Lairge =
Waterford ... 11 E3
Port Laoise ... 11 E3
Port Lincoln .. 62 B2
Port Loko 55 G2
Port MacDonnell 62 C3
Port Macquarie 63 B5
Port Moresby . 61 B8
Port Nelson ... 71 C10
Port Nolloth .. 58 D3
Port Nouveau-
Québec =
Kangiqsualujjuaq
.... 68 C4
Port of Spain .. 87 D7
Port Pegasus . 65 G2
Port Phillip B. . 63 C3
Port Pirie 62 B2
Port Safaga =
Bûr Safâga . 52 C5
Port Said = Bûr
Sa'îd 52 B5
Port Shepstone 59 E6
Port Stanley =
Stanley 95 G5
Port Sudan =
Bûr Sûdân . 53 E6
Port Talbot 11 F5
Port-Vendres .. 13 E5
Port Wakefield 62 B2
Port Weld 36 D2
Porta Orientalis 22 B4
Portachuelo .. 91 G6
Portadown ... 11 D3
Portage La
Prairie 71 D10
Portalegre ... 18 C2
Portile de Fier . 22 B4
Portimão 18 D1
Portland,
N.S.W.,
Australia 63 B4
Portland, Vic.,
Australia 62 C3
Portland, Maine,
U.S.A. 73 C10
Portland, Oreg.,
U.S.A. 80 C2
Portland B. ... 62 C3
Portland Prom. 68 C3
Porto 18 B1
Pôrto Alegre .. 94 C6
Porto Amboim
= Gunza 56 G2
Pôrto de Móz . 92 C3
Pôrto
Empédocle . 21 F4
Pôrto Esperança 91 G7
Pôrto Franco .. 92 D4
Porto Mendes . 94 A6
Pôrto Murtinho 91 H7
Pôrto Nacional 93 E4
Porto Novo ... 55 G5
Pôrto Santo ... 54 B1
Pôrto Seguro .. 93 F6
Porto Tórres .. 20 D2
Pôrto União .. 94 B6
Pôrto Válter .. 91 E4
Pôrto Velho ... 91 E6
Portoferráio .. 20 C3
Portoscuso ... 21 E2
Portovíejo 90 D2

Portree

Portree 10 C3
Portsmouth,
  U.K. 11 F6
Portsmouth,
  U.S.A. 73 F7
Porttipahtan
  tekojärvi 8 E13
Portugal ■ ... 18 C1
Porvenir 95 G2
Posadas 94 B5
Poshan =
  Boshan 35 C6
Poso 39 E2
Posse 93 E4
Possel 56 C3
Possession I. .. 96 B15
Poste Maurice
  Cortier 54 D5
Postojna 20 B5
Potchefstroom . 59 D5
Potenza 21 D5
Poteriteri, L. ... 65 G2
Potgietersrus . 59 C5
Poti 25 E5
Potiskum 55 F7
Potomac → .. 73 E7
Potosí 91 G5
Pototan 38 B2
Potrerillos 94 B3
Potsdam 15 B7
Poughkeepsie . 73 D9
Pouso Alegre .. 93 E2
Považská
  Bystrica 16 D4
Povenets 28 C4
Poverty B. 64 C8
Póvoa de Varzim 18 B1
Powder → .. 76 B2
Powell L. 83 B7
Poyang Hu 35 D6
Požarevac 22 B3
Poznań 16 B3
Pozo Almonte . 91 H5
Pozoblanco ... 18 C3
Pozzuoli 21 D5
Prachuap Khiri
  Khan 36 B1
Prado 93 F6
Prague = Praha 16 C2
Praha 16 C2
Prainha,
  Amazonas,
  Brazil 91 E6
Prainha, Pará,
  Brazil 92 C3
Prairies 71 C9
Prapat 37 D1
Prata 93 F4
Prato 20 C3
Pravia 18 A2
Praya 37 F5
Preparis North
  Channel 41 K9
Preparis South
  Channel 41 K9
Přerov 16 D3
Preservation
  Inlet 65 G2
Presidencia
  Roque Saenz
  Peña 94 B4
Presidente
  Epitácio 93 G3
Presidente
  Hermes 91 F6
Presidente
  Prudente 93 G3
Prešov 16 D5

Prespa, L. =
  Prespansko
  Jezero 23 D3
Prespansko
  Jezero 23 D3
Presque Isle ... 73 A11
Preston 11 E5
Pretoria 59 D5
Préveza 23 E3
Příbram 16 D2
Prichard 74 D3
Prieska 58 D4
Prievidza 16 D4
Prilep 22 D3
Priluki = Pryluky 24 C3
Prime Seal I. .. 62 D4
Prince Albert .. 71 C9
Prince Albert
  Mts. 96 B15
Prince Albert
  Pen. 70 A8
Prince Albert Sd. 70 A8
Prince Charles I. 68 B3
Prince Charles
  Mts. 96 B10
Prince Edward
  I. □ 69 D4
Prince of Wales
  I., Canada ... 70 A10
Prince of Wales
  I., U.S.A. 71 C6
Principe da
  Beira 91 F6
Prins Harald
  Kyst 96 B8
Prinsesse Astrid
  Kyst 96 B7
Prinsesse
  Ragnhild Kyst 96 B8
Pripet → =
  Prypyat → .. 17 C10
Pripet Marshes 17 B9
Pripyat Marshes
  = Pripet
  Marshes 17 B9
Pripyats =
  Prypyat → .. 17 C10
Priština 22 C3
Privas 13 D6
Privolzhskaya
  Vozvyshennost
  .... 24 C6
Prizren 22 C3
Proddatur 43 M11
Progreso 85 C7
Prokopyevsk .. 29 D9
Prokuplje 22 C3
Prome = Pyè .. 41 H10
Propriá 93 E6
Prostějov 16 D3
Proston 63 A5
Provence 13 E6
Providence ... 73 D10
Providencia, I.
  de 86 D3
Provins 13 B5
Provo 81 E8
Prozna → 16 B3
Pruszków 16 B5
Prut → 17 F9
Pruzhany 17 B7
Prydz B. 96 A10
Pryluky 24 C3
Prypyat → .. 17 C10
Przemyśl 17 D6
Przhevalsk ... 29 E8
Psará 23 E5
Pskov 24 B2

Ptich =
  Ptsich → ... 17 B9
Ptsich → 17 B9
Puán 94 D4
Pucallpa 91 E4
Pudukkottai ... 43 P11
Puebla 84 D5
Pueblo 76 F2
Pueblo Hundido 94 B2
Puelches 94 D3
Puente Alto .. 94 C2
Puente-Genil .. 18 D3
Puerto Aisén .. 95 F2
Puerto
  Ayacucho ... 90 B5
Puerto Barrios . 85 D7
Puerto Bermejo 94 B5
Puerto
  Bermúdez ... 91 F4
Puerto Bolívar . 90 D3
Puerto Cabello 90 A5
Puerto Cabezas 86 D3
Puerto Carreño 90 B5
Puerto Chicama 91 E3
Puerto Coig ... 95 G3
Puerto Cortés . 85 D7
Puerto
  Cumarebo .. 90 A5
Puerto del
  Rosario 54 C2
Puerto Deseado 95 F3
Puerto Heath .. 91 F5
Puerto La Cruz 90 A6
Puerto
  Leguízamo .. 90 D4
Puerto Lobos .. 95 E3
Puerto Madryn 95 E3
Puerto
  Maldonado .. 91 F5
Puerto Montt .. 95 E2
Puerto Morelos 85 C7
Puerto Natales 95 G2
Puerto Páez .. 90 B5
Puerto Pinasco 94 A5
Puerto
  Pirámides ... 95 E4
Puerto Plata ... 87 C5
Puerto Princesa 38 C1
Puerto Quellón 95 E2
Puerto Rico ■ . 87 C6
Puerto Sastre . 91 H7
Puerto Suárez . 91 G7
Puerto Wilches 90 B4
Puertollano ... 18 C3
Pueyrredón, L. . 95 F2
Pugachev 24 C6
Puget Sound .. 80 B2
Puigcerdá 19 A6
Pukaki L. 65 F4
Pukapuka 65 L14
Pukekohe 64 B6
Pula 20 B4
Puławy 16 C5
Pullman 80 B5
Pulog 38 A2
Pułtusk 16 B5
Puna 91 G5
Puná, I. 90 D2
Punakha 41 D7
Punata 91 G5
Punch 42 C9
Pune 43 K8
Punjab □, India 42 D9
Punjab □,
  Pakistan 42 D8
Puno 91 G4
Punta Alta ... 94 D4
Punta Arenas . 95 G2
Punta de Díaz . 94 B2

Puntabie 62 B1
Puntarenas ... 86 E3
Punto Fijo 90 A4
Puquio 91 F4
Pur → 28 C8
Purace, Vol. ... 90 C3
Puralia =
  Puruliya 40 F6
Puri 40 H5
Purnia 40 E6
Purukcahu ... 37 E4
Puruliya 40 F6
Purus → 90 D6
Pusan 35 C7
Pushkino 24 C6
Putao 41 D11
Putaruru 64 C6
Puthein Myit → 41 K10
Putignano ... 21 D6
Puting, Tanjung 37 E4
Putorana, Gory 30 C7
Puttalam 43 Q11
Puttgarden ... 15 A6
Putumayo → . 90 D5
Putussibau ... 37 D4
Puy-de-Dôme . 13 D5
Pweto 57 F5
Pwllheli 11 E4
Pyapon 41 J10
Pyasina → ... 30 B6
Pyatigorsk 25 E5
Pyè 41 H10
Pyetrikaw 17 B9
Pyinmana 41 H11
P'yŏngyang .. 35 C7
Pyrénées 19 A6
Pyu 41 H11

Q

Qādib 49 E5
Qā'emshahr .. 44 B3
Qahremānshahr
  = Bākhtarān . 46 D6
Qaidam Pendi . 34 C4
Qalāt 45 C6
Qal'at al Akhḍar 47 E4
Qal'eh Shaharak 42 B4
Qal'eh-ye Now 45 C5
Qamar, Ghubbat
  al 49 D5
Qamruddin
  Karez 42 D6
Qandahār 42 D4
Qandahār □ .. 42 D4
Qapshaghay .. 29 E8
Qāra 52 C4
Qarabutaq ... 29 E7
Qarachuk 46 C5
Qaraghandy ... 29 E8
Qārah 47 E5
Qarataū 29 E8
Qarqan 34 C3
Qarqan He → . 34 C3
Qarqaraly 29 E8
Qarshi 29 F7
Qaşr-e Qand .. 45 E5
Qasr Farâfra .. 52 C4
Qatar ■ 44 E2
Qattâra,
  Munkhafed el 52 C4
Qattâra
  Depression =
  Qattâra,
  Munkhafed el 52 C4
Qāyen 44 C4

142

Qazaqstan =
  Kazakstan ■ . 29 E7
Qazvin 46 C7
Qena 52 C5
Qeshm 44 E4
Qila Safed 42 E2
Qila Saifullāh .. 42 D6
Qilian Shan .. 34 C4
Qingdao 35 C7
Qinghai □ ... 34 C4
Qinghai Hu .. 34 C5
Qinhuangdao . 35 C6
Qinzhou 35 D5
Qiqihar 35 B7
Qitai 34 B3
Qom 44 C2
Qomsheh 44 C2
Qondūz 45 B7
Qondūz □ 45 B7
Qostanay 29 D7
Qu Xian,
  Sichuan,
  China 35 C5
Qu Xian,
  Zhejiang,
  China 35 D6
Quambatook .. 62 C3
Quambone 63 B4
Quan Long ... 36 C3
Quandialla ... 63 B4
Quang Ngai ... 36 A3
Quanzhou ... 35 D6
Quaqtaq 68 B4
Quaraí 94 C5
Quartu
  Sant'Elena .. 21 E2
Quatsino 71 C7
Quba 25 E6
Qüchān 44 B4
Queanbeyan .. 63 C4
Québec 69 D3
Québec □ 69 D3
Queen
  Alexandra Ra. 96 C15
Queen Charlotte
  Is. 70 C6
Queen Charlotte
  Str. 71 C7
Queen Elizabeth
  Is. 66 B9
Queen Mary
  Land 96 B11
Queen Maud G. 70 B9
Queen Maud
  Land 96 B7
Queen Maud
  Mts. 96 C16
Queenscliff .. 63 C3
Queensland □ . 61 E7
Queenstown,
  Australia 62 D4
Queenstown,
  N.Z. 65 F3
Queenstown,
  S. Africa ... 59 E5
Queimadas ... 93 E6
Quela 56 F3
Quelimane ... 59 B7
Quelpart =
  Cheju Do ... 35 C7
Quequén 94 D5
Querétaro ... 84 C4
Quetta 42 D5
Quezon City .. 38 B2
Qui Nhon ... 36 B3
Quibaxe 56 F2
Quibdo 90 B3
Quiberon ... 12 C2
Quilán, C. 95 E2

Quilengues ... 58 A2
Quillabamba .. 91 F4
Quillagua 91 H5
Quillota 94 C2
Quilon 43 Q10
Quilpie 63 A3
Quimilí 94 B4
Quimper 12 B1
Quimperlé ... 12 C2
Quincy 77 F9
Quines 94 C3
Quinga 59 H8
Quintanar de la
  Orden 18 C4
Quintero 94 C2
Quinyambie .. 62 B3
Quipungo 58 A2
Quirindi 63 B5
Quissanga ... 59 G8
Quitilipi 94 B4
Quito 90 D3
Quixadá 92 C6
Qünghirot ... 29 E6
Quondong ... 62 B3
Quorn 62 B2
Qūqon 29 E8
Qûs 52 C5
Quseir 52 C5
Qyzylorda 29 E7

R

Raahe 8 F12
Raba 39 F1
Rába → 16 E3
Rabat, Malta . 21 G5
Rabat, Morocco 54 B3
Rabaul 64 K10
Rābigh 47 G4
Race, C. 69 D5
Rach Gia 36 B3
Racibórz 16 C4
Racine 72 C2
Rădăuţi 17 E7
Radekhiv 17 C7
Radekhov =
  Radekhiv .. 17 C7
Radhwa, Jabal 47 F4
Radom 16 C5
Radomsko ... 16 C4
Radomyshl ... 17 C9
Radstock, C. .. 62 B1
Rae 70 B8
Rae Bareli ... 40 D3
Rae Isthmus .. 68 B2
Raetihi 64 C6
Rafaela 94 C4
Rafai 56 D4
Rafhā 47 E5
Rafsanjān 44 D4
Ragachow ... 17 B10
Ragama 43 R11
Raglan 64 B6
Ragusa 21 F5
Raha 39 E2
Rahad al Bardī 53 F3
Rahaeng = Tak 36 A1
Rahimyar Khan 42 E7
Raichur 43 L10
Raigarh 40 G4
Railton 62 D4
Rainier, Mt. .. 80 B3
Raipur 40 G3
Ra'is 47 G4
Raj Nandgaon . 40 G3
Raja, Ujung ... 37 D1

Raja Ampat,
  Kepulauan .. 39 E3
Rajahmundry .. 40 J3
Rajang → ... 37 D4
Rajapalaiyam .. 43 Q10
Rajasthan □ ... 42 F8
Rajasthan Canal 42 F8
Rajgarh 43 G10
Rajkot 43 H7
Rajpipla 43 J8
Rajshahi 41 E7
Rakaia 65 E5
Rakaia → ... 65 E5
Rakan, Ra's .. 44 E2
Rakaposhi ... 42 A9
Rakata, Pulau . 37 F3
Rakhiv 17 D7
Raleigh 75 B8
Ram Hd. 63 C4
Ramanathapuram
  .... 43 Q11
Ramechhap ... 40 D6
Ramelau 39 F3
Ramgarh, Bihar,
  India 40 F5
Ramgarh, Raj.,
  India 42 F7
Rāmhormoz ... 47 E7
Ramnad =
  Ramanathapuram
  .... 43 Q11
Rampur 42 E11
Rampur Hat .. 40 E6
Ramree I. =
  Ramree Kyun 41 H9
Ramree Kyun . 41 H9
Ramtek 43 J11
Ranaghat 41 F7
Ranau 36 C5
Rancagua 94 C2
Ranchi 40 F5
Randers 9 G10
Rangaunu B. .. 64 A5
Rangia 41 D8
Rangiora 65 E5
Rangitaiki → . 64 B7
Rangitata → .. 65 E4
Rangon → ... 41 J11
Rangoon 41 J11
Rangpur 41 E7
Ranibennur ... 43 M9
Raniganj 40 F6
Raniwara 43 G8
Rankin Inlet ... 70 B10
Rankins Springs 63 B4
Ranong 36 C1
Ransiki 39 E4
Rantau 37 E5
Rantauprapat .. 37 D1
Rantemario ... 39 E1
Rapa 65 M16
Rapallo 20 B2
Rāpch 45 E4
Rapid City ... 76 C3
Rarotonga ... 65 M14
Ra's al Khaymah 44 E4
Ra's al-Unuf ... 52 B2
Ras Bânâs ... 52 D6
Ras Dashen ... 57 B7
Râs Timirist ... 55 E1
Rasa, Punta .. 95 E4
Rashad 53 F5
Rashîd 52 B5
Rasht 46 C7
Rat Islands ... 71 C1
Ratangarh ... 42 E9
Rathenow 15 B7
Ratibor =
  Racibórz 16 C4

Ratlam 43 H9
Ratnagiri 43 L8
Raukumara Ra. 64 C7
Raurkela 40 F5
Rava-Ruska ... 17 C6
Rava Russkaya
  = Rava-Ruska 17 C6
Rāvar 44 D4
Ravenna 20 B4
Ravensburg .. 14 E5
Ravi → 42 D7
Rawalpindi 42 C8
Hawāndūz ... 46 C6
Rawene 64 A5
Rawlins 81 E10
Rawson 95 E3
Ray, C. 69 D5
Rayadurg 43 M10
Rayagada 40 H4
Raymond 71 D8
Raz, Pte. du . 12 B1
Razdel'naya =
  Rozdilna ... 17 E10
Razelm, Lacul . 22 B7
Razgrad 22 C6
Ré, I. de 12 C3
Reading, U.K. .. 11 F6
Reading, U.S.A. 73 D8
Realicó 94 D4
Rebi 39 F4
Rebiana 52 D3
Rebun-Tō ... 32 E12
Rechytsa 17 B10
Recife 92 D7
Reconquista .. 94 B5
Recreo 94 B3
Red →, La.,
  U.S.A. 79 D8
Red →, N. Dak.,
  U.S.A. 76 A6
Red Cliffs 62 B3
Red Deer 71 C8
Red Sea 48 C2
Red Tower Pass
  = Turnu Roşu,
  P. 17 F7
Redcar 11 D6
Redcliffe 63 A5
Redding 80 E2
Redditch 11 E6
Redon 12 C2
Redondela ... 18 A1
Redwood City . 82 B1
Ree, L. 11 E3
Reefton 65 E4
Regensburg ... 15 D7
Réggio di
  Calábria 21 E5
Réggio
  nell'Emília .. 20 B3
Reghin 17 E7
Regina 71 C9
Rehoboth 58 C3
Rehovot 46 E3
Rei-Bouba 53 G1
Reichenbach .. 15 C7
Reidsville ... 75 A8
Reigate 11 F6
Reims 13 B6
Reina Adelaida,
  Arch. 95 G2
Reindeer L. ... 71 C9
Reinga, C. 64 A5
Reinosa 18 A3
Reliance 70 B9
Remarkable, Mt. 62 B2
Remeshk 45 E4
Rendsburg 14 A5
Rengat 37 E2

Reni	17	F9	Ridder	29	D9	Roanoke	73	F6	Rosario,		
Renk	53	F5	Ried	15	D7	Robbins I.	62	D4	Paraguay	94	A5
Renmark	62	B3	Riesa	15	C7	Robertson	58	E3	Rosario de la		
Rennes	12	B3	Rieti	20	C4	Robertson I.	96	A4	Frontera	94	B3
Reno	80	F4	Rig Rig	53	F1	Robertsport	55	G2	Rosário do Sul	94	C6
Reno →	20	B4	Riga	24	B1	Robertstown	62	B2	Rosas, G. de	19	A7
Rentería	19	A5	Riga, G. of	24	B1	Robinvale	62	B3	Roscommon	11	E2
Republican →	76	F6	Rigas Jūras Licis			Roboré	91	G7	Roseau, Domin.	87	C7
Repulse Bay	68	B2	= Riga, G. of	24	B1	Robson, Mt.	71	C8	Roseau, U.S.A.	77	A7
Requena, Peru	90	E4	Rigestān □	42	D4	Roca, C. da	18	C1	Rosebery	62	D4
Requena, Spain	19	C5	Rigolet	68	C5	Rocas, I.	92	C7	Roseburg	80	D2
Resadiye =			Riiser-Larsen-			Rocha	94	C6	Rosenheim	15	E7
Datça	23	F6	halvøya	96	A8	Rochefort	12	D3	Rosetown	71	C9
Resht = Rasht	46	C7	Rijeka	20	B5	Rochester,			Rosetta =		
Resistencia	94	B5	Rimah, Wadi			Minn., U.S.A.	77	C8	Rashîd	52	B5
Reşiţa	17	F5	ar →	47	F5	Rochester, N.Y.,			Roseville	80	F3
Resolution I.,			Rímini	20	B4	U.S.A.	73	C7	Rosewood	63	A5
Canada	68	B4	Rîmnicu Sărat	17	F8	Rock Hill	75	B7	Rosignano		
Resolution I.,			Rîmnicu Vîlcea	17	F7	Rock Island	77	E9	Maríttimo	20	C3
N.Z.	65	F2	Rimouski	69	D4	Rock Springs	81	E9	Rosignol	90	B7
Réthímnon	23	G5	Rinca	39	F1	Rockefeller			Roşiori-de-Vede	22	B5
Réunion ■	51	J9	Rinconada	94	A3	Plateau	96	C18	Roslavl	24	C3
Reus	19	B6	Rinjani	37	F5	Rockford	77	D10	Roslyn	63	B4
Reutlingen	14	D5	Rio Branco,			Rockhampton	61	E9	Ross, Australia	62	D4
Reval = Tallinn	24	B1	Brazil	91	E5	Rocky Mount	75	B9	Ross, N.Z.	65	E4
Revelstoke	71	C8	Rio Branco,			Rocky Mts.	70	C7	Ross I.	96	B15
Rewa	40	E3	Uruguay	94	C6	Rod	42	E3	Ross Ice Shelf	96	C16
Rewari	42	E10	Rio Cuarto	94	C4	Rodez	13	D5	Ross Sea	96	B15
Rey Malabo	56	D1	Rio de Janeiro	93	G5	Ródhos	23	F7	Rossano Cálabro	21	E6
Reykjavík	8	B2	Rio de			Rodney, C.	64	B6	Rossland	71	D8
Reynosa	84	B5	Janeiro □	93	G5	Roes Welcome			Rosslare	11	E3
Rhein →	14	C4	Rio do Sul	94	B7	Sd.	68	B2	Rosso	55	E1
Rhein-Main-			Río Gallegos	95	G3	Rogachev =			Rossosh	24	C4
Donau-			Río Grande,			Ragachow	17	B10	Rosthern	71	C9
Kanal →	15	D6	Argentina	95	G3	Rogagua, L.	91	F5	Rostock	15	A7
Rheine	14	B4	Rio Grande,			Rogatyn	17	D7	Rostov, Don,		
Rheinland-			Brazil	94	C6	Rogoaguado, L.	91	F5	Russia	25	D4
Pfalz □	14	C4	Rio Grande →	78	E3	Rohri	42	F6	Rostov, Yarosl.,		
Rhin =			Rio Grande do			Rohtak	42	E10	Russia	24	B4
Rhein →	14	C4	Norte □	92	D6	Roi Et	36	A2	Roswell	78	C1
Rhine =			Rio Grande do			Rojas	94	C4	Rotherham	11	E6
Rhein →	14	C4	Sul □	94	B6	Rojo, C.	84	C5	Roto	63	B4
Rhineland-			Rio Largo	93	D6	Rokan →	37	D2	Rotondo Mte.	13	E8
Palatinate □ =			Río Mulatos	91	G5	Rolândia	94	A6	Rotorua	64	C7
Rheinland-			Río Muni =			Roma, Australia	63	A4	Rotorua, L.	64	C7
Pfalz □	14	C4	Mbini □	56	D2	Roma, Italy	20	D4	Rotterdam	14	C3
Rhode Island □	73	D10	Rio Negro	94	B7	Roman	17	E8	Rottweil	14	D5
Rhodes =			Rio Verde	93	F3	Romang	39	F3	Rotuma	64	L12
Ródhos	23	F7	Ríobamba	90	D3	Romania ■	22	B5	Roubaix	13	A5
Rhodope Mts. =			Ríohacha	90	A4	Romanovka =			Rouen	12	B4
Rhodopi			Ríosucio,			Basarabeasca	17	E9	Round Mt.	63	B5
Planina	22	D5	Caldas,			Romans-sur-			Roussillon	13	E5
Rhodopi Planina	22	D5	Colombia	90	B3	Isère	13	D6	Rouyn	69	D3
Rhön = Hohe			Ríosucio, Choco,			Romblon	38	B2	Rovaniemi	8	E13
Rhön	14	C5	Colombia	90	B3	Rome = Roma	20	D4	Rovereto	20	B3
Rhondda	11	F5	Rishiri-Tō	32	E12	Rome	74	B5	Rovigo	20	B3
Rhône →	13	E6	Riva del Garda	20	B3	Romorantin-			Rovinj	20	B4
Rhum	10	C3	Rivadavia	94	B2	Lanthenay	12	C4	Rovno = Rivne	17	C8
Riachão	92	D4	Rivera	94	C5	Roncador, Serra			Rovuma →	57	G8
Riasi	42	C9	Riversdale	58	E4	do	93	E3	Rowena	63	A4
Riau □	37	E2	Riverside	82	D4	Ronda	18	D3	Roxas	38	B2
Riau, Kepulauan	37	D2	Riverton,			Rondônia □	91	F6	Roxburgh	65	F3
Riau Arch. =			Australia	62	B2	Rondonópolis	93	F3	Royal		
Riau,			Riverton,			Ronge, L. la	71	C9	Leamington		
Kepulauan	37	D2	Canada	71	C10	Ronne Ice Shelf	96	B3	Spa	11	E6
Ribadeo	18	A2	Riverton, N.Z.	65	G2	Roodepoort	59	D5	Royan	12	D3
Ribeirão Prêto	93	G4	Riviera di			Roorkee	42	E10	Rozdilna	17	E10
Riberalta	91	F5	Levante	20	B2	Roosevelt →	91	E6	Rozhyshche	17	C7
Ribniţa	17	E9	Riviera di			Roosevelt I.	96	B16	Rtishchevo	24	C5
Riccarton	65	E5	Ponente	20	B2	Roquetas de			Ruahine Ra.	64	C7
Richland	80	B4	Rivière-du-Loup	69	D4	Mar	19	D4	Ruapehu	64	C6
Richmond,			Rivne	17	C8	Roraima □	90	C6	Ruapuke I.	65	G3
Australia	63	B5	Rívoli	20	B1	Roraima, Mt.	90	B6	Rub' al Khali	48	D4
Richmond, N.Z.	65	D5	Rivoli B.	62	C3	Rosa	57	F6	Rubio	90	B4
Richmond,			Riyadh = Ar			Rosa, Monte	13	D7	Rubtsovsk	29	D9
Calif., U.S.A.	80	G2	Riyāḍ	47	F6	Rosario,			Rudall	62	B2
Richmond, Va.,			Rize	46	B5	Argentina	94	C4	Rudolf, Ostrov	28	A6
U.S.A.	73	F7	Rizzuto, C.	21	E6	Rosário, Brazil	92	C5	Rufa'a	53	F5
Richmond Ra.	63	A5	Roanne	13	C6	Rosario, Mexico	84	C3	Rufiji →	57	F7

Rufino 94 C4
Rufisque 55 F1
Rugby 11 E6
Rügen 15 A7
Ruhr ⇀ 14 C4
Rukwa L. 57 F6
Rum = Rhum . 10 C3
Rumāḥ 47 F6
Rumania =
  Romania ■ .. 22 B5
Rumbêk 53 G4
Rumia 16 A4
Rumoi 32 F12
Runanga 65 E4
Runaway, C. .. 64 B7
Rungwa 57 F6
Ruoqiang 34 C3
Rupa 41 D9
Rupat 37 D2
Rupert ⇀ 69 C3
Rupert House =
  Waskaganish 69 C3
Rurrenabaque . 91 F5
Rusape 59 B6
Ruschuk = Ruse 22 C5
Ruse 22 C5
Rushworth 63 C4
Russas 92 C6
Russellkonda .. 40 H5
Russkaya
  Polyana 29 D8
Rustavi 25 E6
Rustenburg ... 59 D5
Ruteng 39 F2
Rutshuru 57 E5
Ruwenzori ... 57 D5
Ružomberok .. 16 D4
Rwanda ■ ... 57 E6
Ryazan 24 C4
Ryazhsk 24 C5
Rybache =
  Rybachye ... 29 E9
Rybachye 29 E9
Rybinsk 24 B4
Rybinskoye
  Vdkhr. 24 B4
Rybnitsa =
  Rîbniţa 17 E9
Rylstone 63 B4
Rypin 16 B4
Ryūkyū Is. =
  Ryūkyū-rettō 35 D7
Ryūkyū-rettō .. 35 D7
Rzeszów 16 C5
Rzhev 24 B3

S

Sa Dec 36 B3
Sa'ādatābād .. 44 D3
Saale ⇀ 15 C6
Saalfeld 15 C6
Saar ⇀ 13 B7
Saarbrücken .. 14 D4
Saaremaa 24 B1
Šabac 22 B2
Sabadell 19 B7
Sabah □ 36 C5
Şabāḥ, Wadi ⇀ 47 G7
Sabalān, Kūhhā-
  ye 46 C6
Sábanalarga .. 90 A4
Sabang 36 C1
Sabará 93 F5
Saberania 39 E5
Sabhah 52 C1

Sabinas 84 B4
Sabinas Hidalgo 84 B4
Sablayan 38 B2
Sable, C.,
  Canada 69 D4
Sable, C., U.S.A. 86 A3
Sable I. 69 D5
Sabrina Coast . 96 A12
Sabulubek 37 E1
Sabzevār 44 B4
Sabzvārān 44 D4
Săcele 17 F7
Sachsen □ 15 C7
Sachsen-
  Anhalt □ 15 C7
Sacramento ... 80 F3
Sacramento ⇀ 80 F3
Sacramento
  Mts. 83 D10
Sadani 57 F7
Sadd el Aali ... 52 D5
Sado 33 G11
Sadon 41 E11
Safi 54 B3
Safid Kūh 42 B3
Saga, Indonesia 39 E4
Saga, Japan .. 32 C2
Sagala 55 F3
Sagar 43 M9
Sagil 34 A4
Saginaw 72 C4
Sagīr, Zāb aş ⇀ 46 D5
Saglouc =
  Salluit 68 B3
Sagua la Grande 86 B3
Saguenay ⇀ . 69 D3
Sagunto 19 C5
Sahagún 18 A3
Sahand, Kūh-e 46 C6
Sahara 54 D6
Saharan Atlas =
  Saharien,
  Atlas 54 B5
Saharanpur ... 42 E10
Saharien, Atlas 54 B5
Sahiwal 42 D8
Sa'id Bundas .. 53 G3
Saïda 54 B5
Sa'īdābād 44 D3
Sa'īdīyeh 46 C7
Saidpur 41 E7
Saidu 42 B8
Saigon = Phanh
  Bho Ho Chi
  Minh 36 B3
Saijō 32 C3
Saikhoa Ghat .. 41 D10
Saiki 32 C2
Sailolof 39 E4
St. Andrews ... 10 C5
St. Arnaud ... 62 C3
St-Augustin-
  Saguenay ... 69 C5
St. Augustine . 75 E7
St. Austell 11 F4
St. Boniface ... 71 D10
St.-Brieuc 12 B2
St. Catharines . 69 D3
St.-Chamond . 13 D6
St. Christopher-
  Nevis ■ = St.
  Kitts & Nevis 87 C7
St. Cloud 77 C7
St. Croix 87 C7
St.-Denis 12 B5
St.-Dizier 13 B6
St. Elias, Mt. .. 70 B5
St.-Étienne .. 13 D6
St.-Flour 13 D5

St. Francis, C. . 58 E4
St. Gallen =
  Sankt Gallen 13 C8
St.-Gaudens ... 12 E4
St. George 63 A4
St.-Georges,
  Fr. Guiana .. 92 B3
St. George's,
  Grenada 87 D7
St. George's
  Channel 11 F3
St. Georges Hd. 63 C5
St. Gotthard P
  = San
  Gottardo, P.
  del 13 C8
St. Helena ■ .. 51 H3
St. Helena B. .. 58 E3
St. Helens ... 62 D4
St. Helier 11 G5
St-Hyacinthe .. 69 D3
St. John 69 D4
St. John's,
  Antigua 87 C7
St. John's,
  Canada 69 D5
St. Johns ⇀ .. 75 D7
St. Joseph ... 77 F7
St. Joseph, L. . 69 C1
St. Kilda, N.Z. . 65 F4
St. Kilda, U.K. . 10 C2
St. Kitts & Nevis 87 C7
St.-Laurent 92 A3
St. Lawrence ⇀ 69 D4
St. Lawrence,
  Gulf of 69 D4
St. Lawrence I. 71 B2
St. Leonard ... 69 D4
St.-Lô 12 B3
St-Louis 55 E1
St. Louis 77 F9
St. Lucia ■ .. 87 D7
St. Lucia, L. ... 59 D6
St. Maarten .. 87 C7
St.-Malo 12 B2
St-Marc 87 C5
St. Mary Pk. ... 62 B2
St. Marys 62 D4
St.-Mathieu, Pte. 12 B1
St. Matthews, I.
  = Zadetkyi
  Kyun 36 C1
St.-Nazaire 12 C2
St.-Omer 12 A5
St. Paul 77 C8
St. Peter Port .. 11 G5
St. Petersburg =
  Sankt-
  Peterburg ... 24 B3
St. Petersburg . 75 F6
St.-Pierre et
  Miquelon □ . 69 D5
St.-Quentin .. 13 B5
St. Thomas I. .. 87 C7
St.-Tropez ... 13 E7
St. Vincent, G. . 62 C2
St. Vincent &
  the
  Grenadines ■ 87 D7
Saintes 12 D3
Saintonge ... 12 D3
Saipan 64 H9
Sairang 41 F9
Sairecábur,
  Cerro 94 A3
Sajama 91 G5
Sajó 16 D5
Sakai 32 B4
Sakākah 47 E5

Sakakawea, L. . 76 B4
Sakarya =
  Adapazarı ... 46 B2
Sakarya ⇀ .. 25 E3
Sakata 33 G11
Sakhalin 31 D12
Sakon Nakhon . 36 A2
Sala 9 G11
Sala Consilina . 21 D5
Saladillo 94 D5
Salado ⇀,
  Buenos Aires,
  Argentina ... 94 D5
Salado ⇀,
  La Pampa,
  Argentina ... 94 D3
Salado ⇀,
  Santa Fe,
  Argentina ... 94 C4
Salaga 55 G4
Salālah 49 D5
Salamanca,
  Chile 94 C2
Salamanca,
  Spain 18 B3
Salamís 23 F4
Salar de
  Atacama ... 94 A3
Salar de Uyuni 91 H5
Salaverry 91 E3
Salawati 39 E4
Salayar 39 F2
Saldanha 58 E3
Sale, Australia . 63 C4
Salé, Morocco . 54 B3
Salekhard ... 28 C7
Salem, India .. 43 P11
Salem, U.S.A. . 80 C2
Salerno 21 D5
Salgótarján .. 16 D4
Salihli 23 E7
Salihorsk 17 B8
Salima 59 A6
Salina, Italy ... 21 E5
Salina, U.S.A. . 76 F6
Salina Cruz ... 85 D5
Salinas, Brazil . 93 F5
Salinas, Ecuador 90 D2
Salinas, U.S.A. 82 B2
Salinas Grandes 94 C3
Salinópolis 92 C4
Salisbury,
  Australia 62 B2
Salisbury, U.K. 11 F6
Salisbury, U.S.A. 75 B7
Salluit 68 B3
Salmās 46 C6
Salmon ⇀ .. 80 C5
Salmon River
  Mts. 81 C6
Salon-de-
  Provence ... 13 E6
Salonica =
  Thessaloníki . 23 D4
Salonta 16 E5
Salsk 25 D5
Salso ⇀ 21 F4
Salt Creek ... 62 C2
Salt Lake City . 81 E8
Salta 94 A3
Saltillo 84 B4
Salto 94 C5
Salto ⇀ 20 C4
Salton Sea ... 82 D5
Saltpond 55 G4
Salûm 52 B4
Salûm, Khâlig el 52 B4
Salur 40 H4
Salvador 93 E6

Salwa

Salwa 44 E2
Salween → ... 41 J11
Salyan 25 F6
Salzach → ... 15 D7
Salzburg 15 E7
Salzgitter 14 B6
Salzwedel 15 B6
Sama 28 C7
Sama de
  Langreo 18 A3
Samales Group 38 C2
Samangán □ .. 45 B7
Samar 38 B3
Samara 24 C7
Samarinda 37 E5
Samarkand =
  Samarqand . 29 F7
Samarqand ... 29 F7
Sámarrā 46 D5
Sambalpur 40 G5
Sambar,
  Tanjung 37 E4
Sambas 37 D3
Sambava 59 G10
Sambhal 42 E11
Sambhar 42 F9
Sambiase 21 E6
Sambir 17 D6
Same 57 E7
Samokov 22 C4
Sámos 23 F6
Samothráki,
  Évros, Greece 23 D5
Samothráki,
  Kérkira,
  Greece 23 E2
Sampacho 94 C4
Sampit 37 E4
Sampit, Teluk . 37 E4
Samra 47 F5
Samsun 46 B4
Samui, Ko ... 36 C2
Samut Prakan . 36 B2
Samut
  Songkhram →
  .... 36 B2
San 55 F4
San → 16 C5
San Agustin, C. 38 C3
San Andrés, I.
  de 86 D3
San Andrés
  Tuxtla 85 D5
San Angelo .. 78 D3
San Antonio,
  Chile 94 C2
San Antonio,
  Spain 19 C6
San Antonio,
  U.S.A. 78 E4
San Antonio, C.,
  Argentina ... 94 D5
San Antonio, C.,
  Cuba 85 C8
San Antonio
  Oeste 95 E4
San Benedetto
  del Tronto .. 20 C4
San Bernardino 82 C4
San Bernardino
  Str. 38 B2
San Bernardo . 94 C2
San Bernardo, I.
  de 90 B3
San Borja 91 F5
San Carlos,
  Argentina ... 94 C3
San Carlos,
  Chile 94 D2

San Carlos, Phil. 38 B2
San Carlos,
  Amazonas,
  Venezuela ... 90 C5
San Carlos,
  Cojedes,
  Venezuela ... 90 B5
San Carlos de
  Bariloche ... 95 E2
San Carlos del
  Zulia 90 B4
San Cristóbal,
  Argentina ... 94 C4
San Cristóbal,
  Mexico 85 D6
San Cristóbal,
  Venezuela ... 90 B4
San Diego 82 D4
San Diego, C. . 95 G3
San Felipe, Chile 94 C2
San Felipe,
  Venezuela ... 90 A5
San Felíu de
  Guíxols 19 B7
San Fernando,
  Chile 94 C2
San Fernando,
  La Union, Phil. 38 A2
San Fernando,
  Pampanga,
  Phil. 38 A2
San Fernando,
  Spain 18 D2
San Fernando,
  Trin. & Tob. . 87 D7
San Fernando,
  U.S.A. 82 C3
San Fernando
  de Apure ... 90 B5
San Fernando
  de Atabapo . 90 C5
San Francisco,
  Argentina ... 94 C4
San Francisco,
  U.S.A. 82 B1
San Francisco
  de Macorís .. 87 C5
San Francisco
  del Monte de
  Oro 94 C3
San Gil 90 B4
San Gottardo, P.
  del 13 C8
San Ignacio,
  Bolivia 91 G6
San Ignacio,
  Paraguay ... 94 B5
San Ildefonso,
  C. 38 A2
San Javier,
  Argentina ... 94 C5
San Javier,
  Bolivia 91 G6
San Joaquin → 82 A2
San Jorge, B. de 84 A2
San Jorge, G. . 95 F3
San Jorge, G. de 19 B6
San José,
  Bolivia 91 G6
San José,
  Costa Rica .. 86 E3
San José,
  Guatemala .. 85 E6
San Jose, Phil. 38 A2
San Jose, U.S.A. 82 B2
San Jose de
  Buenovista .. 38 B2
San José de
  Jáchal 94 C3

San José de
  Mayo 94 C5
San José de
  Ocune 90 C4
San José del
  Guaviare 90 C4
San Juan,
  Argentina ... 94 C3
San Juan, Phil. 38 C3
San Juan,
  Puerto Rico . 87 C6
San Juan → .. 86 D3
San Juan, C. . 56 D1
San Juan de los
  Morros 90 B5
San Juan Mts. . 83 B9
San Julián 95 F3
San Justo 94 C4
San Leandro .. 82 B1
San Lorenzo .. 90 C3
San Lorenzo, I. 91 F3
San Lorenzo,
  Mt. 95 F2
San Lucas 91 H5
San Lucas, C. . 84 C2
San Luis 94 C3
San Luis Obispo 82 C2
San Luis Potosí 84 C4
San Marino ... 20 C4
San Marino ■ . 20 C4
San Martín, L. . 95 F2
San Matías ... 91 G7
San Matías, G. 95 E4
San Miguel ... 85 E7
San Miguel → 91 F6
San Miguel de
  Tucumán ... 94 B3
San Narciso ... 38 A2
San Nicolás de
  los Arroyas . 94 C4
San-Pédro 55 H3
San Pedro de
  las Colonias . 84 B4
San Pedro de
  Lloc 91 E3
San Pedro de
  Macorís 87 C6
San Pedro del
  Paraná 94 B5
San Pedro Sula 85 D7
San Pieto 21 E2
San Rafael,
  Argentina ... 94 C3
San Rafael,
  U.S.A. 80 G2
San Ramón de
  la Nueva Orán 94 A4
San Remo 20 C1
San Roque,
  Argentina ... 94 B5
San Roque,
  Spain 18 D3
San Rosendo . 94 D2
San Salvador,
  Bahamas ... 86 B5
San Salvador,
  El Salv. 85 E7
San Salvador de
  Jujuy 94 A4
San Sebastián,
  Argentina ... 95 G3
San Sebastián,
  Spain 19 A5
San Severo ... 20 D5
San Valentin,
  Mte. 95 F2
San Vicente de
  la Barquera . 18 A3

Sana' 49 D3
Sana → 20 B6
Sanaga → ... 56 D1
Sanana 39 E3
Sanandaj 46 D6
Sanco Pt. 38 C3
Sancti-Spíritus . 86 B4
Sancy, Puy de . 13 D5
Sandakan 36 C5
Sandanski ... 22 D4
Sanday 10 B5
Sandgate 63 A5
Sandía 91 F5
Sandıklı 46 C2
Sandoa 56 F4
Sandomierz ... 16 C5
Sandoway 41 H10
Sandusky 72 D4
Sandwip Chan. 41 F8
Sandy C. 62 D3
Sandy L. 71 C10
Sanford, Fla.,
  U.S.A. 75 E7
Sanford, N.C.,
  U.S.A. 75 B8
Sanford, Mt. .. 71 B5
Sanga → 56 E3
Sangamner ... 43 K9
Sangar 31 C10
Sangasangadalam
  .... 37 E5
Sangeang 39 F1
Sangerhausen . 15 C6
Sanggau 37 D4
Sangihe, P. ... 39 D3
Sangkapura ... 37 F4
Sangli 43 L9
Sangmélina .. 56 D2
Sangre de Cristo
  Mts. 78 A1
Sankt Gallen .. 13 C8
Sankt Moritz .. 13 C8
Sankt-Peterburg 24 B3
Sankt Pölten .. 15 D8
Sankuru → ... 56 E4
Sanliurfa 46 C4
Sanlúcar de
  Barrameda .. 18 D2
Sannicandro
  Gargánico .. 20 D5
Sanok 17 D6
Sanshui 35 D6
Santa Ana,
  Bolivia 91 F5
Santa Ana,
  Ecuador ... 90 D2
Santa Ana,
  El Salv. 85 E7
Santa Ana,
  U.S.A. 82 D4
Santa Barbara . 82 C3
Santa Catalina I. 82 D3
Santa
  Catarina □ .. 94 B7
Santa Clara .. 86 B4
Santa Clotilde . 90 D4
Santa Coloma
  de Gramanet 19 B7
Santa Cruz,
  Argentina ... 95 G3
Santa Cruz,
  Bolivia 91 G6
Santa Cruz, Phil. 38 B2
Santa Cruz,
  U.S.A. 82 B1
Santa Cruz → . 95 G3
Santa Cruz de
  Tenerife 54 C1

Santa Cruz do Sul 94 B6
Santa Cruz I. . . 64 L11
Santa Elena . . 90 D2
Santa Eugenia, Pta. 84 B1
Santa Fe, Argentina . . . 94 C4
Santa Fe, U.S.A. 83 C10
Santa Filomena 93 D4
Santa Inés, I. . . 95 G2
Santa Isabel = Rey Malabo . 56 D1
Santa Isabel, Argentina . . . 94 D3
Santa Isabel, Brazil 93 E3
Santa Lucia Range 82 C2
Santa Maria, Brazil 94 B6
Santa Maria, U.S.A. 82 C2
Santa María → 84 A3
Santa Maria da Vitória 93 E5
Santa Maria di Leuca, C. . . . 23 E2
Santa Marta . . 90 A4
Santa Marta, Sierra Nevada de 90 A4
Santa Maura = Levkás 23 E3
Santa Rosa, La Pampa, Argentina . . . 94 D4
Santa Rosa, San Luis, Argentina . . . 94 C3
Santa Rosa, Bolivia 91 F5
Santa Rosa, Brazil 94 B6
Santa Rosa, U.S.A. 80 F2
Santa Rosa de Copán 85 E7
Santa Vitória do Palmar 94 C6
Santai 35 C5
Santana, Coxilha de 94 C5
Santana do Livramento . . 94 C5
Santander . . . 18 A4
Sant'Antíoco . . 21 E2
Santarém, Brazil 92 C3
Santarém, Portugal 18 C1
Santiago, Brazil 94 B6
Santiago, Chile 94 C2
Santiago → . . 90 D3
Santiago de Compostela . 18 A1
Santiago de Cuba 86 C4
Santiago de los Cabelleros . . 87 C5
Santiago del Estero 94 B4
Santo Amaro . . 93 E6
Santo Ângelo . . 94 B6
Santo Antonio . 93 F2
Santo Corazón 91 G7
Santo Domingo 87 C6
Santo Tomás . 91 F4
Santo Tomé . . . 94 B5

Santo Tomé de Guayana = Ciudad Guayana . . . 90 B6
Santoña 18 A4
Santoríni = Thíra 23 F5
Santos 94 A7
Santos Dumont 94 A8
Sanza Pombo . 56 F3
São Anastácio . 94 A6
São Bernado de Campo 93 G4
São Borja 94 B5
São Carlos . . . 94 A7
São Cristóvão . 93 E6
São Domingos 93 E4
São Francisco . 93 F5
São Francisco → 93 E6
São Francisco do Sul 94 B7
São Gabriel . . 94 C6
São João da Madeira 18 B1
São João del Rei 93 G5
São João do Araguaia . . 92 D4
São João do Piauí 92 D5
São José do Rio Prêto 94 A7
São Leopoldo . 94 B6
São Lourenço . 93 G4
São Lourenço → 93 F2
São Luís 92 C5
São Marcos → 93 F4
São Marcos, B. de 92 C5
São Mateus . . 93 F6
São Paulo 94 A7
São Paulo □ . . 94 A7
São Roque, C. de 92 D6
São Sebastião, I. de 94 A7
São Tomé & Principe ■ . . 51 F4
São Vicente, C. de 18 D1
Saône → 13 D6
Saonek 39 E4
Saparua 39 E3
Sapele 55 G6
Saposoa 91 E3
Sapporo 32 F12
Sapulpa 79 B5
Saqqez 46 C6
Sar-e Pol 45 B6
Sar-e Pol □ . . 45 B6
Sar Planina . . 22 C3
Saráb 46 C6
Sarada → 40 D3
Saragossa = Zaragoza . . . 19 B5
Saraguro 90 D3
Sarajevo 20 C7
Saran, G. 37 E4
Sarandí del Yi . 94 C5
Sarangani B. . . 38 C3
Sarangani Is. . . 38 C3
Sarangarh . . . 40 G4
Saransk 24 C6
Sarapul 29 D6
Sarasota 75 F6
Saratov 24 C6
Saravane 36 A3

Sarawak □ 37 D4
Saray 22 D6
Sarayköy 23 F7
Sarbāz 45 E5
Sarbisheh . . . 45 C4
Sarda → = Sarada → . . 40 D3
Sardalas 54 C7
Sardarshahr . . 42 E9
Sardegna □ . . 21 D2
Sardinia = Sardegna □ . 21 D2
Sardis 23 E7
Sargodha 42 C8
Sarh 53 G2
Sārī 44 B3
Sangöl 23 E7
Sarikamiş 46 B5
Sarikei 37 D4
Sark 11 G5
Şarköy 23 D6
Sarlat-la-Canéda 12 D4
Sarmi 39 E5
Sarmiento . . . 95 F3
Sarnia 69 D2
Sarny 24 C2
Sarolangun . . 37 E2
Saronikós Kólpos 23 F4
Sarre = Saar → 13 B7
Sarreguemines 13 B7
Sarro 55 F3
Sarthe → 12 C3
Sartynya 28 C7
Sarvestān . . . 44 D3
Sary-Tash . . . 29 F8
Saryshagan . . 29 E8
Sasabeneh . . . 49 F3
Sasaram 40 E5
Sasebo 32 C1
Saser 42 B10
Saskatchewan □ 71 C9
Saskatchewan → 71 C9
Saskatoon . . . 71 C9
Saskylakh . . . 30 B9
Sasovo 24 C5
Sassandra . . . 55 H3
Sassandra → . . 55 H3
Sássari 21 D2
Sassnitz 15 A7
Sassuolo 20 B3
Sasyk, Ozero . . 17 F9
Sata-Misaki . . 33 D2
Satadougou . . 55 F2
Satara 43 L8
Satmala Hills . . 43 J9
Satna 40 E3
Sátoraljaújhely 16 D5
Satpura Ra. . . . 43 J10
Satu Mare . . . 17 E6
Satui 37 E5
Saturnina → . . 91 F7
Saudi Arabia ■ 47 F6
Sauerland . . . 14 C4
Sault Ste. Marie, Canada 69 D2
Sault Ste. Marie, U.S.A. 72 A3
Saumlaki 39 F4
Saumur 12 C3
Saunders C. . . 65 F4
Sauri 55 F6
Saurimo 56 F4
Sava → 22 B3
Savage I. = Niue 65 L14
Savalou 55 G5
Savanna la Mar 86 C4

Savannah 75 C7
Savannah → . . 75 C7
Savannakhet . . 36 A2
Savanur 43 M9
Savé 55 G5
Save → 59 C6
Sāveh 46 D7
Savelugu 55 G4
Savoie □ 13 D7
Savona 20 B2
Sawahlunto . . 37 E2
Sawai 39 E3
Sawai Madhopur . . 42 F10
Sawara 32 B7
Sawatch Mts. . 83 A9
Sawmills 59 B5
Sawu 39 F2
Sawu Sea 39 F2
Saxony, Lower = Niedersachsen □ 14 B5
Say 55 F5
Sayán 91 F3
Sayan, Zapadnyy . . . 30 D7
Saydā 46 D3
Sayghān 45 C6
Sayhut 49 D5
Saynshand . . . 35 B6
Sazanit 23 D2
Sázava → 16 D2
Sazin 42 B8
Scandicci 20 C3
Scandinavia . . . 8 F10
Scarborough . . 11 D6
Scebeli, Wabi → 49 G3
Schaffhausen . 13 C8
Schefferville . . 69 C4
Schelde → . . . 14 C3
Schenectady . . 73 C9
Schiermonnikoog 14 B4
Schio 20 B3
Schleswig 14 A5
Schleswig-Holstein □ . . 14 A5
Schouten I. . . . 62 D4
Schouten Is. = Supiori 39 E5
Schwäbische Alb 14 D5
Schwaner, Pegunungan 37 E4
Schwarzwald . . 14 D5
Schwedt 15 B8
Schweinfurt . . . 14 C6
Schwenningen = Villingen-Schwenningen 14 D5
Schwerin 15 B6
Schwyz 13 C8
Sciacca 21 F4
Scilla 21 E5
Scilly, Isles of . 11 G3
Scone 63 B5
Scotland □ . . . 10 C4
Scott Glacier . . 96 A12
Scott Inlet 68 A3
Scottsbluff . . . 76 E3
Scottsdale 62 D4
Scranton 73 D8
Scunthorpe . . . 11 E6
Scusciuban . . . 49 E5
Scutari = Üsküdar 25 E2
Seaspray 63 C4

Seattle	80	B2	
Sebastopol =			
Sevastopol	25	E3	
Sebha =			
Sabhah	52	C1	
Şebinkarahisar	46	B4	
Sebta = Ceuta	18	E3	
Sebuku	37	E5	
Sebuku, Teluk	37	D5	
Secretary I.	65	F2	
Secunderabad	43	L11	
Sedalia	77	F8	
Sedan, Australia	62	B2	
Sedan, France	13	B6	
Seddon	65	D6	
Seddonville	65	D5	
Sedhiou	55	F1	
Sedova, Pik	28	B6	
Seeheim	58	D3	
Seferihisar	23	E6	
Segamat	37	D2	
Segesta	21	F4	
Seget	39	E4	
Ségou	55	F3	
Segovia =			
Coco →	86	D3	
Segovia	18	B3	
Segre →	19	B6	
Séguéla	55	G3	
Segura →	19	C5	
Sehitwa	58	C4	
Sehore	43	H10	
Seine →	12	B4	
Seistan	45	D5	
Seistan,			
Daryācheh-ye	45	D5	
Sekayu	37	E2	
Sekondi-			
Takoradi	55	H4	
Selaru	39	F4	
Selçuk	23	F6	
Sele →	21	D5	
Selenga =			
Selenge			
Mörön →	35	A5	
Selenge			
Mörön →	35	A5	
Seletan, Tg.	37	E4	
Sélibabi	55	E2	
Selîma, El			
Wâhât el	52	D4	
Selkirk	71	C10	
Selkirk Mts.	71	C8	
Selma	75	B8	
Selpele	39	E4	
Selu	39	F4	
Selva	94	B4	
Selvas	91	E5	
Semani →	23	D2	
Semarang	37	F4	
Semey	29	D9	
Semiozernoye	29	D7	
Semipalatinsk =			
Semey	29	D9	
Semirara Is.	38	B2	
Semisopochnoi			
I.	71	C1	
Semitau	37	D4	
Semiyarka	29	D8	
Semiyarskoye =			
Semiyarka	29	D8	
Semmering P.	15	E8	
Semnān	44	C3	
Semnān □	44	C3	
Semporna	38	D1	
Semuda	37	E4	
Sena Madureira	91	E5	
Senador			
Pompeu	92	D6	

Senaja	36	C5	
Senanga	58	B4	
Sendai,			
Kagoshima,			
Japan	32	D2	
Sendai, Miyagi,			
Japan	33	G12	
Senegal ■	55	F2	
Senegal →	55	E1	
Senge Khambab			
= Indus →	43	G5	
Sengkang	39	E2	
Senhor-do-			
Bonfim	93	E5	
Senigállia	20	C4	
Senj	20	B5	
Senja	8	E11	
Senlis	13	B5	
Senmonorom	36	B3	
Sennâr	53	F5	
Senneterre	69	D3	
Sens	13	B5	
Senta	22	B3	
Sentani	39	E6	
Seo de Urgel	19	A6	
Seoul = Sŏul	35	C7	
Sepīdān	44	D3	
Sept-Îles	69	C4	
Sequoia			
National Park	82	B3	
Seram	39	E3	
Seram Laut,			
Kepulauan	39	E4	
Seram Sea	39	E3	
Serasan	37	D3	
Serbia □	22	C3	
Serdobsk	24	C5	
Seremban	37	D2	
Serenje	59	A6	
Sereth =			
Siret →	17	F9	
Sergino	28	C7	
Sergipe □	93	E6	
Sergiyev Posad	24	B4	
Seria	36	D4	
Serian	37	D4	
Seribu,			
Kepulauan	37	F3	
Sérifos	23	F5	
Sermata	39	F3	
Serny Zavod	29	F6	
Serov	28	D7	
Serowe	59	C5	
Serpukhov	24	C4	
Serrai	22	D4	
Serrezuela	94	C3	
Serrinha	93	E6	
Sertânia	92	D6	
Serua	39	F4	
Serui	39	E5	
Serule	59	C5	
Sesepe	39	E3	
Sesfontein	58	B2	
Sesheke	58	B4	
Sète	13	E5	
Sete Lagôas	93	F5	
Sétif	54	A6	
Seto	32	B5	
Settat	54	B3	
Setté-Cama	56	E1	
Setúbal	18	C1	
Setúbal, B. de	18	C1	
Seulimeum	36	C1	
Sevan, Ozero =			
Sevana Lich	25	E6	
Sevana Lich	25	E6	
Sevastopol	25	E3	
Severn →,			
Canada	69	C2	

Severn →, U.K.	11	F5	
Severnaya			
Zemlya	30	B7	
Severnyye Uvaly	24	B6	
Severo-			
Yeniseyskiy	30	C7	
Severodvinsk	28	C4	
Sevilla	18	D2	
Seville = Sevilla	18	D2	
Sevlievo	22	C5	
Seward	71	B5	
Seward Pen.	71	B3	
Sewer	39	F4	
Seychelles ■	26	K9	
Seymour	63	C4	
Sfax	52	B1	
Sfîntu Gheorghe	17	F7	
Shaanxi □	35	C5	
Shaba □	57	F4	
Shabunda	57	E5	
Shache	34	C2	
Shackleton Ice			
Shelf	96	A11	
Shackleton Inlet	96	C15	
Shadrinsk	29	D7	
Shāhābād	44	B4	
Shahdād	44	D4	
Shahdād,			
Namakzār-e	44	D4	
Shahdadkot	42	F5	
Shahgarh	42	F6	
Shaḥḥāt	52	B3	
Shahjahanpur	42	F11	
Shahr Kord	44	C2	
Shahrig	42	D5	
Shaikhabad	42	B6	
Shajapur	43	H10	
Shakhty	25	D5	
Shakhunya	24	B6	
Shaki	55	G5	
Shala, L.	53	G6	
Shalqar	29	E6	
Sham, J. ash	44	F4	
Shamīl	44	E4	
Shammar, Jabal	47	F5	
Shamo = Gobi	35	B6	
Shamo, L.	53	G6	
Shamva	59	B6	
Shan □	41	G12	
Shandong □	35	C6	
Shanghai	35	C7	
Shangqiu	35	C6	
Shangrao	35	D6	
Shangshui	35	C6	
Shannon	64	D6	
Shannon →	11	E2	
Shansi =			
Shanxi □	35	C6	
Shantou	35	D6	
Shantung =			
Shandong □	35	C6	
Shanxi □	35	C6	
Shaoguan	35	D6	
Shaowu	35	D6	
Shaoxing	35	C7	
Shaoyang	35	D6	
Shaqra',			
Si. Arabia	47	F6	
Shaqrā', Yemen	49	E4	
Sharjah = Ash			
Shāriqah	44	E3	
Sharon	72	D5	
Sharya	24	B6	
Shashi,			
Botswana	59	C5	
Shashi, China	35	C6	
Shasta, Mt.	80	B2	
Shatt al'Arab →	47	E7	
Shaunavon	71	D9	

Shawan	34	B3	
Shawinigan	69	D3	
Shcherbakov =			
Rybinsk	24	B4	
Shchuchinsk	29	D8	
Shebele =			
Scebeli,			
Wabi →	49	G3	
Sheboygan	72	C2	
Sheffield	11	E6	
Shekhupura	42	D8	
Shelburne	69	D4	
Shelby	75	B7	
Shelbyville	74	B4	
Shellharbour	63	B5	
Shenandoah →	73	E7	
Shendam	55	G6	
Shendî	53	E5	
Shensi =			
Shaanxi □	35	C5	
Shenyang	35	B7	
Sheopur Kalan	42	G10	
Shepetivka	17	C8	
Shepetovka =			
Shepetivka	17	C8	
Shepparton	63	C4	
Sherbro I.	55	G2	
Sherbrooke	69	D3	
Sheridan	81	C10	
Sherman	79	C5	
Sherridon	71	C9	
Shetland Is.	10	A6	
Shibām	49	D4	
Shigaib	53	E3	
Shihchiachuangi			
=			
Shijiazhuang	35	C6	
Shijiazhuang	35	C6	
Shikarpur	42	F6	
Shikoku	32	C3	
Shikoku □	33	H10	
Shikoku-Sanchi	32	C3	
Shilabo	49	F3	
Shiliguri	40	D7	
Shillong	41	E8	
Shilong	35	D6	
Shimada	32	B6	
Shimizu	32	B6	
Shimoga	43	N9	
Shimonoseki	32	C2	
Shinano →	32	A6	
Shīndand	42	C3	
Shingū	32	C4	
Shinyanga	57	E6	
Shipehenski			
Prokhod	22	C5	
Shipki La	42	D11	
Shīr Kūh	44	D3	
Shirane-San	32	A6	
Shīrāz	44	D3	
Shire →	59	B7	
Shiretoko-Misaki	32	F13	
Shiriya-Zaki	32	F12	
Shīrvān	44	B4	
Shirwa, L. =			
Chilwa, L.	59	B7	
Shivpuri	43	G10	
Shizuoka	32	B6	
Shklov =			
Shklow	17	A10	
Shklow	17	A10	
Shkoder =			
Shkodra	22	C2	
Shkodra	22	C2	
Shkumbini →	23	D2	
Shmidta, O.	30	A7	
Sholapur =			
Solapur	43	L9	
Shoshone Mts.	80	F5	

Shoshong	59	C5
Shreveport	79	C7
Shrewsbury ..	11	E5
Shrirampur ...	40	F7
Shu	29	E8
Shuangyashan	35	B8
Shule	34	C2
Shumagin Is. ..	71	C4
Shungnak	71	B4
Shūr →	44	D3
Shurugwi	59	B5
Shūsf	45	D5
Shūshtar	47	D7
Shwebo	41	F10
Shwegu	41	E11
Shweli →	41	F11
Shymkent	29	E7
Shyok	42	B11
Shyok →	42	B9
Si Kiang = Xi		
Jiang → ...	35	D6
Si-ngan = Xi'an	35	C5
Si Racha	36	B2
Siah	47	G6
Siahan Range .	42	F4
Siaksriindrapura	37	D2
Sialkot	42	C9
Siantan, P. ...	37	D3
Siāreh	45	D5
Siargao	38	C3
Siasi	38	C2
Siau	39	D3
Šiauliai	24	B1
Šibenik	20	C5
Siberut	37	E1
Sibi	42	E5
Sibil	39	E6
Sibiti	56	E2
Sibiu	17	F7
Sibolga	37	D1
Sibsagar	41	D10
Sibu	37	D4
Sibuco	38	C2
Sibuguey B. ...	38	C2
Sibut	56	C3
Sibutu	38	D1
Sibutu Passage	38	D1
Sibuyan	38	B2
Sibuyan Sea ..	38	B2
Sichuan □	34	C5
Sicilia	21	F5
Sicily = Sicilia .	21	F5
Sicuani	91	F4
Siddipet	43	K11
Sidéradougou .	55	F4
Sîdi Barrâni ...	52	B4
Sidi-bel-Abbès .	54	A4
Sidley, Mt. ...	96	B18
Sidon = Saydā	46	D3
Sidra, G. of =		
Surt, Khalīj .	52	B2
Siedlce	17	B6
Sieg →	14	C4
Siegen	14	C5
Siem Reap	36	B2
Siena	20	C3
Sieradz	16	C4
Sierra Colorada	95	E3
Sierra Gorda ..	94	A3
Sierra Leone ■	55	G2
Sifnos	23	F5
Sighetu-		
Marmatiei ...	17	E6
Sighişoara	17	E7
Sigli	36	C1
Sigsig	90	D3
Sigüenza	19	B4
Siguiri	55	F3

Sihanoukville =		
Kompong		
Som	36	B2
Siirt	46	C5
Sikar	42	F9
Sikasso	55	F3
Sikhote Alin,		
Khrebet ...	31	E11
Sikhote Alin Ra.		
= Sikhote		
Alin, Khrebet	31	E11
Síkinos	23	F5
Sikkim □	40	D7
Sil →	18	A2
Silchar	41	E9
Silesia = Śląsk	16	C3
Silgarhi Doti ..	40	C3
Silghat	41	D9
Silifke	46	C3
Siliguri =		
Shiliguri	40	D7
Siling Co	34	C3
Silistra	22	B6
Silivri	22	D7
Sillajhuay,		
Cordillera ...	91	G5
Silva Porto =		
Kuito	58	A3
Simanggang ..	37	D4
Simav	23	E7
Simbirsk	24	C6
Simeria	17	F6
Simeulue	37	D1
Simferopol ...	25	E3
Sími	23	F6
Simikot	40	C3
Simla	42	D10
Simplon P.	13	C8
Simpson Desert	60	F6
Simunjan	37	D4
Sinabang	37	D1
Sinadogo	49	F4
Sinai = Es Sînâ'	52	C5
Sinai, Mt. =		
Mûsa, G.	47	E3
Sinaloa de		
Leyva	84	B3
Sināwan	54	B7
Sincelejo	90	B3
Sincorá, Serra		
do	93	E5
Sind □	42	F6
Sind Sagar		
Doab	42	D7
Sindangan	38	C2
Sines	18	D1
Sines, C. de ..	18	D1
Singa	53	F5
Singapore ■ ..	37	D2
Singaraja	37	F5
Singida	57	E6
Singitikós		
Kólpos	23	D5
Singkaling		
Hkamti	41	E10
Singkawang ...	37	D3
Singleton	63	B5
Singora =		
Songkhla ...	36	C2
Sinjai	39	F2
Sinjār	46	C5
Sinkat	53	E6
Sinkiang Uighur		
= Xinjiang		
Uygur		
Zizhiqu □ ...	34	B3
Sinni →	21	D6
Sinnuris	52	C5
Sinop	46	B3

Sintang	37	D4
Sintra	18	C1
Sinŭiju	35	B7
Siocon	38	C2
Siófok	16	E4
Sioma	58	B4
Sion	13	C7
Sioux City	77	D6
Sioux Falls ...	76	D6
Sioux Lookout .	71	C10
Siping	35	B7
Sipura	37	E1
Siquijor	38	C2
Siracusa	21	F5
Sirajganj	41	E7
Sirdaryo =		
Syrdarya →	29	E7
Siret →	17	F9
Sirohi	43	G8
Sironj	43	G10
Síros	23	F5
Sirsa	42	E9
Sisak	20	B6
Sisaket	36	A2
Sisophon	36	B2
Sīstān va		
Balūchestān □	45	E5
Sitapur	40	D3
Sitges	19	B6
Sitía	23	G6
Sitka	71	C6
Sittang Myit →	41	J11
Sittwe	41	G9
Siuri	40	F6
Sīvand	44	D3
Sivas	46	C4
Siverek	46	C4
Sivrihisar	46	C2
Sîwa	52	C4
Siwalik Range .	40	D4
Siwan	40	D5
Sjælland	9	G10
Sjumen =		
Šumen	22	C6
Skadarsko		
Jezero	22	C2
Skagerrak	9	G9
Skagway	71	C6
Skala-Podilska .	17	D8
Skala		
Podolskaya =		
Skala-Podilska	17	D8
Skalat	17	D7
Skardu	42	B9
Skarzysko-		
Kamienna ...	16	C5
Skeena →	70	C6
Skegness	11	E7
Skeldon	90	B7
Skellefte älv →	8	F12
Skellefteå	8	F12
Skíathos	23	E4
Skien	9	G9
Skierniewice ..	16	C5
Skikda	54	A6
Skipton	62	C3
Skíros	23	E5
Skole	17	D6
Skópelos	23	E4
Skopje	22	C3
Skvyra	17	D9
Skye	10	C3
Skyros = Skíros	23	E5
Slamet	37	F3
Śląsk	16	C3
Slatina	22	B5
Slave →	70	B8
Slavgorod	29	D8
Slavonski Brod	20	B7

Slavuta	17	C8
Slavyansk =		
Slovyansk ...	25	D4
Slawharad	17	B10
Sleaford B.	62	B2
Sleeper Is.	68	C2
Sligeach = Sligo	11	D2
Sligo	11	D2
Sliven	22	C6
Slobodskoy ...	24	B7
Slobozia	22	B6
Slonim	17	B7
Slough	11	F6
Slovak Rep. ■ .	16	D5
Slovakia =		
Slovak Rep. ■	16	D5
Slovakian Ore		
Mts. =		
Slovenské		
Rudohorie ..	16	D4
Slovenia ■	20	B5
Slovenija =		
Slovenia ■ ..	20	B5
Slovenská		
Republika =		
Slovak Rep. ■	16	D5
Slovenské		
Rudohorie ..	16	D4
Slovyansk	25	D4
Sluch →	17	C8
Słupsk	16	A3
Slutsk	17	B8
Smara	54	B3
Smarhon	17	A8
Smederevo ...	22	B3
Smith Arm	70	B7
Smithton	62	D4
Smithtown	63	B5
Smoky Bay	62	B1
Smolensk	24	C3
Smolikas, Óros	23	D3
Smolyan	22	D5
Smorgon =		
Smarhon ...	17	A8
Smyrna = İzmir	23	E6
Snake →	80	B4
Snake I.	63	C4
Snake River		
Plain	81	D7
Sneek	14	B3
Sněžka	16	C2
Snøhetta	8	F9
Snowdon	11	E4
Snowdrift	70	B8
Snowtown	62	B2
Snowy →	63	C4
Snowy Mts. ...	63	C4
Snyatyn	17	D7
Snyder	78	C3
Soalala	59	H9
Sobat, Nahr →	53	G5
Sobral	92	C5
Soc Trang	36	C3
Soch'e =		
Shache	34	C2
Sochi	25	E4
Société, Is. de la	65	L15
Society Is. =		
Société, Is. de		
la	65	L15
Sucompa,		
Portezuelo de	94	A3
Socorro	90	B4
Socotra	49	E5
Soda Plains ...	42	B11
Söderhamn ...	8	F11
Sodiri	53	F4
Sodo	53	G6

Sofia

Sofia = Sofiya . 22 C4
Sofia ⟶ 59 H9
Sofiya 22 C4
Sogamoso 90 B4
Sognefjorden . 8 F9
Sohâg 52 C5
Soissons 13 B5
Sokal 17 C7
Söke 23 F6
Sokhumi 25 E5
Sokodé 55 G5
Sokol 24 B5
Sokółka 17 B6
Sokolo 55 F3
Sokolów
    Podlaski 17 B6
Sokoto 55 F6
Solano 38 A2
Solapur 43 L9
Soledad 90 B6
Soligalich 24 B5
Soligorsk =
    Salihorsk . . 17 B8
Solikamsk 28 D6
Solimões =
    Amazonas ⟶ 92 C3
Solingen 14 C4
Sóller 19 C7
Sologne 12 C4
Solok 37 E2
Solomon Is. ■ . 64 K10
Solomon Sea . 61 B9
Solon 35 B7
Solor 39 F2
Solothurn 13 C7
Šolta 20 C6
Solţānābād . . . 44 B4
Solunska Glava 22 D3
Solwezi 59 A5
Soma 23 E6
Somali Rep. ■ . 49 F4
Somalia =
    Somali Rep. ■ 49 F4
Sombor 22 B2
Sombrerete . . 84 C4
Sombrero 87 C7
Somerset East . 59 E5
Somerset I. . . 70 A10
Someş ⟶ 17 E6
Sommariva . . . 63 A4
Somme ⟶ . . . 12 A4
Somosierra,
    Puerto de . . . 18 B4
Somport, Puerto
    de 12 E3
Søndre
    Strømfjord . . 68 B5
Sóndrio 20 A2
Sonepur 40 G4
Song Cau 36 B3
Songea 57 G7
Songhua
    Jiang ⟶ . . 35 B8
Songkhla 36 C2
Songpan 34 C5
Sonipat 42 E10
Sonmiani 42 G5
Sono ⟶ 93 D4
Sonora ⟶ . . . 84 B2
Sonsonate 85 E7
Soochow =
    Suzhou 35 C7
Sopi 39 D3
Sopot 16 A4
Sopron 16 E3
Sør-Rondane . 96 B8
Sorata 91 G5

Sorel 69 D3
Sorgono 21 D2
Soria 19 B4
Sorkh, Kuh-e . . 44 C4
Soroca 17 D9
Sorocaba 94 A7
Soroki = Soroca 17 D9
Sorong 39 E4
Soroti 57 D6
Sørøya 8 D12
Sorrento 63 C3
Sorsogon 38 B2
Sosnowiec 16 C4
Souanké 56 D2
Soúdhas, Kólpos 23 G5
Sŏul 35 C7
Sound, The =
    Øresund 9 G10
Sources, Mt. aux 59 D5
Soure 92 C4
Souris 71 D9
Souris ⟶ . . . 71 D10
Sousa 92 D6
Sousel 92 C3
Sousse 52 A1
South Africa ■ 58 E4
South
    Australia □ . . 62 B2
South Bend . . . 72 D2
South
    Carolina □ . . 75 C7
South China Sea 36 C4
South Dakota □ 76 C4
South East C. . 62 D4
South Horr . . . 57 D7
South I. 65 E3
South
    Invercargill . . 65 G3
South Korea ■ 35 C7
South Magnetic
    Pole 96 A13
South
    Nahanni ⟶ . 70 B7
South Natuna Is.
    = Natuna
    Selatan,
    Kepulauan . . 37 D3
South Orkney Is. 96 A4
South Pagai, I.
    = Pagai
    Selatan, P. . . 37 E2
South Platte ⟶ 76 E4
South Pole . . . . 96 C
South
    Ronaldsay . . 10 B5
South
    Saskatchewan ⟶
    . . . . 71 C9
South Shetland
    Is. 96 A4
South Shields . 11 D6
South Taranaki
    Bight 64 C6
South Uist 10 C3
South West C. . 62 D4
Southampton . 11 F6
Southampton I. 68 B2
Southbridge . . 65 E5
Southend-on-
    Sea 11 F7
Southern Alps . 65 E4
Southern Indian
    L. 71 C10
Southern Ocean 96 A9
Southern
    Uplands 10 D5
Southport 63 A5

Southwest C. . . 65 G2
Soutpansberg . 59 C5
Sovetsk,
    Kaliningd.,
    Russia 24 B1
Sovetsk, Kirov,
    Russia 24 B6
Söya-Misaki . . 32 E12
Soyo 56 F2
Sozh ⟶ 17 C10
Spain ■ 18 C4
Spalding 62 B2
Spanish Town . 86 C4
Sparta = Spárti 23 F4
Spartanburg . . 75 B7
Spárti 23 F4
Spartivento, C.,
    Calabria, Italy 21 F6
Spartivento, C.,
    Sard., Italy . . 21 E2
Spátha, Ákra . . 23 G4
Spence Bay . . . 70 B10
Spencer, C. . . . 62 C2
Spencer G. 62 B2
Spenser Mts. . . 65 E5
Spey ⟶ 10 C5
Speyer 14 D5
Split 20 C6
Spokane 80 B5
Spoleto 20 C4
Sporyy Navolok,
    Mys 28 B7
Spratly I. 36 C4
Spree ⟶ 15 B7
Springbok 58 D3
Springfield, N.Z. 65 E4
Springfield, Ill.,
    U.S.A. 77 F10
Springfield,
    Mass., U.S.A. 73 C9
Springfield, Mo.,
    U.S.A. 79 A7
Springfield,
    Ohio, U.S.A. . 72 E4
Springfield,
    Oreg., U.S.A. 80 C2
Springfontein . 59 E5
Springhill 69 D4
Springhurst . . . 63 C4
Springs 59 D5
Squamish 71 D7
Srbija =
    Serbia □ . . 22 C3
Sre Umbell . . . 36 B2
Srebrnica 20 B7
Sredinnyy Ra. =
    Sredinnyy
    Khrebet 31 D14
Sredinnyy
    Khrebet 31 D14
Srednevilyuysk 31 C10
Śrem 16 B3
Sremska
    Mitrovica . . . 22 B2
Sri Lanka ■ . . . 43 R12
Srikakulam 40 H4
Srinagar 42 B9
Stade 14 B5
Stadlandet 8 F9
Stafford 11 E5
Stakhanov 25 D4
Stalingrad =
    Volgograd . . 25 D5
Staliniri =
    Tskhinvali . . . 25 E5
Stalino =
    Donetsk 25 D4

Stalinogorsk =
    Novomoskovsk
    . . . . 24 C4
Stalowa Wola . 17 C6
Stamford 73 D9
Stanislav =
    Ivano-
    Frankivsk . . . 17 D7
Stanke Dimitrov 22 C4
Stanley,
    Australia 62 D4
Stanley, Canada 71 C9
Stanley, Falk. Is. 95 G5
Stanovoy
    Khrebet 31 D10
Stanovoy Ra. =
    Stanovoy
    Khrebet 31 D10
Stanthorpe . . . 63 A5
Stara Planina . . 22 C4
Stara Zagora . . 22 C5
Starachowice . . 16 C5
Staraya Russa . 24 B3
Starbuck I. . . . 65 K15
Stargard
    Szczeciński . . 16 B2
Staritsa 24 B3
Starogard
    Gdański 16 B4
Starokonstantinov
    =
    Starokonstyantyniv
    . . . . 17 D8
Starokonstyantyniv
    . . . . 17 D8
Staryy
    Chartoriysk . . 17 C7
Staryy Oskol . . 24 C4
State College . . 73 D7
Staten, I. =
    Estados, I. de
    Los 95 G4
Statesville 75 B7
Stavanger 9 G9
Staveley 65 E4
Stavropol 25 D5
Stawell 62 C3
Steenkool =
    Bintuni 39 E4
Stefanie L. =
    Chew Bahir . 53 H6
Stefansson Bay 96 A9
Steiermark □ . . 15 E8
Steinkjer 8 F10
Stellenbosch . . 58 E3
Stendal 15 B6
Steornabhaigh
    = Stornoway 10 B3
Stepanakert =
    Xankändi . . . 25 F6
Stephens Creek 62 B3
Stepnoi = Elista 25 D5
Stepnyak 29 D8
Sterlitamak . . . 29 D6
Stettin =
    Szczecin . . 16 B2
Stettiner Haff . 15 B8
Stettler 71 C8
Steubenville . . 72 D5
Stevenage 11 F6
Stewart 70 B6
Stewart, I. . . . 95 G2
Stewart I. . . . 65 G2
Steyr 15 D7
Stillwater, N.Z. 65 E4
Stillwater,
    U.S.A. 78 A5

Štip 22 D4
Stirling 10 C5
Stockerau 15 D9
Stockholm 9 G11
Stockport 11 E5
Stockton 82 B2
Stockton-on-
Tees 11 D6
Stoke on Trent 11 E5
Stokes Pt. 62 D3
Stolac 20 C6
Stolbovoy,
Ostrov 30 B11
Stolbtsy =
Stowbtsy . . . 17 B8
Stolin 17 C8
Stonehaven . . . 10 C5
Stonewall 71 C10
Stony Tunguska
=
Podkamennaya
Tunguska → 30 C7
Stora Lulevatten 8 E11
Storavan 8 E11
Store Bælt 9 G10
Store Creek . . 63 B4
Storm B. 62 D4
Stormberge . . 59 E5
Stornoway . . . 10 B3
Storozhinets =
Storozhynets 17 D7
Storozhynets . . 17 D7
Storsjön 8 F10
Storuman 8 E11
Stowbtsy 17 B8
Strahan 62 D4
Stralsund 15 A7
Strand 58 E3
Stranraer 11 D4
Strasbourg . . 13 B7
Stratford,
Canada 69 D2
Stratford, N.Z. . 64 C6
Strathalbyn . . . 62 C2
Straubing 15 D7
Streaky B. . . . 62 B1
Streaky Bay . . . 62 B1
Strelka 30 D7
Strezhevoy . . . 29 C8
Strimón → . . 23 D4
Strimonikós
Kólpos 23 D5
Strómboli 21 E5
Stronsay 10 B5
Stroud Road . . 63 B5
Strumica 22 D4
Stryy 17 D6
Strzelecki Cr. → 62 A2
Stuart Ra. 62 A1
Stung Treng . 36 B3
Stutterheim . . . 59 E5
Stuttgart 14 D5
Styria =
Steiermark □ 15 E8
Suakin 53 E6
Subansiri → . 41 D9
Subi 37 D3
Subotica 16 E4
Suceava 17 E8
Suchou =
Suzhou 35 C7
Süchow =
Xuzhou . . . 35 C6
Sucre 91 G5
Sudair 47 F6
Sudan ■ 53 E4
Sudbury 69 D2

Sûdd 53 G4
Sudeten Mts. =
Sudety 16 C3
Sudety 16 C3
Sudirman,
Pegunungan 39 E5
Sueca 19 C5
Suez = El
Suweis 52 C5
Suez, G. of =
Suweis, Khalîg
el 52 C5
Sugluk – Salluit 68 B3
Suhār 44 E4
Suhbaatar . . . 35 A5
Suhl 14 C6
Suihua 35 B7
Sukadana,
Kalimantan,
Indonesia . . 37 E3
Sukadana,
Sumatera,
Indonesia . . 37 F3
Sukaraja 37 E4
Sukarnapura =
Jayapura . . 39 E6
Sukhona → . . 28 C5
Sukhumi =
Sokhumi . . . 25 E5
Sukkur 42 F6
Sukkur Barrage 42 F6
Sula, Kepulauan 39 E3
Sulaiman Range 42 D6
Sulawesi □ . . . 39 E2
Sulawesi Sea =
Celebes Sea . 39 D2
Sulima 55 G2
Sulina 17 F9
Sulitjelma . . . 8 E11
Sullana 90 D2
Sultanpur 40 D4
Sulu Arch. . . . 38 C2
Sulu Sea 38 C2
Suluq 52 B3
Sulzberger Ice
Shelf 96 B17
Sumalata 39 D2
Sumatera □ . . . 37 D2
Sumatra =
Sumatera □ . 37 D2
Sumba 39 F1
Sumba, Selat . 39 F1
Sumbawa 37 F5
Sumbawa Besar 37 F5
Sumbe 56 G2
Šumen 22 C6
Sumgait =
Sumqayıt . . . 25 E6
Summerside . . 69 D4
Sumperk 16 D3
Sumqayıt . . . 25 E6
Sumter 75 C7
Sumy 24 C3
Sunbury 63 C3
Sunda, Selat . . 37 F3
Sunda Str. =
Sunda, Selat 37 F3
Sundarbans,
The 41 G7
Sundargarh . . . 40 F5
Sunderland . . . 11 D6
Sundsvall 8 F11
Sungaigerong . 37 E2
Sungailiat . . . 37 E3
Sungaipakning 37 D2
Sungaipenuh . . 37 E2
Sungaitiram . . . 37 E5

Sungari =
Songhua
Jiang → . . . 35 B8
Sungguminasa 39 F1
Sunghua Chiang
= Songhua
Jiang → . . . 35 B8
Sungurlu 46 B3
Sunnyvale 82 B1
Suntar 30 C9
Supaul 40 D6
Superior 77 B8
Superior, L. . . . 69 D2
Suphan Dağı . . 46 C5
Supiori 39 E5
Sūr, Lebanon . . 46 D3
Sūr, Oman . . . 45 F4
Sura → 24 B6
Surabaja =
Surabaya . . . 37 F4
Surabaya 37 F4
Surakarta 37 F4
Surat, Australia 63 A4
Surat, India . . 43 J8
Surat Thani . . . 36 C1
Suratgarh 42 E8
Surgut 29 C8
Suriapet 43 L11
Surigao 38 C3
Surinam ■ 92 B2
Suriname ■ =
Surinam ■ . . 92 B2
Suriname → . . 92 A2
Surt 52 B2
Surt, Khalīj . . . 52 B2
Suruga-Wan . . 32 B6
Süsangerd 47 E7
Susanville . . . 80 E3
Susquehanna →
. . . . 73 E7
Susques 94 A3
Susunu 39 E4
Susurluk 23 E7
Sutherland Falls 65 F2
Sutlej → 42 E7
Suva 64 L12
Suva Planina . . 22 C4
Suvorov Is. =
Suwarrow Is. 65 L14
Suwałki 17 A6
Suwarrow Is. . 65 L14
Suweis, Khalîg
el 52 C5
Suzdal 24 B5
Suzhou 35 C7
Suzu-Misaki . . 32 A5
Svealand □ . . . 9 G10
Sverdlovsk =
Yekaterinburg 29 D7
Svetlogorsk =
Svyetlahorsk 17 B9
Svetozarevo . . 22 B3
Svishtov 22 C5
Svislach 17 B7
Svyetlahorsk . . 17 B9
Swabian Alps =
Schwäbische
Alb 14 D5
Swakopmund . 58 C2
Swan Hill 62 C3
Swansea,
Australia . . . 63 B5
Swansea, U.K. . 11 F5
Swatow =
Shantou 35 D6
Swaziland ■ . . 59 D6
Sweden ■ 9 G10

Sweetwater . . . 78 C3
Swellendam . . 58 E4
Świdnica 16 C3
Świdnik 17 C6
Świebodzin . . . 16 B2
Świecie 16 B4
Swift Current . . 71 C9
Swindon 11 F6
Swinemünde =
Świnoujście . 16 B2
Świnoujście . . 16 B2
Switzerland ■ . 13 C8
Sydney,
Australia 63 B5
Sydney, Canada 69 D4
Sydra, G. of =
Surt, Khalīj . . 52 B2
Syktyvkar 28 C6
Sylhet 41 E8
Sylt 14 A5
Sym 29 C9
Syracuse 73 C7
Syrdarya → . . 29 E7
Syria ■ 46 D4
Syrian Desert =
Ash Shām,
Bādiyat 47 D4
Syzran 24 C6
Szczecin 16 B2
Szczecinek . . . 16 B3
Szczytno 16 B5
Szechwan =
Sichuan □ . . 34 C5
Szeged 16 E5
Székesfehérvár 16 E4
Szekszárd 16 E4
Szentes 16 E5
Szolnok 16 E5
Szombathely . . 16 E3

Tabacal 94 A4
Tabaco 38 B2
Ṭābah 47 F5
Tabarka 54 A6
Ṭabas,
Khorāsān, Iran 44 C4
Ṭabas,
Khorāsān, Iran 45 C5
Tabatinga, Serra
da 93 E5
Tablas 38 B2
Table B. =
Tafelbaai . . . 58 E3
Table Mt. 58 E3
Tábor 16 D2
Tabora 57 F6
Tabou 55 H3
Tabrīz 46 C6
Tabūk 47 E4
Tacheng 34 B3
Tacloban 38 B2
Tacna 91 G4
Tacoma 80 B2
Tacuarembó . . 94 C5
Tademaït,
Plateau du . . 54 C5
Tadjoura 49 E3
Tadmor 65 D5
Tadoussac . . . 69 D4
Tadzhikistan =
Tajikistan ■ . 29 F8
Taegu 35 C7

Taejŏn

Taejŏn	35	C7
Tafalla	19	A5
Tafelbaai	58	E3
Tafermaar	39	F4
Taft	38	B3
Taga Dzong	41	D7
Taganrog	25	D4
Tagbilaran	38	C2
Tagish	70	B6
Tagish L.	70	B6
Tagliamento →	20	B4
Taguatinga	93	E5
Tagum	38	C3
Tagus =		
Tejo →	18	C1
Tahakopa	65	G3
Tahan, Gunong	36	D2
Tahat	54	D6
Tāherī	44	E3
Tahiti	65	L16
Tahoe, L.	80	F3
Tahoua	55	F6
Tahta	52	C5
Tahulandang	39	D3
Tahuna	39	D3
Taï	55	G3
Tai Hu	35	C7
Taibei	35	D7
T'aichung =		
Taizhong	35	D7
Taidong	35	D7
Taieri →	65	G4
Taihape	64	C6
Tailem Bend	62	C2
Taimyr Peninsula =		
Taymyr, Poluostrov	30	B7
Tain	10	C4
Tainan	35	D7
Taínaron, Ákra	23	F4
T'aipei = Taibei	35	D7
Taiping	36	D2
Taitao, Pen. de	95	F1
Taiwan ■	35	D7
Taïyetos Óros	23	F4
Taiyuan	35	C6
Taizhong	35	D7
Ta'izz	49	E3
Tajikistan ■	29	F8
Tajo = Tejo →	18	C1
Tājūrā	52	B1
Tak	36	A1
Takada	32	A6
Takaka	65	D5
Takamatsu	32	B4
Takaoka	32	A5
Takapuna	64	B6
Takasaki	32	A6
Takatsuki	32	B4
Takaungu	57	E7
Takayama	32	A5
Takefu	32	B5
Takengon	36	D1
Takeo	36	B2
Tākestān	46	D7
Takhār □	45	B7
Takum	55	G6
Talara	90	D2
Talas	29	E8
Talaud, Kepulauan	38	D3
Talaud Is. =		
Talaud, Kepulauan	38	D3
Talavera de la Reina	18	C3

Talayan	38	C2
Talbragar →	63	B4
Talca	94	D2
Talcahuano	94	D2
Talcher	40	G5
Taldy Kurgan =		
Taldyqorghan	29	E8
Taldyqorghan	29	E8
Talesh, Kūhhā-ye	46	C7
Tali Post	53	G5
Talibon	38	B2
Taliwang	37	F5
Tall 'Afar	46	C5
Talladega	74	C4
Tallahassee	75	D5
Tallangatta	63	C4
Tallarook	63	C4
Tallinn	24	B1
Talodi	53	F5
Taltal	94	B2
Talwood	63	A4
Talyawalka Cr. →	62	B3
Tamale	55	G4
Tamanrasset	54	D6
Tamarang	63	B5
Tamaské	55	F6
Tambacounda	55	F2
Tambelan, Kepulauan	37	D3
Tambo de Mora	91	F3
Tambora	37	F5
Tambov	24	C5
Tamburâ	53	G4
Tâmchekket	55	E2
Tamega →	18	B1
Tamenglong	41	E9
Tamgak, Mts.	55	E6
Tamil Nadu □	43	P10
Tammerfors =		
Tampere	8	F12
Tamo Abu, Pegunungan	37	D5
Tampa	75	F6
Tampere	8	F12
Tampico	84	C5
Tamrida =		
Qādib	49	E5
Tamsagbulag	35	B6
Tamu	41	E10
Tamworth	63	B5
Tana →, Kenya	57	E8
Tana →, Norway	8	D13
Tana, L.	53	F6
Tanahbala	37	E1
Tanahgrogot	37	E5
Tanahjampea	39	F2
Tanahmasa	37	E1
Tanahmerah	39	F6
Tanami Desert	60	D5
Tanana	71	B4
Tanana →	71	B4
Tananarive =		
Antananarivo	59	H9
Tánaro →	20	B2
Tandag	38	C3
Tandil	94	D5
Tandil, Sa. del	94	D5
Tando Adam	42	G6
Tandou L.	62	B3
Tane-ga-Shima	33	D2
Taneatua	64	C7
Tanen Tong Dan	41	J12
Tanezrouft	54	D5
Tanga	57	F7

Tanganyika, L.	57	F5
Tanger =		
Tangier	54	A3
Tanggula Shan	34	C4
Tangier	54	A3
Tangshan	35	C6
Tanimbar, Kepulauan	39	F4
Tanimbar Is. =		
Tanimbar, Kepulauan	39	F4
Tanjay	38	C2
Tanjore =		
Thanjavur	43	P11
Tanjung	37	E5
Tanjungbalai	37	D1
Tanjungbatu	37	D5
Tanjungkarang Telukbetung	37	F3
Tanjungpandan	37	E3
Tanjungpinang	37	D2
Tanjungredeb	37	D5
Tanjungselor	37	D5
Tanout	55	F6
Tanta	52	B5
Tantung =		
Dandong	35	B7
Tanunda	62	B2
Tanzania ■	57	F6
Taolanaro	59	K9
Taoudenni	54	D4
Taourirt	54	B4
Tapa Shan =		
Daba Shan	35	C5
Tapah	37	D2
Tapajós →	92	C3
Tapaktuan	37	D1
Tapanui	65	F3
Tapauá →	91	E6
Tapeta	55	G3
Tapi →	43	J8
Tapirapecó, Serra	90	C6
Tapuaenuku, Mt.	65	D5
Tapul Group	38	C2
Taquari →	91	G7
Tara, Australia	63	A5
Tara, Russia	29	D8
Tara →, Montenegro, Yug.	22	C2
Tara →, Russia	29	D8
Tarabagatay, Khrebet	29	E9
Tarābulus, Lebanon	46	D3
Tarābulus, Libya	52	B1
Tarakan	37	D5
Taralga	63	B4
Taranaki □	64	C6
Tarancón	19	B4
Taranga Hill	43	H8
Táranto	21	D6
Táranto, G. di	21	D6
Tarapacá	90	D5
Tararua Ra.	64	D6
Tarashcha	17	D10
Tarauacá	91	E4
Tarauacá →	91	E5
Tarawera	64	C7
Tarawera L.	64	C7
Tarazona	19	B5
Tarbela Dam	42	B8
Tarbes	12	E4
Tarcoola	62	B1
Tarcoon	63	B4
Taree	63	B5

Tarfaya	54	C2
Tarifa	18	D3
Tarija	94	A4
Tariku →	39	E5
Tarim Basin =		
Tarim Pendi	34	C3
Tarim He →	34	C3
Tarim Pendi	34	C3
Taritatu →	39	E5
Tarkhankut, Mys	25	D3
Tarko Sale	28	C8
Tarkwa	55	G4
Tarlac	38	A2
Tarma	91	F3
Tarn →	12	D4
Tarnobrzeg	16	C5
Tarnów	16	C5
Tarnowskie Góry	16	C4
Taroom	63	A4
Taroudannt	54	B3
Tarragona	19	B6
Tarrasa	19	B7
Tarso Emissi	52	D2
Tarsus	46	C3
Tartagal	94	A4
Tartu	24	B2
Tarţūs	46	D3
Tarutung	37	D1
Tasāwah	52	C1
Taschereau	69	D3
Tash-Kömür	29	E8
Tash-Kumyr =		
Tash-Kömür	29	E8
Tashauz =		
Dashhowuz	29	E6
Tashi Chho Dzong =		
Thimphu	41	D7
Tashkent =		
Toshkent	29	E7
Tashtagol	29	D9
Tasman B.	65	D5
Tasman Mts.	65	D5
Tasman Pen.	62	D4
Tasmania □	62	D4
Tatabánya	16	E4
Tatar Republic □ = Tatarstan □	29	D6
Tatarbunary	17	F9
Tatarsk	29	D8
Tatarstan □	29	D6
Tateyama	32	B6
Tathra	63	C4
Tatra = Tatry	16	D4
Tatry	16	D4
Tatta	43	G5
Tatuī	94	A7
Tat'ung =		
Datong	35	B6
Tatvan	46	C5
Taubaté	94	A7
Tauern	15	E7
Taumarunui	64	C6
Taumaturgo	91	E4
Taungdwingyi	41	G10
Taunggyi	41	G11
Taungup	41	H10
Taungup Pass	41	H10
Taungup Taunggya	41	H9
Taunton	11	F5
Taunus	14	C5
Taupo	64	C7
Taupo, L.	64	C6
Tauranga	64	B7
Tauranga Harb.	64	B7

Taurianova ... 21 E6
Taurus Mts. =
  Toros Dağları 46 C3
Tavda 29 D7
Tavda → 29 D7
Taveta 57 E7
Tavira 18 D2
Tavoy 36 B1
Tawau 36 D5
Tawitawi 38 C2
Tay → 10 C5
Tayabamba .. 91 E3
Taylakova 29 D8
Taylakovy =
  Taylakova ... 29 D8
Taymä 47 F4
Taymyr, Oz. ... 30 B8
Taymyr,
  Poluostrov .. 30 B7
Taytay 38 B1
Taz → 28 C8
Taza 54 B4
Tazovskiy 28 C8
Tbilisi 25 E5
Tchad = Chad ■ 53 E2
Tchad, L. 53 F1
Tch'eng-tou =
  Chengdu ... 35 C5
Tchibanga 56 E2
Tch'ong-k'ing =
  Chongqing .. 35 D5
Tczew 16 A4
Te Anau, L. ... 65 F2
Te Aroha 64 B6
Te Awamutu .. 64 C6
Te Kuiti 64 C6
Te Puke 64 B7
Te Waewae B. . 65 G2
Tebakang 37 D4
Tébessa 54 A6
Tebicuary → .. 94 B5
Tebingtinggi .. 37 D1
Tecuci 22 B6
Tedzhen =
  Tejen 29 F7
Tefé 90 D6
Tegal 37 F3
Tegina 55 F6
Tegucigalpa ... 85 E7
Tehachapi 82 C3
Tehrän 44 C2
Tehuantepec .. 85 D5
Tehuantepec, G.
  de 85 D5
Tehuantepec,
  Istmo de 85 D6
Tejen 29 F7
Tejo → 18 C1
Tekapo, L. 65 E4
Tekeli 29 E8
Tekirdağ 22 D6
Tekkali 40 H5
Tel Aviv-Yafo . 46 D3
Tela 85 D7
Telanaipura =
  Jambi 37 E2
Telavi 25 E6
Telekhany =
  Tsyelyakhany 17 B7
Teles Pires → . 91 E7
Telford 11 E5
Télimélé 55 F2
Tellicherry 43 P9
Telsen 95 E3
Teluk Anson . 37 D2
Teluk Betung =
  Tanjungkarang
  Telukbetung . 37 F3

Teluk Intan =
  Teluk Anson . 37 D2
Telukbutun ... 37 D3
Telukdalem ... 37 D1
Tema 55 G4
Temax 85 C7
Temerloh 37 D2
Temir 29 E6
Temirtau,
  Kazakstan ... 29 D8
Temirtau, Russia 29 D9
Temma 62 D3
Temora 63 B4
Tempe 83 D7
Temple 78 D5
Temuco 94 D2
Temuka 65 F4
Tenali 40 J3
Tenasserim ... 36 B1
Tenda, Col di .. 20 B1
Tendaho 49 E3
Tenerife 54 C1
Teng Xian 35 C6
Tengah □ 39 E2
Tengah
  Kepulauan . 37 F5
Tengchong ... 34 D4
Tenggara □ ... 39 E2
Tenggarong ... 37 E5
Tengiz, Ozero . 29 D7
Tenkasi 43 Q10
Tenke 57 G5
Tenkodogo ... 55 F4
Tennessee □ .. 74 B4
Tennessee → .. 72 F1
Tenom 36 C5
Tenryū-
  Gawa → 32 B5
Tenterfield ... 63 A5
Teófilo Otoni .. 93 F5
Tepa 39 F3
Tepic 84 C4
Teplice 16 C1
Ter → 19 A7
Téra 55 F5
Téramo 20 C4
Terang 62 C3
Terebovlya 17 D7
Terek → 25 E6
Teresina 92 D5
Terewah, L. ... 63 A4
Terhazza 54 D3
Teridgerie
  Cr. → 63 B4
Termez =
  Termiz 29 F7
Términi Imerese 21 F4
Termiz 29 F7
Térmoli 20 C5
Ternate 39 D3
Terni 20 C4
Ternopil 17 D7
Ternopol =
  Ternopil 17 D7
Terowie, N.S.W.,
  Australia 63 B4
Terowie,
  S. Austral.,
  Australia 62 B2
Terracina 20 D4
Terralba 21 E2
Terranova =
  Ólbia 20 D2
Terrassa =
  Tarrasa 19 B7
Terre Haute .. 72 E2
Terschelling ... 14 B3

Teruel 19 B5
Teryaweyna L. . 62 B3
Teshio-Gawa → 32 F12
Tesiyn Gol → . 34 A4
Teslin 70 B6
Tessalit 54 D5
Tessaoua 55 F6
Tetas, Pta. ... 94 A2
Tete 59 B6
Teterev → ... 17 C10
Teteven 22 C5
Tetiyev 17 D9
Tétouan 54 A3
Tetovo 22 C3
Teuco → 94 B4
Teun 39 F3
Teutoburger
  Wald 14 B5
Tévere → 20 D4
Tewantin 63 A5
Texarkana 79 C6
Texas 63 A5
Texas □ 78 D4
Texas City ... 79 E6
Texel 14 B3
Teyvareh 45 C6
Tezpur 41 D9
Thabana
  Ntlenyana ... 59 D5
Thabazimbi ... 59 C5
Thailand ■ ... 36 A2
Thailand, G. of 36 B2
Thakhek 36 A2
Thal 42 C7
Thala La 41 C11
Thallon 63 A4
Thames 64 B6
Thames → 11 F7
Thane 43 K8
Thanh Pho Ho
  Chi Minh =
  Phanh Bho Ho
  Chi Minh ... 36 B3
Thanjavur 43 P11
Thar Desert ... 42 F7
Tharad 43 G7
Thargomindah 63 A3
Tharrawaddy .. 41 J10
Thásos 23 D5
Thaton 41 J11
Thaungdut 41 E10
Thayetmyo ... 41 H10
Thazi 41 G11
The Alberga → 62 A2
The Coorong .. 62 C2
The Frome → . 62 A2
The Grampians 62 C3
The Great Divide
  = Great
  Dividing Ra. . 61 E8
The Hague = 's-
  Gravenhage . 14 B3
The
  Hamilton → 62 A2
The
  Macumba → 62 A2
The Neales → . 62 A2
The Pas 71 C9
The Rock 63 C4
The Salt L. 62 B3
The
  Stevenson → 62 A2
The
  Warburton → 62 A2
Thebes = Thívai 23 E4
Theebine 63 A5
Thermaïkós
  Kólpos 23 D4
Thermopylae P. 23 E4

Thessaloníki .. 23 D4
Thessaloniki,
  Gulf of =
  Thermaïkós
  Kólpos 23 D4
Thetford 11 E7
Thetford Mines 69 D3
Thevenard 62 B1
Thiel Mts. 96 C2
Thiers 13 D5
Thies 55 F1
Thika 57 E7
Thimphu 41 D7
Thionville 13 B7
Thíra 23 F5
Thistle I. 62 C2
Thívai 23 E4
Thomas, L. ... 62 A2
Thomasville,
  Ga., U.S.A. . 75 D6
Thomasville,
  N.C., U.S.A. . 75 B7
Thompson 71 C10
Thomson's Falls
  = Nyahururu 57 D7
Thrace 22 D6
Three Hummock
  I. 62 D3
Three Points, C. 55 H4
Thun 13 C7
Thunder Bay .. 69 D2
Thung Song .. 36 C1
Thunkar 41 D8
Thüringer Wald 14 C6
Thurles 11 E3
Thurloo Downs 63 A3
Thurso 10 B5
Thurston I. 96 B2
Thylungra 63 A3
Tia 63 B5
Tian Shan 34 B3
Tianjin 35 C6
Tianshui 35 C5
Tiaret 54 A5
Tiassalé 55 G4
Tibati 53 G1
Tiber =
  Tévere → .. 20 D4
Tiberias, L. =
  Yam Kinneret 46 D3
Tibesti 52 D2
Tibet =
  Xizang □ ... 34 C3
Tibooburra ... 62 A3
Tiburón 84 B2
Tîchît 55 E3
Ticino → 20 B2
Tiddim 41 F9
Tidjikja 55 E2
Tidore 39 D3
Tiel 55 F1
Tierra de
  Campos 18 A3
Tierra del
  Fuego, I. Gr.
  de 95 G3
Tiétar → 18 C2
Tieyon 62 A1
Tiflis = Tbilisi . 25 E5
Tifu 39 E3
Tighina 17 E9
Tignish 69 D4
Tigre → 90 D4
Tigris = Dijlah,
  Nahr → 47 E6
Tigyaing 41 F11
Tih, Gebel el . 52 C5
Tijuana 84 A1
Tikamgarh 43 G11

Tikhoretsk	25	D5
Tikrīt	46	D5
Tiksi	30	B10
Tilamuta	39	D2
Tilburg	14	C3
Tillabéri	55	F5
Tílos	23	F6
Tilpa	63	B3
Tilsit = Sovetsk	24	B1
Timaru	65	F4
Timbedgha ...	55	E3
Timboon	62	C3
Timbuktu =		
Tombouctou	55	E4
Timimoun	54	C5
Timişoara	16	F5
Timmins	69	D2
Timok ─►	22	B4
Timon	92	D5
Timor	39	F2
Tinaca Pt.	38	C3
Tindouf	54	C3
Tingo Maria ...	91	E3
Tinjoub	54	C3
Tinnevelly =		
Tirunelveli ..	43	Q10
Tinogasta	94	B3
Tínos	23	F5
Tintinara	62	C3
Tioman, Pulau .	37	D2
Tipongpani ...	41	D10
Tipperary	11	E2
Tīrān	44	C2
Tirana	22	D2
Tiranë = Tirana	22	D2
Tiraspol	17	E9
Tire	23	E6
Tirebolu	46	B4
Tiree	10	C3
Tîrgovişte	22	B5
Tîrgu-Jiu	17	F6
Tîrgu Mureş ..	17	E7
Tirich Mir	42	A7
Tîrnăveni	17	E7
Tírnavos	23	E4
Tirodi	43	J11
Tirol □	14	E6
Tirso ─►	21	E2
Tiruchchirappalli	43	P11
Tirunelveli	43	Q10
Tirupati	43	N11
Tiruppur	43	P10
Tiruvannamalai	43	N11
Tisa ─►	22	B3
Tisdale	71	C9
Tisza = Tisa ─►	22	B3
Tit-Ary	30	B10
Titicaca, L.	91	G5
Titograd =		
Podgorica ..	22	C2
Titov Veles	22	D3
Titova-Mitrovica	22	C3
Titovo Užice ..	22	C2
Titule	57	D5
Tivaouane	55	F1
Tívoli	20	D4
Tiwī	45	F4
Tizi-Ouzou	54	A5
Tiznit	54	C3
Tjirebon =		
Cirebon	37	F3
Tlaxcala	84	D5
Tlaxiaco	84	D5
Tlemcen	54	B4
Tmassah	52	C2
Toamasina	59	H9
Toay	94	D4
Toba	32	B5
Toba Kakar ...	42	D6

Tobago	87	D7
Tobelo	39	D3
Tobermory	10	C3
Toboali	37	E3
Tobol ─►	29	D7
Toboli	39	E2
Tobolsk	29	D7
Tobruk =		
Tubruq	52	B3
Tobyl =		
Tobol ─► ...	29	D7
Tocantinópolis	92	D4
Tocantins □ ...	93	E4
Tocantins ─► ..	92	C4
Tochigi	32	A6
Tocopilla	94	A2
Tocumwal	63	C4
Tocuyo ─►	90	A5
Todeli	39	E2
Todenyang ...	57	D7
Todos os		
Santos, B. de	93	E6
Togba	55	E2
Togian,		
Kepulauan ..	39	E2
Togliatti	24	C6
Togo ■	55	G5
Toinya	53	G4
Tojikiston =		
Tajikistan ■ .	29	F8
Tojo	39	E2
Tokala	39	E2
Tōkamachi	32	A6
Tokanui	65	G3
Tokar	53	E6
Tokarahi	65	F4
Tokat	46	B4
Tokelau Is.	65	K13
Tokmak	29	E8
Tokushima	32	B4
Tokuyama	32	B2
Tōkyō	32	B6
Tolaga Bay ...	64	C8
Tolbukhin =		
Dobrich	22	C6
Toledo, Spain .	18	C3
Toledo, U.S.A. .	72	D4
Toledo, Montes		
de	18	C3
Tolga	54	B6
Toliara	59	J8
Tolima	90	C3
Tolitoli	39	D2
Tolo	56	E3
Tolo, Teluk ...	39	E2
Toluca	84	D5
Tomakomai ...	32	F12
Tomar	18	C1
Tomaszów		
Mazowiecki .	16	C4
Tombé	53	G5
Tombouctou ..	55	E4
Tombua	58	B2
Tomelloso	18	C4
Tomingley	63	B4
Tomini	39	D2
Tomini, Teluk .	39	E2
Tomorit	23	D3
Tomsk	29	D9
Tonantins	90	D5
Tonawanda ...	73	C6
Tondano	39	D2
Tonekābon ...	44	B2
Tong Xian	35	C6
Tonga ■	65	L13
Tonga Trench .	65	L13
Tongareva	65	K15
Tongchuan ...	35	C5
Tonghua	35	B7

Tongjiang	35	B8
Tongking, G. of		
= Tonkin, G.		
of	35	D5
Tongoy	94	C2
Tongren	35	D5
Tongsa Dzong .	41	D8
Tongue ─► ...	76	B2
Tonk	42	F9
Tonkin, G. of ..	35	D5
Tonlé Sap	36	B2
Toompine	63	A3
Toora	63	C4
Toowoomba ..	63	A5
Topeka	77	F7
Topki	29	D9
Topol'čany ...	16	D4
Topolobampo .	84	B3
Torata	91	G4
Torbalı	23	E6
Torbat-e		
Heydārīyeh .	44	C4
Torbat-e Jām ..	45	C5
Torbay	11	F5
Tordesillas	18	B3
Torgau	15	C7
Torino	20	B1
Torit	53	H5
Tormes ─► ...	18	B2
Torne älv ─► .	8	E12
Torneå = Tornio	8	E12
Torneträsk	8	E11
Tornio	8	E12
Tornquist	94	D4
Toro, Cerro del	94	B3
Toroníios		
Kólpos	23	D4
Toronto,		
Australia	63	B5
Toronto, Canada	69	D3
Toropets	24	B3
Tororo	57	D6
Toros Dağları .	46	C3
Tôrre de		
Moncorvo ...	18	B2
Torre del Greco	21	D5
Torrejón de		
Ardoz	18	B4
Torrelavega ...	18	A3
Torremolinos ..	18	D3
Torrens, L. ...	62	B2
Torrente	19	C5
Torreón	84	B4
Torres	84	B2
Torres Vedras .	18	C1
Torrevieja	19	D5
Tortosa	19	B6
Tortosa, C. de .	19	B6
Țorūd	44	C3
Toruń	16	B4
Tosa-Wan	32	C3
Toscana □ ...	20	C3
Toshkent	29	E7
Tostado	94	B4
Tosya	46	B3
Toteng	58	C4
Totma	24	A5
Totten Glacier .	96	A12
Tottenham	63	B4
Tottori	32	B4
Touba	55	G3
Toubkal, Djebel	54	B3
Tougan	55	F4
Touggourt	54	B6
Tougué	55	F2
Toul	13	B6
Touleupleu ...	55	G3
Toulon	13	E6
Toulouse	12	E4

Toummo	52	D1
Toungoo	41	H11
Touraine	12	C4
Tourane = Da		
Nang	36	A3
Tourcoing	13	A5
Touriñán, C. ..	18	A1
Tournai	14	C2
Tournon	13	D6
Tours	12	C4
Towamba	63	C4
Towang	41	D8
Townsville	61	D8
Toyama	32	A5
Toyohashi	32	B5
Toyonaka	32	B4
Toyooka	32	B4
Toyota	32	B5
Tozeur	54	B6
Trá Li = Tralee	11	E2
Trabzon	46	B4
Trafalgar, C. ..	18	D2
Trail	71	D8
Tralee	11	E2
Trancas	94	B3
Trang	36	C1
Trangan	39	F4
Trangie	63	B4
Trani	20	D6
Transantarctic		
Mts.	96	C3
Transilvania ...	17	F7
Transilvanian		
Alps =		
Carpaţii		
Meridionali ..	17	F7
Transylvania =		
Transilvania .	17	F7
Trápani	21	E4
Traralgon	63	C4
Trasimeno, L. .	20	C4
Traun	15	D8
Travemünde ..	15	B6
Travers, Mt. ..	65	E5
Travnik	20	B6
Trébbia ─► ..	20	B2
Třebíč	16	D2
Trebinje	20	C7
Treinta y Tres .	94	C6
Trelew	95	E3
Tremp	19	A6
Trenčín	16	D4
Trenque		
Lauquen	94	D4
Trent ─►	11	E6
Trento	20	A3
Trenton	73	D8
Trepassey	69	D5
Tres Arroyos ..	94	D4
Três Corações .	93	G4
Três Lagoas ..	93	G3
Tres Montes, C.	95	F1
Tres Puentes ..	94	B2
Tres Puntas, C.	95	F3
Três Rios	93	G5
Treviso	20	B4
Triabunna	62	D4
Trichinopoly =		
Tiruchchirappalli		
....	43	P11
Trichur	43	P10
Trida	63	B4
Trier	14	D4
Trieste	20	B4
Triglav	20	A4
Tríkkala	23	E3
Trikora, Puncak	39	E5
Trinidad, Bolivia	91	F6
Trinidad,		
Colombia ...	90	B4

Trinidad, *Cuba* 86 B3
Trinidad,
  Uruguay 94 C5
Trinidad, *U.S.A.* 78 A1
Trinidad, I. 95 D4
Trinidad &
  Tobago ■ ... 87 D7
Trinity → 79 E6
Trinity B. 69 D5
Trinity Range .. 80 E4
Trinkitat 53 E6
Tripoli =
  Tarābulus,
  Lebanon 46 D3
Tripoli =
  Tarābulus,
  Libya 52 B1
Tripolis 23 F4
Tripura □ 41 F8
Trivandrum ... 43 Q10
Trnava 16 D3
Troglav 20 C6
Trois-Rivières . 69 D3
Troitsko
  Pechorsk 28 C6
Trollhättan 9 G10
Tronador 95 E2
Trondheim .. 8 F10
Trondheimsfjorden
  .... 8 F10
Trout L. 70 B7
Trouville-sur-
  Mer 12 B4
Troy, *Turkey* .. 23 E6
Troy, *Ala.,*
  U.S.A. 74 D5
Troy, *N.Y.,*
  U.S.A. 73 C9
Troyes 13 B6
Trucial States =
  United Arab
  Emirates ■ .. 44 F3
Trujillo,
  Honduras ... 85 D7
Trujillo, *Peru* .. 91 E3
Trujillo, *Spain* . 18 C3
Trujillo,
  Venezuela ... 90 B4
Truk 64 J10
Trundle 63 B4
Truro, *Canada* . 69 D4
Truro, *U.K.* 11 F4
Truskavets ... 17 D6
Trutnov 16 C2
Tsaratanana ... 59 H9
Tsarevo =
  Michurin 22 C6
Tsau 58 C4
Tselinograd =
  Aqmola 29 D8
Tsetserleg ... 34 B5
Tshabong 58 D4
Tshane 58 C4
Tshela 56 E2
Tshikapa 56 F4
Tshofa 57 F5
Tshwane 58 C4
Tsihombe 59 K9
Tsimlyansk Res.
  =
  Tsimlyanskoye
  Vdkhr. 25 D5
Tsimlyanskoye
  Vdkhr. 25 D5
Tsinan = Jinan 35 C6
Tsinghai =
  Qinghai □ .. 34 C4
Tsingtao =
  Qingdao 35 C7

Tskhinvali 25 E5
Tsna → 24 C5
Tsu 32 B5
Tsuchiura 32 A7
Tsugaru-Kaikyō 32 F12
Tsumeb 58 B3
Tsumis 58 C3
Tsuruga 32 B5
Tsurugi-San ... 32 C4
Tsuruoka 33 G11
Tsyelyakhany . 17 B7
Tual 39 F4
Tuamotu Arch.
  = Tuamotu Is. 65 L16
Tuamotu Is. ... 65 L16
Tuamotu Ridge 65 M17
Tuao 38 A2
Tuapse 25 E4
Tuatapere 65 G2
Tubarão 94 B7
Tubau 37 D4
Tübingen 14 D5
Tubruq 52 B3
Tubuai Is. 65 M16
Tucacas 90 A5
Tucson 83 D7
Tucumcari 78 B2
Tucupita 90 B6
Tucuruí 92 C4
Tucuruí, Reprêsa
  de 92 C4
Tudela 19 A5
Tudmur 46 D4
Tuen 63 A4
Tuguegarao ... 38 A2
Tukangbesi,
  Kepulauan .. 39 F2
Tūkrah 52 B3
Tuktoyaktuk ... 70 B6
Tukuyu 57 F6
Tula, *Mexico* .. 84 C5
Tula, *Russia* ... 24 C4
Tulak 45 C5
Tulancingo ... 84 C5
Tulare 82 B3
Tulcán 90 C3
Tulcea 17 F9
Tulchyn 17 D9
Tuli, *Indonesia* 39 E2
Tuli, *Zimbabwe* 59 C5
Tullamore,
  Australia 63 B4
Tullamore,
  Ireland 11 E3
Tulle 12 D4
Tullibigeal ... 63 B4
Tulmaythah .. 52 B3
Tulsa 79 A6
Tulua 90 C3
Tulungagung .. 37 F4
Tum 39 E4
Tumaco 90 C3
Tumatumari .. 90 B7
Tumba, L. 56 E3
Tumbarumba . 63 C4
Túmbes 90 D2
Tumby Bay ... 62 B2
Tumeremo ... 90 B6
Tumkur 43 N10
Tump 42 F3
Tumpat 36 C2
Tumu 55 F4
Tumucumaque,
  Serra 92 B3
Tumut 63 C4
Tuncurry 63 B5
Tunduru 57 G7
Tundzha → .. 22 D6
Tunga Pass ... 41 C10

Tungabhadra →
  .... 43 M11
Tungaru 53 F5
Tunguska,
  Nizhnyaya → 30 C6
Tunis 54 A7
Tunisia ■ 54 B6
Tunja 90 B4
Tunuyán → .. 94 C3
Tunxi 35 D6
Tupelo 74 B3
Tupinambaranas 90 D7
Tupiza 94 A3
Tupungato,
  Cerro 94 C3
Túquerres 90 C3
Tura 30 C8
Turabah 47 E5
Tūrān 44 C4
Turayf 47 E4
Turda 17 E6
Turek 16 B4
Turfan = Turpan 34 B3
Turfan
  Depression =
  Turpan Hami 34 B3
Tūrgovishte ... 22 C6
Turgutlu 23 E6
Turhal 46 B4
Turia → 19 C5
Turiaçu 92 C4
Turiaçu → ... 92 C4
Turin = Torino 20 B1
Turkana, L. ... 57 D7
Turkestan =
  Türkistan ... 29 E7
Turkey ■ 46 C3
Türkistan 29 E7
Turkmenistan ■ 29 F6
Turks & Caicos
  Is. ■ 87 B5
Turku 9 F12
Turnagain, C. .. 64 D7
Turneffe Is. ... 85 D7
Turnhout 14 C3
Tŭrnovo =
  Veliko
  Tŭrnovo 22 C5
Turnu Măgurele 22 C5
Turnu Roşu, P. 17 F7
Turpan 34 B3
Turpan Hami .. 34 B3
Turukhansk ... 30 C6
Tuscaloosa ... 74 C4
Tuscany =
  Toscana □ .. 20 C3
Tuticorin 43 Q11
Tutóia 92 C5
Tutong 36 D4
Tutrakan 22 B6
Tuttlingen 14 E5
Tutuala 39 F3
Tutuila 65 L13
Tuvalu ■ 64 K12
Tuxpan 84 C5
Tuxtla Gutiérrez 85 D6
Tuy 18 A1
Tuz Gölü 46 C3
Tŭz Khurmātū . 46 D6
Tuzla 20 B7
Tver 24 B4
Tweed Heads . 63 A5
Twillingate ... 69 D5
Twin Falls 81 D6
Twofold B. 63 C4
Tyachiv 17 D6
Tychy 16 C4
Tyler 79 C6
Tyre = Şūr 46 D3

Tyrol = Tirol □ 14 E6
Tyrrell → 62 C3
Tyrrell, L. 62 C3
Tyrrhenian Sea 21 E4
Tyumen 29 D7
Tzaneen 59 C6
Tzukong =
  Zigong 35 D5

U

U.S.A. = United
  States of
  America ■ .. 67 F10
Uarsciek 49 G4
Uato-Udo 39 F3
Uatumã → ... 90 D7
Uaupés 90 D5
Uaupés → ... 90 C5
Ubá 93 G5
Ubaitaba 93 E6
Ubangi =
  Oubangi → . 56 E3
Ubauro 42 E6
Ube 32 C2
Ubeda 18 C4
Uberaba 93 F4
Uberlândia ... 93 F4
Ubon
  Ratchathani . 36 A2
Ubort → 17 B9
Ubundu 57 E5
Ucayali → 90 D4
Uchiura-Wan .. 32 F12
Udaipur 43 G8
Udaipur Garhi . 40 D6
Udgir 43 K10
Udhampur 42 C9
Udi 55 G6
Údine 20 A4
Udmurtia □ ... 28 D6
Udon Thani ... 36 A2
Udupi 43 N9
Ueda 32 A6
Uele → 57 D4
Uelzen 14 B6
Ufa 29 D6
Ugab → 58 C2
Ugalla → 57 F6
Uganda ■ 57 D6
Ugljane 20 B5
Ugolyak 30 C10
Uibhist a Deas
  = South Uist 10 C3
Uibhist a Tuath
  = North Uist 10 C3
Uíge 56 F2
Uinta Mts. 81 E8
Uitenhage 59 E5
Ujjain 43 H9
Ujung Pandang 39 F1
Ukerewe I. 57 E6
Ukhrul 41 E10
Ukhta 28 C6
Ukraine ■ 25 D3
Ulaanbaatar .. 35 B5
Ulaangom 34 A4
Ulan Bator =
  Ulaanbaatar . 35 B5
Ulan Ude 30 D8
Ulcinj 22 D2
Ulhasnagar ... 43 K8
Ulladulla 63 C5
Ullapool 10 C4
Ulm 14 D5
Ulmarra 63 A5

Ulonguè

Ulonguè	59 A6	Ures	84 B2	Uvinza	57 F6	Van Gölü	46 C5

Ulonguè 59 A6
Ulster □ 11 D3
Ulubat Gölü . . . 23 D7
Uludağ 23 D7
Ulungur He →. 34 B3
Uluru = Ayers
  Rock 60 F5
Ulutau 29 E7
Ulverstone 62 D4
Ulyanovsk =
  Simbirsk 24 C6
Ulyasutay 34 B4
Umala 91 G5
Uman 17 D10
Umaria 40 F3
Umarkot 43 G6
Umba 28 C4
Umbrella Mts. . 65 F3
Ume älv →. . . 8 F12
Umeå 8 F12
Umera 39 E3
Umm al
  Qaywayn . . . 44 E3
Umm Bel 53 F4
Umm Lajj 47 F4
Umm Ruwaba . 53 F5
Umnak I. 71 C3
Umniati →. . . 59 B5
Umtata →. 59 E5
Umuarama 93 G3
Una →. 20 B6
Unalaska 71 C3
Uncía 91 G5
Underbool 62 C3
Ungarie 63 B4
Ungarra 62 B2
Ungava B. 68 C4
Ungava Pen. . . 68 B3
Ungeny =
  Ungheni 17 E8
Ungheni 17 E8
União da Vitória 94 B6
Unimak I. 71 C3
United Arab
  Emirates ■ . . 44 F3
United
  Kingdom ■ . 11 E5
United States of
  America ■ . . 67 F10
Unnao 40 D3
Unst 10 A6
Ünye 46 B4
Upata 90 B6
Upemba, L. . . . 57 F5
Upington 58 D4
Upper Hutt . . . 65 D6
Upper Volta =
  Burkina
  Faso ■ 55 F4
Uppsala 9 G11
Ur 47 E6
Uracara 90 D7
Ural =
  Zhayyq →. . 29 E6
Ural 63 B4
Ural Mts. =
  Uralskie Gory 28 D6
Uralla 63 B5
Uralsk = Oral . 24 C7
Uralskie Gory . 28 D6
Uranquinty . . . 63 C4
Urawa 32 B6
Uray 29 C7
Urbana 72 D1
Urbino 20 C4
Urbión, Picos de 19 A4
Urcos 91 F4
Urda 25 D6
Urdzhar 29 E9

Ures 84 B2
Urfa = Sanliurfa 46 C4
Urganch 29 E7
Urgench =
  Urganch 29 E7
Uribia 90 A4
Urla 23 E6
Urmia =
  Orūmīyeh . . . 46 C6
Urmia, L. =
  Orūmīyeh,
  Daryācheh-ye 46 C6
Uroševac 22 C3
Uruana 93 F4
Urubamba 91 F4
Urubamba →. . 91 F4
Uruçuí 92 D5
Uruguai →. . . . 94 B6
Uruguaiana 94 B5
Uruguay ■ . . . 94 C5
Uruguay →. . . 94 C5
Urumchi =
  Ürümqi 34 B3
Ürümqi 34 B3
Usakos 58 C3
Usedom 15 B8
Ush-Tobe 29 E8
Ushant =
  Ouessant, I. d' 12 B1
Ushuaia 95 G3
Üsküdar 25 E2
Usman 24 C4
Usoke 57 F6
Uspallata, P. de 94 C3
Uspenskiy 29 E8
Ussuriysk 31 E11
Ust-Aldan =
  Batamay . . . 31 C10
Ust Ilimpeya =
  Yukti 30 C8
Ust Ishim 29 D8
Ust-
  Kamenogorsk
  = Öskemen . 29 E9
Ust-Karenga . . 31 D9
Ust Kuyga 31 B11
Ust Muya 30 D9
Ust Olenek . . . 30 B10
Ust Port 28 C9
Ust Tsilma 28 C6
Ust Urt =
  Ustyurt,
  Plateau 29 E6
Ust Vorkuta . . . 28 C7
Ústí nad Labem 16 C2
Ustica 21 E4
Ustinov =
  Izhevsk 28 D6
Ustye 30 D7
Ustyurt, Plateau 29 E6
Usu 34 B3
Usuki 32 C2
Usumacinta →. 85 D6
Usumbura =
  Bujumbura . . 57 E5
Uta 39 E5
Utah □ 81 F8
Utete 57 F7
Utiariti 91 F7
Utica 73 C8
Utrecht 14 B3
Utrera 18 D3
Utsunomiya . . . 32 A6
Uttar Pradesh □ 42 F11
Uttaradit 36 A2
Uummannarsuaq
  = Farvel, Kap 68 C6
Uusikaupunki . 8 F12
Uvat 29 D7

Uvinza 57 F6
Uvira 57 E5
Uvs Nuur 34 A4
Uwajima 32 C3
Uyuni 91 H5
Uzbekistan ■ . . 29 E7
Uzerche 12 D4
Uzh →. 17 C10
Uzhgorod =
  Uzhhorod . . . 17 D6
Uzhhorod 17 D6
Uzunköprü 22 D6

V

Vaal →. 58 D4
Vaasa 8 F12
Vác 16 E4
Vach →. =
  Vakh →. . . . 29 C8
Vadodara 43 H8
Vadsø 8 D13
Vaduz 13 C8
Váh →. 16 E4
Vahsel B. 96 B5
Vaigach 28 B6
Vakh →. 29 C8
Val d'Or 69 D3
Valahia 22 B5
Valandovo 22 D4
Valcheta 95 E3
Valdayskaya
  Vozvyshennost
  . . . . 24 B3
Valdepeñas . . . 18 C4
Valdés, Pen. . . . 95 E4
Valdez 71 B5
Valdivia 95 D2
Valdosta 75 D6
Valença 93 E6
Valença do Piauí 92 D5
Valence 13 D6
Valencia, Spain 19 C5
Valencia,
  Venezuela . . . 90 A5
Valencia □ 19 C5
Valencia, G. de 19 C6
Valencia de
  Alcántara . . . 18 C2
Valencia I. 11 F1
Valenciennes . . 13 A5
Valentim, Sa. do 92 D5
Valera 90 B4
Valjevo 22 B2
Vall de Uxó . . . 19 C5
Valladolid,
  Mexico 85 C7
Valladolid, Spain 18 B3
Valle de la
  Pascua 90 B5
Valledupar 90 A4
Vallejo 80 F2
Vallenar 94 B2
Valletta 21 G5
Valls 19 B6
Valognes 12 B3
Valona = Vlóra . 23 D2
Valozhyn 17 A8
Valparaíso 94 C2
Vals, Tanjung . 39 F5
Valsad 43 J8
Valverde del
  Camino 18 D2
Van 46 C5
Van, L. = Van
  Gölü 46 C5

Van Gölü 46 C5
Van Rees,
  Pegunungan 39 E5
Vanadzor 25 E5
Vancouver,
  Canada 71 D7
Vancouver,
  U.S.A. 80 C2
Vancouver I. . . 71 D7
Vänern 9 G10
Vanga 57 E7
Vangaindrano . 59 J9
Vännäs 8 F11
Vannes 12 C2
Vanrhynsdorp . 58 E3
Vanua Levu . . . 64 L12
Vanuatu ■ . . . 64 L11
Vapnyarka 17 D9
Varanasi 40 E4
Varangerfjorden 8 D13
Varaždin 20 A6
Varberg 9 G10
Vardak □ 45 C7
Vardar =
  Axiós →. . . . 23 D4
Varese 20 B2
Varna 22 C6
Varzaneh 44 C3
Vasa Barris →. 93 E6
Vascongadas =
  País Vasco □ 19 A4
Vasht = Khâsh 42 E2
Vasilevichi 17 B9
Vasilkov =
  Vasylkiv 17 C10
Vaslui 17 E8
Västerås 9 G11
Västervik 9 G11
Vasto 20 C5
Vasylkiv 17 C10
Vatican City ■ . 20 D4
Vatomandry . . . 59 H9
Vatra-Dornei . . 17 E7
Vättern 9 G10
Vaupés =
  Uaupés →. . . 90 C5
Vawkavysk 17 B7
Vaygach, Ostrov 28 C6
Vedea →. 22 C5
Vega 8 E10
Vegreville 71 C8
Vejer de la
  Frontera 18 D3
Velebit Planina 20 B5
Vélez 90 B4
Vélez Málaga . 18 D3
Vélez Rubio . . . 19 D4
Velhas →. 93 F5
Velika Kapela . 20 B5
Velikaya →. . . 24 B2
Veliki Ustyug . . 24 A6
Velikiye Luki . . 24 B3
Veliko Tŭrnovo 22 C5
Velikonda Range 43 M11
Velletri 20 D4
Vellore 43 N11
Venado Tuerto 94 C4
Vendée □ 12 C3
Vendôme 12 C4
Venézia 20 B4
Venézia, G. di . 20 B4
Venezuela ■ . . 90 B5
Venezuela, G. de 90 A4
Vengurla 43 M8
Venice =
  Venézia 20 B4
Venkatapuram . 40 H3
Ventotene 21 D4
Ventoux, Mt. . . 13 D6

Ventspils 24 B1
Ventuarí ─► ... 90 C5
Ventura 82 C3
Venus B. 63 C4
Vera, *Argentina* 94 B4
Vera, *Spain* ... 19 D5
Veracruz 84 D5
Veraval 43 J7
Verbánia 20 B2
Vercelli 20 B2
Verde ─► 95 E3
Verden 14 B5
Verdun 13 B6
Vereeniging ... 59 D5
Verga, C. 55 F2
Verín 18 B2
Verkhnevilyuysk 30 C10
Verkhniy
Baskunchak . 25 D6
Verkhoyansk .. 31 C11
Verkhoyansk Ra.
=
Verkhoyanskiy
Khrebet 31 C10
Verkhoyanskiy
Khrebet 31 C10
Vermilion 71 C8
Vermont ☐ 73 C9
Vernon, *Canada* 71 C8
Vernon, *U.S.A.* 78 B4
Véroia 23 D4
Verona 20 B3
Versailles 12 B5
Vert, C. 55 F1
Verviers 14 C3
Veselovskoye
Vdkhr. 25 D5
Vesoul 13 C7
Vesterålen 8 E11
Vestfjorden ... 8 E10
Vesuvio 21 D5
Vesuvius, Mt. =
Vesuvio 21 D5
Veszprém 16 E3
Vetlugu ─► ... 28 D5
Vettore, Mte. .. 20 C4
Veys 47 E7
Vezhen 22 C5
Viacha 91 G5
Viamão 94 C6
Viana 92 C5
Viana do
Alentejo 18 C2
Viana do Castelo 18 B1
Vianópolis 93 F4
Viaréggio 20 C3
Vibo Valéntia .. 21 E6
Vicenza 20 B3
Vich 19 B7
Vichy 13 C5
Vicksburg 79 C8
Viçosa 93 D6
Victor 43 J7
Victor Harbor .. 62 C2
Victoria, *Canada* 71 D7
Victoria, *Chile* . 94 D2
Victoria, *Guinea* 55 F2
Victoria,
Malaysia 36 C5
Victoria ☐ 62 C3
Victoria, L.,
Africa 57 E6
Victoria, L.,
Australia 62 B3
Victoria Beach . 71 C10
Victoria de
Durango 84 C4
Victoria Falls . 59 B5
Victoria I. 70 A8
Victoria Ld. ... 96 B14

Victoria
Taungdeik .. 41 G9
Victoria West .. 58 E4
Victorica 94 D3
Vicuña 94 C2
Vidin 22 C4
Vidisha 43 H10
Viedma 95 E4
Viedma, L. 95 F2
Vienna = Wien 15 D9
Vienne 13 D6
Vienne ─► ... 12 C4
Vientiane 36 A2
Vierzon 12 C5
Vietnam ■ 36 A3
Vigan 38 A2
Vigévano 20 B2
Vigia 92 C4
Vigo 18 A1
Vijayawada ... 40 J3
Vikeke 39 F3
Vikna 8 F10
Vila da Maganja 59 B7
Vila de João
Belo = Xai-Xai 59 D6
Vila do Bispo .. 18 D1
Vila Franca de
Xira 18 C1
Vila Machado . 59 B6
Vila Nova de
Gaia 18 B1
Vila Real 18 B2
Vila Real de
Santo António 18 D2
Vila Velha 93 G5
Vilaine ─► 12 C2
Vilanculos 59 C7
Vileyka 17 A8
Vilhelmina 8 F11
Vilhena 91 F6
Vilkitskogo,
Proliv 30 B8
Vilkovo =
Vylkove ... 17 F9
Villa Ahumada 84 A3
Villa Ángela ... 94 B4
Villa Bella 91 F5
Villa Bens =
Tarfaya 54 C2
Villa Colón ... 94 C3
Villa de María . 94 B4
Villa Dolores .. 94 C3
Villa Hayes ... 94 B5
Villa María ... 94 C4
Villa Mazán .. 94 B3
Villa Montes .. 94 A4
Villa Ocampo . 94 B5
Villacarrillo ... 18 C4
Villach 15 E7
Villagarcía de
Arosa 18 A1
Villajoyosa 94 C5
Villahermosa .. 85 D6
Villajoyosa 19 C5
Villalba 18 A2
Villanueva de la
Serena 18 C3
Villanueva y
Geltrú 19 B6
Villarreal 19 C5
Villarrica, *Chile* 95 D2
Villarrica,
Paraguay ... 94 B5
Villarrobledo . 19 C4
Villavicencio .. 90 C4
Villaviciosa .. 18 A3
Villazón 94 A3
Villena 19 C5
Villeneuve-
d'Ascq 13 A5

Villeneuve-sur-
Lot 12 D4
Villingen-
Schwenningen 14 D5
Vilnius 24 C2
Vilyuy ─► 31 C10
Vilyuysk 31 C10
Viña del Mar .. 94 C2
Vinaroz 19 B6
Vindhya Ra. ... 43 H10
Vineland 73 E8
Vinkovci 20 B7
Vinnitsa =
Vinnytsya ... 17 D9
Vinnytsya 17 D9
Virac 38 B2
Viramgam .. 43 H8
Viranşehir .. 46 C4
Virden 71 D9
Vire 12 B3
Vírgenes, C. ... 95 G3
Virgin Is.
(British) ■ .. 87 C7
Virginia ☐ 73 F6
Virginia Beach . 73 F8
Virovitica 20 B6
Virudunagar .. 43 Q10
Vis 20 C6
Visalia 82 B3
Visayan Sea .. 38 B2
Visby 9 G11
Višegrad 20 C7
Viseu, *Brazil* .. 92 C4
Viseu, *Portugal* 18 B2
Vishakhapatnam 40 J4
Viso, Mte. 20 B1
Vistula =
Wisła ─► ... 16 A4
Vitebsk =
Vitsyebsk ... 24 B3
Viterbo 20 C4
Viti Levu 64 L12
Vitigudino ... 18 B2
Vitória, *Brazil* . 93 G5
Vitoria, *Spain* . 19 A4
Vitória da
Conquista ... 93 E5
Vitsyebsk 24 B3
Vittória 21 F5
Vittório Véneto 20 B4
Vivero 18 A2
Vize 22 D6
Vizianagaram . 40 H4
Vjosa ─► 23 D2
Vladikavkaz .. 25 E5
Vladimir 24 B5
Vladimir
Volynskiy =
Volodymyr-
Volynskyy ... 17 C7
Vladivostok .. 31 E11
Vlissingen ... 14 C2
Vlóra 23 D2
Vltava ─► 16 C2
Vogelsberg ... 14 C5
Voghera 20 B2
Vohibinany .. 59 H9
Vohimarina .. 59 G10
Vohimena,
Tanjon' i 59 K9
Vohipeno 59 J9
Voi 57 E7
Voiron 13 D6
Vojvodina ☐ .. 22 B2
Volga ─► 25 D6
Volga Hts. =
Privolzhskaya
Vozvyshennost
.... 24 C6

Volgodonsk ... 25 D5
Volgograd 25 D5
Volgogradskoye
Vdkhr. 24 C6
Volkhov ─► ... 24 A3
Volkovysk =
Vawkavysk .. 17 B7
Volochanka ... 30 B7
Volodymyr-
Volynskyy ... 17 C7
Vologda 24 B4
Vólos 23 E4
Volovets 17 D6
Volozhin =
Valozhyn ... 17 A8
Volsk 24 C6
Volta ─► 55 G5
Volta, L. 55 G5
Volta Redonda 93 G5
Volterra 20 C3
Volturno ─► .. 20 D4
Volzhskiy 25 D5
Voríai
Sporádhes .. 23 E4
Vorkuta 28 C7
Voronezh 24 C4
Voroshilovgrad
= Luhansk . 25 D4
Voroshilovsk =
Alchevsk ... 25 D4
Vosges 13 B7
Vostok I. 65 L15
Vouga ─► 18 B1
Voznesensk ... 25 D3
Voznesenye ... 28 C4
Vrangelya,
Ostrov 31 B15
Vranje 22 C3
Vratsa 22 C4
Vrbas ─► 20 B6
Vrede 59 D5
Vredenburg .. 58 E3
Vršac 22 B3
Vryburg 58 D4
Vryheid 59 D6
Vukovar 20 B7
Vulcan 17 F6
Vulcaneşti ... 17 F9
Vulcano 21 E5
Vulkaneshty =
Vulcaneşti ... 17 F9
Vung Tau 36 B3
Vyatka = Kirov 28 D5
Vyatskiye
Polyany ... 24 B7
Vyazma 24 B3
Vyborg 28 C3
Vychegda ─► . 28 C5
Vychodné
Beskydy 17 D5
Vylkove 17 F9
Vynohradiv .. 17 D6
Vyshniy
Volochek ... 24 B3
Vyškov 16 D3

W

Wa 55 F4
Waal ─► 14 C3
Wabash ─► ... 72 F1
Waco 78 D5
Wad Banda ... 53 F4
Wad Hamid .. 53 E5
Wâd Medanî . 53 F5
Waddington, Mt. 71 C7

Waddy Pt.

Waddy Pt.	63	A5
Wadi Halfa	52	D5
Wafrah	47	E6
Wager B.	68	B2
Wager Bay	68	B1
Wagga Wagga	63	C4
Waghete	39	E5
Wah	42	C8
Wahai	39	E3
Waiau → ...	65	E5
Waibeem	39	E4
Waigeo	39	E4
Waihi	64	B6
Waihou → ..	64	B6
Waikabubak ...	39	F1
Waikari	65	E5
Waikato → ..	64	B6
Waikerie	62	B2
Waikokopu ...	64	C7
Waikouaiti	65	F4
Waimakariri →	65	E5
Waimate	65	F4
Wainganga →	43	K11
Waingapu	39	F2
Wainwright, Canada	71	C8
Wainwright, U.S.A.	71	A3
Waiouru	64	C6
Waipara	65	E5
Waipawa	64	C7
Waipiro	64	C8
Waipu	64	A6
Waipukurau ...	64	D7
Wairakei	64	C7
Wairarapa, L. ..	65	D6
Wairoa	64	C7
Waitaki → ...	65	F4
Waitara	64	C6
Waiuku	64	B6
Wajima	32	A5
Wajir	57	D8
Wakasa-Wan ..	32	B4
Wakatipu, L. ..	65	F3
Wakayama	32	B4
Wakefield	65	D5
Wakema	41	J10
Wakkanai	32	E12
Wakool	63	C3
Wakool → ...	62	C3
Wakre	39	E4
Wałbrzych	16	C3
Walcha	63	B5
Wałcz	16	B3
Wales □	11	E4
Walgett	63	A4
Walgreen Coast	96	B1
Walhalla	63	C4
Walla Walla ...	80	B4
Wallachia = Valahia	22	B5
Wallal	63	A4
Wallaroo	62	B2
Wallerawang ..	63	B5
Wallis & Futuna, Is.	64	L13
Wallowa Mts. .	80	C5
Wallsend	63	B5
Wallumbilla ...	63	A4
Walvisbaai ...	58	C2
Wamba	57	D5
Wamena	39	E5
Wamulan	39	E3
Wana	42	C6
Wanaaring ...	63	A3
Wanaka	65	F3
Wanaka L.	65	F3
Wanapiri	39	E5
Wanbi	62	B3
Wandoan	63	A4
Wangal	39	F4
Wanganella ..	63	C3
Wanganui	64	C6
Wangaratta ...	63	C4
Wangary	62	B2
Wangerooge ..	14	B4
Wangiwangi ..	39	F2
Wanxian	35	C5
Warangal	43	L11
Waratah	62	D4
Waratah B.	63	C4
Warburton	63	C4
Ward	65	D6
Ward →	63	A4
Wardha	43	J11
Wardha → ...	43	K11
Warialda	63	A5
Wariap	39	E4
Warkopi	39	E4
Warmbad, Namibia	58	D3
Warmbad, S. Africa	59	C5
Warner Mts. ..	80	E3
Warracknabeal	62	C3
Warragul	63	C4
Warrego → ..	63	B4
Warren	63	B4
Warrenton ...	58	D4
Warrenville ...	63	A4
Warri	55	G6
Warrina	62	A2
Warrington, U.K.	11	E5
Warrington, U.S.A.	74	D4
Warrnambool .	62	C3
Warsa	39	E5
Warsaw = Warszawa ...	16	B5
Warszawa ...	16	B5
Warta →	16	B2
Warthe = Warta →	16	B2
Waru	39	E4
Warwick	63	A5
Wasatch Ra. ..	81	E8
Wash, The ...	11	E7
Washim	43	J10
Washington ..	73	E7
Washington □ .	80	B3
Washington, Mt.	73	B10
Wasian	39	E4
Wasior	39	E4
Waskaganish ..	69	C3
Wasserkuppe ..	14	C5
Watangpone ..	39	E2
Waterbury	73	D9
Waterford	11	E3
Waterloo, S. Leone	55	G2
Waterloo, U.S.A.	77	D8
Waterton-Glacier International Peace Park .	81	A6
Watertown	73	C8
Waterville	73	B11
Watford	11	F6
Watling I. = San Salvador	86	B5
Watrous	71	C9
Watsa	57	D5
Watson Lake ..	70	B7
Watsonville ...	82	B2
Wattiwarriganna Cr.	62	A2
Watuata = Batuata	39	F2
Watubela, Kepulauan ..	39	E4
Watubela Is. = Watubela, Kepulauan ..	39	E4
Wauchope	63	B5
Waukegan	72	C2
Waukesha	72	C1
Wausau	77	C10
Wauwatosa ..	72	C2
Waverley	64	C6
Wâw	53	G4
Wâw al Kabîr ..	52	C2
Waxahachie ..	79	C5
Wayabula Rau .	39	D3
Wayatinah	62	D4
Waycross	75	D6
Wazirabad	42	C9
We	36	C1
Weda	39	D3
Weda, Teluk ..	39	D3
Weddell I.	95	G4
Weddell Sea ..	96	A4
Wedderburn ..	62	C3
Wee Waa	63	B4
Weemelah	63	A4
Weiden	15	D7
Weifang	35	C6
Weimar	15	C6
Weipa	61	C7
Weir →	63	A4
Wejherowo ...	16	A4
Welbourn Hill .	62	A1
Welkom	59	D5
Wellesley Is. ..	60	D6
Wellington, Australia	63	B4
Wellington, N.Z.	65	D6
Wellington, I. ..	95	F1
Wellington, L. .	63	C4
Wels	15	D8
Welshpool ...	11	E5
Wemindji	69	C3
Wenatchee ...	80	B3
Wenchi	55	G4
Wenchow = Wenzhou ...	35	D7
Wendesi	39	E4
Wensu	34	B3
Wentworth	62	B3
Wenut	39	E4
Wenzhou	35	D7
Werda	58	D4
Werder	49	F4
Weri	39	E4
Werra →	14	C5
Werribee	63	C3
Werrimull	62	B3
Werris Creek ..	63	B5
Wersar	39	E4
Weser →	14	B5
Wesiri	39	F3
West Bengal □ .	40	F7
West Beskids = Západné Beskydy ...	16	D4
West Falkland .	95	G4
West Fjord = Vestfjorden .	8	E10
West Ice Shelf .	96	A11
West Nicholson	59	C5
West Palm Beach	75	F7
West Pt.	62	C2
West Virginia □	72	E5
West Wyalong .	63	B4
Westall Pt.	62	B1
Westbury	62	D4
Westerland → .	14	A5
Western Australia □ ..	60	F3
Western Dvina = Daugava → .	24	B1
Western Ghats	43	N9
Western Sahara ■ ...	54	D2
Western Samoa ■ ..	65	L13
Westerwald ...	14	C4
Westland Bight	65	E4
Weston	36	C5
Weston-super-Mare	11	F5
Westport, Ireland	11	E2
Westport, N.Z. .	65	D4
Westray	10	B5
Wetar	39	F3
Wetaskiwin ...	71	C8
Wetzlar	14	C5
Wexford	11	E3
Weyburn	71	D9
Weymouth	11	F5
Whakatane ...	64	B7
Whale →	68	C4
Whale Cove ..	70	B10
Whales, B. of ..	96	B16
Whangamomona	64	C6
Whangarei	64	A6
Whangarei Harb.	64	A6
Wheeling	72	D5
White →, Ark., U.S.A.	79	C8
White →, Ind., U.S.A.	72	E2
White Cliffs ...	62	B3
White I.	64	B7
White Nile = Nîl el Abyad → .	53	E5
White Russia = Belarus ■ ...	24	C2
White Sea = Beloye More .	28	C4
Whitecliffs ...	65	E4
Whitehaven ...	11	D5
Whitehorse ...	70	B6
Whitemark	62	D4
Whitfield	63	C4
Whitianga	64	B6
Whitney, Mt. ..	82	B3
Whittlesea ...	63	C4
Wholdaia L. ...	70	B9
Whyalla	62	B2
Whyjonta	62	A3
Wichita	78	A5
Wichita Falls ..	78	C4
Wick	10	B5
Wickham, C. ..	62	C3
Wicklow Mts. ..	11	E3
Wieluń	16	C4
Wien	15	D9
Wiener Neustadt	15	E9
Wiesbaden ...	14	C5
Wilcannia	62	B3
Wildspitze	14	E6
Wilhelm, Mt. ..	61	B8
Wilhelm II Coast	96	A11
Wilhelmshaven	14	B5
Wilkes-Barre ..	73	D8
Wilkie	71	C9
Willandra Billabong Creek → ...	63	B4
Willemstad ...	87	D6

William Creek . 62 A2
Williams Lake . 71 C7
Williamsburg . . 73 F7
Williamsport . . 73 D7
Williamstown . . 63 C3
Williston 76 A3
Willowmore . . . 58 E4
Willunga 62 C2
Wilmington,
  Australia . . . 62 B2
Wilmington,
  Del., U.S.A. . 73 E8
Wilmington,
  N.C., U.S.A. . 75 B9
Wilpena Cr. → 62 B2
Wilson 75 B9
Wilson → 62 A3
Wilsons
  Promontory . 63 C4
Wimmera → . 62 C3
Winchester . . . 11 F6
Wind River
  Range 81 D9
Windau =
  Ventspils . . . 24 B1
Windhoek 58 C3
Windsor,
  Australia 63 B5
Windsor, N.S.,
  Canada 69 D4
Windsor, Ont.,
  Canada 69 D2
Windward Is. . . 87 D7
Wingen 63 B5
Wingham 63 B5
Winisk → . . . 69 C2
Winneba 55 G4
Winnipeg 71 D10
Winnipeg, L. . . 71 C10
Winnipegosis L. 71 C9
Winona 77 C9
Winston-Salem 75 A7
Winterthur 13 C8
Winton,
  Australia 61 E7
Winton, N.Z. . . 65 G3
Wirrulla 62 B1
Wisconsin □ . . 77 C10
Wisła → 16 A4
Wismar 15 B6
Witbank 59 D5
Wittenberg 15 C7
Wittenberge . . . 15 B6
Wkra → 16 B5
Włocławek 16 B4
Włodawa 17 C6
Wodonga 63 C4
Wokam 39 F4
Wolfsberg 15 E8
Wolfsburg 15 B6
Wolin 16 B2
Wollaston, Is. . . 95 H3
Wollaston Pen. . 70 B8
Wollongong . . . 63 B5
Wolseley 62 C3
Wolverhampton 11 E5
Wondai 63 A5
Wongalarroo L. 63 B3
Wŏnsan 35 C7
Wonthaggi 63 C4
Woocalla 62 B2
Woodburn 63 A5
Woodenbong . . 63 A5
Woodend 63 C3
Woodland 80 F3
Woodroffe, Mt. . 60 F5
Woods, L. of the 71 D10
Woodstock 69 D4

Woodville 64 D6
Woolamai, C. . . 63 C4
Woolgoolga . . . 63 B5
Woombye 63 A5
Woomera 62 B2
Worcester,
  S. Africa . . . 58 E3
Worcester, U.K. 11 E5
Worcester,
  U.S.A. 73 C10
Workington . . . 11 D5
Worms 14 D5
Worthing 11 F6
Wosi 39 E3
Wou-han =
  Wuhan 35 C6
Wour 52 D2
Wousi = Wuxi . 35 C7
Wowoni 39 E2
Woy Woy 63 B5
Wrangel I. =
  Vrangelya,
  Ostrov 31 B15
Wrangell 71 C6
Wrangell Mts. . 71 B5
Wrath, C. 10 B4
Wrexham 11 E5
Wright 38 B3
Wrigley 70 B7
Wrocław 16 C3
Września 16 B3
Wu Jiang → . 35 D5
Wuhan 35 C6
Wuhsi = Wuxi . 35 C7
Wuhu 35 C6
Wukari 55 G6
Wuliaru 39 F4
Wulumuchi =
  Ürümqi 34 B3
Wum 55 G7
Wuntho 41 F10
Wuppertal 14 C4
Würzburg 14 D5
Wutongqiao . . . 34 D5
Wuwei 34 C5
Wuxi 35 C7
Wuyi Shan 35 D6
Wuzhi Shan . . . 35 E5
Wuzhong 35 C5
Wuzhou 35 D6
Wyandotte 72 C4
Wyandra 63 A4
Wyangala Res. . 63 B4
Wyara, L. 63 A3
Wycheproof . . . 62 C3
Wynbring 62 B1
Wyndham,
  Australia . . . 60 D4
Wyndham, N.Z. 65 G3
Wynnum 63 A5
Wynyard 62 D4
Wyoming □ . . . 81 D10
Wyong 63 B5

X

Xai-Xai 59 D6
Xainza 34 C3
Xangongo 58 B3
Xankändi 25 F6
Xánthi 22 D5
Xapuri 91 F5
Xi Jiang → . . 35 D6
Xiaguan 34 D5
Xiamen 35 D6

Xi'an 35 C5
Xiang Jiang → 35 D6
Xiangfan 35 C6
Xiangtan 35 D6
Xiao Hinggan
  Ling 35 B7
Xiapu 35 D6
Xichang 34 D5
Xigazê 34 D3
Xinavane 59 D6
Xing'an 35 D6
Xingren 35 D5
Xingtai 35 C6
Xingu → 92 C3
Xining 34 C5
Xinjiang Uygur
  Zizhiqu □ . . . 34 B3
Xinjin 35 C7
Xinxiang 35 C6
Xinyang 35 C6
Xinzhu 35 D7
Xique-Xique . . . 93 E5
Xisha Qundao =
  Hsisha
  Chuntao 36 A4
Xixabangma
  Feng 40 C5
Xizang □ 34 C3
Xuanhua 35 B6
Xuchang 35 C6
Xuzhou 35 C6

Y

Ya'an 34 D5
Yaapeet 62 C3
Yabelo 53 H6
Yablonovy Ra. =
  Yablonovyy
  Khrebet 30 D9
Yablonovyy
  Khrebet 30 D9
Yacuiba 94 A4
Yadgir 43 L10
Yagoua 56 B3
Yahuma 56 D4
Yakima 80 B3
Yakutat 71 C6
Yakutsk 31 C10
Yala 36 C2
Yalinga 56 C4
Yalong Jiang → 34 D5
Yalova 22 D7
Yalta 25 E3
Yalutorovsk . . . 29 D7
Yam Ha Melah
  = Dead Sea . 47 E3
Yam Kinneret . 46 D3
Yamagata 33 G12
Yamaguchi . . . 32 B2
Yamal,
  Poluostrov . . 28 B8
Yamal Pen. =
  Yamal,
  Poluostrov . . 28 B8
Yamantau, Gora 29 D6
Yamba, N.S.W.,
  Australia . . . 63 A5
Yamba,
  S. Austral.,
  Australia . . . 62 B3
Yâmbiô 53 H4
Yambol 22 C6
Yamdena 39 F4
Yamethin 41 G11

Yamma-Yamma,
  L. 62 A3
Yamoussoukro 55 G3
Yampil 17 D9
Yampol =
  Yampil 17 D9
Yamuna → . . 40 E3
Yamzho Yumco 34 D4
Yana → 31 B11
Yanac 62 C3
Yanbu 'al Baḥr 47 F4
Yancannia 62 B3
Yanco Cr. → . . 63 C4
Yandoon 41 J10
Yangambi 56 D4
Yangch'ü =
  Taiyuan 35 C6
Yangchun 35 D6
Yangjiang 35 D6
Yangon =
  Rangoon 41 J11
Yangquan 35 C6
Yanji 35 B7
Yanna 63 A4
Yanqi 34 B3
Yantabulla 63 A4
Yantai 35 C7
Yanykurgan . . . 29 E7
Yao 53 F2
Yaoundé 56 D2
Yapen 39 E5
Yapen, Selat . . 39 E5
Yaqui → 84 B2
Yar-Sale 28 C8
Yaraka 61 E7
Yaransk 24 B6
Yardea P.O. . . . 62 B2
Yaremcha 17 D7
Yarensk 28 C5
Yarí → 90 D4
Yarkand =
  Shache 34 C2
Yarkhun → . . 42 A8
Yaroslavl 24 B4
Yarram 63 C4
Yarraman 63 A5
Yarranvale 63 A4
Yarras 63 B5
Yartsevo 30 C7
Yaselda 17 B8
Yasinya 17 D7
Yass 63 B4
Yataǧan 23 F7
Yathkyed L. . . . 70 B10
Yatsushiro 32 C2
Yauyos 91 F3
Yavari → 90 D4
Yavatmal 43 J11
Yavoriv 17 D6
Yavorov =
  Yavoriv 17 D6
Yawatahama . . 32 C3
Yazd 44 D3
Yazd □ 44 C3
Yazdān 45 C5
Yazoo → 79 C8
Ye Xian 35 C6
Yebyu 41 K12
Yecla 19 C5
Yedintsy =
  Ediniţa 17 D8
Yeelanna 62 B2
Yegros 94 B5
Yei 53 H5
Yekaterinburg . 29 D7
Yekaterinodar =
  Krasnodar . . 25 D4
Yelarbon 63 A5

Yelets

Yelets	24	C4
Yelizavetgrad =		
Kirovohrad	25	D3
Yell	10	A6
Yellow Sea	35	C7
Yellowhead Pass	71	C8
Yellowknife	70	B8
Yellowknife →	70	B8
Yellowstone →	76	B3
Yellowstone		
National Park	81	C8
Yelsk	17	C9
Yemen ■	49	E3
Yenangyaung	41	G10
Yenbo = Yanbu		
'al Baḥr	47	F4
Yenda	63	B4
Yenice	23	E6
Yenisey →	28	B9
Yeniseysk	30	D7
Yeniseyskiy		
Zaliv	28	B9
Yenyuka	31	D10
Yeola	43	J9
Yeovil	11	F5
Yerbent	29	F6
Yerevan	25	E5
Yermak	29	D8
Yershov	24	C6
Yerushalayim =		
Jerusalem	47	E3
Yessey	30	C8
Yeu, I. d'	12	C2
Yevpatoriya	25	D3
Yeysk	25	D4
Yezd = Yazd	44	D3
Yiannitsa	23	D4
Yibin	35	D5
Yichang	35	C6
Yichun	35	B7
Yilan	35	D7
Yinchuan	35	C5
Yingkou	35	B7
Yingtan	35	D6
Yining	34	B3
Yinmabin	41	F10
Yishan	35	D5
Yithion	23	F4
Yiyang	35	D6
Yog Pt.	38	B2
Yogyakarta	37	F4
Yokadouma	56	D2
Yokkaichi	32	B5
Yoko	53	G1
Yokohama	32	B6
Yokosuka	32	B6
Yola	53	G1
Yonago	32	B3
Yongji	35	C6
Yonibana	55	G2
Yonkers	73	D9
Yonne →	13	B5
York, U.K.	11	E6
York, U.S.A.	73	E7
York, C.	61	C7
Yorke Pen.	62	B2
Yorkton	71	C9
Yos Sudarso,		
Pulau	39	F5
Yosemite		
National Park	82	B3
Yoshkar Ola	24	B6
Youghal	11	F3
Young	63	B4
Younghusband,		
L.	62	B2
Younghusband		
Pen.	62	C2

Youngstown	72	D5
Yozgat	46	C3
Ysyk-Köl, Ozero	29	E8
Yu Jiang →	35	D6
Yu Shan	35	D7
Yuan Jiang →	35	D6
Yuanling	35	D6
Yuanyang	34	D5
Yuba City	80	F3
Yūbari	32	F12
Yucatán □	85	C7
Yucatán, Canal		
de	85	C7
Yucatán,		
Península de	85	D7
Yucatan Str. =		
Yucatán,		
Canal de	85	C7
Yuci	35	C6
Yugoslavia ■	22	B3
Yukon →	71	B3
Yukon		
Territory □	70	B6
Yukti	30	C8
Yuma	82	D5
Yumen	34	C4
Yun Xian	35	C6
Yungas	91	G5
Yunnan □	34	D5
Yunta	62	B2
Yurgao	29	D9
Yuribei	28	B8
Yurimaguas	91	E3
Yuryung Kaya	30	B9
Yushu	34	C4
Yuzhno-		
Sakhalinsk	31	E12
Yvetot	12	B4

Z

Zabid	49	E3
Zábol	45	D5
Zābol □	45	D6
Zābolī	45	E5
Zabrze	16	C4
Zacapa	85	E7
Zacatecas	84	C4
Zacoalco	84	C4
Zadar	20	B5
Zadetkyi Kyun	36	C1
Zafra	18	C2
Żagań	16	C2
Zagazig	52	B5
Zagorsk =		
Sergiyev		
Posad	24	B4
Zagreb	20	B6
Zãgros, Kũhhã-		
ye	44	C2
Zagros Mts. =		
Zãgros,		
Kũhhã-ye	44	C2
Zãhedãn	45	D5
Zahlah	46	D3
Zaïre ■	56	E4
Zaïre →	56	F2
Zaječar	22	C4
Zakhodnaya		
Dzvina =		
Daugava →	24	B1
Zākhū	46	C5
Zákinthos	23	F3
Zakopane	16	D4
Zalaegerszeg	16	E3

Zalău	17	E6
Zaleshchiki =		
Zalishchyky	17	D7
Zalew Wiślany	16	A4
Zalingei	53	F3
Zalishchyky	17	D7
Zambeze →	59	B7
Zambezi =		
Zambeze →	59	B7
Zambezi	58	A4
Zambia ■	59	B5
Zamboanga	38	C2
Zamora, Mexico	84	D4
Zamora, Spain	18	B3
Zamość	17	C6
Zanaga	56	E2
Zanesville	72	E4
Zanjān	46	C7
Zanjān □	46	C7
Zante =		
Zákinthos	23	F3
Zanzibar	57	F7
Zaouiet El-Kala		
= Bordj Omar		
Driss	54	C6
Zaouiet Reggane	54	C5
Zap Suyu =		
Kabīr, Zab		
al →	46	C5
Zapadnaya		
Dvina	28	D4
Zapadnaya		
Dvina → =		
Daugava →	24	B1
Západné		
Beskydy	16	D4
Zaporizhzhya	25	D4
Zaporozhye =		
Zaporizhzhya	25	D4
Zara	46	C4
Zaragoza	19	B5
Zarand	44	D4
Zaranj	42	D2
Zaria	55	F6
Zaruma	90	D3
Żary	16	C2
Zarzis	52	B1
Zaskar Mts.	42	C10
Zavāreh	44	C3
Zawiercie	16	C4
Zāyandeh →	44	C3
Zaysan	29	E9
Zaysan, Oz.	29	E9
Zbarazh	17	D7
Zdolbuniv	17	C8
Zduńska Wola	16	C4
Zeebrugge	14	C2
Zeehan	62	D4
Zeerust	59	D5
Zeila	49	E3
Zeitz	15	C7
Zelenograd	24	B4
Zémio	57	C5
Zemun	22	B3
Zenica	20	B6
Žepce	20	B7
Zêzere →	18	C1
Zgorzelec	16	C2
Zhabinka	17	B7
Zhailma	29	D7
Zhambyl	29	E8
Zhangagazaly	29	E7
Zhanghua	35	D7
Zhangjiakou	35	B6
Zhangye	34	C5
Zhangzhou	35	D6
Zhanjiang	35	D6
Zhanyi	34	D5

Zhaotong	34	D5
Zhashkiv	17	D10
Zhayyq →	29	E6
Zhdanov =		
Mariupol	25	D4
Zhejiang □	35	D7
Zhengzhou	35	C6
Zhenjiang	35	C6
Zhenyuan	35	D5
Zhezqazghan	29	E7
Zhigansk	30	C10
Zhijiang	35	D5
Zhilinda	30	B9
Zhitomir =		
Zhytomyr	17	C9
Zhlobin	17	B10
Zhmerinka =		
Zhmerynka	17	D9
Zhmerynka	17	D9
Zhodino =		
Zhodzina	17	A9
Zhodzina	17	A9
Zhongdian	34	D4
Zhumadian	35	C6
Zhuzhou	35	D6
Zhytomyr	17	C9
Zibo	35	C6
Zielona Góra	16	C2
Zigey	53	F2
Zigong	35	D5
Zigui	35	C6
Ziguinchor	55	F1
Zile	46	B3
Žilina	16	D4
Zillah	52	C2
Zimbabwe ■	59	B5
Zimnicea	22	C5
Zinder	55	F6
Zion National		
Park	83	B6
Zipaquirá	90	C4
Ziway, L.	53	G6
Zlatograd	22	D5
Zlatoust	29	D6
Zlin	16	D3
Zlītan	52	B1
Zmeinogorsk	29	D9
Znojmo	16	D3
Zolochev =		
Zolochiv	17	D7
Zolochiv	17	D7
Zomba	59	B7
Zongo	56	D3
Zonguldak	46	B2
Zorritos	90	D2
Zouar	52	D2
Zouérate	54	D2
Zrenjanin	22	B3
Zuetina = Az		
Zuwaytīnah	52	B3
Zufar	48	D5
Zug	13	C8
Zugspitze	14	E6
Zula	53	E6
Zumbo	59	B6
Zungeru	55	G6
Zunyi	35	D5
Zürich	13	C8
Zuwārah	52	B1
Zvishavane	59	C6
Zvolen	16	D4
Zwettl	15	D8
Zwickau	15	C7
Zwolle	14	B4
Żyrardów	16	B5
Zyryan	29	E9
Zyryanovsk =		
Zyryan	29	E9
Żywiec	16	D4